CLARENDON LAW

Edited by

PETER BIRKS

CLARENDON LAW SERIES

ADMINISTRATIVE LAW

Fourth Edition

PETER CANE

Australian National University

OXFORD
UNIVERSITY PRESS

OXFORD
UNIVERSITY PRESS

Great Clarendon Street, Oxford OX2 6DP

Oxford University Press is a department of the University of Oxford.
It furthers the University's objective of excellence in research, scholarship,
and education by publishing worldwide in

Oxford New York

Auckland Bangkok Buenos Aires Cape Town Chennai
Dar es Salaam Delhi Hong Kong Istanbul Karachi Kolkata
Kuala Lumpur Madrid Melbourne Mexico City Mumbai Nairobi
São Paulo Shanghai Taipei Tokyo Toronto

Oxford is a registered trade mark of Oxford University Press
in the UK and in certain other countries

Published in the United States
by Oxford University Press Inc., New York

First published 1996
Paperback reprinted 1997, 2000

British Library Cataloguing in Publication Data
Data available

Library of Congress Cataloging in Publication Data
Data available
ISBN 0–19–926898–3

1 3 5 7 9 10 8 6 4 2

Typeset in Ehrhardt
by RefineCatch Limited, Bungay, Suffolk
Printed in Great Britain by
Ashford Colour Press Ltd, Gosport, Hampshire

Contents

Preface

Since the 3rd edition of this book was published in 1996 the landscape of the British constitution has experienced seismic changes. For present purposes, undoubtedly the most significant were the enactment of the Human Rights Act 1998 and its entry into operation in 2001. Other major developments include devolution to Scotland and Wales, the new regime of access to public information introduced by the Freedom of Information Act 2000, and the replacement of the Rules of the Supreme Court by the Civil Procedure Rules and the establishment of the Administrative Court in 2001. It is still far too early to understand or analyse all the implications of these changes—for one thing, the Freedom of Information Act will not be fully operational until 2005. Other reforms on the horizon include rationalization of the tribunal system and more radical recomposition of the House of Lords. Important developments in the common law have occurred in areas such as legitimate expectations and the scope of judicial review.

In addition to taking account of all these developments and general updating, I have taken the opportunity to add a new introductory chapter and to completely rewrite the last chapter to take account of advances in both theoretical and empirical research about judicial review and the impact of administrative law. The discussion of the grounds of judicial review in section B of Part I has been considerably reorganized. The chapter on estoppel has been amalgamated into the discussion of the fettering of discretion in Chapter 8, and the chapters on authority and output in the 3rd edition have been amalgamated into one chapter dealing with substantive review.

The gap of eight years between this edition and the last was partly an unintended result of my moving half-way around the world, and the pressure of other commitments. But in retrospect, I think the delay was probably a good thing. Although the British constitution is still in a state of considerable flux, the main components of the new dispensation can now be clearly discerned. I have no doubt that one of the most significant features of the new order is the increased role of law and legal institutions in the regulation of public power and the resolution of conflicts between governors and governed. There is much to regret in this accretion of power to lawyers and courts. But for students of public law, these are certainly exciting and challenging times. I hope that the considerable struggle required to get my mind around what has happened in the past decade has produced a worthwhile and helpful product.

Many thanks to the production team at OUP, especially Melanie Jackson and Nicola Rainbow. I am particularly grateful to Anna Dziedzic who prepared the tables of cases and legislation, and to Michael Hayes who prepared the index.

Peter Cane
Canberra
January 2004

STOP PRESS

Since I wrote this Preface in January 2004, there have been two major developments that deserve to be noted as they affect what is said in the text at various points. Controversy and uncertainty about further reforms to the composition and functions of the (legislative) House of Lords provide a subtext to both.

1. In March the Constitutional Reform Bill was introduced into the House of Lords. The Bill abolishes the office of Lord Chancellor. Concerns about the impact of this change on judicial independence (see p 413 below) have been addressed by a clause expressly protecting the independence of the judiciary. The Bill also establishes a Supreme Court of the United Kingdom, a Judicial Appointments Commission, and a Judicial Appointments and Conduct Ombudsman. On 9 March, the House of Lords voted to refer the Bill to a special select committee for scrutiny. It is unclear whether the Bill will be enacted before 2005.

2. Section 14(7) of the Asylum and Immigration (Treatment of Claimants etc) Bill amends the Nationality, Immigration and Asylum Act 2000 by inserting a new s.108A that contains detailed and elaborate provisions designed to prevent decisions of the new Asylum and Immigration Tribunal from being challenged by claims for judicial review except on a few grounds, including bad faith and breach of Article 5 of the ECHR. Analogous provisions have been in force in Australia for some years and have elicited various evasive responses from litigants and courts. Clause 14(7) has provoked strong criticism by senior judges and lawyers, and it remains to be seen in what form it will be enacted and how the courts will react to its provisions.

PFC, March 2004

Table of Cases

University of Liverpool Library

Name: Dutton, Lauren
University ID: ******7155

Title: The refugee in international law / Guy S. Goodwin-Gill and Jane McAdam.
Barcode: 01441761B
Due: 03-12-13

Title: Administrative law / Peter Cane.
Barcode: 01391051543
Due: 17-12-13

Total items: 2
Total fines: £3.20
26/11/2013 12:44

Please return your books on due date as given above.

Table of Legislation

Abbreviations

AC	Appeal Cases (1890–)
Admin LR	Administrative Law Reports
ALR	Australian Law Reports
All ER	All England Law Reports
App Cas	Appeal Cases (1875–90)
Brit J of Law & Society	British Journal of Law and Society
CA	Court of Appeal
CBNS	Common Bench New Series (Court of Common Pleas 1856–65)
Ch	Chancery Division Reports
CJR	claim for judicial review
CJQ	Civil Justice Quarterly
CLA	Commission for Local Administration
CLJ	Cambridge Law Journal
CLP	Current Legal Problems
CLR	Commonwealth Law Reports (Australian)
Cm	Command Papers (HMSO)
CMLR	Common Market Law Reports
Cmnd	Command Papers (HMSO)
COD	Crown Office Digest
CPR	Civil Procedure Rules
Crim LR	Criminal Law Review
Cth	Commonwealth
DLR	Dominion Law Reports (Canadian)
DoE	Department of the Environment
DSS	Department of Social Security
DTI	Department of Trade and Industry
EC	European Community
ECHR	European Convention on Human Rights
ECtHR	European Court of Human Rights
ECJ	European Court of Justice

ECR	European Court Reports
ELR	Education Law Reports
Env LR	Environmental Law Reports
European LR	European Law Review
FOI	freedom of information
HC	House of Commons
Harvard LR	Harvard Law Review
HL	House of Lords
HMSO	Her Majesty's Stationery Office ('The Stationery Office')
HRA	Human Rights Act 1998
HSO	Health Service Ombudsman
ICR	Industrial Cases Reports
IMR	Individual ministerial responsibility
J	Mr/Ms Justice
J	Journal
J Env L	Journal of Environmental Law
JPL	Journal of Planning and Environment Law
JR	Judicial Review (journal)
JRP	judicial review procedure
JSWL	Journal of Social Welfare Law
KB (or QB)	King's (or Queen's) Bench Division Reports
L	Law
Law Com	Law Commission (Report)
LGO	Local Government Ombudsman
LGR	Local Government Reports
LJ	Lord Justice
LMCLQ	Lloyd's Maritime and Commercial Law Quarterly
LR HL	House of Lords Appeals (1866–75)
LR Ir	Reports of Irish Cases
LS	Legal Studies
LS Gaz	Law Society Gazette
LQR	Law Quarterly Review
MLR	Modern Law Review
MoD	Ministry of Defence
MR	Master of the Rolls
Monash ULR	Monash University Law Review (Australian)
New LJ	New Law Journal
NILQ	Northern Ireland Legal Quarterly
NPM	New Public Management

NSWR	New South Wales Reports
OJLS	Oxford Journal of Legal Studies
Parl Aff	Parliamentary Affairs
PCA	Parliamentary Commissioner for Administration
P&CR	Property and Compensation Reports
PD	Practice Direction
PI	Planning Inspectorate
PL	Public Law (journal)
PO	Parliamentary Ombudsman
Parl Aff	Parliamentary Affairs
Pol Q	Political Quarterly
Pub Admin	Public Administration
QB (or KB)	Queen's (or King's) Bench Division Reports
Stat LR	Statute Law Review
RSC	Rules of the Supreme Court
RTR	Road Traffic Reports
Sydney LR	Sydney Law Review
TC	Tax Cases
Tort L Rev	Tort Law Review
TLR	Times Law Reports
TSO	The Stationery Office (Her Majesty's Stationery Office)
U of NSWLJ	University of New South Wales Journal
U of Penn LR	University of Pennsylvania Law Review
WLR	Weekly Law Reports

I

Introduction: Getting our Bearings

1.1 WHAT IS ADMINISTRATIVE LAW ABOUT?

There is no universally accepted definition of what is meant by 'administrative law'. If you look at the main textbooks on the subject you will find that although quite a few topics are dealt with in all of them, there are some that are covered in one but not in another, that the common topics are organized in different ways from one book to another, and that they are discussed at different lengths by the various authors. You may also notice amongst the authors different approaches to what administrative law is about. Over the past twenty years, questions such as 'what should administrative lawyers do?' have been the subject of sometimes-acrimonious debates amongst scholars.[1] These debates are important not only as part of the history of scholarly thinking about law, but also because academics' writings may affect the intellectual and ideological climate in which public discussion and judicial thinking about administrative law take place. Scholars may have more immediate impact on the development of the law by participating in political and law-reform activities, and as a result of the citation of their writings by courts. The literature about different 'styles' of administrative law scholarship is not explicitly discussed in this book, partly to avoid its being too long, and partly because a reasonable grasp of administrative law—such as this volume is designed to impart—is a precondition of properly understanding that literature. However, in the spirit of the scholarly debates, this introduction sets out to explain what the book is—and is not—about.

Along with constitutional law, many people think of administrative law as part of 'public law'. This twofold division of public law (into constitutional and administrative law) is of no great significance. It is really just a matter of focus. Whereas constitutional law is concerned with the

---

[1] Key contributions to such debates are C. Harlow and R. Rawlings, *Law and Administration*, 1st edn (1984), chs 1–2; 2nd edn (1997), chs 1–5; M. Loughlin, *Public Law and Political Theory* (1992); B. O'Leary, 'What Should Public Lawyers Do?' (1992) 12 *OJLS* 404; P.P. Craig, 'What Should Public Lawyers Do? A Reply' (1992) 12 *OJLS* 564.

public domain in general, administrative law focuses on the day-to-day handling of public affairs particularly, but by no means exclusively, by what we call 'the executive branch of government'—i.e. Ministers, government departments, executive agencies,[2] local government, and so on. The qualification ('by no means exclusively') is very important, and it needs explanation.

In Britain, administrative law emerged as a distinct subject of study in the latter half of the twentieth century. The first edition of S.A. De Smith's *Judicial Review of Administrative Action* was published in 1959 and the first edition of H.W.R. Wade's *Administrative Law* was published in 1961. An important feature of these books was that rather than being organized around the functions of government—such as the provision of housing and social security, or the regulation of immigration and occupational health and safety—they focused on 'general principles' governing the exercise of governmental powers, such as the rules of natural justice (see 7.3.2) and doctrine of *ultra vires* (see 2.4). Studying government in what is sometimes called a 'sectoral' way inevitably involves focusing on relevant legislation and its day-to-day implementation by administrators. In contrast, the 'general principles' approach to administrative law is primarily court-focused. The general principles in question were made by judges, and they are primarily concerned not with the legislative framework and implementation of government programmes, but rather with the legal accountability of the agencies that run such programmes. Legislative regimes and their implementation continue to be studied sectorally—scholars research and write about immigration law, housing law, social security law, and so on. However, in the 1980s, a new brand of non-sectoral scholarship emerged dealing with 'regulation'. Administrative-law and regulation scholars have many interests in common. But unlike non-sectoral study of administrative law, regulation research is concerned at least as much with legislative frameworks and implementation of regulation as with accountability of regulators. The first texts on the 'general principles' of regulation were published in the 1990s.[3] One important topic that receives much more attention in the regulatory literature than in the administrative law literature is rule-making.[4] This emphasis on rule-making reflects concern with

---

[2] See 12.2.1.

[3] e.g. A.I Ogus, *Regulation: Legal Form and Economic Theory* (Oxford, 1994); R. Baldwin and M. Cave, *Understanding Regulation: Theory, Strategy and Practice* (Oxford, 1999).

[4] e.g. R. Baldwin, *Rules and Government* (Oxford, 1995); J. Black, *Rules and Regulators* (Oxford, 1997).

legislative frameworks and implementation of regulation as opposed to the accountability of regulators.

In the first English administrative law texts, the 'province' of administrative law was understood *institutionally* in terms, primarily, of the organs and agencies of central and local government. Administrative law was seen as concerned, above all, with judicial control (or 'review') of government decision-making. In the 1980s the Thatcher Conservative government initiated an ongoing process of constitutional and institutional reform involving, for instance, privatization of state-owned enterprises (such as the gas and electricity industries) and assets (such as council houses), promotion (and increased regulation) of industry self-regulation (in the financial services sector, for example),[5] contracting-out (or 'out-sourcing') of the provision of public services (such as garbage collection), and the subjection of government agencies (such as the National Health Service and Whitehall departments) to competitive and financial forces analogous to market pressures under which private businesses operate.

A common theme of many of these developments was the desirability of reducing direct government participation in social and economic life.[6] An obvious question raised by this reform agenda concerned the role of administrative law and the courts in the new world of what was compendiously called 'new public management' (NPM). What part would (and should) law and the courts play in controlling the performance of functions that had once been the province of central and local 'government' but which were now to be performed by non-governmental entities, subject only to a greater or lesser degree of supervision or regulation by government?

Coincidentally, at much the same time as these issues were bubbling to the surface, the House of Lords (in the famous *GCHQ* case[7]) held that decisions of central government were reviewable by the courts according to the principles of administrative law regardless of whether the power to make the decision was given by a statute or, on the contrary, was a 'prerogative' power—that is, a power inherited by central government

---

[5] Public regulation of private-sector self-regulation is sometimes called 'meta-regulation'.

[6] Reduction in direct participation has been accompanied by a large increase in indirect participation in the form of regulation, e.g. of the privatized utilities and of industry self-regulatory regimes. For a general account of the rise of the so-called 'new regulatory state' in Britain see M. Moran, *The British Regulatory State: High Modernism and Hyper-Innovation* (Oxford, 2003).

[7] *Council of Civil Service Unions v. Minister for the Civil Service* [1985] AC 374.

from the monarchy in its historical capacity as the executive branch of government. The basic principle underlying this decision was that the reviewability of decisions should depend not on the *source* of the power to make the decision—that is, statute or common law—but on the *substance* or *nature* of the decision. The question was whether the court was the constitutionally appropriate body to review the decision, and whether it was competent, by reason of its procedures and the qualifications of its members, to do so—in other words, whether the decision was 'justiciable'. The seeds of this definition of the scope of administrative law—in what have come to be called 'functional' terms—are probably to be found in an earlier decision of the Court of Appeal (in *ex p. Lain*[8]) in which it was held that decisions of the Criminal Injuries Compensation Board were amenable to judicial review even though the Criminal Injuries Compensation Scheme, which the Board administered, was not contained in either primary or secondary legislation.

The functional approach to the scope of administrative law provided the courts with legal resources for dealing with the constitutional developments initiated by the Thatcher regime. In the ground-breaking *Takeover Panel* (or *Datafin*) case[9] the issue was whether decisions of the City Panel on Takeovers and Mergers were subject to judicial review for compliance with administrative law. The Panel had no statutory or prerogative decision-making power; nor was the decision in question supported by any contractual arrangement between the Panel and the company affected by the decision (Datafin). The Panel's authority was accepted by the financial community generally, but it lacked any formal legal foundation. Equally importantly for present purposes, the Panel was not a government entity. It was set up by and for, and exercised authority over, private financial institutions. In essence, the Court held that the decisions of the Panel were subject to judicial review because the Panel was performing regulatory functions of public importance that significantly affected the interests of individuals, and because its activities were embedded in a framework of statutory regulation of the financial services industry (even though the Panel itself was not operating under a statute). If the Panel had not existed, it was likely that the government would have established a statutory body to do its work.

We can see, then, that within the space of about twenty years there was a fundamental change in the way the province of administrative law and

---

[8] *R v. Criminal Injuries Compensation Board, ex p. Lain* [1967] 2 QB 864.
[9] *R v. Panel on Takeovers and Mergers, ex p. Datafin Plc* [1987] QB 815.

judicial review was defined. In that time, the focus shifted from controlling the *institutions of (central and local) government* to controlling the exercise of *functions of governance* (whatever they may be) whether performed by government or non-government entities.[10] As we will see,[11] the functional approach has not swept all before it. The boundaries of administrative law are set by a messy combination of functional and institutional markers.[12] This is partly because the common law develops slowly: large paradigm shifts can be firmly cemented into the law only by the highest courts—and sometimes only by the higher court. 'Accidents of litigation' play a crucial role in this process.

But it may be that even if it had the opportunity, the House of Lords would not opt for a 'purely functional' definition of the scope of administrative law. A good way to explain this speculation is to look at the Human Rights Act 1998 (HRA). The HRA requires English courts, in various ways, to protect rights conferred by the European Convention on Human Rights (ECHR)—called 'Convention rights' in the HRA. Because the Convention is a treaty between nation-states, the rights it recognizes and the remedies it provides protect citizens against governments. Only states can be defendants to claims before the European Court of Human Rights (ECtHR), and the ECtHR can award remedies only against a State. In other words, only governments (widely defined)[13] are bound by the ECHR. Individuals and non-governmental entities are not bound.[14] In drafting s. 6 of the HRA, the British government tried to reproduce this feature of the ECHR. However, this task was greatly complicated by the constitutional changes already described.[15] The result is a compromise. Section 6 makes it unlawful for a 'public authority' to act incompatibly with a Convention right. Although 'public authority' is not comprehensively defined, s. 6 says two very important things about the term: first, that it 'includes a court or tribunal'; and secondly, that it 'includes any person certain of whose functions are functions of a public nature' but not 'in relation to' a 'private act'.

This rather opaque wording has been interpreted as creating two classes of public authorities called 'core public authorities' and 'hybrid

---

[10] An important set of essays on this topic is contained in M. Taggart (ed.), *The Province of Administrative Law* (Oxford, 1997).

[11] 3.2.2.

[12] J. Black, 'Constitutionalising Self-Regulation' (1996) 59 *MLR* 24.

[13] R. Clayton and H. Tomlinson, *The Law of Human Rights* (Oxford, 2000), para. 5.10.

[14] For an argument that they are (or should be) see A. Clapham, *Human Rights in the Private Sphere* (Oxford, 1993).

[15] See F. Klug, 'The Human Rights Act, *Pepper v. Hart* and All That' [1999] *PL* 246, 255–7.

public authorities' respectively.[16] The basic idea is that core public authorities are governmental entities, and hybrid public authorities are non-
governmental entities performing 'public functions'. Furthermore, s. 6
has been interpreted as meaning that core public authorities are bound by
the HRA in relation to both public and 'private' acts, whereas hybrid
public authorities are bound only in relation to performance of public
acts. Despite the wording of the section, there is a view[17] that the distinction between public and private functions and acts, and between core and
hybrid public authorities, is of no relevance to the scope of application of
the HRA because courts and tribunals are bound to act compatibly with
Convention rights. On this view, a court or tribunal must provide remedies for breaches of Convention rights regardless of whether a private
citizen or a government entity was allegedly responsible for the breach,
and regardless of whether the breach occurred in the course of performance of a public or a private function. However, this is a minority view in
the academic literature, and the relevant cases so far decided under the
HRA are not consistent with it.

Nor does the case law seem to be consistent with a purely functional
interpretation of the application of the HRA to hybrid public authorities.
According to the purely functional approach, the only question to be
asked in relation to an entity 'certain of whose functions are functions of
a public nature' is whether the act alleged to be incompatible with a
Convention right was 'public' or not.[18] If it was public, the HRA would
apply to it, and if it was private the HRA would not apply to it. On this
approach, any entity that performs a public function (or various public
functions) would be bound by the Act in relation to its public acts. This
leaves the question of how to distinguish between public and private
functions and acts. Under a purely functional approach, the answer to
this question would depend solely on the nature or substance of the
function and act in question. However, as we shall see in more detail
later,[19] the courts seem inclined to take a less pure, 'contextual' approach
according to which it is relevant to consider not only what was done but
also who did it. This difference of approach goes to the very heart of the

---

[16] *Aston Cantlow and Wilmcote with Billesley, Warwickshire Parochial Church Council v. Wallbank* [2003] 3 WLR 283; P. Cane, 'Church, State and Human Rights' (2004) 120 *LQR* 41.

[17] Espoused most notably by Sir William Wade: 'Horizons of Horizontality' (2000) 116 *LQR* 217.

[18] P.P. Craig, 'Contracting Out, the Human Rights Act and the Scope of Judicial Review' (2002) 118 *LQR* 551.

[19] See 3.2.2.

constitutional changes described earlier. One interpretation of these changes is that they were designed, at least in part, to free certain activities from control according to the rules and principles of 'public law' (including human-rights law) by transferring them from the public to the private sector. To give effect to this objective, it would be necessary for courts, in defining the scope of operation of public-law controls, to take account not only of what was being done but also of who was doing it. In order to reconcile the purely functional approach with recent constitutional changes, it is necessary to interpret them as motivated by (for instance) the assumption that certain public functions can be performed more 'efficiently' by the private sector, and not by a (legitimate) desire to reduce the reach of public-law controls. According to this approach, the fact that a public function is being performed by a non-governmental body is irrelevant to how its performance should be controlled because the choice between allocating the function to a governmental or non-governmental functionary is purely a matter of 'efficiency' and has nothing to do with 'accountability'.

This book is primarily concerned with the impact on decision-making of the rules and principles of administrative law, not the impact of human rights norms. The scope of application of administrative law may not be (and, perhaps, should not be) the same as that of s. 6 of the HRA. However, in both contexts, the distinction between public and private functions plays an important part: basically, the rules and principles of administrative law apply to the performance of public functions. For present purposes, it is not necessary to choose between the 'purely functional' and the 'contextually functional' approaches to the scope of administrative law (or the HRA). It now seems settled that the province of administrative law is to be defined in terms of some concept of public function. Whether a function is public or not may depend not only on the nature or substance of the function but also (as we will see) on the legal basis of the functionary's powers (statute or contract, for example) and on whether the functionary is or is not part of 'government'.

1.2 WHAT IS THIS BOOK ABOUT?

Our topic, then, is 'accountability' for the performance of public functions. Alternatives to the idea of 'accountability' include 'checking' 'controlling' and 'regulating'. The criteria of accountability with which we are primarily concerned are the rules and principles of administrative law. Most of these rules and principles have been made by, and typically are enforced by, courts.[20] The main mechanism by which the courts control public decision-making is called 'judicial review'. Judicial review is by no means the only form of accountability to which public decision-makers may be subject. Actions in tort, contract, and so on provide another form of 'legal' accountability, and there are various forms of 'non-legal' accountability (such as investigations by Parliamentary committees). The role and significance of judicial review cannot be understood without examining its relationship to such alternative methods of control.

Four important limits on the scope of this book should be noted. First, the court-focused definition of administrative law that is adopted here involves quite a narrow understanding of what counts as 'law'. Some people would define administrative law much more widely to include, for instance, norms developed and applied by what were just referred to as 'non-legal' accountability mechanisms; and to encompass many of the huge array and volume of rules and principles developed by public functionaries to regulate their own behaviour and that of other public functionaries—for instance, Treasury rules and guidelines concerned with public procurement.[21] From this perspective, judge-made administrative law is only the tiny tip of a huge iceberg of norms by which the performance of public functions is framed, influenced, guided, and regulated. This is a point that should be borne in mind when assessing the significance of courts in controlling the exercise of public functions.

Secondly, this book is mainly concerned with English administrative law[22] and with English governmental, legal, and political institutions; although some important issues arising out of Scottish and Welsh devolution will have to be considered. It is also impossible to give an adequate account of English administrative law without discussing the impact of European Community law, and this will receive attention at various points. Equally significant is the impact of the ECHR (via the HRA). Nevertheless, this is not a book on devolution, or on EC administrative law, or on human rights law, but on English administrative law.

---

[20] In Australia, these principles have been codified in the Administrative Decisions (Judicial Review) Act 1977 (Cth). See T.H. Jones, 'Judicial Review and Codification' (2000) 20 *LS* 517.

[21] C. Turpin, *Government Procurement and Contracts* (Harlow, 1989), pp. 64–5.

[22] In legal terms, 'England' means 'England and Wales'. Despite Welsh devolution, England and Wales constitute one 'legal system' (but see T.H. Jones and J.M. Williams, 'Wales as a Jurisdiction' [2004] *PL* 78). Northern Irish administrative law is essentially similar to English. Scottish administrative law is significantly different from English, especially in matters of procedure.

Thirdly, this book is primarily about administrative *law* and about public decision-making *institutions*. However, it should constantly be borne in mind that law and institutions provide only a framework for human activity and, in particular, for political activity. The reader should resist the temptation to treat the law merely as a set of rules and principles or as a set of institutional arrangements, and see it instead as providing a 'normative' framework within which the business of politics and governance is carried on.[23] You might want to think about administrative law as one—but only one—of various tools or techniques for regulating the conduct of public affairs.[24] Judicial review can also be viewed as a resource that may be used to achieve a range of objectives including dispute resolution and influencing public policy.[25]

Fourthly, it should always be remembered that control is a negative and parasitic activity. What citizens most expect of governments is that they should contribute to making society a good place to live. The primary role of laws and legal institutions is to assist the realization of this objective. Their function as tools for controlling government activity is only secondary.[26] It is often argued, for example, that legal controls on public decision-making (such as the requirement to follow certain procedures) may hinder the efficient and effective achievement of desirable social outcomes to such an extent as to cast serious doubt on their overall value. This argument rests on a false contrast because fair procedures in the conduct of public affairs are part of what makes a society a good place to live. Even so, there is a sound underlying point here, namely that however important the negative value of 'legality' might be, it does have costs as well as benefits, and it is not the ultimate justification for government.

---

[23] J. Dearlove, 'Bringing the Constitution Back In: Political Science and the State' (1989) 37 *Political Studies* 521.

[24] For more detailed discussion of the idea of administrative law as a regulatory tool see P. Cane, 'Administrative Law as Regulation' in C. Parker *et al.* (eds), *Regulating Law* (Oxford, 2004).

[25] T. Prosser, *Test Cases for the Poor* (London, 1983), esp. 76–82; C. Harlow and R. Rawlings, *Pressure Through Law* (London, 1992).

[26] C. Harlow and R. Rawlings, *Law and Administration*, 2nd edn (London, 1997), chs 2–4. The authors capture this insight in their famous distinction between red–light and green–light approaches to administrative law. The present book is in the red–light tradition. Studies in the green–light tradition ask how law can be and is used to achieve public objectives, and how it relates to and interacts with other techniques for promoting these objectives. The emphasis is on how law can assist the exercise of public power rather than control it.

1.3   AN IMPORTANT NOTE ON TERMINOLOGY

The 'functional turn' in defining the province or scope of administrative law has generated some terminological difficulties. The word 'government' now tends to be associated with the institutional approach (government is a set of 'public' institutions, not an activity) and has been replaced in the functional approach by the word 'governance'. In this book, the words 'government', 'governmental', 'the government', and so on will be used in the traditional institutional sense. These terms will not be used to describe functions. Instead functions (and decisions and acts and so on) will be referred to as either 'public' or 'private', the term 'public' referring to activities of governance. The terms 'organs ("institutions" and so on) of governance' or 'public functionaries' (or 'bodies' or 'authorities') will be used to refer collectively and generically to entities that perform public (i.e. governance) functions, whether the entities in question are governmental or non-governmental in the institutional sense.

1.4   THE PLAN OF THE BOOK

This book is divided into five parts. The first, and longest part, deals with judicial review.[27] Section 1 of that Part deals with the availability of judicial review, and the remedies and procedures of judicial review. Section 2 examines the 'grounds of judicial review'—i.e. the principles of administrative law which regulate the performance of public functions. Part II examines the law of tort, contract, and restitution as it applies to the performance of public functions. Of course, the aim of the analysis is not to give a detailed account of these areas of the law, but only to discuss what difference it makes that the defendant to a claim in contract, tort or restitution is a public functionary. Part III is concerned with information. Information is critical to accountability, whether legal or otherwise. It is impossible to call a person to account for their conduct without knowing what they have done. Two issues are central to the discussion in this part. First, in what circumstances can public functionaries refuse to disclose information about their activities on the ground that disclosure would not be in 'the public interest'; and secondly, when can citizens be prevented from, and sanctioned for, disclosing such information?

Part IV deals with certain non-judicial avenues for controlling public

---

[27] See 2.4 for a more detailed explanation of what judicial review is.

functionaries. One of the main functions of *Parliament* is to scrutinize the day-to-day conduct of public business. This we might call 'political accountability'. *Ombudsmen* set and enforce standards of 'good administration'. To understand the distinctive contribution of *tribunals* to the accountability process we need to distinguish between applying for 'review' of a decision and 'appealing' from that decision.[28] Tribunals are, basically, appellate bodies. In this Part, judicial review is put in context with other accountability mechanisms.

In Part V judicial control of the performance of public functions is set in a wider landscape. Three topics are discussed. First, we explore the relationship between administrative law and fundamental principles of constitutional design such as separation of powers and ministerial responsibility. Secondly, we look at some aspects of the relationship between law and legal institutions on the one hand, and the political system on the other. Thirdly, there is a discussion of the impact of judicial control on the behaviour of public functionaries.

1.5 THE DISTINCTION BETWEEN PUBLIC LAW AND PRIVATE LAW

Before going further, it is necessary to say something in general terms about the distinction between public law—of which administrative law and constitutional law are elements—and private law. As we have seen, the province of administrative law (and of public law more generally) has come to be defined in terms of the distinction between public and private functions, activities, and acts. The distinction between the public and private sectors of social life assumed an increasingly important role in European legal and political thought in the seventeenth and eighteenth centuries. In France (where it is deeply entrenched) the distinction between public law (governing activities in the public sector) and private law (governing activities in the private sector) is supported by an institutional structure of separate public law and private law courts that developed after the French Revolution.[29] The great Victorian jurist, A.V. Dicey, in his *Introduction to the Study of the Law of the Constitution*, first

---

[28] See 2.4.

[29] J. Allison, *A Continental Distinction in the Common Law: A Historical and Comparative Perspective on English Public Law* (Oxford, 1994); L.N. Brown and J.S. Bell, *French Administrative Law* (Oxford, 1998), ch. 3. Compare the distinction in English law between common law and equity which, until the nineteenth century, was supported by an institutional structure of separate sets of courts.

published in 1885, was strongly critical of the French system, mainly because of a fear that special rules applicable only to government, and different from those applicable to ordinary citizens, would inevitably work to the disadvantage of the latter. For this reason, he argued not only that government and citizen should be 'equal before the law', but also that 'the ordinary courts' should have jurisdiction over claims against government as well as claims against citizens.

Dicey's views had enormous influence on English lawyers and judges in the first half of the twentieth century.[30] As a result, a consciously articulated distinction between public law and private law did not begin to develop in England until the late 1970s when certain procedural changes were made[31] that led, by a long and circuitous route, to the establishment of a special public-law court—the Administrative Court— in 2001.[32] However, no sooner had this development begun than the Thatcher regime launched the programme of constitutional and economic reforms discussed in 1.1. These reforms destabilized the institutional distinction between the public and private sectors by involving non-governmental entities much more in the performance of functions that were identified with government.[33] This led many scholars to argue more or less strongly that the public/private distinction was no longer a helpful way of describing and explaining the organization of social and political life. As we have seen, the courts' response was not to abandon the distinction between public law and private law but rather to reconcep-

---

[30] Perhaps the most famous work in the Diceyan tradition, *The New Despotism* (1929), was written by the then Lord Chief Justice, Lord Hewart. The two most influential critiques of Diceyism were William Robson's *Justice and Administrative Law* (1928) and Ivor Jennings's *Law and the Constitution* (1933). For an accessible history of English administrative law in the twentieth century see J. Jowell, 'Administrative Law' in V. Bogdanor (ed.), *The British Constitution in the Twentieth Century* (Oxford, 2003).

[31] See 6.1.

[32] *Practice Direction (Administrative Court: Establishment)* [2001] 1 WLR 1654.

[33] It should not be thought that non-governmental entities played no significant part in governance before the Thatcher reforms. For instance, professional self-regulation is a centuries-old phenomenon, and there have long been various arrangements that we might now term 'public/private partnerships'. For example, the Board of Deputies of British Jews for many years played an important role in policing certain Sunday Trading laws (G. Alderman, 'Jews and Sunday Trading in Britain: The Private Control of Public Legislation' (1989) 8 *Jewish Law Annual* 221); and the Rowntree Trust (a private charitable organization) has for a long time administered the Family Fund (a public fund to assist families of severely handicapped children). The Thatcher reforms brought these issues to the surface partly because they involved large-scale rapid change and were based on a clearly enunciated ideology which was formulated in reaction to what were seen as excesses of the 'welfare state' (or the 'nanny state' as Margaret Thatcher was fond of calling it)—which was largely a twentieth-century phenomenon.

tualize the province of public law in terms of the distinction between public and private functions and acts: the fact that a function was being performed by a non-governmental entity did not mean that it was not a public function which ought to be performed in accordance with rules and principles of public (administrative) law. Public law, then, was law governing the performance of public functions, whether by government or non-government entities. (Conversely, in this framework private law is understood as law applying to private activities, whether engaged in by government or non-government entities.)

There is a view, propounded most notably by Dawn Oliver,[34] that the distinction between public law and private law is spurious, not because there is no distinction between public and private functions but rather because the principles that regulate public and private decision-making are essentially similar. Here is not the place to examine this claim in detail. There is no doubt that the courts recognize a body of rules and principles of 'administrative law' that are part of 'public law' as opposed to private law, and that apply to public functions but not private activities. Whether these rules and principles are or are not (at some level of generality) similar or identical to analogous rules and principles of 'private law' need not hinder our exploration of them. A question that does deserve attention, however, is why a distinction is drawn between public and private law, public law applying to public activities, and private law applying to private activities.

An obvious but not very informative reply to this question might be: because we want to regulate the performance of public functions in accordance with a different legal regime from that which regulates private activities. By way of explanation, it is possible to suggest a number of reasons for this. First, because institutions of governance have the job of running the country they must have some functions, powers, and duties which private citizens do not have; obvious examples are the waging of war and the issuing of passports. Secondly, because of the very great power governmental institutions can wield over its citizens (most particularly because government enjoys a monopoly of legitimate force), we may want to impose on them special duties of procedural fairness that do not normally apply to private citizens,[35] and special rules about what organs of governance may do and decide. Thirdly, because certain institutions of governance have a monopoly over certain activities and the provision of

---

[34] D. Oliver, *Common Values and the Public–Private Divide* (London 1999).
[35] e.g. *R v. Legal Aid Board, ex p. Donn & Co* [1996] 3 All ER 1.

certain goods and services, it might be thought that the exercise of such powers ought to be subject to forms of 'public accountability' to which the activities of private individuals are usually not subject.[36]

Fourthly, because the courts are themselves organs of governance (i.e. they perform public functions),[37] the view they take of their proper role when dealing with the exercise of public power is different from the way they view their role in relation to purely private matters. In relation to the affairs of private citizens the courts are the primary organs for interpreting, applying, and enforcing the law. By contrast, when they are dealing with matters involving other organs of governance the courts take a more restrained view of their role. Parliament is largely free of judicial control; and under the rules of administrative law other organs of governance enjoy a greater or lesser degree of autonomy from judicial control. This judicial restraint is partly a function of the doctrine of separation of powers, which will be considered in Chapter 20.

A fifth reason for distinguishing between public and private law arises out of the fact that although governments have certain distinctive functions (such as national defence), many of the things they do are also done by private citizens. Governments make (and sometimes break) contracts just as private individuals do; governments own property in the same way as private citizens; governments also sometimes commit torts. The relevant bodies of law—the law of contract, tort, and property—are central areas of private law, developed to regulate dealings between citizen and citizen. Should these regimes of private law apply equally to government contracts, government property, and government torts, or should there be a law of public contracts, public property, and public torts? As we will see in Part II, the answer which the courts have given to this question is neither an unqualified 'yes' nor an unqualified 'no'. There are, for example, some 'public law' rules of liability in contract and tort.

The argument against having a special public law of contract, tort, and so on was most famously put by Dicey.[38] In his view, it was a great strength of English law that government officials were subject to basically the same laws as private citizens to the extent that these covered the

---

[36] In economic terms, this is sometimes put by saying that when there is no possibility of 'exit' (i.e. choosing another supplier of a good or service) consumers/citizens should have a 'voice' about the way the good or service is provided. The possibility of exit is one of the hallmarks of a competitive market.

[37] Remember that courts and tribunals are included in the definition of 'public authority' in s. 6 of the HRA.

[38] *Introduction to the Study of the Law of the Constitution*, ch. 4.

activities of government.[39] In this way the law ensured that the government was given no unfair privileges or advantages over its citizens. An argument which pulls in the opposite direction is this: even when a government agency is, for example, making contracts, it is doing so in some sense as representative of the citizenry at large and must bear the interests of the community as a whole constantly in mind.[40] It might sometimes harm the public interest to subject government to rules designed to deal with cases in which the political responsibilities of government are not at issue. On the other hand, the government is a very powerful institution, and we may feel that private citizens need protection, in their dealings with government, against the operation of this power (even in the absence of abuse) by modification in their favour of the rules which govern the citizens dealings with other citizens when these rules are applied to dealings between citizen's and government. The distinction between public law and private law can, therefore, be used either to accord government special privileges, or to impose on it special responsibilities and duties and to subject it to special controls.

Three examples will illustrate the importance of whether a particular activity is regulated by public law or private law.[41] Take government contracting first. As a general rule, private individuals are free to refuse to buy goods or services from a business on the ground that the business has trading links with a country which is under the control of a government of which they disapprove. This follows from the principle that individuals are free to contract or not to contract with whomever they please. Do (and should) government bodies enjoy the same freedom? We will see in Chapter 12 that as a matter of common law, central government enjoyed the same freedom of contract as a private individual. However, now this freedom to contract is heavily circumscribed by rules based on EC law which, for all practical purposes, prohibit central government and

[39] Remember that Dicey was writing long before the functional turn in understanding the province of administrative law. He conceptualized the public/private distinction in institutional terms.

[40] A major theme of Oliver's book (n. 34 above) is to deny that public functionaries can have interests of their own distinct from the public interest that their function is designed to serve. Although Oliver apparently thinks that this supports her arguments against recognizing a distinction between public and private law, it seems to me to pull in precisely the opposite direction: it requires public functionaries to be treated differently from private citizens, who clearly are recognized by the law as having 'interests of their own'.

[41] Other good examples include *R v. Somerset County Council, ex p. Fewings* [1995] 1 WLR 1037 and *Wandsworth LBC v. A* [2000] 1 WLR 1246.

other 'organs of the state' from refusing to contract with someone for 'non-commercial' or 'non-economic' reasons.

Another illustration is provided by the police. The police, of course, have extensive powers of arrest; but these powers are not unlimited. In particular, a police officer can be sued for wrongful arrest and false imprisonment (which are forms of the tort of trespass to the person) if he or she arrests a person without a justification recognized by law. The application of the law of tort (which is, of course, part of private law) to the police is a reflection of the fact that constitutionally, police officers are not government officials but enjoy independence from the government of the day. On the other hand, police officers are not the same as private security guards, and they enjoy powers of arrest more extensive than those possessed by ordinary citizens. Apparently because of the public nature of policing activities, the House of Lords has held that in a tort action for false imprisonment the question, of whether the police acted reasonably in arresting a person suspected of having committed an arrestable offence, is to be judged according to public law principles of reasonableness.[42] The impact of this decision is to give the police greater freedom to arrest in the public interest and correspondingly to encroach upon the liberty of the individual. It is also clear that decisions and actions of the police can be challenged by way of judicial review.[43]

As a third example, consider the case of *Swain v. Law Society*.[44] The Law Society ran a compulsory liability insurance scheme for solicitors under statutory powers. The Society placed the insurance with commercial insurers and received commission for so doing. It decided not to pay out the sums received as commission to individual solicitors as a sort of dividend but to apply them for the benefit of the profession as a whole. Two solicitors challenged this decision but the House of Lords held that since, in administering the scheme, the Society was acting in a public capacity in the interests of all solicitors and members of the public who employed them, the legality of its decision was to be judged according to principles of public law, not private law; and so judged, what the Society had done was a proper use of its statutory powers. The question of

---

[42] *Holgate-Mohammed v. Duke* [1984] AC 437. For comment see M. Dockray, 'Arrest for Questioning?' (1984) 47 *MLR* 727.
[43] e.g. *R v. Metropolitan Police Commissioner, ex p. Blackburn* [1968] 2 QB 118; *R v. Chief Constable of Devon and Cornwall, ex p. Central Electricity Generating Board* [1982] 1 QB 438. On other ways of controlling the police see A.J. Goldsmith, *Complaints Against the Police: The Trend to External Review* (Oxford, 1991), esp. chs 1 and 5.
[44] [1983] 1 AC 598.

whether, as a matter of private law, individual solicitors were entitled to a pay-out, was irrelevant.

You may be able to think of other reasons for having a special regime of public law that applies to the performance of public functions by organs of governance. Some other reasons are discussed in Chapter 6 (which deals with the judicial review procedure) and Chapters 15 and 16 (dealing with access to information about the performance of public functions). The important point to grasp at this stage is that there is a connection between the reasons for drawing a distinction between public law and private law on the one hand, and defining the province of administrative law on the other. Remember that the scope of application of administrative law is defined in terms of the concept of a 'public function'. The courts have begun to elaborate this concept in the context both of claims under the HRA and of applications for judicial review and we will examine that case-law later.[45] Here it is sufficient to observe that functions do not come labelled as 'public' or 'private'. Nor is publicness like redness— a characteristic that can simply be observed. Rather the distinction between public and private functions is ultimately a political one. This can be appreciated by considering how, in different countries and at different times, the provision of health care, housing, education, and other 'essential' services such as electricity and transport, has been subject to varying degrees of public ownership and control. The 1980s witnessed a significant shifting of the boundary between the public and the private sectors in many Western countries. The precise nature of the shift varied from country to country. In Britain, for instance, sale of state-owned assets ('privatization') was prominent, while in the United States (where there was less direct government involvement in the productive economy) the shift from public to private mainly took the form of reducing government regulation of activities such as air transport ('deregulation'). In Britain, ironically, privatization of state-owned monopolies such as the gas, electricity, and water industries was accompanied by increased government regulation to protect consumers. Reduced public ownership has led to increased public regulation.

Ultimately, then, whether a function is public or not depends, in part at least, on a value judgment about whether its performance ought to be subject to control in accordance with public law principles. The answer to this question, in turn, depends in part on the reasons for drawing the distinction between public and private law. These reasons may vary

---

[45] See 3.2.2.

according to context. Because there are various reasons for distinguishing between public law and private law, there are various criteria for determining whether any particular function is public or not. All of these criteria are complex, and their application to particular cases in the context of litigation may require a court to make difficult and sometimes controversial judgments. The important point to make is that such judgments are not about whether particular functions are public or private but about whether accountability for the performance of particular functions should follow public law or private law rules and principles. Classification of functions as public or private follows this prior judgment about the appropriate accountability regime.[46]

1.6 THE 'GENERAL-PRINCIPLES' APPROACH TO ADMINISTRATIVE LAW

We noted in 1.1 that the emergence of administrative law as a separate topic of scholarly interest involved a shift from studying public law sectorally to studying principles of accountability applicable to most public functions. Of course, these general principles of accountability existed before this change of scholarly emphasis, but they tended to be studied in their application to some particular sector of public activity—such as public housing, or social security or immigration. Legal scholars who study law sectorally focus on the way law is used to implement and to control the implementation of public policy in relation to housing (for instance), or immigration or social security. Their interest in general principles of accountability for the way public power is exercised is subsidiary to this interest in the implementation of public policy and the contribution of law to the achievement of social goals in the sector in question.

These two different approaches are obviously not mutually exclusive. Even so, some people think that administrative law cannot be properly understood unless it is studied in relation to a particular sector of governmental activity. Only in this way, it is argued, is it possible to see how the general rules are used to deal with particular problems.[47] On the other hand, some people think that general rules, such as the rules of natural

---

[46] For further discussion see P. Cane, 'Accountability and the Public/Private Divide' in N. Bamforth and P. Leyland (eds), *Public Law in a Multi-Layered Constitution* (Oxford, 2003).

[47] For a theoretically subtle statement of this view see T.R.S. Allan, 'Doctrine and Theory in Administrative Law: The Elusive Quest for the Limits of Jurisdiction' [2003] *PL* 429.

justice (considered in Chapter 7), which apply across the whole range of administrative activities, can usefully be examined and discussed in their own right, and that doing so may illuminate larger questions of constitutional design better than sectoral studies can. An analogy may be drawn with study of contract law: books are written both on particular types of contract, such as contracts of agency or sale, and on the general principles of the law of contract. This book is based on the view that the general principles of judicial review of administrative action are worth studying in their own right. Indeed, judicial review is relatively so rare and sporadic that there are too few court decisions relating to most areas of government activity to establish a detailed code of judge-made regulation governing those activities. The chief importance of the cases is that they illustrate general principles. This does not mean that the particular context in which the general rules operate can be ignored, and sometimes it will be crucial (see e.g. 11.4). But there is much that can be usefully said about the way in which governmental activities generally are controlled by law, particularly when considering the relationships between different branches of government. One of the main assumptions underlying this book is that a rich understanding of public law generally, and of legal control of government in particular, requires attention to be paid to the interaction between the different branches of government.

Part I

Principles of Judicial Review

SECTION A: THE AVAILABILITY OF JUDICIAL REVIEW

The topics dealt with in this section are: the nature of judicial review (Chapter 2); the scope of judicial review (Chapter 3); who can make a claim for judicial review (Chapter 4); the remedies available in a claim for judicial review (Chapter 5); and the procedure for making judicial-review claims (Chapter 6).

2

The Nature of Judicial Review

2.I TWO FORMS OF JUDICIAL CONTROL

Legal control of the performance of public functions by the courts takes two main forms. Public functionaries, like citizens, are liable to be sued for torts, breaches of contract, breaches of trust, and so on.[1] The main heads of liability are dealt with in Part II. Most public functions are also subject to administrative law and judicial review. This is the main subject of Part I. Both of these forms of judicial control are basically retrospective—they are concerned primarily with cure (dispute resolution), not prevention (dispute avoidance). This is not to say that judicial enforcement of administrative law may not make a contribution to dispute avoidance—i.e. to securing future compliance with administrative law. This possibility is discussed in Chapter 20. However, it seems likely that if administrative law is to impose effective constraints on the exercise of public powers, most public functionaries must be prepared to comply with its demands most of the time regardless of the possibility that enforcement action may be taken if they do not comply. From this perspective, the most significant contribution courts make to controlling the performance of public functions is not *enforcing* rules and principles of administrative law but *making* them. So far as administrative law is concerned, courts are much more important as law-makers than as law-enforcers. Good training of public functionaries, sound management techniques, and careful in-house monitoring of performance are likely to be much more effective than judicial review in ensuring that public functionaries act lawfully.[2]

---

[1] Concerning the criminal liabilities of public functionaries see P. Cane, *Responsibility in Law and Morality* (Oxford, 2002), ch. 8, esp. paras 8.4.2 and 8.5.2.

[2] J. Mashaw, *Bureaucratic Justice* (New Haven, 1983).

2.2 FORMAL AND INFORMAL CONTROL

Judicial review, like nearly all of the techniques considered in this book for controlling government and redressing grievances are formal, institutionalized, and 'external' to the entity being reviewed. In one sense this presents a misleading picture because only a small fraction of complaints about the performance of public functions is handled through such channels. Many more complaints are dealt with more or less informally (and often much more cheaply and quickly) within the organization responsible for the decision in question as a result of a complaint by the aggrieved citizen,[3] or by some body on his or her behalf such as an MP,[4] local councillor, union, interest group, or other NGO.[5] Nevertheless, there are various reasons why the techniques discussed in this book are more important than the frequency of their use would suggest. First, because formal institutionalized procedures may attract more publicity than informal ones, the outcome of individual cases can influence the outcome of other complaints or potential complaints. Secondly, formal decisions about the legality or propriety of past action may influence the way public functionaries deal with similar cases in the future; and the threat of publicity may contribute further to the deterrent effect of formal complaints procedures. Thirdly, the respect in which the courts are held gives their decisions an influence out of proportion to the number of cases they deal with. This factor is particularly important in relation to what might be called 'high-profile' judicial review claims. By this I mean claims[6] that concern issues of wide public interest and, perhaps, of political controversy; that involve decisions made by (or close to) high-ranking elected members of elected government; and that are typically made by NGOs in pursuit of a political agenda rather than by individuals acting

---

[3] Such 'internal reviews' may be regulated by statute. For a valuable empirical study of internal reviews of homelessness decision-making see D. Cowan and S. Halliday, *The Appeal of Internal Review* (Oxford, 2003).

[4] P. Norton, ' *"Dear Minister . . ."*: The Importance of MP-to-Minister Correspondence' (1982) 35 *Parliamentary Affairs* 59; R. Rawlings, 'The MP's Complaints Service' (1990) 53 *MLR* 22 and 149.

[5] F.F. Ridley, 'The Citizen Against Authority: British Approaches to the Redress of Grievances' (1984) 37 *Parliamentary Affairs* 1; P. Birkinshaw, *Grievances, Remedies and the State*, 2nd edn (London, 1994), pp. 70–85. Even so, the number of judicial review claims has increased more than tenfold since 1977, to 4,372 in 2001.

[6] Such as *M v. Home Office* (see 5.2.5); *R v. Secretary of State for the Home Department ex p. Fire Brigades Union* (see 4.2.2) and *R v. Secretary of State for Foreign and Commonwealth Affairs ex p. World Development Movement* (see 4.2.2).

on their own behalf and in their own interests. The high prestige of the Administrative Court is essential for its ability to control the upper of echelons of government, especially central government.

Fourthly, because decisions of the courts are often elaborately reasoned and reported in law reports, they are crucially important in developing the concepts, principles and rules of administrative law. The courts do not hear a large number of cases, but they are the major source, apart from Parliament, of the law governing the performance of public functions. Legal rules are a very important part of the 'instructions' according to which public functionaries are required to exercise their powers. Legal rules are by no means the whole of the instructions—internal policy guidelines, for example, play a large part—but legal rules have distinctive importance because they are binding and authoritative in a way that other types of rules are not.

2.3 WHAT IS JUDICIAL REVIEW ABOUT?

Could a taxi driver be deprived of his licence to operate at Heathrow because of misconduct, without being given a chance to put his side of the story? Could parents force a local authority to keep schools open during a strike of ancillary workers? When is the Home Office entitled to change policy guidelines concerning the release of prisoners on licence, or the admission to Britain of immigrant children wanted for adoption here? Could the government ban union membership amongst civil servants working at its intelligence headquarters without consulting union leaders? Could Spanish owners of fishing vessels force the government to allow their vessels to fish in British waters pending a decision as to whether they were entitled to do so under European Community law? Could campaigners for the preservation of the remains of Shakespeare's Rose theatre challenge a decision not to register the remains as an historic monument? Could the government lawfully ban transmission of the voices of members of terrorist organizations? Could the Equal Opportunities Commission challenge an Act of Parliament on the ground that it was inconsistent with EC law? Could an individual worker do so? Could a trade union challenge a change in the rules under which compensation is paid to victims of crime? Could an interest group challenge a government decision to use some of the overseas aid budget to help build a dam in Malaysia? Could a resident of a nursing home prevent it being closed on the ground that she had been promised that it would be her 'home for life'?

These are just a few of the issues that have arisen in judicial-review claims that will be discussed in this book. They show how diverse and important are the matters with which the rules and principles of administrative law deal. Many judicial-review claims concern situations of immediate importance to ordinary people—for instance, whether the Home Office could prevent people buying a new TV licence, before their current one had expired, in order to avoid a licence fee increase; whether an immigrant will be allowed to enter Britain or will be sent back whence he or she came; whether a landowner will be allowed to build on their land. But many cases also raise constitutional and political issues of the most fundamental importance. For example, the case about criminal injuries compensation (mentioned above) concerned the relationship between the government and Parliament, and in particular whether the Home Secretary could introduce a non-statutory compensation scheme which was inconsistent with a statutory scheme which was on the statute book but which had never been brought into operation. In another case the question was whether a Minister of central government could be held to be in contempt of court for failing to comply with a court order. In the 1980s in particular there was a great deal of judicial review litigation concerning relationships between central and local government. Judicial review applications may raise issues about the impact of EC law and of the ECHR in the UK, and about the powers of the Scottish Parliament. And so on.

2.4 WHAT IS JUDICIAL REVIEW?

In a general sense, 'judicial review' refers to judicial control of public decision-making in accordance with rules and principles of administrative law.[7] These are examined in Section B of this Part. The mechanism for seeking judicial review in this sense is by making a 'claim for judicial

---

[7] In US law (for instance) a distinction is drawn between judicial review of primary (i.e. Parliamentary) legislation and judicial review of other public decision/rule making. Traditionally in Britain the courts have lacked the power to review primary legislation to ensure its compliance with some 'higher law'. Now, however, English courts can invalidate Parliamentary legislation that is inconsistent with EC law, and can make a declaration that Parliamentary legislation infringes Convention rights protected by the HRA. Judicial review of legislation is usually treated as an aspect of constitutional law, not administrative law. This distinction rests on a conception of the province of administrative law in terms of the threefold separation of governmental functions into legislative, executive (or 'administrative') and judicial, and an identification of the executive function with the executive branch of government. Because of what we might call 'the functional turn' in administrative law, in this book judicial review of primary legislation is treated as part of administrative law.

review' (CJR).[8] In Rule 54.1 of the Civil Procedure Rules (CPR) the claim
for judicial review is defined as 'a claim to review the lawfulness of (i) an
enactment; or (ii) a decision, action or failure to act in relation to the
exercise of a public function'. The reference to 'an enactment' establishes
the CJR as the mechanism for challenging primary legislation on the
grounds of inconsistency with EC law or incompatibility with a Convention right (under the HRA). CPR Part 54[9] contains a (but not the only)
procedure for making a CJR. It is called 'the judicial review procedure'
(JRP) and it is dealt with in Chapter 6. Most judicial review claims are
made by judicial review procedure, and these claims are made to the
Administrative Court, which is part of the High Court.[10] The next three
chapters are concerned with claims for judicial review.

The court's power of judicial review is sometimes referred to as its
'supervisory jurisdiction'. This jurisdiction is 'inherent'; that is to say, it
was not conferred on the courts by statute but was invented by the judges
themselves. Supervisory jurisdiction is to be contrasted with 'appellate
jurisdiction'. The common law (i.e. the courts) never developed mechanisms for appeals as we understand them today, and all appellate powers
are statutory in origin.

What are the main differences between appeal and review? The first
relates to the power of the court: in appeal proceedings the court may
substitute its decision on the matters in issue for that of the body appealed
from.[11] For example, if an appeal court thinks that the victim of a motor
accident has been awarded too small a sum of damages for injuries
inflicted by the defendant's negligence, it can increase the award. In
review proceedings, on the other hand, the court's basic power is to
'quash' the challenged decision, that is, to hold it to be invalid. If any of
the matters in issue have to be decided again, this must be done by the
original deciding authority and not by the supervising court. If the
authority was under a duty to make a decision on the matters in issue

---

[8] As we shall see, issues about whether a public functionary has complied with rules of
administrative law can also arise 'collaterally' in the course of other types of proceedings,
such as a criminal prosecution: see 6.6. A claim that a statute is incompatible with a
Convention right or with EC law may be made in any type of proceeding, as may a claim
that a public authority has acted incompatibly with a Convention right (HRA, s. 7(1)(b)).

[9] More accurately, CPR Part 8 as modified by CPR Part 54.

[10] *Practice Direction (Administrative Court: Establishment)* [2000] 1 WLR 1654. The
Administrative Court is the successor to the Crown Office List, an administrative arrange-
ment under which certain judges were nominated to hear judicial-review cases within the
Queen's Bench Division of the High Court.

[11] Unless the appeal takes the form of an application for a new trial in cases where the
proceedings under appeal were tried by jury.

between the parties, this duty will revive when the decision is quashed, and it will then be for the authority to make a fresh decision. It is also open to the court, in appropriate cases, to issue an order requiring the authority to go through the decision-making process again.

Another course open to the Administrative Court when it quashes the decision of a governmental body is to remit the matter to the agency with a direction to reconsider it in accordance with the findings of the Administrative Court.[12] The difference between this and the two previous outcomes is that under this procedure, the agency does not have to go through the whole decision-making process again. For example, it might be that all the relevant facts have already been ascertained and the findings of the Administrative Court concern only their legal significance. In that situation, a complete reconsideration of the case, including the taking of evidence and the finding of facts, would be a waste of time and money, and so the court can remit the case and direct the authority to reconsider the facts in the light of the law as laid down by the Administrative Court. This procedure is different from an appeal in only a very formal sense. On the other hand, remission would not be appropriate where, for example, the authority is found to have been biased.[13] Then a complete rehearing before a differently constituted body would be needed in order for justice to be seen to be done. The distinction between appeal and review is even harder to discern in cases in which the Administrative Court (under CPR Rule 54.19(3)) can itself remake the quashed decision 'if it considers that there is no purpose to be served by remission and the relevant statute allows it'. But it is not clear under what circumstances this power could appropriately be exercised.[14]

The second main distinction between appeal and review relates to the 'subject matter' of the court's jurisdiction. This distinction can be put briefly by saying that an appellate court has power to decide whether the decision under appeal was 'right or wrong', while a court exercising supervisory jurisdiction only has power to decide whether or not the decision under review was 'legal' (or 'lawful', as it is put in CPR Rule 54.1). If the decision is illegal it can be quashed; otherwise the court cannot intervene, even if it thinks the decision to be wrong in some respect. Conversely, if a decision is illegal—for instance, because the decision-maker did not follow proper procedures—it may be quashed

---

[12] CPR Rule 54.19(2); Supreme Court Act 1981, s. 31(5).
[13] See 7.3.2.1.
[14] A. Proops, 'The Substitutionary Remedy under CPR 54.19(3)' [2001] *JR* 216; J. Campbell, 'The Substitutionary Remedy under CPR 54.19(3)—A Response' [2002] *JR* 72.

even if the court thinks that the decision was right as a matter of law and fact. Discussion of the notion of illegality is made tricky by the fact that a number of different terms are used to convey the idea of illegality. The question of whether a decision was 'legal or not' is sometimes put in terms of whether it was made 'within or without jurisdiction' or whether it is *'intra vires'* or *'ultra vires'* (i.e. literally, 'within or beyond power').[15] *'Intra vires'* and *'ultra vires'* are widely used as synonyms for 'legal' and 'illegal' respectively. The concept of jurisdiction is much more difficult (see 9.6.1), and its use is perhaps best avoided since acting without jurisdiction is just one example of acting illegally.

Appeals to courts[16] constitute an important alternative to judicial review as a form of judicial control of public decision-making.[17] Very many statutes make provision for appeals from decisions of public functionaries.[18] Commonly, such appeals are limited to 'points of law', but they may extend further—to issues of fact, for instance. Also, the concept of 'error of law' has been given a very wide meaning that includes, for instance, making perverse or irrational findings of fact and ignoring relevant considerations (both of which are 'grounds' of judicial review). Indeed, it has been said that the powers of the county court under s. 204 of the Housing Act 1996 (creating a right of appeal on a point of law) are in substance the same as those of the Administrative Court in judicial

---

[15] Use of the term *'ultra vires'* is also complicated by the fact that it is used in a different and narrower sense in recent debates about 'the constitutional foundations of judicial review'. (Many of the main contributions to this debate are collected in C. Forsyth (ed.), *Judicial Review and the Constitution* (Oxford, 2000). A helpful brief statement of the opposing views can be found in P. Craig and N. Bamforth, 'Constitutional Analysis, Constitutional Principle and Judicial Review' [2001] *PL* 763.) In these debates, the *'ultra vires'* theory of judicial review is the view that the ultimate foundation of judicial review is the will or intention of Parliament, and that when a court holds a decision to be illegal it is giving effect to the will of Parliament. Contrasted with the *ultra vires* theory is the 'common law' theory which finds the foundation of judicial review in the concept of the rule of law.

[16] Concerning appeals to tribunals see 18.2.

[17] For instance, in the area of homelessness decision-making by local authorities, a right of appeal to the county court on a point of law was introduced by s. 204 of the Housing Act 1996. Before that, decisions of local authorities under the homelessness legislation could only be challenged by a claim for judicial review. Between January 1987 and March 1991, 35 per cent of all judicial review claims against local authorities related to homelessness decisions: L. Bridges, G. Meszaros, and M. Sunkin, *Judicial Review in Perspective* (London, 1995), 44.

[18] See Law Commission Consultation Paper 126, *Administrative Law: Judicial Review and Statutory Appeals* (1993), ch. 18; Law Com. No. 226, *Administrative Law: Judicial Review and Statutory Appeals* (1994), Part XII.

review proceedings.[19] It has also been said that there is normally little practical difference between a 'full appeal' (in which the court can reconsider the whole case from scratch)[20] and an appeal on a point of law.[21] These points, added to the fact that an appeal court may (as under s. 204 of the Housing Act) have power to quash—as well as to 'confirm or vary'—the decision under appeal, might lead us to the conclusion that the most important difference between appeal and review lies not in the power of the court or the subject matter of the jurisdiction, but more prosaically in the court's identity: claims for judicial review are the business of the Administrative Court whereas appeals will go to some other court such as the county court.[22] Because all rights of appeal are statutory, creation of a right of appeal provides a means by which the legislature can restrict the availability of judicial review: if there is a right of appeal, a claimant will normally be required to exercise it rather than making a claim for judicial review. In this way, the resources and expertise of the Administrative Court can be reserved for cases in which they are most appropriate and needed.

2.5 THE IMPORTANCE OF REMEDIAL LAW

It may surprise the reader that the availability of judicial review is being discussed before the grounds on which decisions may be reviewed. The reason for this is that the law of judicial review is more 'remedies-oriented' than private law. In contract or tort, for example, the first question to be asked is whether the claimant has suffered some legally recognized wrong at the hands of the defendant. Only if such a wrong has been suffered is it worthwhile considering what, if any, remedy would be suitable or available. On the other hand, it is necessary for the applicant for judicial review from the start to give at least as much attention to questions of remedies as to the question of whether the respondent has committed a legal wrong. An applicant for judicial review may lose the case no matter how sound it might be as a matter of substantive (as opposed to remedial) law if, for example, he or she pursues the wrong

---

[19] *Nipa Begum v. Tower Hamlets LBC* [2000] 1 WLR 306; cited with approval in *Runa Begum v. Tower Hamlets LBC* [2003] 2 WLR 388 at [7] *per* Lord Bingham of Cornhill and [98] *per* Lord Millett.

[20] Or 'by way of rehearing'.

[21] *Runa Begum* [2003] 2 WLR 388 at [47] *per* Lord Hoffmann; [99] *per* Lord Millett.

[22] However, the distinction between appeal and review may be important in relation to Art. 6 of the ECHR: see 7.3.2.1.

procedure for seeking a remedy or does not satisfy the rules of standing (see Chapter 4). What is the explanation for this emphasis on remedial law? One possibility is the following. Private law primarily concerns the rights and obligations of citizens against and towards one another. So it is clear that private citizens are the proper persons to 'enforce' private law. At the other end of the scale, although in many cases it is open to private individuals to prosecute for breach of the criminal law, for various reasons, it is usually thought best for public prosecutors to take such action. When it comes to ensuring that public functionaries act in accordance with the rules and principles of administrative law, we find some uncertainty about how the law ought to be enforced. Should private individuals be given a remedy through the courts, or should it, rather, be left to some public official, such as the Attorney-General, or to Parliament or an ombudsman, or to someone within government itself, to supervise the activities of public functionaries? For a long time English law embodied the idea that the rights of individuals to challenge governmental action should be quite limited.[23]

The idea that it is particularly appropriate that control of 'inferior' public bodies and officers should be in the hands of government is reflected in the history of what are now called 'quashing orders', 'prohibiting orders', and 'mandatory orders' but which, until recently, were known as the 'prerogative orders', (and before that the prerogative 'writs') of (respectively) *certiorari*, prohibition, and mandamus.[24] These remedies were called 'prerogative' because the function of controlling the exercise of governmental authority was initially 'regarded as a royal prerogative'.[25] For this reason, the title of applications for prerogative orders took the form: *R* (*Regina*, the Crown, the nominal claimant) *v. A* (defendant) *ex p.* (on behalf of) *B* (the real claimant). This was nothing but form because the real claimant initiated the proceedings for a prerogative order, conducted them in their entirety, and was liable for the costs of the action. However, the form did serve as a reminder of uncertainty about the extent to which private citizens are the most appropriate persons to initiate action in the courts to challenge public

---

[23] There is an interesting discussion of this issue by McHugh J in *Bateman's Bay Local Aboriginal Land Council v. The Aboriginal Community Benefit Fund Pty Ltd* (1998) 194 CLR 247, 275–80.

[24] J.H. Baker, *An Introduction to English Legal History*, 4th edn (London, 2002), pp. 143–50. For more detail about these remedies see Ch. 5 below.

[25] Baker, *Introduction to English Legal History*, p. 143.

decision-making. This uncertainty remains in the title of applications for quashing, prohibiting and mandatory orders: *R. (A) v. B*, A being the real claimant.

This uncertainty about the appropriateness of 'private enforcement' of administrative law is also reflected in the requirement that a litigant who makes a claim for judicial review under CPR Part 54 must first seek 'permission' from the court to do so. The alleged function of this requirement is to protect public functionaries from harassment by citizens bringing cases that have no reasonable chance of success.[26] The defendant does not have to take part in permission proceedings. In a private law action, by contrast, it is for the defendant to take action to have the claimant's case struck out if it is without substance. The permission procedure focuses attention on remedies (more than on the merits of the claimant's case) because the 'permission' is to apply for a remedy. Another factor which draws attention to remedies is that all judicial review remedies are discretionary.[27] There are principles governing the exercise of the discretion whether or not to award a remedy, but no public law litigant can afford to ignore the fact that usually there is no right to the remedy sought, however strong their case may be on its merits.

[26] See further 6.2.   [27] See further 5.4.

3

The Scope of Judicial Review

3.1 DEFENDANTS

As we saw in Chapter 1, the scope of judicial review is defined in terms of the concept of 'public function'. The origins of this definition of the scope of administrative law can be found in *ex p. Lain*[1] (1967) in which it was held that the Criminal Injuries Compensation Board (CICB) had to comply with administrative law (or, in other words, was subject—or 'amenable'—to judicial review) essentially because the function it was performing was very similar to the (public) function performed by courts of law when they award damages in tort for personal injuries. In the landmark *Takeover Panel* case[2] in 1987 it was held that the City Panel on Takeovers and Mergers was amenable to judicial review because it was exercising a public function or a power with a public element. The CICB was a non-statutory public body whose powers derived from 'the prerogative'. The Takeover Panel was a private body whose powers did not derive from statute, the prerogative, or contract. Indeed, it was said that the Panel 'lacked visible means of legal support'. It exercised '*de facto*' (as opposed to '*de iure*') power merely as a result of the acquiescence of those subject to its decisions. These cases establish the general principle that the amenability of a body (whether public or private) to judicial review depends neither on the body's identity or status, nor on the source of its power, but rather on the nature of the functions it performs. This general principle must, however, be qualified in at least four ways.

First, although it is a public body and exercises public functions, the High Court is not subject to judicial review.[3] An obvious explanation for this is that it is the High Court that invented and exercises judicial review jurisdiction. Technically, the rule can be explained by saying that the

---

[1] *R v. Criminal Injuries Compensation Board ex p. Lain* [1967] 2 QB 864.
[2] *R v. Panel on Takeovers and Mergers ex p. Datafin Plc* [1987] QB 815.
[3] *R v. Visitors of the Inns of Court ex p. Calder* [1994] QB 1. The Crown Court is not subject to judicial review in respect of 'matters relating to trial on indictment' (Supreme Court Act 1981, s 29(3)). R. Ward, 'Judicial Review and Trials on Indictment: Section 29(3) of the Supreme Court Act 1981' [1990] *PL* 50.

High Court is a 'superior' court of unlimited jurisdiction. In theory, the purpose of judicial review is to police limits of power (or jurisdiction). So 'inferior' courts of limited jurisdiction (such as magistrates' courts and the county court) are subject to judicial review, but the High Court is not. The standard procedure for challenging decisions of the High Court is by way of appeal to the Court of Appeal and the House of Lords.

A second qualification to the basic principle about the scope of judicial review relates to Parliament. Traditionally, in accordance with the constitutional doctrine of Parliamentary sovereignty (or 'supremacy'), Parliamentary (that is, 'primary') legislation is not subject to judicial review because—despite the fact that Parliament is, of course, a public body performing public functions—there are no *legal* limits to the legislative power of Parliament. Courts interpret and apply legislation, but they cannot question its legal validity. As a result of Britain's membership of the EU, this traditional rule is now subject to an important exception: Parliamentary legislation that is inconsistent with EC law is subject to being invalidated by an English court. There is a second exception to the traditional rule. For the purposes of s. 6 of the HRA, Parliament is not a 'public authority'[4] that must act compatibly with Convention rights. However, under s. 4 of the HRA, certain courts have power to make a 'declaration of incompatibility' in relation to a provision of primary legislation that is judged to be incompatible with a Convention right. Such a declaration 'does not affect the validity, continuing operation or enforcement of the provision in respect of which it is given' (HRA s. 4(6)(a)),[5] but it does establish that the provision is inconsistent with the 'higher law' contained in the ECHR, and in that limited sense 'illegal'.

A third qualification to the general principle about the scope of administrative law relates to the proposition that the source of a body's power is irrelevant to whether its decisions are subject to judicial review. In particular, there is considerable confusion about the amenability to judicial review of bodies whose existence and powers are based on a contract. Typical examples of such bodies are trade unions and trade associations. On the one hand, it has been held that such a body may be subject to administrative law principles in its dealings with a party to the

---

[4] Indeed, neither House of Parliament (whether acting in a legislative capacity or not) is a public authority; nor is any 'person exercising functions in connection with proceedings in Parliament'.

[5] It is for the government to decide what to do about the legislation in the light of the declaration: HRA s. 10.

empowering contract, such as an officer of a trade union;[6] and also in dealings with an individual who wishes to become a party to the empowering contract, such as an applicant for a horse-trainer's or boxing licence.[7] The basis of such decisions is that bodies of this sort exercise great, and often monopoly, power over some area of social or economic activity in which not only participants in the activity but also the wider public have an interest. On the other hand, in several cases it has been held that bodies which derive their existence and powers from a contract are not amenable to judicial review, at least at the suit of parties to that contract.[8] The basis of these decisions appears to be that the effect of the contract is to make the conduct of the body a matter to be judged purely by principles of private (contract) law,[9] even if the body operates within a statutory framework and is subject to a public regulatory regime.[10] Julia Black argues that decisions such as this rest on a failure to distinguish between contract as 'an instrument of economic exchange' and as 'an instrument of governmental or non-governmental organisation and regulation'.[11] She thinks that if a body exercises 'regulatory power', its exercise of that power should be subject to judicial review regardless of its source—whether in statute, the prerogative or a contract—because regulation is a public function. But the law has not yet got to the point where the source of power is completely irrelevant to its classification as public or private.

The fourth qualification relates to a very important difference between the scope of judicial review and the scope of s. 6 of the HRA. Whereas the scope of judicial review is defined in terms of the concept of a 'public function', the scope of s. 6 is defined in terms of the concept of a 'public

---

[6] *Stevenson v. URTU* [1977] 2 All ER 941.

[7] *Nagle v. Fielden* [1966] 2 QB 633.

[8] *R v. Disciplinary Committee of the Jockey Club ex p. Aga Khan* [1993] 1 WLR 909; *R v. Lloyd's of London ex p. Briggs* [1993] 1 Lloyd's Rep 176; *R v. Football Association ex p. Football League* [1993] 2 All ER 833; *R v. Panel of the Federation of Communication Services ex p. Kubis* (1999) 11 Admin LR 43.

[9] It appears, for instance, that admission and exclusion decisions made by State schools are amenable to judicial review, but that such decisions made by private schools are not: *R v. Governors of Haberdashers' Aske's College Trust ex p. Tyrell* [1995] ELR 350; *R v. Muntham House School ex p. R* [2000] LGR 255; unless the decision was made in relation to admission under the statutory 'assisted places scheme': *R v. Cobham Hall School ex p. S* [1998] ELR 389.

[10] *R v. Fernhill Manor School ex p. Brown* (1992) 5 Admin LR 159. In other words, the fact that the performance of a function is subject to a public regulatory regime does not make it a public function. Where the function that is subject to a regulatory regime is itself a regulatory function, the regime may be referred to as 'meta-regulation'—that is, regulation of regulation.

[11] J. Black, 'Constitutionalising Self Regulation' (1996) 59 *MLR* 24, 41–2.

authority'. There are two types of public authorities: core public author-ities and hybrid public authorities. A hybrid public authority is an entity certain of whose functions are public functions. Hybrid public authorities are covered by s. 6 only in relation to performance of their public acts and not in relation to 'private acts'. Core public authorities, by contrast, are covered in relation to both their public and their private acts. In other words, core public authorities must act compatibly with Convention rights in all their activities, whether public or private. The distinction between core and hybrid public authorities is not part of the law of judicial review outside the HRA context. Non-HRA judicial review applies and applies only to the performance of public functions, regardless of who the defendant is.

3.2 REVIEWABLE DECISIONS AND ACTS

3.2.1 THE DISTINCTION BETWEEN DECISIONS AND ACTS

Both decisions and acts can be illegal in a public law sense, and in this respect there is no particular reason to distinguish between them. But the distinction between acting and deciding to act can be important from the point of view of available remedies. If a public functionary has decided to do an act which is allegedly illegal but has not yet done it then, of course, the claimant will want to challenge the decision so as to obtain an order to quash the decision or instructing the functionary not to carry out its decision. If the functionary has decided not to perform some duty, the claimant will often be satisfied with an order requiring it to act. If the functionary has already acted and the act can be easily undone, the claim-ant can challenge the decision to act and seek an order requiring the functionary to undo its action. For example, if a local authority has granted planning permission to A but building has not yet started, B might be able to get the permission revoked. But if the authority's decision has inflicted irreparable damage on the claimant—for example, if the authority had the claimant's house pulled down in pursuance of an invalid demolition order—the remedies of public law will be much less satisfactory for the applicant. Judicial-review remedies will enable the illegality of the order to be established; but, unless the claimant can take advantage of some statutory provision for compensation (such as s. 8 of the HRA), an entitlement to damages in private law will have to be shown if the damage is to be made good by monetary compensation. Judicial review remedies are not of much use to the citizen who has suffered actual injury (whether physical or economic) as opposed to one who has an intangible grievance.[12]

3.2.2 PUBLIC FUNCTIONS

A decision (or act) is subject to judicial review if it was made (or done) in exercise of a public function. (Conversely, private decisions (and acts)—made (or done) in exercise of private functions—are not subject to judicial review.) This was established in the *Takeover Panel* case,[13] which concerned a private body that regulated commercial takeover activity in the City of London under what is often called 'a scheme of industry self-regulation'. But what is a public function? In relation to non-governmental agents, this question has been answered in two different ways.[14] One answer is that a function is public if the government would make provision for its exercise if it was not being performed by the functionary in question.[15] The other answer is that a function is public if the functionary operates as an integral part of a public statutory scheme of regulation or service provision.[16] Both factors were taken into account in the *Takeover Panel* case: the government had apparently made a conscious decision to encourage the setting up of the Panel, and the Panel operated against the background of a network of statutory provisions relevant to its activities. It will be noticed that neither criterion refers specifically to the nature of the function being performed or the substance of the decision being challenged. Rather, both direct attention to the context within which the function was being performed.

In terms of a distinction introduced in 1.1, we can say that both criteria provide a contextually functional, as opposed to a purely functional, approach to defining the scope of administrative law. In a contextually functional approach, certain factors other than the nature or substance of the function in question can be taken into account in deciding whether the function is public or not. The distinction between the purely and contextually functional approaches has been brought into sharp focus by recent cases arising in two distinct areas: s. 6 of the HRA (in which the definition of 'public authority' includes 'any person certain of whose

---

[12] On the question of whether there ought to be more public-law compensation remedies see 5.5.1.

[13] [1987] QB 815.

[14] Black, 'Constitutionalising Self Regulation' (1996) 59 *MLR* 24, 41–2.

[15] e.g. *R v. Chief Rabbi of the United Hebrew Congregations of Great Britain and the Commonwealth ex p. Wachmann* [1992] 1 WLR 1036.

[16] e.g. *R v. Disciplinary Committee of the Jockey Club ex p. Aga Khan* [1993] 1 WLR 909 *per* Hoffmann LJ.

functions are functions of a public nature'; and CPR Part 54 (dealing with judicial review procedure) which applies to claims 'to review the lawfulness of . . . a decision, action or failure to act in relation to the exercise of a public function' (amongst others). The cases in question concern functions central to 'the welfare state' as it was developed in Britain after the Second World War, such as the provision of residential accommodation for the aged (*Servite Houses, Leonard Cheshire*),[17] of public housing (*Poplar*)[18] and of hospitals (*Partnerships in Care*).[19] *Poplar* is perhaps the most important of these cases in terms of the principles it contains. Tower Hamlets Council set up a housing association (a non-governmental entity) in order to transfer to it a substantial proportion of the Council's stock of public housing. Tenants of the association included people to whom the council owed a statutory obligation to provide housing. The issue in *Poplar* was whether the association was exercising a public function (for the purposes of the HRA) when it issued proceedings to obtain possession of a property on the basis that the council no longer owed the occupant a statutory housing obligation and the property was required for other purposes.

The Court of Appeal rejected a purely functional approach to this issue: providing accommodation for rent—even for the underprivileged—was not, by its nature, a public function. The Court apparently accepted that performance by the council of its statutory housing obligations was a public function (for the purposes of the HRA). But it did not follow that provision of housing by a private property owner to persons owed such an obligation by the council was a public function,[20] even if the private provider was a non-profit charitable organization,[21] and was subject to a regime of public regulation (as providers of 'social

---

[17] *R v. Servite Houses ex p. Goldsmith* [2001] LGR 55; *R (Heather) v. Leonard Cheshire Foundation* [2002] 2 All ER 936.

[18] *Poplar Housing and Regeneration Community Association Ltd v. Donoghue* [2002] QB 48.

[19] *R (A) v. Partnerships in Care Ltd* [2002] 1 WLR 2610.

[20] This was the conclusion reached (reluctantly) by the judge in *Servite*. In *R (A) v. Partnerships in Care Ltd* the claimant was detained under statute in a private psychiatric hospital. It was held that in changing the nature of the care provided, the hospital authorities were exercising a public function because statutory obligations for the care of patients were imposed directly on the hospital.

[21] As in *Leonard Cheshire* where the Court of Appeal held that provision by a large charity of residential care for the disabled was not a public function even in relation to persons to whom a local authority owed a statutory obligation to provide accommodation at public expense.

welfare' services typically are).[22] Nevertheless, the Court decided that the association's act in seeking possession of the property was public because its activities were 'closely enmeshed with' and 'assimilated to' the public housing functions of the council.

Various aspects of the institutional context in which the association operated were referred to by the Court in support of this decision: the association was set up by the council to own and manage the housing stock; five members of its board were also members of the council; the occupant was a sitting tenant at the time the property was transferred to the association; the act in question was 'authorized by statute'. Such a 'multi-factor' approach recognizes the institutional complexity of many of the arrangements under which welfare and other social functions are performed.

This decision can be contrasted with that in *Servite*, in which a local authority arranged to fulfil its statutory obligation to house old people by contracting-out the provision of accommodation to the proprietor of a private residential home rather than by providing accommodation itself. The issue was whether the proprietor's decision to close the home was amenable to judicial review under CPR Part 54.[23] The judge held that it was not, because the proprietor was entitled to close the home under the terms of its contract with the local authority, which gave no rights to the claimants. In *Leonard Cheshire* the Court of Appeal took the view that the scope of application of the HRA and the scope of judicial review are not necessarily the same.[24] It may be, for instance, that the technique of contracting-out is more effective to exclude administrative law controls than to exclude human rights norms. However, there are too many factual differences between *Servite* and *Partnerships in Care* (which deal with the scope of judicial review) on the one hand, and *Poplar* and *Leonard Cheshire* (which deal with the scope of the HRA) on the other to enable anything more to be said with confidence about this. We do not yet know what view the courts will take of the policy considerations respectively

---

[22] The principle that a function is not public merely because its performance is subject to a regime of public regulation is particularly important in relation to privatization of utilities, which was accompanied by the establishment of strong statutory regulatory regimes.

[23] In *Hampshire CC v. Beer* [2003] EWCA Civ 1056 the CA took an approach to this issue very similar to that taken in *Poplar* to the reach of human rights law. It was held that a decision to exclude a trader from a public market, made by a private company established by a local authority to run markets, was amenable to judicial review. The scope of application of Part 54 is strictly a different issue from the scope of administrative law because it is not only in claims for judicial review under Part 54 that administrative law may be applicable. However, these two issues are generally not distinguished in the cases.

[24] See also *Aston Cantlow and Wilmcote with Billesley Parochial Church Council v. Wallbank* [2003] 3 WLR 283 at [52]–[55] *per* Lord Hope and [87] *per* Lord Hobhouse.

relevant in the two contexts.[25] What we can say, however, is that the courts have refused to treat contracting-out simply as a mechanism for the provision of *public* services and the performance of *public* functions. Rather, they have interpreted it (like privatization) as motivated partly at least by a policy of reducing the reach of public forms of accountability and, thus, itself relevant to the task of classifying functions as public or private. There may legitimately be disagreement about whether this approach is desirable or not. But if one believes that courts, in developing the common law, should be sensitive to legislative policies, the position they have taken is certainly defensible.[26]

Three other points deserve to be made by way of comment on these cases. First, it will be noticed that they all adopt the 'integration' criterion of publicness (was the function integral to, or enmeshed in, or assimilated to, a public statutory scheme of regulation or service provision?) rather than the 'necessity' criterion (would the government make provision for the performance of the function if it was not being performed by the respondent?). It should not be concluded from this that the necessity criterion has been abandoned in favour of the integration criterion. The integration criterion was appropriate in these cases because in all of them a governmental body owed a statutory obligation to the applicant to provide the service that the respondent was delivering. But the necessity criterion might, for instance, be relevant to classifying as public or private a service (such as one provided by a private/privatized utility company) that no governmental body has a statutory obligation to provide to citizens.

The second point is that no matter what criterion of publicness is adopted, its application in any particular case will usually involve the court in making a judgment about the desirable scope of administrative law. This is obviously true of the purely functional criterion. Functions are not public or private as a matter of their inherent nature, but because we choose to treat them as such for various purposes. A good illustration of this point is provided by a case in which the London Borough of Greenwich sought to challenge by judicial review the distribution by the government of a leaflet explaining the poll tax. The Borough argued that

---

[25] It is important to note that in determining the scope of s. 6 the HRA (but not of judicial review), English courts are required to take account of relevant decisions of the ECtHR. Article 34 of the ECHR prevents 'governmental organisations' from complaining of infringements of the Convention. As a result, the scope of human-rights law has a stronger institutional flavour than the scope of judicial review.

[26] For a contrary view see Paul Craig, 'Contracting Out, the Human Rights Act and the Scope of Judicial Review' (2002) 118 *LQR* 551.

the leaflet was inaccurate and, therefore, that its distribution was illegal.[27] The court decided that the leaflet was not sufficiently misleading to justify finding in the Borough's favour; but implicit in the court's decision is a holding that the court had jurisdiction to decide the issue of legality— in other words, that the decision to distribute the leaflet was amenable to judicial review. This aspect of the case provoked a vigorous correspondence in *The Times*.[28] Some argued, in effect, that the decision to distribute was not subject to judicial review because the distribution of information is not a public function but one which any individual is entitled to do. Against this, it was argued that government bodies which use public money to provide information to the public are under a special public law obligation to ensure that the information is accurate; and this obligation, being a public law one, was properly enforceable by judicial review.[29]

Application of contextually functional criteria of publicness also requires a value judgement about the scope of administrative law. Integration can take various forms and is, anyway, a question of degree. There is no objective or mechanical test of how integrated into a public statutory scheme a function must be in order to qualify as public. Normally, too, there will be no conclusive evidence relevant to answering the hypothetical question whether the government would provide for the performance of a particular function if it was not already being performed by a non-governmental organization. Ultimately, the court must decide whether the performance of the function *should* be subject to administrative law controls.

A third point to make concerns what it means to say that the performance of a function is subject to administrative law controls. As we will see in Section B of this Part, administrative law contains various rules and principles that provide resources for judicial control of public functionaries. We will also see that being subject to administrative law does not always mean being subject to all of those rules and principles. For instance, courts are generally more willing to control the procedure of public decision-making than the substance of public decisions; and in general, they are more willing to control public decision-making in the name of legality than of rationality. In some contexts, courts are more

---

[27] *R v. Secretary of State for the Environment ex p. Greenwich LBC*. Noted by C.R. Munro, 'Government Advertising and Publicity' [1990] *PL* 1, 7–8.

[28] 18, 20, 25, 26, 27 May 1989.

[29] For a similar debate about the disciplinary functions of universities see H.W.R. Wade, 'Judicial Control of Universities' (1969) 85 *LQR* 468; J. Garner, 'Students: Contract or Status?' (1974) 90 *LQR* 6.

willing to control decision-making by unelected than by elected bodies; and in general they exercise less control over central government than over other public bodies. In other words, administrative law is not an indivisible package of controls which either applies in its entirety or not at all. Moreover, the demands that the various rules and principles of administrative law impose on public functionaries may vary according to the identity of the functionary in question and to the circumstances in which the function is being performed. Such flexibility in the law allows account to be taken of institutional complexity in arrangements for the performance of social functions. In the *Takeover Panel* case, for instance,[30] the Court of Appeal combined its holding that the Panel was amenable to judicial review with a context-sensitive approach to the application of the various heads of judicial review to decisions of the Panel.[31]

Although for most purposes the concept of 'public function' serves well enough to define the scope of judicial review, there are some qualifications and complications that need to be noted. It is to these that we now turn.

3.2.3 LEGISLATIVE, ADMINISTRATIVE, AND JUDICIAL FUNCTIONS

The institutions of government are traditionally divided into three: the legislature, the executive (or 'the administration'), and the judiciary. Corresponding to this tripartite division of institutions is a tripartite classification of functions: legislative, administrative, and judicial. Legislation might be defined as the making of general rules to govern future conduct. Under this definition, Public Acts of Parliament are the central case of legislation. Administration is considerably more difficult to define briefly, but for our purposes may be taken to mean the application of general rules to particular cases by the making of some order (for example, a demolition order) or some decision (for example, that an immigrant is entitled to refugee status), or by performing some action (e.g., making a payment of social security benefit). The central case of the judicial function is the final and binding resolution of bipartite (i.e. two-party or 'bipolar') disputes as to facts, or as to the existence or scope of

[30] [1987] QB 815.
[31] Institutional context may also be relevant to deciding what constitutes action incompatible with the various Convention rights. Greater sensitivity to human rights may be demanded of some institutions than of others.

legal rights or duties, by means of finding facts, deciding what the law is, and applying the law to the facts.

None of these definitions is entirely straightforward because borderline cases can easily be found. For example, Private Acts of Parliament are treated as legislation even though they may regulate the conduct of only a single individual; on the other hand, an 'administrative order' affecting a large number of people may be difficult to distinguish from a legislative act. Again, it is not easy to be dogmatic in answer to the question whether a court is exercising a judicial function when it entertains a reference from the Attorney-General as to what the law is on a particular point.[32] Another complication arises from the fact that the same term may have different meanings in different contexts. For example, the definition of the judicial function may vary according to whether we are concerned with rules about contempt of court,[33] absolute privilege in the law of defamation,[34] judicial immunity from actions in tort,[35] or the applicability of the rules of natural justice.[36] Because of such difficulties, too much weight should not be put on these distinctions.[37]

Nevertheless, despite the complications, each of these types of function has a relatively clear central core, and the distinction between them is of importance in several areas of administrative law. It should be noted, however, that it is by no means true that each function is performed only by the branch of government with the corresponding name. In particular, the executive exercises all three types of function. For example, a great deal of legislation is made by Ministers under statutory powers delegated by Parliament.

Another point to note is that, at certain times in the history of administrative law, a distinction has been drawn between 'judicial' and 'quasi-judicial' functions. The distinction was drawn in the following terms: both types of function involved the resolution of a dispute, but whereas the former involved resolution by recourse to law, the latter allowed and often required recourse to considerations of public policy. Quasi-judicial

[32] Under the Criminal Justice Act 1972, s. 36 following acquittal of a criminal defendant: T. Ingham, *The English Legal Process*, 9th edn (Oxford, 2002), pp. 228–9.
[33] C.J. Miller, *Contempt of Court*, 3rd edn (Oxford, 2000), paras 3.09–3.24.
[34] *Trapp v. Mackie* [1979] 1 WLR 377.
[35] P. Cane, *Tort Law and Economic Interests*, 2nd edn (Oxford, 1996), pp. 232–3.
[36] See 7.2.3.
[37] In legal systems, such as Australia, which have a written constitution that entrenches the distinction between the three branches of government and allocates the judicial function to the judiciary, the definition of 'judicial power' may be of great importance in deciding precisely what the judicial and the executive branches respectively may and may not do.

functions, it was thought, were best performed by politically responsible Ministers rather than by courts because ultimately the required decision had to be made on policy grounds. This distinction was heavily criticized, chiefly on the basis that courts, when exercising judicial functions, often cannot resolve a dispute simply by applying the law but must sometimes exercise discretion on policy grounds to fill gaps in the law. So the need to have recourse to policy was no reason not to commit a decision to a body which would deal with it in a fully 'judicial' way. This criticism is part of a wider attack on the use of classification of functions as a criterion for deciding issues such as the availability of judicial remedies to control administrative action (the remedy of *certiorari*[38] was at one time said to be available only if the decision-maker was under a duty to act 'judicially'),[39] or the applicability of the rules of natural justice in particular circumstances (sometimes said to apply only to 'judicial functions').[40] Classification of functions fell into disrepute because the classifications were often applied mechanically and without asking whether a particular remedy ought to have been available, or whether the rules of natural justice ought to have applied as a matter of fairness or policy. A turning-point came in the case of *Ridge v. Baldwin*[41] in which it was held that the distinction between administrative and judicial functions was of no relevance to deciding whether a decision-maker ought to comply with the rules of natural justice or to the availability of judicial review remedies. The important thing was not whether the decision-maker was performing a judicial or an administrative function but whether the decision made affected the rights of those subject to it.

As we will see later (see 7.3.2.2.2), the judicial/administrative distinction has not been completely removed from the law of natural justice. So far as the availability of judicial review (remedies) is concerned, the distinction was used in cases decided after *Ridge* to provide a basis for denying, for example, that disciplinary decisions of prison governors (as opposed to boards of prison visitors) were subject to judicial review.[42] In a subsequent case, however, the House of Lords made it clear that the scope of judicial review depended not on any distinction between judicial and administrative functions but on whether the challenged decision

---

[38] Now called a 'quashing order'. See 5.2.1.
[39] *R v. Electricity Commissioners ex p. Electricity Joint Committee Co (1920) Ltd* [1924] 1 KB 171 *per* Atkin LJ.   [40] See 7.2.3.   [41] [1964] AC 40.
[42] *R v. Hull Prison Visitors ex p. St Germain* [1979] QB 425; *R v. Deputy Governor of Camphill Prison ex p. King* [1985] QB 735.

affects the claimant's rights or legitimate expectations[43] and on arguments about the suitability and propriety of judicial review of the decision in question.[44] This case was decided before the full significance of the 'functional turn' in administrative law had become clear. So what is the relationship between the idea that the scope of judicial review depends on whether rights or legitimate expectations are at stake, and the idea that it depends on whether the respondent was performing a public function? The first thing to say is that making general rules, applying them and resolving disputes about their application—i.e. legislation, administration and adjudication—are not necessarily public functions. For instance, within a purely private family context parents may engage in each of these activities in relation to their children. So performance of any of these functions will be subject to judicial review only if the function was performed publicly. However, public performance of any of these functions will only be subject to judicial review if it affected the claimant's legal rights or legitimate expectations. In other words, while a decision or action will be subject to judicial review only if it was made or done in performance of a public function, this by itself will not guarantee that it is subject to judicial review. Judicial review will not be available if the public decision or act does not adversely affect the legal rights or legitimate expectations of the claimant.

So far as the performance of public legislative (or 'rule-making') functions are concerned, another major limitation on the availability of judicial review is that Parliamentary (or 'primary')[45] legislation (i.e. 'statutes') cannot, because of the doctrine of Parliamentary supremacy, be challenged in a court of law except on the ground that it is inconsistent with European Community law or a 'Convention right' as defined in the HRA. Rule-making by bodies other than Parliament[46] may be subject to judicial review on a various additional grounds, as we will see in due course. If a court holds that a statutory provision is inconsistent with EC law, that provision is deprived of legal force. By contrast, a declaration of incompatibility under the HRA does not affect the legal validity of the provision in question. Rather it is for the government to decide what to do in response to the declaration.

---

[43] See 7.3.2.2.1.

[44] *Leech v. Deputy Governor of Parkhurst Prison* [1988] AC 533.

[45] Note that under s. 21(1) of the HRA, the term 'primary legislation' has a wider meaning than this.

[46] In this book the words 'Parliament', 'Parliamentary' and so on are used to refer to the Westminster Parliament. The Scottish Parliament will be referred to as such.

Non-parliamentary legislation can be usefully divided into a number of categories.[47] First, there are statutory instruments that are subject to the provisions of the Statutory Instruments Act 1946. To be subject to the Act, the rules must meet the definition of a 'statutory instrument' contained in s. 1 of the Act. All such rules are made either by a Minister or the Queen-in-Council in exercise of powers conferred by statute, and they must normally be published. Commonly the statute under which particular rules are made provides that they must be laid before Parliament and, in many cases, approved (or, at least, not disapproved) by one or both Houses. The 1946 Act regulates the procedure for laying. Secondly, there are legislative documents that are made in exercise of statutory powers to make rules but which are not subject to the 1946 Act. This category includes what is sometimes called 'sub-delegated legislation',[48] that is rules made by B in exercise of a power to make rules conferred by statute on A and delegated by A to B in exercise of an express or implied power to delegate. Also included in this category are by-laws made by local authorities. Instruments in this category may be (but equally may not be) subject to a statutory requirement of laying before Parliament or publication or both, contained in the statute conferring the power to make rules.

Thirdly, there are rules made by governmental bodies but not in exercise of any statutory or common law ('prerogative') power to make rules. Such rules go by a variety of names: 'quasi-legislation',[49] 'administrative rules',[50] 'tertiary rules',[51] 'administrative guidelines', 'circulars', 'informal rules', 'codes of practice' 'soft law', and so on. Such rules do not have to be, and often are not, published, and they do not have to be laid before or approved by Parliament. The constitutional and legal status of many such rules is a matter of controversy. Take 'extra-statutory tax concessions', for example. These are non-statutory rules made by the Inland Revenue stipulating when full tax liability will not be enforced. There is a basic constitutional principle, embodied in the Bill of Rights of 1688/9, that the levying of taxes must be authorized by statute; and so there is an argument for saying that non-statutory rules made by the Revenue which effectively determine a taxpayer's liability to tax are 'unconstitutional'.

---

[47] For a wide-ranging discussion of government rule-making see R. Baldwin, *Rules and Government* (Oxford, 1995). See also J. Black, *Rules and Regulators* (Oxford, 1997).

[48] See *Blackpool Corporation v. Locker* [1948] 1 KB 349.

[49] G. Ganz, *Quasi-Legislation Recent Developments in Secondary Legislation* (London, 1987).

[50] R. Baldwin and J. Houghton, 'Circular Arguments: The Status and Legitimacy of Administrative Rules' [1986] *PL* 239.

[51] Baldwin, *Rules and Government.*

On the other hand, it has been recognized that such concessions can, if applied fairly and without discrimination, aid the efficient administration of the tax system.[52] A different criticism is that non-statutory rules are undesirable if they are used as a substitute for legislation to achieve ends which might encounter political opposition in Parliament.[53] Nevertheless, the courts have recognized the value of informal rules in a variety of contexts, and it is now quite clear that such rules may be subject to judicial review on a number of grounds (as we will see later). One manifestation of the functional turn in administrative law has been this willingness of courts to extend judicial review to cover rules that 'lack visible means of legal support'. The relevant question is not whether the rule-maker was exercising a legal power to make rules. Rather the courts ask whether the rule-maker was performing a public function and whether the rules affect rights or legitimate expectations.

Fourthly, there are rules made by non-governmental bodies that exercise public functions but enjoy no statutory or common law power to make rules to regulate the conduct of members of the public.[54] Such rules, too, may be subject to judicial review[55] even if both the rules themselves and the body making them 'lack visible means of legal support'.

It is sometimes said that rules in the last two categories 'lack the force of law', by which is meant that they are not enforceable in a court. This statement is an oversimplification. The phrase 'having the force of law' has no precise meaning but is an amalgam of features which different rules may possess to a greater or lesser extent. For example, although the Immigration Rules (which fall into the second category described above) have statutory backing, there is considerable doubt about the extent to which departure from them renders decisions liable to be quashed. Again, it has been held that the Prison rules are merely 'regulatory' and that breach of them cannot give rise to a cause of action for damages, although it may found an application for judicial review.[56] In fact, the legal force of any particular rule depends partly on the source of its authority (essentially, whether it is supported by statute or not); partly on the way it is drafted (rules which are drafted in precise technical language

---

[52] *R v. Inspector of Taxes, Reading ex p. Fulford-Dobson* [1987] QB 978, 985–8.

[53] Ganz, *Quasi-Legislation*, pp. 13–14.

[54] If the body owes its existence to a contract, it may have contractual power to make rules. Such rules would be legally binding only on parties to the contract conferring the rule-making power.

[55] *R v. Panel on Takeovers and Mergers ex p. Datafin Plc* [1987] QB 815.

[56] *R v. Deputy Governor of Parkhurst Prison ex p. Hague* [1992] 1 AC 58.

are more likely to be given some legal force than are rules drafted loosely and non-technically); and partly on its contents.[57]

3.2.4 POWERS AND DUTIES

Another way of classifying public functions is into the categories of powers and duties. In this context, the word 'power' is used in three senses. First, to say that a body has a (legal) power to do X may mean that it is (legally) entitled to do it. In this sense there is nothing wrong with saying that a body has both the (legal) power and a (legal) duty to do X because, of course, if a body is required by law to do X, then it is legally entitled to do X. Secondly, we need to distinguish between legal powers and what we might call '*de facto*' powers. Legal powers derive either from statute or from common law: the legislature and the courts are the only sources of law recognized in the English legal system. If a body has a legal power to do X, it has authority to do it. By contrast, a body may have the ability to do X without having legal authority to do it: the doing of X may lack visible means of legal support. Ability without legal authority is *de facto* power. As we have already seen, the exercise of *de facto* power may be subject to judicial review.

So far as ordinary citizens and non-governmental bodies are concerned, the background principle of English law is that a person or body may do anything that the law does not prohibit. In some respects, governmental bodies enjoy the same freedom of action. For example, in *Malone v. Metropolitan Police Commissioner*[58] it was held that since there was no law against telephone tapping and it did not amount to any common law wrong, it was not unlawful for the police to engage in it. Again, at common law central government traditionally enjoyed freedom to make contracts as extensive as that enjoyed by private individuals.[59] But in other respects, government bodies are more restricted. For example, taxes may not be levied and public money may not be expended without the authority of an Act of Parliament;[60] an individual may not be deprived of personal liberty without positive legal authority;[61] private property

---

[57] For example, Baldwin and Houghton say that procedural rules are relatively unlikely to be held to create legally enforceable rights: *op cit.* n. 50 above, pp. 262–4.

[58] [1979] Ch 344. For an account of the current law on interception of communications, see D. Feldman, *Civil Liberties and Human Rights in England and Wales*, 2nd edn (Oxford, 2002), pp. 660–83.

[59] See further 12.1.2.

[60] But see J.F. McEldowney, 'The Contingencies Fund and the Parliamentary Scrutiny of Public Finance' [1988] *PL* 232.

[61] G. Robertson, *Freedom, the Individual and the Law*, 7th edn (London, 1993), p. 3.

may not be seized[62] or searched[63] by government except with legal authority. But there is no identifiable general principle determining which acts of government require positive legal authorization in order to be lawful.[64] It should be noted, too, that government conduct can be authorized by 'prerogative' powers which depend for their existence on recognition by the courts. It is now accepted that new prerogative powers cannot be created, but the scope of many established prerogative powers is unclear. If a court feels that a particular act which is not authorized by statute requires positive legal authorization, it may be able to achieve this by extending an existing prerogative power into a new area.[65]

The third meaning of the word 'power' is 'discretion'. The concept of discretion is a complex one,[66] but for our purposes we can say that the essence of a discretion is choice. In this sense of the word, a body cannot have both a power and a duty in respect of the same action. A duty is something black and white: once we know what it is that a body has a duty to do and what it actually did, we can say either that the authority has performed its duty or that it has not. Furthermore, it is not for the duty-bearer to decide what action the duty requires; some other (superior) body, will decide exactly what the body has to do.

Discretionary powers are quite different. They give the power-holder a choice. That choice is not unlimited; as we will see, it is limited by various principles of administrative law. But within the limits laid down by those principles, it is for the power-holder to decide what to do. Failure to act in a particular way will not be an abuse of power unless the decision not to act in that way is beyond the limits of the discretion given to the power-holder. The discretion given to a power-holder may relate to one or more aspects of an activity. It may be a choice as to whether to do X or not, or as to whether to do X, Y, or Z or as to how or when to do X.

The distinction between discretions and duties is not so clear in practice as it is in theory. As we have seen, the notion of a duty entails that someone other than the duty-bearer must decide what action the duty requires. The

---

[62] *Burmah Oil Ltd v. Lord Advocate* [1965] AC 75.

[63] Robertson, *Freedom, the Individual and the Law*, p. 128.

[64] See A. Lester and M. Weait, 'The Use of Ministerial Powers without Parliamentary Authority: the Ram Doctrine' [2003] *PL* 415: government operates on the basis that ministers can decide for themselves when Parliamentary authorisation should be sought for the exercise of common law and prerogative powers.

[65] On one view, this is what was done in *R v. Secretary of State for the Home Department ex p. Northumbria Police Authority* [1989] QB 26, noted by R. Ward, 'Baton Rounds and Circulars' [1988] *CLJ* 155.

[66] D. Galligan, *Discretionary Powers* (Oxford, 1986), ch. 1.

legislature may do this by couching the duty in clear, concrete, and specific terms. But many statutory duties are couched in more-or-less vague terms that leave it unclear what the duty-bearer must do in concrete situations. For example, fire authorities have a 'target duty'[67] to 'make provision for fire-fighting services';[68] and road authorities have a duty 'to take such measures as appear to . . . be appropriate to prevent accidents'.[69] Courts are generally wary of deciding what specific actions are required by target duties. The assumption seems to be that legislature intended the uncertainty inherent in such duties to be resolved by the duty-bearer, not by the court. Typically, performance of target duties involves decisions (which may be politically contentious) about the deployment of scarce resources, and courts are unwilling to tell statutory authorities how to allocate their limited budgets between competing activities (see 8.5.1). This situation creates the theoretically paradoxical outcome that the duty-bearer is allowed to decide what the duty requires it to do.

The way the courts have resolved this paradox is effectively to interpret target duties as an amalgam of mandatory and discretionary elements. Take, for example, the provision that imposes a duty on local authorities to provide 'sufficient schools'. Courts have interpreted this provision as requiring local authorities to provide minimum educational facilities; and the court will decide what this minimum is. But beyond that minimum it will be left to the authority to decide what to provide. For example, in *Meade v. Haringey LBC*[70] the issue was whether the council had breached its duty by closing its schools during a strike of ancillary workers. The court said that the decision whether to close the schools was within the area of discretion left to the authority. This technique of interpreting a duty as a duty-coupled-with-a-discretion, although strictly illogical (how can a duty be discretionary?), is a useful device to enable courts to avoid making decisions that they feel uncomfortable about making for one reason or another. The mandatory element in such cases may be defined in terms of the concept of 'unreasonableness':[71] was the authority's failure to take the particular action in question so unreasonable that no reasonable authority would have failed to do it? If so, it was under a duty to take that action. If not,

---

[67] This useful term was coined by Woolf LJ in *R v. Inner London Education Authority ex p. Ali* (1990) 2 Admin LR 822, 828.
[68] *Capital and Counties Plc v. Hampshire CC* [1997] QB 1004, 1026.
[69] *Larner v. Solihull MBC* [2001] LGR 255.   [70] [1979] 1 WLR 637.
[71] See 9.8.1.

the failure to take the action was within the area of discretion given to the authority by the legislation.

3.2.5 STATUTE, PREROGATIVE, AND JUSTICIABILITY

In *Council of Civil Service Unions v. Minister for the Civil Service*[72] one of the issues was whether so-called 'prerogative' powers of the Crown (which is another name for central government)[73] were subject to judicial review. Prerogative powers include the power to wage war, the power to make treaties, the power to conduct foreign relations, the power to regulate the Civil Service, and the power to award honours. The position before this case was that if a power was properly classifiable as a prerogative power, the courts could decide what the extent of the power was and whether a proper occasion for its exercise had arisen, but they could not decide whether it had been exercised unreasonably or unfairly. In this respect, the law drew a clear distinction between prerogative and statutory powers: the basic rule was that the exercise of statutory powers was subject to judicial review on grounds of unreasonableness and unfairness. In other words, the source of the power (statute or common law) was relevant to its reviewability. In the *GCHQ* case, the House of Lords held that there was no general rule that prerogative powers were not subject to judicial review on grounds of unreasonableness and unfairness. Whether any particular exercise of a prerogative power was subject to review depended on the content of the power in question and the circumstances in which it was exercised. The question was whether there was any reason, based on the content of the power or the circumstances of its exercise, why it should not be subject to review for unreasonableness or unfairness.[74]

The decision in the *GCHQ* case added considerable momentum to the functional turn in administrative law. In the case, Lord Roskill gave several examples of prerogative powers that would not be reviewable on grounds of unreasonableness and unfairness: 'those relating to the making

---

[72] The '*GCHQ* case' [1985] AC 374.

[73] *Town Investments Ltd v. Department of Environment* [1978] AC 359.

[74] Note that under s. 21(1) of the HRA, exercises of prerogative powers by Order in council (a form of non-Parliamentary legislation) are classified as 'primary legislation' for the purposes of the Act. This means that they are reviewable under ss. 3 and 4 of the Act but not under s. 6. To this extent, the source of power is relevant to reviewability. See further D.B. Squires, 'Judicial Review of the Prerogative after the Human Rights Act' (2000) 116 *LQR* 572; P. Billings and B. Pontin, 'Prerogative Powers and the Human Rights Act: Elevating the Status of Orders in Council' [2001] *PL* 21.

of treaties,[75] the defence of the realm,[76] the prerogative of mercy,[77] the grant of honours, the dissolution of Parliament and the appointment of ministers'.[78] Another is the power of the Attorney-General to 'lend his or her name to relator proceedings'.[79] Nor can the grounds on which payments of *ex gratia* compensation are made or refused be questioned in a court,[80] unless criteria for the payment of such compensation are published.[81] On the other hand, it has been held that exercises of the power to issue passports can be questioned in a court[82] unless, for example, the particular case involves matters of national security. Also reviewable are decisions of prosecuting authorities (other than the Attorney-General)[83] whether or not to institute proceedings, although the available grounds of review may be limited.[84]

It is clear, too, that the exercise of statutory powers (and the performance of statutory duties) might be unreviewable in a court if the particular case raised issues, such as matters of national security, which were considered unsuitable for judicial review. This follows from the basic proposition that the nature and content of a power rather than its source determines whether it is reviewable or not.

Decisions and acts which are unreviewable in a court are sometimes called 'non-justiciable'.[85] The idea of non-justiciability is a complex one,[86] but may be said to involve an amalgam of several related ideas. The first concerns what might (following American terminology) be called

---

[75] *Blackburn v. Attorney-General* [1971] 1 WLR 1037; *R v. Secretary of State for Foreign and Commonwealth Affairs ex p. Rees-Mogg* [1994] QB 552.

[76] i.e. national security. This was held to be in issue in the *GCHQ* case itself. See also *R v. Secretary of State for the Home Department ex p. McQuillan* [1995] 4 All ER 400.

[77] But see *R v. Secretary of State for the Home Department ex p. Bentley* [1994] QB 349; *Lewis v. Attorney-General of Jamaica* [2000] 1 WLR 1785.

[78] [1985] AC 374, 418.

[79] *Gouriet v. Union of Post Office Workers* [1978] AC 435. See also *R v. Solicitor General ex p. Taylor* (1996) 8 Admin LR 206 (criticized by D.J. Feldman and C.J. Miller, 'The Law Officers, Contempt and Judicial Review' (1997) 113 *LQR* 36).

[80] *R v. Secretary of State for the Home Department ex p. Harrison* [1988] 3 All ER 86.

[81] *R v. Criminal Injuries Compensation Board ex p. Lain* [1967] 2 QB 864; *R v. Secretary of State for the Home Department ex p. Chubb* [1986] *Crim LR* 806.

[82] *R v. Secretary of State for Foreign and Commonwealth Affairs ex p. Everett* [1989] QB 11.

[83] *R v. Solicitor General ex p. Taylor* (1996) 8 Admin LR 206.

[84] *R v. Director of Public Prosecutions ex p. C* [1995] 1 Cr App R 136; *R v. Inland Revenue Commissioners ex p. Mead* [1993] 1 All ER 772; Y. Dotan, 'Should Prosecutorial Discretion Enjoy Special Treatment in Judicial Review? A Comparative Analysis of the Law in England and Israel' [1997] *PL* 513.

[85] Colloquially, 'no-go areas'.

[86] G. Marshall in A.G. Guest (ed.), *Oxford Essays in Jurisprudence, First Series* (Oxford, 1961), ch. 10.

'political questions': because courts are neither representative bodies nor responsible to the electorate, they should not pronounce on the reasonableness of decisions which raise issues of 'high policy'.[87] For example, the duty of the Secretary of State for Health under the National Health Service Act 1977 to promote the establishment of a comprehensive health service is, no doubt, non-justiciable: this duty could be enforced, if at all, only by the political process.

This example also illustrates a second idea which is sometimes referred to as 'polycentricity'. This concept was worked out in detail by the American jurist Lon Fuller in a famous article first written in 1957 but not published widely until 1978.[88] A polycentric issue is one which involves a large number of interlocking and interacting interests and considerations. Fuller gave several examples of polycentric problems: how to divide a collection of paintings between two art galleries in equal shares; the task of establishing levels of wages and prices in a centrally planned economy; how to decide the positions in which members of a football team will play. By this definition, the question of what would count as a comprehensive health service could be said to be a polycentric one. Fuller argued that court proceedings and the judicial process ('adjudication') were not suitable for the resolution of polycentric issues and disputes.

The essential feature of the judicial process which makes it unsuitable to deal with polycentric problems is its bipolar and adversary nature. It is designed for one party to put forward a proposition which the other party denies or opposes. For example, the claimant asserts that he or she owns a piece of land and the defendant denies it; or the claimant asserts that he or she is entitled to compensation for personal injuries from the defendant and the latter denies it. None of Fuller's examples lends itself to being dealt with in this all-or-nothing way. For example, one of the galleries might want the Picasso if it also gets the Cezanne but not the Turner; but it would not insist on the Picasso if it got the Turner; but would want both if it did not get the Cezanne. The other gallery might have an equally complex set of preferences, and the greater the number of works involved, the more complex the preference sets might become. The workers in an industry might claim a wage increase of £X and their employers might resist it and offer £Y; but the interests of another part of the economy might be affected in such a way by either proposal that neither

---

[87] For a discussion of the reviewability of Cabinet decisions see M.C. Harris, 'The Courts and the Cabinet: "Unfastening the Buckle"? [1989] *PL* 251.

[88] L.L. Fuller, 'The Forms and Limits of Adjudication' (1978) 92 *Harvard LR* 353.

is acceptable.[89] It might be impossible to decide whether Joanna should play in a particular position on the football field without knowing where other players are going to be: the permutations are numerous and interdependent. In all these cases some form of consultation of all interested parties and groups, and mutually acceptable or advantageous adjustment of the competing possibilities in as wide a context as possible is desirable.

A good example in the administrative law context of a polycentric problem is provided by a motorway inquiry.[90] The ramifications of the decision whether to build a motorway or not are enormous. At stake are not only the interests of potential motorway users and of persons whose land might be compulsorily acquired to provide a route for the motorway. Also involved are the inhabitants of villages and towns which will be relieved of through-traffic by the motorway. The railways may have an interest in inhibiting the development of alternative means for the transport of goods. Improved transport and communications facilities provided by the motorway may benefit some businesses at the expense of others; and motorways have, of course, serious environmental effects which lovers of the countryside and people who live near the proposed route will be anxious to avoid. Not only would accommodation and compromise between these various interests be desirable, but also it may be that the best solution would be some alternative to a motorway, or some alternative route not already considered. The complexity of the issues involved makes the model of bipolar adversary presentation of fixed positions by parties in conflict seem inappropriate to the sound resolution of the issues involved.

It is important to realize, however, that problems do not present themselves pre-labelled as polycentric or not. It depends on how they are viewed. Many problems which we are prepared to treat as bipolar have ramifications that could be taken into account if they were thought to be as important as the impact of the decision on the two contestants. For

[89] An example of this sort of difficulty in English law is *Launchbury v. Morgans* [1973] AC 127 in which the House of Lords declined to extend the vicarious liability of the owner of a car for negligence of its driver because it lacked information about the impact this would have on the insurance industry. Many issues with which governments have to grapple are so complex that no matter how well-informed the decision-maker, it is not possible confidently to predict all the likely consequences or knock-on effects of any particular decision. The courts are particularly handicapped in dealing with such issues.

[90] e.g. *Bushell v. Secretary of State for the Environment* [1981] AC 75. See also *Ridge v. Baldwin* [1964] AC 40, 72, 76 *per* Lord Reid; and R. Baldwin, *Regulating the Airlines* (Oxford, 1985), chs 10 and 11. See also *Marcic v. Thames Water Utilities Ltd* [2003] UKHL 66 (court not a suitable body to assess the reasonableness of a water undertaking's strategy for increasing the capacity of a large sewerage system).

example, the decision in *Paris v. Stepney BC*,[91] in which it was decided that the employer of a one-eyed motor mechanic had a special duty of care to provide him with goggles to protect his good eye, may have had the perhaps-unexpected and certainly-undesired consequence of making it harder for disabled workers to get jobs in which they need special protection. The wider interests of disabled people could not easily have been taken into account in that case, but they were undoubtedly relevant.

Similarly, we could decide the question of whether a motorway should be built solely by considering whether landowners, whose property is to be acquired, will be properly compensated; but to do so would be to ignore a large number of other important interests. Very many court decisions have an impact far beyond the interests of the litigants, if only because the doctrine of precedent makes them relevant to the affairs of others. The bipolar adversary process often involves paying little attention to these wider interests. Furthermore, polycentricity is a matter of degree. How many of the ramifications of a particular decision ought to be explicitly taken into account by the decision-maker?

A third idea underlying the concept of justiciability is related to the second. As one might expect, the procedures followed by courts are designed to deal with bipolar disputes in an adversary way. We will consider some of the implications of this later (see 7.2.1, 7.2.4). The point to make here is that the logic of adversary adjudication is that the decision of the court should be based on the case put to it by the parties in dispute and not on material or information supplied by third parties; and rules of evidence are designed to achieve this result. On the other hand, polycentric disputes can be satisfactorily resolved only if the solution takes account of the interests of all affected parties and if the decision-maker has access to all relevant information and opinions from whatever quarter they come. In other words, court procedures are not well-adapted to resolving polycentric disputes. This fact provides another good reason why courts should decline to entertain polycentric disputes.[92] However, this is not always easy to do because, as I have already said, most disputes are more or less polycentric. Some people would argue that many applications for judicial review which are heard by courts in fact involve wider political and administrative issues; and that the rules of evidence and procedure in such cases should be changed to allow interested third parties to intervene in the proceedings and to allow relevant information

---

[91] [1951] AC 367.
[92] J. Allison, 'The Procedural Reason for Judicial Restraint' [1994] *PL* 452.

to be given about the likely impact of a decision one way or the other on the administrative process and on the public at large.[93] On the one hand, such proposals seem no more than simple common sense: why should courts decide disputes without being aware of the wider ramifications of what they are deciding. But they also raise important issues about the role of the judiciary which can only be assessed in the light of a consideration of the functions of judicial review, which will be undertaken in Part V.

A fourth idea implicit in the concept of non-justiciability is that of expertise: a court might decline to review a decision or action if it felt it lacked the skill, expertise, or experience to judge the issues raised by the dispute. For example, courts have refused to review decisions about the grading of examination papers by university examiners,[94] a decision to remove a person from a list of approved foster parents on grounds of reputation, character, and temperament,[95] and a 'run-of-the-mill management' decision to terminate a police officer's secondment to a special investigation unit.[96] This approach should not be taken too far. The thing that judges are expert in is law: they are very often not expert in the subject matter of the disputes which come before them. This does not relieve courts of the need to decide technical issues arising in litigation: expert witnesses are called and courts are often required to choose between the conflicting testimony of expert witnesses called by opposing parties. Nevertheless, in some cases at least, an argument from lack of expertise might well support a refusal by a court to hear a particular dispute.

It is important to distinguish the idea of non-justiciability from the idea of judicial restraint in reviewing performance of public functions. If a decision is held to be non-justiciable the court will decline jurisdiction over it. For example, if the government alleges that what it did was done in the interests of national security and the court accepts this, the aggrieved party's action will simply be dismissed. However, the arguments which underlie the concept of justiciability can also be used to support the idea that in reviewing decisions over which the courts are prepared to exercise control, they should award remedies to aggrieved parties only in cases where it can be said that the public functionary has gone wrong in some fairly extreme way. If a decision is non-justiciable, it is not subject to judicial review; but even if it is 'justiciable', the arguments which underlie the concept of non-justiciability also restrain the courts in

[93] e.g. J.A.G. Griffith, 'Judicial Decision-Making in Public Law' [1985] *PL* 564, 580–2.
[94] *Thorne v. University of London* [1966] QB 237.
[95] *R v. Wandsworth LBC ex p. P* (1989) 87 LGR 370.
[96] *R (Tucker) v. Director General of the National Crime Squad* [2003] ICR 599.

awarding judicial remedies. What this means in detail we will see in Section B of this Part.

This section can be simply summarized: performance of a public function (whether prerogative or not) will not be amenable to judicial review if, by reason of its content or the circumstances in which it was exercised, the decision or action in question is classified by the court as nonjusticiable.

3.2.6 VARIETIES OF PUBLIC FUNCTIONS

Public functions can be usefully divided into a number of different categories, and it is illuminating to ask how likely it is that decisions in some of these categories are likely to be subjected to scrutiny in the courts.

A significant proportion of public expenditure and a smaller proportion of public revenue arises from the making by government of contracts for the purchase and sale of goods and services. In the case of purchase, this function is known as 'public procurement'. Contracting by central government, as we shall see (see 12.1.2), has traditionally been quite well protected from judicial review because in law, central government possesses the same contracting powers as private persons. The contractual freedom of local authorities is less because their contractual powers are statutory in origin and are limited by statute. Judicial review can be used to enforce those statutory limits. This example illustrates a general point, namely that the more heavily regulated by statute a public function is, the more likely it is to be amenable to judicial review. Court actions for breach of contract against government agencies are very rare because other means of resolving contractual disputes (such as arbitration) are seen as preferable to litigation. Where the alleged breach consists of the exercise of a contractual power in a particular way, it is unclear to what extent principles of public law (as opposed to the ordinary law of contract) can be used as criteria for judging whether the action taken was an abuse of the power.[97]

Another important area of government activity is what might loosely be called 'regulation'. The government regulates a great many aspects of economic and social life to a greater or lesser extent. A significant increase in public regulation of social and economic life has occurred in Britain in the past thirty years.[98] Some areas of regulatory activity attract much more judicial attention than others. For example, a significant proportion of

---

[97] T. Daintith, 'Regulation by Contract: The New Prerogative' [1979] *CLP* 41, 53–8.
[98] M. Moran, *The British Regulatory State: High Modernism and Hyper-Innovation* (Oxford, 2003).

judicial review actions arises out of regulation of the movement of persons (i.e. immigration control). This is partly because of the importance of the interests at stake in immigration decisions: personal safety and liberty. Land use planning decisions also generate a considerable volume of litigation, once again partly because of the value of what is at stake and partly because of dissatisfaction with the system of planning appeals.[99] The value of what is at stake and the availability of alternative remedies can both have an effect on the likelihood that the courts will be asked to review particular government decisions. On the other hand, although in recent times the regulation of the financial services industry has generated a lot of judicial review claims against regulatory bodies, the courts have discouraged these, largely because they do not want court proceedings to be used as tactical weapons to delay financial transactions by parties disappointed by the failure of a regulatory body to give the applicant the protection it sought from financial predators.[100] Relatively little use has been made of judicial review in relation to regulation of the privatized utilities. As we will see in Chapter 13, the courts have also gone to great lengths to make it difficult to bring tort actions against regulatory bodies.

Thirdly, consider the raising and spending of revenue. Taxes must be authorized by an Act of Parliament, and the question of whether a particular charge levied by government without such authorization is a tax may be raised in a court. Questions about an individual's liability to pay tax rarely arise in judicial review proceedings because there is an adequate system for appealing against decisions about tax liability. Disputes about the legality of extra-statutory tax concessions may be dealt with by judicial review, but normally only at the suit of the taxpayer directly affected. Third parties are unlikely to be able to challenge concessions granted to a taxpayer.[101] The raising of revenue by local authorities generated a lot of litigation in the 1980s as authorities sought to challenge the legality of caps imposed by central government on levels of local taxes. As far as government spending decisions are concerned, a decision needs to be drawn between 'macro' and 'micro' spending decisions. For example, every decision to pay a social security benefit is a 'micro' spending deci-

---

[99] See further 7.7.
[100] P. Cane, 'Self Regulation and Judicial Review' [1987] *CJQ* 324, 342–7. M. Hopper, 'Financial Services Regulation and Judicial Review: The Fault Lines' in J. Black, P. Muchlinski and P. Walker (eds), *Commercial Regulation and Judicial Review* (Oxford, 1988), ch. 3.
[101] *R v. Inland Revenue Commissioners ex p. National Federation of Self-Employed and Small Businesses Ltd* [1982] AC 617.

sion. But because there is an extensive non-judicial appeals system and because the amounts at stake for any one individual are typically small, there is very little judicial activity in this area. Over the years, however, the Child Poverty Action Group has made considerable use of judicial review as a way of attacking what they see as wider faults in the social security system, of which individual benefit decisions are only a symptom.[102] The relaxation of standing rules has facilitated this development.[103] The legality and regularity of micro spending decisions is a major concern of the National Audit Office (for central government) and the Audit Commission (for local government).[104] Only relatively rarely[105] do such issues find their way into a court.

In relation to macro decisions about the allocation of scarce resources between competing social groups, interests and needs, a distinction has to be drawn between central and local government. Individuals who contribute to local authority finances through local taxes can challenge an authority's spending decisions by judicial review because local authorities are said to owe a 'fiduciary duty' towards their taxpayers.[106] On the other hand, central government owes no such duty to taxpayers who cannot, directly at least, challenge in the courts the way government decides to use tax revenue: the control of public expenditure policy is a matter primarily for Parliament.[107]

I have not attempted to give an exhaustive or systematic account of the variety of government functions. The four broad types I have mentioned account for a very large proportion of governmental activity, but each could be divided up into a number of smaller functions. The point to make is that light can be thrown on the role of judicial control of government activity by looking at how it operates in relation to particular areas of government activity, and although I will not attempt to do so in any systematic way in this book, the reader would do well to bear this in mind.

---

[102] T. Prosser, *Test Cases for the Poor* (London, 1983).

[103] See 3.2.2.

[104] See generally F. White and K. Hollingsworth, *Audit, Accountability and Government* (Oxford, 1999).

[105] e.g. *R v. Her Majesty's Treasury ex p. Smedley* [1985] QB 657; *R v. Secretary of State for Foreign and Commonwealth Affairs ex p. World Development Movement* [1995] 1 WLR 115; I. Harden, F. White and K. Hollingsworth, 'Value for Money and Administrative Law' [1996] *PL* 661; White and Hollingsworth, *Audit, Accountability and Government*, pp. 67–71.

[106] See 8.5.1.

[107] J. McEldowney, 'The Control of Public Expenditure' in J. Jowell and D. Oliver (eds), *The Changing Constitution*, 4th edn (Oxford, 2000), ch. 8; T. Daintith and A. Page *The Executive in the Constitution: Structure, Autonomy and Internal Control* (Oxford, 1999), chs 5 and 6.

4

Claimants

4.1 STANDING

To be entitled to challenge performance of a public function by way of judicial review a claimant must have sufficient standing (or *locus standi*). The requirement of standing may be understood as indicating that the primary concern of administrative law is not simply to control the performance of public functions but rather to exercise control in the interests of persons affected in particular ways.

4.1.1 PUBLIC LAW WRONGS AND PRIVATE LAW WRONGS

The requirement of standing applies only to cases in which the claimant alleges that a public functionary has committed a 'public law wrong'. Breaches of the rules and principles of administrative law are public law wrongs in this sense. Standing is not normally a requirement for bringing a 'private law claim'—for instance, a claim in tort or for breach of contract—against a public functionary. There are certain private law concepts that resemble rules of standing: for example, duty of care in the tort of negligence, the principle that breach of a statutory duty will be actionable *in tort* only if the duty is owed to the claimant as an individual (as opposed to the public generally), and the doctrine of privity of contract. However, these are not seen as separate from the rules that define the relevant wrong, but as part of the definition of the wrong. In administrative law, on the other hand, rules of standing are seen as rules about entitlement to complain of a wrong rather than as part of the definition of the wrong. The explanation for this may be that public law wrongs are first and foremost wrongs against the public; they infringe the public's right to be lawfully governed. Thus the wrong is defined in terms of the public interest whereas the right to sue in respect of it is described in terms of the claimant's interest in the matter. This explanation fits in with the 'prerogative' nature of the original public law remedies of *certiorari*, prohibition, and mandamus.[1] It also explains why the Attorney-General, as representative of both government and people, always has standing to protect public rights (although in practice the Attorney is reluctant to sue where the defendant is a department of central government).

One area of private law where a standing requirement does apply is the tort of public nuisance. This is because a public nuisance is defined as an interference with a public right—such as freedom of passage along a highway. In order to sue for damages for, or an injunction to restrain, a public nuisance, a private claimant must show that the interference with the public right also interfered with some private law right of the claimant, or caused the claimant 'special damage'. Typical legal rights are property rights and contractual rights. In general terms, special damage is damage over and above that suffered by the public at large, or by some significant section of it affected by the decision. For example, blocking of a highway adversely affects everyone who might wish to use the highway. It would inflict special damage on a business located on the highway to which the blockage prevented public access, thus reducing its income. Another way of stating the special damage requirement is to say the claimant must have a special or personal interest in the claim over and above the public's interest.

This principle, that the claimant must establish that the defendant's conduct interfered with a private law right of the claimant or caused the claimant special damage, was relevant in the famous case of *Gouriet v. Union of Post Office Workers*.[2] The claimant sought an injunction to restrain the union from instructing its members to boycott mail to South Africa in protest against the South African government's policy of apartheid. If carried out, the boycott would have constituted a breach of the criminal law; so the injunction the claimant was seeking was directed at a threatened breach of the criminal law. Although citizens may, in principle, prosecute criminal offences, an injunction to restrain a threatened breach of the criminal law can normally be sought only by the Attorney-General or by a local authority[3] on behalf of the public. There is, however, a procedure (called the 'relator procedure') by which a citizen can obtain the Attorney-General's permission to enforce public rights—such as the right that the criminal law be complied with—regardless of whether

---

[1] See 5.2.1–5.2.3.   [2] [1978] AC 435.
[3] e.g. under s. 222 of the Local Government Act 1972, as in *Stoke-on-Trent CC v. B & Q Retail Ltd* [1984] AC 754. Concerning injunctions to enforce land-use planning controls see *Wrexham County BC v. Berry* [2003] 2 AC 558.

interference with the public right would also interfere with a private right of the claimant or cause the claimant special damage. In a relator action, the Attorney General is the nominal claimant, but it is the relator who actually conducts and bears the costs of the claim. Gouriet sought the Attorney-General's permission, but it was refused; and the House of Lords held that this refusal was not subject to judicial review. The relator procedure has been rendered more or less defunct by 'liberalization' of the rules of standing, which make it much easier for citizens to enforce public rights and to complain of breaches of administrative law by public functionaries, regardless of whether their private law rights have been interfered with or they have suffered special damage. But even so, it is unlikely that a claim such as Gouriet's would succeed. The basic principle of English criminal law, that a person should be presumed to be innocent until proven to have committed a criminal offence, underpins another principle to the effect that except in very special cases, an injunction will not be granted to restrain threatened breaches of the criminal law. Such an injunction will be granted only when offences have been committed in the past and it appears that mere prosecution will not deter further breaches of the law in the future.[4]

4.2 STANDING FOR JUDICIAL REVIEW

4.2.1 PERSONAL STANDING

Before 1978 the standing requirement for judicial review varied according to the remedy sought by the claimant—one of the prerogative orders, for instance, or a declaration or injunction. Rule 3(7) of Order 53 of the Rules of the Supreme Court—the predecessor to CPR Part 54—introduced (in 1978) a common standing rule applicable to all judicial review claims brought under that Order, namely that the claimant was required to have 'a sufficient interest in the matter to which the application[5] relate[d]'. This formulation gave the courts more or less unfettered discretion to rewrite the standing rules, and its effect was to render the existing rules more or less defunct. Although, strictly, this rule applied only to judicial review claims brought under Order 53, it was widely assumed that it would apply to all judicial review claims. This standing rule was repeated in s. 31(3) of the Supreme Court Act 1981. CPR Part 54 makes no mention of standing, but the Supreme Court Act provision is still in force.

---

[4] *B & Q Retail* [1984] AC 754.
[5] Under Ord. 53, judicial review proceedings were called 'applications' rather than 'claims'.

The leading case on the meaning of the 'sufficient interest' test is *R v. Inland Revenue Commissioners, ex p. National Federation of Self-Employed and Small Businesses Ltd* (the *Fleet Street Casuals* case).[6] In this case the applicant (a trade association) challenged a tax amnesty granted by the Revenue to casual workers in the newspaper industry: the Revenue had agreed not to seek to recover unpaid tax provided the workers ceased their tax-evading tactics in the future. It was held that the applicants lacked a sufficient interest in the matter because the Revenue had acted within the discretion permitted to it in the day-to-day administration of the tax system. Some of the judges thought that one effect of rule 3(7) was to abolish the distinction, so far as standing is concerned, between the various prerogative orders; but at least two of their Lordships were less certain on this point. The later case of *R v. Felixstowe Justices, ex p. Leigh*[7] clarified this point: standing is related to the claimant's interest and not to the remedy sought. In that case it was held that a journalist lacked standing for a mandatory order requiring the chair of the justices to reveal the names of the magistrates who had heard a particular case, but that he did have standing for a declaration that a policy of not disclosing the names of justices who heard certain types of cases was contrary to the public interest and unlawful. The point was that the journalist's investigative purpose was sufficiently served by the declaration, and that he did not need to know (and had no sufficient interest in knowing) the identities of the justices who had heard the particular case. The implication of this decision is that whether or not a claimant has standing does not depend on which remedy is sought. It so happened that two different remedies were sought in this case, but the decision on the issue of standing would have been the same even if the applicant had sought two declarations in different terms.

Other important points emerge from the *Fleet Street Casuals* case. First, the question of what is a sufficient interest is partly a matter of legal principle—what do earlier cases say about standing?—and partly a question to be decided in the light of the circumstances of the case before the court. So it will often be impossible to be sure, in advance of litigation, whether any particular applicant has a sufficient interest. Secondly, the question of sufficient interest has to be judged in the light of relevant statutory provisions—what do they say or suggest about who is to be

---

[6] [1982] AC 617. At the time of this case, many national newspapers had their premises in Fleet Street.

[7] [1987] QB 582.

allowed to challenge decisions made under the statute? For example, suppose a statute gives a Minister two different but related powers. Suppose further that the statute provides that before the Minister exercises power A, he or she must consider representations made by 'any person', and that before the Minister exercises power B he or she must consult a particular government body with responsibility for some relevant aspect of government policy. It could be argued that these provisions would justify allowing any person to challenge exercises of power A, but also applying a more restrictive standing rule (perhaps something like 'special interest') to challenges to exercises of power B on the ground that Parliament had intended the government body in question to be the prime guardian of the public interest in the exercise of power B.

Thirdly, sufficient interest has to be judged in the light of the substance of the claimant's complaint. Looking at the substance of the complaint has a number of purposes. There is no point granting leave to a person with sufficient interest if it is clear, for example, that the case is a hopeless one on its merits and is bound to fail for that reason; or that the case raises only non-justiciable issues. The *Felixstowe Justices* case illustrates another way in which standing is related to the substance of the claim: just as the journalist had a sufficient interest only in the general policy of secrecy and not in its application to a particular case, so the remedy to which he was entitled related only to the general policy. In other words, whatever the claimant's interest in the subject matter of the application may be, that interest not only determines whether the claimant has standing, but also dictates the nature and terms of the relief which the applicant can expect.

Finally, whether the claimant's interest is sufficient depends to some extent on the seriousness of the alleged breach of administrative law. Whatever the claimant's interest, the more serious the breach, the more likely that interest is to be sufficient. This last point raises a fundamental question about the nature and function of standing rules. There is a sense in which standing is a preliminary question, separate from that of the substance and merits of the claim: standing rules determine entitlement to raise and argue the claim, and it makes little sense to say that entitlement to argue the claim depends on whether the claim is a strong one. Only if the chance of failure at the end of the day approaches certainty should the likely outcome affect the question of access to the court.

This argument assumes that there is some value in separating the issue of entitlement to apply for judicial review from the question of entitlement to a remedy at the end of the day. A counter-argument might be that standing rules are just one mechanism for weeding out hopeless or frivolous cases at an early stage and protecting public functionaries (rightly or wrongly) from harassment by 'professional litigants' or 'busy-bodies'[8] meddling in matters which do not really concern them. If this assertion is correct, then it would not matter if the standing requirement was abolished entirely, provided some other mechanism was put in its place for weeding out hopeless and crank cases. The requirement of obtaining the court's 'permission to proceed' with a judicial review claim under CPR Rule 54.4 performs this function. In this regard, it may be significant that whereas under Order 53, 'leave' (i.e. permission) was not to be granted unless the claimant had a sufficient interest, under Part 54 the granting of permission is not expressly subject to standing— although, no doubt, standing is a relevant issue to be considered at this stage.[9] We might conclude that there is no need to have stringent standing rules (or, indeed, any standing rule at all) if other means to weed out hopeless and vexatious cases are provided. The 'sufficient interest' test as interpreted in the *Fleet Street Casuals* case can be seen as giving partial effect to such an argument.

This interpretation of *Fleet Street Casuals* assumes that the requirement of sufficient interest is a liberal standing rule in the sense that it makes access to the courts to challenge administrative action easy, and so shifts the burden of weeding out weak cases to other mechanisms. Do the cases support this assumption? This question is made somewhat difficult to answer because one of the effects of the emphasis on the facts and merits of the particular case in *Fleet Street Casuals* is that the issue of standing now often receives little or no attention from the courts and is sometimes the subject of concessions by the defendant. Judges often try to avoid the issue of standing by resolving the substance of the claim first.

Nevertheless, there are some cases decided since *Fleet Street Casuals* which throw light on the issue. It has been held, for example, that a gypsy living on a caravan site provided by a local authority under statute has sufficient interest to challenge a decision by the authority no longer to provide the site or any alternative; and to challenge a decision by the Minister not to exercise a statutory default power.[10] Of considerable importance is a series of cases which introduce the concept of 'legitimate

---

[8] Who else would expend the time and resources necessary to mount a hopeless case?

[9] In *R v. Somerset CC, ex p. Dixon* [1998] Env LR 111 Sedley J said that provided the claimant had an arguable substantive case, leave should not be refused on the basis of lack of standing unless the claimant was a 'busybody' or a 'troublemaker'.

[10] *R v. Secretary of State for the Environment, ex p. Ward* [1984] 1 WLR 834.

expectation' into the law of standing. A legitimate expectation may arise when a public functionary, by its words or conduct, leads a citizen reasonably to expect that it will act in a particular way. If the functionary then acts differently, it may be held to have acted unfairly and illegally, at least if it has not given the citizen a chance to make representations as to why he or she should be treated in the way expected.[11] It has been held in a number of cases that if a person claims to have a legitimate expectation, this will give that person standing to make an application for judicial review unless the claim is totally frivolous. These cases are significant because they illustrate one of the ways in which standing is related to the substance of the claim. The notion of legitimate expectation concerns whether the claimant has a case against the defendant; but the claim that such an expectation exists, provided it is not prima facie ludicrous, will give the claimant standing to argue the merits of the claim.

These cases seem to indicate that the effect of the introduction of the sufficient interest test has been to liberalize the law of standing at least in relation to applicants who claim a personal interest in the subject matter of the application.[12] But the best test of the liberality of a regime of standing rules is how it deals with might be called 'representative standing', to which we now turn.

4.2.2 REPRESENTATIVE STANDING

A representative claimant is one who comes to court not to protect their own interests but to represent the interests of other parties not before the court. Three different types of representative standing can usefully be distinguished: surrogate standing, associational standing, and citizen standing.[13] Surrogate standing refers to a situation in which the claimant purports to represent an individual with a personal interest in the claim. Unless there was some good reason why that individual should not make the claim personally (such as the individual's age or mental condition), a court would be unlikely to accord standing to a surrogate.[14] Associational standing refers to a situation in which the claimant purports to represent

---

[11] See 8.3.4.

[12] Indeed, it has been said that 'almost invariably if an applicant can establish a case which deserves to succeed, standing will not constitute a bar to the grant of a remedy': *Broadmoor Hospital Authority v. R* [2000] 2 All ER 727, 733 *per* Lord Woolf MR.

[13] For more detailed discussion see P. Cane, 'Standing, Representation and the Environment' in I. Loveland (ed), *A Special Relationship? American Influences on Public Law in the UK* (Oxford, 1995), ch. 5.

[14] *R v. Legal Aid Board, ex p. Bateman* [1992] 1 WLR 711.

a group of individuals who have a personal interest in the claim.[15] There are some good reasons why courts should, in principle, allow associational claims: they may facilitate access to justice by making it easier for groups (especially the poor and unorganized) to invoke the judicial process; and they may promote the efficient conduct of litigation by allowing numerous bilateral disputes, which raise similar issues, to be resolved in one set of proceedings.

Citizen (or 'public interest') standing refers to a situation in which the claimant purports to represent 'the public interest' as opposed to the interests of any particular individual(s). Citizen standing can be supported by arguing that because Parliament is under the effective control of the government,[16] the courts can and should provide an alternative forum for the airing of widely held grievances about the way the country is being run and for ensuring that public functionaries observe the law. On the other hand, it might be said that the more the courts are opened up to arguments about the interests of the public or of sections of the public rather than of individuals, the more likely are the judges to be drawn into debates that ought to be held in the political arena and not in courts. The courts, it might be said, should not provide a 'surrogate political process' in which battles that have been fought and lost elsewhere can be reopened. A middle path might be to distinguish between, on the one hand, public interests that are quite uncontroversial and, in some sense, of fundamental constitutional importance (for instance, that there be 'no taxation without Parliamentary approval'); and on the other, interests which are sectional or politically controversial. It might be thought appropriate that the courts should protect basic principles on which our society and government is based when asked to by ordinary citizens, but not that they should mediate between sectional and contested points of view about the way government and society should operate.[17]

Whatever the justification for citizen standing, it is clear that English courts are now prepared to entertain 'citizen' or 'public interest' actions. In the *Felixstowe Justices* case (mentioned earlier) it was held that the claimant journalist was entitled to represent the public interest as a 'private Attorney-General'. It has also been held that a taxpayer would have

---

[15] A representative claimant cannot have standing unless the persons represented have a sufficient interest in the subject matter of the claim: *R v. Secretary of State for the Environment, ex p. Rose Theatre Trust Ltd* [1990] 1 QB 504.

[16] See 16.1.

[17] P. Cane, 'Open Standing and the Role of Courts in a Democratic Society' (1999) 20 *Singapore LR* 23.

standing to challenge the legality of an Order in council authorizing the payment of public money to the European Community.[18] In one case a citizen with a 'sincere concern for constitutional issues' was held to have standing to challenge ratification of the Maastricht Treaty on European Union;[19] and in another a mother was allowed to challenge government guidelines to doctors about the giving of contraceptive advice to girls under the age of 16.[20] In none of these cases did the individual claimant allege a personal interest in the outcome of the litigation. Organizations and groups may also bring public interest actions. For example, a trade union was allowed to challenge a decision by the Home Secretary to change the basis on which criminal injuries compensation was awarded;[21] and a non-governmental organization was allowed to challenge a decision to provide funding for the building of a dam in Malaysia out of the foreign aid budget.[22] Statutory bodies may also be accorded public interest standing: for instance, the Equal Opportunities Commission was allowed to challenge legislation on the basis of inconsistency with EC law.[23]

English courts also seem willing to recognize associational standing. The applicant in the *Fleet Street Casuals* case was a trade association which purported to represent its members, but the House of Lords did not consider this a reason not to accord the applicant standing—indeed, the representative nature of the applicant was not mentioned. It has also been held that the Child Poverty Action Group (a non-governmental

---

[18] *R v. Her Majesty's Treasury, ex p. Smedley* [1985] QB 657.

[19] *R v. Secretary of State for Foreign and Commonwealth Affairs, ex p. Rees-Mogg* [1994] QB 552. In *R (Feakins) v. Secretary of State for the Environment, Food and Rural Affairs* [2003] EWCA Civ 1546 it was held (obiter) that an individual might not be granted standing to raise an issue of public interest if the claim is motivated by 'ill-will or some other improper purpose' (at [23]) as opposed to a genuine desire to protect the public. The question of whether and when a claimant's motives ought to affect the success of the claim is a complex one. This holding might suggest, for instance, that organizations are more likely than individuals to be granted public-interest standing because they are, perhaps, less likely to be driven by unacceptable motives.

[20] *Gillick v. West Norfolk and Wisbech AHA* [1986] AC 112.

[21] *R v. Secretary of State for the Home Department, ex p. Fire Brigades Union* [1995] 2 AC 513.

[22] *R v. Secretary of State for Foreign and Commonwealth Affairs, ex p. World Development Movement Ltd* [1995] 1 WLR 115.

[23] *R v. Secretary of State for Employment, ex p. Equal Opportunities Commission* [1995] 1 AC 1. Ironically, it was held that an individual co-claimant, who had a personal interest in the claim, lacked standing on the basis that the proper way for her to challenge the legislation was in an action for compensation before an employment tribunal. The only case that casts significant doubt on the commitment of the courts to allowing public interest actions is *R v. Secretary of State for the Environment, ex p. Rose Theatre Trust Co Ltd* [1990] 1 QB 504. This decision is out of line with more recent decisions.

organization that purports to represent the interests of social security claimants) has standing to make applications for judicial review of decisions in the area of social security.[24] Greenpeace—the non-governmental environmental organization—has been accorded standing to challenge authorizations for the discharge of nuclear waste from a reprocessing plant at Sellafield in Cumbria partly on the basis that it had some 2,500 'supporters' in the affected area.[25]

It must be said, however, that the courts have not drawn the distinction between associational and public interest standing; and in the *Greenpeace* case, at least, there is some doubt about whether the claimant was accorded standing as a representative of personally interested individuals or as a representative of the public. Nevertheless, the distinction is important for two reasons. First, the sort of arguments which could be used to support a challenge to a decision in the name of the public may be different from the arguments which could be used on behalf of a group of personally interested individuals. In other words, the public's interest in a decision may be different from that of a group of individuals or a discrete section of the public. Secondly, it may be argued that a claimant can plausibly purport to represent particular individuals, and should be allowed to do so before a court, only if the claimant has taken adequate steps to ascertain the views of those individuals and whether they want the claim to be made on their behalf. In no application for judicial review brought before an English court by a representative claimant has the question of whether the claimant had a 'mandate' from the represented been raised.

Apart from this issue of mandate, have the English courts looked for any other qualifications in representative claimants? In the case of public interest actions brought by individuals, the courts seem prepared to grant

---

[24] *R v. Secretary of State for Social Services, ex p. Child Poverty Action Group* [1990] 2 QB 540, 556.

[25] *R v. Inspectorate of Pollution, ex p. Greenpeace Ltd (No. 2)* [1994] 4 All ER 329. For more detailed discussion of these cases see P. Cane, 'Standing up for the Public' [1995] *PL* 276. An alternative to this type of representative claim is the test case. A test case is an individual claim sponsored by an organization and chosen because it raises issues common to a group of individual claims. Compared with a representative claim, a test case carries a risk that the individual claimant might be 'bought off' by the defendant with an out-of-court settlement, or that the claim might be decided on issues personal to the claimant rather than common to the group. On the other hand, legal aid for a judicial review claim can be granted only for the benefit of individuals. Judicial review claims (and claims for damages against public authorities) form a priority category for funding under the legal aid scheme: see Legal Services Commission, *The Funding Code: Decision Making Guidance*, parts 16 and 17 (see also part 6 on HRA claims).

standing to anyone who is genuinely concerned about the subject-matter of the application. By contrast, in cases where courts have granted standing to non-governmental organizations, they have remarked upon the respectability of the claimant, its experience, expertise, and financial resources, thus implying that standing might not be granted to a group or organisation which the court thought 'unsuitable' in some sense. In my view, if an organization or group claims standing on an associational basis, it should be required to demonstrate that it has an appropriate mandate from those it purports to represent;[26] but if it can do this, no other qualifications should be required. So far as public interest actions are concerned, if they are to be allowed at all, then in my view, any genuinely concerned individual or group should be allowed to represent the public interest.

The concern shown, especially in public interest actions, that the claimant should be suitably qualified perhaps springs from three worries. One is that the claimant may in fact be seeking to further its own interests or a sectional interest rather than the 'public interest'. This concern can be met by allowing public interest actions only in cases where the court believes that the public interest is genuinely at stake and by requiring the applicant to restrict its case to that interest. A second worry is that the claimant may not be able to pay the defendant's costs if the application is unsuccessful. This worry should be addressed through rules as to costs and the funding of litigation, not through the rules of standing.[27]

A third worry is that the claimant may not be able to present the case effectively if it lacks adequate resources, knowledge and experience. This is not a consideration that the courts take into account in ordinary litigation, and it suggests that they see the judicial role in public interest litigation as being different from that in other types of litigation. This suggestion finds support when we turn from the issue of standing to

---

[26] For a different view see C. Harlow, 'Public Law and Popular Justice' (2002) 65 *MLR* 1, 4–5.

[27] In *R v. Lord Chancellor, ex p. Child Poverty Action Group* [1999] 1 WLR 347 public interest claimants asked the court to make a 'pre-emptive costs order' that they would not be liable for the defendant's costs if they were unsuccessful. The judge refused to make the order but accepted that he had the power to do so and that in an appropriate case, it would be right not to order an unsuccessful public interest claimant to pay the defendant's costs. It may be that a better way to finance public interest actions would be to establish a special legal aid fund for such cases. Under the present legal aid rules, it counts in favour of the granting of aid that a claim raises issues of wide public interest. But only individuals—and not representative claimants—can obtain legal aid. See generally S. Chakrabati, J. Stephens, and C. Gallagher, 'Whose Cost the Public Interest? [2003] *PL* 697.

initiate a judicial review claim to the related issue of intervention in judicial review proceedings initiated by someone else.

4.2.3 RIGHTS OF INTERVENTION

In an adversary system such as the British, litigation is basically a two-sided affair. In general, interested third parties are not given the opportunity to intervene and express to the court their point of view about the matters in dispute between the claimant(s) and the defendant(s) even if their contribution would assist the court in achieving a sound resolution of the dispute. While it may be reasonable that third parties should not, in general,[28] be allowed to intervene in cases in which the claimant seeks to protect their own personal interests or the interests of some other individual(s), it seems much less reasonable to prevent members of the public, other than the claimant and the defendant, from intervening in cases in which the claimant seeks to protect the public interest. Unless one takes the (implausible) view that the public interest is monolithic and obvious, it would seem unwise to give one person a monopoly on its protection. In a public interest action the main difficulty may be to identify exactly what the public's interest in the matter is. The public interest may, in fact, be many-faceted ('polycentric')[29] and contested, and the claimant may be promoting a sectional interest rather than the public interest. Moreover, even if a public interest claimant has expertise and experience relevant to the subject matter of the claim (and especially if it does not), it seems hard to argue that the court should be deprived of the wisdom and knowledge of other expert or experienced parties.

On the other hand, it is not obviously a good idea to allow extensive rights of public interest intervention. As a result, court proceedings might become very much more complex, costly, and lengthy. The nature of the judicial process might be significantly changed so that courts hearing public interest judicial review claims, instead of resolving cases by adjudicating upon the rights and obligations of the litigating parties, would do so by formulating public policy on the basis of consultations with the litigating parties and interveners. Such transformation of judicial proceedings might undermine the legitimacy of the courts by opening them to accusations of straying beyond their proper legal domain

---

[28] An exception might be made for third parties who have a personal interest in the claim: S. Hannett, 'Third Party Interventions: In the Public Interest?' [2003] *PL* 128, 130–1.

[29] See 3.2.5.

into the political sphere.[30] Here, then, is a dilemma: once the law allows 'public interest claims', the case for allowing 'public interest interventions' becomes a strong, if not an irresistible, one. At the same time, however, the potential disadvantages of too readily allowing public interest interventions may argue against allowing public interest claims in the first place.

At present the law says very little about rights of intervention in applications for judicial review. Under CPR Rule 54.7 the judicial review claim form must be served on 'any person the claimant considers to be an interested party'; and under CPR Rule 54.17 'any person may apply for permission (a) to file evidence; or (b) to make representations at the hearing of the judicial review'. An 'interested party' is a person (other than the claimant or the defendant) 'who is directly affected by the claim' (CPR Rule 54.1(f)); and it seems that the term 'directly affected' covers only those with a personal interest in the claim.[31] As a result, a person may apply for permission to intervene even if they were not entitled to receive the claim form. So far as concerns permission to intervene either in writing or orally, a recent survey found a significant increase in recent years in the number of applications (made mainly by organizations rather than individuals) to intervene in cases before the House of Lords.[32] However, as in the case of representative standing, no distinction has been drawn between associational and public interest interveners; and no principles have been developed about when interventions will be allowed, who will be allowed to intervene, or the form the intervention should take.

It has been proposed that in exercising its discretion to allow interventions, the court should consider whether the intervention would be likely to assist the court and whether it would cause undue delay or otherwise prejudice the rights of the parties to the action. Interventions would

---

[30] 'Interest group politics'—consultation of interested parties and groups—is a defining feature of so called 'participatory' (as opposed to 'representative') democracy. Traditionally, courts—even in relation to public law matters—have not been seen as democratic policy-making institutions. The danger inherent in a very liberal regime of standing and intervention rules is that courts may come to be seen as illegitimately providing a forum of political contestation for parties disappointed by the outcome of the mainstream policy-making process. To what extent should courts act as umpires in the 'great game' of interest-group politics? Should standing and intervention rules be used to prevent the over-politicization of the judicial process? For a supportive assessment of intervention see M. Arshi and C. O'Cinneide, 'Third-Party Interventions: the Public Interest Reaffirmed' [2004] *PL* 69.

[31] *R v. Legal Aid Board, ex p. Megarry* [1994] COD 468; *R v. Liverpool CC, ex p. Muldoon* [1996] 1 WLR 1103; *R v. Broadcasting Complaints Commission, ex p. British Broadcasting Commission* (1995) 7 Admin LR 575.

[32] Hannett, op cit. n. 28 above.

normally take the form of relatively short written submissions.[33] The court could attach conditions to a grant of leave to intervene (concerning the payment of costs, for instance), and it would specify the date by which the written submission would have to be filed. The makers of these proposals think that they strike a reasonable balance between the advantages and disadvantages of public interest intervention which were canvassed above. Whether you agree may depend on your view about the proper role of the courts in regulating the performance of public functions.

4.2.4 WHAT IS A SUFFICIENT INTEREST?

The guidance given in the *Fleet Street Casuals* case as to the meaning of the term 'sufficient interest' is very abstract. Can anything more concrete be said on this topic? This question has two parts. First, what can be said about when an individual has a sufficient interest in the subject matter of a claim?[34] Secondly, what can be said about when the public has an interest to support a public interest claim? An individual would obviously have a sufficient interest in a decision that adversely affected the claimant's health or safety. A person would also have a sufficient interest in a decision that affected his or her property or financial well-being. For instance, neighbours have sufficient interest to challenge planning decisions in respect of neighbouring land. Producers and traders have standing to challenge the grant of a licence or other benefit to a competitor;[35] and a taxpayer might have standing to complain about the favourable treatment of a competitor by the Revenue.[36] The expenditure of time, energy and skill in caring for a particular species of wildlife or some feature of the natural environment could give a person a sufficient interest in a decision adversely affecting that species or feature.[37] An aesthetic interest in the built environment may also generate a sufficient interest.[38]

---

[33] Justice/Public Law Project, *A Matter of Public Interest* (London, 1996). See also D. Smith, 'Third Party Interventions in Judicial Review' [2002] *JR* 10.

[34] This question is relevant both to claims by individuals on their own behalf and to 'associational' claims on behalf of other individuals.

[35] *R v. Thames Magistrates' Court, ex p. Greenbaum* (1957) 55 LGR 129.

[36] *R v. Attorney-General, ex p. Imperial Chemical Industries Plc* [1987] 1 CMLR 72.

[37] *R v. Poole BC, ex p. Beebee* [1991] COD 264.

[38] *Covent Garden Community Association Ltd v. Greater London Council* [1981] *JPL* 183; *R v. Hammersmith & Fulham LBC, ex p. People Before Profit Ltd* [1981] *JPL* 869; *R v Stroud DC, ex p. Goodenough* [1992] *JPL* 319.

What about public interests? It seems clear that the public has a sufficient interest in the observance of basic constitutional principles such as 'no taxation or expenditure without Parliamentary approval'.[39] The public also has an interest that governmental powers such as that to ratify treaties,[40] or to set up a non-statutory compensation scheme,[41] or to issue informal guidance on medical matters (for instance)[42] should be exercised in accordance with law. The public has an interest that UK legislation should comply with EC law.[43] It also has an interest in freedom of information.[44] Normally the public would not have a sufficient interest in the way an individual was treated by government, but it may in a case, for instance, of exercise of planning powers in relation to a site of great public importance.[45]

So far as concerns challenges by citizens to government spending decisions, the law seems to draw a distinction between central and local government. It has long been clear that ratepayers (now council tax payers) have standing to challenge a wide variety of decisions, including expenditure decisions, by local authorities; whereas the *Fleet Street Casuals* case suggests that taxpayers would not normally have standing to challenge spending decisions by central government. Local authorities owe a fiduciary duty to their ratepayers in the use of rate revenue,[46] and the right of ratepayers to challenge local authority spending decisions is a corollary of this duty. Central government, by contrast, owes no legal duties to taxpayers as such relating to the use of the 'tax pound'. There has been quite a bit of litigation in the United States in which taxpayers have sought to challenge some use to which taxes have been put. The American cases draw a distinction between a genuine personal interest (which gives a right to sue) and generalized grievances about the way the country is being run (which do not). English law does not, of course, require a claimant for judicial review to have a personal interest, but

---

[39] *R v. Her Majesty's Treasury, ex p. Smedley* [1985] QB 657; *R v. Secretary of State for Foreign and Commonwealth Affairs, ex p. World Development Movement Ltd* [1995] 1 WLR 386.

[40] *R v. Secretary of State for Foreign and Commonwealth Affairs, ex p. Rees-Mogg* [1994] QB 552.

[41] *R v. Secretary of State for the Home Department, ex p. Fire Brigades Union* [1995] 2 AC 513.

[42] *Gillick v. West Norfolk and Wisbech AHA* [1986] AC 112.

[43] *R v. Secretary of State for Employment, ex p. Equal Opportunities Commission* [1995] 1 AC 1.

[44] *R v. Felixstowe Justices, ex p. Leigh* [1987] QB 582.

[45] *Save Britain's Heritage v. No. 1 Poultry* [1991] 1 WLR 153.

[46] See 8.5.1.

courts in this country are almost certain to take the view that the way taxes are spent is a political question which the courts are not the proper bodies to consider, and that no taxpayer has sufficient interest to raise this matter in court. Is the difference between the challengeability of central and local government spending decisions justified?

4.3 STANDING UNDER THE HUMAN RIGHTS ACT

Under s. 7(1) of the HRA a person may make a claim against a public authority on the ground that the authority has acted incompatibly with a Convention right (contrary to s. 6) only if the person is (or would be) a 'victim' of the allegedly unlawful action. Section 7(3) provides that if the claim is made is for judicial review, the claimant has 'sufficient interest' in the claim only if the claimant is (or would be) a victim of the action.[47] Furthermore, under s. 7(1)(b), only a victim can 'rely on' a Convention right in legal proceedings in which it is alleged that a public authority has acted in a way made unlawful by s. 6. The victim test of standing is copied from Article 34 of the ECHR (HRA s. 7(7)). It appears to be much narrower than the sufficient interest test as it has been developed and applied in the non-HRA judicial review case-law.[48] It would certainly rule out associational and public interest claims in respect of action incompatible with a Convention right. But it would not prevent a corporation, organization, or group making a claim if the corporation, organization, or group itself was a victim.

The adoption of the victim test has been much criticized. Some people think it undesirable that the standing rule should differ according to whether or not the claim is based on s. 6 of the HRA. The strength of this objection depends on what the respective functions of administrative law and human rights law are considered to be. Liberalization of standing for judicial review may be seen as involving a reorientation of judicial review away from the protection of individual rights and interests against undue

---

[47] J. Miles, 'Standing under the Human Rights Act 1998: Theories of Rights Enforcement and the Nature of Public Law Adjudication' [2000] *CLJ* 133.

[48] Ibid., 137–8; R. Clayton and H. Tomlinson, *The Law of Human Rights* (Oxford, 2000), paras 22.27–36. Under Art. 34 of the ECHR governmental organizations cannot complain of infringements of the Convention. The standing rule under EC law applicable to judicial review of acts of Community institutions is also more restrictive than the English rule: T.C Hartley, *The Foundations of European Community Law*, 5th edn (Oxford, 2003), ch. 12; A. Albors-Llorens, 'The Standing of Private Parties to Challenge Community Measures: Has the European Court Missed the Boat?' [2003] *CLJ* 72.

interference by public functionaries and towards regulation of the performance of public functions and deterrence of 'illegal' conduct. Sedley LJ expressed this view neatly when he said that administrative law is 'at base about wrongs, not rights'.[49] From this perspective, it might seem entirely unproblematic that the victim test should provide the standing rule for human *rights* claims. This argument is slightly complicated by the fact that many Convention rights (such as freedom of speech and the right to a fair trial) are also protected by the common law, and breach of such common law rights may provide grounds for a non-HRA judicial-review claim. However, although the sufficient interest test applicable to judicial review claims can be applied widely, it could also be interpreted more narrowly along the lines of the victim test in cases where this seems appropriate. Claims based on breaches of human rights might be such cases.

It should be noted also that under s. 7, the victim test applies only to claims that a public authority has acted contrary to s. 6. It does not, expressly at least, apply to an application for a declaration under s. 4 that a provision of primary (or subordinate)[50] legislation is incompatible with a Convention right. Nor, apparently, would it prevent a non-victim from 'relying on' a Convention right in legal proceedings by alleging that some provision of primary (or subordinate) legislation was incompatible with the right.[51]

Despite the narrowness of the victim test of standing, the ECHR (Art 36.2) gives the ECtHR power to allow interventions (both oral and written) by 'any person concerned'.[52] This combination of a narrow standing rule and a potentially generous approach to inteventions suggests a view of the latter not as a corollary of a generous approach to standing but as a counterbalance to restricted rights of claim-initiation.

4.4 THE FUNCTION OF STANDING AND INTERVENTION RULES

What is the function of standing rules? A common answer is that they restrict access to judicial review. But why restrict access? One suggested

---

[49] *R v. Somerset CC, ex p. Dixon* [1998] Env LR 111, 121.

[50] Note that subordinate legislation can also be attacked under s. 6 as an act of a public authority. Primary legislation cannot be so attacked because the Houses of Parliament are expressly excluded from the definition of 'public authority' in s. 6(3). See also s. 6(2).

[51] M. Elliott, 'The Human Rights Act and the Standard of Substantive Review' [2001] *CLJ* 302, 322–34.

[52] The HRA says nothing about intervention except that the government is entitled to be joined as a party to a claim for a declaration of incompatibility: s. 5.

reason is to protect public bodies (and the courts) from vexatious litigants ('busybodies') with no real interest in the outcome of the case but just a desire to make things difficult for public functionaries.[53] It is highly doubtful that many such litigants exist in real life, and if they do, the requirement to obtain permission to make a judicial review claim should be adequate to deal with them. Other reasons for restricting access have been suggested: to reduce the risk that civil servants will behave in over-cautious and unhelpful ways in dealing with citizens for fear of being sued if things go wrong; to ration scarce judicial resources;[54] to prevent the conduct of government business being unduly hampered and delayed by 'excessive' litigation; to ensure that the argument on the merits is presented in the best possible way and by a person with a real interest in presenting it;[55] to ensure that people do not meddle paternalistically in the affairs of others.[56]

Arguably, each of these aims could be furthered by standing rules; but there are probably other ways in which each of them could be achieved. What is distinctive about standing rules is that they direct attention to the interest of the claimant in the outcome of the claim. The sort of interest the judicial review claimant is required to have will depend on what we think judicial review is for. So far as personal standing is concerned, if the aim of judicial review is seen as being the protection of individuals (whether people or corporations), this would suggest and justify standing rules which require the claimant to have been specially affected by what was done or decided.[57] If judicial review is seen as going further and being concerned with the protection of groups as well as individuals, standing rules should only require that the claimant share some personal interest with others. If the prime function of judicial review is seen as being to provide remedies against unlawful behaviour by government, then there should be no requirement of personal interest.

So far as representative standing is concerned, the prime function of associational standing is to facilitate the protection of what might be called 'diffuse interests', that is interests shared by many people. If each member of a group has a personal interest which has been interfered

---

[53] See, e.g., *Broadmoor Hospital Authority v. R* [2002] 2 All ER 727, 733 *per* Lord Woolf MR.

[54] These two reasons were suggested by Schiemann J in the *Rose Theatre Case* [1990] 1 QB 504].

[55] But quality of presentation and personal interest do not always go together.

[56] A requirement that an associational claimant be able to show that it has a mandate from the represented parties would reduce the risk of paternalism.

[57] T.R.S. Allan, *Law, Liberty and Justice* (Oxford, 1993), pp. 223–36.

with, the protection of that interest by court action is made much easier if one person can bring an action as representative of the group. Associational applications are particularly useful when the impact of the challenged action on any particular individual is too slight to justify litigation, but the aggregate impact on all members of the affected group is considerable. Viewed in this way, associational standing is a sort of substitute for a class or representative action,[58] that is an action in which a large number of litigants can consolidate their claims into one for the purposes of having it decided by a court.

The function of public interest standing is to facilitate the enforcement of legal limits on public powers. The two main questions in a public interest action are whether the public functionary has acted illegally and whether the public has a justiciable interest in the subject matter of the claim—that is, an interest which the court should protect. If we were to say that the public always has a justiciable interest that the government should act legally, there would, in effect, be no issue of standing in such cases—the only question would be whether the respondent acted legally or not. As a test of standing, the requirement of public interest performs two functions: it marks the boundary between decisions in which the public has a legitimate interest and decisions in which only affected individuals have a legitimate interest; and it marks the boundary between public interests which are, and those which are not, suitable for protection by the judicial process. An illustration of the former function is the principle (derived from the *Fleet Street Casuals* case), that the general body of taxpayers normally has no legitimate interest in dealings between the Inland Revenue and any individual taxpayer. In performing the latter function, public interest standing is really indistinguishable from the idea of justiciability.

Whereas standing rules regulate the initiation of claims that public functionaries have acted contrary to law, intervention rules regulate participation in claims initiated by others. The standard justification for allowing interventions is to assist the court to resolve the claim in the best possible way. Thus interventions can be allowed even though neither of the parties to the claim consents. Third party interventions are most likely to be helpful in this way when the court conceives the issue facing it as having wide social or political ramifications. A liberal attitude to interventions is likely to go hand-in-hand with a public-interest standing

---

[58] See CPR Part 19.II.

rule.[59] Interventions are less likely to be helpful in cases where the issues at stake are understood and defined more narrowly in terms of the claimant's personal interests.

As we noted earlier, one of the main arguments against a regime of broad public-interest standing and intervention rules is that it might fundamentally change the nature of the judicial process.[60] However, rather than viewing such a change as an undesirable side-effect, we could say that bringing about such a change was the very reason for adopting such a regime of standing and intervention rules. From this point of view, the fundamental issue concerns the role of courts in the constitutional set-up. Once that has been resolved, standing and intervention rules fall into place as a corollary of the judicial function. This line of thought might lead us to reject the idea with which this section began—namely that the function of standing rules is to restrict access to judicial review. Instead, we might see standing rules as facilitating the presentation of a certain class of disputes to the courts for resolution; and, in conjunction with intervention rules, providing the court with sources of information and opinions for the appropriate resolution of those disputes. On this interpretation, the significant differences between regimes of standing and intervention rules relate to the types of disputes they respectively allow to be brought before courts and the types of information and opinions they allow to be presented.

[59] From this perspective, the combination under the ECHR of the narrow victim test of standing and a wide discretion to allow interventions seems odd. It might suggest that the prime function of the victim test is not to focus attention on individual claimants but rather to discourage human-rights organizations from using the judicial process to further their political objectives. Nevertheless, by locating human rights issues within the concrete context of a breach of a particular individuals rights, the victim test might enable the court to prevent the intervention process from becoming unmanageably wide-ranging and unfocused.

[60] See 4.2.3.

5

Remedies

5.1 USES AND AVAILABILITY

Judicial-review remedies (i.e. remedies for breaches of public law) fall into two broad groups. On the one hand there are 'public law remedies'. These used to be known as the 'prerogative orders' of *certiorari*, prohibition, and mandamus. They are now called 'quashing orders', 'prohibiting orders', and 'mandatory orders' respectively.[1] On the other hand there are the 'private law' remedies of declaration, injunction, and damages.[2] Leaving damages aside, these remedies perform four main functions: ordering something to be done is the function of the mandatory order and the (mandatory) injunction; ordering that something not be done is the function of the prohibiting order and the (prohibitory) injunction; depriving a decision of legal effect is the function of the quashing order; and stating legal rights or obligations is the function of the declaration.

5.2 PUBLIC LAW REMEDIES

5.2.1 QUASHING ORDERS

A quashing order deprives a decision of legal effect. There is a theoretical problem here because a decision which is illegal in the public law sense is usually said to be void or a nullity, which means that the decision is treated as never having had any legal effect. A decision which has never had any legal effect cannot be deprived of legal effect. On this view, when we say that an order quashes an illegal decision, what we really mean is

[1] Into this category also fall injunctions under s. 30 of the Supreme Court Act 1981 restraining a person from acting in an office in which the person is not entitled to act: see CPR Rule 54.2(d). The remedy of *habeas corpus* is extremely important in the context of immigration control. The procedure for claiming the remedy is contained in RSC Order 54 (contained in Schedule 1 to the CPR). There is some reason to think that the rules governing the availability of *habeas corpus* are more restrictive than those governing the other judicial review remedies. For discussion see Law Com. No. 226, *Administrative Law: Judicial Review and Statutory Appeals*, Part XI.

[2] Restitution, which is a private law remedy, is dealt with in Ch. 13.

that the order formally declares that from the moment it was purportedly made ('*ab initio*') the decision had no effect in law. Thus anything done in execution of it is illegal. This is the declaratory view of the effect of a quashing order. An alternative view is that an illegal decision is valid until a court decides that it is illegal, at which point it can quash it with retrospective effect.[3] On this view, a quashing order has a constitutive rather than a purely declaratory effect.

Even if the declaratory view of the quashing order is theoretically correct, and illegal decisions never have legal effect, it may not be possible or wise for a person just to ignore such a decision, especially if it authorizes the government to act to that person's detriment. Apart from the fact that it is often unclear, as a matter of law, whether a decision is illegal or not (and so it would be unsafe just to ignore it), it is not the case that a void decision is forever void. However illogical it may seem, a void decision will become valid unless it is challenged, within any time limit for challenges, by an claimant with standing, and unless a court exercises its discretion to award a remedy to the claimant.[4] Once the decision 'matures into validity' as it were, acts already done in execution of it also mature into legality because maturity is retrospective.[5] So whatever the position in theory, in practice, quashing orders are not just declaratory in effect.

5.2.2 PROHIBITING ORDERS

The prohibiting order, as its name implies, performs the function of ordering a body amenable to it to refrain from illegal action. Its issue presupposes that some function of the body remains to be performed, and this sets an internal time limit after which the order could not issue (although an applicant can be denied the order because of undue delay even before the expiry of this time).

It used to be the law that quashing and prohibiting orders were available only against decision-makers who had a duty to act judicially.[6] The meaning of this phrase was never very clear, but it now seems that whatever it meant, the availability of these two remedies is not limited in this way.

---

[3] See M. Taggart, 'Rival Theories of Invalidity in Administrative Law: Some Practical and Theoretical Consequences' in M. Taggart (ed.), *Judicial Review of Administrative Action in the 1980s* (Auckland, 1986).

[4] See 5.4 for discussion of the remedial discretion.

[5] In the constitutive view of the effect of quashing orders, illegal decisions are valid until quashed, and acts done under them are legally valid until the decision that supports them is quashed.

[6] *R v. Electricity Commissioners, ex p. Electricity Joint Committee Co* [1924] 1 KB 171, 205 *per* Atkin LJ.

5.2.3 MANDATORY ORDERS

Quashing and prohibiting orders are concerned with control of the exercise of discretionary powers whereas the mandatory order is designed to enforce the performance of duties. Breach of statutory duty can take the form either of nonfeasance (i.e. failure to perform the duty) or misfeasance (i.e. substandard performance). In certain circumstances,[7] a person who suffers damage as a result of a breach of statutory duty by a public functionary can bring an action in tort for damages or an injunction. Public authorities can also be attacked for nonfeasance by being required to perform their duty. The mandatory order (or a mandatory injunction) is the remedy for this purpose. A mandatory order sometimes issues in conjunction with a quashing order to require a public functionary whose decision has been quashed to go through the decision-making process again. In many cases of this type, the duty which the mandatory order enforces is not a statutory one but the common law duty, which every power-holder has, to give proper consideration to the question of whether or not to exercise the power.

5.2.4 QUASHING, PROHIBITING, AND MANDATORY ORDERS ARE PUBLIC LAW REMEDIES

Quashing, prohibiting, and mandatory orders are not available against decision-makers who derive their powers solely from contract.[8] This limitation is technical and historical. It is concerned with defining the scope of judicial review. As we have seen,[9] it is not clear to what extent contractual bodies are subject to judicial review; but to the extent that they are, there is no good reason why they should not be amenable to a quashing order. Immunity from the prohibiting order is of no practical importance because the function of this remedy is also performed by the injunction, to which contractual bodies are amenable.

It is not clear whether a mandatory order is available in respect of any and every failure by a statutory authority to perform a statutory duty. Probably it is available only in respect of public duties. If this were not so a claimant could, by seeking a mandatory order, evade the restrictive rule that an action in tort for an injunction to restrain breach of statutory duty

---

[7] See 11.3.1.
[8] *R v. Criminal Injuries Compensation Board, ex p. Lain* [1967] 2 QB 864, 882 *per* Lord Widgery CJ. They may be available against decision-makers that 'lack visible means of legal support': *R v. Panel on Takeovers and Mergers, ex p. Datafin Plc* [1987] QB 815.
[9] See 3.1.

will lie only if the duty is owed to the claimant individually—as we have seen, a person claiming a mandatory order only needs to have a 'sufficient interest' in the performance of the duty.

5.2.5 THE CROWN AND THE PUBLIC LAW REMEDIES

The traditional rule was that prerogative orders of *certiorari*, prohibition, and mandamus (now quashing, prohibiting, and mandatory orders respectively) were not available against 'the Crown' (i.e. in modern parlance, central government)[10] or any servant or officer of the Crown acting in his or her capacity as such.[11] The appropriate remedy against the Crown was the declaration. Now, however, it is clear that in judicial review proceedings, these remedies can be awarded against ministers of the Crown acting in their official capacity because ministers are constitutionally responsible for the conduct of government business.[12] Moreover, if an officer of the Crown disobeys a mandatory or prohibiting order, that officer personally may be held to be in contempt of court; and a Minister may be held to be in contempt of court in his or her official capacity if such an order is disobeyed by an officer of the Crown for whom the Minister is responsible. In the former case, the officer can be punished for the contempt; but in the latter case the Minister cannot be punished because of a legal principle[13] that court orders cannot be 'executed' (that is, enforced) against the Crown. The effect of this principle is that as against the Crown, prohibiting and mandatory orders have only declaratory or admonitory (i.e. non-coercive) force.

[10] In English public law, the concept of 'the Crown' is loaded with terminological ambiguity and historical baggage. It is often said that English law lacks a concept of 'the State', and uses the concept of the Crown instead. But such statements are additionally plagued by terminological uncertainties surrounding the concept of the State. They are typically used to support criticism of some aspect or rule of English public law. It is not clear what advantages would accrue from substituting 'State' for 'Crown'. See generally M. Loughlin, 'The State, the Crown and the Law' and P. Craig, 'The European Community, the Crown and the State' in M. Sunkin and S. Payne (eds), *The Nature of the Crown: A Legal and Political Analysis* (Oxford, 1999).

[11] *R v. Secretary of State for War* [1891] 2 QB 326, 334. This is a complicated topic. For a helpful exploration of some of the complexities see T. Cornford, 'Legal Remedies against the Crown and its Officers Before and After *M*' in M. Sunkin and S. Payne (eds), *The Nature of the Crown: A Legal and Political Analysis* (Oxford, 1999).

[12] *M v. Home Office* [1994] 1 AC 377; S. Sedley, 'The Crown in its Own Courts' in C. Forsyth and I. Hare (eds), *The Golden Metwand and the Crooked Cord: Essays on Public Law in Honour of Sir William Wade* (Oxford, 1998). To appreciate the full significance of this development it is necessary to know that at the time, although the declaration—which was available against the Crown—provided an alternative form of final relief, there was no such thing as an interim declaration. There is now: CPR Rules 54.6(1)(c) and 25.1(1)(b).

[13] See RSC Order 77.15 (contained in Schedule 1 to the CPR).

Why is central government immune from the execution of court orders? Historically, the reason is that central government inherited most of the powers of the Monarch. This is why it is called 'the Crown'. Because the Monarch was also seen as the 'fount of justice' and the courts were seen as the Monarch's, it was felt inappropriate that the courts should be able to coerce the Monarch's heir, the Crown, into complying with its orders or punish it for failure to do so.[14] Now, the courts take the view that central government can and should be trusted to obey their orders. Perhaps the judges fear that in any serious confrontation with the government, the courts would suffer. Certainly, the increasingly active and even aggressive use in recent years by the courts of their judicial review powers against central government has not been without its critics. At the end of the day, it may be that the strength of the courts must lie in the esteem they can command from government and people rather than in the power to fine or imprison for disobedience of their orders.

5.3 PRIVATE LAW REMEDIES

The private law remedies are so called because they were originally used only in private law and only later came to be used in public law.

5.3.1 INJUNCTION

The injunction may perform either a prohibiting or a mandatory function. The injunction found its way into public law partly as a means of enforcing public law principles, especially the rules of natural justice, against non-governmental regulatory bodies that derived their powers from contract and so were not amenable to orders of prohibition or mandamus. This use of the injunction is now subject to the doubts noted earlier about the applicability of public law principles to the conduct of contractual bodies.[15]

The other context in which injunctions are important in public law is that of 'interim relief'. When a party challenges the validity of a public decision, the claimant's interests might be irreparably damaged if, pending the hearing and resolution of the case by the court, it was open to the decision-maker to act on or execute the decision. The main function of interim relief is to prevent this happening by ordering the defendant to

---

[14] A. Tomkins, *Public Law* (Oxford, 2003), ch. 2, esp. pp. 51–60.   [15] See 3.1.

refrain from giving effect to its decision pending the trial of the action.[16] When a claimant seeks permission to make a judicial review claim, CPR Rule 54.10(2) allows the court to order 'a stay of the proceedings to which the claim relates'. Such a stay of proceedings can be ordered against any defendant amenable to these orders, including the Crown.[17] However, the precise nature and effect of a stay of proceedings is unclear,[18] and as a result its usefulness as an interim remedy is limited.

The most important form of interim relief in both public and private law is the interim injunction. Traditionally, injunctions (whether final or interim) could not be awarded in proceedings against the Crown. Now, the position differs according to whether the proceedings are 'civil proceedings' or judicial review proceedings. Actions for torts, breaches of contract, and other private law wrongs are civil proceedings for this purpose, while judicial review claims under CPR Part 54 are judicial review proceedings.[19] The rules governing the availability of injunctions against the Crown in civil proceedings are explained later (see 10.2). In judicial review proceedings injunctions, both final and interim, are available against Ministers of the Crown either in respect of their own conduct or in respect of conduct of servants or officers of the Crown for which they are constitutionally responsible. This position was first established in relation to interim injunctions in a case involving an alleged breach of EC law;[20] and it was later extended to injunctions generally and to breaches of English law.[21] A Minister or other officer of the Crown who failed to comply with an injunction could be held to be personally in contempt of court and could be punished for the failure. A Minister could be held in contempt in respect of failure to comply on the part of any servant or officer of the Crown for whose conduct the Minister was constitutionally

---

[16] An alternative to award of an interim injunction for protecting the interests of the claimant pending trial is to allow claims to be made for monetary compensation for loss inflicted by implementation of the challenged decision if the decision is ultimately held to have been illegal. In *R v. Secretary of State for Transport, ex p. Factortame Ltd (No. 2)* ('*Factortame No. 2*') Lord Goff considered the likely unavailability of damages as a consideration in favour of awarding an interim injunction: [1991] 1 AC 603, 673. Concerning damages generally see 5.5.

[17] *R v. Secretary of State for Education, ex p. Avon CC* [1991] 1 QB 558.

[18] See Law Commission Consultation Paper No. 126, *Administrative Law: Judicial Review and Statutory Appeals*, paras 6.8–12.

[19] It is not clear how to categorize judicial review claims not brought under CPR Part 54, as to which see 6.1.

[20] *R v. Secretary of State for Transport, ex p. Factortame Ltd (No. 2)* [1991] 1 AC 603.

[21] *M v. Home Office* [1994] 1 AC 377.

responsible; but the Minister could not be punished for such a contempt.[22]

A claimant who seeks an interim injunction is normally required to give an undertaking to compensate the defendant for irreparable monetary loss suffered as a result of compliance with the injunction in case the defendant wins at the hearing and the injunction is not made permanent but is discharged; but the court has a discretion not to require an 'undertaking as to damages'. If the defendant is a government body, an undertaking may not be required if any damage likely to be suffered will be intangible or unquantifiable injury to the public. Where a government body seeks an injunction against a private individual or corporation, an undertaking is less likely to be required if the purpose of the action is to enforce the law than if its purpose is to protect the government's proprietary or contractual interests.[23] A relevant factor is whether, if no undertaking is required and the legal rule being enforced is ultimately found to have been unlawful, the defendant will nevertheless be able to recover for any loss suffered as a result of the award of the injunction by suing the government. If so, it is less important to demand an undertaking. It is not clear whether this distinction between law–enforcement and other actions is consistent with EC law.[24]

The decision of the House of Lords in *Factortame (No. 2)*, that interim injunctions are available in respect of breaches of EC law, was necessitated by a ruling of the European Court of Justice to the effect that English courts are under an obligation to ignore any rule of English law which stands in the way of the award of such an injunction in a case involving an alleged breach of EC law. The decision created a glaring anomaly between the rule governing breaches of EC law and the rule governing breaches of English law (namely, that injunctions were not available against the Crown). The House of Lords took an early opportunity to remove this anomaly (in *M v. Home Office*). However, the incident has wide implications for English public law. The basic principle of EC law is that the provision of remedies for the enforcement of rights in EC law against Member States is a matter for the legal systems of the Member States (although, of course, EC law itself provides remedies for

---

[22] See 5.2.5.

[23] *Kirklees MBC v. Wickes Building Supplies Ltd* [1993] AC 227.

[24] Ibid. Wickes alleged that statutory Sunday trading provisions were inconsistent with EC law. The House of Lords held that no issue of EC law arose because if Wickes was right, any obligation to pay compensation under EC law would fall on central government and not on the defendant, a local authority.

breaches of EC law by the Community's own legal institutions).[25] This principle creates the possibility that remedies for breaches of EC law by Member States might vary significantly from Member State to Member State, and from the remedies available in respect of breaches of EC law by EC institutions. The European Court views large divergences of this sort as undesirable, and in recent years has laid down various principles to be followed by Member States in designing remedies for breaches of EC law.[26] To the extent that such principles make the remedies available for breaches of EC law by the UK government more generous to claimants than the remedies available for analogous breaches of English law by the government, serious anomalies may arise within English public law. This is what happened in respect of interim injunctions. Such anomalies may appear hard to justify,[27] and as a result, developments in EC law may precipitate analogous 'spillover' developments in English law to bring the two into line.[28]

5.3.2 DECLARATION

The declaration is a non-coercive remedy, which means that failure to comply with a declaration does not amount to a contempt of court.[29] Originally a private law remedy, the declaration proved useful in public law as an alternative to the injunction, which was not available against the Crown. Like the injunction, it became popular in the 1960s and 1970s because it was free of certain procedural limitations that applied to the prerogative orders until 1978. The declaration is an attractive remedy in any situation where the seeking of a coercive remedy might be thought unnecessarily aggressive, and where the claimant is confident that the defendant will do the right thing once a court says what it is. In more recent years the declaration has been used in public interest actions where it often serves the claimant's purpose at least as well as any other remedy.

The declaration, as its name implies, only declares what the legal position of the parties is; it does not change their legal position or rights.

---

[25] See T.C. Hartley, *Foundations of European Community Law*, 5th edn (Oxford, 2003), part IV.

[26] For more details see Hartley, *Foundations of European Community Law*, pp. 229–35.

[27] Even so, the principles governing the award of interim injunctions differ as between English and EC law: *R v. Secretary of State for Health, ex p. Imperial Tobacco Ltd* [2002] QB 161.

[28] See 5.5.2 and 5.6.3. It might also be thought that the difference between the standing rule for judicial review under the HRA and in non-HRA cases is anomalous: see 4.3.

[29] A coercive order may be obtained if the defendant deliberately refuses to comply with a declaration: *Webster v. Southwark LBC* [1983] QB 698.

A declaration (which we might call a 'surrogate declaration') can provide a non-coercive alternative to one of the other judicial review remedies. By granting a declaration that a decision is invalid a court may give guidance to future decision-makers[30] or enable a person to avoid some negative consequence of the decision[31] even in cases where the court is, for some reason, unwilling to quash the decision. But a surrogate declaration could not be awarded in a case where the court had no power to award the 'primary' remedy. Moreover, a declaration (which might be called an 'autonomous declaration') can be awarded even when no other remedy would be available. For example, a declaration is the only remedy available in a case where primary legislation is challenged for inconsistency with EC law—the High Court has no power to issue certiorari to quash an unlawful provision in a statute.[32] A third type of declaration is the so-called 'declaration of incompatibility'. This is the remedy available under the HRA for establishing that a provision of primary or subordinate legislation is incompatible with a Convention right.[33]

The Law Commission has recommended that the High Court have power to award 'advisory' declarations.[34] An advisory declaration is one which does not resolve any existing dispute. A court may be willing to make such a declaration even though the parties are no longer in dispute[35] if, by doing so, it can give useful guidance for the future on a matter of public interest.[36] It is less clear that a court would, or should, make a declaration about an issue over which no dispute has yet arisen—the courts are not a legal advisory service.[37] Particular caution should be

[30] *R v. Secretary of State for Social Services, ex p. Association of Metropolitan Authorities* [1986] 1 WLR 1.
[31] *R v. Panel on Takeovers and Mergers, ex p. Datafin plc* [1987] QB 815, 842. See further C. Lewis, 'Retrospective and Prospective Rulings in Administrative Law' [1988] *PL* 78.
[32] *R v. Secretary of State for Employment, ex p. Equal Opportunities Commission* [1995] 1 AC 1. For further discussion of declarations see P. Cane, 'The Constitutional Basis of Judicial Remedies in Public Law' in P. Leyland and T. Woods (eds), *Administrative Law Facing the Future: Old Constraints and New Horizons* (London, 1997), pp. 262–8.
[33] The other remedies are also available under the HRA: HRA s. 8.
[34] Law Com. No. 226, paras 8.9–14.
[35] Or as it is sometimes put, if the issue is 'moot'.
[36] *R v. Secretary of State for the Home Department, ex p. Salem* [1999] 1 AC 450; *R v. Board of Visitors of Dartmoor Prison, ex p. Smith* [1987] QB 106.
[37] Nor will a court make a declaration of incompatibility under the HRA simply in order to 'chivvy Parliament into spring-cleaning the statute book': *R v. Attorney-General, ex p. Rusbridger* [2003] 3 WLR 232, at [36] *per* Lord Hutton. But note that under both the Government of Wales Act 1998 and the Scotland Act 1998 devolution issues can be raised independently of any legal dispute: P. Craig and M. Walters, 'The Courts, Devolution and Judicial Review' [1999] *PL* 274, 278, 285–6.

exercised in cases where the question the court is asked is highly abstract in the sense that it has very little factual background. The basic function of the courts is adjudication, not the making of abstract statements of law in the nature of legislation.

5.4 THE DISCRETION TO REFUSE A REMEDY

Quashing, prohibiting, and mandatory orders, declarations and injunctions are all discretionary remedies. This means that even if the claimant has standing, has made the application in good time, and can establish that the defendant has acted illegally, relief may be denied if the court thinks, for some reason, that it should not be granted.[38] The fact that a decision is void or that some action or inaction is illegal does not impose on the court any obligation to award a remedy to the claimant. This discretion can also be used to justify refusal of permission to proceed with a claim for judicial review under CPR Part 54; and so it is sometimes said that the whole judicial review jurisdiction is discretionary, not just the remedies.

One aspect of this remedial discretion relates to the time limit for making an application for judicial review under CPR Part 54. CPR Rule 54.5 provides that a claim for judicial review must be commenced 'promptly and in any event not later than 3 months after the grounds to make the claim first arose' unless some other enactment specifies a shorter time limit. Section 31(6) of the Supreme Court Act 1981 allows the court to refuse permission or to refuse relief if there has been undue delay in making the application and the granting of relief would, amongst other things, be 'detrimental to good administration'. Another aspect of the remedial discretion allows a court to refuse a remedy if some suitable alternative avenue of redress was open to the claimant; this is considered in detail later in this chapter (see 5.6.2). The use of the discretion is particularly controversial in the context of review on the basis of procedural impropriety (see 7.3.2.2.1).

The general idea underlying the remedial discretion seems to be that a court should not award a judicial review remedy if to do so would cause (*query* serious)[39] damage to the 'public interest' such as would outweigh the injury which the claimant would suffer as a result of refusal of a remedy. This principle is hopelessly vague. Do the cases give any more

---

[38] T. Bingham, 'Should Public Law Remedies be Discretionary?' [1991] *PL* 64.
[39] See *R v. Attorney-General, ex p. Imperial Chemical Industries Plc* [1987] 1 CMLR 72.

concrete guidance as to how this discretion might be exercised? In one case it was said that courts must show 'a proper awareness of the needs of public administration':[40] a court should be wary of striking down a decision if it is clear that the same decision would have been made even if the decision-maker had not acted unlawfully; or if doing so would unduly delay the conduct of government business;[41] or if members of the public are likely already to have relied on the challenged decision; or if the court thinks that the claimant's motivation in making the application was improper or vexatious or frivolous. Several of these points were taken up in the *Takeover Panel* case[42] in which Lord Donaldson said that the court should be wary of allowing judicial review to be used as a tactical or delaying device by a company which is the target of a takeover bid or by one of several rival bidders.[43]

It has been said that a mandatory order ought not to be made if the defendant is doing all that can reasonably be done to remedy the breach of duty.[44] Another factor was raised in a case in which the government did not properly consult local authorities (as required by statute) before making regulations: by the time the application to revoke the regulations was heard, they had been in operation for some time and to revoke them would have caused considerable administrative inconvenience which could not be justified given that no real complaint was made about the substance of the regulations.[45] But the judge was prepared to award a declaration that the government had not complied with the obligation to consult. This shows that even if a court is not prepared to award one remedy, it may be prepared to give another instead.[46] Relief has also been refused on the ground that the claimant has in the past behaved badly in dealings with the defendant and so is undeserving of assistance;[47] and on

---

[40] *R v. Monopolies and Mergers Commission, ex p. Argyll Group Plc* [1986] 1 WLR 763, 774–5.

[41] This consideration is distinct from the question of whether the claim has been made within the time limit.

[42] [1987] QB 815.

[43] This principle would not prevent award of a declaratory remedy after the takeover battle was over. Judicial review will not normally be allowed before the decision-maker has completed consideration of the case: *R v. Association of Futures Brokers and Dealers Ltd, ex p. Mordens Ltd* (1991) 3 Admin LR 254.

[44] *R v. Inner London Education Authority, ex p. Ali* (1990) 2 Admin LR 822.

[45] *R v. Secretary of State for Social Services, ex p. Association of Metropolitan Authorities* [1986] 1 WLR 1.

[46] See also *Chief Constable of North Wales v. Evans* [1982] 1 WLR 1155.

[47] H.W.R. Wade and C.F. Forsyth, *Administrative Law*, 8th edn (Oxford, 2000), p. 689.

the ground that the remedy sought would achieve no practical benefit for the applicant.[48] The discretion to refuse relief (and permission) raises a number of very important issues. First, is it right that a remedy should be refused because the defendant would have made the same decision even if it had not acted illegally? At first sight it certainly seems wasteful in such circumstances to require the decision-maker to decide again, and in some cases refusal of relief might be justifiable. The danger is that if relief is too often refused on such grounds it may give decision-makers the signal that it does not really matter whether they act within the law or not, so long as the decision is 'right'. This risk is particularly great in relation to procedural impropriety, and we shall discuss it again in that context.[49] A way of avoiding the problem would be for the court, instead of refusing relief completely, to grant a declaration which would not impugn the decision affecting the claimant but would state a rule or principle applicable to future cases.

Secondly, is it right that relief should be refused because the court disapproves of the claimant personally or of the motives behind the making of the claim? In extreme cases perhaps it is; but relief should not be refused unless the claimant's conduct or motive makes it inappropriate to award the relief sought in *this* case. Courts should not refuse relief in order to penalize a claimant for bad conduct unrelated to the relief sought.

Thirdly, it can be argued that the discretion creates unacceptable uncertainty and unpredictability in the law because it allows a person to be refused relief on unexpected and ill-defined grounds. This argument assumes that the rules of judicial review which can be waived by appealing to the discretion are themselves clear and certain; but, as we will see, this is very far from the case. On the other hand, remedial discretion should not be seen as a substitute for defining the grounds of judicial review more carefully and narrowly. For example, if it is thought that an error of law or fact or a breach of natural justice should justify quashing only if it can be said that but for the error or breach, the decision would have been different, this should be built into the definition of the relevant ground of review and not dealt with as a matter of remedial discretion. Nor should remedial discretion be used as a way of discouraging claims for judicial review in order to reduce waiting lists in the courts.

---

[48] *R v. Governors of St Gregory's Roman Catholic Aided High School and Appeals Committee, ex p. M* [1995] ELR 290.
[49] See 7.3.2.2.1.

It is certainly essential that the grounds on which the discretion to refuse relief can be exercised should be spelled out as clearly as possible, and that those grounds should be supportable by rational argument. The courts will always wish to retain a residual and undefined discretion to deal with unexpected cases, but the scope for its operation must be kept as narrow as possible.

5.5 MONETARY REMEDIES

5.5.1 ENGLISH LAW

5.5.1.1 Damages a Private Law Remedy

Unlike the declaration and the injunction, which are private law remedies (i.e. remedies for the redress of private law wrongs) which have been extended to redress public law illegality, damages is a purely private law remedy.[50] What this means is that in order to obtain an award of damages it is necessary[51] that the claimant has suffered a 'private law wrong' such as a tort or a breach of contract. Damages cannot be awarded simply on the basis that a governmental body has acted illegally.[52] The relevance of the remedy in public law is that public functionaries can commit private law wrongs, and so damages is a remedy available against public functionaries. For example, damages for breach of contract can be obtained against a government department. Conversely, whereas a declaration or injunction is available to restrain a breach of natural justice or to declare the invalidity of a decision made in breach of the rules of natural justice, damages are not available for breach of natural justice as such, because this is a wrong recognized only in public law. If a breach of natural justice also amounted to a breach of contract, damages might be available for the breach.[53]

---

[50] *R v. Northavon DC, ex p. Palmer* (1996) 8 Admin LR 16. Concerning restitution (as opposed to damages) see Ch. 13; and P. Cane, 'The Constitutional Basis of Judicial Remedies in Public Law' in P. Leyland and T. Woods (eds), *Administrative Law Facing the Future: Old Constraints and New Horizons* (London, 1997), pp. 257–8.

[51] In the absence of a statutory right to compensation for unlawful conduct such as those created by the Regulation of Investigatory Powers Act 2000, s. 67(7).

[52] Contrast restitution: see Ch. 13 below. At common law, the government is not allowed to confiscate property without paying compensation. This rule is not an exception to the statement in the text because it deals with lawful confiscation; unlawful confiscation would normally be actionable in private law. There is legislation dealing with lawful confiscation.

[53] See further E. Campbell, 'Liability to Compensate for Denial of a Right to a Fair Hearing' (1989) 15 *Monash ULR* 383.

It is not clear why the remedy of damages is not available for public law wrongs. Why should a citizen who is injured in a pecuniary sense by a public law wrong have to be satisfied with having the decision reversed if reversal does not undo the pecuniary injury? The explanation may lie in the fact that all the remedies we have so far considered are discretionary. On the other hand, the remedy of damages is not discretionary, and so the courts do not have as much control over the award of this remedy as over the judicial review remedies. Another possible explanation is related to the nature of judicial review. One of the characteristics of judicial review is that the supervising court does not substitute its decision for that of the public authority; rather it leaves it to the body to make good its illegal behaviour by making a fresh decision which complies with the requirements of the law. To award damages, on the other hand, is in a sense to substitute a decision for that of the public authority. A strict analogy with judicial review would perhaps give the decision-maker a power (and a duty) to award compensation after it had re-made its decision, if it turned out that the claimant had suffered loss as a result of the initial illegal decision (although there are difficulties in this solution which we will consider in a moment).

Should damages be made available as a remedy in public law, and if so, on what basis? There seems no good reason why damages should not, at least in some cases, be a suitable remedy in public law.[54] The second question is, therefore, the more important of the two. There are two main theories which have been suggested as providing a suitable basis for an award of damages: the illegality theory and the risk theory.

5.5.1.2 Damages for Illegality

Under the illegality theory, as the name implies, the ground for the award of damages is that the defendant has acted illegally. The main problem with this theory is that because of the nature of judicial review for illegality it would, in many cases, be extremely difficult, if not theoretically impossible, for a claimant to prove a causal link between the illegal action and the loss suffered. Suppose a claimant suffers loss as a result of an illegal administrative decision. The decision is quashed and the authority makes a fresh and legal decision. That decision might be the same as the first one and cause the claimant the same loss. In fact, one would expect a public authority always to be inclined to search for a way to reach the same decision legally the second time round, if only to save face; and the

---

[54] P. Cane, 'Damages in Public Law' (1999) 9 *Otago LR* 489.

incentive to do so would be even greater if it were likely to be required to pay damages should it decide that its earlier loss-causing decision ought to be changed.

Many grounds of public law illegality do not rule out the making of the same decision again. A decision can be illegal because, for example, it was made in contravention of the rules of natural justice; or because relevant considerations were ignored in making it; or because the authority was unduly influenced by some external factor, such as the opinion of some other authority or an agreement with a third party. None of these grounds of illegality rules out the possibility that exactly the same decision might be reached even if natural justice were complied with, or all relevant considerations were taken into account, or the authority were to ignore all impermissible influences on its decision. So, until the decision is made again, it is not possible to say whether the loss would not have been suffered but for the illegal decision. A solution might be to postpone the decision on the issue of damages until after the authority has deliberated again. The danger of this is that the fear of an award of damages against it would unduly encourage the authority to reach the same decision again, thus creating an appearance of bias.[55] Whether this is a real practical difficulty depends on whether the desire to save face would not anyway have this effect of encouraging the same decision to be made again, even if there were no risk of a damages award.

On the other hand, public authorities do not usually commit illegal acts deliberately, and if an atmosphere of opinion were created in which compensation for illegality were seen as being simply compensation for loss and not as carrying any stigma of fault or as being designed to perform the function of deterring illegal conduct, public authorities might be able to ignore the chance of an award when deciding the claimant's case the second time round.[56] There is a danger of viewing compensation for illegality too much in terms of a traditional tort model rather than in terms of fair distribution of the financial ill-effects of governmental 'mistakes'. In a less than perfect world it is inevitable that public functionaries will sometimes act illegally, and there may be a lot to be said for bringing the 'loss distribution' insights of modern tort theory to bear on the way we perceive public law compensation. The fact that a public functionary pays the compensation should not lead us to think of public functionaries

---

[55] On bias see 7.3.2.1.

[56] Although an award of damages might still have an adverse effect on the authority's finances.

as ordinary defendants. We could see compensation for breaches of public law as providing insurance against loss caused by (typically) unintentional failure to keep within the bounds set by the principles of public law. On the other hand, it may be that this is wishful thinking and that, in practical terms, the award of damages for illegality is incompatible with the theory of judicial review because it cannot be reconciled with the idea that the ultimate decision must usually be left to the public functionary.

However, sometimes the ultimate question is only in theory left to the decision-maker; for example, in some cases of review for errors of law or fact[57] in which it is clear that if the decision-maker had got the law or the facts right, its decision would have been different and could only have been one way. Again, if the court holds that a particular decision was unreasonable, *that* decision could not lawfully be made again. In such cases the claimant may be able to show that if the defendant had not acted unlawfully, no loss would have been suffered.

There are certain other circumstances in which this problem of unduly encouraging an authority to reach a particular decision does not arise and in which a scheme of compensation might be feasible and desirable: where there is no question of a decision being re-made, notably where the time-limit for challenging an allegedly illegal decision has run out (through no fault of the claimant); or where a citizen has suffered loss by relying on a representation by a public functionary that it will act in a particular way, in circumstances where the law will not require the functionary to make good its representation because it has undertaken to act illegally;[58] or where a court exercises its discretion not to quash an illegal decision. In such cases the problem of causation does not exist because the decision in question will not be reconsidered. The problem with drawing distinctions between cases in this way is that the chance circumstance that a particular case falls into one of these categories does not seem to justify the difference between compensation and no-compensation for illegality.

5.5.1.3 Damages for Risk

The risk theory operates independently of any concept of fault or illegality. The idea here is that citizens would be entitled to damages in respect of

---

[57] On these see 9.6 and 9.7.
[58] See 8.3.1.1. The Parliamentary Ombudsman may recommend that compensation be paid in such cases: P. Brown, 'The Ombudsman: Remedies for Misinformation' in G. Richardson and H. Genn (eds), *Administrative Law and Government Action* (Oxford, 1994), ch. 13.

harm resulting from a particular activity regardless of whether that activity was conducted legally or illegally, in a faulty way or absolutely blamelessly—simply on the basis that the harm was a 'risk of the activity'. In terms of the law of tort, the risk theory contemplates either a strict liability scheme of compensation, in which the government would bear the initial burden of compensation, or a no-fault scheme in which the individual is insured against loss by some form of insurance (perhaps tax-based). Under the risk theory, therefore, compensation might be awarded for public law wrongs, but it might also be awarded for action which is perfectly legal in the public law sense.

There are situations in which, by statute, compensation is already payable on a risk theory. For example, under the Land Compensation Act 1973 property owners are entitled to compensation for depreciation in the value of their land caused by such things as noise, vibration, smells, and fumes resulting from public works. The underlying reasoning is that since the public is presumed to benefit greatly from the building of a motorway (for example), private citizens who suffer as a result of its construction should not have to bear their loss for the sake of that wider public interest. The risk theory, therefore, requires an important value judgment in relation to any particular public activity: if that activity inflicts loss on private individuals, should those individuals be expected to bear it or should the public purse pick up the bill? A court might not be thought to be a particularly suitable body to make such a decision because, in many situations, the decision, whichever way it goes, will be politically highly contentious.

It is worth noting, however, that one of the ideas behind the risk theory, namely that losses should be borne by the party best able to absorb them with least dislocation and disruption, is a very popular one in the (private) law of tort. Since government is responsible for, or influences in important ways, a very large number of activities, there may be sound political arguments for thinking seriously about a more extensive and rationalized set of 'risk theory schemes' of compensation for loss caused by public action. It may be, of course, that what we really want is that some losses so caused should be compensated for if they result from illegal action, and some other losses compensated for regardless of whether they result from illegal action or not. The category into which particular losses are put will depend on the value we put on the interests which the public action in question has interfered with, weighed against the value we put on the end which the public action was designed to serve. In some cases we might be happy for courts to do the weighing exercise involved and, to the extent that we are, we could have a 'common law' of public-law compensation. But if the decisions involved are perceived as being too politically sensitive for the courts, some legislative intervention might be necessary to establish the desired framework of value judgements.

5.5.1.4 Voluntary Compensation Schemes

Finally, it should be noted that central government may voluntarily pay '*ex gratia*'[59] compensation to injured individuals without being held liable to do so and even when legal liability to do so may be doubtful or nonexistent. This may happen when a government department settles a case out of court or when compensation is paid as a result of a recommendation of an ombudsman.[60] For example, over £150 million was paid out to investors in a failed investment group after an adverse report by the Parliamentary Commissioner for Administration on the role of the Department of Trade in the affair.[61] The Government has accepted as a general principle that when a person has suffered financial loss as a direct result of maladministration, compensation should be paid to put the person in the position they would have been in if the maladministration had not occurred.[62]

If there is a large group of potential claimants, the government may formalize the awarding of compensation. Sometimes this is done by statute.[63] In other cases the government may establish a non-statutory scheme; for

---

[59] That is, grace and favour, without admission of liability. See C. Harlow, *Compensation and Government Torts* (London, 1982), pp. 119–43.

[60] M. Amos, 'The Parliamentary Commissioner for Administration, Redress and Damages for Wrongful Administrative Action' [2000] *PL* 21. Concerning compensation for 'misinformation' see P. Brown, 'The Ombudsman: Remedies for Misinformation' in G. Richardson and H. Genn, *Administrative Law and Government Action* (Oxford, 1994), ch. 13.

[61] R. Gregory and G. Drewry, 'Barlow Clowes and the Ombudsman' [1991] *PL* 192 and 408. See also R. James and D. Longley, 'The Channel Tunnel Link, the Ombudsman and the Select Committee' [1996] *PL* 38.

[62] Government Response to the First Report from the Select Committee on the Parliamentary Commissioner for Administration 1994–5, Maladministration and Redress (1994–5, HC 316), pp. iv, vi. Payment of compensation for failure to meet published standards of service was a feature of the Citizen's Charter, which became the Service First programme (C. Scott, 'Regulation inside government: re-badging the Citizen's Charter' [1999] *PL* 595) and then the Striving for Better Public Services programme. Central responsibility for such matters appears to have passed to the Prime Minister's Office of Public Service Reform. See also D. Fairgrieve, *State Liability in Tort: A Comparative Study* (Oxford, 2003), pp. 250–3, 259–60.

[63] e.g. Vaccine Damage Payments Act 1979; Criminal Justice Act 1988, s. 133 (compensation for victims of miscarriages of justice).

instance, there is a scheme for compensating people who suffer loss as a result of maladministration by officials handling National Insurance contributions. *Ex gratia* compensation schemes of this sort are attractive to governments because the identity of the beneficiaries and the amounts paid out are under their direct control. On the other hand, such schemes inevitably create anomalies: chosen beneficiaries are often no more 'worthy' of compensation than other victims of government action who are not covered by a similar scheme. The creation of such schemes is more often a reaction to political pressure than the result of a coherent approach to the issue of compensation for the effects of government action. The administration of non-statutory, *ex gratia* compensation schemes may be subject to judicial review to ensure that the provisions of the scheme are properly interpreted and applied.[64] The provisions of a scheme may also be challenged on the ground that they are 'unreasonable'[65] or otherwise contrary to law. It can be argued that such schemes should be embodied in statutes so as to put their administration and the principles of compensation on a firm legal footing.

Local authorities have no general power to make *ex gratia* payments, but may do so on the recommendation of the local government ombudsman.[66]

5.5.2 EUROPEAN COMMUNITY LAW

In certain circumstances, monetary compensation is available in EC law as a remedy against governmental institutions of the Community for the equivalent of what, in English law, would be called public law wrongs.[67] The European Court of Justice (ECJ) has also developed principles under which Member States can be held liable in national courts for breaches of EC law. Such principles were first developed in relation to non-implementation of EC directives. The basic rule is that a directive can create rights and obligations enforceable in the courts of a Member State only if it has been implemented by that Member State. However, if the provisions of a directive are clear, unambiguous, and unconditional, it may be enforceable in national courts by citizens of Member States

---

[64] *R v. Criminal Injuries Compensation Board, ex p. Lain* [1967] 2 QB 864; *R v. Secretary of State for the Home Department, ex p. Harrison* [1988] 3 All ER 86; *R (Mullen) v. Secretary of State for the Home Department* [2002] 1 WLR 1857.

[65] *R v. Ministry of Defence, ex p. Walker* [2000] 1 WLR 806; *R (Association of British Civilian Internees, Far East Region) v. Secretary of State for Defence* [2002] 3 WLR 80.

[66] Local Government Act 2000, s. 92.

[67] T. Hartley, *Foundations of European Community Law*, 5th edn (Oxford, 2003), pp. 462–77.

against organs of the State[68] even though the directive has not been implemented at all or has been wrongly implemented by the State in question. Provisions enforceable in this way are called 'directly effective'. If damages for breach of the directive would have been available against the State if the directive had been implemented, damages can be obtained even though the directive has not been implemented.[69] Although such damages are for breach of the directive, the basis on which they are awarded is that the Member State has failed in its obligation under EC law to implement the directive properly. Furthermore, if a citizen suffers loss as a result of failure by a Member State properly to implement a directive, the citizen may be entitled to recover damages for that loss from the State even if the relevant provisions of the directive are not directly effective and even if, had the directive been implemented, the citizen would have been entitled to damages from another citizen rather than from the State.[70]

More importantly, the ECJ has also held that a Member State can be liable to pay damages for loss directly resulting from a serious breach of any provision of EC law so long as the provision was intended to confer rights on individuals.[71] Such liability can arise out of the actions of any branch of government, whether the legislature, the executive, or the judiciary.[72] It is for national courts to create a head of liability to give effect to this principle; but the rules governing Member-State liability for breach of EC law must be no less favourable to claimants than the rules relating to similar domestic claims, and they must not be such as to make it impossible or excessively difficult to obtain compensation. The ECJ held that any rule requiring malice on the part of the Member State would fall foul of this latter requirement; as would any rule which totally excluded liability for purely economic loss and any rule that required fault greater than a serious breach of EC law.

This decision of the ECJ will require English courts to award damages for serious breaches of EC law by organs of the UK government (including the legislature and the courts) regardless of whether such breaches amount to a wrong in English private law. It has thus created the potential for significant divergence between the liability of governmental bodies for

---

[68] The concept of State organs (or 'emanations') is functionally equivalent to that of 'public authority' under s. 6 of the HRA.

[69] *Foster v. British Gas Plc* [1991] 1 QB 405; [1991] 2 AC 306.

[70] *Francovich v. Italy* [1991] ECR I-5357.

[71] *R v. Secretary of State for Transport, ex p. Factortame Ltd (No. 4)* [1996] QB 404. See also *Dillenkofer v. Federal Republic of Germany* [1997] QB 259. For more detailed discussion see Hartley, *Foundations of European Community Law*, pp. 235–40.

[72] Including the highest court: *Köbler v. Austria* [2003] 3 CMLR 1003.

breaches of EC law and their liability for breaches of English public law. Such divergence will probably, sooner or later, generate pressure to bring EC law and English law into line.[73]

5.5.3 HUMAN RIGHTS LAW

Article 41 of the ECHR provides that if the internal law of a State which is a party to the Convention 'allows only partial reparation' for a violation of the Convention, the ECtHR 'shall, if necessary, afford just satisfaction to the injured party'. Under s. 8 of the HRA, damages may be awarded for breaches of s. 6 of the HRA (i.e. conduct by a public authority unlawful by reason of incompatibility with a Convention right); but no award of damages is to be made unless 'the court is satisfied that the award is necessary to afford just satisfaction'. In deciding whether to award damages, and the amount of any such award, the court must take into account principles developed by the ECtHR under Article 41.[74] In theory, damages under the HRA/ECHR are fundamentally different from damages in English law in that the court has a discretion whether or not to award the former,[75] but no discretion in relation to the latter. However, it is not clear how much difference this makes in practice. Under both regimes, a claimant will not be awarded substantial damages unless substantial harm has been suffered;[76] and if it has, a court is likely to consider that an award of substantial damages is necessary to provide just satisfaction.[77]

The possibility of obtaining a monetary remedy under the HRA/ECHR clearly creates an incentive for claimants to argue that particular acts of public authorities that cause harm are not only unlawful as a matter of English public law, but are also in breach of s. 6 of the HRA.[78] It also creates the possibility that damages may be recoverable under the

---

[73] For further discussion see Cane, op cit. n. 50 above, pp. 258–60.

[74] See generally *Anufrijeva v. Southwark LBC* [2003] EWCA Civ 1406; Law Com. No. 266, *Damages under the Human Rights Act 1988* (2000); D. Fairgrieve, 'The Human Rights Act 1988, Damages and Tort Law' [2001] *PL* 695.

[75] It is said that under the ECHR/HRA damages are a remedy of last resort to be awarded only when necessary taking into account the interests of the complainant and the public.

[76] This is why English law has the concept of 'nominal damages'. Such an award respects the claimant's entitlement to damages while also recognizing that substantial damages are not appropriate because no (substantial) harm has been suffered.

[77] An award of common law damages (e.g. in a tort action for nuisance) may satisfy the requirement of just satisfaction for any breach of the ECHR involved in the conduct for which damages are awarded: *Marcic v. Thames Water Utilities Ltd* [2002] QB 929 (reversed by HL on other grounds: [2003] UKHL 66). Exemplary damages are not available under the ECHR/HRA: *Anufrijeva v. Southwark LBC* [2003] EWCA Civ 1406.

[78] e.g. *R (Bernard) v. Enfield LBC* [2003] LGB 423.

HRA for harm caused by conduct that is not unlawful as a matter of English public or private law.[79]

5.6 EXCLUSION OF JUDICIAL REVIEW

5.6.1 EXPRESS EXCLUSION

The courts have generally taken an uncompromising attitude towards express legislative provisions designed to exclude judicial review. Judicial review is seen as a basic right of all citizens which the legislature will be taken to have excluded only by the very clearest words. It cannot be excluded by implication.[80] This attitude seems to be the result of viewing judicial review as chiefly designed to protect the rights of the individual from unlawful interference by government. So it has been held that a provision in a statute that regulations made under the statute will take effect as if enacted in the statute (i.e. they will be unchallengeable as if they were made by Parliament) does not prevent the courts holding the regulation to be *ultra vires*.[81] A provision that a decision shall not be subject to appeal (or that it shall be 'final') does not exclude judicial review.[82] In *Anisminic Ltd v. Foreign Compensation Commission*[83] it was held that a statutory provision that decisions of the Commission were not to be 'called in question in any court of law' was ineffective to exclude the quashing of a decision affected by 'jurisdictional' error of law: its only effect was to prevent a decision being quashed for 'non-jurisdictional' error of law.[84] The excluding provision was drafted in what appeared to be very clear and unambiguous terms, and the decision indicates that the House of Lords saw the role of the courts in judicial review proceedings as being of great importance.

Of course, *Anisminic* is authority only in relation to the precise wording of the provision in issue in that case, and it would not prevent a court interpreting different wording more favourably to the decision-maker. So,

---

[79] e.g. *Anufrijeva v. Southwark LBC* [2003] EWCA Civ 1406 (damages for maladministration).

[80] *R (Sivasubramaniam) v. Wandsworth County Court* [2003] 1 WLR 475.

[81] *Minister of Health v. R (on the Prosecution of Yaffe)* [1931] AC 494; such provisions are no longer used.

[82] *R v. Medical Appeal Tribunal, ex p. Gilmore* [1957] 1 QB 574.

[83] [1969] 2 AC 147; see 9.6.1.

[84] See also *R v. Maidstone Crown Court, ex p. Harrow LBC* [2000] QB 719 (provision excluding judicial review of matters arising out of trials on indictment ineffective where it is alleged that the trial court lacked jurisdiction and there is no other remedy); *R v. Secretary of State for the Home Department, ex p. Fayed* [1997] 1 All ER 228.

for example, more recent authority suggests that a provision to the effect that the issuing of a certificate 'shall be conclusive evidence' that the conditions for the issue of the certificate had been satisfied would normally be effective to exclude judicial review of the decision to issue the certificate.[85] The scope and effectiveness of statutory exclusion clauses are matters of statutory interpretation, and it is open to the courts, by interpreting such clauses more or less strictly, to regulate access to judicial review. After a period when the insertion into statutes of clauses of the *Anisminic* type fell out of favour, their use increased again. A variety of wording is used[86] and it is difficult to be certain how such clauses will be interpreted.

Another important type of statutory exclusion clause is one that sets a time-limit on judicial review. It has been said by the courts that there are good reasons of public policy to enforce such time-limits: public programmes ought not to be suspended or held up indefinitely for fear of a challenge at some later date.[87] The most common statutory period for the challenge of administrative decisions is six weeks.[88] There can be no sound objection to time limits of some sort, but six weeks seems an unnecessarily and even unfairly short time. Such limits might be acceptable if the only persons entitled to challenge governmental action were persons directly affected. But as we have seen, the law in some cases allows anyone with a genuine interest to make an application for judicial review, and it may take such persons a considerable time to find out about the decision they want to challenge.

5.6.2 IMPLIED OUSTER BY ALTERNATIVE REMEDIES

The basic principle here is that because judicial review remedies are discretionary, they will not be awarded if an equally or more 'convenient, beneficial and effectual' alternative remedy is available.[89] The mere

---

[85] *R v. Registrar of Companies, ex p. Central Bank of India* [1986] QB 1114. The court was told that there were some 300 such clauses on the statute book.

[86] For example, Telecommunications Act 1984, s. 18(3): 'shall not be questioned by any legal proceedings whatever'; Regulation of Investigatory Powers Act 2000, s. 67(8): 'decisions of the Tribunal . . . (including any decisions as to their jurisdiction) shall not be subject to appeal or liable to be questioned in any court.'

[87] *R v. Secretary of State for the Environment, ex p. Ostler* [1977] QB 122.

[88] CPR Rule 54(5) imposes a three-month time limit on applications for judicial review, but this limit operates subject to any statutory time limit. See also Supreme Court Act 1981, s. 31(7) and 6.2.

[89] *R v. Paddington Valuation Officer, ex p. Peachey Property Corporation Ltd* [1966] 1 QB 380; *R v. Hillingdon LBC, ex p. Royco Homes Ltd* [1974] QB 720; *Scott v. National Trust* [1998] 2 All ER 705.

existence of an alternative remedy does not exclude judicial review.[90] For example, it is in the discretion of the court whether or not to award mandamus to enforce the performance of a statutory duty despite the existence of a statutory default power.[91] However, it has often been said that judicial review will be allowed in the face of an alternative remedy only in exceptional cases.[92] Judicial review might be refused on the ground that the alternative dispute-settling body possessed relevant expertise which the court lacked; or that the case raised issues which could be considered by the alternative body but not by the court on judicial review;[93] or that the alternative body's procedure was better suited to resolving the case than judicial review procedure;[94] or that the alternative procedure was likely to be more speedy than judicial review.[95]

Even so, permission may be given for judicial review, despite the existence of an alternative remedy, if the claimant alleges bias or procedural irregularity,[96] malice on the part of the decision-maker,[97] lack of jurisdiction, or breach of human rights.[98] Even in cases where the claimant has pursued the alternative remedy, permission for judicial review may be

---

[90] *Leech v. Deputy Governor of Parkhurst Prison* [1988] AC 533; *R v. Bedwellty Justices, ex p. Williams* [1997] AC 225; *R v. Director of Public Prosecutions, ex p. Kebeline* [2000] 2 AC 26. But the fact that the claimant has no remedy alternative to judicial review does not necessarily mean that permission will be granted to make a CJR: *R (Tucker) v. Director-General of the National Crime Squad* [2003] ICR 599.

[91] *R v. Inner London Education Authority, ex p. Ali* (1990) 2 Admin LR 822; *R v. Secretary of State for the Environment, ex p. Ward* [1984] 1 WLR 834. The exercise of default powers is itself subject to judicial review: e.g. *Secretary of State for Education and Science v. Tameside MBC* [1977] AC 1014. The existence of a statutory default power can also affect the availability of private law causes of action such as nuisance: *Marcic v. Thames Water Utilities Ltd* [2003] 3 WLR 1603.

[92] e.g. *R v. Chief Constable of Merseyside Police, ex p. Calveley* [1986] QB 424, 433 *per* Lord Donaldson MR; *R v. Panel on Takeovers and Mergers, ex p. Guinness Plc* [1990] 1 QB 146, 178; *R (Sivasubramaniam) v. Wandsworth County Court* [2002] 1 WLR 475. See also *R (Cowl) v. Plymouth City Council* [2002] 1 WLR 803; *Anufrijeva v. Southwark LBC* [2003] EWCA Civ 1406 at [81] (claim for damages for maladministration under the HRA).

[93] The rules of judicial review might not, for example, allow a thorough investigation of the merits of the claim.

[94] Because, for example, the claim raises significant factual questions for the resolution of which judicial review procedure is not designed: *R v. Falmouth and Truro Port Health Authority, ex p. South West Water Ltd* [2000] 3 All ER 306. On judicial review and fact-finding see 6.2.

[95] *R v. Birmingham City Council, ex p. Ferrero Ltd* (1991) 3 Admin LR 613; *R v. Falmouth and Truro Port Health Authority, ex p. South West Water Ltd* [2000] 3 All ER 306.

[96] *R v. Hereford Magistrates' Court, ex p. Rowlands* [1998] QB 110.

[97] *R v. Birmingham City Council, ex p. Ferrero Ltd* (1991) 3 Admin LR 613.

[98] *R (Sivasubramanian) v. Wandsworth County Court* [2003] 1 WLR 475; *Leech v. Deputy Governor of Parkhurst Prison* [1988] AC 533.

granted if the alternative procedure appears unlikely to produce a satisfactory outcome;[99] or if it has become seriously delayed.[100]

5.6.3 THE IMPACT OF EC AND HUMAN RIGHTS LAW

Mrs Johnston was a reserve officer in the Royal Ulster Constabulary. Her
contract of employment was not renewed because there was a policy that
women officers should not carry arms and, as a result, there were enough
full-time women officers in the RUC to do all the jobs open to women.
Mrs Johnston made a claim to an industrial tribunal that she had been a
victim of sex discrimination; but the Secretary of State issued a certificate
(which the relevant statute said was 'conclusive') that she had been dismissed on grounds of national security. This certificate deprived the
tribunal of jurisdiction. Sex discrimination in employment is a matter
dealt with by EC law, and the tribunal referred a number of questions to
the ECJ which held, *inter alia*, that the Order in Council under which the
certificate was issued was inconsistent with a requirement of EC law that
the right of men and women to equal treatment recognized by EC law
should be effectively protected by national legal systems.[101]

It is clear, therefore, that rules of English law which restrict access to
courts, tribunals, and remedies may fall foul of EC law; and the greater the
restriction, the more likely is it to do so. Being required to have recourse
to one remedy rather than another would not be contrary to EC law
unless the latter gave significantly less-effective protection to the aggrieved
party than the former. But very short time limits may be vulnerable to
attack.[102]

So far as human rights law is concerned, time limits, provisions excluding judicial remedies, and rules about the effect of alternative remedies
may be incompatible with Article 6 of the ECHR (right to a fair hearing
by an independent and impartial tribunal),[103] or with Article 13 (right to
an effective remedy for breaches of the ECHR).[104] Article 6 applies to

---

[99] *R v. Ealing LBC, ex p. Times Newspapers Ltd* (1985) 85 LGR 316, 331.

[100] *R v. Chief Constable of Merseyside Police, ex p. Calveley* [1986] QB 424.

[101] *Johnston v. Chief Constable of Royal Ulster Constabulary* [1987] QB 129.

[102] In *Matra Communications SAS v. Home Office* [1999] 1 WLR 1646 the CA held that a
requirement (contained in regulations giving effect to an EC directive) that proceedings be
brought 'promptly and in any event within three months' was not contrary to EC law. On
the other hand, in *Emmott v. Minister for Social Welfare* [1993] ICR 8 the ECJ held that a
Member State cannot rely on a time-limit provision in answer to a claim based on the
provisions of an EC directive that the State has failed to implement properly.

[103] R. Clayton and H. Tomlinson, *The Law of Human Rights* (Oxford, 2000), paras
11.185–203, 11.321A.

[104] Ibid., paras 21.156–179.

many administrative procedures as well as to court proceedings. In certain types of case, lack of independence or impartiality in an administrative decision-maker may be cured if the decision is subject to judicial review.[105] In such cases, availability of judicial review is effectively a precondition for the compliance of an administrative decision-making regime with Article 6.

5.6.4 THE CONSTITUTIONAL SIGNIFICANCE OF RULES ABOUT EXCLUSION OF REMEDIES

In theory, the effect of a statutory exclusion clause is simply a matter of statutory interpretation. Interpeting the words of a statute is often not a simple matter, and an exclusion clause may admit of more than one possible meaning. If so, and if the different meanings leave more or less scope for the award of judicial remedies, then the courts have a limited power to give effect to their view of the importance of judicial control of government. Judicial views on this matter are likely to vary from judge to judge and from time to time: some judges favour more rather than less judicial review; others less rather than more. Ultimately, the balance is a question of individual judgment guided, perhaps, by some notion of the function of judicial review. Also, the factors identified above as relevant to deciding the effect of alternative remedies may be relevant to deciding the effect of a statutory exclusion clause which is open to more than one interpretation. Relevant, too, are the views of individual judges about the role of the courts in interpreting and applying legislation: some judges may be more prepared to find an ambiguity in statutory language than others or even to interpet a statute 'purposively'[106] in order to achieve a desired result. Individual judges may give more or less weight to the fact that it is the government, rather than Parliament, which drafts legislation and decides what it shall contain. Some may wonder why the government should be able to stipulate the limits of judicial control of the government by enacting exclusion provisions in statutes which courts are, by virtue of the doctrine of Parliamentary supremacy, bound to apply.

So far as alternative remedies are concerned, if the alternative is provided by statute, deference to Parliamentary intention can be called in aid of requiring recourse to the alternative. Alternative remedies raise quite directly questions about the suitability of the judicial process as opposed

---

[105] *R (Alconbury Developments Ltd) v. Secretary of State for the Environment, Transport and the Regions* [2003] 2 AC 295.

[106] See 19.1.2.

to other avenues open for the control of governmental action. For example, if a claim for a judicial review remedy raises politically contentious matters, a court might be inclined to say that an alternative political form of control, such as a ministerial default power, is the only one available. As we have seen, questions of expertise and speed are also relevant. Once again, judicial views about the function and importance of judicial remedies, even if unexpressed, are bound to underlie decisions about the effect of alternative remedies. In one case an immigrant who was present in Britain was denied judicial review of a decision not to give him leave to enter the country because of the existence of a right of appeal which could only be exercised if the immigrant left Britain.[107] This decision seems to me very harsh, but this is a value-judgement with which others could reasonably disagree. Views about the proper role and function of judicial remedies to control government activity are inevitably political in nature in the sense that they concern the allocation of decision-making power in society. We will explore these themes in more detail in Chapter 19.

It has also been suggested that requiring recourse to an alternative remedy is used as a way of reducing the number of judicial review cases and the strain on the judicial resources available to hear such cases.[108] It is questionable whether this is a good way to deal with lack of judicial resources. At all events, the rules about alternative remedies introduce another large element of discretion into the award of judicial review remedies, making the outcome of the process of seeking judicial review extremely unpredictable. Indeed, Lord Donaldson once said that the circumstances in which the court will allow judicial review in the face of an alternative remedy 'defy definition'.[109]

---

[107] *R v. Secretary of State for the Home Department, ex p. Swati* [1986] 1 WLR 477.

[108] N. Collar, 'Judicial Review and Alternative Remedies—An Analysis of Recent English Decisions' (1991) 10 *CJQ* 138, 142–3.

[109] *R v. Panel on Takeover and Mergers, ex p. Guinness Plc* [1990] 1 QB 146, 147.

6

The Mechanics of Judicial Review

The subject matter of this chapter is technical and complex. But it is worth careful attention because under the surface are two issues of considerable practical and theoretical importance. One issue is whether claims relating to the performance of public functions should be dealt with by procedures that are, in certain respects, more advantageous to the defendant than those applicable to other types of claims. The second issue is whether such claims should be channelled to a specialist forum for resolution.

6.1 THE CLAIM FOR JUDICIAL REVIEW AND THE JUDICIAL REVIEW PROCEDURE

One result of the emphasis on remedies in administrative law[1] is that the procedure for applying for those remedies is central to an understanding of the position of the public law litigant. The procedure for applying for quashing, prohibiting and mandatory orders (called 'the judicial review procedure' (JRP)) is contained in Part 8 of the Civil Procedure Rules (CPR) as modified by CPR Part 54. (For convenience, in this chapter, these orders will be referred to collectively as 'the new prerogative orders'.)[2] These rules lay down a procedure for what are called claims for judicial review (CJRs). A CJR is 'a claim to review (i) the lawfulness of an enactment; or (ii) a decision, action or failure to act in relation to the exercise of a public function' (CPR Rule 54.1(2)(a)). JRP (as laid down in CPR Parts 8 and 54) must be used for making a CJR in which any one of the new prerogative orders is sought (whether or not any other remedy is sought in addition or in the alternative). For making a CJR in which the

---

[1] See 2.5.

[2] Strictly, the new prerogative orders are the 'old' prerogative orders of *certiorari*, prohibition, and mandamus under different names. But in practice it seems likely that the name change will free these remedies of such of the technical rules as still govern their availability. In other words, the name change is likely to shift attention away from the remedies as such and on to the rights and obligations that they are designed to protect.

remedy sought is a declaration or an injunction, JRP *may* be used (and *must* be used if any one of the new prerogative orders is sought in the alternative or in addition). A CJR made by JRP 'may include a claim for damages but may not seek damages alone' (CPR Rule 54.3(2)).[3] For making a CJR that does not have to be made by JRP, the claimant can choose between the procedure laid down in CPR Part 8 (unmodified by Part 54) (which the CPR calls 'the alternative procedure' for making claims) and that laid down in CPR Part 7 (which, for convenience, will be referred to in this chapter as 'the basic procedure'). So there are two procedural routes available for making a CJR—JRP, and either the basic or the alternative procedure at the claimant's option. Which route is appropriate depends on the remedy (or remedies) sought by the claimant.

This complicated two-track procedural regime was first introduced in 1978 by amendments to the predecessor of CPR Part 54, Order 53 of the Rules of the Supreme Court (RSC). The basic aim of these amendments was to establish RSC Order 53 as the procedure for making applications for judicial review (as they were then called) regardless of the remedy sought by the applicant (as the claimant was then called). Because the remedies of declaration and injunction continued to be available in private law as well as in public law, Order 53 contained a provision (Rule 1(2)) about when it would be appropriate for declarations and injunctions to be sought and awarded in applications made under Order 53. In essence, that provision allowed a declaration or an injunction to be awarded if the conditions for the award of one of the 'old' prerogative orders (i.e. *certiorari*, prohibition, or mandamus)[4] were satisfied. In more modern jargon, we can say that this provision defined the scope of application of Order 53 procedure, and the availability of declarations and injunctions under that procedure, in terms of the rules governing the availability of *certiorari*, prohibition, and mandamus. This provision was also enacted in s. 31(2) of the Supreme Court Act 1981; and although Order 53 has now been replaced by CPR Rule 54, s. 31(2) is still in force and is expressly referred to in CPR Rule 54.3 as setting out the circumstances in which the court may grant a declaration or injunction in a claim for judicial review. This means that in theory, at least, the law about the availability of the old prerogative orders is relevant to determining the availability of declarations and injunctions under CPR Part 54.

In practice, however, the availability of a declaration or injunction in a claim made by JRP under CPR Part 54 is likely to depend on whether the

---

[3] See also Supreme Court Act 1981, s. 31(4).   [4] See n. 2 above.

claim is a CJR as defined in CPR Rule 54.1(2). Before 1978, judicial review and administrative law were basically understood in terms of the rules governing the availability of *certiorari*, prohibition, and mandamus; and this was reflected in the way the scope of Order 53 (and the availability of declarations and injunctions under Order 53) was defined in the 1978 amendments. However, as a result of the functional turn in administrative law (described in Chapter 1), to which the 1978 amendments to Order 53 made a significant contribution, the scope of judicial review and of administrative law is now understood primarily in terms of the concept of a public function. Declarations and injunctions, like the new prerogative orders, are remedies for breaches of administrative law thus understood, and the CJR is the main formal vehicle for complaining of such breaches. If a claim falls within the definition of a CJR, a declaration or injunction (like the new prerogative orders) will be available to satisfy that claim. The difficult question is not when declarations and injunctions are available as remedies in a CJR made by JRP, but rather when a CJR (in which the remedy sought is a declaration or injunction) may appropriately be made by the basic (Part 7) or alternative (Part 8) procedure as opposed to the JRP.

Before addressing that question, it is necessary to outline the chief differences between the basic procedure and JRP.

6.2 THE BASIC/ALTERNATIVE PROCEDURES AND JRP CONTRASTED

The first important difference is that under Part 54 the claimant must first seek 'permission to proceed' with a CJR.[5] JRP, therefore, has two stages: the 'permission stage' and the 'hearing stage'. At the permission stage the court decides whether the claim should proceed, and at the hearing stage it decides whether it should succeed. In theory, any matter which is relevant to whether the claimant should be awarded a remedy at the hearing stage is also relevant to the decision, at the permission stage, whether the claim should be allowed to proceed. In other words, permission to proceed can be refused on any ground on which a remedy could be refused at the hearing stage. Conversely, the fact that a claimant is given permission to proceed does not (in principle, at least) prevent the court at the hearing stage deciding, for example, that the claim should fail because

---

[5] Concerning the compatibility of the permission requirement with ECHR Article 6 see R. Clayton and H. Tomlinson, *The Law of Human Rights* (Oxford, 2000), para. 11.320.

of undue delay, even if the issue of delay was argued and expressly decided in the claimant's favour at the permission stage.[6] The permission requirement gives the court control over the proceedings from the very start, and because the defendant does not have to take part in a permission hearing,[7] it may be relieved of the need to take any steps to secure refusal of permission to proceed with a weak claim.[8] By contrast, in claims brought under the basic or alternative procedure, the defendant has to take positive steps to have the claim struck out if there is some ground for doing so.

A practice direction supplementing CPR Part 54 (PD 54, 8.4) says that the court will generally, in the first instance, consider the question of permission without a hearing. Even when there is a hearing in order to clarify issues, permission proceedings are meant to be brief. The basic idea is that the court should give only cursory consideration to the claimant's case at the permission stage, and that permission proceedings should not be used as a surrogate for a full hearing in order to test the strengths and weaknesses of the parties' respective cases as an aid to settlement out-of-court.[9] The function of the permission requirement is not spelled out in Part 54. But it has been said that it is designed to weed out cases which are prima facie unarguable and so have no real chance of success; or which might be called 'frivolous' or 'vexatious' in the sense of being brought, not out of a genuine interest in the outcome, but for some

---

[6] *R v. Lichfield DC and Williams, ex p. Lichfield Securities* [2001] EWCA Civ 304.

[7] Unless ordered by the court to do so. A defendant who takes part in a permission hearing will normally have to bear the cost of doing so: R. McCracken and G. Jones, '*Leach* and Permission Costs' [2002] *JR* 4.

[8] To be allowed to take part in a permission hearing, the defendant must file an acknowledgement of receipt of the claim form by which the claim process is started. But failure to do so does not, by itself, prevent the defendant taking part in the *hearing* of the claim if permission is granted. On the other hand, once permission has been granted, the defendant cannot apply to have it set aside.

[9] Indeed, it has been said that a court may be justified in refusing permission to proceed in order to provide an incentive for the resolution of the dispute, without recourse to litigation, by some form of 'alternative dispute resolution' (ADR) even though the alternative method does not amount to an 'alternative remedy' in the strict sense (see 5.6.2.): *R (Cowl) v. Plymouth City Council* [2002] 1 WLR 803. The relationship between permission and settlement is ill-understood. But it is known that a significant proportion of CJRs are settled or withdrawn after permission to proceed has been granted. See generally L. Bridges, G. Meszaros, and M. Sunkin, 'Regulating the Judicial Review Caseload' [2000] *PL* 651. Whether or not this gives cause for concern depends in part on views about the function of judicial review: M. Sunkin, 'Withdrawing: A Problem of Judicial Review?' in P. Leyland and T. Woods, *Administrative Law Facing the Future: Old Constraints and New Horizons* (London, 1997), pp. 221–41.

ulterior motive such as to make things difficult for the defendant.[10] The arguability test is reasonable, but the idea that 'frivolous or vexatious' claims should not be allowed to proceed is more problematic. Legal proceedings are often brought for a variety of reasons: not just to obtain a favourable outcome, but also in order, for example, to obtain publicity, or to force a reconsideration of a contentious decision or policy, or as a bargaining tactic. It might be argued that so long as one of the claimant's motives is to obtain a favourable outcome, permission should be granted provided the claim is not unarguable.[11] However, it has been said, in the context of applications for judicial review of decisions of bodies exercising powers to regulate company takeovers, that a remedy would not normally be given until after the takeover process was complete; and that such a body should 'ignore any application for leave[12] . . . since to do otherwise would enable such applications to be used as a mere ploy in takeover battles'.[13] Underlying this approach is a fear that judicial review will be used for tactical purposes to cause delay and ultimately defeat the takeover bid.

If the basic function of the permission requirement is to weed out unarguable or vexatious cases it might be expected that only a small proportion of cases would fail at this stage. However, it seems that permission is refused in more than a third of all CJRs, and this might suggest that the permission requirement is performing some other function such as keeping the number of pending CJRs down,[14] so that the delay between the granting of leave and the hearing is not too great. If this is happening, it is surely a misuse of the permission procedure, and it reveals a lack of judicial resources to meet demand. Ironically, the permission procedure itself is liable to exacerbate any shortage of judicial resources: a two-stage procedure inevitably requires more judicial resources than would a single-stage procedure. Also, it may be that the relative cheapness and speed of the permission procedure encourages applications to be made for

---

[10] *R v. Inland Revenue Commissioners, ex p. Federation of Self-Employed and Small Businesses Ltd* [1982] AC 617. Concerning permission in human rights cases see Clayton and Tomlinson, *Law of Human Rights*, para. 22.99.

[11] *R v. Monopolies and Mergers Commission, ex p. Argyll Group Plc* [1986] 1 WLR 763, 773–4 *per* Lord Donaldson MR. But see *Ex p. Ewing* [1991] 1 WLR 388.

[12] As permission was called at this time.

[13] *R v. Panel on Takeovers and Mergers, ex p. Datafin Plc* [1987] QB 815, 840.

[14] See e.g. *R v. Panel on Takeovers and Mergers, ex p. Guinness Plc* [1990] QB 146, 177–8. Between 1981 and 1999 the number of applications for permission increased about ninefold. But researchers have found 'no consistent relationship between the overall volume of judicial review applications and [permission] grant rates': Bridges, Meszaros, and Sunkin, op. cit. n. 9 above, 666.

tactical reasons (e.g. to increase the chance of a favourable settlement) despite the absence of any serious expectation that permission will be granted. In other words, the requirement of permission may encourage the very sort of applications it is designed to weed out, especially given the very short time limit within which a CJR has to be commenced: it is safer to seek permission even if the claimant expects to settle the claim without further litigation. In this light, the high failure rate of permission applications would not be as surprising as it first seems.[15]

The second noteworthy feature of JRP is that CPR Rule 54.5 imposes a short time-limit in which a CJR must be made: the claim must be made promptly and at any event within three months from the date when the grounds to make the claim arose.[16] By contrast, the time limit for private law claims (in tort and contract, for instance) is at least three years; and for CJRs made by the basic or alternative procedure, there is no fixed time limit. Rather, delay in applying is a factor to be taken into account when the court exercises its discretion whether or not to award a declaration or injunction. The chief functions of the short time-limit under CPR Part 54 are to prevent public programmes from being unduly held up by litigation challenging their legality;[17] and to prevent steps already taken in execution of challenged decisions having to be reversed long after the decision was acted upon.

The time limit in Part 54 suffers from three major defects. First, the period of three months is too short (and may be vulnerable to attack under EC law[18] or ECHR Article 6[19]). Secondly, not even the three months is an entitlement: a case may be struck out for undue delay even if brought within three months.[20] Thirdly, while the three-month period cannot be extended by agreement between the parties (CPR Rule

---

[15] There is also an important, but ill-understood, relationship between legal aid and rates of applications for permission: Bridges, Meszaros, and Sunkin, op. cit. n. 9 above, pp. 658–64. In certain types of case, the Funding Code allows legal aid to be granted for applications for permission that have only a 'borderline' chance of success.

[16] For a consideration of the law as to time limits see *R v. Dairy Produce Tribunal, ex p. Caswell* [1990] 2 AC 738; Law Com. No. 226, paras 5.23–30.

[17] And sometimes to promote certainty in commercial matters: *R v. Registrar of Companies, ex p. Central Bank of India* [1986] QB 1114 (reversed on unrelated grounds by the CA). A power to give advisory opinions might be useful in this context: H. Woolf, *Protection of the Public—A New Challenge* (London, 1990), pp. 46–50.

[18] But see *Biggs v. Somerset CC* [1996] 2 All ER 735, 744f per Neill LJ.

[19] *R (Burkett) v. Hammersmith and Fulham LBC* [2002] 1 WLR 1593, esp. at [49] and [53].

[20] Supreme Court Act 1981, s. 31(6).

54.5(2)), the court has a discretion to allow more time (CPR Rule 3.1(2)(a)); but no criteria for the exercise of this discretion are given, thus creating uncertainty.[21] It would be better if, as in private law, there were a longer fixed period that could be extended only in exceptional cases on stated and reasonably precise grounds.

The Part 54 time limit does not apply when another enactment specifies a shorter time limit for the claim in question. On the other hand, s. 7(5) of the HRA lays down a longer time limit for claims that a public authority has acted incompatibly with a Convention right in contravention of s. 6 of the HRA: '12 months from the date on which the act complained of took place, or such longer period as the court . . . considers equitable in all the circumstances of the case.' This longer time limit does not apply when another rule specifies a shorter time limit for 'the procedure in question'. The HRA does not lay down a procedure for s. 6 claims, but contemplates that such claims will be made by some appropriate existing procedure. Commonly, a s. 6 claim will take the form of a CJR. If the particular CJR is one that can be, and is, made by the basic procedure, the twelve-month time limit will apply because no time limit is laid down for CJRs made by basic procedure. But if the claim is one that must be (or is) made by JRP, the Part 54, three-month time limit will apply.

The third notable feature of JRP relates to fact-finding. JRP under Part 54 is a modified version of the alternative procedure in CPR Part 8. Part 8 procedure is designed for cases which are 'unlikely to involve a substantial dispute of fact' (CPR Rule 8.1(2)(a)). Under this procedure (in contrast to the basic procedure), relevant factual evidence is normally given in writing. Under Rule 8.6(2) and (3) the court has power to permit oral evidence to be given at a hearing, and witnesses to be cross-examined (see also Rule 32(7)). Although it has sometimes been said that such an order should be no less readily made in judicial review proceedings than in other types of proceedings brought under the alternative procedure,[22] in practice a more restrictive approach has often been taken.[23] It should also be noted that under the basic procedure, each party is entitled to require the other to disclose relevant documents that are in the other's control (see CPR Part 31), whereas under JRP disclosure is required only if the

---

[21] Clayton and Tomlinson, *Law of Human Rights*, para. 22.64.
[22] *R v. Inland Revenue Commissioners, ex p. J. Rothschild Holdings Plc (No. 1)* (1987) 61 TC 178.
[23] Law Com. No. 226, Part VII.

court so orders (PD 54, 12.1).[24] There is, of course, good reason to provide an alternative, streamlined procedure for cases in which there is unlikely to be a substantial dispute of fact. But normally the claimant can choose between the alternative procedure and the basic procedure on the basis of which seems more appropriate; whereas in certain cases, a CJR has to be made by JRP regardless of whether or not the claim is likely to involve a substantial dispute of fact. This may possibly be justified by appeal to a public interest in preventing the exercise of public functions being unduly delayed by litigation. However, it might be argued in reply that fair resolution of factual disputes is a basic requirement of justice that should be sacrificed for speed only when the case for expedition is overwhelming.[25] In the case of a CJR that has been, but did not have to be, made by JRP, the Administrative Court can order that the claim continue as if it had not been made by JRP (CPR Rules 30.5 and 54.20). Such an order would allow the claim to proceed according to the basic procedure if the claimant so chose. But in cases where JRP has to be used, proper resolution of factual disputes depends on the court making appropriate orders to this end.

6.3 APPLICATIONS FOR DECLARATIONS AND INJUNCTIONS IN A CJR

As stated above, there are two procedural routes available for applying for declarations and injunctions in a CJR: JRP under CPR Parts 8/54, and basic or alternative procedure under CPR Parts 7 and 8. By choosing the latter rather than the former an applicant might be able to avoid restrictive features of JRP. The Law Commission, which first suggested the introduction of the predecessor to the CJR—the application for judicial review—contemplated that claimants would have a free choice between the two procedural paths. Moreover, both CPR Rule 54.3(1) and section 31(2) of the Supreme Court Act 1981 provide that JRP 'may' be used to seek a declaration or injunction in a CJR, and that a declaration or injunction may be granted in a CJR made by JRP if the court considers that it would be just and convenient to do so. Expressly at least, these provisions do not require a claimant for such remedy ever to use JRP. However, in

---

[24] But see the Judicial Review Pre-Action Protocol, §16(d).

[25] 'The limited availability of disclosure of documents and cross examination . . . are unlikely to satisfy the requirements of [ECHR] Article 6 where the applicant disputes the underlying facts . . .': Clayton and Tomlinson, *Law of Human Rights*, para. 11.322; see also paras 22.102–12.

O'Reilly v. Mackman[26] the House of Lords held that because the procedural regime laid down in the 1978 version of RSC Order 53 (the predecessor of CPR Part 54) was more advantageous to claimants than that under the pre-1978 version and struck a sound balance between the interests of claimants and defendants, in certain cases it would be an 'abuse of the process of the court' for a claimant seeking a declaration or an injunction in a CJR not to use JRP. This ruling—that in certain types of case a CJR in which a declaration or injunction was sought had to be made by JRP—became known as the 'exclusivity principle'. According to this principle, in certain types of case JRP is the only procedure that may be used for seeking a declaration or injunction in a CJR. Although *O'Reilly v. Mackman* was strictly concerned with matters of procedure, its effect was to introduce into English law a new substantive distinction between public law and private law. Viewed in this way, the exclusivity principle states that (what we might call) 'public CJRs' (as opposed to 'private CJRs') must be made by JRP regardless of whether the remedy sought in the claim is one of the new prerogative orders, or a declaration or injunction. Under the exclusivity principle, the scope of application of JRP depends not on the remedy sought but on the substance of the CJR. The principle prevents certain 'public law' issues being raised by *any* procedure other than JRP. So understood, the exclusivity principle can be seen as one move in the functional turn in administrative law described in Chapter 1. In institutional terms, the principle requires such public law issues to be litigated in the Administrative Court (which is the only court in which a CJR may be made by JRP). They cannot be raised in, for instance, a claim before a county court or a tribunal. So what are public CJRs?

6.4 PUBLIC CJRS

In *O'Reilly v. Mackman* the House of Lords held that a prisoner who was seeking (on the ground of breach of natural justice) to challenge a decision of a Board of Prison Visitors (the effect of which was to deprive him of a remission of sentence) had to use Order 53 procedure because he had no private law right to a remission but only a legitimate expectation that the remission would be granted if no disciplinary sentence of forfeiture of remission had been made against him. This legitimate expectation was recognized only in public law and not in private law. This decision

[26] [1983] 2 AC 237.

established the general rule that if a judicial review claimant seeks to protect rights or interests recognized only in public law, he or she must do so by JRP. In *Cocks v. Thanet DC*[27] the House of Lords applied this rule and held that an applicant who wanted to challenge a decision of a local authority to the effect that he was intentionally homeless and so not entitled to be housed, had to use Order 53 procedure because his only rights in respect of the decision were public law rights, namely that the decision would be made in accordance with rules of public law. By contrast, in the same case it was held (obiter) that once the council had decided that the applicant was entitled to be housed, the right to be housed was a private law right that did not have to be enforced by Order 53 procedure but could be enforced in a tort action for breach of statutory duty in the county court. This latter proposition was rejected in *O'Rourke v. Camden LBC*:[28] the statutory right of a homeless person to be housed by a local authority is a public law right that can be enforced only by JRP.

To be contrasted with these cases is *Wandsworth LBC v. Winder*.[29] The council passed a resolution increasing council house rents. The applicant thought that it was *ultra vires* and refused to pay the increased rent. When the council sought to evict him for non-payment of the extra rent he pleaded in defence that the resolution was invalid. The House of Lords held, in effect, that since the applicant was arguing that he had a contractual right under his lease to remain at the lower rent, he was asserting a private law right and so could raise the defence in the possession proceedings in the county court and did not have to raise it in an application for judicial review. In *Roy v. Kensington and Chelsea and Westminster Family Practitioner Committee*[30] the applicant challenged a decision of the respondent to withhold part of his basic practice allowance. The House of Lords held that the case did not have to be brought under Order 53 because Dr Roy's relationship with the respondent (i.e. the defendant), whether contractual or statutory, conferred on him a private law right in respect of payment of the practice allowance.

The distinction between public law and private law interests seems to rest on the assumption that the latter are in some way more important and more worthy of protection than the former. JRP incorporates certain procedural protections for public functionaries, and the rule that a claimant asserting public law interests can only use JRP puts him or her

---

[27] [1983] 2 AC 286.   [28] [1998] AC 188.
[29] [1985] AC 461; applied in *Wandsworth LBC v. A* [2000] 1 WLR 1246.
[30] [1992] 1 AC 624; see also *Mercury Communications Ltd v. Director General of Telecommunications* [1996] 1 WLR 48.

at a disadvantage which is justifiable only on the assumption that public law interests do not matter as much as private law rights and, therefore, do not deserve as much legal protection. When one considers the subject matter of some of the public law interests which have generated litigation (e.g. remission of sentence, obtaining council housing) this assumption appears ill-founded. The fact that the public law claimant is usually challenging the exercise of a discretionary power does not mean that what is at stake is any less important than the sort of interests protected by private law. This is obviously true where the basis of the claim is that the defendant has acted incompatibly with a Convention right; and it may well be that the exclusivity principle does not apply to such a claim.[31]

Furthermore, determining whether JRP must be used by reference to the nature of the claimant's interest may sit uneasily with the fact that JRP is designed to deal with cases that do not raise substantial disputes of fact. In *Trustees of Dennis Rye Pension Fund v. Sheffield City Council*[32] this feature of JRP led Lord Woolf rather unconvincingly to distinguish *O'Rourke v. Camden LBC* (see above) in order to allow a claimant to use the basic procedure to assert a claim that turned mainly on issues of fact. It is true both that a private law claim may raise no substantial issue of fact (and so might suitably be made under CPR Part 8) and that a public law claim may raise substantial issues of fact for the resolution of which JRP would not be suitable. There is no necessary correlation between the nature of the claimant's interest (public or private?) and whether the claim raises disputed issues of fact.

6.5 PROTECTING PRIVATE LAW RIGHTS BY JRP

Assuming that the underlying rationale of the distinction between public law and private law interests is to force certain claimants to use the less advantageous JRP, it might seem to follow that a claimant would be free to choose JRP to protect private law rights. And in some cases this is undoubtedly so: if he had wished, Dr Roy could have challenged the decision of the Family Practitioner Committee by an application for judicial review under Order 53. Public law is not only concerned with the protection of public law rights but also with the protection of private law rights against illegal interference by public functionaries. However, in some instances, private law rights cannot be protected in this way. In the

---

[31] Clayton and Tomlinson, *Law of Human Rights*, para. 22.53.
[32] [1998] 1 WLR 840. See also *Steed v. Secretary of State for the Home Department* [2000] 1 WLR 1169.

first place, JRP cannot be used for making a CJR against a body that owes its existence to contract.[33] This rule seems to be a hangover from the time when the only judicial review remedies were the (old) prerogative orders: these were (and are) not available against contractual bodies, but there seems no good reason of policy or principle why a declaration or injunction should not be sought against such a body by JRP.

Secondly, the contractual rights of an employee, even against a government employer, cannot be enforced by JRP unless those rights are 'underpinned by statute' or by some constitutional principle[34] in a way that injects a 'public element' into the employment relationship.[35] A policy basis for this rule might be that the preferable way to protect employment rights is by an action for unfair dismissal before an Industrial Tribunal or by an ordinary action for breach of contract; and that in cases with no clear public element recourse should be had to such alternative remedies and not to a CJR in the Administrative Court.[36] This rule adds a consideration to those already discussed as being relevant to the scope of application of JRP, namely whether the Administrative Court or the alternative forum is more expert in dealing with the type of issue in question or better equipped to resolve it. Judges of the Administrative Court who regularly hear CJRs are, presumably, expert in the law of judicial review[37] but not in employment law, which industrial tribunals deal with regularly. Of course, this consideration can only be relevant if there is an alternative forum available; if there is not, then the Administrative Court may hear the claim unless there is some statutory provision which precludes this, even if the rights in issue are essentially ordinary employment rights.[38]

---

[33] *R v. Disciplinary Committee of the Jockey Club, ex p. Aga Khan* [1993] 1 WLR 909; *Law v. National Greyhound Racing Board* [1983] 1 WLR 1302. It may be, however, that this rule only applies where there is a contractual relationship between the claimant and the defendant: *R v. Jockey Club, ex p. RAM Racecourses Ltd* (1991) 3 Admin LR 265, 292–3 *per* Simon Brown J.

[34] Such as the desirability of preserving the independence of Crown prosecutors: *R v. Crown Prosecution Service, ex p. Hogg* (1994) 6 Admin LR 778.

[35] *R v. East Berkshire Health Authority, ex p. Walsh* [1985] QB 152; *R v. British Broadcasting Corporation, ex p. Lavelle* [1983] 1 WLR 23.

[36] See esp. *R v. Civil Service Appeal Board, ex p. Bruce* [1988] 3 All ER 686, affirmed by CA [1989] 2 All ER 907.

[37] One of the aims of the 1978 version of RSC Order 53 was to channel judicial review cases to the Divisional Court which, at the time, heard applications for the prerogative orders under the old Order 53. The Administrative Court is the successor to the 'Crown Office List' which was in turn, the successor to the Divisional Court as the forum for CJRs.

[38] *R v. Secretary of State for the Home Department, ex p. Benwell* [1985] QB 554.

The question which these cases raise concerning the proper forum for protecting the employment rights of government employees has generated a large volume of litigation, and the resulting law is complex and unsatisfactory. The underlying problem is that cases concerning the employment rights of public employees often raise both public law and private law issues which are not easily separable, if at all. It has been argued that all public employment cases should be dealt with by the same forum, which could resolve all the issues raised.[39]

It is unclear whether or not the rule that private employment rights are not enforceable in CJR made by JRP is an application of a wider principle that contractual rights cannot be protected by JRP unless they possess a sufficient 'public element'. Of course, any definition of 'sufficient public element' is bound to be complex and controversial.

6.6 EXCEPTIONS TO THE EXCLUSIVITY PRINCIPLE

In *O'Reilly v. Mackman*[40] Lord Diplock said that there were two exceptions to the exclusivity principle. First, JRP need not be used when none of the parties objects to the use of the basic or alternative procedure. The rationale of this exception is that there is no reason to protect a defendant who does not wish to be protected by the restrictive features of JRP. On the other hand, it could be argued that these features of JRP are in the public interest and should not be waivable. Also it is strange that an action which is an abuse of court process can be allowed to proceed simply because no party to the action objects.

The second exception arises where the challenge to the contested decision or action is *collateral*—that is, it arises out of and incidentally to a some other legal claim. The challenge to the council's resolution in *Wandsworth LBC v. Winder* was collateral in two ways: it was made in answer to a claim for possession of the premises by the council,[41] and it was incidental to an assertion of a contractual right under the lease. Does a case fall within the exception only if it is collateral in both senses? There is no simple answer to this question.

---

[39] S. Fredman and G. Morris, 'Public or Private? State Employees and Judicial Review' (1991) 107 *LQR* 298.
[40] [1983] 2 AC 237.
[41] See also *Pawlowski v. Dunnington* (1999) 11 Admin LR 565.

On the one hand, it would seem that if a claim can be framed as one in contract, tort, or restitution,[42] or if it concerns a private legal right,[43] it need not be made by JRP even if the very ground on which the defendant's action is alleged to be an unlawful interference with a private law right is that it was illegal in a public law sense. It is not an abuse of process to assert private law rights by a private action even if the action raises or turns on public law issues.[44] Of course, if a claim in tort or contract against a public functionary does not turn on any issue of public law, it need not be made by JRP.[45] On the other hand, it has been held that gypsies who camp on public land cannot argue, in defence to a claim for an eviction order by a council, that the council has failed to fulfil its statutory obligation to provide camping sites, because the gypsies had no legal right to the land on which they were camping.[46] So it would seem that even a defence may be an abuse of process if it is not based on private rights. One might conclude from these cases that the collateral attack exception is in fact a restatement of the public law right/private law right distinction. However, in some cases at least it is permissible to argue, in defence to a prosecution for breach of a statute, regulation or administrative order, that the relevant statutory provision, regulation or order is *ultra vires*.[47] It is difficult to see how this involves assertion of a 'private law right': there is no private law right not to be prosecuted (as opposed to a right not to be prosecuted maliciously).[48]

The 'collateral attack' exception raises a number of problems. First, consider *Winder* again: the council sought to evict Winder years after the challenged resolution was passed. If Winder's challenge to the resolution succeeded this would mean that all the council's tenants would be in a position to refuse to pay the increased rent, and maybe to claim return of overpaid rent.[49] Such an outcome would have caused a great deal of trouble for the council, which could have been largely avoided if the

---

[42] *British Steel Plc v. Customs and Excise Commissioners* [1997] 2 All ER 366.

[43] *Roy v. Kensington and Chelsea and Westminster Family Practitioner Committee* [1992] 1 AC 624.

[44] But see *G v. Hounslow LBC* (1987) 86 LGR 186.

[45] *Davy v. Spelthorne BC* [1984] AC 264.

[46] *Waverley DC v. Hilden* [1988] 1 WLR 246. People in this situation may be able to claim that the decision to institute eviction proceedings was illegal in the public law sense, but such a claim would have to be made by JRP: *Avon CC v. Buscott* [1988] QB 656. They might also seek mandamus but only, of course, by JRP.

[47] *Boddington v. British Transport Police* [1999] 2 AC 143; *Howker v. Secretary of State for Work and Pensions* [2002] EWCA Civ 1623.

[48] Malicious prosecution is actionable in tort.

[49] On this see Ch. 13.

resolution had been directly challenged in an application for judicial review soon after it was made. The short time limit under CPR Part 54 is designed to deal with just such cases.[50] By contrast, although the claimant in *O'Reilly v. Mackman* had also delayed well beyond the judicial review time limit in bringing his claim, this delay would have caused no undue problem for the defendant. This suggests that there may be a mismatch between the rationale for protecting defendants by a short time limit and the criteria used to decide whether or not JRP must be used by the claimant. We will return to this point soon. It also raises the general issue of whether collateral attacks should be subject to the procedural limitations attaching to CJRs; and if not, why not.

A second difficulty posed by the collateral attack exception relates to claims for damages. CPR Rule 54.3(2) provides that a CJR made by JRP may include a claim for damages[51] but may not seek damages alone; and s. 31(4) of the Supreme Court Act 1981 provides that damages may be awarded in a CJR if the claim for damages arises from any matter to which the CJR relates (and the claimant is entitled to damages). If a claim for damages is based on an allegation that a public functionary has acted illegally in a public law sense, why should the claim not have to be made by JRP regardless of whether any other remedy is sought?[52] The obvious answer is that claims for damages often raise substantial disputes of fact. But if that is the case, why should it be permissible to hook a damages claim onto a CJR?

This last question raises a third and larger difficulty with the collateral attack exception (which was mentioned at the end of 6.4). Many collateral attacks are likely to raise factual issues. We have seen that JRP is not designed for cases that are likely to give rise to substantial disputes of fact. However, despite what Lord Diplock seemed to believe,[53] it is not the case that direct challenges to public decisions by CJR are unlikely to raise factual issues: in particular, challenges based on breach of natural justice, on error of fact, and, perhaps most significantly, on infringements of

---

[50] In fact, Winder had applied for leave to apply for judicial review but it had been refused. See also *Wandsworth LBC v. A* [2002] 1 WLR 1246, 1259.

[51] Monetary claims other than claims for damages cannot be included in a CJR made by JRP. This was one of the reasons why Dr Roy was not required to proceed by JRP. The Law Commission recommended that it should be possible to make restitutionary claims and claims for a liquidated sum by JRP: Law Com. No. 226, paras 8.5–7.

[52] In *Anufrijeva v. Southwark LBC* [2003] EWCA Civ 1406 at [81] the Court of Appeal suggested that although free-standing claims for damages under the HRA could not be made by JRP, they should be 'brought to the Administrative Court by an ordinary claim'.

[53] *O'Reilly v. Mackman* [1983] 2 AC 237, 282.

Convention rights,[54] may well raise difficult and complex issues of fact. There is no direct correlation between whether or not a challenge is collateral and whether or not it is likely to raise issues of fact.

More generally, there is no direct correlation between the justifications for the restrictive features of JRP and the criteria relevant to deciding when JRP must be used (notably that based on the distinction between public law and private law rights). The permission requirement is designed to weed out frivolous, vexatious, or hopeless cases; but there is no reason to think that claims based on private law rights will not sometimes be frivolous, vexatious, or hopeless, or that claims based on public law rights are particularly prone to be frivolous, vexatious, or hopeless. Nor is there any reason to think that claims based on private law rights will not sometimes hold up public programmes if they are allowed to be brought after the short Part 54 time-limit; or that claims based on public law rights will necessarily cause trouble if brought after that time limit has expired. Finally, claims based on public law rights might well raise factual issues more suited to resolution by basic procedure than by JRP;[55] conversely, claims based on private law rights may well raise no such issues—which is why CPR Part 8 procedure is available as an alternative to the basic procedure. This produces a tension within the JRP scheme: on the one hand, CJRs may raise factual disputes that take time to resolve properly and fairly; on the other hand, JRP is designed to be speedy.

In short, there is no reason to think that the JRP is ideally suited for all claims based on public law rights or, conversely, that the basic procedure is necessary for all claims based on private law rights. The exclusivity principle, therefore, seems to be based on a false premise, namely that JRP is necessary and desirable for dealing properly with all public CJRs.

The House of Lords has recognized a third exception to the exclusivity principle. In *Chief Adjudication Officer v. Foster*[56] the applicant challenged refusal of a social security benefit on the ground that the regulation that justified the refusal was *ultra vires*. The House of Lords held that under the relevant legislation, the Social Security Commissioners (the highest tribunal in the social security appeals system) had jurisdiction to decide

---

[54] Clayton and Tomlinson, *Law of Human Rights*, paras 22.105–12.

[55] See, e.g., *R v. Chief Constable of the Warwickshire Constabulary, ex p. Fitzpatrick* [1998] 1 All ER 65, 80 *per* Jowitt J.

[56] [1993] AC 754.

the legality of the regulation even though the legality of secondary legislation is quintessentially a public law issue. There were two main reasons for this decision. One was that the Commissioners are especially well equipped to decide such an issue by reason of their 'great expertise in this somewhat esoteric area of the law'; and secondly, to require the applicant in such a case to raise the issue of legality by JRP would create 'a cumbrous duplicity of proceedings[57] which could only add to the already overburdened list of applications for judicial review awaiting determination'.[58] This case raises fundamental issues which are also relevant to the collateral attack exception to the exclusivity principle: are Administrative Court judges necessarily the best equipped to decide public law issues, which can arise in a great diversity of factual contexts?[59] Is there good reason why any court or tribunal before which a public law issue arises should not have jurisdiction to decide the issue? 'Decentralization' of the judicial review jurisdiction would be a way of coping with the steady increase in public law litigation, which is unlikely to abate. Public law issues which arose in proceedings brought before courts or tribunals other than the Administrative Court, but which were thought to justify or require the 'judge-power' of the Administrative Court, could be referred to it (rather in the way that matters of European law can be referred to the European Court of Justice by courts of Member States)[60] or, as the Law Commission has recommended, transferred to the High Court at an early stage.[61] Both the Government of Wales Act 1998 and the Scotland Act 1998 contain provisions for referral of 'devolution issues' by tribunals and lower courts to higher courts.[62] These provisions could, with suitable modifications, form the basis of a system of referral of public law issues to the Administrative Court.

---

[57] If the Social Security Commissioners could not determine the issue of legality, the claimant's appeal would have to have been adjourned while a CJR was made to resolve that issue.

[58] [1993] AC 754, 766–7.

[59] *Wandsworth LBC v. A* [2002] 1 WLR 1246, 1259.

[60] T.C. Hartley, *The Foundations of European Community Law*, 5th edn (Oxford, 2003), ch. 9.

[61] C. Emery, 'Public Law or Private Law?—The Limits of Procedural Reform' [1995] *PL* 450; 'Transfer of Cases Between Public and Private Law Procedures: the English Law Commission's Proposals' [1992] *CJQ* 308; Law Com. No. 226, paras 3.22–3. The Law Commission proposal apparently applies only to cases begun in the county court, and it does not deal with cases in which public law issues are raised by way of defence.

[62] P. Craig and M. Walters, 'The Courts, Devolution and Judicial Review' [1999] *PL* 274, 279, 286–7. Cases raising devolution issues can also be transferred from the forum in which they arose to the Privy Council: ibid. 278, 286.

In this context, it is worth noting that 'human rights' issues can be raised in any proceedings to which they are relevant and in any court or tribunal before which such proceedings can be brought. This does not mean that any court or tribunal can entertain any and every human rights claim. For instance, only the High Court can hear a claim for a declaration of incompatibility; and the rules about when JRP has to be used seem to apply to human rights claims as to other types of claim.[63] However, it does cast doubt on the value of the policy of channelling public law claims to the Administrative Court. It should also be noted that the CPR Part 30 contains flexible provisions for the transfer of cases from one court to another, which could form the basis for a regime to deal with public law claims, that would be less rule-bound than that to which the decision in *O'Reilly v. Mackman* has given rise.

Decentralization of the adjudication of public law issues would seriously undermine the procedural rationale for the exclusivity principle for two reasons: first, it would not be possible or desirable to saddle the adjudication of public law issues, wherever this took place, with the restrictive features of JRP.[64] Secondly, the arguments for decentralization suggest that the procedural rules by which any particular adjudicator operates are only one factor to be taken into account in allocating public-law disputes to different adjudicators, and that equally important are the qualifications, expertise, and suitability of the adjudicator for deciding the dispute in question. It should be noted that whereas the initial discussion of the exclusivity principle in this chapter was in terms of a choice between making a CJR by JRP on the one hand, or by the basic or alternative procedure on the other, the issue of the proper forum before which to raise public law issues, with which the exclusivity principle is concerned, is much wider and has to be considered not in terms of a choice between different divisions of the High Court but in terms of a choice between the Administrative Court and any one of a wide range of other courts and tribunals before which public law issues might arise. So long as the choice of initial forum is between two divisions of the High Court, it can be seen as turning on procedural differences only. This approach makes much less sense when the choice may lie between two very different forums; then questions of expertise may appear to be at least as important as questions of procedure.

---

[63] Clayton and Tomlinson, *Law of Human Rights*, 2nd Updating Supplement, 2003, para. 22.53.

[64] But note that permission is needed to make a CJR by JRP whether the claim is started by JPR or transferred to the Administrative Court: CPR Rule 54.4.

6.7 LET THE CLAIMANT BEWARE!

At the time *O'Reilly v. Mackman* was decided, the exclusivity principle created a procedural minefield. In principle, at least, a litigant who should have made an application for judicial review under RSC Order 53 but did not would lose regardless of the merits of the claim. There was no provision under which the case could continue as if begun in the correct way. The position of a litigant who wrongly made an application for judicial review was different because under RSC Order 53, rule 9(5) the court had a discretion to allow the case to continue as if it had been started by the correct procedure. Now, under the CPR (Rules 54.20 and 30.5) claims wrongly started by the basic or alternative procedure can be transferred to the Administrative Court (subject to permission to proceed), and claims wrongly begun by JRP can be transferred to another division of the High Court and carried on as if begun by basic or alternative procedure. Cases can also be transferred from the High Court to the county court and vice versa (CPR Rule 30.3(1)(a)). Claims that should have been started by JRP can also be dealt with by other mechanisms that do not focus merely on the fact that it was not started in the correct way.[65] Even so, on balance it is still probably safer to use JRP if there is doubt about whether or not it should be used. But this course of action brings with it the restrictive features of JRP. For instance, it is still open to the court to hold that a claim that should have been brought by JRP cannot now continue in the Administrative Court simply because of expiry of the short Part 54 time limit.

Furthermore, these arrangements for transfer of cases within the High Court and between the High Court and the county court do not deal with all of the difficulties generated by the exclusivity principle. It is still the case, for instance, that a collateral challenge to a public decision will simply fail if it should have been brought by JRP regardless of its merits. Similarly, cases cannot be transferred from a tribunal to the Administrative Court even if this would be the best way of dealing with public law issues to which the case gives rise.

---

[65] See *Clark v. University of Lincolnshire and Humberside* [2000] 1 WLR 1988.

6.8 FURTHER PROCEDURAL REFORMS

One option for further reform of judicial review procedure would be to repeal CPR Part 54 and to allow the claimant to choose between commencing a CJR under CPR Part 7 or Part 8.[66] The main argument for this reform is that public functionaries should not enjoy special procedural protections. This argument has acquired added force since the enactment of the HRA. It is at least arguable that some of the restrictive features of JRP are vulnerable to attack on two grounds: first, that CJRs made by JRP do not provide an effective remedy as required by ECHR Article 13; and secondly, that JRP does not satisfy the fair hearing requirements of ECHR Article 6.[67] While Article 13 only applies to claims based on breaches of human rights, Article 6 applies to CJRs generally and, indeed, to all court proceedings involving 'the determination of . . . civil rights and obligations or of any criminal charge'.

The case for some such reform is further strengthened the more the law allows public law issues to be decided by forums other than the High Court (by allowing collateral challenges, and direct challenges in tribunals and inferior courts), because the differences between JRP on the one hand, and the basic and alternative procedures on the other, really only make sense on the assumption that all public law issues will be decided by the High Court.

The reality is that public law issues can arise in many contexts and before many forums, just as issues of EC law and human rights law can arise in many contexts and before many forums. It seems desirable that any forum before which an issue of public law arises should have the jurisdiction to deal with it, but also a discretion to refer (or transfer) it to the Administrative Court if this seems appropriate. If it is thought that public functionaries should enjoy special procedural protections when their decisions and actions are challenged on public law grounds, such protections should be available in whatever forum the public law issue arises. In particular, if it is thought that there should be a short time limit within which public law issues can be raised, such a limit should apply in whatever forum the issue arises and whether the party raising it is

---

[66] D. Oliver, 'Public Law Procedures and Remedies—Do We Need Them?' [2002] *PL* 91.
[67] I. Leigh and L. Lustgarten, 'Making Rights Real: The Courts, Remedies and the Human Rights Act' [1999] *CLJ* 509, 522–6.

the claimant or the defendant. However, it is also important that the applicability of any special procedural protection should be decided by reference to whether that protection is necessary or appropriate in the case at hand to protect the public interest, and not according to some non-procedural criterion such as whether the citizen is asserting only public law rights.

Several other procedural reforms have been suggested. They are designed to cope with the fact that public law actions often raise complex issues of public policy and administrative practice which go well beyond the interests of the parties to the action and of the applicant in particular. One idea is that public law procedure should be more 'inquisitorial' and should allow the court or tribunal to take a more active part in the finding of facts and the calling of evidence relevant to wider issues raised by the case but which the parties themselves might have no strong incentive to call. The adversarial system of procedure currently in use confines the adjudicator to a passive umpiring role and gives no real scope for the gathering of evidence which the parties (and any intervenors who are allowed to take part) do not wish to present.[68]

Another idea is that there should be an official—perhaps called a Director of Civil Proceedings (DCP)—who would have the power to initiate court proceedings if this was in the public interest and to intervene in proceedings initiated by others to represent the public interest. The DCP would be to public law rather what the Director of Public Prosecutions is to the criminal law. Such an official would be able to bring before a court or tribunal the sort of evidence which the proposal for inquisitorial procedure is designed to elicit. The DCP would also be able to initiate the sort of actions which, under the present system, might never be brought because of lack of funds or problems of co-ordination, or because prospective applicants, by reason of social deprivation or lack of education, do not have the human resources to speak for themselves.[69]

The former proposal could be seen as just a way of improving the quality of decision-making in public law proceedings. The second proposal seems to contemplate an expanded role for the judicial branch of government as a way of controlling the executive (in particular); and increasing the sources of information available to the courts in the way

---

[68] J.A.G. Griffith, 'Judicial Decision-Making in Public Law' [1985] *PL* 564; J. Allison, 'The Procedural Reason for Judicial Restraint' [1994] *PL* 452.

[69] H. Woolf, *The Protection of the Public: A New Challenge* (London, 1990), pp. 109–13.

contemplated by the first proposal might so change perceptions of the judicial role that it, too, would lead to an expanded conception of the role of the judicial branch in controlling the exercise of public power. Whether or not such an expansion is desirable is a question the reader must decide for himself or herself after reading the rest of this book.

SECTION B: GROUNDS OF JUDICIAL REVIEW

This section is concerned with grounds on which exercises of public power can be held unlawful. The rules and principles that define these grounds can be viewed as a set of norms that regulate the performance of public functions, or alternatively as providing a set of norms of good public decision-making. For the sake of convenience of analysis, the various grounds of judicial review can be divided into three categories. One category is concerned with what in the United States is often called 'administrative procedure'. This topic is dealt with in Chapter 7. A second category is concerned with what might loosely be called 'decision-making'. Relevant issues here include who should make the decision, and what matters should be taken into account. It is dealt with in Chapter 8. The grounds of review discussed in these two chapters can be seen as dealing with a broader topic that is sometimes described in terms of 'process' (as opposed to the narrower concept of 'procedure'). A third category of grounds of review is concerned with the substance of public decisions and rules. This topic is dealt with in Chapter 9.

7

Procedural Grounds of Review

7.1 GENERAL INTRODUCTION

In this chapter we will consider grounds of judicial review that relate to the procedure followed in the making of public decisions and rules. In some cases, public decision and rule making is governed by statutory rules of procedure. As we will see later, failure to comply with such statutory rules does not necessarily render a decision or rule invalid. Public decision-makers are also subject to a set of common law procedural rules that are known collectively as the 'rules of natural justice'. The rules of natural justice embody two main principles, one concerned with the decision-maker and the other concerned with the person who is the subject of the decision. The rule against bias requires that a person must not be judge in their own cause (*nemo iudex in sua causa* in Latin); and the 'fair hearing rule' (*audi alteram partem* in Latin) embodies a set of procedural requirements designed to protect the interests of the subject of the decision.

The term 'natural justice' might be thought to suggest that these principles have some objective validity and that through them the law is simply giving effect to self-evident principles about how decisions ought to be made. There is a certain amount of truth in this. There is good reason to be suspicious of a decision for or against a party made by a person who has an interest, financial or otherwise, in the decision. It is not necessarily the case, of course, that an interested decision-maker will, because of that interest, make an unfair decision. The decision-maker may succeed in standing back from the situation and decide purely on the merits of the case. However, the point of this rule is not just that 'justice' should be done but also that it should be seen to be done. What matters is not whether the decision-maker was actually biased but whether there was an appearance of bias. On the other hand, the appearance of justice does not guarantee that justice will be done, any more than the appearance of bias necessarily leads to a biased decision. But while the appearance of impartiality carries no guarantee of a fair decision, it does increase the chance of that outcome.

The rule against bias is designed to foster and maintain confidence in decision-making processes, and it is basic to our idea of what it means to treat individuals fairly when decisions are made which affect them. It is only in very special circumstances (where, for example, a party has freely waived the right to an impartial decision-maker, or where all suitable decision-makers might appear to be biased) that observance of the rule can be dispensed with.

The rule requiring a fair hearing might be thought to be equally basic. It seems clear that no decision unfavourable to anyone ought to be made without that person being given a fair chance to make a case, and in this way to participate in the decision-making process.[1] But in various ways courts have indicated that they accord to the fair hearing rule somewhat less importance than we might at first be inclined to attribute to it. Indeed, statements can be found in some cases which suggest that the demands of natural justice can sometimes be satisfied without giving a hearing at all, provided only that the rule against bias is not breached. Less dramatically, it has always been said that the requirements of a fair hearing are not fixed in advance but must be moulded to the circumstances of each particular case.

A great many things might be demanded in the name of a fair hearing—notification of the date, time, and place of the hearing, notification in more or less detail of the case to be met, adequate time to prepare one's case in answer, access to all material relevant to one's case, the right to present one's case orally or in writing or both, the right to examine and cross-examine witnesses (including one's opponent), the right to be represented (perhaps by a qualified lawyer), the right to have a decision based solely on material which has been available to (and so answerable by) the parties, the right to a reasoned decision which takes proper account of the evidence and addresses the parties' arguments. The courts have never been prepared to concede all these things as a matter of automatic right in every case; indeed, the very status of legal representation and a reasoned decision as requirements of natural justice is uncertain, as we shall see.

Why have the courts found the fair hearing rule more problematic than the rule against bias? A number of reasons may be suggested, and they take us to the very heart of the basic theory of natural justice. The first and perhaps most obvious reason why the courts have not been prepared to accord all the rights enumerated above in every case is that hearings are

---

[1] G. Maher, 'Natural Justice as Fairness' in N. McCormick and P. Birks (eds), *The Legal Mind* (Oxford, 1986), ch. 6.

expensive of both time and money. So, for example, it was held in *Re HK*[2] that an airport immigration officer—given the circumstances in which the officer worked and the fact that the officer had to make an on-the-spot decision whether to allow the person to enter the country—could not be expected to conduct a full scale inquiry in the nature of a trial as a preliminary to deciding whether a person claiming a right to enter the UK was over 16 years of age. All that could be required was that the officer should tell the immigrant that they were suspected of being over 16 years of age and give the immigrant a chance to dispel the suspicion. In general terms it seems reasonable that the right to a hearing should not be seen as something to be secured at any cost. Speed and economy in the conduct of government business are important. Nor should we forget the adage that 'justice delayed is justice denied'. On the other hand, the fair hearing rule is partly designed to improve the chance that the best possible decision will be made, and good decision-making is itself an aspect of efficient government.

A second reason why the courts have found the fair hearing rule difficult is that the traditional notion of a fair hearing embodies an adversarial style of decision-making, and courts have expressed and given effect to doubts about whether an adversarial style is always the most appropriate. We will return to this point in detail later (see 7.2.1). Thirdly, giving a fair hearing often requires the government to disclose information which it would rather keep secret, and the real or supposed demands of government secrecy have, in some contexts, played an important part in justifications for limiting the right to a hearing. Fourthly, it is clear that the courts are not prepared to require elaborate procedures for the deciding of relatively unimportant matters.[3] The elaborateness of the hearing to which a person is entitled depends in no small measure on what is at stake for that person: the importance of the interest which the person is seeking to protect and the seriousness of the consequences of an adverse decision.

A final reason why the fair hearing rule has often appeared problematic is that the courts have always experienced difficulty in working out the relationship between it and statutory procedural rules. Suppose a statute prescribes a procedure which is less protective of the individual than the rules of natural justice would be. Should the statutory procedure be treated as exhaustive of the individual's procedural rights or should the common law reinforce the statutory protection by requiring a fair

---

[2] [1967] 2 QB 617.   [3] e.g. *McInnes v. Onslow-Fane* [1978] 1 WLR 1520.

hearing? There is no simple answer to this question because it can often be argued that there are good reasons why the statutory protection is less than that which the common law could provide. Once again, it is not clear that the common law notion of a fair hearing is always the most appropriate procedural standard to apply.

Besides statutory procedural regimes and the common law of natural justice, another increasingly important source of procedural norms is Article 6 of the ECHR, which provides (in part) that 'in the determination of his civil rights . . . or of any criminal charge against him, everyone is entitled to a fair . . . hearing . . . by an independent and impartial tribunal'. The concept of 'determination of civil rights' covers many exercises of public power. The concept of a 'fair hearing' is analogous to the fair hearing rule in English law; but the jurisprudence of the ECtHR provides an external standard against which to measure domestic principles. The concept of an 'independent and impartial tribunal' includes ideas expressed in the rule against bias. But as we will see, it goes rather further, and has provided the basis for reassessing administrative decision-making structures, and the role of courts and other review mechanisms in regulating the relationship between citizens and public functionaries.

7.2 THEORETICAL CONSIDERATIONS

7.2.1 THE RULES OF NATURAL JUSTICE AND THE ADVERSARY SYSTEM

As implied above, one source of difficulty in relation to the fair hearing rule is that the rules of natural justice are, in essence, a skeletal version of the elaborate rules of judicial procedure to be found in their fullest form in the Civil Procedure Rules (CPR). English judicial procedure takes the form it does because our courts operate under what is called the 'adversary system' (which is usually contrasted with an 'inquisitorial (or "investigatory") system'). The basic idea underlying the adversary system is that the truth is best discovered by allowing parties who allege conflicting versions of what happened (or of what the law is) each to present, in its strongest possible form, their own version of the truth, and leave it to an impartial third party to decide which version more nearly approximates to the truth.[4] An inquisitorial system depends much more

---

[4] In many administrative contexts, there will be only two parties: the decision-maker and the citizen applying for some benefit or potentially subject to some adverse decision or action. Some features of the adversary system will be inapplicable in two-party situations,

on the third party making investigations and, by questioning each of the parties and other relevant persons, deciding where the truth lies.[5]

While impartiality is equally important in both systems, the rules of procedure which determine how the case is to be presented and decided will be rather different according to whether a combative or a non-combative mode of discovering the truth is adopted. In particular, under the adversarial model the decision-maker contributes very little to the fact-finding process whereas under an inquisitorial system, his or her input is much greater. Procedural rules will reflect this difference. Furthermore, whereas the adversary system tends to operate in a rather formal and technical way (partly because people in conflict usually want to stand on their rights), inquisitorial methods of fact-finding can be (although they are not always) more informal. The fact-finder can foster a spirit of cooperation in the search for truth which is inimical to the adversary system.[6] The activities of ombudsmen[7] provide a good example of non-combative inquisitorial fact-finding methods.

The adversary model embodied in the fair hearing rule has other important features. It involves authoritative imposition of a decision or a solution to a dispute. This feature it shares with certain other decision-making mechanisms, notably legislation, non-legislative (administrative) orders (sometimes called 'managerial direction'), and arbitration. By contrast, there are forms of dispute settlement which involve the parties reaching a solution by mutual agreement. Sometimes impartial third parties may be called upon to assist. In conciliation the third party is essentially a facilitator: their role is to help the parties see each other's point of view and to emphasize points of agreement. It is not for the conciliator to suggest or promote particular solutions to the conflict. In mediation, too, the third party is a facilitator, but in addition may promote agreement by suggesting a solution and pointing out its advantages. All of these alternatives to the adversarial model have been used in the English administrative process[8] and it is not difficult to see the attractions of each which would encourage their use in certain circumstances.

but the basic point is the same: the fair hearing rule is only one possible means of discovering the truth.

[5] For a judicial discussion see *R v. Secretary of State for the Home Department, ex p. Cheblak* [1991] 1 WLR 890, esp. 903–8 *per* Lord Donaldson.

[6] On the costs of adversarial behaviour see C. Menkel-Meadow, 'Will Managed Care Give Us Access to Justice?' in R. Smith (ed.), *Achieving Civil Justice: Appropriate Dispute Resolution for the 1990s* (London, 1996), p. 103.

[7] See Ch. 17 below.

[8] G. Ganz, *Administrative Procedures* (London, 1974).

It is central to the adversary model not only that each party should have a fair opportunity to put their case and to know the other party's case, but also that the final decision should be based on, and be justifiable in terms of, the arguments presented by the parties. It follows that issues of fact must be resolved only on the basis of evidence which the parties choose to put before the decision-maker, and that the decision must be based on rules, principles or policies binding on or accepted by both parties. In this respect, the fair hearing required by adversarial adjudication is different from 'consultation'. A body under an obligation to consult must reveal in more or less detail what it proposes to do and why, and must give parties with a right to be consulted a fair opportunity to express views about and objections to the proposed course of action. However, the body's decision about what to do does not have to be justified in terms of what the consulted parties say; it must not close its mind to what they say, but the obligation to consult does not require it to take what they say into account in any particular way in reaching its decision or to be impartial as between competing outcomes. As we will see, consultation is a very important procedure in public decision-making contexts.

Consultation between government and non-governmental entities may be part of or may develop into 'negotiation' if the government thinks that by offering some benefit or concession to a particular group it can, in return, gain aid in the implementation of its policy objectives. Consultation will turn into negotiation only when the government is dealing with one or a very few entities, or where the government chooses to deal with one person or group, to the exclusion of other interests competing for influence on government policy. Consultation, by contrast, may involve hundreds or even thousands of competing individuals and groups. There is no doubt that bargaining plays a very important role in the government of Britain; but the way it is conducted is, rightly or wrongly, largely beyond judicial control because the rules of natural justice are not applicable to such activity.[9]

The adversary model of adjudicative decision-making has some obvious disadvantages. The available options for dealing with any issue are limited to those presented by the parties. Because the adversary system is geared to dealing in black and white terms with rights and obligations it tends to accentuate difference and disagreement, rather

---

[9] In the US, 'negotiated rule-making' is recognized and regulated by law: T. Ziamou, 'Alternative Modes of Administrative Action: Negotiated Rule-Making in the United States, Germany and Britain' (2000) 6 *European Public Law* 45; and see 7.6.2.2.

than to concentrate on points of agreement and encourage the parties to reach a willing accommodation on their points of disagreement. Even when parties settle their differences without resort to litigation, they often do so within an adversary framework (but the rule-based decision of an authoritative third party is replaced by a decision largely moulded according to the relative bargaining strengths of the parties). The adversary system also promotes formality. This not only makes the system expensive and time-consuming, but it also tends to intimidate people who have only occasional contact with law and legal processes.

The important point to note is that the adversary model embodied in the rules of natural justice is not the only possible model of decision-making procedure. This goes some way to explaining an unwillingness on the part of the courts to require all administrative decisions to be made in accordance with these rules. In some cases it might be more appropriate to utilize inquisitorial or investigative methods of fact-finding, or non-adversary methods of conflict resolution; or to limit the involvement of individuals to consultation, or to reach a negotiated agreement.

7.2.2 FAIR PROCEDURE AND NATURAL JUSTICE

All the models of decision-making which have been mentioned can be abused. Rules of fair procedure, different for each model and expressing the ideal mode of operation of that model, could be developed, just as the rules of natural justice have been developed for the adversary model. Indeed, the courts have made some rules about how statutory duties to consult must be performed. In cases where there is no procedure prescribed by statute, the courts have interpreted their function as being only to enforce the rules of natural justice to the extent appropriate in particular cases; and in some cases this has led to decisions that the rules of natural justice do not apply at all. The courts have not seen fit, in the absence of statute, to impose procedural requirements which do not reflect the adversarial mode of decision-making. So, for example, the courts have not developed a common law duty resting on administrative rule-makers to consult interested parties before making rules.

It should be noted, however, that in deciding whether and when to waive compliance with rules of natural justice, the courts are making decisions about the sort of circumstances in which such rules are appropriate. Such questions, when raised in Parliament in various contexts, have often proved contentious.[10] There is no simple answer to the

---

[10] G. Ganz, 'Allocation of Decision-Making Functions (Part I)' [1972] *PL* 215, 216–19.

question of which procedure is relevant in which circumstances or to which decisions. There is no necessary relationship between particular models of procedure and particular types of issue. The question of which issues ought to be decided according to which procedure is one of policy. For example, the guilt or innocence of an alleged murderer could be decided by the toss of a coin,[11] or by trial by ordeal, or by a closed court in the absence of the accused, or by the most scrupulously conducted criminal trial. A more or less convincing justification could be given in support of most of these methods. Again, a variety of procedures could be contrived for deciding whether a particular stretch of motorway should be built—ministerial fiat, wide public consultation, legislation, technical studies of traffic flows, and so on. What is crucial in choosing a procedure is that those affected by the decision should as far as possible feel confidence in, and willingly accept the validity and authority of the outcome of, whatever procedure is adopted. What we need to ask is which procedure seems most fair and suitable for deciding particular questions.

7.2.3 THE DUTY TO ACT JUDICIALLY

An early attempt of the courts to decide the proper ambit of the rules of natural justice was contained in the (now much-criticized) notion of the duty to act judicially. According to this approach, a decision-maker ought to comply with the rules of natural justice (and so behave in a more or less adversarial fashion) if he or she is under a duty to act judicially. This concept is a very vague one. In the first place, the notion of judicial duty, and the related concepts of judicial function and judicial power, play a part in a number of very diverse areas of the law: for example, contempt of court;[12] absolute privilege in the law of defamation; immunity from liability in tort; as well as in the law of natural justice. It may be that there is no single notion of judicial function that is used in these diverse areas.

Secondly, even in the context of natural justice, there are at least three meanings which could be given to the statement that an agency is under a duty to act judicially. First, it might refer to a duty to follow a certain procedure conceived of as being judicial or appropriate to a court. This seems to have been the sense adopted by the Privy Council in *Nakkuda*

---

[11] Chance procedures are sometimes used to resolve polycentric issues: e.g. a college-room ballot, or conscription for jury or military service. See generally N. Duxbury, *Random Justice* (Oxford, 1999).

[12] *Attorney-General v. British Broadcasting Corporation* [1981] AC 303; *General Medical Council v. British Broadcasting Corporation* [1998] 3 All ER 426.

Ali v. Jayaratne[13] when, in deciding whether the rules of natural justice were applicable, it looked to the legislation under consideration for some indication, express or implied, that the Controller of Textiles was required to give notice of his intention to revoke the applicant's licence; or to hold an inquiry before revoking it; or that the applicant had a right of appeal from his decision. The obvious difficulty with this meaning, as a test of whether the rules of natural justice must be complied with, is that the duty to act judicially in this sense is essentially synonymous with the duty to observe the rules of natural justice. So the 'test' is circular.

A second possible meaning of the duty to act judicially is that the decision-maker, although not necessarily exercising judicial functions in the sense to be discussed below, must bring to bear on the performance of his or her functions 'a judicial mind—that is, a mind to determine what is fair and just in respect of the matters under consideration'.[14] This meaning hardly makes sense as a test for deciding when particular rules of *procedure* have to be complied with; but, as we will see in due course, there are indications in the cases that in some situations the requirement of natural justice might be satisfied by this non-procedural idea of fairness.

Thirdly, and most importantly, the notion of the duty to act judicially might arise out of the fact that the agency performs functions usually associated with a court or judge. 'Judicial function' in this sense refers to a situation in which there is a dispute between two parties (often referred to in Latin as a *lis inter partes*) as to their respective rights and obligations, which is resolved by adjudicating upon disputes of fact and applying to the facts as found rules of law determined to exist by the court. The decision of the court will bind the parties for the future and the court will often have power to enforce its decision. In other words, the traditional view is that the adversary system of procedure as embodied in the rules of natural justice is best suited to resolving disputes of fact and law as they relate to rights and obligations.

This sort of approach was adopted in 1932 by the Committee on Ministers' Powers (the Donoughmore Committee).[15] The Committee recommended that a distinction ought to be observed between judicial functions (which involve the finding of facts and the application of law to facts) and what it called 'quasi-judicial' functions (which involve the use of discretion by administrators in applying policy rather than law). The

---

[13] [1951] AC 66, 78–9.
[14] *Royal Aquarium etc Society v. Parkinson* [1892] 1 QB 431, 452 *per* Lopes LJ.
[15] Cmnd. 4060.

former should ideally be committed to courts or other bodies following judicial procedures, while the latter should be left to administrators. The approach came under very heavy fire[16] partly on the ground that it failed to recognize that the judicial function very often involves the exercise of discretion both in finding facts and in determining law, and that such exercises of discretion often depend on matters of policy. For example, in novel tort cases such as *Donoghue v. Stevenson*[17] or *Hedley Byrne v. Heller*[18] the court, in imposing a new liability, exercises a certain amount of discretion on the basis of arguments of policy, even though it may be constrained in what it can do by precedents and rules.

It seems, therefore, that there is no clear-cut distinction between rules and principles on the one hand, and policy and discretion on the other, which would enable us to decide when a court rather than an administrator should decide a question and the extent to which adversary procedures are appropriate. What we have to decide is which policy questions we are prepared to leave to courts and other bodies following adversary procedures, and which we want decided by some other method. The main shortcoming of adversary procedures for deciding many policy questions is that the adversary system concentrates on the interests of the parties before the court, whereas policy questions often concern a much larger class of persons who have no say in the judicial process. Procedures, such as class actions, which enable the representation of large interest groups in litigation and which are quite highly developed in the United States, are rare in this country. This is partly because they may lead to changes in the role of the judge and the judicial process: they may tend to turn judges into administrators by requiring them to construct and police the implementation of remedial 'schemes' which will deal with the grievances of many people.[19]

Another shortcoming of the adversary system (as we have seen) is that the decision-maker has to choose between the outcomes contended for by the litigants, and cannot consider and investigate other and possibly better alternative outcomes. Methods of consultation and investigation are more suited to examining multiple alternatives than is the adversary trial. In general, the more controversial and wider-ranging the issues in a case are, the less appropriate is it that the case should be decided by adversarial procedures.

---

[16] W.A. Robson, *Justice and Administrative Law* (London, 1951).
[17] [1932] AC 562.   [18] [1964] AC 465.
[19] A. Chayes, 'The Role of the Judge in Public Law Litigation' (1976) 89 *Harv LR* 1281.

Given this idea of judicial function and the limitations of the judicial process, it can be argued that one of the basic ideas underlying the legal concept of the duty to act judicially as a device for limiting the scope of the applicability of judicial procedures is the recognition that since adversary procedures are of limited usefulness, and since a court would not be a suitable body to decide certain types of issues, it is also inappropriate that a court should have a supervisory power to review a decision on such an issue by a decision-maker following a different and more suitable procedure and, possibly, to strike the decision down because the decision-maker did not comply with the (inappropriate) rules of natural justice. On the other hand, it could be argued that there is no good reason why courts should not develop non-adversarial procedural models and require decision-makers to comply with such models as and when appropriate. Indeed, as noted earlier, the courts have started to do this in relation to consultation.

7.2.4 POLYCENTRICITY AND NATURAL JUSTICE

Perhaps the best-known non-judicial attempt to identify the sort of question for which the judicial adversary process is most appropriate is that of the American jurist Lon Fuller who put forward the idea that judicial procedure was not suitable for dealing with what he called 'polycentric' disputes. We have already discussed the notion of polycentricity in detail.[20] Adversarial procedure is ill-suited to the resolution of polycentric disputes because the adversarial model of decision-making requires issues to be treated as bipolar. The legal concept of the duty to act judicially and the theoretical notion of polycentricity both embody the same basic idea: that some matters do not lend themselves to adversarial treatment because they involve issues and interests more numerous, complex, and diverse than could be properly considered in the context of an ordinary judicial trial 'fairly' conducted.

7.3 THE RULES OF NATURAL JUSTICE

The detailed rules which we must now consider are directed to two questions: do the rules of natural justice apply at all to the particular case; and if so, what procedural steps do those rules dictate in that case?

---

[20] See 3.2.5.

7.3.1 CASES IN WHICH THE RULES OF NATURAL JUSTICE ARE INAPPLICABLE

7.3.1.1 The Rule against Bias

The rule against bias may be excluded by statute;[21] and a party can waive the right to have a tribunal which appears to be unbiased.[22] The acceptance of a tribunal which could reasonably be suspected of bias would only bind a person if that person had a free choice,[23] and probably only if the tribunal was not in fact biased. In some cases, necessity may justify disregard of the rule if all the available qualified decision-makers could reasonably be suspected of bias.[24] This would not mean, however, that if it could be shown that the decision-maker had in fact acted with partiality, the decision would not be invalidated.

7.3.1.2 The Fair Hearing Rule

7.3.1.2.1 Delegated Legislation

Failure to comply with the rules of natural justice in the course of making delegated legislation does not invalidate the legislation.[25] The reasons for this are fairly obvious: delegated legislation tends to affect large numbers of people, and if all had a right to be heard the system would grind to a halt for lack of time and money. Furthermore, the process of making delegated legislation is seen as part of the political rather than of the judicial system. Political modes of consultation and control are considered more appropriate since delegated legislation very often deals with contentious polycentric issues. Judicial techniques of decision-making are not always superior to political ones.

7.3.1.2.2 Exclusion by Statute

When will a statutory scheme of procedure oust the common law rules of natural justice? As a practical matter, it is worth noting that the enactment of a set of procedural rules which parties feel to be fair can go a long way to reducing the volume of complaints on the ground of procedure.

---

[21] See 7.3.1.2.2.

[22] *Locabail (UK) Ltd v. Bayfield Properties Ltd* [2000] QB 451.

[23] *Jones v. DAS Legal Expenses Insurance Co Ltd* [2003] EWCA Civ 1071.

[24] Concerning the interaction between the doctrine of necessity and Art. 6 of the ECHR see *Kingsley v. UK* (2002) 35 EHRR 177; I. Leigh, 'Bias, Necessity and the Convention' [2002] *PL* 407.

[25] *Bates v. Lord Hailsham* [1972] 1 WLR 1373. The rules do not, of course, apply to the Parliamentary legislative process. Delegated legislation is discussed further at 7.6.2.2.

The relative dearth of cases concerning tribunal procedure is probably a tribute to the sound drafting of procedural rules.

Statutes sometimes specifically allow a person to act as a decision-maker despite having some interest in the outcome. A specific ouster of the fair hearing rule is less common. Instead, the question is whether the statutory scheme was intended to be exhaustive of the procedural rights of the claimant. The statute might, in theory, explicitly provide that the statutory code is to apply to the exclusion of rules of natural justice. In the absence of such express provision, the more detailed the statutory scheme the more likely it is that the rules of natural justice will not operate. On the other hand, it has been recognized for over a hundred years that the common law can 'make good the omission of the legislature';[26] and if the statutory scheme provides the claimant with less procedural protection than the common law, the rules of natural justice can be used to fill the gap. In the end, whether the procedural safeguards provided by the statutory scheme are considered adequate or not will depend on whether and to what extent the model of judicialized procedure is thought appropriate to the sort of decision in question.[27]

7.3.1.2.3 Exclusion by Contract

There is authority to support the view the rules of natural justice may apply to the activities of 'domestic tribunals', such as trade unions or private licensing bodies, whose powers are derived solely from a contract between the body and its members rather than from a statute.[28] Subject to what is said below about employment contracts, if such a body exercises powers of discipline or expulsion against one of its members or refuses an applicant a licence to engage in some activity controlled by it then, provided something of sufficient value, such as the applicant's ability to exercise a trade or profession, is at stake, the courts may imply into the contract a term requiring compliance with the rules of natural justice in the exercise of such powers. What if such a contract purports to exclude the rules of natural justice? Although the law is not clear on the point, there are indications, at least where a person's livelihood is at stake, that such a provision could be held invalid on grounds of public policy.[29] The notion of public policy (as opposed to contractual agreement) is important

---

[26] *Cooper v. Wandsworth Board of Works* (1863) 14 CBNS 180.

[27] See, e.g., *Local Government Board v. Arlidge* [1915] AC 120; *Selvarajan v. Race Relations Board* [1967] 1 WLR 1686; *R v. Commission for Racial Equality, ex p. Cottrell & Rothon* [1980] 1 WLR 1580.

[28] But see 3.1.

[29] See *Edwards v. SOGAT* [1971] Ch 354.

in this context because technically there is no contract, between an applicant for a licence and the licensing body, until a licence is granted; nevertheless the courts have been prepared to exercise control over licensing
activities of private bodies which control entry to a trade or profession in
the absence of a contract.[30] By extension, there may be limits, imposed by
public policy, on the ability of a domestic body to exclude the operation
of the rules of natural justice by contractual provision.

7.3.1.2.4 *Employment Cases*

According to the common law of contract, an employee can be dismissed
without being given a hearing.[31] One reason for this appears to be that an
employee owes duties only to the employer and not to the public at large,
and so there is no relevant public interest which would justify an application of the requirements of natural justice, which are seen as part of
public law. By contrast, an employee (sometimes called an 'officer') who
does have responsibilities towards the public as well as towards the
employer (e.g. a police officer) cannot be removed from office without a
fair hearing. It is by no means easy to decide in some cases whether
the public's interest in a particular activity is strong enough to justify
treating a practitioner of that activity as a public officer. We have already
noted, when discussing the claim for judicial review, that much litigation
has been launched to determine whether the treatment of particular
public employees by their employers raised issues of public law.[32]

   The idea that mere employees are not entitled to the protection of the
rules of natural justice, because they owe no duties to the public, is
somewhat difficult to reconcile with the cases discussed in the previous
section which suggest that at least where a body has some sort of monopoly power over employment in a particular trade or profession, it must
comply with the rules of natural justice regardless of any particular public interest in the applicant's job. The public interest in such cases seems
to be a wider one of preventing abuse of monopolistic powers which
affect a person's 'right to work'. Especially at times when unemployment
is high and dismissal from one job may sentence the dismissed employee
to long-term unemployment, it seems hard to justify allowing any
employer to dismiss an employee without giving the employee a chance to
put their side of the case.

---

[30] *Nagle v. Fielden* [1966] 2 QB 633. This was not a natural justice case, but it was relied
on in relation to natural justice in *McInnes v. Onslow-Fane* [1978] 1 WLR 1520.
[31] *Ridge v. Baldwin* [1964] AC 40.
[32] See 6.5.

A stronger explanation of the rule is that the law is unwilling, for good practical reasons, to enforce a contract of service by requiring an employer to go on employing an employee they no longer want. To hold a dismissal invalid for breach of natural justice amounts to an order for reinstatement. The trouble with this explanation is that it proves too much: even if the dismissed person is an officer, there may be good reasons not to require the employer to take the employee back which will lead a court to decline to order reinstatement.[33] Sometimes this difficulty does not arise because the employee's interest is not in reinstatement but, for example, in preserving pension rights that are dependent on the worker's not having been validly dismissed,[34] or in clearing his or her reputation.

At all events, the line between dismissals of purely private concern and those of sufficiently public concern is a very hazy one. Further, it seems clear that although at common law the dismissal of an employee cannot be challenged for failure to comply with the rules of natural justice, such a failure can make a dismissal 'unfair' under statutory provisions concerning unfair dismissal.[35] Since the court has power under the legislation either to award compensation for unfair dismissal or to order reinstatement,[36] there seems little to justify adherence by the common law to its traditional distinction between servants and officers.[37] More generally, although the rules of natural justice have usually been seen as part of public law, it may be that the principles which underlie them are so basic that the courts will be prepared to apply them to many cases where a decision by one private citizen affects another, provided the interest of the latter in the decision is sufficiently great.

7.3.1.2.5 Decisions Requiring Expertise and Judgment
Courts are unlikely to hold breach of the rules of natural justice to be an available ground for challenging decisions about issues such as whether a student ought to be admitted to an educational institution or to a course, or should be awarded a scholarship; or whether a student's examination script has been given the right mark. Such decisions require a high degree of expert or professional judgment and not just the application of objective criteria of merit which might be subjected to scrutiny by adjudicative

---

[33] e.g. *Chief Constable of North Wales v. Evans* [1982] 1 WLR 1155.
[34] e.g. *Ridge v. Baldwin* [1964] AC 40.
[35] Employment Rights Act 1996, Part X.
[36] See generally *Polkey v. Dayton* [1988] AC 344.
[37] *R v. British Broadcasting Corporation, ex p. Lavelle* [1983] 1 WLR 23, 31–6.

techniques. On the other hand, it is clear that if an institution decided, for example, to expel a student on non-academic grounds, such as misbehaviour, the rules of natural justice would apply.[38] Similarly, it has been held that if a person were removed without a hearing from a local authority's list of approved foster parents on grounds of reputation, character, or temperament there would be no basis for quashing the decision for breach of natural justice; but that a court would require a hearing if the ground of removal was misbehaviour towards, or abuse of, a fostered child.[39]

A further relevant consideration in the case of medical treatment, for example, is that judicial techniques might not be thought particularly appropriate for the making of what have been called 'tragic choices',[40] that is, choices about the allocation of scarce resources between highly desirable human goals such as health and education; although whether such choices should be made on technical (as opposed to political) grounds may also be contentious. It is probably felt, too, that professionals ought to be accorded a high degree of autonomy in making professional and technical judgments; and, given the choice, the courts prefer to stay out of highly technical areas. Besides, if all of life's choices became judicialized, ordinary activities would grind to a halt and an unhealthy spirit of litigious antagonism would be encouraged.

7.3.1.2.6 Preliminary Decisions

A decision will not generally be invalidated for failure to give a hearing if the decision is merely preliminary to a later decision for which a hearing must be given; 'preliminary' in the sense that no issue will be conclusively settled by the earlier hearing in such a way as to prevent its being raised at the later hearing.[41] A related rule is that in cases of emergency, a decision may be made, for example, to remove an officer from office without a hearing pending investigations;[42] but the person cannot, of course, be finally removed from office without being heard. There is good sense in the general position—it avoids unnecessary duplication of hearings and undue interference with timely administration.

On the other hand, even preliminary recommendations may influence later decisions, and this fact argues in favour of some procedural protection

---

[38] e.g. *Glynn v. Keele University* [1971] 1 WLR 487.
[39] *R v. Wandsworth LBC, ex p. P* (1989) 87 LGR 370.
[40] G. Calabresi and P. Bobbitt, *Tragic Choices* (New York, 1978). See further 8.5.1.
[41] *Pearlberg v. Varty* [1972] 1 WLR 534; but contrast *Wiseman v. Borneman* [1971] AC 297; *Norwest Holst Ltd v. Department of Trade* [1978] ch 201.
[42] *Lewis v. Heffer* [1978] 1 WLR 1061.

even in relation to preliminary decisions. So it has been held that proceedings before advisory panels (with no power of decision) may be challenged for breach of natural justice.[43] On the other hand, the procedural protection required may be limited.[44]

7.3.2 THE REQUIREMENTS OF NATURAL JUSTICE

7.3.2.1 The Rule against Bias

If a person can show that a decision has actually been affected by bias on the part of the decision-maker that person is, of course, entitled to have the decision quashed. A decision-maker is actually biased 'if motivated by a desire to favour one side or disfavour the other'[45] 'for reasons unconnected with the merits of the issue',[46] such as 'prejudice, predilection or personal interest'.[47] A decision-maker who is actually a party to the matter to be decided, or who has a financial interest—or, exceptionally, a non-financial interest—in the decision to be made is 'automatically disqualified' as a decision-maker, and their decision will be invalid.[48] In any other case where the claimant relies on the rule against bias, 'the court must first ascertain all the circumstances that have a bearing on the suggestion that the [decision-maker] was biased . . . then ask whether those circumstances would lead a fair-minded and informed observer to conclude that there was a real possibility . . . that the tribunal was biased'.[49] In both 'automatic disqualification' and 'real possibility' cases, the concern is not about actual bias (whether justice was done), but about the appearance of bias (whether justice was seen to be done). In cases of automatic disqualification, it does not matter that the decision-maker did not know of the interest at the time the decision was made because the basis of the disqualification is the existence of the interest, not its potential effect on the decision-maker's mind. By contrast, in other cases the ground of invalidity is the 'real possibility', objectively judged, that the

---

[43] *R v. Secretary of State for the Home Department, ex p. Cheblak* [1991] 1 WLR 890.

[44] 'at the low end of the duties of fairness': *R v. Secretary of State for Transport, ex p. Pegasus Holdings (London) Ltd* [1988] 1 WLR 990.

[45] *R v. Gough* [1993] AC 646, 659 *per* Lord Goff of Chieveley.

[46] *R v. Inner West London Coroner, ex p. Dallaglio* [1994] 4 All ER 139, 151 *per* Simon Brown LJ.

[47] Ibid. 162 *per* Sir Thomas Bingham MR.

[48] *R v. Bow Street Metropolitan Stipendiary Magistrate, ex p. Pinochet Ugarte* [2000] 1 AC 119.

[49] *In re Medicaments and Related Classes of Goods (No. 2)* [2001] 1 WLR 700 at [85] (CA); *Porter v. Magill* [2002] 2 WLR 37 at [103] *per* Lord Hope. This formula is considered to comply with Art. 6 of the ECHR.

decision was biased—which could only happen if the decision-maker was aware of the circumstances giving rise to the possibility.

In automatic disqualification cases, the crucial question is whether the court considers the interest in question to be of such a nature as to justify automatic invalidation of the decision. For instance, in the notorious *Pinochet* case,[50] the House of Lords held that one of the Law Lords was automatically disqualified by reason of involvement with a charity that had been allowed to intervene in criminal proceedings to secure the extradition of a former president of Chile to stand trial for alleged abuses of human rights. In 'real possibility' cases, the critical factor is how the court interprets and understands the concept of the 'fair-minded and informed observer'.[51] For instance, in one case it was said that 'the informed observer can be expected to be aware of the legal traditions and culture of this jurisdiction' such as 'the practice of judges and advocates lunching and dining together at the Inns of Court'![52] In another case it was said that 'the observer may . . . be credited with knowledge that a Recorder, who in a criminal case has sat with jurors, may not subsequently appear as counsel in a case in which one or more of those jurors serve'![53] A realistic approach might be that the concept of the 'fair-minded and informed observer' simply provides a fig-leaf of legitimation to the court's own assessment of the circumstances and merits of the case before it.

It is not clear that automatic disqualification performs any function—other than a symbolic one, perhaps—that could not just as well be performed by the real-possibility test.[54] The fair-minded person would surely see a real possibility that a decision-maker, who was a party to or had a financial interest in the matter to be decided, might not act impartially. Unfortunately, too, the automatic-disqualification rule may be difficult to apply because it requires concepts, such as 'being a party to a matter' and having a 'non-financial interest in a matter', to be defined;

[50] See n. 48 above.
[51] '[O]ne is entitled to conclude that such an observer will adopt a balanced approach': *Lawal v. Northern Spirit Ltd* [2003] ICR 856 at [14]. See further S. Attrill, 'Who is the "Fair-Minded Observer"? Bias after *Magill*' [2003] *CLJ* 279 (arguing that the test should be understood as involving judicial balancing of the considerations for and against disqualification).
[52] *Taylor v. Lawrence* [2002] 3 WLR 640 at [61] (CA).
[53] *Lawal v. Northern Spirit Ltd* [2003] ICR 856 at [21].
[54] A.A. Olowofoyeku, 'The *Nemo Judex* Rule: The Case Against Automatic Disqualification' [2000] *PL* 456.

and this, as *Pinochet* itself shows, may not be straightforward.[55] Indeed, taken together the concepts of 'financial interest' and 'non-financial interest' seem wide enough potentially to bring any case of interest within the automatic–disqualification principle. This problem is illustrated by cases in which what might be called 'indirect' or 'remote' or 'insignificant' financial interests have been held not to fall foul of the rule against bias, apparently as a result of applying the fair-possibility test.[56] It is not obvious that *any and every* financial interest, however slight, should lead to automatic disqualification. Still less is it obvious which non-financial interests should lead to automatic disqualification; although some circumstances—such as being closely related to one of the parties,[57] or hearing an appeal from one's own decision—provide a strong case for disqualification independently of any appeal to what the 'fair-minded person' would think.

As noted in 7.1, the right to a fair trial before an independent and impartial tribunal, guaranteed by Art. 6 of the ECHR, covers some of the same ground as the rule against bias. However, whereas the common-law rule is typically used to question the involvement of particular individuals as decision-makers on the basis of some personal interest in the outcome,[58] Art. 6 is now being used to question the fairness of institutional structures of decision-making regardless of any question of personal interest.[59] The common-law approach to this latter issue is illustrated by *Franklin v. Minister of Town and Country Planning*,[60] which concerned a proposal for the establishment of a new town. Under the relevant legislation, the department had responsibility for initiating the proposal, and the Minister had the final power of deciding whether it would be adopted. The Minister made certain public statements which, it was argued, indicated that the government was determined that the particular proposal

---

[55] Particularly difficult are instances in which the decision-maker is known to have opinions or views generally relevant, but not specific, to the matter in issue: *Locabail (UK) Ltd v. Bayfield Properties Ltd* [2000] QB 451.

[56] *R v. Mulvihill* [1990] 1 WLR 438; *Jones v. DAS Legal Expenses Insurance Co Ltd* [2003] EWCA Civ 1071. The latter case is the more troublesome because it post-dates *Pinochet*.

[57] e.g. *Metropolitan Properties (FGC) Ltd v. Lannon* [1969] 1 QB 577.

[58] This may be changing: e.g. *Lawal v. Northern Spirit Ltd* [2003] ICR 856.

[59] In *Taylor v. Lawrence* [2002] 3 WLR 640 the CA appears to have turned an issue of personal interest into one of institutional structure. Art. 2 of the ECHR (right to life) also imposes significant procedural obligations on States: *R v. Secretary of State for the Home Department, ex p. Amin* [2003] 3 WLR 1169; *R. (Khan) v. Secretary of State for Health* [2003] EWCA Civ 1129; *Davies v. Her Majesty's Deputy Coroner for Birmingham* [2003] EWCA Civ 1739.

[60] [1948] AC 87.

should go ahead regardless of objections. It was held that provided the Minister complied with the statutory procedure for processing such proposals, his adoption of the proposal could not be challenged on the ground of bias. The relevant question was not whether the Minister appeared to be biased against the objectors, but whether he had in fact genuinely considered their objections. There was no evidence that he had not done this. In another case it was held that a land-use planning decision of a local authority could not be attacked under the rule against bias simply because the majority group on the council had previously adopted a policy in relation to it, provided the issues at stake were given proper consideration.[61] In these cases, the alleged bias arose not out of a personal interest of the decision-maker, but from what might be called an 'institutional' interest in furthering the decision-making body's policy in relation to the subject matter of the decision.

In *R (Alconbury Developments Ltd) v. Secretary of State for the Environment, Transport and the Regions*[62] it was argued (in effect) that the statutory power of the Secretary of State to make various land-use planning decisions was incompatible with Art. 6 of the ECHR because the Minister (acting in his statutory capacity) was not an independent and impartial tribunal. Interpreting and applying jurisprudence of the ECtHR, the House of Lords held that although the challenged decisions involved a 'determination of civil rights', and although the Minister was not an independent and impartial tribunal, the requirements of Art. 6 were met because the Minister's decisions were subject to judicial review. This decision rests on a general principle that a decision-making process in which the initial decision-maker is not an independent and impartial tribunal[63] can nevertheless comply with the requirements of Art. 6

---

[61] *R v. Amber Valley DC, ex p. Jackson* [1985] 1 WLR 298; see also *R v. Secretary of State for the Environment, ex p. Kirkstall Valley Campaign Ltd* [1996] 3 All ER 304; 8.3.5. It would be different if the local authority had a financial interest in the decision: *Steeples v. Derbyshire CC* [1985] 1 WLR 256 (but see *R (Alconbury) v. Secretary of State for the Environment, Transport and the Regions* [2003] 2 AC 295 at [55] *per* Lord Slynn; [130] *per* Lord Hoffmann). For a discussion of the constitutional context of these cases see I. Leigh, *Law, Politics and Local Democracy* (Oxford, 2000), pp. 187–95. Similar issues can arise in non-governmental contexts, as where a significant proportion of the members of a professional complaints or disciplinary body are members of the profession: *Re S (A Barrister)* [1981] QB 683.

[62] [2003] 2 AC 295. A. Layard, 'Comment' (2001) 13 *J Env L* 349.

[63] Or in which the claimant has been denied a fair hearing: *R (Adlard) v. Secretary of State for the Environment, Transport and the Regions* [2002] 1 WLR 2515. For the analogous common law rule see *Calvin v. Carr* [1980] AC 574 (an appeal can cure a breach of natural justice at the initial hearing if, overall, the process is 'fair').

provided the decision is subject to review by an independent and impartial tribunal that has 'full jurisdiction' to deal with the case. What constitutes 'full jurisdiction' depends on the nature of the decision and the decision-making process that is being challenged. In this case, the House held, it did not matter that judicial review of the Minister's decisions would be limited to the issue of 'legality' and could not address the 'merits' of the decisions,[64] because the Minister was accountable to Parliament and, ultimately, to the electorate.

For present purposes, it is not necessary to examine in detail the concepts of 'civil rights', 'independent and impartial tribunal' and 'full jurisdiction'. The most important point to make is that as a result of the decision in *Alconbury*, judicial review (whether in the form of review, strictly understood, or an appeal), is more than an external check on public decision-making to ensure that fair decision-making procedures are followed. In addition, it may be an integral component of the design of decision-making structures, necessary to ensure their compatibility with Art. 6 of the ECHR. In a loose sense, it might be said that the effect of *Alconbury* is to 'entrench' judicial review into the UK constitution.[65] Put differently, we might say that the impact of Art. 6 of the ECHR (as demonstrated in *Alconbury*) is to judicialize public decision-making. This is a result of the fact that the independence of 'courts' staffed by 'judges' is very well protected and jealously guarded under British constitutional arrangements, and so a court can always meet the need for an 'independent and impartial tribunal' to secure compliance with Art. 6 of the ECHR. The extent of this judicialization will depend on the scope of application of Art. 6 and, in particular, on the extent to which the concept of 'civil rights' is interpreted to cover interests that are the subject of public decision-making powers.[66]

In broad constitutional terms, a likely impact of Art. 6 will be to give the concept of separation of powers increased prominence in

---

[64] The use of the distinctions between legality and merits, and law and policy, deserves special notice. It signals the importance of the concept of separation of powers in this context. See further nn. 67–9 below and text.

[65] This is not the only context in which judicial review may have constitutional significance. In *R v. Shayler* [2003] 1 AC 247 the availability of judicial review supported a decision that ss 1 and 4 of the Official Secrets Act 1989 are not incompatible with Art. 10 of the ECHR. See also *Marcic v. Thames Water Utilities Ltd* [2003] UKHL 66 (judicial review of decision of water industry regulator satisfies Art. 8).

[66] *Runa Begum v. Tower Hamlets LBC* [2003] 2 WLR 388 at [5]–[6] *per* Lord Bingham of Cornhill. See also P. Craig, 'The Human Rights Act, Article 6 and Procedural Rights' [2003] *PL* 753, 754–60.

administrative law thinking.[67] This is because of the underlying logic of Art. 6, which is that certain decisions ('determinations of civil rights') should be made by 'tribunals' that enjoy the degree of 'independence' traditionally associated with the judicial branch of government. Because such independence implies distance from the executive, officials implementing statutes and public policy are much less likely than courts to qualify as independent tribunals for the purposes of Art. 6. Put crudely, Art. 6 assumes a relatively sharp distinction (or 'separation') between adjudication by courts on the one hand, and by 'administrators' on the other. In both the US and Australia, this distinction is entrenched in a written constitution which provides that 'judicial power' is to be vested in 'courts' as defined by the constitution.[68] Because administrative (as opposed to judicial) adjudication is such a common feature of modern government activity, ways have had to be found, consistently with the constitutional text, of allowing bodies, that are not 'courts' in the relevant sense, to perform adjudicatory functions traditionally associated with courts. This involves striking a workable balance between the adjudicatory roles of administrators and judges respectively. This is precisely the process at work in the Art. 6 case-law we have just examined.[69]

7.3.2.2 Fair Hearing Rule

As we have noted, a great many procedural steps could be demanded in the name of a fair hearing. It is not appropriate in a book of this size to consider in detail each of these steps. Instead, we will consider the general approach of the courts to the question of what steps are required to satisfy the obligation to give a fair hearing.

[67] See, e.g., the judgment of Lord Hoffmann in *Runa Begum v. Tower Hamlets LBC* [2003] 2 AC 430; *R (Anderson) v. Secretary of State for the Home Department* [2003] 1 AC 837 at [48]–[57] *per* Lord Steyn.

[68] These constitutions also provide that executive power is to be vested in the executive branch of government and legislative power on the legislative branch. In both countries the courts have had little difficulty in reconciling 'administrative legislation' with the constitution.

[69] The solution towards which the English courts are working is more similar to that adopted in the US than to that adopted in Australia. See generally P. Cane, 'The Making of Australian Administrative Law' in P. Cane (ed.), *Centenary Essays for the High Court of Australia* (Sydney, 2004).

7.3.2.2.1 The Nature of the Applicant's Interest

In *Ridge v. Baldwin*[70] Lord Reid said that any body having the power to make decisions affecting rights[71] was under a duty to give a fair hearing. Unfortunately, the term 'rights' is a vague one. Clearly, it covers property rights;[72] and (at least some) statutory rights.[73] It does not necessarily include contractual rights because, as we have seen (see 7.3.1.2.4), a mere employee (holding no office) is not entitled at common law to a hearing before being dismissed, even if the employer is a public body. On the other hand, it appears that there may be an obligation to observe the rules of natural justice even in the absence of a contract between the claimant and the decision-maker, if the claimant's livelihood is at stake.[74] The 'right to work' is a right in the relevant sense for the purposes of Lord Reid's formula even though it is not enforceable against any particular individual but is in the nature of a 'fundamental human right'.[75]

In *McInnes v. Onslow-Fane*[76] Megarry VC drew a distinction between three types of case according to the nature of the interest at stake. In what he called the 'forfeiture cases' the claimant is deprived of some right or position which he or she already holds; where, for example, a person is expelled from a society or an office. In such cases the claimant is entitled to a high degree of procedural protection. A high degree of protection would also be due in cases where the claimant was complaining of having been the victim of some serious wrong, such as unlawful racial discrimination;[77] or where a person is facing a serious charge of misconduct. In 'legitimate expectation cases' the claimant seeks the renewal or confirmation of some licence, membership, or office already held. In such cases, apparently, the claimant would be entitled to be told, before being refused renewal or confirmation, the grounds on which the application was to be refused so that he or she could say something in reply or defence. Thirdly, in 'application cases' a person merely seeks a licence, membership, or office which has not previously been held. Here the decision-maker's only

---

[70] [1964] AC 40.

[71] A person may have a right to be heard even if they are not the subject of the decision, if they will be indirectly affected by it: *R v. Life Assurance Unit Trust Regulatory Organisation, ex p. Ross* [1993] QB 17.

[72] e.g. *Cooper v. Wandsworth Board of Works* (1863) 14 CBNS 180.

[73] e.g. the right to complain of unlawful racial discrimination: *R v. Army Board of the Defence Council, ex p. Anderson* [1992] QB 169.

[74] *McInnes v. Onslow-Fane* [1978] 1 WLR 1520.

[75] See *Heatley v. Tasmanian Racing and Gaming Commission* (1977) 137 CLR 487; *Forbes v. New South Wales Trotting Club* (1979) 143 CLR 242 (freedom of contract and movement).

[76] [1978] 1 WLR 1520.

[77] *R v. Army Board of the Defence Council, ex p. Anderson* [1992] QB 169.

obligation is to act 'fairly'. It must reach its decision honestly and without bias or caprice (i.e. without abusing its decision-making power); but provided it does so, it is under no duty to tell the claimant even the gist of the reasons for its refusal of the application, or to give the claimant a chance to address it unless, perhaps, the refusal of the licence would cast a slur on the claimant's character (as in the *Gaming Board* case below).

This exposition raises difficulties of fundamental importance. First, the distinction between expulsion, expectation, and application cases seems to run counter to ideas such as the right to work. In each of these types of case a person's livelihood may be at stake. The same objection can be levelled at the concept of a privilege. In *R v. Gaming Board for Great Britain, ex p. Benaim & Khaida*[78] the claimants sought to challenge the refusal of a certificate necessary to support an application for a licence to run a gaming establishment. Lord Denning said that since the claimants were seeking a privilege rather than to enforce a right, the Board had no duty to give them detailed reasons for the refusal of the certificate, but only had to tell them their impressions and give them a chance to disabuse the Board if the impression was wrong. Yet the grant of the certificate was essential to the applicants' ability to earn their living by running a lawful casino. It is undesirable that the law concerning procedure should contain within it concepts which will pull in opposite directions and which can be appealed to as the court sees fit to produce a result which accords with its view of the merits. It would be better to tailor the right to procedural protection according to the effects on the applicant of denial of the application, regardless of whether the claimant's interest be technically a right or a legitimate expectation or a 'mere privilege.'[79] If a person's livelihood or reputation is at stake they deserve a proper hearing.

A second unfortunate aspect of Megarry VC's approach in *McInnes* is its use of the concept of legitimate expectation. This concept has at least three different senses. First, it may refer to an interest (e.g. in being granted parole,[80] or in having a licence renewed, or in not having an immigration entry permit revoked before its expiry date)[81] which is less than a right but more substantial than the mere hope of a favourable exercise of a discretion. A legitimate expectation in this sense is an interest which is protected by the claimant's right to be told the gist of the case

---

[78] [1970] 2 QB 417.
[79] See e.g. *R v. Norfolk CC, ex p. M* [1989] QB 619.
[80] *O'Reilly v. Mackman* [1983] 2 AC 237.
[81] *Schmidt v. Secretary of State for the Home Department* [1969] 2 Ch 149.

against them and to be given a chance to meet that case before a decision is made which adversely affects the interest. In Megarry VC's exposition, a legitimate expectation seems to require and deserve less procedural protection than certain more important interests, but in other cases no conclusion has been drawn from the fact that the claimant's interest is a legitimate expectation about the degree of procedural protection due. In this first sense, the term 'legitimate expectation' is redundant: the basis of procedural protection is the claimant's interest, and calling it a legitimate expectation does not make the interest any stronger.

Secondly, the term may refer to a situation in which an agency gives an undertaking,[82] or adopts and publishes a policy guideline,[83] or follows a course of conduct,[84] which justifies a person dealing with the agency in expecting that they will be given some sort of hearing before being treated in a particular way.[85] In this sense, the term 'legitimate expectation' is not redundant. It expresses the idea that a person may be entitled to some sort of hearing before a decision is made even if that person's interest in the decision, considered in isolation, might not require or justify a hearing.

The term 'legitimate expectation' has also been used in a third sense to refer to whether the claimant can legitimately expect a hearing. In this sense a person has a legitimate expectation only if they deserve a hearing or if a hearing would do some good. A clear illustration of this meaning is found in Lord Denning's judgment in *Cinnamond v. British Airports Authority*[86] where the authority sought to prohibit taxi-drivers, who had been prosecuted on numerous occasions for loitering and touting for business on airport property, from entering the airport. The drivers claimed that they ought to have been given a hearing before being excluded. Clearly something of considerable importance was at stake for them (in fact, in terms of Megarry VC's classification, the case looks like a forfeiture case, not a legitimate expectation case), but Lord Denning held that because of their repeated misconduct, and because of the fact that they must have known that this was why they were being banned, and since a hearing would have done them no good, they had no legitimate

---

[82] *R v. Liverpool Corporation, ex p. Liverpool Taxi Fleet Operator's Association* [1972] 2 QB 299; *Attorney-General of Hong Kong v. Ng Yuen Shiu* [1983] 2 AC 629.

[83] *R v. Secretary of State for the Home Department, ex p. Khan* [1984] 1 WLR 1337.

[84] *Council of Civil Service Unions v. Minister for the Civil Service* [1985] AC 374.

[85] There may be cases in which a person legitimately expects to be treated in a particular way rather than to be heard before being treated in a particular way: see 8.3.4.

[86] [1980] 1 WLR 582. See also *Glynn v. Keele University* [1971] 1 WLR 487.

expectation of being heard. This is an objectionable use of the concept of legitimate expectation because it enables the court, in the name of procedural fairness, to judge the merits of the case.

There is, you might think, a lot to be said for avoiding the time and expense involved in a hearing when it seems clear that the hearing will not affect the outcome. If a decision is clearly good in substance, why should a claimant be able to improve an unmeritorious case by seeking to have the decision quashed on procedural grounds? There are four important objections to such an approach.[87] The first is that it gives insufficient weight to the important idea that justice should not only be done but also be seen to be done: procedural rules are not just instrumentally important in producing fair decisions but also independently important in expressing respect for individuals whose interests are affected by decisions and in maintaining confidence in the decision-making process. Secondly, it assumes that the claimant will have nothing to say in his or her favour. Yet it cannot be concluded from the fact that there are certain things which the claimant could not say that there is nothing which they could say, even if only in mitigation of penalty. Thirdly, if courts give to inferior decision-makers a message that their decisions are not liable to be quashed for procedural defects if the decision itself is clearly 'right', such decision-makers may be tempted to dispense with proper procedure in any case in which they think that the right answer is obvious. The trouble with this is that what seems obvious to one person is not necessarily obvious to another, especially without the benefit of hearing both sides. Good procedure aids good decision-making, and insisting on good procedure has a symbolic and hortatory effect which is independent of the merits of any particular case.

Fourthly, by pronouncing on the merits of cases the courts are taking upon themselves a power of decision which has been entrusted to another body, either by statute or contract. The classic position is that a court exercising supervisory jurisdiction should not, when presented with a challenge on procedural grounds, concern itself with the merits of the case. This principle was reaffirmed by the House of Lords in *Chief Constable of North Wales v. Evans*.[88] Unfortunately it is not clear that the courts will be prepared to exercise such restraint in cases where they are not in sympathy with the claimant.

---

[87] *R v. Chief Constable of Thames Valley Police, ex p. Cotton* [1990] IRLR 344, 352 *per* Bingham LJ.

[88] [1982] 1 WLR 1155; applied in *Modahl v. British Athletic Federation Ltd* [2002] 1 WLR 1192.

The confusion of procedural and substantive fairness is even more obvious in another aspect of Megarry VC's reasoning in *McInnes v. Onslow-Fane*. He held that a decision-maker could act fairly without giving a hearing provided that the decision reached was bona fide and honest; or, in other words, provided the decision-maker did not abuse or exceed his or her powers. This may be true, but it assumes that the only function of procedure is to produce results which are in fact fair; it ignores the importance of creating a situation where those who are in fact treated fairly feel that they have been treated fairly and where this appears to be the case.

The temptation to pronounce on the merits of a case can take subtle forms. In *Calvin v. Carr*[89] the Privy Council had to decide when an appeal properly conducted in accordance with the rules of natural justice will make good a defect in procedure at the original hearing. The case concerned a contractual decision-making power and the question was whether, as a matter of interpretation of the contract, the claimant was entitled to have two proper hearings or whether he must be taken to have agreed to accept the result of a proper hearing on appeal, despite an earlier improper one. The Privy Council said that this depended on 'whether, at the end of the day, there has been a fair result, reached by fair methods, such as the parties may fairly be taken to have accepted when they joined the association'. In other words, whether a proper hearing mends an improper one depends, in part, on whether the appeal produces what the court considers to be a substantially fair result.

Objections to the confusion of procedural and substantive fairness are not confined to procedure in the sense of natural justice. Fair procedure is important in its own right no matter what procedural model is used.

7.3.2.2.2 *Natural Justice and Fairness*
It will be noticed that the words 'fairness' and 'fair hearing' have been used frequently in discussion so far. In fact, the term 'fairness' is now used much more frequently than the traditional term 'natural justice'. A great deal of ink has been spilt in attempts to elucidate the relationship between fairness and natural justice. Sometimes they appear to be equated, as when natural justice is described as 'fair play in action'.[90] On

---

[89] [1980] AC 574.
[90] *Wiseman v. Borneman* [1971] AC 297, 309 *per* Lord Morris. For early uses of the term 'fairness' see *Local Government Board v. Arlidge* [1915] AC 120, 133 *per* Viscount Haldane LC; *Board of Education v. Rice* [1917] AC 179, which is the origin of the seductive statement that 'the duty to act fairly . . . lies on everyone who decides anything'.

the other hand, there are dicta which suggest that natural justice is the standard of procedure appropriate to judicial functions, while fairness is a lesser standard applicable to the performance of non-judicial functions;[91] or that there is a continuum from natural justice to fairness and from judicial to administrative functions.[92] There are two ways of viewing such dicta. One is that the notion of fairness has encouraged courts to exercise some degree of control over the procedure of bodies or officers over whom they would not formerly have exercised control (e.g. immigration officers, the Gaming Board,[93] Companies Act inspectors).[94]

The other interpretation is that the idea of fairness has enabled courts to evade the full implications of Lord Reid's dictum in *Ridge v. Baldwin* (that anyone having the power to make decisions affecting rights must comply with the requirements of natural justice), by holding that some lesser 'rights' deserve lesser procedural protection. This second interpretation of the development of the concept of fairness is particularly supported by those cases in which it has been said that a decision can be fair even if not preceded by a hearing, and that in some circumstances undeserving claimants are not treated unfairly even if they are not given a hearing (although the first emergence of these ideas predates the modern introduction of the notion of fairness). These cases give to fairness a substantive connotation which is at variance with the traditional concept of natural justice.

Some writers suggest that fairness is merely a more flexible version of natural justice. It has always been recognized that the requirements of natural justice vary according to the facts, but cases have traditionally been divided into classes or types according to their facts (e.g. according to the type of function being performed, or the type of interest at stake). Fairness, on the other hand, is seen, on this view, as more closely dependent on the detailed facts of particular cases. Categorization of cases is frowned upon as mechanical. The result of this emphasis on detailed facts often[95] seems to be that fairness can be satisfied by lower procedural standards than the traditional notion of natural justice implied. This has frequently had the result that the requirement of a hearing has been given a truncated meaning, or has been subordinated to the idea of substantive

---

[91] e.g. *Pearlberg v. Varty* [1972] 1 WLR 534, 547 *per* Lord Pearson.
[92] *McInnes v. Onslow-Fane* [1978] 1 WLR 1520.
[93] *R v. Gaming Board for Great Britain, ex p. Benaim and Khaida* [1970] 2 QB 417.
[94] *Re Pergamon Press* [1971] Ch 388; *Maxwell v. Department of Trade and Industry* [1974] QB 523.
[95] But not always: e.g. *R v. Army Board of the Defence Council, ex p. Anderson* [1992] QB 169.

fairness. On the other hand, the notion of fairness has facilitated the development of procedural protections not traditionally seen as part of the requirements of natural justice, notably the obligation to give reasons for a decision (see 7.3.2.2.5). The notion of fairness has been used both to augment and to truncate the traditional notion of natural justice.

It is worth noting that while the traditional notion of the right to be heard consists of a 'menu' of procedural requirements which decision-makers must comply with as and when appropriate, the notion of fairness relates to the quality of the procedure used (was it fair?) rather than to the procedural steps actually followed (for instance, was the claimant allowed to cross-examine witnesses?). Viewed in this way, fairness offers a radically different approach to procedure from that embodied in the rules of natural justice. Indeed, there may be circumstances in which adherence to the adversarial model reflected in the rules of natural justice might itself be unfair: if, for example, one of the parties in dispute is much less able than the other to present a coherent case. Or again, since the classic adversarial model refers to two competing parties and a third party adjudicator, some aspects of that model might be inappropriate to situations involving only two parties—a government official and a citizen, for instance. In such cases a non-adversarial model of procedure might be fairer.

If the courts viewed fairness in this broader way, they might see their role as being to specify in any particular case what procedure would be most fair, whether it were an adversarial trial, an inquisitorial investigation, consultation, mediation or any other possible approach to decision-making. In fact, what the courts have actually done is to use the notion of fairness to give themselves the freedom to pick and choose appropriate procedural steps from only a rather narrow menu of possibilities based on the traditional model of an adversarial trial. The notion of fairness has also been used, via the doctrine of legitimate expectations (which, I believe, is based on that notion) both to expand and to restrict the incidence of the right to be heard. In other words, as used by the courts, the notion of fairness is not a version of natural justice but an evaluative concept used to provide flexibility in applying the notion of natural justice to particular cases.

Finally, it should be noted that the issues discussed in this section have counterparts in the developing jurisprudence under Art. 6 of the ECHR. Article 6 (it will be recalled) guarantees (amongst others) a right to a fair hearing before an independent and impartial tribunal in the determination of a person's civil rights. This provision raises several issues: how closely tied to the adversarial model of adjudication is the concept of a 'fair hearing'? how closely tied to traditional understandings of a court is the concept of an 'independent and impartial tribunal'? and what is meant by the term 'civil rights'? *Runa Begum v. Tower Hamlets LBC*[96] makes the important point that if the term 'determination of civil rights' is given a broad meaning covering a wide range of public decision-making contexts, there is a danger that public decision-making procedures will be 'over-judicialized'—in other words, that public decision-makers will be required to follow court-like procedures in circumstances where this is thought inappropriate. Just as the courts have injected flexibility into the concept of natural justice by using the concept of fairness, so they will need to prevent Art. 6 becoming a procedural straitjacket that requires all public decisions to be made according to 'judicial' methods. This danger might be thought particularly acute in a system of norms (such as the ECHR) that is based on the concept of fundamental individual human rights. Within this ideological framework, it may be especially difficult to give due weight to values that compete with those associated with 'due process'.

7.3.2.2.3 *The Circumstances of the Decision*

A factor relevant in deciding what natural justice (or fairness) requires in particular cases is the factual background against which the decision falls to be made. For example, in *R v. Secretary of State for the Home Department, ex p. Cheblak*[97] the claimant challenged the validity of a deportation order made against him on the ground that he had not been told in detail why it had been made. The court held that since the information relevant to the making of the order was highly sensitive from the point of view of national security, the normal requirement of disclosure of the case against the claimant did not apply. However, the court also made it clear that the authorities had to act fairly; but in this case fairness only required that the immigrant be allowed to make representations to the Home Secretary's advisory panel set up to consider appeals against deportation orders. In the *GCHQ* case[98] the House of Lords held that the demands of national security relieved the government of any obligation of consultation before banning employees at the government's intelligence headquarters from belonging to unions.

---

[96] [2003] 2 AC 430.
[97] [1991] 1 WLR 890. See also *R v. Secretary of State for the Home Department, ex p. Hosenball* [1977] 1 WLR 766.
[98] [1985] AC 374.

There are other situations in which the disclosure of information by the decision-maker may be wholly or partly dispensed with. For example, in the *Gaming Board* case[99] it was held that the claimants were entitled to know the gist of the case against them but not the details: the court was concerned that otherwise, confidential sources of valuable information would dry up or be put in danger.[100] In another case it was held that a prisoner was entitled to be told only the gist of reports prepared in connection with the annual review of his security classification, because the decision was 'administrative' in character, was subject to review, and was important not only to the prisoner but also for the general running of the prison.[101] In some cases the need to act quickly as a matter of emergency may justify dispensing with a full hearing. For example, in one case it was held that a permit to carry passengers by air could be provisionally suspended with only a minimum of procedural protection if the safety of passengers was in issue.[102] In *Re HK*[103] the court was clearly influenced by the impracticability of requiring an airport immigration officer to mount a full hearing in the physical surroundings of an airport and given the volume of entrants to be processed.

7.3.2.2.4 Legal Representation

Many people who are affected by administrative decisions do not have the training or ability to put their case in its most convincing form. This is true whether the 'hearing' is oral or in the form of written submissions. In theory it would not seem difficult, in cases where the adversary model of procedure is appropriate, to justify a right to representation (i.e. to have another present one's case in person) as part of the right to have one's side of the story fairly heard. A right to representation is, perhaps, less easily justified in cases in which the decision-maker takes a more active role in the proceedings, although even here it may not be possible or appropriate for the decision-maker to do as much to facilitate the presentation of the claimant's case as a representative would. Even if representation is not appropriate in every procedural model, it is certainly appropriate in the adversary model (at least in serious cases), and so should be one of the requirements of natural justice.

The arguments in favour of a right to representation are reinforced by

---

[99] [1970] 2 QB 417.

[100] The issue of protecting sources is examined in greater detail at 15.2.

[101] *R v. Secretary of State for the Home Department, ex p. McAvoy* [1998] 1 WLR 791.

[102] *R v. Secretary of State for Transport, ex p. Pegasus Holdings (London) Ltd* [1988] 1 WLR 990.

[103] [1967] 2 QB 617. See also *Wandsworth LBC v. A* [2000] 1 WLR 1246.

research into the workings of four different types of tribunals which shows that representation significantly increases the claimant's chance of success.[104] It does not follow from this that there should always be a right to be represented by a lawyer. The presence of lawyers tends to make proceedings longer and more formal and legalistic, and in some cases this may be undesirable. Indeed, the research just mentioned suggests that non-legal representatives who specialize in welfare law have higher success rates on behalf of clients appearing before social security tribunals than do lawyers.

Where a person is facing a criminal charge, Art 6(3)(c) of the ECHR confers a right to *legal* 'assistance'.[105] A right to legal (or other) representation may also be conferred by statute.[106] In cases to which neither such a statute nor the ECHR applies, the decision-maker has a discretion whether or not to allow legal representation.[107] There is (somewhat old) authority that a provision in a contract purporting to exclude the right to legal representation would not, for that reason, be contrary to public policy;[108] and that regulations which excluded such a right would not, on that ground, be unreasonable and *ultra vires*.[109] But a litigant before a court is entitled, as a matter of procedural fairness, to reasonable assistance in presenting his or her case.[110] This right does not require the court to allow the assistant to address the court unless he or she has a 'right of audience' (i.e. unless the assistant is a qualified lawyer). It is not clear whether the right to assistance applies to proceedings before bodies other than courts.

It might be thought unnecessary to insist on establishing certain rights to representation when, by virtue of the general principle that a decision-making body is master of its own procedure, it has a discretion to allow representation. But the whole point of the rules of natural justice is that they constitute a framework of procedural rights that limit the discretion

---

[104] H. Genn and Y. Genn, *The Effectiveness of Representation at Tribunals* (Lord Chancellor's Department, 1989). For useful summary and discussion see T. Mullen, 'Representation at Tribunals' (1990) 53 *MLR* 230.

[105] *Ezeh and Connors v. United Kingdom* (2002) 35 EHRR 691.

[106] e.g. *Bache v. Essex County Council* [2000] 2 All ER 847.

[107] *R v. Board of Visitors of Her Majesty's Prison, The Maze, ex p. Hone* [1988] AC 379.

[108] *Pett v. Greyhound Racing Association Ltd* [1968] 2 All ER 545; [1969] 2 All ER 221; *Enderby Town Football Club v. Football Association Ltd* [1971] Ch 591; *Maynard v. Osmond* [1977] QB 240.

[109] *Maynard v. Osmond* [1977] QB 240.

[110] *R v. Leicester City Justices, ex p. Barrow* [1991] 2 QB 260. But it may not always be 'in the interests of justice' to allow a litigant to bring an assistant to court: *R v. Bow County Court, ex p. Pelling* [1999] 1 WLR 1807.

of decision-makers to control their own procedure. Given the importance of the clear and effective presentation of a party's case, representation ought not, as a general rule, to be a matter of discretion.

While a right to representation is very important, it is by itself of little value if, for lack of available representatives or of funds, a claimant cannot secure representation. As a general rule, legal aid is not available for hearings before administrative tribunals, and there is no organized system of funding lay representatives. This represents a serious limitation on access to justice.

7.3.2.2.5 *Reasons*

Here we are concerned not with informing a claimant of the case to be answered but with the giving of reasons for the decision once it has been made.[111] If the right to be heard is to have any real meaning, it must entail a duty on the part of the decision-maker to take account of the claimant's arguments in reaching the decision and to address, and either to accept or reject in a reasoned way, the points made by the claimant. Furthermore, unless reasons for the decision are given, parties are deprived of a proper chance to challenge the decision if it is thought to be wrong. For example, it is only if reasons are given that a party can know whether a decision-maker took account of some irrelevant consideration.

A decision-maker may be under a statutory duty to give reasons for its decisions.[112] If there is no statutory duty to give reasons, the common law may, in the name of procedural fairness, impose such a duty, although there is no 'general' common law duty to give reasons. A duty to give reasons may arise if the body in question has, by its words or conduct, generated a legitimate expectation that reasons will be given.[113] In the absence of such an expectation, reasons may be required if the claimant's interest in the decision is sufficiently weighty;[114] or if, given the circumstances of the case, the decision appears odd and in need of explanation.[115] However, the nature of the decision may make the giving of

---

[111] G. Richardson, 'The Duty to Give Reasons: Potential and Practice' [1986] *PL* 437. The distinction drawn in the text was critical in *R v. Secretary of State for the Home Department, ex p. Fayed* [1997] 1 All ER 228.

[112] e.g. Tribunals and Inquiries Act 1992, s. 10; Local Government Act 1988, s. 20. See A.P. Le Sueur, 'Legal Duties to Give Reasons' (1999) 52 *CLP* 150.

[113] *R v. Civil Service Board, ex p. Cunningham* [1991] 4 All ER 310.

[114] e.g. *R v. Secretary of State for the Home Department, ex p. Doody* [1994] 1 AC 531; *R v. Corporation of the City of London, ex p. Matson* [1997] 1 WLR 765; *R v. Ministry of Defence, ex p. Murray* [1998] COD 134.

[115] *R v. Civil Service Appeal Board, ex p. Cunningham* [1991] 4 All ER 310.

reasons inappropriate—for instance, if it is a pure exercise of academic judgment.[116]

The issue of the relationship between procedural safeguards and the merits of individual decisions (which was discussed in 7.3.2.2.1) is relevant in this context. The question is whether, in a case where reasons are required by statute or the common law, failure to give reasons is a ground of judicial review in itself; or whether failure to give reasons will justify the court's intervention only if the failure supports a conclusion that the decision-maker had no legally satisfactory or relevant reason for the decision, or did not consider the matter properly, with the result that the decision itself is *ultra vires*.[117] There is high authority for the proposition that a decision will be quashed on account of inadequacy of (as opposed to total failure to give) reasons only if the applicant can convince the court that the gap in the reasons raises a substantial doubt as to whether there was a flaw in the decision which would justify quashing it on some other ground than failure to give reasons.[118] If this is the law, failure to give adequate reasons, in and of itself, would not invalidate a decision.[119] On the other hand, it has been said that where the subject matter of the decision is sufficiently important and serious, or of great public interest, failure to give reasons may justify quashing of the decision regardless of whether the decision itself is unlawful.[120] It might be thought that this should be the general approach because of the difficulty of determining whether a decision is lawful or not in the absence of reasons. One of the justifications for reason-giving is to allow the quality of the decision to be assessed. It is perverse to require a person to establish that a decision is unlawful as a precondition of being entitled to reasons for the decision. Reason-giving is also important in its own right as a means of showing respect to a person adversely affected by a decision.

Where there is a duty to give reasons, the reasons must satisfy a minimum standard of clarity and explanatory force, and must deal with all the substantial points which have been raised.[121]

---

[116] *R v. Higher Education Funding Council, ex p. Institute of Dental Surgery* [1994] 1 WLR 242. See also *Gupta v. General Medical Council* [2002] 1 WLR 1691 (credibility of witnesses and reliability of evidence).

[117] *R v. HEFC, ex p. Institute of Dental Surgery* [1994] 1 WLR 242, 257–8.

[118] *Save Britain's Heritage v. Number 1 Poultry Ltd* [1991] 1 WLR 153.

[119] See also *Crake v. Supplementary Benefits Commission* [1982] 1 All ER 498.

[120] *R v. Director of Public Prosecutions, ex p. Manning* [2001] QB 330.

[121] *Re Poyser and Mills' Arbitration* [1964] 2 QB 467; *R v. Criminal Injuries Compensation Board, ex p. Cook* [1996] 2 All ER 144.

Even if a decision-maker is under no statutory or common law duty to give reasons, once its decision is challenged it will be forced to explain itself to a greater or lesser extent.[122] It is, however, obviously undesirable that a person should have to challenge a decision in order to discover the grounds on which it was made.

7.4 THE EFFECT OF BREACH OF NATURAL JUSTICE

In theory, breach of natural justice renders a decision invalid and a nullity. On the other hand, this bald statement needs to be qualified in at least three ways. First, a party who loses the right to be heard through his or her own fault or that of a legal adviser, cannot complain of breach of natural justice.[123] Secondly, it is probably the case that the only person who would have standing to challenge a decision for breach of natural justice would be the person denied a hearing or whose case was heard by a biased tribunal. Thirdly, as we have seen (see 7.3.2.2.1), courts are prepared to deny a remedy for breach of natural justice if they consider that the breach caused no real prejudice because, for example, a hearing would have done no good.

7.5 NATURAL JUSTICE AND THE FUNCTION OF JUDICIAL REVIEW

The rules of natural justice (and the analogous requirements of Art. 6 of the ECHR) embody the idea that the function of judicial review is to protect the (procedural) rights of the individual. By contrast, modern departures from and dilution of natural justice tend to be informed by the idea that the role of judicial review is to give effect to the public interest in good and efficient government.[124] In some respects this is a sound development as it may lead to a recognition that in relation to decisions to which individual rights are not crucial, the individual needs and deserves less procedural protection. It also prevents the judicialization of the whole administrative process. There are, however, dangers in this. Court-like procedure tends to be slow and expensive, and there is a risk that the interests of individuals in procedural fairness will be sacrificed to a public

---

[122] *R v. Lancashire CC, ex p. Huddleston* [1986] 2 All ER 941.
[123] *R v. Secretary of State for the Home Department, ex p. El-Mehdawi* [1990] 1 AC 816.
[124] See Ch. 19 for further discussion of the 'protection of the individual' and 'public interest' 'models' of judicial review.

interest in economical and efficient public decision-making processes. We need to be confident that proposed alternatives to court-like procedure will be fair and produce good decisions (rather than being just quicker and cheaper) before we abandon judicial procedure. In some respects the development of the public interest view of procedural protection is to be deplored; it has in some cases led to the denial of individual procedural rights in situations acknowledged to fit into the adversary model, on the basis that no substantial injustice or illegality has been done. It is good to recognize that different procedural models can be fair, but bad to move from this to the idea that procedural unfairness can be cured by substantive fairness.

As we have seen in this chapter, the rules of natural justice are concerned primarily with the *ex post facto* settlement of disputes between individuals and administrative bodies.[125] They do not apply to the legislative process, and they have not been used as the basis for securing group participation in the public policy-making process.[126] It may be that there are good grounds for this approach: the expertise and constitutional position of the courts may well justify concentration on protecting the rights of the individual. However, an important result is that the judicial process is irrelevant to important areas of administrative activity, and offers no procedural framework for many interactions between individuals (and groups) and the administration.[127]

The common law rules of natural justice must, therefore, be seen as limited in at least three important ways: they are primarily concerned with the protection of individuals; they are based on an adjudicative model of dispute settlement; and they have little or nothing to say about interactions between citizens (and groups) and the administration which are concerned with providing a framework for future conduct and relations and with avoiding (as opposed to resolving) disputes.

---

[125] But the rules may also protect one governmental institution which is affected by a decision of another governmental institution 'which is based upon their having acted, or which necessarily implies that they have acted, unlawfully or discreditably': *R v. Secretary of State for the Environment, ex p. Hammersmith and Fulham LBC* [1991] 1 AC 521, 598. See also *R v. Secretary of State for the Environment, ex p. Brent LBC* [1982] QB 593.

[126] See further 19.3.1 on the 'interest representation' model of judicial review.

[127] P. Cane, 'The Constitutional and Legal Framework of Policy-Making' in C. Forsyth and I. Hare (eds), *The Golden Metwand and the Crooked Sword: Essays on Public Law in Honour of Sir William Wade* (Oxford, 1998).

7.6 STATUTORY PROCEDURAL REQUIREMENTS

7.6.1 EFFECT OF NON-COMPLIANCE

The traditional approach is that failure to comply with a statutory procedural requirement does not render a decision invalid if the requirement is 'directory' rather than 'mandatory'. The nature of any particular provision is ultimately a matter of statutory interpretation. Since the statute will usually not identify the nature of the requirement, the court will normally have to classify the requirement in the light of all the facts of the case including the terms of the statute; the seriousness of the procedural defect and the seriousness of its effects on the claimant and the public; and, possibly, the merits of the case. In general, it seems that the courts will consider it in their discretion to choose the classification that achieves 'justice' in all the circumstances of the case.[128] This position produces considerable uncertainty and allows courts to pronounce on the merits of a case in the name of procedural review in a way similar to that noted in the context of natural justice.

Even if a statutory procedural requirement is classified as being 'mandatory', failure to comply may not result in invalidity if the court is prepared to hold that there was 'substantial' compliance. Alternatively, because judicial review remedies are discretionary, the court may simply refuse, in its discretion, to quash the decision in order to avoid what it considers to be 'unjust and unintended consequences'.[129] The fact that so many escape routes have been devised illustrates a fundamental tension in administrative law:[130] although it is often said that judicial review is primarily concerned with administrative procedure rather than with the substance of administrative decisions and rules, courts tend to be unwilling to quash administrative decisions and rules merely for procedural irregularity unless something seems to be wrong with the decision itself.

It would not be appropriate in a book of this nature to consider in detail the sorts of procedural requirements which are commonly imposed by statute. But there are a few which do deserve some attention.[131]

---

[128] *London & Clydeside Estates Ltd v. Aberdeen DC* [1980] 1 WLR 182, 189–90. See also 8.3.1.1.2.

[129] *R v. Secretary of State for the Home Department, ex p. Jeyeanthan* [2000] 1 WLR 354, 358–9, 362 *per* Lord Woolf MR.

[130] See also 7.3.2.2.1.

[131] Concerning statutory duties to give reasons see 7.3.2.2.5.

7.6.2 PARTICULAR STATUTORY REQUIREMENTS

7.6.2.1 Statutory Instruments Act 1946

The Statutory Instruments Act 1946 requires that statutory instruments which are subject to its provisions, once they have been made, be printed and put on sale to the public. It is not clear whether failure to comply with the statutory requirement renders a statutory instrument unenforceable. Because the Act does not say anything about this, it depends on the position at common law. There is disagreement about whether at common law delegated legislation becomes enforceable as soon as it is made (in the case of statutory instruments this is when the instrument is laid before or approved by Parliament) or only when it is published.[132] The latter would seem preferable as a general rule, although there may be cases where it would be desirable for regulations to come into force as soon as they are made so as to minimize the possibility of large-scale evasive conduct in anticipation of a change in the law. It seems highly desirable that the matter be resolved by legislation.

Statutory instruments subject to the Act, as well as other governmental rules, are often required by statute to be laid before Parliament. It appears that failure to satisfy such a requirement would not render an instrument invalid.[133]

7.6.2.2 Consultation

It is not uncommon for a statute to provide that before a Minister or other governmental body makes a particular decision, order or (especially) a set of rules it should (or may) consult[134] interested parties or a specified body (such as an advisory committee set up for the purpose, or a non-departmental, governmental body (quango) or both).[135] Consultation is a type of procedure appropriate for making decisions and rules which affect large numbers of people. The common law recognizes no 'general' obligation to consult parties before making decisions or rules

---

[132] D. Lanham, 'Delegated Legislation and Publication' (1974) 37 *MLR* 510; A.I.L. Campbell, 'The Publication of Delegated Legislation' [1982] *PL* 569.

[133] A.I.L. Campbell, 'Laying and Delegated Legislation' [1983] *PL* 43.

[134] See 7.2.1 concerning the nature of consultation.

[135] J. Garner, 'Consultation in Subordinate Legislation' [1964] *PL* 105; A.D. Jergensen, 'The Legal Requirements of Consultation' [1978] *PL* 290; A.G. Jordan and J.J. Richardson, *Government and Pressure Groups in Britain* (Oxford, 1987), ch. 6.

which will affect them.[136] However, the common law may impose an obligation to consult before making a decision that will deprive a group of individuals of some significant benefit.[137] If a public body has published policy guidelines, the doctrine of legitimate expectation may prevent it from departing from its policy without (at least) first consulting affected parties.[138] Also, if a public body has in the past followed a practice of consulting particular individuals or bodies before making rules on certain topics, it may be held to have acted illegally if it abandons that practice.[139]

Statutory duties (as opposed to powers) to consult will normally be held to be mandatory, and failure to comply will render a decision or rule invalid.[140] On the other hand, the effects of invalidity may be limited: if the decision or rule affects a number of parties some of whom were consulted and others not, the decision or rule may be invalid only as it applies to the parties who ought to have been, but were not, consulted.[141] Furthermore, a court may decline to exercise its discretion to make a quashing order if the claimant makes no real complaint about the substance of the decision or rule but only about lack of consultation; or if the court thinks that to revoke the decision or rule would generate undue administrative inconvenience;[142] or would have a significant detrimental impact on the interests of third parties but minimal impact on the interests of the applicant.[143] The use of remedial discretion in this way makes a mockery of the requirement of consultation.

A body may fail to comply with a duty to consult not only by total inaction, but also by consulting inadequately. Consultation must take place at a time when proposals are still at a formative stage; all those entitled must be consulted; the consultation must cover all relevant issues and the consulting party must give adequate information about what it proposes to do and why;[144] the consulted party must be given sufficient

---

[136] *Bates v. Lord Hailsham* [1972] 1 WLR 1373 (rule-making). For an argument that it should see G. Richardson in G. Richardson and H. Genn (eds), *Administrative Law and Government Action* (Oxford, 1994), ch. 5.

[137] e.g. *R v. Devon CC, ex p. Baker* [1995] 1 All ER 73 (closure of an old people's home).

[138] See 8.3.2. [139] See 8.3.4.

[140] e.g. *Howker v. Secretary of State for Work and Pensions* [2003] ICR 405.

[141] *Agricultural, Horticultural and Forestry Training Board v. Aylesbury Mushrooms Ltd* [1972] 1 WLR 190.

[142] *R v. Secretary of State for Social Services, ex p. Association of Metropolitan Authorities* [1986] 1 WLR 1.

[143] *R v. Secretary of State for the Environment, ex p. Walters* (1998) 10 Admin LR 265.

[144] *R v. Secretary of State for Health, ex p. United States Tobacco International Inc* [1992] QB 353, 371 *per* Taylor LJ; *R v. Devon CC, ex p. Baker* [1995] 1 All ER 73, 91 *per* Simon Brown LJ.

time to consider the proposals and formulate a response to them; and the 'product of the consultation must be conscientiously taken into account in finalising any . . . proposals'.[145]

Although statutory obligations resting on public bodies to consult interested parties before making rules are by no means uncommon, they are certainly not universal. We might ask, therefore, whether there is a case for greater use of mandatory publicity and consultation in this context.[146] One of the most obvious features of the Parliamentary legislative process is that proposed legislation is usually subjected to a considerable amount of public discussion and scrutiny both inside and outside Parliament. Before and during the drafting process the government will usually consult interested groups[147] and will often publish discussion documents (Green Papers) and White Papers (firmer statements of policy) on the subject matter of the legislation which Parliament and members of the public can discuss and comment on. Although the content of the legislation will be largely decided by the government, Parliamentary and concerted public pressure can sometimes force changes even in legislation which is at an advanced stage of its progress though the legislative machine.

The process of non-Parliamentary rule-making is usually not so public as this. It is certainly the case that the government often consults widely amongst interested groups before making rules even when it is not required to do so by statute.[148] Such consultation can serve a number of functions: to obtain information and to explore policy options; to provide information about government plans; to legitimate government action; to avoid unnecessary dissatisfaction with the rules made and to reduce the chance of legal challenges to rules in the future. But much government rule-making does not pass through any significant public stage. Local authority by-laws will no doubt often be subjected to a certain amount of local scrutiny; but they have to receive ministerial approval before they come into force, and often this procedure is short-circuited by local authorities adopting model by-laws drafted by central government departments. Much central government legislation has to be laid before Parliament but, as we will see later,[149] most receives little or no discussion

---

[145] *R v. Devon CC, ex p. Baker* [1995] 1 All ER 73, 91.

[146] R. Baldwin and J. Houghton, 'Circular Arguments: The Status and Legitimacy of Administrative Rules' [1986] *PL* 239, 272–4; P.P. Craig, *Public Law and Democracy* (Oxford, 1990), pp. 160–82.

[147] D. Miers and A.C. Page, *Legislation*, 2nd edn (London, 1990), pp. 39–43.

[148] Ibid. 113; R. Baldwin, *Rules and Government* (Oxford, 1995), pp. 74–80, 111–19.

[149] See 16.2.4.

in Parliament. Furthermore, many rules are not made in exercise of statutory rule-making powers and are probably made without any significant consultation of interests outside government; such rules are not even required to be laid before Parliament, let alone scrutinized by it.

It would seem, therefore, that despite the volume and importance of non-Parliamentary rule-making, much of it is subject to relatively little public scrutiny, and such consultation as takes place is largely at the initiative of the law-maker and with bodies of its choice. This, coupled with the low-key nature and the infrequency of judicial control of rule-making, might lead one to expect considerable dissatisfaction with the system—but there isn't.

By contrast, in the 1960s and 1970s US courts developed an elaborate body of law to regulate rule-making by government agencies.[150] Yet administrative rule-making in the United States is a matter of acute and continuing controversy. It is worthwhile considering briefly why this might be so.[151] Much rule-making in the United States is done by agencies set up to regulate economic and social activity. These agencies are staffed largely by technical experts and are designed to be relatively independent of political influence and control. They have had considerable difficulty in establishing their legitimacy as rule-makers. There are two main reasons for this. First, many have felt that while technical expertise is necessary to ensure that government regulations establish a regime of governmental control which is practicable and efficient, at the end of the day the extent to which, and the way in which, government should control the activities of its citizens is a political issue. Technical expertise does not help in the choice between different regulations which are equally acceptable on technical grounds; and sometimes there may be sound political reasons for preferring a technically inferior scheme.

The limited relevance of technical expertise also gives rise to a second reason for discontent. If governmental regulation does involve political choices, then it is undesirable that the decision-makers should be independent of the political process. The more politically contentious the matters with which the authority has to deal, the more dissatisfaction

---

[150] R.B. Stewart, 'The Reformation of American Administrative Law' (1975) 88 *Harvard LR* 1669. For an elegant and powerful defence of the US system see M. Shapiro, 'Trans-Atlantic: Harlow Revisited' in P. Craig and R. Rawlings (eds), *Law and Administration in Europe: Essays in Honour of Carol Harlow* (Oxford, 2003), ch. 12.

[151] M. Asimow, 'Delegated Legislation: United States and United Kingdom' (1983) 3 *OJLS* 253; R. Baldwin, *Regulating the Airlines* (Oxford, 1985), pp. 242–50. See also T. Ziamou, 'Alternative Modes of Administrative Action: Negotiated Rule-Making in the United States, Germany and Britain' (2000) 6 *European Public Law* 45.

there is likely to be with the technical solution, whatever it is. An intrusive and detailed system of judicial control over rule-making by regulatory agencies may plausibly be seen as a response to worries about the legitimacy of agency rule-making. Requiring agencies to publicize their proposals and to hear and take account of objections injects a popular and political element into the law-making process. Judicial control adds a further element of publicity, as well as giving a say to groups which may not have been properly consulted earlier. Procedural requirements and judicial control are legitimizing techniques.

The position in Britain is very different. Here most statutory rule-making powers reside in officials or bodies which are not, and are not seen as being or required to be, politically independent.[152] Although rule-makers no doubt have the benefit of expert advice when deciding what rules to make, their function is seen as that of putting flesh on the bones of the policy objectives laid down by Parliament in the enabling legislation. In other words, rule-making by government is seen very much as a political activity. The legitimacy of political decision-makers in our system tends to derive more from the mode of their selection than from the substance of the decisions they make. We expect the government to make rules that give effect to declared policies, and we are not so concerned with influencing or controlling particular decisions so long as we feel that the electoral process is reasonably fair and democratic.

Another reason that may account for the lack of any real dissatisfaction with our system of control over government rule-making is that rule-making plays a smaller part in British governmental arrangements that it does in the US. Although British governments make a great many rules, much governmental regulation of economic and social life is conducted not through rule-making but through more individualized (and discretionary) modes of decision-making.[153] In Britain too, regulatory agencies have traditionally been much more involved in monitoring and enforcing compliance with the law by individuals than in making rules. At the most abstract level, both the American desire for rules and the concern to control rule-making may reflect a deep-seated distrust of government which the British do not feel.

The main advantages of a more formalized procedure of rule-making are said to be that it gives the citizen a greater chance to participate in

---

[152] For a discussion of rule-making by British regulators see T. Prosser, *Law and the Regulators* (Oxford, 1997), pp. 277–86; also pp. 50–1, 84–6.

[153] D. Vogel, *National Styles of Regulation: Environmental Policy in Britain and the United States* (Ithaca, NY, 1986).

decision-making and that it improves the quality of the rules made. However, unless participation leads to greater satisfaction with and acceptance of the rules themselves, it is of doubtful value. If the participants object to the rules made, despite extensive involvement, and feel that participation has only 'worked' if the result they favour is reached, then participation by itself may be of limited value. The formalized procedures used in the United States do not seem to have reduced dissatisfaction with the administrative rule-making. It may be that Americans are much less happy than the British about having their lives regulated by government at all, and that this, rather than the actual content of the regulation, is the main source of discontent. No amount of formalized procedure can overcome this problem.

As for the second alleged advantage, the concept of increased quality of rule-making is a very difficult one to pin down. If quality refers to technical matters such as drafting, participation of non-experts may not improve quality. On the other hand, consultation of those whose interests will be affected may assist the rule-maker, in designing a rule that will effectively and efficiently achieve desired policy objectives, by providing detailed information about the circumstances in which the rule will operate. If 'quality' is really a surrogate for political acceptability, then once again there may be reason to doubt that increased popular participation will make rules more acceptable to those who dislike them.

There are considerable problems associated with more formal participatory forms of rule-making. They take a lot of time and money; and so groups with the greatest resources tend to have an advantage over less well-endowed interest groups. It is unlikely that statutory obligations to consult would overcome such inequalities in resources. Furthermore, it is not clear that hearing a wide diversity of conflicting views makes it easier to frame a rule; the result may just be that the rule finally formulated fails to satisfy many of those views. On the other hand, consultation at an early stage may at least increase levels of compliance later on and reduce the chance that those dissatisfied with any rules made will seek actively to challenge them.

7.7 PUBLIC INQUIRIES

Several of the themes of this chapter are well illustrated by an examination of the institution of the public inquiry. Public inquiries are an important feature of the British administrative process. Their most significant, but by no means their only, use is as part of the land-use planning

system. (Other areas in which public inquiries play a part include housing, agriculture, health, and aviation.) By contrast with the process of
much governmental rule-making, the land-use planning system is highly
formalized and allows interested individuals and groups to have a say
before decisions are made that will affect their rights and interests.

More than 20,000 land-use planning inquiries are held each year; most
are run by the Planning Inspectorate.[154] The largest group of inquiries
concerns planning applications, but a significant number deal with compulsory acquisition of land, and some are concerned with local development plans.[155] Inquiries are conducted by 'inspectors', most of whom are
employed by the Planning Inspectorate (PI), although independent persons (e.g. a QC or judge) are engaged to conduct large and contentious
inquiries. There are about 300 inspectors.

7.7.1 SMALL-SCALE INQUIRIES

Public inquiries concerning land use perform two main functions. First,
they play an important part in the planning appeal process. If, for
example, a landowner appeals to the Minister against a decision of a local
authority[156] refusing planning permission or making a compulsory purchase order, the public inquiry performs the function of ascertaining the
relevant facts, hearing objections from interested third parties,[157] and
assessing the local conditions relevant to the particular decision. In such
cases, the inquiry will usually be concerned essentially with establishing
facts relevant to evaluating the strength of the cases for and against the
local authority's decision. The inquiry will often not raise important
matters of national policy but will involve a small-scale dispute between a
landowner and a local authority. Such inquiries are usually concluded
without an oral hearing (in which case third parties have certain statutory
rights to make representations) or after an informal hearing.

When the main aim of the inquiry is to gather facts, it seems only
reasonable and fair that the Minister should not be entitled to take
account of factual material which did not come out at the inquiry and
which the applicant has not had a chance to challenge; and this is the

---

[154] Some 150 appeals a year are 'called in' or 'recovered' to be decided by the Secretary of
State. These procedures were the subject of the *Alconbury* case discussed in 7.3.2.1.

[155] B. Webster and A Lavers, 'The Effectiveness of Public Local Inquiries as a Vehicle for
Public Participation in the Plan-Making Process' (1991) *JPL* 803.

[156] Local authorities are the first-instance decision-makers in the planning system.

[157] The legal right of third parties to be heard at inquiries is limited, but in practice
inspectors typically allow any interested party to appear.

basic legal position embodied in statutory procedural rules. The inspector at such inquiries operates as a sort of planning appeal tribunal, finding facts and applying rules and principles of planning law, and policy guidelines laid down in planning circulars. Indeed, in the great majority of such cases it is the inspector, rather than the Minister, who decides the appeal.

7.7.2 LARGE–SCALE INQUIRIES

In other cases, however, the function of an inquiry is very different. Classic examples are motorway or other major-infrastructure inquiries.[158] In such cases the Minister's role is not appellate: the government is the initiator of the scheme involving the proposed land use and also the Minister is the member of the government with whom lies the power of decision as to whether the scheme will be put into effect.[159] Here the inquiry performs the function of allowing local views to be expressed about a development that has much more than local importance. The ultimate decision about whether the motorway or other infrastructure will be built or not must be taken at the central government level because it affects many people in many areas and is of general economic and social importance.

Planning appeals also sometimes raise issues of national importance and questions of relevance to many groups and interests. A good example is an appeal in relation to planning permission to build a nuclear waste reprocessing plant or an airport terminal. Such an appeal may raise ecological, economic, and energy-policy questions of deep and wide significance. Indeed, there is no clear line between inquiries that raise issues of wide public significance and those that do not. It is all a matter of degree. I have drawn an artificially sharp distinction between the two types only for discussion purposes.

In one sense the decision whether or not to build a motorway on a particular route or to allow a nuclear power station to be constructed is a legislative one: it affects a large number of people and has wide-ranging and long-term effects. It is to some extent a question of technique, although a very important question of technique, whether such decisions are made by means of primary legislation,[160] delegated legislation, or administrative decision (involving local inquiries). It is a curious feature

---

[158] J. Popham and M. Purdue, 'The Future of the Major Inquiry' [2002] *JPL* 137.

[159] Concerning the compatibility of such arrangements with the ECHR see 7.3.2.1.

[160] Concerning 'private' and 'hybrid' acts of Parliament, see Popham and Purdue, op. cit. n. 158 above, pp. 142–5.

of our governmental system that there appear to be no general constitutional principles relevant to deciding which decision-making technique will be used for any particular type of decision, even though the choice has important ramifications for the way decisions are made. What is clear is that proposals for such mammoth schemes of development ought ideally to be subjected to a considerable amount of public scrutiny before the final decision, whether or not to proceed, is made.

It is a matter of debate what the function of public inquiries is in relation to large-scale developments of national importance. One view is that inquiries are designed to ensure that the best possible decision is made in the public interest. This aim requires that local objections to the development should be aired so that they can be weighed against the public benefit to be achieved by the scheme in a sort of cost–benefit analysis. Associated with this idea is the notion that inquiries are designed to 'inform the mind of the Minister' as to relevant local conditions and views. This view of the function of local inquiries suggests that the procedure at local inquiries should not be designed to protect the rights of those affected by the planned development but rather to maximize the sources of information available to the Minister. In practice, however, large-scale inquiries tend to be conducted along formal adversarial lines.

A second approach says that the local inquiry is a statutory and institutionalized version of the fair hearing required by natural justice. This approach (which is usually traced back to the Report of the Franks Committee on Administrative Tribunals and Inquiries (1957)) sees public inquiries as designed to protect the rights of affected individuals. It is reflected in the fact that procedure at inquiries tends to be formal and to incorporate many features of court procedure. Statutory procedural rules governing the conduct of inquiries make detailed provision about the giving of notice that an inquiry is to be held and about the steps that parties must take to inform other parties of the case that will be put at the inquiry. If important and relevant new material emerges after the inquiry has finished, it may have to be reconvened.[161] The report of the inspector is invariably published even when this is not required by law. Section 10 of the Tribunals and Inquiries Act 1992 requires reasons to be given for the Minister's ultimate decision. All of these features of inquiry procedure have contributed to the 'judicialization' of the system. On the other hand, in *Bushell v. Secretary of State for the Environment*[162] Lord

---

[161] *Rea v. Minister of Transport* (1984) 48 P & CR 239.
[162] [1981] AC 75.

Diplock warned that a public inquiry ought not to conducted like a piece of civil litigation. So it is unclear to what extent an inquiry ought to be seen as a formalized version of the fair hearing.[163]

A third view would see public inquiries as a formalized mechanism for consultation designed to inject an element of public participation into administrative decision-making. The optimistic version of this view sees inquiries as giving citizens a real opportunity to influence government policy even though they give no guarantee of any particular outcome because the inspector can only make recommendations which the Minister is free to accept or reject. The pessimistic version treats public inquiries as no more than a public-relations exercise (and often a very lengthy one, costly in time and money for both government and objectors) designed to assuage and defuse the strong feelings of the objectors.

There is considerable room for doubt as to whether large-scale inquiries perform a useful function, whichever of these views of their role is preferred. In the first place, since the project under consideration will usually be of national significance, the views and objections of people living in one particular area can only be of limited importance or impact; at the end of the day the national interest will usually prevail over the local interest. Even in relation to questions which are of mainly local significance, such as the exact route of the motorway, so much planning will have gone into the question of the route before the inquiry is even held that it is likely that only the most compelling arguments will sway the decision-makers even on such issues. It is unlikely that they will not have contemplated most of the objections in advance and the inquiry will often do no more than provide the objectors with a chance of airing their views without any real hope of influencing the outcome. Inquiries occur too late in the decision-making process in such cases to have any very significant impact.

A second and related problem arises out of the fact that in relation to large-scale national projects, central government not only makes the final decision but is also often the initiator of the proposals which the inquiry considers. This means that the Minister will usually be so committed to

---

[163] Ad hoc investigatory inquiries, such as the Scott inquiry into the arms to Iraq affair and the Saville inquiry into Bloody Sunday, may also generate controversy about procedure: Sir R. Scott, 'Procedures at Inquiries: The Duty to be Fair' (1995) 111 *LQR* 596; Lord Howe, 'Procedure at the Scott Inquiry' [1996] *PL* 445; *R v. Lord Saville of Newdigate, ex p. A* [2000] 1 WLR 1855; *R (A) v. Lord Saville of Newdigate* [2002] 1 WLR 1249; L. Blom-Cooper, 'Public Interest in Public Inquiries' [2003] *PL* 578; *Persey v. Secretary of State for the Environment, Food and Rural Affairs* [2002] EWHC 371 (Admin) (whether inquiry need be held in public).

the initial proposals that departure from those proposals as a response to what is said at an inquiry is relatively unlikely.

Thirdly, the law itself recognizes a distinction between matters of national policy and matters of local concern: inquiries should not be used as a forum for discussing matters of national policy.[164] This is a difficult distinction to maintain in practice,[165] and large-scale inquiries often focus as much on broad as on local issues. However, the distinction does provide a flexible tool for limiting the participation which inquiries allow to citizens in the decision-making process.

Finally, even at the local level, the issue of the building of a motorway, for example, is a classic example of a polycentric issue. Environmentalist groups, business associations, inhabitants of nearby villages and towns, motorists' associations, rail operators, truckers' associations, and so on, might all have different arguments for and against particular routes. It is perhaps unlikely that any formalized inquiry procedure would be very successful in generating a solution to such an issue which was acceptable to all parties.

For all these reasons, there is some ground for thinking that the large-scale public inquiry is unlikely to be very satisfying for those opposed to the proposals being considered. This view is confirmed by the amount of dissatisfaction with the public inquiry system,[166] particularly amongst environmental groups. The basic problem is that objectors have unrealistic expectations about the functions and possibilities of public inquiries. Although inquiries have the appearance of allowing interest groups to participate in the decision-making process, they do not in fact do this because there is no necessary relationship between what the interest groups say at the inquiry and the final decision. Most of the material put forward at large-scale public inquiries will be of a technical and expert nature of which the government is already aware, or the validity of which is contested; or else it will consist of contestable assessments of the balance between various uncontested but opposing factors. It is relatively unlikely that the inquiry will actually produce material that the government feels is such as to compel a change of decision. Interest groups are allowed to participate but only by making their views known. True participatory democracy involves participation in the making of decisions. Our public decision-making system is basically representative, not

---

[164] *Bushell v. Secretary of State for the Environment* [1981] AC 75 (no cross-examination on matters of national policy).

[165] *R v. Secretary of State for Transport, ex p. Gwent CC* [1988] QB 429, 437 *per* Woolf LJ.

[166] e.g. J. Lucas, *Democracy and Participation* (Harmondsworth, 1976), pp. 276 ff.

participatory, and the inquiry system has not led to any significant shift in the allocation of decision-making power.

Furthermore, this dissatisfaction with inquiries on the part of objectors should be set alongside the point of view of the government and those who favour the proposed development. Large-scale inquiries are often extremely expensive and time-consuming. For example, the inquiry into the building of Britain's first pressurized water reactor at Sizewell (1983–5) cost about £25 million, lasted 340 days, and took evidence from 120 witnesses.[167] The inquiry in *Bushell v. Environment Secretary*[168] lasted for 100 days; and by the time the proceedings had been through the court system the decision-making process lasted about five years. The most resource-hungry inquiry so far—that into the proposal for Heathrow Terminal 5—lasted for four years, cost in the region of £80 million, and generated a significant amount of litigation along the way. It was eight years from the date of the planning application until approval of the project. Such delay and expense is bound to generate frustration, and opposition to the whole inquiry process, amongst government officials involved, and amongst private citizens who will benefit from the planned development, and contractors who will be involved in its construction. The length and cost of many major inquiries also means that it is difficult for individuals or unorganized groups of objectors with small resources to participate.[169] Even organized pressure groups may have difficulty in raising the large sums needed to employ the staff and legal advisers necessary to make effective contributions to large public inquiries. In some cases Ministers have power to pay the costs of the parties involved in inquiries, and the costs of successful objectors are usually met as a matter of administrative practice. But this only deals partially with the problem. Taking public participation seriously means that it should be made financially possible even if it does not result in a change in the proposed plan, provided it is not frivolous.

The fact that inquiries give people the opportunity to be heard but very little prospect of affecting the substantive result provides the key to another reason why inquiries are unsatisfactory. Many of the land-use decisions which inquiries precede relate to projects which are in

---

[167] T. O'Riordan, R. Kemp, and M. Purdue, *Sizewell B: An Anatomy of an Inquiry* (London, 1988).

[168] [1981] AC 75.

[169] M. Purdue and R. Kemp, 'A Case for Funding Objectors at Public Inquiries?' [1985] *JPL* 675; Environment, Transport and Regional Affairs Select Committee, *The Planning Inspectorate and Public Inquiries*, Thirteenth Report, 1999/2000, paras 34–7, 78.

themselves highly contentious. For example, there is a great deal of opposition to the building of motorways and airport terminals. When the goals to which decision-making mechanisms are directed are very contentious, it is unlikely that procedures which give objectors a say, but no vote in the substantive outcome, will satisfy these objectors. The choice of the public inquiry mechanism pushes contentious land-use issues out of the political arena and forces the political debate into the forum of the supposedly non-political public inquiry. The law has set its face against the use of inquiries for political purposes; and anyway, even to the extent that political debate can be conducted at inquiries, the fact that they are no more than forums for debate and that they give the objectors no vote in the substantive outcome means that no matter how extensive the opportunities are for objectors to put their case at inquiries, they are bound to be an unsatisfactory substitute for the political process.

7.7.3 INSPECTORS

Finally, a word should be said about the inspectors who conduct inquiries.[170] As we have already noted, most inquiries are conducted by inspectors employed by the Planning Inspectorate, which is an executive government agency. The main argument for this is that PI employees are likely to be more in touch with governmental policy than are independent inspectors. This argument rests on the view that inquiries are administrative machinery for informing the mind of the Minister prior to the making of a policy decision. In contrast to tribunals, inquiries are not seen as independent machinery for adjudication. And yet, in the case of many planning appeals, the inquiry does perform an essentially adjudicatory function. The inspector arbitrates between the local authority and the landowner; often there are no third-party objectors and no issues of national policy are at stake (which would give the government a direct interest in the outcome); the inspector makes the final decision in the majority of such cases (about 70 per cent). It is not clear why there should not be a planning appeals tribunal to deal with such cases. It does not, of course, follow from this that procedure in such cases should be essentially adversarial. Questions of planning might be thought particularly suitable to resolution by negotiation and compromise with the help of an independent third-party conciliator or mediator.

---

[170] For an inspector's view of inquiries see F. Layfield, 'The Planning Inquiry: An Inspector's Perspective' [1996] *JPL* 370. See also Environment, Transport and Regional Affairs Select Committee, *The Planning Inspectorate and Public Inquiries*, Thirteenth Report, 1999/2000.

The cases in which independent inspectors are appointed tend to be those involving large-scale inquiries into projects of national importance where the final decision will be made on policy grounds, and in which some government department is directly interested. The contentious nature of many such inquiries clearly means that it is in the interest of the department which has proposed, and will ultimately decide the fate of, the development under consideration, to distance itself from the outcome by appointing an independent inspector. On the other hand, the political nature of the ultimate decision really makes such distancing impossible, and the attempted appearance of impartiality is a sham. This is the essential dilemma of the large-scale public inquiry: it is a non-political mechanism for dealing with essentially political issues.

7.7.4 CONCLUSION

This brief consideration of inquiries illustrates some of the difficulties in developing suitable procedures for public decision-making. The more multi-faceted and politically contentious the issues involved, the less likely are trial-like procedures to be appropriate for their resolution. Nor do the finer points of trial-like procedures (such as cross-examination) make much sense when the final decision need not be based on any particular set of rules, guidelines, or standards which can form the basis of argumentation between the parties. Furthermore, because trial-like procedures are very expensive and time-consuming, it is not enough to provide groups having only limited resources with the mere opportunity to participate. Given these difficulties, the promotion of consultation and participation is, at worst, prone to breed frustration and cynicism amongst those who do not like the outcome; and, at best, it will produce passive and resigned acceptance of government decisions rather than any positive sense of satisfaction based on a feeling of real involvement in the decision-making process. It is not clear that the cost of large-scale public inquiries is worth such results. By contrast, when the number of parties affected by a planning decision is small and there is a body of rules, principles, and policies relevant to judging the propriety of the decision under review, an essentially adjudicatory appeal mechanism seems appropriate and acceptable.

The basic idea that people who will be affected by a decision should be told in advance what is proposed and be given a chance to express their views seems to be of universal validity. But the way that basic idea receives practical and detailed expression must vary from situation to situation according to such factors as the nature of the issues involved, the numbers of people affected, and the criteria according to which the decision is to be made.

8

Making Decisions and Rules

Central to the concept of making decisions and rules is choice or 'discretion'. If a person has, in relation to some conduct or other, no choice about what to do, or about when or how to do it, we would not normally say that the person has a decision to make whether or not, or when or how, to engage in that conduct. In this chapter we first examine limitations which the law imposes on the decision-making and rule-making powers of public functionaries in order to preserve the essential element of choice. We then go on to look at what the law says about the matters that may be taken into account in making public decisions and rules.

8.1 CONTROLLING DISCRETION

Discretion (which is a synonym of 'choice') lies at the heart of administrative activity.[1] As we will see in Chapter 9, discretion is a feature not only of 'policy' decisions but also of decisions on questions of fact and law, which often have no 'right answer' but several 'reasonable' answers between which the decision-maker must choose. Discretion as to the procedure to be followed in making a decision can also have an important impact on the decision itself. Discretion is central not only to the making of individual decisions but also to the making of rules. Discretion may be the product of a deliberate grant, or it may exist simply as a by-product of the power (perhaps *de facto*) to make decisions or rules.

The essence of discretion is choice; the antithesis of discretion is duty. The idea of 'decision-making' implies an element of choice: duty does away with the need to make decisions. Duty removes discretion; but discretion may also be limited without being entirely removed, by standards or guidelines or critieria which the decision-maker is to take into account in exercising discretion. Discretion can also be limited by the specification of ends or purposes which the decision-maker is to pursue in exercising discretion. Duties impose rigid limits on the exercise of

---

[1] See generally D. Galligan, *Discretionary Powers* (Oxford, 1986).

discretion whereas standards, guidelines, criteria, and the specification of purposes to be achieved impose flexible limits which preserve some choice to the decision-maker.

It is a basic tenet of the rule of law (as expounded by the famous nineteenth-century jurist A.V. Dicey) that discretionary power should be controlled: uncontrolled (or in Dicey's terminology, 'absolute') discretion is an evil to be avoided in most contexts.[2] This idea is still central to administrative law. There are two main legal techniques[3] for controlling discretion. One is to impose *ex post facto* (or 'retrospective') checks in the form of complaints mechanisms, appeals or judicial review; the other is to regulate the exercise of discretion in advance (or 'prospectively').[4] Imposing prospective controls on the exercise of discretion is sometimes loosely called 'rule-making'. But the line between prospective and retrospective control is not clear-cut because the process of retrospective control may generate rules that can give prospective guidance to decision-makers. This is sometimes referred to as 'adjudicative rule-making'; and it is, of course, a basic feature of the common law technique of resolving disputes.

An American jurist, K.C. Davis,[5] identified two types of prospective controls: confining and structuring discretion. Confining discretion involves setting the limits of discretion by the use of rules that rigidly define the area in which the decision-maker's choice is to operate.[6] Structuring discretion involves controlling the way in which the choice is made by the administrator between alternative courses of action that lie within

---

[2] Conversely, controlling discretion helps to legitimate its exercise: J. Jowell, 'The Rule of Law Today' in J. Jowell and D. Oliver, *The Changing Constitution*, 4th edn (Oxford, 2000), ch. 3.

[3] Law is only one of the many influences on the way discretionary powers are exercised, only one technique by which discretion is controlled and only one factor in the legitimation of discretionary decisions. See generally K. Hawkins (ed), *The Uses of Discretion* (Oxford, 1992), esp. chs 1 (Hawkins), 3 (Bell), 4 (Baumgartner), and 11 (Lacey); K. Hawkins, *Law as Last Resort* (Oxford, 2002).

[4] Achieving a suitable balance between prospective and retrospective controls may be a very complicated task: R. Baldwin and K. Hawkins, 'Discretionary Justice: Davis Reconsidered' [1984] *PL* 570.

[5] *Discretionary Justice: A Preliminary Inquiry* (Urbana, Ill, 1977). For a critical discussion of Davis's approach see R. Baldwin, *Rules and Government* (Oxford, 1995), pp. 16–33.

[6] However, rules need to be interpreted and applied by the decision-maker, and this involves an element of discretion. Also, rules often have unanticipated gaps that need to be filled. So the distinction between discretionary and rule-based decisions is not clear-cut. Rules can leave plenty of room for choice: R. Sainsbury, 'Administrative Justice: Discretion and Procedure in Social Security Decision-Making' in K. Hawkins (ed.), *The Uses of Discretion*.

the limits of the discretion. This can be done in two ways: first, by laying down flexible standards (and so on) to guide the exercise of discretion;[7] and secondly, by laying down procedural rules which the administrator must observe in exercising the discretion.

Discretion can be structured by flexible standards in a number of ways. For example, the standard may lay down a general purpose or policy which the decision-maker is to aim at in exercising the discretion; or it may list factors to be taken into account in exercising the discretion.[8] A discretion may also be structured by providing that it should be exercised 'reasonably'. This gives the decision-maker a degree of freedom because people may fairly disagree about what is reasonable, but it rules out certain results as unacceptable.

Discretion has both advantages and disadvantages,[9] and the purpose of controlling discretion should be to preserve the advantages to the greatest degree consistent with minimizing the disadvantages. Discretion has the advantage of flexibility; it allows the merits of individual cases to be taken into account. Discretion is concerned with the spirit, not the letter of the law, and it may allow government policies to be more effectively implemented by giving administrators freedom to adapt their methods of working in the light of experience. It is useful in new areas of government activity as it enables administrators to deal with novel and perhaps unforeseen circumstances as they arise. On the other hand, discretion puts the citizen much more at the mercy of the administrator, especially if the latter is not required to tell the citizen the reason why the discretion was exercised in the particular way it was.[10] Discretion also opens the way for inconsistent decisions, and demands a much higher level of care and attention on the part of the decision-maker exercising it; discretion is expensive of time and money. In political terms, the conferral of discretion may be used as a technique for off-loading onto front-line administrators difficult and politically contentious policy choices as to the way a public programme ought to be carried out and as to the objectives of the programme. In this way, political debate and opposition may be avoided. But if, as a result, the aims and purposes of the programme are never

---

[7] Rigidity and flexibility are matters of degree. They depend partly on the style in which a rule is drafted and partly on the perceived 'authoritativeness' of the rule.

[8] For a discussion of the use of guidelines by the Civil Aviation Authority see R. Baldwin, *Regulating the Airlines* (Oxford, 1985), esp. ch. 11.

[9] C.E. Schneider, 'Discretion and Rules: A Lawyer's View' in K. Hawkins (ed.), *The Uses of Discretion*.

[10] On reason-giving see 7.3.2.2.5.

stated clearly, judicial control of the exercise of the relevant discretion may become very difficult, and itself a source of political controversy. When judges and civil servants are thus forced to make contentious political choices, the legitimacy of their decisions may be threatened.

Rules, by contrast, make for certainty and uniformity of result, and they facilitate retrospective control by giving a standard against which decisions can be judged. Rules may also make the administrative process more efficient in the sense that the fewer choices there are to be made, the less the time that needs to spent on each case. Rules can create rights and entitlements for citizens dealing with the administration. This is often thought particularly important in the area of social welfare—many think that citizens should receive the basic necessities of life from the State as a matter of entitlement, not as a matter of gift or charity. On the other hand, rules are less flexible and more rigid than discretion: they may make it more difficult to take account of the details of particular cases. Rules may lead to impersonal administration which has little concern for the citizen as an individual.

Social security law provides a good illustration of this general discussion. At one stage an important part of the social security system was that persons claiming 'supplementary benefit' could, in certain circumstances, be given discretionary extra payments to cover extraordinary needs. The exercise of the discretionary power to make extra payments was under the control of the Supplementary Benefits Commission which, over the years, developed a long and detailed code of practice governing the award of discretionary benefits. According to Professor David Donnison[11] (who was at one time chair of the Commission), in some local social security offices extra rules of thumb were applied to cut down the number of cases which had to be considered for discretionary payments. Neither the code nor the informal accretions to it were published.

Professor Donnison thought that the discretionary system and the code suffered from a number of serious defects: it was often degrading for applicants to have to ask for help; it was inefficient because the payments involved were usually small; because the code was not published claimants did not know where they stood; the system generated a very large number of appeals; it required experienced staff to operate it well and doing so often caused staff to become harassed. Donnison was of the view that much of the discretion needed to be taken out of the system. Discretion to deal with hardship created by urgent and unforeseeable needs should

[11] *The Politics of Poverty* (London, 1982), pp. 91–2.

be clearly defined and limited. Payments to meet extraordinary needs should be clearly defined and should be a matter of rule-based entitlement, not discretionary charity. When social situations arose which the scheme had never had to deal with before, there would be a need for some discretion at first, but it should be quickly limited by legislation and judicial review. Donnison considered that discretion is often positively harmful. In a few exceptional cases it is positively beneficial, but experienced staff and careful planning are needed to deal with these cases.

In due course much of the discretionary element was purged from the supplementary benefits system and was replaced by legally binding regulations.[12] One of the aims in doing this was to limit the amount spent on special payments. Perhaps predictably, these regulations came in for criticism—they were said to be difficult to understand and unduly complex; it was also said that they did not expel discretion from the system but just relocated it in the rule-makers and thereby weakened external control of its exercise.[13] Before long, the system swung back again: the making of special payments (out of what is called 'the Social Fund') to people in receipt of income support (as the successor of supplementary benefit is called) now involves, with some exceptions,[14] a significant element of discretion.[15] The exercise of the discretion is controlled by the *Social Fund Manual*, which contains detailed guidance and directions issued by the Secretary of State which are, in practice, not all that different from the regulations which they replaced.[16] The discretion of Social-Fund decision-makers is also affected by the fact that the Social Fund is subject to a cash limit. The new system was heavily criticized on the grounds that it subjected front-line decision-makers to a very high level of ministerial control; that the exercise of this control was itself subject to very little external check; and that there was no adequate system of external check of Social-Fund decision-making.[17]

This illustration makes two points very clearly. The first is that the

---

[12] Social Security Act 1980.

[13] C. Harlow, 'Discretion, Social Security and Computers' (1981) 44 *MLR* 546.

[14] Funeral and cold-weather payments.

[15] Social Security Act 1986.

[16] The system of directions and guidance was unsuccessfully challenged: *R v. Secretary of State for Social Services, ex p. Stitt* (1991) 3 Admin LR 169; D. Feldman, 'The Constitution and the Social Fund: A Novel Form of Legislation' (1991) 107 *LQR* 39.

[17] NJW 'Reviewing Social Fund Decisions' (1991) 10 *CJQ* 15. There is no right of appeal to a social security tribunal in respect of Social-Fund decisions. Instead, decisions can be reviewed by a Social Fund Inspector in the Independent Review Service, and decisions of SFIs are subject to judicial review: M. Sunkin and K. Pick, 'The Changing Impact of Judicial Review: The Independent Review Service of the Social Fund' [2001] *PL* 736.

ideal balance between discretion and rules is very difficult to find.[18] The second is that although rules can offer certain benefits to citizens, they are also a very important means by which central governmental authorities can exercise control over large and geographically decentralized administrative networks.

In theory, in English law, rigid rules that confine discretion must be contained in legislation made either by Parliament or a delegate of Parliament, such as a Minister, exercising a statutory power to make such rules. On the other hand, standards and guidelines which flexibly structure the exercise of discretions in a way which nevertheless allows the circumstances of particular cases to be taken into account may be laid down in documents which do not have statutory force. The *Social Fund Manual* (mentioned above), which is made in exercise of statutory powers, is a mixture of rigid 'directions' and flexible 'guidance'. As might be expected, the more flexible a rule, the less likely a court will strike down a decision on the basis that it does not conform with the rule.

Flexible standards may be laid down in advance or they may be developed by decision-makers incrementally in the course of exercising their powers. The law, as we will see (see 8.3.2), is prepared to allow decision-makers to develop and apply flexible guidelines to structure the exercise of their discretionary powers, provided they are not used rigidly so as to exclude the essence of discretion, namely a readiness to deal with each case individually. The importance of such self-created guidelines is difficult to overestimate because there is a tendency on the part of all decision-makers to attempt to structure their discretionary powers. Also, no organization of any size can operate efficiently without the exercise of management control through the use of policy guidelines and the specification of working practices. Good management and the efficient pursuit of desired ends requires managers to find a workable a mix of freedom for and control of front-line decision-makers. There is a limit to the extent to which any organization can be managed from the outside (e.g. by the laying down of policies and working practices in regulations or statutes). To a great extent, the role of ensuring that an organization achieves its goals effectively and efficiently must rest inside the organization itself.[19]

---

[18] R. Baldwin, *Rules and Government* (1995) approaches this issue by asking when rule-making is the best strategy for achieving governmental policy objectives. There are different types of rules, and choosing the most appropriate may be a very complex task: J. Black, ' "Which Arrow?" Rule Type and Regulatory Policy' [1995] *PL* 94.

[19] J. Mashaw, *Bureaucratic Justice* (New Haven, 1983) explores this general theme in the context of a particular US government activity.

These facts raise the possibility of conflicts between externally imposed rules and a decision-maker's self-imposed policy guidelines and working practices. There is a large body of literature which illustrates how externally imposed rules are regularly disobeyed, ignored, or modified in practice by regulators in areas such as the control of pollution and health and safety at work.[20] Such failures of compliance with rules should not necessarily be seen as deliberate lawlessness. Rather they may illustrate the limits of rule-making as a means of controlling the exercise of public functions, or they may result from defects in the rule-making system and in the rules themselves. In many (but by no means all) cases, non-compliance by a decision-maker with an externally imposed rule may be challengeable by judicial review or some other court procedure. In relative terms, this very rarely happens, and the most important questions for policy-makers concern the optimal balance between rules and discretion, and how rules can be drafted so as to maximize the chance that they will be complied with by decision-makers and enforced *vis-à-vis* the persons being dealt with by the decision-maker.

8.2 JUDICIAL REVIEW OF DISCRETION

In Davis's terminology, some of the principles of judicial review confine discretion while others structure it. Rules of procedure, which were considered in Chapter 7, structure discretion. Most of the other rules confine discretion: they define when the decision-maker can be said to be acting within the limits of its discretion or, as it is put, '*intra vires*', or 'legally'; and when the decision-maker can be said to have stepped outside the limits of the discretion and to have acted '*ultra vires*', or 'illegally'.

A distinction is sometimes made between abusing a discretionary power and exceeding it. For instance, to take an irrelevant consideration into account or to exercise power for an improper purpose might be said to amount to an abuse of discretion, whereas making an unreasonable decision might be said to involve exceeding the limits of the discretion. When we are considering judicial review this distinction is not of much importance because abusing and exceeding a discretion have the same legal result—they make the decision or action taken illegal or *ultra vires*.

Discretion is by its very nature a power to choose. However acceptable in substance a decision may be, if it is not the result of an exercise of free choice by the decision-maker, it is not an exercise of that person's

---

[20] R. Baldwin, 'Why Rules Don't Work' (1990) 53 *MLR* 321.

discretion. Even the fact that the decision-maker would have reached exactly the same decision if free discretion had been exercised does not make the decision *intra vires*, if it was not freely chosen. Moreover, choice is a personal thing: my choice may not be the same as your choice. If I hire Juliet to paint my portrait, I would not be happy if she subcontracted the job to Harriet. The law reflects this in the basic rule that discretion must be exercised by the person to whom it is given and not by anyone else. These two elements—freedom of choice and personal exercise—can be said to define the concept of discretion in administrative law. They can be encapsulated by saying that decision-making power must not be fettered and that it must not be transferred. We will consider these principles in turn.

8.3 DISCRETION MUST NOT BE FETTERED

Limits on discretion do not, as such, constitute unlawful fetters. This section is concerned with drawing the line between lawful and unlawful constraints on public decision-makers' freedom of choice.

8.3.1 DECISIONS[21]

The general question to be considered here concerns the extent to which a public decision-maker's freedom of choice is lawfully constrained by its own previous decisions. It is necessary to consider illegal decisions and legal decisions separately.

8.3.1.1 Illegal Decisions

Suppose that a public authority purports to exercise a statutory power to provide a benefit (such as planning permission) for one of its citizens, and that this exercise of power is *ultra vires* on some ground or other; but that the citizen could not reasonably be expected to have known this. The basic rule, of course, is that *ultra vires* decisions are neither binding nor enforceable. Therefore, a strict application of the principle of *ultra vires* would force us to say that the authority would act illegally if it provided the promised benefit and that it could not be forced to provide it, no matter how unfair this might seem to the citizen involved and no matter

---

[21] Readers familiar with previous editions of this book may recognize the material in this section as having been formerly included in a chapter on 'estoppel'. Following the lead set by Lord Hoffmann in *R (Reprotech (Pebsham) Ltd) v. East Sussex CC* [2003] 1 WLR 348 at [33]–[35], in this edition I have reconceptualized this topic in terms of the limits of discretion. See also *South Bucks DC v. Flanagan* [2002] 1 WLR 2601 at [16] *per* Keene LJ.

how much loss he or she might have suffered in reliance on the purported exercise of power. To what extent is the law prepared to relieve parties of the strict consequences of the doctrine of *ultra vires*?

It must be said that most of the cases display a distinct unwillingness to allow any exceptions to the principle of *ultra vires* beyond those which are necessary to deal with the most obvious cases of injustice. Those exceptions that are recognized were largely the work of Lord Denning, and they have only been accepted with a greater or lesser degree of reluctance by other judges. The House of Lords is yet to give comprehensive consideration to the matter. Why is there this reluctance? The first reason seems obvious enough: the logic of any distinction between the strict legal position and exceptions to or relief from strict law in the name of 'fairness' or 'justice' requires that the exceptions be kept within relatively narrow and well-defined limits if they are not to threaten the general principle with extinction.

There are other reasons that relate more specifically to the position of public functionaries. First, most public decision-making powers are statutory in origin and, thus, limited in scope by the terms of statute. In fact, one of the basic ideas behind the doctrine of *ultra vires* is that all statutory powers have limits and that the power to decide those limits must reside in some person or body other than the power-holder. It would make a nonsense of the idea of powers limited by statutory provision if the courts had too extensive a power to dispense with those limits in the name of some idea of (non-statutory) justice. A second reason is implicit in the first and it relates to the idea of separation of powers.[22] The doctrine of *ultra vires* serves to define the boundary between the powers of the legislature, the courts and the executive to decide what governmental decision-makers can and cannot do. If the courts could freely dispense with the requirements of the doctrine of *ultra vires* this would entail a considerable shift of power to the courts and away from the legislature and the executive. For example, suppose that a planning officer of a local authority purports to grant planning permission even though there is no authority to do so. The council later refuses permission. It might be thought that the aggrieved citizen ought to use the statutory method of appeal to the Secretary of State against refusal of planning permission rather than go to the courts and seek to have the purported grant by the officer upheld on the basis that 'fairness' requires the decision to be

---

[22] See further 9.1.4.

enforced. An appeal would allow the merits of the application for planning permission to be properly considered.

Thirdly, it is basic to the very structure of public law that sometimes the interests of private individuals must suffer at the expense of some larger public interest. Therefore, it cannot be a ground for attacking a conduct of a public functionary simply that it caused injury to a private citizen. Conversely, it could not be a ground for waiving the doctrine of *ultra vires* simply that not to do so would cause injury to the claimant. If the doctrine is to be waived, there must be some additional ground. This need to find some additional ground itself produces a bias in favour of a narrow range of exceptions to the basic principle that illegal decisions are neither binding nor enforceable.

Fourthly, and related to the last reason, the mere fact that a private citizen will suffer injury if the doctrine of *ultra vires* is not waived in their favour cannot by itself justify such waiver, because to allow an *ultra vires* decision or action to stand might inflict injury on the public interest (which the doctrine of *ultra vires* is designed to serve), or on specific third parties. If an *ultra vires* grant of planning permission is allowed to stand, persons who own property adjacent to or near the claimant's land may suffer by not having planning law enforced. A fundamental difference between the way we perceive private law and the way we perceive public law is that private law situations are basically bipolar, whereas public law ones involve interests beyond those of the two parties (the public decision-maker and the citizen) actually in dispute. It is true, of course, that the resolution of private law disputes does often affect third parties; but we are generally prepared to ignore these external effects as unimportant. In public law, however, the public interest and the interest of particular third parties always have to be considered of great importance in any dispute between a citizen and a public functionary.

8.3.1.1.1 The 'Delegation' Exception

In *Western Fish Products Ltd v. Penwith DC*[23] Megaw LJ said that there are two exceptions to the basic principle that an *ultra vires* decision is unenforceable. The first exception deals with cases in which the power to make a decision resides in one officer or body, but the decision is made by another officer on behalf of that body or officer and the claimant reasonably thinks that the officer has the power to make the decision on behalf of the superior. In some cases, public functionaries have authority to

---

[23] [1981] 2 All ER 204.

delegate their powers.[24] If this has been duly done, then the decision of the delegate is as binding on the authority as would be the same decision made by the delegator. If the functionary has no authority to delegate its decision-making power, or has such authority but has not properly exercised it, the doctrine of *ultra vires*, in the form of the rule against delegation, renders the decision of the supposed delegate illegal and not binding on the principal body.

There is authority,[25] which was accepted in *Penwith*, for the proposition that if there is evidence of a well-established practice of (unlawful) delegation which would justify a person dealing with the delegate in thinking that the delegate had the power to make the decision, the delegator could be bound by the delegate's decision. It is not enough that the decision was made by a person holding a senior office; this by itself would not justify a person in assuming that the officer had authority. There would have to be some more positive ground for making this assumption. The Court of Appeal rejected wide dicta of Lord Denning MR[26] to the effect that any person dealing with officers of a government department or a local authority is entitled to assume that they have the authority which they appear to have to make the decisions which they purport to make.

Two points should be made about this rule. First, the exception is sometimes referred to in terms of whether the officer had 'ostensible', or 'apparent', or 'usual' authority to make the decision in the claimant's favour. These phrases come from the private law of agency and refer to situations in which a principal can be bound by the acts of an agent (who had no actual authority to bind the principal) because the principal represented or put the agent in a position where the agent could make it appear that they had the authority claimed. There is a clear difficulty in applying these agency rules to the exercise of statutory powers in public law situations: they potentially conflict with the rule that the repository of a statutory power (the '*delegatus*') may not ('*non potest*'), in the absence of express or implied statutory authority, further delegate ('*delegare*') that power: *delegatus non potest delegare*. In public law terms, an agent who exercises a statutory power but has no actual (i.e. express or implied statutory) authority to do so is (subject to exceptions) an unlawful delegate; in public law, appearances are irrelevant and cannot make good a lack of

---

[24] See 8.4.2.

[25] *Lever (Finance) Ltd v. Westminster Corporation* [1971] 1 QB 222.

[26] Similar dicta appear in *Robertson v. Minister of Pensions* [1949] 1 KB 227, disapproved in *Howell v. Falmouth Boat Co* [1951] AC 837.

actual authority. It is better, therefore, not to use the language of agency
to describe this exception to the strict application of the rule against
delegation, but rather to define the exception simply in terms of the
conditions which have to be fulfilled to establish it.

The second point to make is this: as just noted, the exception allows
citizens to rely on appearances only in a very limited class of cases. This
might be satisfactory when the citizen in question is a well-educated
and articulate individual or a corporation, and can make the inquiries
necessary to confirm that the officer in question has the authority they
claim or appear to have. But the ordinary citizen dealing with a government department or local authority would not necessarily think to
question the authority of a front-line officer or know how to ascertain
the true position. It was this, perhaps, which led Lord Denning MR in
Robertson[27] to make the sweeping statements he did. There a citizen
relied, to his detriment, on an assurance by a government department
(which it had no power to make) that he was entitled to a military
pension.

8.3.1.1.2 The 'Formality' Exception

The second exception is exemplified by *Wells v.* *Minister of Housing and
Local Government*[28] in which a planning authority was not allowed to rely
on the fact that a particular procedural requirement for the grant of
planning permission had not been complied with because the authority
itself had waived that requirement by initially ignoring non-compliance
with it. In *Penwith*[29] Megaw LJ said that the operation of this exception
would depend on the construction of the statute. By saying this, he may
have wanted to convey the idea that whether a procedural requirement
could be waived or not would depend on the importance of that requirement in the total context of the statutory scheme of procedure. A similar
idea is embodied in the distinction between mandatory and directory
procedural requirements.[30] It should be noted, however, that if the
requirement waived is merely directory, then the breach of it does not
invalidate the decision and so enforcement of the decision does not
involve a departure from the strict principles of *ultra vires*. The distinction between mandatory and directory requirements is a vague one and
depends on all the circumstances of the case. This flexibility enables the
courts, by classifying procedural requirements as being merely directory,

---

[27] [1949] 1 KB 227.   [28] [1967] 1 WLR 1000.
[29] [1981] 2 All ER 204.   [30] See 7.6.1.

to evade the doctrine of *ultra vires* without actually having to create exceptions to it. It can be seen that this second exception deals with a rather different situation from the first. Here the issue is not one of the authority of an officer acting on behalf of another but the more immediate issue of the validity of the decision. The first exception assumes that the only defect in the decision is that it was made by the wrong person, and that if it had been made by the authority itself it would have been valid. On the other hand, it should be noted that in the case of each exception, the ground of invalidity in issue is a procedural one. There is no suggestion in the cases that a decision which is *ultra vires* on some non-procedural ground may be binding. The problems associated with too wide a power to dispense with the doctrine of *ultra vires* are much more acute in relation to non-procedural grounds of illegality than they are in relation to procedural grounds.

8.3.1.1.3 Further Exceptions
The law, then, appears to recognize two rather limited exceptions to the doctrine of *ultra vires*. Beyond this, however, it does not go. So, for example, a local planning authority cannot be bound to grant planning permission by the fact that a clerk has mistakenly issued a notice saying that permission has been granted,[31] or has issued a notice of grant of permission in order to forestall litigation against an authority which has, in fact, refused permission; or by the fact that the signature of a local authority clerk has been forged on a fake notice of grant of permission or that a notice of grant has been signed by a subordinate official without authority.[32] It may be possible for the aggrieved citizen to sue the clerk personally if he or she has been fraudulent or negligent (or sue the council vicariously;[33] or personally, if it has been negligent or fraudulent). But to succeed it would not, of course, be enough for the citizen to show that they had been injured by a false appearance of validity. It would be necessary to show that this was the result of fraud or negligence on the part of the authority or its agents.

A possible explanation for this unwillingness to recognize further exceptions to the *ultra vires* principle is that front-line officials might become over-cautious in dealing with the public if they thought that any statement or decision they made would bind their employer even if it

---

[31] *Norfolk CC v. Secretary of State for the Environment* [1973] 1 WLR 1400.
[32] *Co-operative Retail Services Ltd v. Taff Ely BC* (1980) P & CR 223.
[33] *Lambert v. West Devon BC* (1997) 96 LGR 45.

turned out to be wrong. Front-line officials should be encouraged, to some extent at least, to be creative and spontaneously helpful, rather than always going exactly 'by the book'. On the other hand, there is no empirical evidence of the 'chilling effect' of litigation to support this argument.

8.3.1.1.4 Detriment
There is authority for the rule that a public functionary can be bound by an *ultra vires* decision only if the claimant suffered detriment as a result of acting in reliance on a false appearance of validity or finality.[34]

8.3.1.1.5 A Balancing of Interests Approach
There is a quite different approach which could be taken to these cases.[35] Instead of adhering to the doctrine of *ultra vires* as the benchmark of enforceability of decisions, it would be possible to go to the heart of the matter and recognize that what these cases involve is a conflict between individual interests on the one hand, and government policy and public interest on the other.

On this approach, the basic question to be answered would be whether, balancing the various interests involved, the authority should be allowed to assert the invalidity and unenforceability of its decision or that of its officer, despite the claimant's reliance on its validity. A decision would be enforceable by a citizen, despite the fact that it was *ultra vires*, if not to enforce it would inflict injury on the individual without any countervailing benefit to the public (apart from the fact that an *ultra vires* decision would not be enforced). On the other hand, if enforcement of the decision would damage the public interest in a significant way, this would justify allowing the authority to plead its illegality, despite the fact that the claimant would be injured by the non-execution of the decision. For example, in *Robertson v. Minister of Pensions*[36] the claimant sought to enforce against the defendant an *ultra vires* assurance that he was entitled to a pension. Clearly the impact on Robertson of not receiving the pension would be very considerable, whereas the impact on the public purse involved in paying it would be imperceptible. By contrast, the interests of particular third parties, and of the public generally, will often be significantly injured if *ultra vires* grants of planning permission are allowed to stand. Furthermore, such third parties will have no chance to put their

---

[34] *Norfolk* case [1973] 1 WLR 1400.
[35] P.P. Craig, 'Representations by Public Bodies' (1977) 93 *LQR* 398. A similar approach is taken in EC law: S. Schønberg, *Legitimate Expectations in Administrative Law* (Oxford, 2000), pp. 96–102. It remains to be seen whether it will spill over into English law.
[36] [1949] 1 KB 227.

side of the story if the disappointed landowner seeks to enforce the decision by court action.

It appears to be implicit in this 'benefit-maximizing' or 'utilitarian' approach that it would only apply to situations in which an individual who has detrimentally relied on an *ultra vires* decision seeks to enforce the decision against the maker of it. It does not seem to be contemplated that a functionary, whose decisions are directly challenged by application for judicial review, should be entitled to appeal to the balancing of interests approach to argue that its decision, though *ultra vires*, ought not to be quashed because it inflicts no appreciable injury on the person challenging it. (It will be recalled, however, that there are (controversial) natural justice cases in which just such an approach has been adopted by the courts in favour of public bodies; these are cases in which a breach of natural justice has been held not to invalidate a decision because no substantial injustice to the applicant has resulted from the decision.[37] But it is also noteworthy that these are cases involving procedural *ultra vires*. Indeed, they rest on an assertion of the substantive correctness of the decision in question.)

Unlike the approach in *Western Fish* which seeks to mitigate the harshness of the *ultra vires* principle by creating two narrow procedural exceptions to it, this approach contemplates a 'substantive' exception to the principle: it involves looking at the substance of the decision in order to decide whether it ought to be allowed to stand or not. An important implication of this approach is that it may not be enough to ask whether the authority's decision ought to be executed or not. There is another theoretically possible remedy for an aggrieved citizen who has suffered loss by reliance on a false appearance of validity: monetary compensation for the loss.[38] So, even if a court decides, as a result of balancing the interests involved, that a particular decision ought not to be allowed to stand, there may be no reason of public policy why the aggrieved citizen ought not to be compensated out of public funds for the loss. Conversely, it may be that if an *ultra vires* decision (for example, an *ultra vires* planning decision as in *Lever*) is allowed to stand, third parties who have to put up with the existence of the unauthorized development should be compensated for having to do so, for in that case they will have suffered injury as the result of an *ultra vires* decision.

---

[37] See 7.3.2.2.1.
[38] For detailed discussion of this option see, Schønberg, *Legitimate Expectations in Administrative Law*, chs 5 and 6.

There are two problems with this approach. In the first place, the task of balancing public and private interests in the unstructured way which the approach contemplates is not one which the courts are likely to be willing to undertake. Is a court likely to be prepared to decide whether the loss to a developer, who has to abandon a development for which *ultra vires* approval was given, is greater than the loss which would be suffered by neighbours and the public at large if the development went ahead? On the other hand, it must be admitted that many of the rules and principles of judicial review require the courts to balance interests in a way not dissimilar to what is contemplated here.

Secondly (and more seriously) when would this balancing approach be used? Would it only be appropriate where the decision in question was *ultra vires* on one of the two procedural grounds discussed in the *Penwith* case? Or would it apply in any case where an individual sought to enforce an *ultra vires* decision? Suppose, for example, that a grant of planning permission is successfully challenged by a third party on the ground that it was made as the result of taking into account an irrelevant consideration.[39] The person to whom the grant was made could surely not then argue that despite the fact that the decision was based on an irrelevant consideration (and not just made by a wrong procedure), nevertheless the balance of public and private interests was such that the decision ought to be allowed to stand. The doctrine of *ultra vires* embodies principles which deserve to be protected in their own right regardless of the economic desirability of allowing the decision to stand. Unless exceptions to the *ultra vires* principle are few and narrow, the whole doctrine of *ultra vires* is liable to be subverted. The principles of *ultra vires* should be waivable only where the defect in the decision issue is procedural and where refusing to enforce the decision would reward unmeritorious insistence by the decision-maker on the strict technical letter of the law.

Once this restriction is stated, however, it appears difficult to justify. Why should balancing of interests justify dispensing with the doctrine of *ultra vires* in some cases but not in others? Why *not* substitute balancing of interests for the heads of *ultra vires* as the test of legality and enforceability in public law? The answer is implicit in what has already been said: once balancing of interests is made the test of enforceability in some cases, there seems no reason why it should not be the test in all cases; and not just where an individual seeks to have a decision enforced, but also where they seek to have it invalidated. For this very reason, the courts are

---

[39] See 8.5.1.

unlikely to be prepared to adopt a test which threatens to subvert the whole doctrine of *ultra vires* because that doctrine embodies, in theory at least, a principle of judicial restraint in reviewing administrative action which the balancing of interests test does not.

8.3.1.2 Legal Decisions

The public always has some interest that an unlawful decision should not be enforced; but it may have no interest in the non-enforcement of a lawful decision. So, the basic principle is that *intra vires* decisions are legally effective and binding on the body that makes them.[40] This rule is sometimes put in terms of the principle of *res judicata*: once a matter has been determined, it cannot (subject to some statutory exceptions) be re-opened before the same body, or before another body of equivalent status. The use of this phrase is apt to mislead because it is confined to rule-based decisions about the existence of legal rights.[41] In relation to 'policy' decisions it is recognized that a certain amount of flexibility has to be allowed to take account of the fact that the public interest may change over time in a way which would justify revoking a lawful decision to the detriment of a private citizen.[42] But the values of certainty and predictability in dealings between individual citizens and public functionaries demand that such flexibility be severely limited.

A public functionary may, therefore, be allowed to change a lawful decision. What the court has to decide is whether the public interest in changing the decision outweighs the interest of the claimant in not having it changed; or, in the words of Lord Denning MR in *Laker Airways Ltd v. Department of Trade*[43] whether the change inflicts injury on the claimant without any countervailing benefit to the public. In *Rootkin v. Kent CC*[44] it was held that the defendant could reverse a decision to grant the plaintiff's daughter a free bus pass when it discovered that the distance between the family home and the daughter's school had been wrongly

---

[40] As a general rule, a public functionary will be allowed to rely on a decision adverse to an individual once (but only once) that decision has been communicated to the affected person: *R (Anufrijeva) v. Secretary of State for the Home Department* [2003] 3 WLR 252.

[41] *Thrasyvoulou v. Secretary of State for the Environment* [1990] 2 AC 273.

[42] In *Rootkin v. Kent CC* [1981] 1 WLR 1186 it was said that this rule applies only to decisions concerning a person's 'existing rights' and not to 'policy' decisions about future rights. If this were true as a general proposition, it would be impossible to rely with confidence on any policy decision made by a public functionary.

[43] [1977] QB 643, 707; see also *HTV v. Price Commission* [1976] ICR 170, 185.

[44] [1981] 1 WLR 1186.

measured. The court also relied on the fact that no detriment had been suffered in reliance on the decision.

8.3.2 NON-STATUTORY RULES

A public decision-maker must, of course, comply with any applicable statutory rules, whether contained in primary or subordinate legislation. Much public decision-making is also regulated by non-statutory rules.[45] The term 'non-statutory' does not signify that the existence of such rules may not be recognized or even authorized by statute, but only that the rules lack the peremptory legal force of primary and subordinate legislation. Such rules may be made by the decision-maker itself or by some other rule-maker authorized to regulate the way the decision-maker exercises its powers. Such non-statutory rules may deal with the same matters as are covered by the statutory provisions that confer the decision-making powers and by statutory rules made under that legislation—although a non-statutory rule will, of course, be unlawful if, and to the extent that, it is inconsistent with such primary or secondary legislation. Non-statutory rules may be indistinguishable in form and content from rules made under statutory rule-making powers, although non-statutory rules are often drafted in a more flexible and less formalistic and precise way than statutory rules, thus leaving more leeway in their application. This is one reason why they are often loosely called 'soft law'.[46]

There are certain controls, over the making of statutory rules that fall within the Statutory Instruments Act 1946,[47] that do not apply to non-statutory rules. And yet such rules play a very important part in public administration, both in giving citizens guidance as to their as to how they are likely to be dealt with by public authorities, and in guiding public decision-makers in the exercise of their powers. It is, therefore, surprising that there are no legal rules which determine when a body, invested with a statutory power to make rules on a particular subject, must exercise that power, and when (by contrast) it may make (non-statutory) rules on the same subject without exercising that power. There are considerable advantages for the decision-maker in making non-statutory rules rather

---

[45] See 3.2.3; Baldwin, *Rules and Government*, pp. 80–119.

[46] Soft law plays a central role in British constitutional arrangements more generally in the form, for instance, of constitutional conventions and devolution 'concordats' (R. Rawlings, 'Concordats of the Constitution' (2000) 116 *LQR* 257; J. Poirier, 'The Functions of Intergovernmental Agreements: Post-Devolution Concordats in Comparative Perspective' [2000] *PL* 134).

[47] See 7.6.2.1.

than statutory ones. Although such rules may be published, normally publication is not required by law;[48] and this, obviously, disadvantages the citizen. Non-statutory rules are more easily changed than statutory rules to meet changing circumstances and increased knowledge of the matters with which the rules deal. The conventions of statutory drafting do not apply to non-statutory rules; so they can be more loosely worded.[49] Because non-statutory rules will normally not be scrutinized by Parliament, they may be used to implement policies that the government fears might be controversial if subjected to public debate.

In this light one might expect courts to be somewhat wary of non-statutory rules. To what extent does the law allow decision-makers to structure their discretion with (lawful) non-statutory rules or 'policies' (as they are sometimes called)? In *British Oxygen Co Ltd v. Minister of Technology*[50] the Board of Trade refused an application for an investment grant to pay for a large number of gas containers because it had a policy of not awarding grants for the purchase of items individually costing less than £25, however many such items were bought at once. The containers cost on average £20 each, but BOC had spent more than £4 million on them over a period of three years. The House of Lords held that the decision not to make a grant was *intra vires*. Lord Reid said that where an authority has to deal with a large number of similar applications there can be no objection to its forming a policy for dealing with them, provided that authority is willing to listen to 'anyone with something new to say' and to change or waive its policy in appropriate cases.[51] Viscount Dilhorne thought that it would be 'somewhat pointless and a waste of time' for the Board of Trade not to have a policy, but that representations could be made to the Board that the policy should be changed.

An obvious advantage of policies is that they save time and promote certainty and uniformity. But they must not be applied without regard to

---

[48] *Open Government Code of Practice on Access to Government Information*, 2nd edn (1997), Part I, para. 3, 'commits' bodies subject to it to publish 'such rules, procedures, internal guidance to official, and similar administrative manuals as will assist better understanding of departmental action in dealing with the public'. Under s. 19 of the Freedom of Information Act 2000, public authorities subject to the Act are required develop 'publication schemes' in order actively to promote public access to government information. Such schemes will eventually replace the Code.

[49] Although there is no legal or logical reason why statutory rules should not be loosely and flexibly drafted.

[50] [1971] AC 610; see also *R v. Port of London Authority, ex p. Kynoch Ltd* [1919] 1 KB 176.

[51] A non-statutory rule may be quashed if it fails to make provision for exceptional cases: *R v. North West Lancashire Health Authority, ex p. A* [2000] 1 WLR 977.

the individual case. If the claimant raises some relevant matter that the authority did not take into account in forming its policy, it must listen and be prepared not to apply its policy if it turns out to be irrelevant or inappropriate to the particular case. In other words, policies and non-statutory rules must be applied flexibly, not rigidly. Viscount Dilhorne's approach perhaps allows policies to be applied in too rigid a way: he seems to contemplate that once made, a policy should be applied unless and until it is changed. On the other hand, if a policy is going to be of any use in structuring discretion, it must apply unless some good reason can be shown why it should not apply. There must be a bias in favour of a policy.[52] Policies and non-statutory rules strike a compromise between unregulated discretion and rigid rules.[53] They help the decision-maker by saving time and resources; and provided they are published, they can also help the citizen by giving guidance about how to present their case and about its likely outcome.

The application of a policy may, therefore, be held to have been unlawful if insufficient account was taken of facts of the particular case which render the policy inappropriate to it. On the other hand, a citizen cannot normally complain of the *non-application* of a policy or non-statutory rule even if it would have operated for his or her benefit if it had been applied. However, by publishing a policy a public authority may be held to have given a person a 'legitimate expectation' of being treated in accordance with the terms of the policy.[54] The authority may then be held to have acted unfairly (and hence illegally) if it departs from the policy without giving adequate notice of the change. In one case the Home Office was held to have acted unfairly in laying down conditions for the issue of entry certificates to immigrant children whom UK residents wished to adopt, and then adding further conditions without notice.[55] It seems that in some cases this rule will only require the decision-maker to give the citizen a chance to put a case for being treated in accordance with the

---

[52] D. Galligan, 'The Nature and Function of Policies within Discretionary Power' [1976] *PL* 332.

[53] The concept of fettering does not apply to bodies whose powers are non-statutory. Even so, rules made by such bodies to regulate their decision-making may be a mixture of the rigid and the flexible, and this may affect the way the courts approach judicial review of their activities: P. Cane, 'Self-Regulation and Judicial Review' [1987] *CJQ* 324, 331–3, 344–5. Should it ever be unlawful to adopt a policy? Or not to adopt a policy? See C. Hilson 'Judicial Review, Policies and the Fettering of Discretion' [2002] *PL* 111.

[54] Where there is no legal obligation to publish, this rule may have the undesirable effect of discouraging publication.

[55] *R v. Secretary of State for the Home Department, ex p. Khan* [1984] 1 WLR 1337.

original policy.[56] In other cases, however, the citizen may be entitled to be dealt with in accordance with the original policy or may be awarded a declaration that they should have been dealt with in that way.[57] On the other hand, since legitimate expectations generated by the publication of policies limit the exercise of discretionary powers, not every change of published policy will be illegal. The very nature of a discretionary power requires that its holder be given considerable freedom in deciding what to do in exercise of it; and this includes a power, in suitable circumstances, of changing direction and replacing existing policies with new ones.[58] Provided there is a good enough reason for the change of published policy, it will not be held to be unfair or illegal.

An important feature of these legitimate expectation cases is that, viewed in isolation, the original policy statement was valid; and so also was the new policy. But put side by side, two policies lawful in themselves can create unfairness if the authority making them can give no good reason for changing its mind, having created a legitimate expectation that it would act in a particular way. The idea of having (and giving) good reasons for decisions is of central importance in judging the validity of the use and alteration of policy guidelines. All discretionary powers are given for particular purposes, and authorities must be able and prepared to give reasons for their decisions which explain how their decisions further (or, at least, do not frustrate) those purposes. The idea of unfairness implies not only that decisions must be reasoned but also that any reason given for a decision must be properly related to the purposes for which the power was given—an authority could not repel a charge of unfairness by giving a totally spurious or irrelevant reason, or by giving a claimant a hearing and then ignoring the reasons put forward as to why the claimant should be treated in the way expected.

At first sight, there may seem to be a conflict between the *British Oxygen* principle and the doctrine of legitimate expectation: does the latter not allow, in effect, a fettering of the decision-maker's discretion? Two points need to be made. The first is that a legitimate expectation will arise only if the court thinks that there is no good reason of public policy

---

[56] See 7.3.2.2.1.

[57] e.g. *R v. Secretary of State for the Home Department, ex p. Ruddock* [1987] 1 WLR 1482. In this case the defendant had failed to comply with its own telephone-tapping guidelines. It would have made no sense to protect the claimant's expectation that the guidelines would be followed by saying that the defendant should have consulted the claimant before fixing the tap. Failure to notify a person in advance that they are the target of secret surveillance does not constitute a breach of the ECHR: *Klass v. Federal Republic of Germany* (1978) 2 EHRR 214.

[58] *In re Findlay* [1985] AC 318, 338.

why it should not. This is why the word 'legitimate' is used rather than the word 'reasonable': the matter is not to be judged just from the claimant's point of view. The interest of the claimant in being treated in the way expected has to be balanced against the public interest in the unfettered exercise of the decision-maker's discretion; and it is the court which must ultimately do this balancing. Secondly, the *British Oxygen* principle is concerned with ensuring that policies are properly applicable to the particular case at hand, whereas the legitimate expectation principle is designed to prevent the alteration of a policy which the citizen accepts as applicable.[59]

There may be a conflict between the legitimate expectation principle as applied to non-statutory rules and the principles governing the revocation of lawful decisions (see 8.2.1.1.2). The cases on revocation of decisions suggest that an individual will be entitled to complain of a change of policy only if detriment has been suffered as a result of reliance on the decision. However, the cases we considered above about non-statutory rules make no mention of this requirement, and some of them[60] are inconsistent with a detrimental reliance requirement. Regardless of the position in respect of individual decisions, it is suggested that no such requirement should be necessary in this context. Public authorities should normally be required to stand by their published policies simply in the name of legality and for the sake of predictability in dealings between governors and governed.[61]

8.3.3 CONTRACTS

Because valid contracts create legally enforceable rights, they provide public bodies with means by which they can achieve their ends in a way that may be less open to reversal by successors than legislative and administrative measures.[62] In *Stringer v. Minister of Housing and Local Government*[63] a local authority agreed with Manchester University that it would discourage development in a particular area so as to protect Jodrell Bank telescope from interference. In pursuance of this agreement it rejected a development application. Cooke J held that this refusal was *ultra vires* because in honouring the agreement the authority had ignored

---

[59] For a detailed analysis of this point see Y. Dotan, 'Why Administrators Should be Bound by Their Policies' (1997) 17 *OJLS* 23.
[60] e.g. *R v. Secretary of State for the Home Department, ex p. Ruddock* [1987] 1 WLR 1482.
[61] J. Raz, *The Authority of Law* (Oxford, 1979), pp. 214–15.
[62] e.g. *Verrall v. Great Yarmouth BC* [1981] 1 QB 202.
[63] [1979] 1 WLR 1281.

considerations which the statute said were relevant to the fate of the planning application.

Four points are worth noting about this decision. First, it was held to be irrelevant whether the agreement between the authority and the university was legally binding or not; the important point was the effect it had on the consideration by the council of the application. It follows that an undertaking by a public functionary to act in a particular way may not be binding even if it is contained in a contract. On the other hand, it might be thought that the fact that an undertaking has contractual force should provide *a* reason for enforcing it, additional to whatever other reasons (if any) there may be for doing so. Secondly, the fact that the authority's refusal of permission on the basis of the agreement was illegal did not mean that protection of the telescope was not a relevant consideration on the basis of which, and without reference to the agreement, the Minister could uphold the refusal of permission on appeal. Thirdly, the agreement in this case related expressly and directly to the way a particular discretion would be exercised in the future. The relevance of this point will be taken up in a moment.

Fourthly, in *Stringer* the attack by the claimant (who was not a party to the agreement) was on the exercise of the discretion. Sometimes, in cases such as this, the attack might be on the contract itself by one of the parties to it. For example, a successor of the original contracting authority might want to get out of the contract, as happened in *Ayr Harbour Trustees v. Oswald*,[64] where the Trustees wanted to be free of a covenant, given by their predecessors, not to build on Oswald's land. A mirror image of such a case (where it is the other contracting party who objects to the contract) is *William Cory & Son Ltd v. London Corporation*.[65] Cory contracted with the Corporation to remove garbage in its barges; later the Corporation passed new health regulations making it more expensive for Cory to perform its contract. Cory argued that a term ought to be implied into the contract to the effect that the Corporation would not exercise its power to make by-laws in such a way that the contract became more expensive for Cory to perform. The Court of Appeal held that since such a clause, if put expressly into the contract, would be void as a fetter on the Council's power to make health regulations, it could not be implied into the contract so as to protect Cory. Indeed, in one case it was held that a term should be implied into a lease to the effect that, in making the lease,

---

[64] (1883) 8 App Cas 323.   [65] [1951] 2 KB 476.

the Crown (the lessor) was not undertaking not to exercise its power to requisition the premises should they be needed in case of war emergency.[66] It might be thought that the willingness of courts to enforce (or imply) discretion-constraining undertakings might vary according to the identity of the party seeking to constrain the agency's freedom of action. It is one thing for the beneficiary of an undertaking to seek to enforce it against the agency that made it, but quite another for the agency to seek to enforce it against a third party who argues that it is a void fetter on the agency's powers.

It is clear that not all contracts which in some way limit the exercise of statutory discretionary powers are, for that reason, void as fetters on the discretion. The difficult task is to identify those that are void. In the first place, it might be useful to draw a distinction between contracts which are specifically intended[67] to regulate the exercise of a discretion, as in *Stringer* (above), and those which aim not to limit an authority's action but, on the contrary, to exercise one of its powers. At first sight it might be thought that contracts of the first type would be more likely to be void, and in some cases such contracts have indeed been held void. For example, in the *Ayr Harbour* case (above) the covenant not to build on Oswald's land was held to be a void fetter on the powers of the Trustees to build. Contrast *Birkdale District Electric Supply Co Ltd v. Southport Corporation*.[68] In this case the company agreed not to raise the price of its electricity above the price charged for power supplied by the Corporation. When the company tried to raise its prices and the Corporation attempted to stop it doing so, the company argued that the agreement was a void fetter on its power to fix prices. The House of Lords rejected this argument on the ground that the agreement did not run counter to the intention of the legislature in setting up the company. It was not intended that it should make a profit, and there was no reason to think that any of the statutory functions of the company had been or would be adversely affected by compliance with the agreement.

So it would appear that the question of incompatibility of a contract with a discretionary power is a question of statutory interpretation—has the contract already seriously limited, or is it reasonably likely in the future seriously to limit, the authority in the exercise of its statutory powers or the performance of its statutory functions? Ultimately the court has to make a choice: what is more important in this case, the

---

[66] *Commissioners of Crown Lands v. Page* [1960] 2 QB 274.
[67] Intention is judged objectively.   [68] [1926] AC 355.

interest of the other party to the contract and the principle that contracts should be kept, or the public interest in the exercise of the statutory power? There can be no general answer to such a question; it all depends on the facts of the particular case. And although the terms of the statute provide the basic material for answering this question, the terms of statutes often leave considerable choice to courts in interpreting them. Seen in this light the question gives the court a heavy responsibility to make policy choices between public and private interests. No analytical formula will solve the problem; the court must make a value judgement.

Two cases will serve to illustrate the type of case in which the contract is intended primarily as an exercise of discretion rather than a limitation of it.[69] In *Stourcliffe Estates Co. Ltd v. Bournemouth Corporation*[70] the Corporation bought some land for a public park and covenanted to build on it only a band-stand or such like structure. On its face the contract was designed to acquire land for a park, which the council had power to do. When the council sought to exercise a statutory power to build public conveniences by putting them in the park, the claimant was awarded an injunction to restrain the building. The court rejected the argument that the covenant was a void fetter. In *Dowty Boulton Paul Ltd v. Wolverhampton Corporation*[71] the Corporation conveyed to the plaintiff for ninety-nine years certain land for use as an aerodrome. Some years later, when use of the aerodrome had somewhat dropped off, the council sought to exercise a power to re-acquire the land for development on the ground that it was no longer required for use as an airfield. Pennycuick VC held that the company was entitled to keep the airfield and that the contract was not a void fetter.

The crucial difference between the contracts in these two cases and that in *Stringer*, for example, is that the contracts in the former two cases were made as part of a genuine exercise of a statutory power other than the one which the contract adversely affected. In *Stourcliffe* the council was validly exercising a power to acquire land; in *Dowty* the council was exercising a power to dispose of land. Each contract was an unexceptionable way of exercising the power in question. In both cases it was pointed out that to hold the contract void would be to put an unreasonable restriction on the power of the authority to enter into contracts relating to land. It might have been different if the statutory power to build conveniences

---

[69] See also *R v. Hammersmith and Fulham LBC, ex p. Beddowes* [1987] QB 1050.
[70] [1910] 2 Ch 12.   [71] [1971] 1 WLR 204.

or to re-acquire had related only to the specific piece of land involved, because then it might have been said that the contract was a specific attempt to fetter that power. But since the powers related to land generally, to hold such contracts to be void fetters on the powers would be to put an excessive limitation on the contract-making power. When two powers impinge on each other in this way some compromise adjustment has to be found. Should the contract-making power prevail to the benefit of the citizen, or should the public interest in the exercise of the conflicting power be protected? In all these cases, at the end of the day, the court is called upon to balance the public and private interests involved and to decide which deserves more weight.

8.3.4 NON-CONTRACTUAL PROMISES, UNDERTAKINGS, AND REPRESENTATIONS

We have noted that in *Stringer*, Cooke J said that the important question was not whether or not the undertaking had contractual force but rather the effect it had on the decision-maker's deliberations. This implies not only that an undertaking may not bind the decision-maker even it is contractual, but also that an undertaking may, in principle at least, be binding even if it is non-contractual. The doctrine of 'legitimate expectation' has been used to justify giving legal effect to non-contractual promises, undertakings, and representations as to how powers will be exercised, despite their constraining effect on decision-making freedom.[72] In one case a local authority undertook that it would not increase the number of taxi licences issued by it until certain legislation was passed. The Court of Appeal held that the authority ought to have consulted the taxi-owners' association before going back on its assurance.[73] In another case, the Hong Kong immigration authorities were held to have acted illegally in reneging on an explicit assurance that illegal immigrants would be given a hearing before being deported.[74] If the Inland Revenue gives a lawful undertaking[75] as to how a particular taxpayer will be treated, it may not be

---

[72] The representation or undertaking must have been made or given by someone with authority to do so: *South Bucks DC v. Flanagan* [2002] 1 WLR 2601.

[73] *R v. Liverpool Corporation, ex p. Liverpool Taxi Fleet Operators' Association* [1972] 2 QB 299.

[74] *Attorney-General of Hong Kong v. Ng Yuen Shiu* [1983] 2 AC 629.

[75] It seems that unlawful representations, promises and undertakings (i.e. that an agency will act in a way that it has no power to act) cannot give rise to a legitimate expectation. In 8.3.1.1 we saw that there are two exceptions to the rule that unlawful decisions are not binding. It is not clear whether the principles on which these exceptions are based, or any

allowed to go back on its representation unless, for example, the taxpayer did not reveal all relevant information to the Revenue, or new relevant facts come to light subsequent to the giving of the undertaking,[76] or the undertaking is withdrawn before the taxpayer has relied on it.[77] There are also related cases in which public authorities have been held to have acted unfairly in not following relevant past practices adopted by the authority.[78] In such cases it may be said that by consistently following a particular practice, the authority impliedly represents that the practice will be followed in the future.

A legitimate expectation will arise only if the conduct on which it is based clearly and unequivocally supports the claimant's interpretation of it.[79] A general statement of policy, that makes no reference to individual circumstances, about how a class of individuals will be treated will not normally be interpreted as giving rise to a legitimate expectation on the part of any particular individual of being treated in accordance with the policy regardless of their particular circumstances.[80] In some contexts, even a clear, express undertaking that a particular individual will be treated in accordance with the terms of an existing policy will not give rise to a legitimate expectation on the part of the individual of being treated in that way rather than in accordance with a later and less advantageous policy.[81] More generally, a compelling public interest can prevent a legitimate expectation arising from promises, undertakings, representations, and practices.[82] So, for instance, undertakings will not be enforced

other such principles, are relevant in this context. For an argument that unlawful representations, etc, should be capable of giving rise to legitimate expectations, see Schønberg, *Legitimate Expectations in Administrative Law*, pp. 163–6.

[76] *R v. Inland Revenue Commissioners, ex p. Preston* [1985] AC 835; *R v. Inland Revenue Commissioners, ex p. MFK Underwriting Agents Ltd* [1990] 1 WLR 1545. See also *Re 56 Denton Road, Twickenham* [1953] Ch 51.

[77] *R v. Inland Revenue Commissioners, ex p. Matrix Securities Ltd* [1994] 1 WLR 334, 346–7 *per* Lord Griffiths.

[78] *R v. Inland Revenue Commissioners, ex p. Unilever Plc* (1996) 68 TC 205; *HTV v. Price Commission* [1976] ICR 170; *Council of Civil Service Unions v. Minister for the Civil Service (GCHQ* case) [1985] AC 374.

[79] e.g. *R (Wagstaff) v. Secretary of State for Health* [2001] 1 WLR 292; *R (Association of British Civilian Internees, Far East Region) v. Secretary of State for Defence* [2003] 3 WLR 80.

[80] *R v. Secretary of State for Education and Employment, ex p. Begbie* [2000] 1 WLR 1115.

[81] *R v. Secretary of State for the Home Department, ex p. Hargreaves* [1997] 1 All ER 397.

[82] *R v. Secretary of State for Health, ex p. United States Tobacco International Inc* [1992] QB 353: government free to ban oral snuff despite earlier encouraging the claimant to manufacture it in Scotland.

at the expense of unduly limiting the freedom of successive governments to depart from the policies of their predecessors.[83]

The relationship between general policies and individualized promises and representations is clearly one of the most difficult issues in this emerging area of the law.[84] As we have seen (see 8.2.1.2), policy statements and non-statutory rules can give rise to legitimate expectations. However, this creates the risk of unduly constraining the freedom of public authorities either to change their policies or to tailor them to take account of the facts of individual cases, and in this way fettering discretion and giving policies and non-statutory rules the force of statutory rules. For this reason, courts are wary of reading promises or representations to individuals into general (non-individualized) statements of policy.[85] It is not yet clear how this tension will be resolved. One possible approach would be that a general policy or rule could generate a legitimate expectations only if it was quite detailed and specific or, perhaps, limited in its operation to a relatively small class of people.[86] Even then, of course, a compelling public interest could prevent a legitimate expectation from arising.

In *R v. North and East Devon Health Authority, ex p. Coughlan*[87] it was said that a legitimate expectation generated by conduct of a public functionary may be protected in one of three ways. First, the functionary may be required to give the expectation due weight as a relevant consideration in making its decision.[88] This obligation would not require the agency to act in any particular way, but only to take proper account of the expectation in deciding what action to take. Secondly, the authority may be required not only to take account of the expectation, but also to consult the beneficiary of the expectation[89] before reaching its decision in order to give the beneficiary an opportunity to persuade the agency that it should fulfil the expectation. Thirdly, the functionary may be required to fulfil

---

[83] *Laker Airways Ltd v. Department of Trade* [1977] QB 643, 707, 708–9, 728. This is also true of contracts: *R v. Hammersmith and Fulham LBC, ex p. Beddowes* [1987] QB 1050, esp. 1074–5 *per* Kerr LJ (dissenting).

[84] See *R v. North and East Devon Health Authority, ex p. Coughlan* [2001] QB 213 at [82].

[85] e.g. *R v. Ministry of Defence, ex p. Walker* [2000] 1 WLR 806.

[86] e.g. *R (Abbasi) v. Secretary of State for Foreign and Commonwealth Affairs* [2002] EWCA Civ 1598 (policy statements about providing diplomatic protection to British citizens in certain circumstances held to give rise to a legitimate expectation). This may be what the court was getting at in *Coughlan* in an obscure passage at [71].

[87] [2001] QB 213. What follows is an interpretation rather than description of what was said. The judgment is, unfortunately, unclear in various respects.

[88] See 8.5.1.

[89] Or, more accurately, perhaps, give the beneficiary a hearing.

the expectation by actually making a decision consistent with its promise, undertaking, representation, or previous practice.[90] In *Coughlan*, the difference between the second and third of these alternatives was put in terms of a distinction between 'procedural' and 'substantive' expectations. But this is a little misleading.

It may be helpful to distinguish between the content of expectations and modes of protecting expectations. The threefold classification in *Coughlan* relates to modes of protection of expectations, not to their content. Let us call the first the 'relevant-consideration' mode, the second the 'procedural' mode, and the third the 'substantive' mode of protection. So far as content is concerned, let us call an expectation (for instance) that an illegal immigrant will be given a hearing before being deported, a 'procedural expectation'; and an expectation (for instance), of having a 'home for life' in a local authority facility for the disabled, as in *Coughlan*, a 'substantive expectation'. It is obvious that a 'substantive' expectation could be protected either procedurally or substantively (as well as in the first 'relevant consideration' mode). But it is also possible, in principle at least, to protect a procedural expectation either procedurally or substantively. Suppose that an agency has generated a legitimate expectation that a person will be given a court-like hearing before being treated in a particular way; and that the agency has changed its mind and wants to give a much less elaborate hearing instead.[91] The expectation could be protected substantively by requiring the agency to give the promised hearing, or procedurally by requiring it to consult the claimant before deciding whether to stand by its promise or whether, instead, to give a less elaborate hearing.

Unfortunately, the court gave relatively little guidance about how to decide the mode of protection appropriate to any particular expectation. *Coughlan* itself concerned a substantive expectation, and the issue was whether it deserved substantive protection. The court decided that it did. Normally, it said, substantive expectations will normally be protected substantively only in cases where only one or a few people expect to be

---

[90] A fourth possible form of protection would be compensation payable where a person relies to their detriment on a representation etc. which generated a legitimate expectation which the court is unwilling to enforce: see Schønberg, *Legitimate Expectations in Administrative Law*, p. 234.

[91] In *R (Wagstaff) v. Secretary of State for Health* [2001] 1 WLR 292 the issue was whether an inquiry into deaths of patients of a GP should be held in public and whether relatives should be given legal aid. It was held that no legitimate expectation arose on the facts of the case.

treated in the promised way,[92] where the content of the promise is 'important', and where satisfying the expectation only needs the expenditure of money.[93] As the court recognized, protecting substantive expectations substantively is more problematic than protecting substantive expectations procedurally, and more problematic than protecting procedural expectations substantively, because of the relatively greater restriction it imposes on the agency's freedom of action, and because it involves the court telling the agency what decision to make rather than how to go about making a decision. It is for such reasons that courts in Australia and the US, for instance, have generally refused to protect substantive expectations substantively. It remains to be seen how the limits of substantive protection of substantive expectations will be defined.

It is clear from *Coughlan* that in deciding whether an expectation deserves substantive protection, the question to be asked is not whether failing to fulfil the expectation would be *unreasonable* but whether it would be *unfair*. What this means is that if an authority refuses to fulfil an expectation, it is ultimately for a court to decide whether it has acted unlawfully by weighing for itself the factors for and against fulfilling the expectation. It is no answer for the authority to say to the court: even though you would have fulfilled the expectation if you had been in our shoes, nevertheless our failure to fulfil it was not unreasonable. The same approach also applies to deciding whether an expectation deserved procedural protection but perhaps not to the relevant-consideration mode of protection which, in practice, only requires the agency to convince the court that its decision was consistent with having given some weight to the expectation.[94]

As we saw earlier (see 8.2.1.1.2), there is authority for the proposition that whether or not a person has relied to their detriment on an individualized lawful decision is relevant to whether the decision-maker is free to revoke the decision. We have also seen (see 8.2.1.2) that a non-statutory rule may give rise to a legitimate expectation regardless of whether the claimant has detrimentally relied on the rule. What is the

---

[92] In *R (Abbasi) v. Secretary of State for Foreign and Commonwealth Affairs* [2002] EWCA Civ 1598 it was held that a legitimate expectation could be created by the ratification of a treaty. It is highly unlikely that such an expectation would be substantively protected.

[93] The third of these criteria is, perhaps, the most difficult. In what sense was keeping the home open, rather than closing it and sending the claimant to a different institution, merely a financial matter? More importantly, expenditure of money on an activity that an agency has decided should be abandoned, will inevitably have an impact on its capacity to fund other activities. In what sense is this merely a financial matter?

[94] See further 8.5.1.

position in relation to promises, representations, and so on? There is a clear difference between saying that an authority should act in a particular way because a person has detrimentally relied on the agency's decision or policy or promise that it would so act, and saying that an authority should act in a particular way because it has decided, announced or promised that it will act in that way (with the result that it is legitimate for a person to think that the authority will so act). Under the first approach, the authority's obligation is based on action by the claimant in response to conduct of the authority, whereas under the second approach the obligation rests directly on the conduct of the authority. So it makes no sense to say that the legitimacy of an expectation may depend on whether the conduct that gave rise to it has been relied upon.[95] If, as a result of an authority's conduct, a person legitimately expects that it will act in a particular way, and if 'legitimate expectation' is recognized as a ground of legal obligation, it is irrelevant to the existence of the obligation whether the claimant has or has not detrimentally relied on the authority's conduct. It follows that reliance is irrelevant to the doctrine of legitimate expectation. If it is relevant in relation to individualized decisions, this shows that some doctrine of detrimental reliance, and not the doctrine of legitimate expectation, underpins that area of the law.

8.3.5 POLITICAL COMMITMENTS

At the national level[96] the party system operates in such a way that it is perfectly acceptable for MPs to vote in accordance with the instructions of the party whips and to do so without the benefit of hearing or taking serious acccount of arguments against their party's position. By contrast, although local government is politicized more-or-less along the same party lines as national government,[97] the common law does not allow the party system to operate as rigidly at local government as at central government level.[98] Members of local authorities must not, by agreeing in

---

[95] The converse is not true, of course. If detrimental reliance is required, that reliance must be reasonable, which is another way of saying that it must be the product of a legitimate expectation that the agency would act in the way it said it would.

[96] In this context, this phrase covers the Westminster and Scottish Parliaments and, perhaps, the Welsh Assembly. The hesitation arises from the fact that the legal position of the Welsh Assembly is closer to that of a local government authority than of a national Parliament.

[97] I. Leigh, *Law, Politics and Local Democracy* (Oxford, 2000), pp. 183–7.

[98] This is not to say that the courts take no account of the role of party politics in local government: e.g. *R v. Greenwich LBC, ex p. Lovelace* [1991] 1 WLR 506.

advance to vote a particular way on an issue, effectively close their minds on the issue: party policy and the instructions of the whips are factors which councillors may take into account, but not to the exclusion of other relevant factors.[99] Except in extreme cases, however, it would in practice be very difficult to prove that a councillor had ignored every factor but party policy. Nor is it clear as a matter of political principle that the law should treat members of local authorities differently from MPs in this respect.

A related question is whether governmental bodies are free to put policies into operation solely because the policy was part of the government party's election manifesto. Once again, the law differentiates between central and local government: at central level the election manifesto is accepted, in political terms, as an important source of legitimacy for government conduct. It is generally not a criticism of a government to say that it has given effect to its manifesto; and failure to fulfil manifesto promises may attract serious criticism. On the other hand, it would probably be thought constitutionally improper for a government to be formally bound by a manifesto, especially if members of the non-parliamentary wing of the party had a hand in its formulation.[100] In legal terms, however, the doctrine of Parliamentary supremacy provides central government with a powerful weapon (namely, the enactment of its policies in a statute) for protecting its conduct from scrutiny in the courts whether on the ground that it failed, in formulating its legislative policy, to consider all relevant factors, or on any other ground.

At local government level the mandate performs a similar political function as at central level. In legal terms, the extent to which local authorities are entitled to follow manifesto policies is somewhat unclear as a result of apparently conflicting dicta.[101]

8.4 DISCRETION MUST NOT BE TRANSFERRED

8.4.1 ACTING UNDER DICTATION

In *R v. Stepney Corporation*[102] a local authority had a statutory duty to pay a redundant clerk compensation for the loss of his part-time job. Instead

---

[99] *R v. Waltham Forest LBC, ex p. Baxter* [1988] QB 419. For discussion of the constitutional context of this case see Leigh, *Law, Politics and Local Democracy*, pp. 195–9.

[100] D. Oliver, 'The Parties and Parliament: Representative or Intra-Party Democracy?' in J. Jowell and D. Oliver (eds), *The Changing Constitution*, 2nd edn (Oxford, 1989), pp. 126–32.

[101] Ibid.   [102] [1902] 1 KB 317.

of calculating the compensation themselves taking into account the considerations laid down in the statute, they asked the Treasury how they calculated compensation for the loss of a part-time office and then applied that formula. The authority was ordered to exercise its discretion to calculate the compensation, applying the statutory criteria. It is worth noting that under the statute the claimant was entitled to appeal to the Treasury if he was dissatisfied with the council's decision on compensation; but this did not mean that the council was not under an obligation to decide the matter in exercise of its own discretion first; an appeal is not a substitute for a first instance decision.

In *H. Lavender & Son Ltd v. Minister of Housing and Local Government*[103] the Minister refused the applicant permission to develop land as a quarry just because the Ministry of Agriculture objected. Willis J said that it was acceptable for the Minister to hear the views of the Ministry of Agriculture and even to adopt the policy of always paying careful attention to those views. What he must not do was to allow the Ministry of Agriculture in effect to make the planning decision for him, by always and automatically yielding to its objections. It is worth noting that the refusal of planning permission was quashed even though the judge thought it unlikely that the applicant would be able to establish that the refusal was unreasonable as a matter of substance.

There are three strands of reasoning in these decisions: not only must the agency not allow itself to be dictated to in the exercise of its statutory discretions, but also it must not adopt rigid criteria for the exercise of its discretion; and it must not allow someone else to make its decision for it. So the cases reveal a mix of concerns about procedure and legitimacy.

8.4.2 THE RULE AGAINST DELEGATION: '*DELEGATUS NON POTEST DELEGARE*'

The rule against delegation is closely related to the rule against acting under dictation. They are both designed to ensure that when a specific person or body is given a statutory discretion, the discretion is exercised by that person or body, and not by someone else. The rule does not impose an absolute prohibition on delegation. It usually operates as a principle of statutory interpretation: a statutory power will be delegable if the statute so provides or the power to delegate is clearly implied. Power to delegate will, perhaps, more likely be implied in relation to individual decision-making than in relation to rule-making.

---

[103] [1970] 1 WLR 1231.

In *Barnard v. National Dock Labour Board*[104] the Board had power to suspend workers who breached a disciplinary code. It passed a resolution that effectively gave the power to suspend to the London port manager. A worker suspended by the manager successfully challenged his suspension. It was held that not only had the Board no power to delegate the suspending function, but also that it had no power to ratify a suspension by the port manager since 'the effect of ratification is . . . equal to a prior command'. It would have been permissible for the Board to receive a recommendation from its subordinate and then to decide, in exercise of its discretion, whether to accept the recommendation or not. It was not entitled simply to rubber-stamp what someone else had decided. This makes clear the link between this rule and that against acting under dictation.

In addition to conferring a power to delegate, a statute may also make provision about which persons the power may be delegated to, and about formalities to be observed in delegating the power. There are, therefore, three ways in which the non-delegation rule may be breached: an authority may purport to delegate a function which it has no statutory power to delegate; or a function may be delegated to an inappropriate person; or the delegator may fail to observe some formality required to be observed if a function is to be lawfully delegated. In any of these cases the decision of the delegate will be unlawful.

There is a qualification to the non-delegation rule that rests on the principle of ministerial responsibility. In *Carltona Ltd v. Commissioner of Works*[105] a senior official in the Ministry of Works and Planning, in purported exercise of emergency powers, wrote a letter to Carltona requisitioning premises occupied by Carltona. Carltona challenged the requisitioning. The Court of Appeal held that independently of statute, delegation of functions by Ministers of State to officials within their department is both permissible and necessary because it would be physically impossible for the Minister to exercise personally all the powers vested in the Minister in his or her official capacity. The Minister is responsible to Parliament if things go wrong, or if a decision is delegated to an unsuitable official, or if a decision is delegated which the Minister ought to have made personally. So it is unnecessary and inappropriate (so the reasoning goes) for the courts to enforce the principle of non-delegation in this case as they do in the case of public bodies which are

---

[104] [1953] 2 QB 18.   [105] [1943] 2 All ER 560.

not under the direct control of Ministers, and so do not fall under the umbrella of Parliamentary accountability. It has been suggested that part of the reason for this decision was the traditional reluctance of the courts to review the exercise of emergency powers in wartime. But it is clear that the principle is not limited in its operation to emergency situations.[106]

The main difficulty with the *Carltona* decision is that it relies on an unrealistic view of the effectiveness of ministerial responsibility as a vehicle of political accountability. Moreover, it is not clear whether or how the *Carltona* principle applies to decisions made by civil servants employed in executive agencies as opposed to traditional ministerial departments.[107] On the other hand, unless it is anchored in the doctrine of ministerial responsibility, the scope of the principle becomes unclear. For instance, it has been held that it does not apply as between a commissioner of police and a superintendent because the former is not in the same position as a Minister so far as accountability to Parliament is concerned.[108] More recently, however, this reasoning was rejected in a case in which the principle was applied to delegation by a Chief Constable to officers on the basis that the former was *legally answerable* for decisions of the officers.[109] Interpreted in this way, the *Carltona* principle has the potential to swallow the rule against delegation.

Apparently related to the *Carltona* principle is the idea that the Crown, in the sense of central government, is a single indivisible entity.[110] In one case this idea was applied to support a holding that a statutory decision, made by a government department which had no power to make it, could bind another department, which did have the power to make it, because both departments were part of the Crown.[111] By contrast, local authorities have only such powers of delegation as are expressly or impliedly conferred by statute. Section 101 of the Local Government Act 1972 allows local authorities to delegate the discharge of any of their functions to a committee, sub-committee, officer, or other local authority.

---

[106] *R v. Skinner* [1968] 2 QB 700; *R v. Secretary of State for the Home Department, ex p. Oledahinde* [1991] 1 AC 254.

[107] M. Freedland, 'The Rule Against Delegation and the *Carltona* Doctrine in an Agency Context' [1996] *PL* 19.

[108] *Nelms v. Roe* [1969] 3 All ER 1379.

[109] *R (Chief Constable of the West Midlands Police) v. Birmingham Justices* [2002] EWHC 1087 (Admin)

[110] *Town Investments Ltd v. Department of the Environment* [1978] AC 359; M. Freedland, 'The Crown and the Changing Nature of Government' in M. Sunkin and S. Payne (eds), *The Nature of the Crown: A Legal and Political Analysis* (Oxford, 1999).

[111] *Robertson v. Minister of Pensions* [1949] 1 KB 227, 232.

Delegation is a public law notion. It is related to agency, which is basically a private law concept; but the relationship between the two is rather obscure. Since the non-delegation principle is basically one of statutory interpretation, it is often said that the term 'delegation' only properly applies to transfers of power authorized expressly or impliedly by statute. For instance, it would seem that the notion relevant to analysing the exercise of common-law contracting powers by employees and officers of central government is agency, not delegation. It is also possible to argue that the *Carltona* case is not concerned with delegation because the internal organization of departments of State is not regulated by statute but by non-statutory rules of law or merely by administrative practice. This would make the relationship between Minister and official more like that of principal and agent than of delegator and delegate.

Often a person is made an agent of another by a contract between them defining what the agent is empowered to do on behalf of the principal. The powers of an agent are not limited to those actually given by the contract. They may extend to powers which, as a result of conduct of the principal, the agent appears or can pretend to have (this is called 'apparent' and 'ostensible' authority). Whereas the limits of delegation are in theory defined by statute (i.e. by the legislature), the limits of agency and of the *Carltona* principle are defined ultimately by the common law (i.e. by the courts) which can extend the limits of the agency as defined in the contract between the parties and can determine when the *Carltona* principle is applicable. The force of saying that matters of internal organization are not strictly matters of delegation is presumably that this gives the courts more power to say who can do what within government agencies.

This distinction between agency and delegation can be important. Suppose an official does an act (such as granting planning permission) the doing of which the employing authority has no power to delegate to the official, or has not properly delegated. Suppose, too, that the authority has acted in such a way that it appears the official has authority to do the act, for example by always rubber-stamping what the official does. According to the public law principle of non-delegation, the act is illegal; but if the principles of agency were applied a court might hold the authority bound by what the official had done.[112]

[112] See 8.3.1.1.1.

8.5 THE BASIS OF THE DECISION

In this section we are concerned with what the law says about the matters that may be taken into account in making public decisions and rules. Our focus is not on the decision itself but on certain aspects of the reasoning processes by which it was reached.

8.5.1 RELEVANT AND IRRELEVANT CONSIDERATIONS

It is a reviewable error either to take account of irrelevant considerations or to ignore relevant ones, provided that if the relevant matter had been considered or the irrelevant one ignored, a different decision or rule might (but not necessarily would) have been made.[113] So this head of challenge could be used, for example, to attack decisions or rules which discriminated unfairly between people in similar situations or failed to take account of relevant differences between different people. This head of challenge is closely related to other heads of review. For example, many errors of law and fact[114] involve ignoring relevant matters or taking account of irrelevant ones. Again, when a body by its conduct creates a legitimate expectation that it will act in a particular way, it has an obligation (at least) to take that expectation into account in deciding what to do.[115] Ignoring relevant considerations or taking account of irrelevant ones may make a decision or rule unreasonable or not in accordance with statutory policy,[116] and this may justify quashing of the decision or rule.[117]

Sometimes statutes or other rules list relevant considerations. Very often, however, the statute conferring a power does not expressly or unambiguously state what considerations are relevant to its exercise. In extreme cases this may lead a court to hold that this head of review does not apply.[118] More often the court will attempt to lay down criteria of relevance by extracting what implied guidance it can from the legislation or from other relevant documents, such as delegated legislation or circulars (non-statutory rules). The search for criteria of relevance becomes even more elusive when the power in question is a common law one or a

---

[113] *R v. Secretary of State for Social Services, ex p. Wellcome Foundation Ltd* [1987] 1 WLR 1166, 1175 *per* Sir John Donaldson MR. For an application of this head of challenge to non-statutory rules see *R v. North West Lancashire Health Authority, ex p. A* [2000] 1 WLR 977.

[114] See 9.1–9.7.

[115] See 8.3.4.

[116] e.g. *R v. Somerset CC, ex p. Fewings* [1995] 1 WLR 1037.

[117] See 9.8.

[118] *R v. Barnet and Camden Rent Tribunal, ex p. Frey Investments Ltd* [1972] 2 QB 342.

de facto power which has no identifiable legal source other than the principle that everything is permitted which is not prohibited (see 3.2.4). But powers always exist for the achievement of certain purposes, and such purposes ultimately provide the criteria of relevance.

The number and scope of the considerations relevant to any particular decision or rule will depend very much on the nature of the decision or rule. For example, licensing authorities are normally required to consider not only the interests of the applicant and of any objectors but also of the wider public. By contrast, for example, decisions about individual applications for social security benefits are usually to be made solely on the basis of considerations personal to the applicant.[119] It should be noted, however, that English courts have not traditionally engaged in 'hard-look' review (as it is called in the United States).[120] Hard-look review requires decision-makers to show that they have considered all relevant available evidence and that the decision made is, in the light of that evidence, a rational way of achieving desired policy goals. By contrast, English courts have traditionally done no more than decide whether the particular consideration(s) specified by the claimant ought or ought not to have been taken into account.[121] Thus applied, this head of review only requires the decision-maker to show that specified considerations were or were not adverted to.[122] It does not require them to conduct comprehensive pre-decision inquiries or to justify the decision made in the light of the relevant and available material. Some people have argued that English courts should adopt something like the hard-look approach,[123] and it may be that English law is moving in that direction under the influence of EC and human rights law.[124]

The classic English example of a case where a decision was struck down for taking irrelevant considerations into account is *Roberts v. Hopwood*.[125] A decision was made by the Poplar Borough Council (under a power to pay its employees such salaries and wages as it thought fit) to

---

[119] D. Galligan, *Discretionary Justice* (Oxford, 1986), pp. 188–95.

[120] Ibid. 314–20.

[121] *Cannock Chase DC v. Kelly* [1978] 1 All ER 152.

[122] Strictly, the onus of proof is on the claimant. But in practice, the defendant will have to provide some evidence about what factors were or were not taken into account and how they affected the decision. A mere catalogue of factors ignored or considered may not be enough: *R v. Lancashire CC, ex p. Huddleston* [1986] 2 All ER 941.

[123] I. Harden and N. Lewis, *The Noble Lie* (London, 1986), esp. pp. 272–8; criticized by P.P. Craig, *Public Law and Democracy in the United Kingdom and the United States of America* (Oxford, 1990), pp. 182–7.

[124] See further 9.8.3, 9.9.   [125] [1925] AC 578.

pay its employees uniform wage increases considerably greater than the rate of inflation, and unrelated to the sex of the employee and to the nature of the work done. In a famous statement Lord Atkinson said that the Council had allowed itself 'to be guided by some eccentric principles of socialistic philanthropy or by a feminist ambition to secure equality of the sexes in the matter of wages in the world of labour', rather than by ascertainment of what was fair and reasonable remuneration for services rendered. This case is important not only as an illustration of reasoning in terms of irrelevant considerations. It also shows how relative to changing political and social views the judgment of relevance can be. Discretionary powers typically can be used to achieve different ends favoured by groups with divergent political views. Very often the legislation does not rule out all but one of such ends, and so the courts must decide which ends are permissible and which are not. In this way the courts inevitably become involved in politics.

Roberts v. Hopwood also rests on the narrower principle that since a local authority is dealing with funds contributed by local-tax payers, it owes them a 'fiduciary' duty to consider their interests as well as those of the intended beneficiaries of any spending programme before deciding how to spend the proceeds of local taxes.[126] The classic example of the fiduciary-duty reasoning is *Prescott v. Birmingham Corporation*.[127] Birmingham Council had power to charge such fares for public transport as it thought fit. It introduced a scheme of free travel for senior citizens which was invalidated by the court on the ground that the council was in effect making a gift to one section of the public at the expense of local-tax payers. The effect of this decision was subsequently negated by statute, but the principle on which it rests remains: local authorities must take proper account of the interests of local-tax payers in making spending decisions.

The basis of the fiduciary-duty principle seems to be that whereas most central-tax payers can vote in central government elections, paying taxes to a local authority and being entitled to vote for it do not by any means always go together. A significant proportion of voters does not (directly) pay taxes to the authority for which they are entitled to vote. Moreover, many local-tax payers are commercial concerns that cannot vote. The individuals who comprise those concerns often live in a different

---

[126] Leigh, *Law Politics and Local Democracy*, pp. 131–9; M. Loughlin, *Legality and Locality: The Role of Law in Central-Local Relations* (Oxford, 1996), ch. 4.

[127] [1955] 1 Ch 210.

local authority area, where they in turn pay local taxes and can vote. So commercial concerns often do not have a voice in local government elections, while spending decisions often affect them. This is not, however, a conclusive argument because it is also true that companies pay taxes to central government and yet have no vote as to how those taxes will be spent. On the other hand, those who own and run such companies do have a vote. The fiduciary duty principle is designed to make good the 'democratic deficit' which these facts are seen to produce.

By contrast, central government does not owe a fiduciary duty to the body of taxpayers. Political parties campaign at elections on the basis of certain policies and if elected into government they put those policies more or less into effect, raising and using taxes for that purpose. In modern political practice the idea of the electoral mandate is used to legitimize spending, subject of course to Parliamentary approval in the form of Finance and Appropriation Acts. It seems that the idea of the electoral mandate is not perceived as having the same legitimizing force at the local level.[128] Local government election campaigns turn at least in part on schemes for local spending programmes. A notorious example— the Greater London Council's 'Fares Fair' scheme for reduced fares on London Transport[129]—was a major issue in the elections which preceded the introduction of the scheme. Nevertheless, local authorities are required to pay continuing attention to the interests of local-tax payers in moulding their policies and may even be required, in fulfilment of their fiduciary duty, to give up some policy which they were apparently elected to put into effect. It is not difficult to argue that the use by the courts of the fiduciary duty notion is an attempt to exercise control of local authority policy-making in the name of a doctrine which has a spurious air of legal certainty and legitimacy. To say that local authorities owe a fiduciary duty to local-tax payers stacks the cards against the authority in any dispute about expenditure.

The fiduciary duty of local authorities to their taxpayers is reinforced by the rule of standing that local-tax payers as such have standing to challenge local authority spending decisions whereas central-tax payers apparently have no right to challenge central government spending decisions.

---

[128] Leigh, *Law, Politics and Local Democracy*, pp. 71–4.
[129] See *Bromley LBC v. Greater London Council* [1983] 1 AC 768; *R v. London Transport Executive, ex p. Greater London Council* [1983] QB 484. The former decision was extremely controversial: see J.A.G. Griffith, *The Politics of the Judiciary*, 5th edn (London, 1997), pp. 126–33; *Judicial Politics Since 1920: A Chronicle* (Oxford, 1993), pp. 154–7.

A particularly difficult issue concerns the relevance of an agency's available financial resources to decisions about provision of public welfare services. Much will depend on the precise wording of the relevant statutory provisions. It has, for instance, been held that in assessing the 'needs' of an elderly person for domestic assistance, a local authority is entitled to balance the degree of need and the cost of providing the needed services against available resources;[130] that a local authority may take resources into account in deciding whether to provide accommodation for a 'child in need';[131] that a road authority may take resources into account in considering the merits of a proposal to build a footpath;[132] and that a Chief Constable may take account of resources in deciding how many police to commit to a particular operation.[133] By contrast, it has been held that in deciding what would be a 'suitable education' for a disabled child, a local education authority may not take available resources into account.[134] Even if an agency may take resources into account in deciding whether criteria of entitlement to the service are met, once an agency has decided that a person meets the criteria, it cannot rely on lack of resources as an excuse for not providing the service.[135] The key to understanding these cases appears to lie in the distinction between duties and discretionary powers.[136] If a statute is interpreted as imposing on an agency a duty to provide a particular service (such as 'suitable education'),[137] the agency will not be allowed to take resources into account in deciding what service to provide (i.e. what would be a suitable education in the circumstances of the particular case). By contrast, if the statute is interpreted as conferring on an agency a discretion about the particular services to be provided in the circumstances of the case (e.g. to meet a person's domestic 'needs'), the agency is allowed to take resources into account in deciding what service(s) to provide (i.e. what the person's 'needs' are). In reviewing the

---

[130] *R v. Gloucestershire CC, ex p. Barry* [1997] AC 584 (Chronically Sick and Disabled Persons Act 1970, s. 2(1)).

[131] *R v. Barnet LBC, ex p. G(FC)* [2003] 3 WLR 1194 (Children Act 1989, s. 17(1)).

[132] *R v. Norfolk CC, ex p. Thorpe* (1998) 96 LGR 597 (Highways Act 1980, s. 66).

[133] *R v. Chief Constable of Sussex, ex p. International Trader's Ferry Ltd* [1999] 2 AC 418 (this case concerned the performance of the common-law obligation to keep the peace).

[134] *R v. East Sussex CC, ex p. Tandy* [1998] AC 714 (Education Act 1993, s. 298); applied in *R v. Birmingham CC, ex p. Mohammed* [1999] 1 WLR 33 (Housing Grants, Construction and Regeneration Act 1996).

[135] *R v. Sefton MBC, ex p. Help the Aged* [1997] 4 All ER 532.

[136] *R v. Barnet LBC, ex p. G(FC)* [2003] 3 WLR 1194 at [10]–[15] *per* Lord Nicholls.

[137] The fact that a statute refers to a function as a 'duty' is not conclusive because some so–called 'duties' ('target duties') leave the functionary with considerable discretion: see 3.2.4.

exercise of such a discretion, the relevant principle is that the court should not second-guess decisions about the allocation of scarce resources.[138] Only if such a decision is 'unreasonable'[139] (or, presumably, *ultra vires* on some other ground) will it be liable to be quashed.[140] Although this distinction is dressed up as depending on legislative intent, its practical effect in many instances will be to allow the courts to decide when to set spending priorities for service-providers and when to leave them relatively free to decide how to allocate available resources between competing demands.

8.5.2 IMPROPER PURPOSES

The issue of whether a decision-maker or a rule-maker has ignored a relevant consideration or taken account of an irrelevant one does not raise any question about the decision-maker's intention or motive in choosing what to base the decision on. The subjective purpose or motive of the decision-maker or rule-maker may provide grounds for challenging the decision if the agency consciously pursued an improper purpose.[141] The word 'improper' does not necessarily imply dishonesty or corruption, although actual dishonesty or fraud can, of course, invalidate a decision or rule.[142] The word indicates that the decision-maker or rule-maker consciously pursued a purpose identifiably different from the purpose for which the power to decide or to make rules was conferred. For example, Leicester City Council was held to have acted improperly when it banned Leicester Football Club from using a recreation ground owned by the council as a punishment for the club's failure to oppose participation by some of its players in a tour to South Africa.[143] As this case demonstrates, like the judgment as to what considerations are irrelevant, the judgment as to what ends are impermissible may require courts to make delicate and controversial political judgments.

An area in which questions of improper purposes frequently arise is

---

[138] *R v. Cambridge HA, ex p. B* [1995] 1 WLR 898; *R v. North West Lancashire Health Authority, ex p. A* [2000] 1 WLR 977.

[139] See 9.8.1.

[140] See *R v. East Sussex CC, ex p. Tandy* [1998] AC 714, 749 *per* Lord Browne-Wilkinson.

[141] Of course, these two heads of review overlap: deliberate pursuit of an improper purpose involves taking an irrelevant consideration into account—but more as well. In theory, at least, a power can be conferred in such wide terms that it could be used for *any* lawful purpose, with the result that this head of review would not apply.

[142] *Porter v. Magill* [2002] 2 AC 357 (improper for a local authority to use statutory powers to promote the electoral advantage of the political party in control of the council: [19]–[21] *per* Lord Bingham).

[143] *Wheeler v. Leicester City Council* [1985] AC 1054.

that of government contracting: government bodies may wish to use their economic power to award contracts for the provision of goods and services with a view to achieving ends over and above simply acquiring the goods or services in question. We will discuss this area of the law in detail in Chapter 12.

An authority may have more than one purpose in mind when it acts. In *R v. Brixton Prison Governor, ex p. Soblen*[144] an order for the deportation of Soblen to the United States was not invalidated even though it would deliver Soblen into the hands of the United States government, which sought his extradition for a non-extraditable offence. The court was satisfied that the Minister's prime motive was deportation of an unwelcome alien. The fact that the Minister was happy thereby to be able to help the US government did not render the order illegal. The proper question is, what was the dominant motive or purpose? Because motives are often (if not usually) multiple and mixed, the vague concept of dominance gives the court significant leeway in deciding whether or not invalidate decisions on this ground.

---

[144] [1963] 2 QB 302.

9

Substantive Review

9.1 INTRODUCTION

This chapter is concerned with grounds of review that focus on the substance or content of decisions and rules, as opposed to the procedure by which they were made or the agency's motivations or reasons for making a particular decision or rule. Of central importance here are distinctions between issues of law, issues of fact, and matters of policy. A decision or rule may be unlawful because it is inconsistent either with some rule of law binding on the agency or with the purposes (or 'policies') supporting the agency's powers, or because the agency made an error of fact. As we will see, whether a particular decision or rule is unlawful or not depends, in part, on whether the issue at stake is classified as one of law, fact, or policy, because different tests of unlawfulness are applied to each category. The distinction between issues of law and issues of fact is also important in the context of appeals to the High Court from decisions of public functionaries. There are numerous statutory provisions for appeals on (and limited to) points of law, the most general of which is s. 11 of the Tribunals and Inquiries Act 1992. It is necessary, first, to say something about these distinctions between law, fact, and policy.

9.2 LAW, FACT, AND POLICY

Courts see themselves, both in terms of constitutional role and expertise, as the ultimate arbiters of questions of law. On this view, the prime function of courts is to enforce, and to preserve the force of, the law. The concept of 'the rule of law', although extremely abstract, is the bedrock justification for judicial review of the exercise of public functions: if judicial review has any legitimate function it is to ensure that public functionaries comply with the law. Courts are not so willing to assume ultimate control over resolution of issues of fact; but they undoubtedly see themselves as well equipped to do so, by reason of expertise and the nature of court procedure, when this seems appropriate. By contrast, courts tend to be much more wary of interfering with performance of public functions on grounds of policy. This is partly because judges are not elected by or directly answerable to the people; and partly because court procedures are not seen as the most appropriate way of making policy decisions.

9.3 LAW AND FACT

Unfortunately, however, the distinctions between law, fact, and policy are by no means always easy to draw. Consider, first, the distinction between law and fact and, in particular, questions about whether particular legal rules or concepts apply to particular sets of facts. There are two main approaches to distinguishing between questions of law and questions of fact in this type of case. These might be called the analytical approach and the pragmatic approach. According to the analytical approach, a question of fact is a question as to the existence of some phenomenon in the world about us; a legal question is any question about the legal significance of such phenomena. This distinction is not always easy to apply. For example, in *Edwards v. Bairstow*[1] the question was whether a joint venture to purchase a spinning plant was 'an adventure in the nature of trade' within the Income Tax Act. On the analytical approach, the details of the joint venture are matters of fact, and the meaning of the phrase 'adventure in the nature of trade' is a matter of law. But how are we to classify the composite question of whether the factual arrangement entered into by the taxpayer satisfied the legal definition of an adventure in the nature of trade? Some judges take the view that such composite questions about whether particular facts fall within particular statutory language (sometimes called 'mixed questions of fact and law') are questions of law.[2] Other judges, however, point out that in many cases different opinions can reasonably be held about how to answer such questions. For example, reasonable people may differ about whether a flat is 'furnished', or about whether a house is 'unfit for human habitation', or about whether a particular piece of land is 'part of a park'. In *Edwards v. Bairstow* Lord Radcliffe said that any reasonable decision on such an issue should be treated as a decision on a question of 'fact and degree' rather

---

[1] [1956] AC 14; see also *O'Kelly v. Trusthouse Forte Plc* [1984] QB 90.
[2] e.g. Lord Denning MR in *Pearlman v. Keepers and Governors of Harrow School* [1979] QB 56. For a clear exposition of the analytic approach see E. Mureinik, 'The Application of Rules: Law of Fact?' (1982) 98 *LQR* 587.

than as a decision on a question of law.[3] Similarly, some judges (but not all) say that when a word in a statute bears its 'ordinary' meaning, the application of it to a particular case is a question of fact, not law.[4]

According to the analytical approach, the court first asks whether an issue is one of law or of fact. Only when it has answered this question analytically can it decide which is the appropriate test of unlawfulness, or whether an appeal lies under a provision for appeals on 'points of law'. It is clear, however, that different judges may disagree about whether to classify particular issues as issues of law or issues of fact. An attempt could be made to iron out such differences of classification by making the definitions of questions of law and questions of fact respectively more detailed and complex. But this is not, I think, the best approach. For example, there is, *ex hypothesi*, no obvious way of deciding whether mixed questions of fact and law are questions of law or questions of fact. Nor is there an obvious way of deciding whether a word in a statute is being used in its 'ordinary' meaning so that its application to particular facts is a question of fact rather than law.

Points such as these form the foundation of the second approach to the law/fact distinction, namely the pragmatic approach. According to this approach, the court first decides, on the basis of the values that justify judicial review or appeals on points of law, whether or not it ought to intervene. It then classifies the issue before it as one of law or fact in order to justify this decision in terms of legal categories. In other words, the distinction between questions of law and questions of fact is a tool for regulating the incidence of judicial review and appeals on points of law. For example, where the form of the proceeding is an appeal on a question of law, as in *Edwards v. Bairstow*, the result of adopting the 'fact and degree' classification is that the court will decline to overturn the original decision unless it thinks it was 'unreasonable'—that is, so unreasonable that no reasonable decision-maker properly understanding its powers could have reached it. The mere fact that the court might not agree with the decision will not be enough to justify intervention. On the other hand, classifying a question as one of law can be used to justify overturning it just on the ground that the court would have decided the issue otherwise. This approach may result in more frequent intervention by

---

[3] See also *Moyna v. Secretary of State for Work and Pensions* [2003] 1 WLR 1929.
[4] *Brutus v. Cozens* [1973] AC 854. The term 'question of fact' is used in two senses: (1) questions about whether particular phenomena exist in the world about us; and (2) questions the answer to which are not statements of law. In this context, it is the second of these senses that is in play. In 9.5, it is the first sense that is being used.

superior courts. The fact that the courts rarely admit that they use the 'law' and 'fact' categories to give effect to value judgements about the appropriate level of judicial control of public decision-making is not thought to disprove the pragmatic approach because English judges are generally loath to admit that their decisions are based on such value-judgements.

One value said to support more rather than less judicial intervention is the desirability of ensuring that different public decision-makers reach the same decision on major issues. Ensuring uniformity may be seen as particularly important where decisions on the same issue will have to be made by a number of officials or agencies working independently of one another. Especially where there is no developed system for reporting and publishing decisions of such bodies, courts can play a role in ensuring uniformity of result where this is desirable. To treat like cases alike is, of course, a basic requirement of justice, and this gives uniformity of result a high value in our legal system. An argument often used to justify less rather than more judicial intervention is that public functionaries may have more experience of and expertise in the matters they deal with than the court has. Such experience and expertise may be important when interpreting and applying legislation. A person with a mature under-standing of the problems the legislation was designed to deal with and the factual background against which it operates is likely to be able to give it the meaning and operation which will best achieve the policy goals of the legislator.

Of course, the argument from uniformity and the argument from expertise and experience pull in different directions, and it is up to indi-vidual judges to decide which is stronger in particular cases. There is a danger that the argument, 'Uniformity on this point is desirable', may be turned into the argument, 'The court's view on this point is to be pre-ferred to that of the decision-maker'; and that the interpretation put on the statute by the court will not reflect the expert knowledge of front-line agencies. On the other hand, one of the functions of the courts (perhaps their main function) is to develop and give effect to general principles of justice and constitutional propriety which ought to be respected by any decision-maker whatever the subject matter of the decision.

The pragmatic approach seems desirable not only because it acknow-ledges the difficulty in many cases of distinguishing between law and fact in an analytically watertight way, but also because it allows (and, indeed, requires) the courts to give effect to arguments about the appropriate division of functions between the courts and decision-makers subject to judicial review. However, the pragmatic approach makes it crystal clear that the courts have considerable power to decide for themselves how active they will be in exercising control over administrative decision-makers. Such decisions will be made on the basis of individual judges' personal assessments of the strength of the various reasons for and against judicial control of public decision/rule-making.[5] This is inevitable because statutory law often gives only vague guidance to judges about their role in controlling public decision/rule-makers. The result is that judges may be open to criticism from people who have different views about what that role should be. For example, it has been argued that in dealing with questions of land clearance, the courts have shown themselves more willing to intervene to protect the rights of landowners than to further the public interest or the cause of greater public participation in land-use decisions.[6] It has also been suggested that courts are more willing to require some groups (such as immigrants) than others (such as police officers) to exhaust alternative remedies;[7] and more willing to place a narrow interpretation on the powers of the Commission for Racial Equality than on the powers of the Monopolies and Mergers Commission.[8] More generally, Griffith has argued that the judiciary as a group tend to espouse conservative rather than radical political views and that this creates a consistent, although not an invariable, bias in their dealings with the government.[9]

Of course, judges would never publicly admit to such biases (even if they have them), but one of the advantages of the pragmatic approach is

---

[5] Contrary to the suggestion of T. Endicott, 'Questions of Law' (1998) 114 *LQR* 292, the pragmatic approach supported here does not involve the court deciding whether or not to intervene according to its judgment about which party deserves to win in the case before it. Rather, it involves assessing arguments for and against judicial control of the type of decision and type of decision-maker involved. Endicott calls this a 'normative' approach, and it is the one he favours. The main difference between his approach and mine appears to be terminological: for him, both the analytic and the pragmatic approaches, as I use the terms, are 'analytic'. But the former is an unsound analytic approach (because it does not pay attention to the norms underlying the use of the terms 'law' and fact'—i.e. why we distinguish between the two types of issue), whereas the latter is a sound analytic approach (because it does). Endicott defines a question about the application of law to facts as a question of law if 'the law requires it to be answered in a particular way'. In effect, what this means is that a question of law is a question that the court thinks it should answer for itself rather than allowing the agency in question to answer provided it does so reasonably.

[6] P. McAuslan, *The Ideologies of Planning Law* (Oxford, 1980), pp. 84 ff.

[7] S. Sedley, 'Now You See It, Now You Don't: Judicial Discretion and Judicial Review' (1987) 8 *Warwick Law Working Papers*, No. 4, 4.

[8] J.A.G. Griffith, *The Politics of the Judiciary*, 4th edn (London, 1991), p. 139.

[9] Ibid., 5th edn (London, 1997), chs 4, 8, and 9. See also *Judicial Politics Since 1920: A Chronicle* (Oxford, 1993).

to make clear that the existence of the appellate and supervisory powers of the courts over public decision-makers often requires the courts to make choices about the amount of control they will exercise, and that the choices made may be controversial. But, at the end of the day, someone has to decide where power should lie, and so long as the courts can be asked to intervene they will have to decide whether to do so or not. Even a decision not to intervene decides something about where the decision-making power on the points in issue lies, namely that it does not lie with the courts. Legislation could never exhaustively define the limits of judicial review; and so, unless we abolish it altogether, the courts will have to make decisions about where decision-making power should lie. This is one reason why it is worthwhile to study the general principles of administrative law. Such a study concentrates attention on the aspect of the courts' work which involves making decisions about the distribution of public decision-making power.

Another advantage of the pragmatic approach is that it alerts us to the fact that often, in order to understand a case properly, we must pay close attention to its subject matter: planning, immigration, housing, etc. The study of general principles is not enough in itself, and this should be borne constantly in mind. The question of where the power of decision should lie depends in part on the nature of the issues at stake. The general constitutional and political principles on which this book concentrates present only part of the picture.

9.4 LAW AND POLICY

The term 'law' bears a different meaning in this context from the last. Here, to make a decision 'according to law' is to make it by applying a rule or principle derived from legislation or common law; whereas to make a decision 'on policy grounds' is to make it on the basis of some political, social or economic value, not a legal rule. 'Policy' in this context refers to the goals, values, and purposes which governments and other public functionaries seek to promote. Law is one means for promoting policies, and courts play a central role in applying and enforcing (policies which have been embodied in) legal rules and principles. But courts not only apply law, they also make it; and the process of making (common) law (and of authoritatively interpreting statutes) involves the embodiment of policies in legal form.

Courts play a much greater role in controlling decisions about issues of law made by public agencies than in controlling decisions they make on policy grounds. However, because the distinction between law and policy is often unclear it can, like the law/fact distinction, be used by the courts to regulate the amount of judicial control of governmental decision-making. The vagueness of the distinction is easily demonstrated. Many applications for judicial review turn on issues of statutory interpretation: what does the statutory provision (the legal rule) which governs this case mean? When the relevant statutory rule is open to more than one interpretation, the process of deciding what it means by choosing between the two possible interpretations cannot just involve applying the statute. The choice must be made on the basis of some external factor: which meaning will best give effect to the purpose of, or the values underlying, the statutory provision? The choices open to the court in giving a meaning to the statutory provision will be constrained by the words of the statute, but those words will not dictate one choice rather than another. In other words, many questions of statutory interpretation are 'mixed questions of law and policy'.

Conversely, public decisions of may be challenged on the ground that the decision does not give proper effect to the goals and purposes of the statute under which it was made. Such challenges are often treated as raising questions of policy, not law. But since the relevant goals and purposes can, in theory at least, only be discovered by reading and interpreting the statute, such challenges might be treated as raising questions of law or, in other words, of statutory interpretation. Whether a question of statutory purpose is treated as one of law or as one of policy probably often depends on how explicitly the legislation spells out the criteria according to which the particular decision is to be made. The more explicit and detailed the statutory instructions given to the decision-maker, the more likely is a court to treat any question of statutory purpose as being one of law to be decided by interpretation of the words of the statute. If the statute gives only vague instructions, the court will assume that the decision-maker should be left fairly free to decide how the statute should be implemented. This approach is consistent with the general attitude of English courts that their basic function in applying statutes is to give effect to the terms of the legislation. It is important to realize that questions of law often cannot be neatly distinguished from questions of policy because law embodies policy. But it often does so only imperfectly so that applying the law often requires the law-applier first to decide what the law is; and this is essentially the same activity as making law, that is, as giving (legal) effect to policy.

9.5 FACT AND POLICY

There are two distinct types of factual error which a decision-maker might commit. One is reaching a conclusion of fact which is unsupported by evidence; and the other is failing to take due account of a relevant fact or taking account of an irrelevant fact.[10] In relation to both types of error, the distinction between questions of fact and questions of policy can often be unclear.[11] A good example in relation to the first type of error is the question of whether a worker is an 'employee' or an 'independent contractor'.[12] This question is, indeed, a mixed question of fact, law, and policy, although the courts usually do not admit the policy element. Whether a worker is an employee or not depends partly on the factual details of the relationship between the worker and the employer; and partly on legal principles, such as the 'control test'. The classification of the employee is also influenced by policy factors. This is made clear by the existence of the rule that the parties to a contract cannot conclusively stipulate that the worker is not an employee and thereby, for example, deprive the worker of protections enjoyed by employees but not by independent contractors. The courts reserve the right to decide, on policy grounds, whether such protections should be made available to the worker by classifying him or her as an employee.

This frequent mingling of fact and policy issues is one reason why the courts are often unwilling to interfere with decisions on questions of fact. The argument for deference to decisions of inferior bodies based on experience and expertise recognizes that questions of fact can often not be decided simply by collecting raw factual data (such as the details of the relationship between employer and employee). Such data often has to be interpreted and its significance assessed in order to reach a factual conclusion which best fits the policy aims of the relevant legislation. A body with relevant experience and expertise may be better placed than the court to interpret the raw factual data in a way that best furthers the policy aims of the legislation.

The second type of factual error involves the application of a more general principle requiring decision-makers not to take account of

---

[10] As to the latter see, e.g., *R v. Criminal Injuries Compensation Board, ex p. A* [1999] 2 AC 330; and generally T. Jones, 'Mistake of Fact in Administrative Law' [1990] *PL* 507.

[11] D. Galligan, *Discretionary Powers* (Oxford, 1986), pp. 314–20.

[12] *O'Kelly v. Trusthouse Forte Plc* [1984] QB 90.

irrelevant factors and not to ignore relevant ones.[13] It is not possible to distinguish between relevant factors and irrelevant ones without first deciding the policy ends or aims by reference to which relevance is to be judged. Conversely, all policy decisions are made in a particular factual context: particular powers are given to deal with particular situations. Policy-making involves applying values to factual premises to produce statements of purpose. So a court may, by emphasizing the factual element, be able to deal with a case under the rubric of fact rather than policy.

Apart from the mixed fact/policy content of many decisions, another important reason why the courts are often deferential to decisions on questions of fact is in order to conserve scarce judicial resources for dealing with issues that are significant for a large number of cases. Questions of law are typically relevant to classes of case whereas questions of fact are typically relevant only to one case (this is why decisions on questions of law can create precedents but decisions on questions of fact cannot).

The distinctions between questions of law, questions of fact, and issues of policy play a central role in the law of judicial review. The way an issue is classified is an important determinant of how likely it is that the court will award the applicant a judicial review remedy. The task of classification is performed by the court; and as we have seen, the available categories are unstable. This fact gives the courts very considerable discretion in deciding the appropriate level of control of public decision-making.

9.6 ERRORS OF LAW

In 9.3 the focus was on questions about the interpretation of legal rules and concepts and their application to particular fact situations. We saw that courts treat some such questions as questions of law, but some are not treated as questions of law. In that context, to make an error of law is to give a wrong answer to a question of interpretation/application that the court classifies as a question of law. But the term 'error of law' is not applied only to wrong answers to such questions. Sometimes, it is used very broadly to include reaching a factual conclusion on no (or inadequate) evidence,[14] wrongful admission or exclusion of evidence, and

---

[13] See 8.5.1.

[14] Reaching a factual conclusion in the absence of probative evidence is sometimes classified as a breach of natural justice: *Mahon v. Air New Zealand* [1984] AC 808; *R v. Criminal Injuries Compensation Board, ex p. A* [1999] 2 AC 330.

a number of forms of abuse of discretion, such as ignoring relevant considerations or taking irrelevant considerations into account. In other words, 'error of law' may be used as a loose synonym of 'illegal action'.[15] This usage is too inclusive of the grounds of judicial review to be of much use.

On the other hand, it is not necessary to confine use of the concept of error of law to the type of issue discussed in 9.3. An agency may also commit an error of law by purporting to make a decision or a rule that it had no legal authority to make, or by making a decision or rule that conflicts with some legal rule binding on the decision/rule-maker. For instance, an administrative decision, a non-statutory rule,[16] or a provision of delegated legislation, may be held invalid because it conflicts with some statutory provision, or with a basic constitutional principle such as the rule that taxes may not be levied without the consent of Parliament.[17] Any of these, as well as a provision of Parliamentary legislation, may be invalid because it conflicts with some provision of EC law.[18] So we can say that to make an error of law is to act inconsistently (in any of these ways) with some legal rule binding on the decision/rule-maker.

There is one sense, however, in which this concept of error of law is too narrow. This is because the principles that we are about to discuss may also be relevant to conduct that is inconsistent with rules that are not binding rules of *law* in a strict sense because they were not made in exercise of legal power to make rules.[19] Acting inconsistently with a rule may provide a basis for judicial review even if the rule is not strictly a rule of *law*. At the same time, there is another sense in which this concept of error of law is too broad, because the legal status of some rules made in exercise of legal rule-making power, such as the Immigration Rules[20] or

---

[15] J. Beatson, 'The Scope of Judicial Review for Error of Law' (1984) 4 *OJLS* 22.
[16] See 3.2.3.
[17] e.g. *Congreve v. Home Office* [1976] QB 629. See also *R v. Lord Chancellor, ex p. Witham* [1998] QB 575 (constitutional right of access to the courts); *Attorney-General v. Wilts United Dairy* (1921) 37 TLR 884 (constitutional principle that jurisdiction of the courts may not be ousted).
[18] *R v. Secretary of State for Transport, ex p. Factortame Ltd (No. 2)* [1991] 1 AC 603. Primary legislation that is incompatible with a Convention right is not, for that reason, invalid; but a declaration of incompatibility may be made under s. 4 of the HRA. Concerning the relationship between EC law and the HRA see A. O'Neill, 'Fundamental Rights and the Constitutional Supremacy of Community Law in the United Kingdom after Devolution and the Human Rights Act' [2002] *PL* 724.
[19] *R v. Criminal Injuries Compensation Board, ex p. Lain* [1967] 2 QB 864; *R v. Panel on Takeovers and Mergers, ex p. Datafin Plc* [1987] QB 815; P. Cane, 'Self-Regulation and Judicial Review' [1987] *CJQ* 324, 331–3, 343–4.
[20] S. Legomsky, *Immigration and the Judiciary* (Oxford, 1987), pp. 50–67.

the Social Fund Manual[21] is sufficiently unclear to make it uncertain in particular cases whether acting inconsistently with the rules would be a ground of judicial review. For most purposes, however, the statement, that to make an error of law is to act inconsistently with some relevant legal rule, is accurate enough.

In order to understand the law relating to review for error of law, it is first necessary to give an account of what is called the 'theory of jurisdiction'.

9.6.1 THE THEORY OF JURISDICTION

The leading case on review for error of law is *Anisminic Ltd v. Foreign Compensation Commission.*[22] Before this case a distinction was drawn between errors of law 'going to jurisdiction' and errors of law 'within jurisdiction'. Suppose, for example, as in *Anisminic*, a tribunal denies a claimant compensation, for nationalization of its property by a foreign government, because the claimant's successor-in-title is not a British national when, as a matter of law, entitlement to compensation does not depend on the nationality of the successor-in-title or, indeed, on anything to do with successors-in-title. There are two ways of analysing this situation. The pre-*Anisminic* approach was to ask whether the question of law (i.e. about whether the issue of nationality was relevant) went to jurisdiction or not. A question which went to jurisdiction (sometimes called a 'collateral question') was one on which the existence of the tribunal's jurisdiction (or 'power to decide', in this case the power to award compensation) depended. In other words, a question of law going to jurisdiction was a question about the decision-maker's authority to decide. If, as a result of answering such a question wrongly, a tribunal (or other administrative body) concluded that it had jurisdiction (or power to decide) which it went on to exercise, it could be ordered not to act, and any decision it made in exercise of its functions (in *Anisminic*, to award compensation) was illegal and could be quashed. If the decision-maker decided wrongly that it had no jurisdiction it could be ordered to exercise the jurisdiction it legally had.[23] Things done as a result of a wrong decision on a collateral question of law were said to have been done 'without jurisdiction'.

---

[21] R. Drabble and T. Lynes, 'Decision-Making in Social Security: The Social Fund— Discretion or Control? [1989] *PL* 297, 305–9.

[22] [1969] 2 AC 147.

[23] e.g. *R v. West Yorkshire Coroner, ex p. Smith* [1983] QB 335 (coroner wrongly decides that jurisdiction is limited to deaths occurring in the UK).

On the other hand, if the question of law was one 'within jurisdiction', the mere fact that the tribunal answered the question incorrectly did not entitle the court to quash the decision. The tribunal had limited power to answer questions of law within its jurisdiction rightly or wrongly.[24] Furthermore, a wrong answer to a question of law within the tribunal's jurisdiction did not make the tribunal's decision illegal.

Lord Morris, who dissented in *Anisminic*,[25] adopted this traditional approach and held that the effect of the Commission's error in inquiring into the nationality of the applicant's successor-in-title was not that it had no jurisdiction to decide the issue of compensation. The error fell within jurisdiction and so the Commission's decision was wrong as a matter of law, but it was not illegal.

The main problem with the distinction between the two types of questions of law lay in the lack of a consistent criterion for drawing it. Rarely do statutes, in conferring functions on administrative authorities, give much guidance as to whether giving a correct answer to any relevant questions of law is a precondition of the existence of the power to exercise those functions. The statute in the *Anisminic* case gave no clear guidance as to whether the status of the successor-in-title was relevant to whether the Commission had power to act at all, or whether it was merely one of the factors which might come up in the process of reaching the decision whether or not to award compensation. The distinction did not lend itself to being applied analytically.[26]

The approach of the majority in *Anisminic* rendered the distinction between questions of law which did, and those which did not, go to jurisdiction to an extent unnecessary, although it was not clear to what extent. The traditional way of drawing the distinction had a temporal ring about it. The decision-maker first had to decide whether it had power to act at all in the circumstances; 'jurisdictional' questions of law related to this issue. If it did have this power it could go on and exercise it. 'Non-jurisdictional' questions of law were those which arose in the course of exercising the power. The majority in *Anisminic* rejected this temporal image and held that an error of law could be treated as going to jurisdiction even though it was an error made in the process of exercising

---

[24] For discussion of the limits see 9.6.2.

[25] Lord Pearson also dissented on the ground that the Commission had not made an error of law.

[26] For another example of this difficulty see *Pearlman v. Keepers and Governors of Harrow School* [1979] QB 56.

the power rather than an error in deciding whether the power existed. So, even though the question about the successor-in-title was one which arose in the course of exercising a power (to award compensation) which the Commission had, nevertheless the Commission had to answer the question correctly if its decision was to be legal. An agency could act illegally not only by deciding a question of law wrongly in such a way as to give itself power which it did not really have, but also by answering a question wrongly and in this way reaching a wrong result on a matter which it had power to decide—in *Anisminic*, the question of whether compensation ought to be awarded.

Anisminic, therefore, blurred the distinction between the legality and the correctness of administrative decisions, and in this way blurred the distinction between appeal and review. A decision-maker may have power or jurisdiction to decide and yet act illegally by reaching a wrong decision.

It should be said that the terminology used in this area can be treacherous. The usual word for 'power to decide' is 'jurisdiction'. Thus, a question relevant to whether an authority has power to decide is a jurisdictional question. Questions which arise in the course of exercising that power lie within jurisdiction. Before *Anisminic*, to act without jurisdiction was to act illegally; making a mistake of law within jurisdiction was not illegal. *Anisminic* said that going wrong within jurisdiction could be illegal. This led to the use of the word 'jurisdictional' in a wide sense to cover all errors of law which entailed illegality. It should be remembered, however, that the word covers two sources of illegality, namely acting without power and giving wrong answers to questions of law which arise in the course of exercising power.

The ultimate issue at stake in *Anisminic* was not whether the Commission had acted illegally or not but whether an 'ouster clause' in its empowering statute[27] prevented the court declaring that its decision was invalid because of the error of law it made. The approach of the courts to interpreting such provisions rests on a presumption that in the absence of clear indication to the contrary, Parliament does not intend that administrative bodies should be free to extend their jurisdiction by answering jurisdictional questions wrongly. Applying this presumption, the House of Lords in *Anisminic* held that the ouster clause in question would be effective to prevent the award of a judicial review remedy only if

---

[27] Determinations of the Commission 'shall not be called into question in any court of law'.

the error of law was within jurisdiction. So the effect of expanding the definition of 'jurisdictional error of law' was to reduce the effect of statutory ouster clauses and to expand the limits of judicial review. At no stage did the House of Lords expressly confront the issue of whether, in policy terms, this approach to statutory ouster clauses was the best one.

Anisminic did not decide that all questions of law, which administrative agencies have the power to decide, go to jurisdiction. Are there any questions of law that fall within jurisdiction, or does any and every error of law result in illegality? In the years following the decision, three views developed on this question. Some judges and commentators took the view that as a result of *Anisminic*, all errors of law went to jurisdiction. Other judges said that the distinction between jurisdictional and non-jurisdictional questions of law was still relevant, but there was very little discussion of how it was to be drawn. A middle way was that of Lord Diplock in *Re Racal Communications Ltd*.[28] In his view, the effect of *Anisminic* was to render the distinction irrelevant in relation to the activities of administrative authorities but not in relation to the activities of inferior courts (such as magistrates' courts or county courts). This approach was later rejected by a Divisional Court and, apparently, by Lord Diplock himself.[29]

The first of these views was adopted as being generally correct by the House of Lords in *R v. Hull University Visitor, ex p. Page*.[30] However, a majority held that the distinction between jurisdictional and non-jurisdictional errors of law (and fact) is still relevant in relation to decisions of university visitors:[31] provided the visitor, in exercising his or her powers, does not exceed the jurisdiction of the office, the visitor's decisions on questions of law (and fact) are unchallengeable in the courts. The reason given for this exception to the general rule was that the visitor applies the 'domestic law' of the university (which applies only to its members), not the general law of the land, so that decisions of the visitor

---

[28] [1981] AC 374.

[29] *R v. Greater Manchester Coroner, ex p. Tal* [1985] QB 67; *O'Reilly v. Mackman* [1983] 2 AC 237, 278.

[30] [1993] AC 682. There are, however, hints of the second view in Lord Browne-Wilkinson's judgment (at 703).

[31] And also in relation to decisions of other types of 'visitor', that is a person appointed to settle disputes arising out of the application of the 'domestic laws' of an 'eleemosynary charitable foundation' or other society (such as the Inns of Court: *R v. Visitors to the Inns of Court, ex p. Calder* [1994] QB 1).

within jurisdiction[32] cannot be erroneous 'in law' in the relevant sense (that is, 'contrary to the general law of the land').[33]

This distinction between domestic and general law is problematic for two reasons: first, institutions with visitors may operate within a statutory framework, and disputes presented to the visitor may raise mixed issues of domestic and general law. Secondly, not all decision-makers amenable to judicial review who apply rules, which are not part of the law of the land and the application of which is limited to a specific group of people, fall within the *Page* approach.[34] Difficult questions about the precise scope of the *Page* rule remain to be resolved.

There are several justifications for the basic rule that all errors of law go to jurisdiction—or, in other words, that any and every error of law provides a ground of judicial review: the courts are the law experts; uniformity on questions of law is desirable; Parliament has often shown its desire to entrust questions of law to the courts by making provision for appeals on questions of law; and the adversary system of judicial procedure is well designed to facilitate the resolution of disputed questions of law.

9.6.2 ERROR OF LAW ON THE FACE OF THE RECORD

Before *Anisminic*, the fact that an error of law fell within the decision-maker's jurisdiction did not mean that the decision could not be quashed. Decisions affected by non-jurisdictional error of law could be quashed if the error of law was apparent 'on the face of the record'.[35] This power entitled the court to quash a decision simply because it was legally wrong and even though the authority had not exceeded its jurisdiction in answering the question of law wrongly. It was first used in recent times in 1952.[36] The court could quash the decision only if the error could be seen simply by examining the record. Historically, the record consisted of the documents by which the proceedings were started; the pleadings, if any; and the formal decision. It did not include the evidence. It could contain

---

[32] A question goes to the jurisdiction of a visitor if it relates to whether 'the visitor has power under the regulating documents to enter into the adjudication of the dispute' ([1993] AC 682, 702). A visitor with such power has 'jurisdiction in the narrow sense'.

[33] There are also suggestions in the judgments of Lords Griffiths and Browne-Wilkinson that a statutory provision to the effect that a decision was to be 'final and conclusive' would immunize that decision from being quashed for error of law within jurisdiction even if the decision-maker was not a visitor.

[34] *R v. Visitors to the Inns of Court, ex p. Calder* [1994] QB 1, 50 *per* Stuart-Smith LJ.

[35] Such errors were sometimes called 'patent' errors of law.

[36] *R v. Northumberland Compensation Appeal Tribunal, ex p. Shaw* [1952] 1 KB 338.

the reasons for the agency's decision if it chose to incorporate them into the record. Further, the parties could, by unanimous agreement, raise issues of law that did not appear on the face of the record by swearing affidavits which disclosed the points of law.

In the years following 1952 the scope of the record was expanded. It was held that reasons for a decision were part of the record even if they were given orally and were only proved by an affidavit which had not been approved by all the parties.[37] Secondly, s. 12 of the Tribunals and Inquiries Act 1971 (now s. 10 of the Tribunals and Inquiries Act 1992) imposed an obligation on many tribunals to give reasons for their decisions if requested to do so; it also provided for these reasons to form part of the record. Finally, it was held that the reasons for decision of an agency not covered by this provision would, nevertheless, be treated as part of the record by analogy with the statutory provision.[38] Since relevant errors of law most often appear in the reasons for decision, these developments were of considerable importance.

As a result of the decision in the *Page* case, however, it seems that the power to quash for error of law on the face of the record is defunct. In relation to most decision-makers who are subject to judicial review, any error of law will be jurisdictional. In those few types of case in which the distinction between jurisdictional and non-jurisdictional errors of law is still relevant, it appears that an error of law within jurisdiction will not justify quashing even if it is on the face of the record.[39] In such a case, a decision affected by an error of law within jurisdiction could be challenged only if there was a statutory right of appeal on points of law.

9.6.3 WHAT IS AN ERROR OF LAW?

As a general rule, then, a decision made by a decision-maker who is subject to judicial review can be quashed if the decision is affected by an error of law. What is an error of law? Perhaps surprisingly, the courts have not given a consistent answer to this question. In relation to jurisdictional errors of law the courts have usually taken the view that questions of law have one and only one right answer; and that it is for the reviewing court to decide what the correct answer is. On this view, an error of law is an answer to a question of law different from the answer the reviewing court

---

[37] *R v. Chertsey Justices, ex p. Franks* [1962] 1 QB 152.

[38] *R v. Knightsbridge Crown Court, ex p. International Sporting Club (London) Ltd* [1982] QB 304.

[39] This would certainly be true if the decision was protected by a 'final and conclusive' clause.

thinks is correct. By contrast, in relation to non-jurisdictional errors of law, courts sometimes said that a decision should be quashed only if the error of law was 'gross' or of general importance, or if the error rendered the decision so unreasonable that no reasonable decision-maker could have made it.[40] The idea that decisions affected by error of law should be quashed only if the error is 'serious' achieves an effect similar to classifying questions as ones of fact and degree rather than of law: it gives the original decision-maker a degree of freedom in deciding the case or, in other words, in deciding what the relevant law is.

It is clearly more realistic to allow that questions of law sometimes admit of more than one reasonable answer than to insist that a question of law can only ever have one right answer. It is now widely accepted that in 'hard cases' the courts often have to choose between competing answers to questions of law not on the basis that one is right and the other(s) wrong, but because, for policy reasons, one is better or more acceptable than the other(s). In other words, there is no clear line between questions of law and questions of policy. Judges of the Court of Appeal and Law Lords who dissent on questions of law are not thought irrational because they dissent. In fact the views of dissenters often receive considerable approval. Further, as we have seen (see 9.3), many questions about the legal significance of facts are questions of degree—whether a flat is furnished; whether an alteration to a house is a structural improvement; whether a commercial deal is an adventure in the nature of trade. There may be no 'right' answer, in the normal sense, to such questions.[41] The 'right' answer is simply that answer which appeals to the body with the last word on the question.

Why, then, do courts ever adopt the less realistic view that questions of law have one right answer? In the context of the theory of jurisdiction the reason was the view that inferior decision-makers with limited powers must not be allowed to extend (or restrict) those powers by deciding jurisdictional questions of law wrongly, and that it is one of the jobs of the courts to police the limits of those powers. Another more general reason is that English judges have traditionally seen their role as finding out what the law actually is rather than as saying what it reasonably ought to be. A third reason relates to the role of the courts as 'guardians' of the law: if an inferior decision-maker can be said to have answered a question of law

---

[40] e.g. *R v. Preston Supplementary Benefits Appeal Tribunal, ex p. Moore* [1975] 1 WLR 624; *R v. National Insurance Commissioner, ex p. Michael* [1977] 1 WLR 109.

[41] *R v. Monopolies and Mergers Commission, ex p. South Yorkshire Transport Ltd* [1993] 1 WLR 23.

wrongly, then it is the court's duty to say what the right answer is. If it is accepted that the answer which the authority gave is only one of a set of possible answers, the court may only be justified in intervening if the answer given is unreasonable in a rather extreme sense. In other words, the 'right answer' thesis justifies more judicial intervention than the 'reasonableness' doctrine, which gives administrative authorities more freedom in choosing answers to questions of law—more freedom, that is, to make law. In practical terms, under the right answer thesis the reviewing court's view of the law will prevail, whereas under the reasonableness doctrine the original decision-maker's view of the law is much more likely to prevail.

Of these three reasons, the best justification for the 'right-answer' approach to questions of law is the first: the theory of jurisdiction. Now that the distinction between jurisdictional and non-jurisdictional errors of law is generally defunct, perhaps the courts should abandon the right-answer theory of review of questions of law and instead subject all questions of law decided by administrative agencies to review according to a standard of reasonableness.[42] The most important effect of this approach would probably be to reduce the overall level of judicial control of the administration, as the courts would not interfere just because they disagreed with a decision on a point of law, but only if it was unreasonable. So whether you find this proposal attractive or not will depend on your view of the proper scope of judicial review of inferior decision-makers.

9.7 ERRORS OF FACT

The distinction between jurisdictional and non-jurisdictional questions of law is paralleled by a distinction between jurisdictional and non-jurisdictional questions of fact. The classic exposition of this latter distinction is found in *R v. Nat Bell Liquors Ltd.*[43] The Privy Council in *Nat Bell* made it clear that the court could not quash a decision which the decision-maker had power to make simply because it was unsupported by

---

[42] This approach would not prevent a court holding that the view it preferred was the only reasonable one. But it should be wary of so holding where the decision-maker has greater expertise than the court relevant to answering the question of law. For a discussion of the approach of the US Supreme Court to this issue see P. Craig, 'Jurisdiction, Judicial Control and Agency Autonomy' in I. Loveland (ed.), *A Special Relationship? American Influences on Public Law in the UK* (Oxford, 1995).

[43] [1922] 2 AC 128; see also *R v. Fulham, Hammersmith and Kensington Rent Tribunal, ex p. Zerek* [1951] 2 KB 1.

the evidence.[44] It could interfere if the decision-maker had made an error of fact on which its jurisdiction depended but not if it made an error of fact in exercising a jurisdiction that it undoubtedly had. In *White & Collins v. Minister of Health*[45] a local authority had power to acquire land compulsorily, but not if it was part of a park. The power to make a compulsory acquisition order was held to depend on whether, as a matter of fact, the land in question was part of a park. On the other hand, in *Dowty Boulton Paul Ltd v. Wolverhampton Corporation (No. 2)*[46] a local authority had leased an airfield to the claimant; the authority sought to exercise a power to re-acquire the airfield for development on the ground that it was no longer required for use as an airfield. The Court of Appeal held that the question whether the land was still required as an airfield was a question of degree and comparative need, and was for the authority to make. It has also been held by a majority of the Court of Appeal that a decision may not be quashed merely because fresh evidence has been discovered since the hearing.[47] Both the power to overturn decisions unsupported by evidence and the power to consider fresh evidence are possessed by appeal courts but not, according to these cases, by the High Court exercising its supervisory jurisdiction.

The courts have for a very long time recognized the difficulties of the fact-finding process. Appeal courts are unwilling to interfere with findings of fact by courts of first instance unless they are convinced that the findings are wrong. Very often direct evidence of what happened will be lacking or inadequate, and so inferences will have to be drawn about what actually happened; in other words, circumstantial evidence will often be important. Assessing evidence, both direct and circumstantial, often depends a great deal on seeing the witness giving the evidence in person in order to assess his or her credibility. This an appeal court never does, and so it is at a disadvantage which leads to caution in reversing the findings of the court which actually saw the witnesses. This is, no doubt, one of the reasons why courts exercising powers of judicial review of administrative action are often unwilling to review questions of fact. Furthermore, as we have seen, judicial review procedure is not primarily designed to deal with factual disputes.[48]

---

[44] *R v. Secretary of State for Scotland* [1999] 2 AC 512, 541–2 *per* Lord Clyde.
[45] [1939] 2 KB 838.   [46] [1976] Ch 13.
[47] *R v. West Sussex Quarter Sessions, ex p. Albert and Maud Johnson Trust Ltd* [1974] QB 24.
[48] See 6.2.

There are also other reasons for this deference to inferior decision-makers on questions of fact. Two were suggested above:[49] a desire to ration scarce judicial resources and a recognition that questions of fact often involve not just the collection and processing of raw factual data but also the interpretation of that data in the light of policy considerations. The first of these two reasons may have influenced the House of Lords in *R v. Hillingdon LBC, ex p. Puhlhofer*[50] where it was held that it was for local authorities to decide whether the factual preconditions of entitlement to public housing were satisfied and that a court should only very rarely interfere with such decisions.

The second reason is well illustrated by the case of *R v. Secretary of State for the Home Department, ex p. Bugdaycay*.[51] This appeal involved two separate decisions made by immigration authorities: one was that certain asylum-seekers ought not to be given leave to enter Britain; and the other was, in effect, that an immigrant would not be in physical danger if he was deported. The House of Lords held that decisions as to whether particular immigrants were refugees should only be interfered with in extreme cases, partly because such decisions often raise difficult issues of foreign policy and diplomacy which courts are not suited to resolve.[52] The second decision turned on whether the Home Office had given sufficient weight to a letter which indicated that the immigrant might be maltreated if he was returned to his country of origin. The House of Lords decided that sufficient weight had not been given to this letter. This decision could be reached without delving into delicate political questions.[53]

Yet another reason for deference to decisions on questions of fact is that the courts have been willing to recognize that questions of fact often do not admit of one correct answer and that more than one interpretation of the evidence might be equally reasonable. An important case in this context is *Zamir v. Home Secretary*[54] in which the question of fact at issue was whether an immigrant's entry certificate had been obtained by fraud.

---

[49] See 9.5.

[50] [1986] AC 484; applied in *R v. Secretary of State for Education, ex p. Avon CC* (1990) 88 LGR 737.

[51] [1987] AC 514.

[52] See also *Secretary of State for the Home Department v. Rehman* [2003] 1 AC 153 (deportation on grounds of national security).

[53] See also *R v. Secretary of State for the Home Department, ex p. Turgut* [2001] 1 All ER 719. The CA pointed out that this approach is required by Art. 3 of the ECHR (prohibition of torture and inhuman or degrading treatment).

[54] [1980] AC 930.

In the first instance, this question had to be answered by an immigration officer at the point of entry into Britain. Lord Wilberforce stated the distinction between jurisdictional and non-jurisdictional questions of fact in the following terms: in some cases 'the exercise of power, or jurisdiction, depends on the precedent establishment of an objective fact. In such a case it is for the court to decide whether that precedent requirement has been satisfied'. In other cases, however, of which this was an example, all the High Court can do is 'to see whether there was evidence on which the immigration officer, acting reasonably, could decide as he did'.[55]

This approach is important for a number of reasons. First, it establishes, contrary to what was said in *Nat Bell*, that courts can sometimes quash decisions affected by non-jurisdictional error of fact. Secondly, it acknowledges that the issue with which the theory of jurisdiction is essentially concerned is that of who should ultimately decide particular questions of fact. Thirdly, it recognizes that the issue of substance is not whether the finding of fact is correct but whether it is reasonable. Where the question of fact is a precondition of jurisdiction, the court's task is not well described as finding the correct answer, but as choosing the answer that seems to it most reasonable. Finally, Lord Wilberforce explicitly stated the reasoning which led him to the result he adopted: the immigration officer has to take into account several factors of varying and contestable weight. When the court reviews an officer's decision it is limited as to the amount of material it can consider, and so the procedure of judicial review is not well suited to resolving questions of fact.

The actual application in *Zamir* of the principles laid down by Lord Wilberforce is now considered to have been wrong. In *R v. Secretary of State for the Home Department, ex p. Khawaja*[56] it was held that where, as in *Zamir*, the claimant for judicial review is challenging an order that he or she be personally detained, the court must decide for itself the factual issues on which the validity of the order depends. Personal liberty is too important an issue to be left to the decision of immigration officers, subject only to the requirement of reasonableness. Similarly, in *Bugdaycay* (mentioned above) it was said that a decision whether to accord refugee status should be interfered with only if it was unreasonable, whereas the

---

[55] An unreasonable decision is one that is, either literally or to all intents and purposes, wholly unsupported by the evidence. See the judgments of Lord Denning MR in *Ashbridge Investments Ltd v. Minister of Housing and Local Government* [1965] 1 WLR 1320 and *Coleen Properties Ltd v. Minister of Housing and Local Government* [1971] 1 WLR 433.

[56] [1984] AC 74.

court would interfere with a decision as to whether an immigrant was in danger of life or limb if it (the court) was of the opinion that the decision-maker had, for example, given too much (or too little) weight to some piece of evidence which was available to him or her or had misunderstood the force of some piece of evidence.[57] We could say that the effect of these decisions is to classify questions of fact relevant to issues of personal liberty or safety as jurisdictional questions of fact. However, it seems better to recognize that in some cases the courts will be prepared to quash decisions affected by non-jurisdictional errors of fact even though the decision could not be said to be 'unreasonable' in the strong sense used in administrative law (namely 'so unreasonable that no reasonable decision-maker could have reached it': see 9.8.1.).

It would seem, therefore, that the law recognizes three categories of factual questions: jurisdictional questions of fact which the court has power to decide for itself; non-jurisdictional questions of fact which are subject to judicial review on the unreasonableness standard; and non-jurisdictional questions of fact in relation to which the court will seek to ensure that the decision-maker has given proper weight to the available evidence.[58] In relation to errors of this third type the court will, in effect, invite the decision-maker to reconsider the evidence. It is sometimes suggested that the courts are moving towards what is called a 'substantial evidence' rule. This rule would replace the theory of jurisdictional fact and would provide that all decisions of fact by administrative authorities would be liable to be upset if they were not supported by substantial evidence. The proponents of this rule contemplate that it would lead to more judicial intervention; but this would depend very much on how the rule was applied. It seems clear from *Bugdaycay* that what would qualify as 'substantial evidence' in one context and on one issue might not be sufficient on some other issue. The greater the evidence required, the less leeway for 'error' would decision-makers have.

Finally, it should be noted that the immunity from judicial review established in *R v. Hull University Visitor, ex p. Page*[59] extends to errors of fact.

---

[57] See also *Secretary of State for Education and Science v. Tameside MBC* [1977] AC 1014, 1047 *per* Lord Wilberforce.

[58] Also, wrongful admission or refusal to admit evidence may give grounds for quashing a decision on a non-jurisdictional question of fact.

[59] [1993] AC 682.

9.8 POLICY MISTAKES

This section is concerned with grounds on which decisions and rules can be held invalid on the basis of their relationship to the policies or purposes for which the decision/rule-making power was conferred.

9.8.1 WEDNESBURY UNREASONABLENESS

In the *GCHQ* case Lord Diplock said (somewhat imprecisely) that the grounds of judicial review were concerned with three types of defect: illegality (by which he meant 'errors of law' including, for example, taking account of irrelevant considerations), procedural impropriety (by which he referred to matters discussed in Chapter 7), and irrationality.[60] 'Irrationality' is more often referred to as 'unreasonableness'. The inherent vagueness in this term makes it difficult to understand the law on this topic: how 'unreasonable' must a decision or rule be before it is liable to be quashed? The classic answer to this question is that of Lord Greene MR in *Associated Provincial Picture Houses Ltd v. Wednesbury Corporation*:[61] the challenged decision or rule must be 'so unreasonable that no reasonable authority could ever have come to it'. The court does not decide what the reasonable authority *would* do, but only what *no* reasonable authority *could* do. In other words, a court should not strike down a decision or rule on this ground just because it does not agree with it. In *GCHQ* Lord Diplock said that an irrational decision is one 'so outrageous in its defiance of logic or of accepted moral standards that no sensible person who had applied his mind to the question to be decided could have arrived at it'. Applied literally, these definitions are so stringent that unreasonable decisions in this sense are likely to be a very rare occurrence in real life.[62]

Not all definitions of *Wednesbury* 'unreasonableness' are so uncompromising, however. For example, Lord Donaldson MR once said that an unreasonable decision is one of which it can be said, 'my goodness, that is certainly wrong'.[63] It has also been said that a decision can be held unreasonable even though there are arguments in its favour, if the court thinks that the arguments against the decision are 'over-

---

[60] [1985] AC 374, 410–11.
[61] [1948] KB 223. For a more recent statement see *R v. Secretary of State for the Home Department, ex p. Brind* [1991] 1 AC 696, 757 *per* Lord Ackner.
[62] A possible example is *R v. Secretary of State for the Home Department, ex p. Sinclair* (1992) 4 Admin LR 613.
[63] *R v. Devon CC, ex p. G* [1989] AC 573, 583H.

whelming'.[64] Even when a court purports to quash a decision because it is '*Wednesbury* unreasonable', it may be applying a standard of unreasonableness less stringent than that specified by Lord Greene.[65] The concept of 'unreasonableness' is a flexible one and can be adapted to different types of decisions. In fact, whether a decision is unreasonable or not appears to depend ultimately on the court's assessment of the arguments for and against it and on the extent to which it can be said to give effect to the policies and purposes in aid of which the decision-making power was given.[66] The court's willingness to hold a decision unreasonable may also depend on its subject matter and the context in which it was made. According to Sir Thomas Bingham MR, '[t]he greater the policy content of a decision, and the more remote the subject matter of the decision from ordinary judicial experience,[67] the more hesitant the court must necessarily be in holding a decision to be irrational.'[68] Indeed, it has been held that decisions made in exercise of powers to formulate and implement 'national economic policy' or which concern 'the appropriate level of public expenditure and public taxation' are matters of 'political opinion', and that there are no 'objective criteria' by which they can be judged. Such decisions and rules cannot be struck down as *Wednesbury* unreasonable, at least if they have been debated and approved by Parliament; but they may be vulnerable under other heads of *ultra vires*.[69]

The same general point applies to the notion of unreasonableness applied in relation to rule-making.[70] In this context, the degree of control exercised under this head may vary according to the identity of the rule-maker. If it is a commercial or unelected body the court, it has been said, should 'jealously watch' the exercise of its rule-making powers to 'guard against their unnecessary or unreasonable exercise to the public

---

[64] *West Glamorgan CC v. Rafferty* [1987] 1 WLR 457, 477 *per* Ralph Gibson LJ.

[65] e.g. *R v. Cornwall CC, ex p. Cornwall and Isles of Scilly Guardians ad Litem and Reporting Officers Panel* [1992] 2 All ER 471.

[66] e.g. *R (Asif Javed) v. Secretary of State for the Home Department* [2002] QB 129.

[67] For instance, if it is 'policy-laden, esoteric or security-based'.

[68] *R v. Ministry of Defence, ex p. Smith* [1996] QB 517.

[69] *R v. Secretary of State for the Environment, ex p. Hammersmith and Fulham LBC* [1991] 1 AC 521, 595–7. See also *Marchiori v. Environment Agency* [2002] EWCA Civ 03 (national defence policy).

[70] Statutory rules are very rarely challenged under this head. This may be partly the result of the fact that interested parties are often consulted before such rules are made. Examples of challenges under this head to non-statutory rules include *R v. Ministry of Defence, ex p. Walker* [2000] 1 WLR 806; *R (Assocation of British Civilian Internees, Far East Region) v. Secretary of State for Defence* [2003] QB 1397.

disadvantage'.[71] By contrast, if the rules were made by a public represen-tative body, such as a local authority, the court would be slow to condemn the legislation as unreasonable unless it was 'partial or unequal in [its] operation as between different classes. . .[or] manifestly unjust. . .[or] disclosed bad faith. . .[or] involved such oppressive or gratuitous inter-ference with the rights of those subject to [it] as could find no justification in the minds of reasonable men'.[72] Even so, it is not clear that all of the items in this list satisfy Lord Green's narrow criterion. Furthermore, it seems that when the courts are judging the validity of non-statutory rules, they may apply a loose purpose-based test: does the particular rule further the permitted policy goals of the rule-maker?[73]

While there is no doubt that the courts recognize unreasonableness as an available ground of judicial review, its precise role is harder to discern. In the *Wednesbury* case Lord Greene MR seems to have seen this head of challenge as a last resort which might enable a court to strike down a decision which could not be said to fall foul of any of the other heads of judicial review such as irrelevant considerations.[74] As an independent ground of review, unreasonableness means something like extreme inconsistency or incompatibility with relevant policy objectives or pur-poses. Viewed in this way, unreasonableness is unlikely to play a signifi-cant role because if a decision or rule can be described as unreasonable in an extreme sense it will typically fall foul of one of the other heads of judicial review. On the other hand, the fact that a court could not fit a case into one of the other heads of judicial review would normally not prevent it invalidating the decision or rule if it felt it could be described as unreasonable in the *Wednesbury* sense.[75]

Instead of viewing unreasonableness as an independent ground of review, it might be interpreted as a standard of review. The idea here would be, for instance, that a decision or rule could be held invalid on the ground of taking an irrelevant consideration into account only if that failure could be described as unreasonable in the extreme *Wednesbury* sense.[76] Understood in this way, the concept of unreasonableness gives

---

[71] *Kruse v. Johnson* [1898] 2 QB 91, 99.   [72] Ibid.

[73] See e.g. *R v. Inspector of Taxes, Reading, ex p. Fulford-Dobson* [1987] QB 978, esp. 988D; P. Cane, 'Self-Regulation and Judicial Review' [1987] *CJQ* 324, 343–4.

[74] This also seems to have been the view of the House of Lords in *R v. Secretary of State for the Environment, ex p. Hammersmith and Fulham LBC* [1991] 1 AC 521, 597.

[75] e.g. *R v. Lord Saville of Newdigate, ex p. A* [2000] 1 WLR 1855.

[76] There is an inconclusive discussion of this point in *Pickwell v. Camden LBC* [1983] QB 962. But it seems to be the approach adopted in *R v. North and East Devon Health Authority,*

effect to a more general principle of 'judicial restraint' or 'deference' to the policy choices of the decision/rule-maker.

These two different approaches to the role of unreasonableness, although both supported by authority, are incompatible with one another. Perhaps the main argument for the restraint embodied in the second more general approach is that if courts are too ready to invalidate decisions and rules on policy grounds, they will open themselves to criticism and compromise their independence. It is for Parliament to exercise political control over institutions of governance and for the courts to ensure that the legal limits of public power are observed. Even so, opinions can differ about where the outer limits of reasonable discretion should be set, and courts may be subject to criticism even when they try to exercise restraint as they see it. This is a danger from which there is no escape. When we allow courts to decide that certain decisions are unreasonable we give them power to make value judgements on matters which may be politically contentious. It is unrealistic to expect that a court will be able to give an apolitical or value-free answer to a disputed political question, for no such answer exists.

Even if the distinction between the two different understandings of *Wednesbury*-unreasonableness is clear in principle, it is of little practical significance. This is because even under the second, standard-of-review approach, it is clear that unreasonableness is not the appropriate standard of review for grounds such as error of law and breach of natural justice. So under both approaches, the fundamental issue is when a highly deferential standard of review is appropriate and when, instead, the court should adopt a less deferential and more intrusive attitude to the control of public decision-making.

9.8.2 UNREASONABLENESS IN A BROAD SENSE

Matters are made even more confusing[77] by reason of the fact that the term 'unreasonable' is sometimes used in relation to statutes which confer powers, for example, on a Minister to act if he 'has reason to believe' or 'is satisfied' that, or if 'in his opinion', something is the case; or to take such steps as he thinks 'fit'. In this sense, a decision or rule may be unreasonable if it fails to further the purposes of the power under which

---

ex p. Coughlan [2001] QB 213 in relation to the first mode of protection of legitimate expectations: see 8.3.4.

[77] As was recognized by Lord Bridge in *R v. Secretary of State for the Environment, ex p. Hammersmith and Fulham LBC* [1991] 1 AC 521, 597.

it was made or if it conflicts with some other superior rule of law, even though it is not unreasonable in the *Wednesbury* sense.[78]

Phrases such as those listed above immediately raise the question whether the challenged action is to be judged according to the authority's own sense of reasonable belief (or satisfaction or fitness) or by some more objective standard. We might think that the notion of unreasonableness could only be applied objectively and that there is hardly any point in applying a subjective test because very rarely will an authority act in a way which it does not honestly (if mistakenly) believe to be reasonable. However, in a few cases a subjective approach has been adopted. The most famous is *Liversidge v. Anderson*[79] which was an action for false imprisonment. The Home Secretary had power to detain any person whom he had reasonable cause to believe to be of hostile origins or associations. A majority of the House of Lords held that the Home Secretary's action in detaining the complainant would be justified provided he had acted in the honest belief that there was reason to think that the detainee was hostile. A somewhat similar case is *McEldowney v. Forde*.[80] This case involved a challenge to a regulation (which proscribed republican clubs and like organizations in Northern Ireland) made under a power 'to make regulations . . . for the preservation of peace and the maintenance of order'. A majority of the House of Lords held that the power gave the Minister a very wide discretion which would only be interfered with if it could be shown that the Minister had not acted honestly, or if the regulation bore no relation to the purposes for which the power had been given. These cases are exceptional and are probably to be explained by the fact that both concerned the preservation of peace and security.

The leading authority for the proposition that even subjective statutory language ought to be given an objective interpretation is *Padfield v. Minister of Agriculture, Fisheries, and Food*.[81] In that case the Minister had power to refer to an investigation committee complaints about decisions of the Milk Marketing Board fixing milk prices. It was held that the Minister was under a duty to give proper consideration to the question whether to refer the complaint, and that any such decision had to be based on good reasons. Moreover, if the Minister gave no reason for a refusal to refer, the court would consider for itself whether there were

---

[78] e.g. *R v. Barnet LBC, ex p. Johnson* (1990) 89 LGR 581 (conditions condemned as *Wednesbury* unreasonable even though they were simply beyond the statutory power in question).

[79] [1942] AC 206.   [80] [1971] AC 632.   [81] [1968] AC 997.

good reasons.[82] Another important case is *Secretary of State for Education and Science v. Tameside MBC*.[83] The Minister had power to give directions to a local authority as to the performance of its statutory functions if he was satisfied that the local authority was acting or was proposing to act unreasonably.[84] The issue at stake was the highly contentious one of the 'comprehensivization' of schools: a Conservative local authority decided to reverse a scheme, worked out by its Labour predecessor and approved by the Secretary of State, for the abolition of selective schools in its area. It was made clear in this case that the test to be applied in judging the Ministers satisfaction was an objective, not a subjective, one: was the opinion which the Minister had formed about what the local authority had done or was about to do, one which a reasonable person could entertain? In this case much turned on evidence concerning the amount of disruption to the school system which the proposed reversion to the selective entry criteria would cause.

Planning and land–use legislation often contains provisions empowering authorities to attach such conditions as they see fit to the grant of planning or land–use permission. Five of the many cases on such provisions will provide us with a useful case–study.[85] In *Pyx Granite Co. Ltd v. Ministry of Housing and Local Government*[86] Lord Denning made it clear that although the phrase in the legislation was 'such conditions as they think fit', the conditions imposed had to relate fairly and reasonably to the permitted development of the land and must not be imposed for some ulterior motive; and that it was for the court to police this restriction. In *Fawcett Properties Ltd v. Buckingham CC*[87] the council gave permission for the erection of two cottages on the condition that they were to be reserved for farm workers and not to be let to city-dwellers. This condition was held to be a fair and reasonable, if imperfect, way of giving effect to the valid policy of preserving the green belt. In *R v. Hillingdon LBC*,

---

[82] But failure to give reasons where there is no obligation to do so raises no presumption that the decision-maker had no good reason for the decision: *R v. Secretary of State for Trade and Industry, ex p. Lonrho Plc* [1989] 1 WLR 525.

[83] [1977] AC 1014.

[84] Which was held the mean '*Wednesbury*-unreasonably'. This holding has been criticized on the ground that the restraint embodied in the *Wednesbury* test is designed to regulate the relationship between the courts and the executive, not that between one governmental body and another.

[85] For more detailed consideration of these cases see P. McAuslan, *The Ideologies of Planning Law* (Oxford, 1980), pp. 162 ff.

[86] [1958] 1 QB 554.   [87] [1961] AC 636.

ex p. Royco Homes Ltd[88] the Divisional Court struck down conditions attached to the grant of permission to build flats. The reason given was that the conditions in effect required the developer to fulfil, at its own expense, a significant part of the duty of the local authority as housing authority to provide public housing.

The next two cases concerned the grant of a licence to run a caravan site. The relevant legislation stated a number of matters which the authority could regulate by attaching conditions to the site licence—they related chiefly to the State and layout of the site. In *Chertsey UDC v. Mixnam's Properties Ltd*[89] the authority sought, by imposing conditions, to regulate relations between the site owner and the caravan owners on matters such as security of tenure. The House of Lords struck down the conditions as being insufficiently related to the purposes for which the statute intended conditions to be imposed namely, regulating the State of the site. In another case[90] it was held that in deciding what conditions could be imposed about the use of the site, general considerations of the effect of the site on the surrounding community could be taken into account. For example, if too many caravans were allowed on the site this might overload local educational and other facilities, and this would affect the caravan owners as much as other local inhabitants. On the other hand, in granting a site licence, as opposed to planning permission, preservation of the green belt was not a relevant consideration.

The basic issue raised by all of these cases is whether it is permissible to use conditions to achieve specific ends. The preservation of the green belt is a permissible end in some cases but not in others; protection of the amenities of the community around the caravan site is permissible but regulating relations between the site owner and the caravan owners is not; the provision of housing for persons on a local authority housing list is not a permissible use of planning conditions. These cases make clear the essentially evaluative nature of the judgment of unreasonableness. The legislation in question did not in any of these cases dictate the result or even give a clear indication as to what it should be. It left the planning authorities quite free to decide how to implement the statutory scheme. Is it right that courts should have the power, in effect, to substitute their views about the policy aims of the legislation for that of planning authorities? At one level, the answer to this question is simple: so long as courts

---

[88] [1974] QB 720. See also *Hall & Co Ltd v. Shoreham-by-Sea UDC* [1961] 1 WLR 240.
[89] [1965] AC 735.
[90] *Esdell Caravan Park Ltd v. Hemel Hempstead RDC* [1965] 3 All ER 737.

are involved in reviewing decisions of governmental bodies they will inevitably be required to make policy decisions which may prove contentious. In some contexts the courts seek to minimize their role by applying the notion of *Wednesbury* unreasonableness, but they do not do this universally. This inconsistency generates uncertainty and opens judges to accusations of being more willing to protect some interests against government interference than others.

9.8.3 PROPORTIONALITY

In the *GCHQ* case,[91] Lord Diplock contemplated the possibility that English law might at some time adopt the concept (found in French law, for instance) of 'proportionality'. This term is slightly misleading because what it refers to are cases in which a decision or rule is a *dis*proportionate response to a particular problem or a *dis*proportionate way of giving effect to a policy objective.

As in the case of '*Wednesbury*-unreasonableness', there are two different ways of understanding this concept. As a *ground* of judicial review, proportionality captures the colloquial injunction against using a sledgehammer to crack a nut. According to this understanding, over-reacting to a situation is one, but only one, sort of policy mistake. In the late 1980s the British government banned broadcasts of voices of members of proscribed terrrorist organizations. In the *Brind* case, the ban was challenged on the ground (amongst others) that it was disproportionate to the object of the empowering legislation. The House of Lords held that the ban would be unlawful only if it was unreasonable in the *Wednesbury* sense (which it was held not to be).[92] This does not mean that a measure that was disproportionate to the end to be achieved could not be unlawful, but only that it would not be unlawful for that reason unless it was so disproportionate that no reasonable authority could have thought it an appropriate response.

Another understanding of the concept of proportionality treats it not (just) as a ground of review but (also) as a competitor to *Wednesbury*-unreasonableness as a specification of the degree of unacceptability necessary to justify holding a decision or rule unlawful on policy grounds. In this sense, a decision or rule could be unlawful, even if it was not *Wednesbury*-unreasonable, provided that it was lacked 'proportionality'. As a standard of review, proportionality would not necessarily be limited

---

[91] See n. 60 above.
[92] *R v. Secretary of State for the Home Department, ex p. Brind* [1991] 1 AC 696.

in operation to proportionality as a ground of review. In *Brind*, the House of Lords rejected this use of proportionality on the basis that it would license excessive judicial interference with public decision/rule-making by allowing judges to pronounce on the 'merits' (as opposed to the 'legality') of decisions and rules. Given that *Wednesbury* unreasonableness, as much as proportionality, is concerned with the substance or content of decisions and rules, this objection amounts to no more than saying that the latter would license too much judicial interference and allow lack of due deference. The distinction between the merits of a decision and its substance is illusory. So is the distinction between merits and legality — error of law is a substantive ground of review but also the core instance of 'illegality'.

As a standard of review, the principle of proportionality is well established in EC law, for instance.[93] But it is difficult to say whether or to what extent it licenses the degree of judicial interference that the House of Lords feared, not least because the difference between lack of proportionality and *Wednesbury* unreasonableness is impossible to quantify in the abstract and independently of particular circumstances. We have also seen that *Wednesbury* unreasonableness is a flexible concept that can be used to justify various degrees of judicial interference; and the same is true of proportionality.[94] In fact, both concepts are typically used simply to provide justificatory frameworks for particular decisions by courts whether or not to invalidate particular decisions and rules. English courts always have and always will decide whether or not a decision or rule is invalid because of a policy mistake in a flexible and fact-sensitive way regardless of the conceptual framework in which the issue is considered.[95]

Even if English courts accept proportionality as the appropriate standard of review in certain types of case,[96] it is unlikely that they would, for instance, interpret it as requiring a strongly evidence-based cost–benefit analysis,[97] as opposed to a somewhat impressionistic and normative

---

[93] T.C Hartley, *Foundations of European Community Law*, 5th edn (Oxford, 2003), pp. 151–3.

[94] S. Boyron, 'Proportionality in English Administrative Law: A Faulty Translation' (1992) 12 *OJLS* 237 (discussing French law).

[95] For instance, courts will be highly deferential to decisions on defence or macroeconomic policy regardless of whether the standard of review adopted is *Wednesbury*-unreasonableness or proportionality.

[96] For a recent discussion see *R (Association of British Civilian Internees, Far East Region) v. Secretary of State for Defence* [2003] 3 WLR 80 at [32]–[37].

[97] Recall that judicial review procedure is not designed to resolve factual disputes: see 6.2. But it may, as a result, be incompatible with ECHR Art 6: 6.8. It is often said, however, that proportionality requires a more 'structured' inquiry than *Wednesbury* unreasonableness

assessment, of the relationship between the challenged decision or rule and its objective. It also seems certain that if English courts adopt the principle of proportionality, they will do so selectively, and only apply it to cases in which it is thought appropriate or necessary for courts to exercise a more intrusive style of scrutiny of public decisions and rules than could convincingly be justified by reference to the concept of 'unreasonableness'.

9.9 BREACH OF HUMAN RIGHTS

English courts conduct substantive review of decisions and rules in a fact-sensitive way. One of the relevant facts is the nature and content of the interest with which the claimant alleges the challenged decision or rule has unduly interfered. One of the most significant developments in English public law in the last decade has been increasing recognition of 'fundamental human rights'. This development started before, but has been considerably advanced by, the coming into force of the HRA. Fundamental human rights, as the name implies, are considered to be particularly important interests that deserve specially powerful legal protection; and amongst fundamental rights, some (such as the right not to be tortured under Art. 3 of the ECHR) are given more unqualified protection than others.[98] The HRA protects 'Convention rights' in various ways. The common law also recognizes fundamental rights (or 'constitutional rights' as they are sometimes called),[99] such as freedom of speech, personal liberty, and access to the courts, and accords them a measure of importance greater than that accorded to other common law rights and interests.[100] One of the ways in which fundamental rights are given special legal protection is by a rule that primary and subordinate legislation will not be read as authorizing infringement of human rights unless it does so

does: e.g. *R (Daly) v. Secretary of State for the Home Department* [2001] 2 AC 532 at [27] *per* Lord Steyn. For an example of a structured inquiry conducted in the language of unreasonableness see *R (Wagstaff) v. Secretary of State for Health* [2001] 1 WLR 292.

[98] Many rights are expressed to be subject to such qualifications as are, for instance, 'necessary in a democratic society'. In the case of unqualified rights, the role of the court is not to decide whether the challenged decision, action or rule is an unreasonable or disproportionate interference with the right, but whether it is an infringement, full stop: I. Leigh, 'Taking Rights Proportionately: Judicial Review, the Human Rights Act and Strasbourg' [2002] *PL* 265, 282–7.

[99] J. Jowell, 'Beyond the Rule of Law: Towards Constitutional Judicial Review' [2000] *PL* 671.

[100] This may be of considerable practical importance for entities that cannot satisfy the narrow test of standing under the HRA (see 4.3).

expressly.[101] Another way in which (qualified)[102] rights are specially protected, both at common law and under the HRA (s. 6), is by applying
what is sometimes called 'anxious scrutiny' to public decisions and
rules that are challenged on the ground of interference with such
rights.[103] What this means is that the more serious the interference with
human rights, the greater the justification needed to make it lawful.
In cases involving Convention rights, the degree of scrutiny applied by
English courts (or, in other words, the strength of the reasons required
to justify the challenged conduct) must be at least as great as that
applied by the ECtHR in relation to the right in question.[104] In cases
involving common law rights that are not also protected by the ECHR,
English courts are free to decide for themselves the appropriate degree
of scrutiny and, conversely, the appropriate degree of deference to the
decision-maker.[105]

This principle is of relevance to all the grounds of judicial review, but
especially to those considered in this chapter.[106] Whenever the claimant's
fundamental human rights are at stake, the court must bear this in mind
in deciding whether the relevant ground of review has been established. It
should not be assumed, however, that the requirement of anxious scrutiny
necessarily favours the language of proportionality over that of unreasonableness.[107] Both concepts only provide packaging for fact-dependent

---

[101] *R v. Secretary of State for the Home Department, ex p. Simms* [2000] 2 AC 115. Section 3
of the HRA requires courts, if possible, to interpret legislation in a way compatible with the
protection of Convention rights.

[102] In the case of unqualified rights, once the content of the right has been established, *any*
interference with it will constitute an unlawful infringement. In these cases, the balancing of
interests inherent in the concepts of unreasonableness and proportionality takes place as
part of deciding what the content of the right is—e.g. what 'torture' means.

[103] Concerning the common law, see *R v. Ministry of Defence, ex p. Smith* [1996] QB 517.

[104] e.g. in *Smith and Grady v. UK* (1999) 29 EHRR 493 the ECtHR held that the English
courts in *R v. Ministry of Defence, ex p. Smith* (previous note) had not scrutinized the
challenged decision closely enough.

[105] For suggestions about factors relevant to deciding how much deference is appropriate
see M. Hunt, 'Sovereginty's Blight: Why Contemporary Public Law Needs the Concept of
"Due Deference" in N. Bamforth and P. Leyland (eds) *Public Law in a Multi-Layered
Constitution* (Oxford, 2003), pp. 353–4. Hunt argues that proper protection of individual
rights requires abandonment of the idea that some issues are beyond judicial control and
non-justiciable.

[106] For instance, challenges, on the ground of error of fact, to decisions of immigration
authorities on asylum applications frequently involve assertions that the asylum-seeker's
rights to life (ECHR Art. 2) and not to be tortured (ECHR Art. 3) are at stake.

[107] See, e.g., *R (Wagstaff) v. Secretary of State for Health* [2001] 1 WLR 292.

judicial judgments; and, it seems, the more anxious the scrutiny the more detailed the attention the court will give to the facts of the case.[108]

9.10 VAGUENESS

There is one other ground of substantive review that deserves brief mention. It seems that non-Parliamentary rules can be struck down if they are so vague either that they do not give those subject to them adequate guidance as to what their legal rights and obligations are, or that it is impossible to say whether they are properly related to the purposes for which the law-making power was conferred.[109] It may be argued that the requirement of clarity is a desideratum of valid law independent of any notion of reasonableness and that vagueness is, therefore, an independent ground of judicial review.

[108] e.g. *R (Wilkinson) v. Broadmoor Special Hospital Authority* [2002] 1 WLR 419. JRP is not designed for detailed investigation of facts, and this is one reason why it may not comply with ECHR Art. 13 which requires an effective domestic remedy for infringements of rights protected by the ECHR: See 6.8.

[109] *McEldowney v. Forde* [1971] AC 632.

Part II

Liability of Public Functionaries

10

Starting Points

10.1 GENERAL PRINCIPLE

So far we have been concerned with rules of 'public law'. In this Part we will consider the way in which rules of private law can be used to challenge and control the activities of officials and bodies exercising public functions and, in particular, the way in which these rules are modified in their application to public functionaries.

There is a strong tradition in English law of seeing private law rules as the paradigm governing not only relations between citizens but also relations between citizens and the government. According to the nineteenth-century constitutional lawyer, A.V. Dicey, the 'rule of law' requires that public functionaries should be answerable for their actions to the same extent and according to the same rules as private individuals. It is clear that this approach is inadequate as a complete theory of governmental liability if for no other reason than that there are grounds of public law illegality which have no application or relevance to the conduct of private individuals. But we might defend Dicey from further criticism by saying that his theory primarily concerned the application to the activities of public functionaries of private law rules of liability for loss or damage.

At the time Dicey was writing, this view of the liability of governmental bodies was not entirely implausible; and so influential has Dicey's approach been that it is probably true to say that rules of private law liability apply to the activities of public functionaries in the same way and to the same extent as they apply to the activities of private citizens, unless some good reason can be found why they should not. It seems clear, as we will see later, that private law rules are not always appropriate in an unqualified form as controls on the exercise of public functions. But it may well be that the best starting-point is a presumption that they do apply, leaving it to the defendant to adduce some good reason why they should not. In some instances, the legitimate demands of public policy may require that bodies exercising public functions be subject to lesser obligations than private individuals who have no responsibilities to the public generally.

There is another side to the 'public interest' coin. In relation to the making of contracts, for example, the government wields such economic and psychological power that it may be argued that ordinary citizens dealing with the government require greater protection from the effects of inequality of bargaining power than they do when they are dealing with each other. This might imply that in some cases the government should be subject to greater restrictions than private citizens, not lesser.[1] Power and privilege, it might be thought, should not exist without countervailing responsibilities. At this level of generality such arguments are very difficult to assess, and it is only by discussing specific areas of the law that their force or lack of it can be appreciated.

Perhaps the most important point to make at this stage is that the traditional Diceyan view rests on what might now be thought a rather outdated picture of the nature of government and the way it operates. It sees government as made up of a collection of rather autonomous and personally responsible individuals who differ from private citizens only in the respect that when a government official acts, he or she does not do so on his or her own behalf but on the behalf of others, as a sort of agent. Today, on the other hand, we view government much more as a corporate entity which stands over against individuals and, to some extent, operates antagonistically to them on behalf of a set of interests that are often opposed to the interests of individuals as perceived by themselves. Government is seen as rather impersonal and sometimes hostile, whereas Dicey seems to have conceived of it as a more personal and benign force. This change is not unrelated to the dramatic increase, during the last 100 years or so, in the scope of governmental activities in the social and economic spheres. Government is now very intrusive in the lives of ordinary citizens and this fact throws doubt on the value of Dicey's approach as a complete theory of governmental liability. At the same time, there seems no reason to abandon the basic premise that in the absence of countervailing considerations bodies exercising public functions should be at least as liable in contract, tort, and so on, as private citizens.

---

[1] An application of this idea in a slightly different context is the rule that government bodies *Derbyshire CC v. Times Newspapers Ltd* [1993] AC 534) and political parties (*Goldsmith v. Bhoyrul* [1998] QB 459) cannot sue for defamation in respect of their public activities.

Dicey's picture is also anachronistic because it obviously has nothing to say about recent changes in the geography of governance resulting from privatization, contracting-out, and so on. As we saw in Chapter 1, these developments led to the functional turn in administrative law, and the articulation of the public/private distinction as a counterpoint to Dicey's principle of equality, which was based on an essentially institutional understanding of government and governance.

10.2 THE SPECIAL POSITION OF THE CROWN

Some of the rules relating to the civil liability of public functionaries are couched in terms of and apply to 'the Crown'.[2] This term does not by any means embrace all governmental bodies, let alone all public functionaries. It is important to understand what the term means because the Crown enjoys certain privileges and immunities that other organs of government do not enjoy. For example, under section 21 of the Crown Proceedings Act 1947 a court cannot, in civil proceedings,[3] grant an injunction or make an order of specific performance against the Crown.[4] Secondly, by virtue of section 25 of the 1947 Act, money judgments cannot be executed against the Crown: the claimant must be satisfied with a certificate of the amount due (backed up by a statutory duty to pay). The disbursement of money by central government is lawful only if authorized by Parliament. In practice, however, a specific appropriation for the purpose of paying damages would not usually be necessary: expenditure is typically authorized in large amounts and in respect of broadly defined heads of government activity. Thirdly, section 40(2)(f) of the same Act preserves the principles of statutory interpretation that the Crown may take the benefit of a statute even if the statute does not expressly (or by necessary implication) mention the Crown as a beneficiary; and that the Crown is not subject to any statutory obligation or burden even if the statute does not expressly (or by necessary implication) relieve it of the obligation or burden.[5]

In European law, a directive can bind organs of a Member State (but

---

[2] Concerning the criminal liability of the Crown see M. Sunkin, 'Crown Immunity from Criminal Liability in English Law' [2003] *PL* 716.

[3] For our purposes, this phrase refers to actions for private law wrongs such as torts and breaches of contract.

[4] See 5.2.5 and 5.3.1 for discussion of the availability of judicial-review remedies against the Crown.

[5] See also *Lord Advocate v. Dumbarton DC* [1990] 1 AC 580.

not private individuals) even if it has not been implemented by the State.[6] For this purpose, the definition of 'state organ' is much wider than the definition of the 'Crown'.[7] It is possible to conceive of circumstances in which the rule that a statute does not bind the Crown unless expressed to do so might conflict with EC law, in which case an English court would have to create an appropriate exception to the rule.

The Crown's liability in tort is also limited in several ways. Limitations worth noting are that the Crown is not liable for breach of statutory duty unless the duty in question also rests on persons other than the Crown and its officers;[8] and that statutory immunities or limitations of liability accruing to any government department or officer also accrue for the benefit of the Crown.[9]

10.3 DEFINITION OF THE CROWN

The privileged position of the Crown dates from a period when the Monarch personally wielded a great deal of political and governmental power. When, as a result of the constitutional changes of the seventeenth and later centuries, many of the powers of the Monarch were transferred to Parliament and to Ministers, a distinction developed between the Crown in a personal sense (the Monarch), and the Crown in an impersonal, governmental sense. This would suggest that in historical terms at least, the Crown in this latter sense encompasses all persons and bodies who exercise powers which were at some time exercised by the Monarch. However, the term in its modern sense clearly does not extend this far. For example, Her Majesty's judges of the High Court in theory dispense royal justice, but judges are not thought of as being comprehended by the term 'the Crown'. And because of the development of the doctrine of Parliamentary supremacy over all other organs of government including the Monarch, Parliament is not thought of as being a part of the Crown even though it was a major beneficiary of the shift of powers from the Monarch.

This leaves the executive branch of central government (local government has always been subordinate to and separate from central government, whether in its present form or in its monarchical form). By the 'executive branch of central government' is meant Ministers of State and the departments for which they are constitutionally responsible. There

---

[6] See 5.5.2.   [7] *Foster v. British Gas Plc* [1991] 2 AC 306.
[8] Crown Proceedings Act 1947, s. 2(2).   [9] Ibid., s. 2(4).

are dicta that support exactly this definition of the Crown.[10] At the same time, however, it is clear that servants and officers of the Crown (including Ministers) may, for instance, be sued personally for torts committed in the course of performing their public functions, and that such an action would not count as an action against the Crown.[11] The 'Crown' is to be understood in a corporate sense as referring to departments of central government and to Ministers as the individuals who are constitutionally responsible (to Parliament) for the conduct of those departments. It follows that there is a distinction between the Crown, and servants and officers of the Crown. For example, 'common law' and 'prerogative' powers belong to central government by virtue of its being the Crown, while statutory powers conferred by Parliament on Ministers do not.[12] Thus, in *Town Investments Ltd v. Department of Environment*[13] it was held that a contract made with a Minister acting in his official capacity is made with the Crown, not with the Minister.

10.4 THE APPLICATION OF STATUTORY PROVISIONS TO PUBLIC BODIES

A context in which the issue of defining the Crown often arises is whether a statutory provision applies to a particular non-departmental or quasi-governmental body: remember that the Crown is not subject to statutory obligations unless the statute expressly (or by necessary implication) provides that it applies to the Crown, but that it can take the benefit of a statute even if not expressly (or by necessary implication) mentioned as a beneficiary. This issue is particularly important in relation to non-departmental governmental bodies and private bodies performing public functions.

A number of factors emerge from the cases as being important in determining whether particular statutory provisions apply to particular bodies. First, the degree of control which the organs of central government

---

[10] *Town Investments Ltd v. Department of Environment* [1978] AC 359, 381 *per* Lord Diplock.

[11] *M v. Home Office* [1994] 1 AC 377. The personal liability of government officials was, of course, central to Dicey's theory of the rule of law.

[12] See A. Lester and M. Weait, 'The Use of Ministerial Powers Without Parliamentary Authority: the Ram Doctrine' [2003] *PL* 415: government operates on the basis that ministers can decide for themselves when Parliamentary authorization should be sought for the exercise of common law and prerogative powers.

[13] [1978] AC 359.

exercise over the body has to be considered. For example, in *British Broadcasting Corporation v. Johns*[14] it was held that the BBC does not enjoy Crown immunity from taxation. The Court of Appeal stressed the fact that the BBC was set up as an independent entity and that this was, no doubt, exactly for the purpose of avoiding both the appearance and the actuality of central government control over its activities. Conversely, in *Pfizer Corporation v Ministry of Health*[15] it was held, in effect, that the supply of drugs to the NHS is supply 'for the services of the Crown'. The question in this case was whether the NHS had certain rights under patent legislation, and the fact that the decision benefited the NHS financially may have been an important factor in leading the court to it. It was also relevant that although the NHS was made up of a system of statutory corporations, these were subject to a high degree of central government control and were directly, and almost entirely, dependent on the government for finance. Statutory corporations that operate in a commercial way would be unlikely to be treated as part of the Crown in any sense.

A second factor relates to the nature of the function that the body performs. For example, in *BBC v. Johns* the court rejected the BBC's argument that wireless telegraphy was a public function. In the light of the functional turn in administrative law (see Chapter 1), the argument, that the nature of the function being performed is relevant to whether the functionary counts as part of the Crown, seems to rest on a confusion of categories. 'The Crown' is an institutional concept, and a function of the Crown is not necessarily public merely by virtue of belonging to the Crown. Conversely, the fact that a body performs public functions does not determine its institutional status. Bodies that perform public functions may not be governmental, let alone part of the Crown (which is a sub-category of governmental bodies). A functional interpretation of the BBC's argument might involve asking whether, given the nature and purpose of the particular immunity or benefit, a body performing the function in question is an appropriate recipient of the immunity or the benefit. Take the *Pfizer* case, for instance. It could be argued that, since the provision of basic health care is thought to be a function of great public importance, there is a good case for relieving the NHS of any statutory obligation to pay royalties to private drug manufacturers for the

---

[14] [1965] Ch 32.
[15] [1965] AC 512. Since this case was decided, the organization of the NHS has changed significantly, and it is unclear what conclusion would be reached if a similar issue arose now.

use of drug patents. However, if such an argument is valid, its validity is not dependent on whether or not the NHS is part of the Crown.

A third factor is the relationship between the claimed benefit or immunity and the particular ground on which it is claimed. For example, in *Tamlin v. Hannaford*[16] it was held that the British Transport Commission was an independent commercial entity and not part of the Crown. Thus, it was not entitled to ignore the provisions of the Rent Acts in ejecting a tenant from its premises. But even if the Commission had been held to be an arm of central government, there would be a good case for arguing that it should not be allowed to ignore legislation designed for the protection of tenants. The Commission did not need such immunity for the proper conduct of its statutory functions. In an Australian case[17] the question was whether a statutory body charged with the job of investing the assets of a superannuation fund for government employees had to pay stamp duty in respect of transactions entered into by it in pursuance of its statutory functions. One judge drew a distinction between this issue and the question of whether, for example, landlord and tenant legislation would apply to acquisition by the Investment Trust of office accommodation. He seems to have thought that the latter was less central to the functions of the Trust and, therefore, less likely to give rise to entitlement to any immunity or benefit.

Finally, a specific statutory provision can decide the issue of immunity. Thus, s. 60 of the National Health Service and Community Care Act 1990 stripped the NHS of many Crown privileges. Again, the Act which establishes the Advisory, Conciliation, and Arbitration Service (ACAS) provides that the functions of the service are performed on behalf of the Crown notwithstanding the fact that, in the performance of its central functions, it is to be free of ministerial direction.[18] This led Lord Scarman in *UKAPE v. ACAS*[19] to say that injunctive relief was not available against the service. This is an interesting case because, given the nature of the service and the functions it performs, it is, as the legislation recognizes, highly desirable that the service should be independent and free from outside influence so that it can truly mediate between the parties in dispute. Judged by the criterion of central government control, ACAS would not qualify as a Crown body. On the other hand, the conciliatory nature of the service's activities makes the use of injunctive relief in

---

[16] [1950] 1 KB 18.
[17] *Superannuation Fund Investment Trust v. Commissioner of Stamps* (1979) 145 CLR 330.
[18] Employment Protection Act 1975, Schedule 1, para. 11(1).
[19] [1980] 1 All ER 612, 619.

connection with them wholly inappropriate. Agreement between the parties, not coercion by one of them, is the essence of the exercise. So there are good grounds for according the Service immunity from injunctive relief, but they are not captured by the formula that ACAS 'performs its functions on behalf of the Crown'.

The conclusion to be drawn from all this is that there may sometimes be good grounds for relieving a public body of some obligation (such as an obligation to pay tax) or for giving it some immunity (such as freedom from injunctive relief). But these grounds have little to do with the fact that the body is or is not part of central government, or that it is or is not subject to central government control. They have much more to do with the nature of the activity or function in question and its relationship to the benefit or immunity claimed. It is, therefore, not helpful to express a conclusion, about the application of a statutory provision to a particular body's activities, in terms of whether the body is or is not part of the Crown. It would be better if the terminology were jettisoned and the real issues underlying it were faced squarely. Such an approach would also be consistent with the functional turn in administrative law, with which the special position of the Crown is extremely difficult to reconcile. Historically, the Crown, understood as the executive branch of central government, was in a special position because of its identification with the Monarch. The fundamental principle underlying the functional turn is that the scope of administrative law rules and remedies depends not on the source of power (whether common law, the prerogative, or statute) or on the identity of the functionary, but on whether the challenged decision or action is public in nature and a suitable subject for judicial review. It has to be admitted, however, that such a radical shift in legal thinking is unlikely to occur quickly because the concept of the Crown is deeply entrenched in the British constitution and in English law.

Tort

II.I THE BASIC PRINCIPLE

Section 2 of the Crown Proceedings Act 1947 provides (subject to a number of exceptions and qualifications)[1] that the Crown shall be liable in tort to the same extent 'as if it were a private person of full age and capacity' in respect of vicarious liability, employers' liability, and occupiers' liability. The assumption underlying this general provision is that prior to the Act the Crown enjoyed a general immunity from liability in tort. Governmental bodies other than the Crown never enjoyed such an immunity;[2] nor did (or does)[3] the immunity of the Crown prevent an action being brought against the Crown servant or agent who committed the tort. The general principle now is that all governmental bodies may be sued and held liable in tort in the same way and to the same extent as private individuals and corporations.[4] Consistently with the functional turn in administrative law, the question addressed in this chapter concerns the application of the law of tort to the performance of public functions, whether by governmental or non-governmental[5] entities.

---

[1] For instance, the Crown is not liable in respect of the exercise of judicial functions (Crown Proceedings Act 1947, s 2(5)); nor are the judges themselves: P. Cane, *Tort Law and Economic Interests*, 2nd edn (Oxford, 1996), pp. 228–33.

[2] *Mersey Docks Trustees v. Gibbs* (1866) LR 1 HL 93; *Geddis v. Proprietors of Bann Reservoir* (1878) 3 App Cas 430. Although these cases concerned liability for negligence, they are applications of a more general principle. They were actions against non-governmental statutory corporations, but they are now treated as having established a general rule governing the exercise of statutory functions by governmental as well as non-governmental bodies.

[3] *M v. Home Office* [1994] 1 AC 377.

[4] US law starts from the opposite position. 'The United States is immune from suit except so far as it has waived its sovereign immunity': H.M. Goldberg, 'Tort Liability for Federal Government Actions in the United States: An Overview' in D. Fairgrieve, M. Andenas, and J. Bell (eds.), *Tort Liability of Public Authorities in Comparative Perspective* (London, 2002).

[5] e.g. *Watson v. British Boxing Board of Control Ltd* [2001] QB 1134 (non-governmental, non-statutory regulator).

11.2 LIABILITY FOR EXERCISE OF PUBLIC FUNCTIONS

11.2.1 NEGLIGENCE: *X V. BEDFORDSHIRE CC*

There are, however, two important difficulties in applying this general principle to the exercise of public functions. The first concerns the relationship between liability in tort and the doctrine of *ultra vires*. To say that someone has committed a tort is to say that they have acted unlawfully in a private law sense. To say that a body has acted *ultra vires* is to say that it has acted unlawfully in a public law sense. A body can be held to have acted unlawfully in a public law sense only if it has acted *ultra vires*. However, it is possible, in theory at least, that a body might commit a tort even though what it did was not *ultra vires*; and so the question arises: could a governmental body be liable in tort even though its tortious conduct was, in a public law sense, *intra vires*? In summary terms, is *ultra vires* a precondition of holding a public functionary liable in tort?

The second difficulty is caused by the fact that in some contexts at least, the courts exercise considerable restraint in awarding judicial-review remedies in respect of governmental policy decisions. This inevitably raises the question of whether courts should show similar restraint in awarding remedies in tort in respect of acts done in execution of policy decisions. Such restraint is most clearly manifested in the concept of unreasonableness in the strong *Wednesbury* sense of 'so unreasonable that no reasonable authority could have made it' (see 9.8.1). In 'private' tort law, 'unreasonableness' is understood in a weaker sense in terms of what, all things considered, a reasonable authority would (or would not) have done. The question is whether the stronger concept of *Wednesbury* unreasonableness should be used instead of the weaker sense of unreasonableness in tort actions against public functionaries.

The courts have been grappling with these difficulties for more than thirty years.[6] But to understand the current law, we can start with the 1995 decision in *X v. Bedfordshire CC*.[7] In this case, Lord Browne-Wilkinson offered general guidance as to when a public authority could be held liable in the tort of negligence in respect of the performance of a statutory function. The first requirement was that the private law

---

[6] Important early decisions were *Dorset Yacht Co Ltd v. Home Office* [1970] AC 1004; *Anns v. Merton LBC* [1978] AC 728.

[7] [1995] 2 AC 633.

conditions for the existence of a duty of care must be satisfied. These (as laid down in *Caparo Industries Plc v. Dickman*)[8] are that the defendant ought to have foreseen that the claimant might suffer injury or damage if the defendant acted negligently; that there was a sufficient relationship of proximity between the claimant and the defendant; and that it would be just and reasonable to impose a duty of care on the defendant. The concept of proximity has been used as the basis for refusing to impose a duty of care in several cases where it was alleged that by negligence in performing its functions, a regulatory or law-enforcement authority failed to prevent the claimant suffering loss or damage as a result of conduct of a third party:[9] the authority's function, it was said, was to protect the public as a whole, not specific individuals.[10] It is generally conceded that the concept of proximity is simply a cover for giving effect to value-judgements about the desirable scope of tort liability. Two principles relevant in many actions against public authorities are, first, that the law of tort in general and the tort of negligence in particular are mainly concerned to compensate for personal injury and property damage, and only marginally and exceptionally for economic loss; and secondly that tort liability for failure to prevent loss occurring (as opposed to causing it) should be exceptional.[11]

In relation to the exercise of statutory functions, *X v. Bedfordshire CC* seemed to establish that the third condition ('justice and reasonableness') has three elements. The first is that a duty of care will be imposed only if it would be compatible with the provisions and purposes of the statute in

---

[8] [1990] 2 AC 605.

[9] See esp. *Yuen Ku Yeu v. Attorney-General of Hong Kong* [1988] AC 175; *Hill v. Chief Constable of West Yorkshire* [1989] AC 53. Contrast *Watson v. British Boxing Board of Control Ltd* [2001] QB 1134 (sporting regulator owes duty of care to participants in the sport); see further J. George, '*Watson v. British Boxing Board of Control*: Negligent Rule-Making in the Court of Appeal' (2002) 65 *MLR* 106.

[10] However, if the authority had dealings with the claimant in particular, this might forge a sufficient relationship of proximity: e.g. *T v. Surrey CC* [1994] 4 All ER 577; *Welsh v. Chief Constable of the Merseyside Police* [1993] 1 All ER 692; *Swinney & Swinney v. Chief Constable of Northumbria* [1997] QB 464, (1999) 11 Admin LR 811; *Costello v. Chief Constable of Northumbria* [1999] ICR 752.

[11] e.g. failure by a highway authority to remove a danger created by someone else is much less likely to attract liability than a failure by the authority to remove a danger it has created: *Kane v. New Forest DC* [2002] 1 WLR 312. Emergency services owe no duty to take care to respond to calls for help; and if they do respond, their only duty is to take care not to make matters worse: *Capital and Counties Plc v. Hampshire CC* [1997] QB 1004; *OLL Ltd v. Secretary of State for Transport* [1997] 3 All ER 297. But for these purposes, the ambulance service is not an emergency service. It has a duty of care to respond, and in responding, to calls: *Kent v. Griffiths* [2001] QB 36 (Lord Woolf's rationalization of this distinction between various services is unlikely to convince everyone).

question.[12] This element is relevant whether or not the statutory function in question is a 'discretion'. It appears that in this context, 'discretion' does not simply mean 'power' or 'choice'. For instance, in *X v. Bedfordshire CC* Lord Browne-Wilkinson said that 'the decision to close a school . . . necessarily involves the exercise of a discretion' whereas 'the actual running of a school' does not,[13] even though running a school confronts those responsible with a multitude of choices. Rather, the distinction between discretionary and non-discretionary decisions seems to parallel a distinction drawn in the earlier case of *Anns v. Merton LBC*[14] between 'policy' (or 'planning') and 'operational' decisions. Under the *Anns* scheme, policy decisions were accorded special deference by the courts, and an allegedly negligent policy decision would be actionable in tort only if the decision-maker had acted *ultra vires* in reaching the decision. On the other hand, negligence in making an operational decision could, in itself, justify the award of a tort remedy (provided other conditions of liability were satisfied). Operational decisions could be challenged in a negligence action according to ordinary private law principles of tort law. In other words, *Anns* established a 'policy defence' to an action in negligence which, if successful, would immunize the defendant from liability for *intra vires* policy decisions. As a result of *Anns*, a finding of *ultra vires* was, in cases of 'negligence at the policy level', a precondition of liability in the tort of negligence in respect of the exercise of a statutory function. The principles laid down by Lord Browne-Wilkinson in *X v. Bedfordshire CC* concerning liability for negligent exercise of a statutory *discretion* apparently relate to what, under the *Anns* scheme, were called 'policy decisions'. So we can rephrase the third sentence of this paragraph as follows: the compatibility condition has to be satisfied whether or not the negligence claim is in respect of a policy or an operational decision.[15]

However, *X v. Bedfordshire CC* also established that the compatibility condition of negligence liability has to be satisfied whether the function in question was a 'power' or a 'duty'. Here, 'power' is used synonymously with 'discretion' in the sense of 'choice', rather than in the narrower sense just explained. In *Stovin v. Wise*[16] Lord Hoffmann said that the compatibility condition is less likely to be satisfied in relation to powers

---

[12] An analogous requirement applies to non-statutory functions: e.g. *Hill v. Chief Constable of West Yorkshire* [1989] AC 53 (prevention and investigation of crime). See also *Leach v. Chief Constable of Gloucestershire* [1999] 1 WLR 1421.

[13] [1995] 2 AC 633, 735.   [14] [1978] AC 728.

[15] See also *Stovin v. Wise* [1996] AC 923, 951–2 *per* Lord Hoffmann.

[16] [1996] AC 923.

than in relation to duties. He also interpreted the condition more strongly than Lord Browne-Wilkinson by saying that only in exceptional cases would a statute be interpreted as being compatible with the imposition of liability for negligent exercise (or, even more, non-exercise) of a statutory duty or power.

Lord Browne-Wilkinson's judgment in *X v. Bedfordshire CC* further indicated that in relation to the exercise of statutory discretions—in the sense of 'policy decisions'—the 'justice and reasonableness' requirement has two elements in addition to compatibility with the statutory scheme. First, a duty of care would arise only if the discretion had been exercised unreasonably in the *Wednesbury* sense.[17] Secondly, a duty of care would not be imposed if, in order to decide whether it had been breached, the court would have to consider 'non-justiciable issues'. Putting these three elements together, the resulting principle would be that a public authority would owe a duty of care in the tort of negligence in respect of the exercise of a statutory discretion only if the imposition of such a duty would be compatible with the statute, if the discretion was exercised unreasonably in the *Wednesbury* sense, and if the issue of breach of the duty would raise no non-justiciable issues. Let us examine each of these three elements in a little more detail.

11.2.1.1 Compatibility

The compatibility issue requires the court to decide whether the imposition of a duty of care would be consistent with the general scheme and particular provisions of the relevant statute.[18] For instance, in *Governors of Peabody Donation Fund v. Sir Lindsay Parkinson & Co. Ltd*[19] it was held that the powers of local authorities under public health

---

[17] See also *Stovin v. Wise* [1996] AC 923. Lord Hoffmann was critical of the policy/ operational distinction, and his judgment can be read as meaning that the 'unreasonableness' condition applies to any and every exercise of (or failure to exercise) a statutory power regardless of whether is raises issues of 'policy'. On the other hand, *Stovin v. Wise* is often treated as establishing the unreasonableness condition only in relation to failure to exercise a statutory power or, in other words, failure to prevent harm occurring (as opposed to causing harm). See also *Larner v. Solihull MBC* [2001] LGR 255. For an argument that all exercises of public power should be immune from negligence liability see B. Feldthusen, 'Failure to Confer Discretionary Public Benefits: The Case for Complete Negligence Immunity' [1997] *Tort L Rev* 17.

[18] Analogous issues may arise in non-statutory contexts: e.g. soldiers owe no duty of care to fellow soldiers when engaging the enemy in battle, nor is the army under a duty to provide a safe system of work on the battlefield: *Mulcahy v. Ministry of Defence* [1996] QB 737.

[19] [1985] AC 210. The decision in this case must be read in the light of *Murphy v. Brentwood DC* [1991] 1 AC 398. See also *Reeman v. Department of Transport* [1997] 2 Lloyd's Rep 648; *Harris v. Evans* [1998] 1 WLR 1285.

legislation to inspect buildings in the course of construction were designed to protect the health and safety of *occupants*; so a developer could not recover from a local authority the cost of replacing faulty drains (even if they constituted a danger to the health of prospective occupants). Similarly, in *Yuen Kun Yeu v. Attorney-General of Hong Kong*[20] it was held to be no part of the statutory functions of the Commissioner of Deposit-Taking Companies to monitor the day-to-day activities of registered companies to ensure that they continued to be financially sound. It has also been held that the purpose of the Prison Act 1952, and of the Prison Rules made under it, is to regulate the internal affairs of prisons, and that breach of provisions of the Act or the Rules would not be actionable in tort.[21]

In *X v. Bedfordshire CC* local authorities were sued in respect of the way their social services departments had handled allegations of child abuse. The House of Lords refused to impose a duty of care on the grounds that to do so 'would cut across the whole statutory system set up for the protection of children at risk'; that civil litigation would be likely to have a detrimental effect on the relationship between social worker and client; and that the statute provided full procedures for the investigation of grievances.[22] In the same case, local education authorities were sued in respect of providing for children alleged to have special educational needs. Once again, the House refused to impose a duty of care on the grounds that the parents of the children were involved in the statutory process of deciding what provision to make for their children; that there was a statutory appeals mechanism; and imposition of a duty of care would have an inhibiting effect on the performance of the statutory functions.[23] By contrast, the House held that an education authority that provided a psychological advisory service to parents could owe a duty of care in respect of the conduct of that service.[24]

The reference to the statutory appeals mechanism raises the issue of

---

[20] [1988] AC 175.

[21] *R v. Deputy Governor of Parkhurst Prison, ex p. Hague* [1992] 1 AC 58. Of course, statutes may contain express provisions relevant to the availability of actions in tort, but typically they do not.

[22] [1995] 2 AC 633, 749, 750 and 752 respectively.   [23] Ibid. 760–2.

[24] Whether a public functionary owes a duty of care (or, as it is sometimes put, whether the functionary is 'directly liable') must be distinguished from the issue of whether the functionary is vicariously liable for the negligence of servants or agents. See *Phelps v. Hillingdon LBC* [2001] 2 AC 619. As a general rule, there is no vicarious liability for the negligence of independent contractors. This rule is particularly important in relation to contracting-out of the provision of public services to private-sector providers.

the relevance of availability of alternatives to a tort action. It is sometimes said that a tort action is a last resort which should not be allowed if there is a suitable alternative remedy available. For example, the existence of a 'statutory default power' (effectively, a right of appeal to a Minister) may preclude an action in tort for damages for failure by a public functionary to perform a statutory duty.[25] In *Jones v. Department of Employment*[26] it was held that a negligence action could not be brought in respect of loss suffered as a result of refusal of unemployment benefit because there was an adequate statutory appeal mechanism.[27] One of the reasons why the House of Lords declined to impose a duty of care on the police in *Hill v. Chief Constable of West Yorkshire*[28] was that victims of crime may be able to recover compensation from the Criminal Injuries Compensation Board. In *Cullen v. Chief Constable of the Royal Ulster Constabulary*[29] one of the reasons why the House of Lords refused to allow an action for breach of a statutory duty to allow an accused access to a lawyer was that judicial review provided a better remedy.

On the other hand, the mere existence of an alternative remedy will not preclude a tort action. It has been recognized that judicial review or other complaints mechanisms will not provide an adequate alternative to an action in tort unless the adverse effects of the challenged decision can thereby be reversed or damages can thereby be obtained for irreversible loss or damage suffered.[30] For instance, the fact that JRP is not designed for detailed investigation of facts may make it an unsuitable alternative to a tort claim.[31]

The fear expressed by Lord Browne-Wilkinson that tort liability might detrimentally affect the relationship between social worker and client echoes what Lord Keith in *Rowling v. Takaro Properties Ltd*[32] called 'the danger of overkill'. The idea is that the fear of being sued might cause public bodies to take 'unnecessary' action, or to refrain from

---

[25] e.g. *Watt v. Kesteven CC* [1955] 1 QB 408; *Cumings v. Birkenhead Corporation* [1972] Ch 12; *Pasmore v. Oswaldtwistle UDC* [1898] AC 387.

[26] [1989] QB 1.

[27] This aspect of the decision is problematic because the court treated the tort action as being an alternative to an appeal against refusal of unemployment benefit. Since the claimant had successfully appealed against the refusal, it is not surprising, viewed in this way, that his tort action failed. In fact, however, what the claimant sought to recover in the tort action (damages representing the cost of the appeal and for mental distress) could not be secured by appealing.

[28] [1989] AC 53.   [29] [2003] 1 WLR 1763.

[30] *West Wiltshire DC v. Garland* [1995] Ch 297, 309.

[31] *Waters v. Metropolitan Police Commissioner* [2000] 1 WLR 1607, 1613 *per* Lord Slynn.

[32] [1988] AC 473.

taking action, merely in order to minimize the risk of being sued and not because this was in the best interests of the public in general or of affected individuals in particular. For example, in *Calveley v. Chief Constable of Merseyside*[33] the House of Lords refused to impose a duty of care on police officers conducting an internal disciplinary inquiry partly on the ground that to do so might inhibit free and fearless conduct of the investigation. A major problem with this argument is that its use is rarely based on any (reliable) empirical evidence about the effect of potential tort liability.[34] In the absence of such evidence, an equally plausible speculation is that the risk of incurring liability might improve standards to the benefit of all involved. Furthermore, the force of the overkill argument as a reason not to impose a common law duty of care is weakened in cases where the allegedly tortious conduct may also constitute a breach of a Convention right for which a monetary remedy may be available, at least if it is assumed that the risk of incurring tort liability would be likely to have no significant 'chilling' effect over and above that produced by the risk of incurring liability for breach of the Convention right.[35]

11.2.1.2 Unreasonableness

As noted above, under the *Anns* scheme, negligence liability could arise out of the exercise of a policy discretion only if the discretion was exercised *ultra vires*. There was no discussion in *Anns* of whether any and every head of *ultra vires* could attract negligence liability or whether only some could. In *X v. Bedfordshire CC* Lord Browne-Wilkinson expressly stated that the only head of *ultra vires* that could attract tort liability for negligence was *Wednesbury* unreasonableness.[36] In other words, the only way of challenging the exercise of a statutory discretion in a negligence action is to attack its substance; the decision-making process followed by the functionary is not open to attack in a negligence action.[37] An important

---

[33] [1989] AC 1228; See also *Elguzouli-Daf v. Commissioner of Police of the Metropolis* [1995] QB 335.

[34] P. Cane, 'Consequences in Judicial Reasoning' in J. Horder (ed.), *Oxford Essays in Jurisprudence, Fourth Series* (Oxford, 2000). For a contrary point of view see R. Bagshaw, 'The Duties of Care of Emergency Service Providers' [1999] *LMCLQ* 71, 90–1.

[35] *D v. East Berkshire Community Health NHS Trust* [2003] EWCA Civ 1151 at [79]–[85].

[36] [1995] 2 AC 633, 736–7.

[37] Contrast *Rowling v. Takaro Properties Ltd* [1988] AC 473 in which it was alleged that a policy decision had been reached by a negligent procedure. The Privy Council held that the procedure had not been negligent, but did not say that procedural defects could not form the basis of a negligence action.

result of this surprising limitation is that the standard of care in a negligence action in respect of the exercise of a statutory discretion is *Wednesbury* unreasonableness: unless the claimant can satisfy the court that the defendant acted in a way so unreasonable that no reasonable authority could have so acted, an action in negligence will fail. On the other hand, if the claimant can satisfy the court that the defendant acted unreasonably in the *Wednesbury* sense, the defendant's conduct will automatically satisfy the weaker test of unreasonableness used in the tort of negligence, namely whether the defendant acted in a way a reasonable authority would not have acted. At this point, however, it is important to refer back to the discussion of the concept of *Wednesbury* unreasonableness in Chapter 9. There we saw that its inherent vagueness and flexibility softens the contrast between it and the weaker sense of unreasonableness.[38]

11.2.1.3 Non-Justiciability

Assuming that the imposition of a duty of care would not be incompatible with the relevant statute and that the defendant acted unreasonably in the *Wednesbury* sense, still (according to *X v. Bedfordshire CC*) a duty of care would not be imposed if assessment of the defendant's conduct required consideration of non-justiciable issues. This would mean that while some policy decisions could form the basis of a negligence action provided they were *Wednesbury*-unreasonable, others could not form the basis of a negligence action even if they were *Wednesbury*-unreasonable.

In *X v. Bedfordshire CC* Lord Browne-Wilkinson explained the concept of non-justiciability in several ways. He spoke of 'matters of social policy', 'the determination of general policy', 'the weighing of policy factors' and decisions about the 'allocation of finite resources between different calls made upon them or . . . the balance between pursuing desirable social aims against the risk to the public inherent in so doing'[39] as being non-justiciable. From this it would seem that the term 'non-justiciable' bears a different meaning in this context from that which it bore in the *GCHQ* case.[40] In the *GCHQ* sense, a non-justiciable decision is one that cannot be challenged in a court either by way of judicial review

---

[38] It has been suggested that the EC-law concept of 'serious breach' (see 5.5.2) would provide a better basis for liability (both in negligence and for breach of statutory duty) than *Wednesbury* unreasonableness: P. Craig, 'The Domestic Liability of Public Authorities in Damages: Lessons from the European Community?' in J. Beatson and T. Tridimas (eds.), *New Directions in European Public Law* (Oxford, 1998), pp. 83–9; but see J. Allison, 'Transplantation and Cross-Fertilisation' in ibid., pp. 176–82.

[39] [1995] 2 AC 633, 737, 748, 749 and 757 respectively.   [40] See 3.2.5.

or by way of an action for damages. By contrast, in Lord Browne-
Wilkinson's sense, a non-justiciable decision is one which is not actionable in tort or, at least, in negligence. This difference of meaning is
important because a decision which is not actionable in negligence by
reason of being non-justiciable may, nevertheless, be challengeable by way
of an application for judicial review. For example, 'decisions about the
allocation of finite resources' are not, as such, immune from judicial
review.[41] The judicial-review cases indicate that whether a court will be
prepared to interfere with a decision about how to use finite resources
depends on the substance of the decision itself. For instance, courts are
very unwilling to decide whether a patient should be treated in a particular way or what resources the police should commit to a particular operation; but they may be willing to require a local authority to provide basic
care for a disabled person. The central issue is not the fact that the
decision has resource implications, but whether the court should second-
guess the original decision-maker in respect of the subject matter of the
decision. It may be that such an approach is what Lord Browne-
Wilkinson had in mind in *X v. Bedfordshire CC*. If so, it is unclear what
types of decision he would consider non-actionable in negligence on the
ground that they raise non-justiciable issues about the allocation of scarce
resources (for instance). However, there are certain types of decision
which we can confidently assert would be 'non-justiciable in negligence',
namely decisions about national economic and defence policy. This is
because it has been held that such decisions could be quashed in judicial-
review proceedings only if they were contrary to law, and not on the
ground of *Wednesbury* unreasonableness.[42] In other words, even if such a
decision was *Wednesbury*-unreasonable, it could not, on that ground
alone, be quashed. *A fortiori*, such a decision would be non-justiciable
in tort.

11.2.1.4 Negligence Law and the ECHR

The conceptual scheme set up by Lord Browne-Wilkinson in *X v.
Bedfordshire CC* to limit the negligence liability of public functionaries
focused on the duty-of-care element of the tort of negligence: it involved

---

[41] See 8.5.1. A nice illustration of this point is *Marcic v. Thames Water Utilities Ltd* [2003]
3 WLR 1603. The House of Lords held that a regulatory body rather than a court was the
appropriate entity to assess the reasonableness of a water undertaking's strategy for dealing
with overloading of its sewerage system; but also that the regulator's assessment was subject
to judicial review.

[42] See 9.8.1 (n. 74).

immunizing public functionaries from negligence liability by providing that a duty of care would not arise unless certain conditions, additional to those applicable to ordinary private-law tort claims, were satisfied. In *Osman v. UK*[43] the ECtHR held that this approach to the liability of public functionaries was incompatible with the right to a fair hearing created by Art. 6 of the ECHR. The basic idea underlying the *Osman* decision was that the duty-of-care technique did not pay sufficient attention to the facts of individual cases in the way that consideration of the issues of breach and causation inevitably would if a duty of care were held to arise. The decision in *Osman* apparently influenced the outcome of *Barrett v. Enfield LBC*,[44] in which the House of Lords refused to accept a local authority's argument that it owed no duty of care in respect of the way it looked after children in its care. In *X v. Bedfordshire* it had been held that no duty of care was owed in respect of decisions whether or not to take children into care. Instead of overruling that decision, the House in *Barrett* drew a distinction between deciding whether or not to take a child into care (in relation to which no duty of care was owed) and decisions about the welfare of a child already in care (in respect of which a duty could be owed).[45]

The main impact of the *Barrett* approach appears to be that the issues of compatibility, unreasonableness, and justiciability are (in some cases, at least) to be decided in the context of considering whether the defendant has breached the duty of care rather than in the context of deciding whether a duty of care was owed.[46] *Barrett* does not mean that these issues are no longer relevant to the negligence liability of public functionaries, but only that they may, and in some cases should, be considered in the context of the detailed facts of individual cases, and not at the more abstract level and in the less fact-specific way suggested by the approach in *X v. Bedfordshire*. If the court thinks that the imposition of negligence liability would be incompatible with the relevant statutory scheme, or that the defendant should not be held liable because it did not act unreasonably in the strong, *Wednesbury* sense, or that the claim raises non-justiciable

---

[43] (2000) 29 EHRR 245.   [44] [2001] 2 AC 550.

[45] This distinction has nothing in its favour except the doubtful advantage of saving the House of Lords from the embarrassment of departing from one of its own recent decisions. In *D v. East Berks Community Health NHS Trust* [2003] EWCA Civ 1151 the Court of Appeal rejected the distinction and held that in dealing with child-abuse allegations and deciding whether to take care proceedings, local authorities owe a common law duty of care to the child but not to the parents (because their interests may conflict with those of the child, which are 'paramount').

[46] *W v. Essex CC* [2002] 2 AC 592.

issues, the claim will fail. The way this result is rationalized—i.e. whether in terms of duty of care, breach of duty,[47] or causation—is of secondary importance.[48] At the same time, however, *Barrett* may not only represent a change of judicial technique, but also signal a greater willingness to impose tort liability on public functionaries.

No sooner had the House of Lords modified its approach to the negligence liability of public functionaries to accommodate the reasoning in *Osman*, than the ECtHR changed its mind about the incompatibility of the duty-of-care technique with Art. 6.[49] This is not to say, however, that the shift of approach was unnecessary because the ECtHR also held that although the duty-of-care technique was not incompatible with Art. 6, it was incompatible with Art. 13 of the ECHR, which requires an 'effective remedy before a national authority' for breaches of the Convention.[50] Where a claimant makes an 'arguable' case of infringement of a right protected by the ECHR (other than that protected by Art. 13), the right to an effective remedy requires that the claimant's allegations be properly investigated. To the extent that a holding, that no duty of care was owed to the claimant, precludes such investigation, it is incompatible with Art. 13, and the claimant is entitled to an award of just satisfaction[51] on account of the infringement of Art. 13. It seems that the modified approach in cases such as *Barrett* would satisfy the requirements of Art. 13.[52]

It is true, of course, that Art. 13 (unlike Art. 6) is relevant only in cases involving alleged breaches of some other article of the ECHR. But the House of Lords seems likely to take the sensible view that the way tort

---

[47] Concerning the relevance or resources to the standard of care in medical negligence cases against the NHS see C. Witting, 'National Health Service Rationing: Implications for the Standard of Care in Negligence' (2001) 21 *OJLS* 443.

[48] This is also true of the foreseeability and proximity elements of the *Caparo* test.

[49] *TP and KM v. UK* (2002) 34 EHRR 42; *Z v. UK* (2002) 34 EHRR 97; *DP and JC v. UK* (2003) 36 EHRR 183. See also *Matthews v. Ministry of Defence* [2003] 1 AC 1163: statutory exclusion of tort liability not inconsistent with Art. 6.

[50] Art. 13 is not given effect by the HRA partly because it (Art. 13) is drafted from a supra-national point of view.

[51] In accordance with Art. 41.

[52] It is unclear whether the duty-of-care technique could ever comply with Art. 13 in a case of arguable allegations of an infringement of the ECHR. The judgments of the ECtHR could be read as saying that whether the duty-of-care technique offends Art. 13 depends on which other Convention rights are in issue: the more important the right, the more demanding the requirement of an effective remedy. In *McGlinchey v. UK* (2003) 37 EHRR 41 the ECtHR awarded compensation under Art. 13 for non-pecuniary loss suffered by a prisoner and her relatives in respect of a breach of Art. 3 (inhuman or degrading treatment). The conduct constituting the breach of Art. 3 was, in effect, negligent failure to care adequately for a sick prisoner. The Court held that Art. 3 had been breached even though there was no allegation that the negligence had caused the prisoner's suffering and ultimate death.

claims against public authorities are handled should be the same regardless of whether human rights are in issue. It should be noted, too, that the claims which were the subject of the decisions of the ECtHR that we have just considered were all decided by English courts before the HRA came into operation. Section 8 of the HRA now provides a domestic remedy for breaches of Convention rights that did not exist when these claims were considered by English courts, and which would very likely satisfy Art. 13. However, the measure of damages under s. 8 of the HRA is 'just satisfaction'. It is possible, in theory at least, that damages in tort in a particular case might exceed just satisfaction for any breaches of Convention rights entailed by the relevant tortious conduct, thus giving the claimant an incentive to sue in tort rather than under the HRA.

11.3 LIABILITY IN TORTS OTHER THAN NEGLIGENCE

11.3.1 BREACH OF STATUTORY DUTY

Although the *Bedfordshire* case was concerned primarily with liability in the tort of negligence, the principles it establishes could apply to any tort. For instance, a tort action for damages (or an injunction) for breach of statutory duty[53] will lie only if the statute can be interpreted as giving rise to individual rights of action in people in the claimant's position and in respect of the sort of injury or damage suffered by the claimant.[54] This requirement is indistinguishable from the principle of compatibility. Indeed, in *X v. Bedfordshire CC* the reasons which led the court to conclude that a duty of care would not be compatible with the relevant statutes were very similar to the reasons why it also held that no action would lie for breach of the defendants' duties under those statutes. The principle that the exercise of a discretion will only be actionable if it was *Wednesbury* unreasonable can also apply to an action for breach of statutory duty. For

---

[53] As opposed to a negligence action for breach of a common law duty of care arising out of breach of a statutory duty.
[54] e.g. *Wentworth v. Wiltshire CC* [1993] QB 654; *KA & SBM Feakins Fashions Ltd v. Dover Harbour Board* (1998) 10 Admin LR 665; *O'Rourke v. Camden LBC* [1998] AC 188 (criticized by R. Carnwath, 'The *Thornton* Heresy Exposed: Financial Remedies for Breach of Public Duties' [1998] *PL* 407); *Kirvek Management and Consulting Services Ltd v. Attorney-General of Trinidad and Tobago* [2002] 1 WLR 2792. An action for damages for breach of statutory duty will lie only where the claimant has suffered some pecuniary or non-pecuniary harm. Breach of statutory duty is not actionable *per se: Cullen v. Chief Constable of the Royal Ulster Constabulary* [2003] 1 WLR 1763.

example, in *Meade v. Haringey LBC*[55] the question was whether the council had breached its statutory duty to provide sufficient schools by closing schools in its area during a cleaners' strike. This duty is an open-textured one which leaves considerable discretion to local authorities.[56] The court held, in effect, that it was up to the council to decide how to handle strikes provided only that any action it took was not *ultra vires*. In other words, the decision how to handle a strike was a policy one which could only be challenged in a tort action for breach of statutory duty if it was *ultra vires*.

In light of the close analogy between the rules about the actionability in tort of breaches of statutory duty and the duty-of-care technique adopted in *X v. Bedfordshire CC*, it may be that English law on this topic will be found to be incompatible with Art. 13 of the ECHR.

11.3.2 NUISANCE

Consider next the tort of private nuisance. Private nuisance is an unreasonable interference with a person's use and enjoyment of their land. One defence to an action for nuisance is that the nuisance was authorized by statute. If a statute authorizes (or requires) the doing of a specific act, and the doing of that act necessarily or inevitably creates a nuisance no matter how carefully it is done, then the nuisance is authorized and cannot form the subject of a successful tort action. But if the nuisance is the result of negligence in doing the authorized act then an action in nuisance may lie because the nuisance will not be inevitable. If (as will usually be the case) a statute authorizes a class of acts and leaves it up to the authority to decide which of those acts it will perform (in other words, if the statute gives the authority a choice), and if the choice could have been exercised in such a way as not to create a nuisance, then an action for damages (or an injunction) may lie if a nuisance is created by the chosen course of action.[57] It is not clear what the phrase 'could have been exercised in such a way as not to create a nuisance' means. It has the effect, at least, that if the nuisance is the result of negligent exercise of a statutory power a plea of statutory authorization would fail.

There is no reason why the *Bedfordshire* principles should not apply here: if a defendant pleads statutory authorization, then if the nuisance-creating action was at the operational level the defendant would have to

---

[55] [1979] 1 WLR 624.   [56] See 3.2.4.

[57] *Managers of Metropolitan Asylum District v. Hill* (1881) 6 App Cas 193; *Allen v. Gulf Oil Ltd* [1981] AC 1001.

prove that it acted without negligence. If the action was at the policy level, then provided it was not *Wednesbury*-unreasonable, the defence would succeed. If it was *Wednesbury*-unreasonable the defence would fail because a *Wednesbury*-unreasonable action would also, *ex hypothesi* be unreasonable in the negligence sense.

Even if a defence of statutory authorization is not available, a common-law action for nuisance resulting from the performance of statutory functions will lie only if such an action would be compatible with the statutory scheme. In *Marcic v. Thames Water Utilities Ltd*[58] it was held that an action for nuisance would not lie in respect of repeated flooding caused by over-loading of a sewerage system because the statute created a regulatory mechanism more suitable than litigation for dealing with the complex issues of public interest involved in deciding how best to solve the problem.

11.3.3 TRESPASS

Finally, consider the tort of trespass. In the old case of *Cooper v. Wandsworth Board of Works*[59] the claimant successfully sued the defendant in tort for trespass to land when it demolished part of a house in pursuance of an invalid demolition order. If the order had been *intra vires* the action would not have succeeded; but since the defendant had failed to comply with the rules of natural justice in making the order the defendant had no legal authority for the demolition of the house. This case illustrates the role of *ultra vires* in tort actions in respect of the exercise of policy-based discretions.[60] It is possible to conceive of cases of 'operational trespass' in which the ordinary principles of trespass law would apply regardless of whether the impugned action was *ultra vires* or not: for example, if peripatetic workers employed by a public authority mistakenly and without authority or permission set up camp on private land rather than on land owned by the authority.

11.4 CRITICISMS OF THE POLICY–OPERATIONAL DISTINCTION

The use of the distinction between policy and operational (or discretionary and non-discretionary) functions and decisions as a basis for limiting the tort liability of public authorities has been criticized on three main

---

[58] [2003] 3 WLR 1603. [59] (1863) 14 CBNS 180.
[60] However, doubt may be cast on the result in *Cooper* by Lord Browne-Wilkinson's statement in *X v. Bedfordshire* that breach of natural justice 'ha[s] no relevance to the question of negligence': [1995] 2 AC 633, 736.

grounds. In the first place it is said that there is no non-circular way of classifying decisions as policy or operational: a policy decision is simply one which can lead to liability in negligence only if it is also *Wednesbury*-unreasonable, whereas an operational decision is one to which this condition does not apply, and it is ultimately up to the court, according to its own willingness to award a tort remedy, to decide into which category to place any particular decision.[61]

At first sight, this criticism might seem exaggerated. In some cases the policy-operational distinction seems intuitively attractive and relatively easy to apply. For example, in the *Dorset Yacht Co* case[62] a distinction could be drawn between, on the one hand, a decision to have a system of low-security penal institutions for young offenders which raised important issues of policy; and, on the other, an 'operational' decision by guards to relax security procedures for their own convenience for which no policy justification could be found. Again, in a case like *Anns v. Merton LBC*[63] a distinction could plausibly be drawn between, on the one hand, a (policy) decision on financial grounds only to inspect every third building site; and, on the other, an (operational) decision by an inspector to have only a cursory glance at a particular site because he or she trusted the builder. It is also easy to see a decision about how to handle a strike[64] as a policy decision; and the issuing of an inaccurate certificate by a land registry clerk,[65] or failure to provide a safe system of work for employees,[66] or failure by the police to protect a prisoner from suicide,[67] or nuisance consisting of failure to remove tree roots,[68] as operational lapses.

---

[61] Note that the distinction between policy and operational decisions is not a distinction between the making of decisions and the execution of decisions. For example, a decision to establish a system of low-security prisons for the sake of rehabilitation might be held to be a policy decision. If a prisoner escaped as a result of the execution of that decision (by setting up a low-security prison), an allegation that the execution of the decision was an unreasonable course of action would raise exactly the same policy issues as an allegation that the decision was unreasonable. Conversely, if executing a particular decision is an operational matter, so is the decision itself. The distinction between policy and operations turns on whether the claimant's allegations of tortious conduct raise issues that are inappropriate to be judged according to the ordinary private law of tort.

[62] [1970] AC 1004.

[63] [1978] AC 728.

[64] As in *Meade v. Haringey LBC* [1979] 1 WLR 624.

[65] As in *Ministry of Housing and Local Government v. Sharp* [1970] 2 QB 223.

[66] e.g. *Walker v. Northumberland CC* [1995] ICR 702; *Waters v. Metropolitan Police Commissioner* [2000] 1 WLR 1607.

[67] *Orange v. Chief Constable of West Yorkshire Police* [2002] QB 347.

[68] *Delaware Mansions Ltd v. Westminster City Council* [2002] 1 AC 321.

However, other cases are much more difficult. For example, in *Bird v. Pearce*[69] road markings that indicated traffic priorities at an intersection were obliterated when the road was resurfaced. The markings were not repainted immediately and the council had decided 'as a matter of policy' not to erect temporary priority signs at intersections in such circumstances. But the council was held liable on ordinary negligence principles for creating a danger of physical injury and damage and not taking reasonable steps to remove it. Similarly, in *Reffell v. Surrey CC*[70] a child was injured when her hand went through a glass swing-door which she was trying to control. It was held that the school authority was in breach of its statutory duty to ensure that school premises are safe. This duty is rather open-textured and could be interpreted so as to leave to school authorities a considerable degree of discretion to decide how much to spend on safety and the level of safety to be aimed at. It was held, however, that the duty was 'absolute' in the sense that it was for the authority to secure the safety of pupils, and that the test of breach was objective in the sense that it was for the court, not the authority, to decide what 'reasonable safety' meant. There was no evidence in the case as to whether the council which, according to the judge, appreciated the risk presented by such doors (which existed in a number of older schools), had consciously decided for reasons of economy or otherwise not to replace such doors or modify them to render them safe. The judge surmised that the council simply waited for a major refurbishment of old schools or for a breakage before replacing such doors. Such an approach may have been *ultra vires*, but the clear implication of the judgment is that even if the council had genuinely decided not to replace all such doors immediately, an action for breach of statutory duty would still have lain because the authority's duty was to secure safety, not to make a valid decision whether to secure it or not. These cases show that it is ultimately for the court to decide whether an impugned decision raises policy issues which it is prepared to leave to the defendant authority to decide subject only to the requirement that the decision not be *ultra vires*.[71]

The problematic nature of the policy-operational distinction is also illustrated by *Rigby v. Chief Constable of Northamptonshire*[72] in which a decision not to acquire a particular type of CS-gas canister (the use of which did not create a fire risk) was held to be a policy decision, whereas a

[69] [1979] RTR 369.   [70] [1964] 1 WLR 358.
[71] See also *Vicar of Writtle v. Essex CC* (1979) 77 LGR 656.
[72] [1985] 1 WLR 1242.

decision on a particular occasion to use a canister of a type which did create a fire risk, even though a fire-engine was not present, was an operational decision. It could be argued that decisions about how to deal with particular situations should be left to the police[73] to at least the same extent as a decision to purchase one type of canister rather than another.

It has been said[74] that decisions as to the allocation of scarce resources (e.g. a decision on financial grounds to reduce policing levels at a protest site) or decisions deliberately to take risks (e.g. by establishing low-security penal institutions for the sake of rehabilitation) are policy decisions. But the cases we have just considered suggest that there are certain interests (such as the safety of persons or property) which the courts may not allow governmental bodies to jeopardize for the sake of economy; and the *Rigby* case suggests that courts will not always allow public bodies to take risks which endanger persons or property. Whether financial stringency or the benefits of risk-taking will protect a defendant from tort liability depends on how much weight the court gives to the interests thereby put in jeopardy relative to the interests served by the decision being challenged. The more weight the court gives to the interests served by the decision the more likely it is to classify it as a policy decision.

The second ground on which the use of the policy/operational distinction has been criticized is that it rests on an illogicality. According to *Anns*, a policy decision could form the basis of a negligence action if it was *ultra vires*. The purpose of the *ultra vires* requirement was to ensure that courts would not interfere unduly with the discretion of public authorities by making judgments about the propriety, from a policy point of view, of their decisions. On the other hand, once the *ultra vires* condition was met, it appeared to be open to a court to decide that the decision was negligent or, in other words, that in making it the authority had not struck a reasonable balance between the interest of the claimant in being free from injury or damage and the public interest in what the authority had decided to do. But surely in doing this the court was doing exactly what the legislature had intended the authority to do, namely to balance the interests of private individuals against the public interest. The difficulty with the *Anns* formula was that it made *ultra vires* a precondition of liability but not the ground of liability. It may have been with this

---

[73] See also *Hill v. Chief Constable of West Yorkshire* [1989] AC 53, 63 *per* Lord Keith; *R v. Chief Constable of Sussex, ex p. International Trader's Ferry Ltd* [1999] 2 AC 418.

[74] e.g. by Lord Browne-Wilkinson in *X v. Bedfordshire CC*.

criticism in mind that Lord Browne-Wilkinson held in the *Bedfordshire* case that the exercise of a statutory discretion could be actionable in negligence only if it was *Wednesbury*-unreasonable: the effect of this requirement is that *Wednesbury* unreasonableness is both a precondition of liability for negligence in the exercise of a statutory discretion and also the definition of negligence in the exercise of a statutory discretion. Once the court has decided that a discretion was exercised unreasonably in the *Wednesbury* sense it has also decided that it was exercised negligently. Whether intentionally or not, Lord Browne-Wilkinson seems to have met this second criticism of the *Anns* scheme by imposing as a precondition of actionability in negligence a ground of public law illegality that implies negligence.

The third criticism which has been directed at the *Anns* scheme is that the policy-operational distinction is unnecessary because it adds nothing to the ordinary concepts of the tort of negligence. The test for negligent . conduct (that is, basically, unreasonableness) is, according to this view, flexible enough to overcome the difficulties with which the distinction was designed to deal: in deciding whether a public authority has acted reasonably the court can take account of its responsibilities to the public interest.[75] A good illustration of this point is provided by a nuisance case, *Page Motors Ltd v. Epsom & Ewell BC*.[76] A group of gypsies had camped in a field owned by the council beside which ran a road that gave access to the claimant's automotive garage. The claimant's business suffered because the behaviour of the gypsies discouraged customers from using the access road. The council obtained an eviction order against the gypsies, but delayed for five years in enforcing it because of political pressure from the county council and from Westminster to await a wider-ranging solution to the gypsy 'problem'. It was apparently argued on behalf of the council, in effect, that their decision not to enforce the eviction order was a policy decision which should only be actionable if it was *ultra vires*. The Court of Appeal rejected this argument and held that the liability of the council as occupier had to be judged according to the ordinary principles of the tort of nuisance: had their actions interfered unreasonably with the use and enjoyment of the claimant's land? However, the court then proceeded to hold that because the council was a public body, it was reasonable for it to go through the 'democratic process of

---

[75] S.H. Bowman and M.J. Bailey, 'The Policy/Operational Dichotomy—A Cuckoo in the Nest' [1986] *CLJ* 430; 'Public Authority Negligence Revisited' [2000] *CLJ* 85.

[76] (1982) 80 LGR 337.

consultation' before deciding when and how to abate the nuisance; and so the council was justified in delaying longer before acting than a private landowner would have been (although not five years). Another relevant way in which the concept of unreasonable conduct in the tort of negligence is helpfully flexible is that it is sometimes (notably in actions against doctors) given a meaning very similar to *Wednesbury* unreasonableness. So it is not necessary to introduce the policy/operational distinction in order to introduce the idea of *Wednesbury* unreasonableness into the tort of negligence.

The thrust of this third criticism is not that the law of tort should apply to public bodies in exactly the same way as it applies to private individuals. It allows that there might be some policy decisions of public bodies for which there ought not to be liability in tort. Rather it argues that the policy-operational distinction is an unnecessarily inflexible way of providing the desirable level of non-liability.

There seems little doubt that understood as a sharp dichotomy, or as a basis for creating areas of complete immunity form tort liability, the policy/operational distinction is open to serious objection. On the other hand, the basic idea that the distinction captures is of continuing normative attraction. This is the judgment that in certain areas courts should exercise restraint in holding public functionaries liable to pay tort damages. Attempts (most notably in *X v. Bedfordshire CC*) to lay down abstract principles to give effect to this judgment have been largely unsuccessful. Under the influence of the ECtHR, the House of Lords has adopted a more fact-sensitive approach which perhaps meets the major criticisms of the policy/operational distinction. The result may be that in order to understand the tort liability of public functionaries we need to focus on the way the law of tort applies to particular functions rather than on general principles of tort liability. This may be an area in which the 'general-principles' approach to administrative law (see 1.5) has little to teach us.

11.5 MISFEASANCE IN A PUBLIC OFFICE

All the torts we have considered so far have their origin in and derive their basic characteristics from private law. There is one tort that can be called a public law tort because it applies only to the activities of public functionaries. This tort is called 'misfeasance in a public office'. There has been considerable academic discussion of its origins and status and of technical matters such as the meaning of the term 'public office'. The only point which needs to be made here is that the tort is only committed if either (1) a public power is exercised with the intention of injuring the claimant; or (2) the official knew that the conduct complained of was *ultra vires* and would probably injure the claimant[77] or, at least, cause an injury of the type the claimant suffered.[78] As a result, the tort is of quite limited value and importance as a means of controlling the ordinary run of inadvertent governmental illegality. In *R v. Secretary of State for Transport, ex p. Factortame Ltd (No. 4)*[79] the ECJ decided that the government could be held liable to pay damages to individuals for loss suffered as a result of serious breaches of EC law. The court also held that any requirement of fault (such as that for misfeasance in a public office) over above the requirement of a serious breach of EC law was inconsistent with EC law. It remains to be seen whether this decision will have any impact on the rules of governmental damages liability in purely domestic cases. Past experience suggests that pressure will sooner or later build up to bring domestic law into line with EC law.

It should also be noted in this context that one of the few grounds on which exemplary damages may be awarded in a tort action is where a body or official has been guilty of 'oppressive, arbitrary or unconstitutional action'[80] in exercise of a governmental (or 'public') function.[81] For example, exemplary damages are sometimes awarded against the police in actions for false imprisonment or malicious prosecution; and they can be awarded in a suitable case of misfeasance in a public office.[82]

---

[77] *Three Rivers DC v. Bank of England (No. 3)* [2003] 2 AC 1.
[78] *Akenzua v. Secretary of State for the Home Department* [2003] 1 WLR 741.
[79] [1996] QB 404. [80] *Rookes v. Barnard* [1964] AC 1129.
[81] *Bradford City MC v. Arora* [1991] 2 QB 507.
[82] *Kuddus v. Chief Constable of Leicestershire Constabulary* [2002] 2 AC 122.

12

Contract

In order to understand the role of the legal concept of contract and of the law of contract in the performance of public functions, it is helpful to distinguish between contract as a medium of exchange and contract as a technique of governance or regulation. In relation to the former, the main topics to be discussed are 'public procurement'—that is, the process of acquisition of goods and services for public purposes—and the application of rules of contractual liability to public functionaries. Examples of contracting used as a technique of governance include 'NHS contracts' (i.e. arrangements between 'providers' and 'purchasers' within the National Health Service) and 'framework documents' that regulate the relationship between government departments (such as the Department for Work and Pensions) and their executive agencies (such as Jobcentre Plus). The main focus of contract as a form of governance is regulation of the provision of public services to citizens, as opposed to the acquisition of goods and services by public functionaries. However, the distinction between these two notions of contract and contracting is not watertight. From a legal point of view, the similarities between them are as important as the differences. The significance of both will become clearer as the discussion progresses.

12.1 CONTRACT AS A MEDIUM OF EXCHANGE

Public procurement is big business. Non-military procurement by central government is worth some £13 billion a year. When military procurement and procurement by local authorities and other publicly funded entities is taken into account, the figure is very much higher. Contracts for public works and for purchase of goods and services by public authorities and public utilities account for around 14 per cent of the gross domestic product of the European Union. The main objectives of public procurement policy are value-for-money through competition, and efficiency in the procurement process.[1] Because contract is the legal form of procurement activity, these goals have to be pursued within the framework of contract law, as well as EC public procurement law. This section is concerned with that framework.

12.1.1 THE BASIC PRINCIPLE

The principle that government should be subject to the ordinary law of the land lies at the bottom of the law of public contracts, both in respect of contracts made with public bodies generally and in respect of contracts made with central government (the Crown) in particular. Prior to 1947 the fiat (or leave) of the Attorney-General had to be obtained by a litigant who wished to bring an action for breach of contract against the Crown, but this special procedural protection for the Crown was abolished by s. 1 of the Crown Proceedings Act 1947. Section 17 of the Act overcomes technical obstacles to suit which may arise if the department of central government which the claimant wishes to sue is not strictly a legal person (i.e. if it is not incorporated). The 1947 Act has, therefore, removed procedural obstacles to suing central government for breach of contract.

12.1.2 PRECONTRACTUAL NEGOTIATIONS AND THE MAKING OF CONTRACTS

The traditional attitude of the English common law to the making of contracts[2] is embodied in the phrase 'freedom of contract': parties are entitled, subject to any relevant legal limitations, to make what contracts they like with whomever they choose, or not to contract at all. This common law principle applies as much to public contracting parties as to private citizens; and it applies as much to the statutory contracting powers of public bodies as to the common law contracting power of the Crown. This laissez-faire approach of the common law has had some very important consequences. The first is that as a general principle, the common law contracting power of the Crown has traditionally not been subject to judicial review. In this respect, it was treated like a prerogative power. However, we have seen that common law powers of the Crown may now be subject to judicial review,[3] and it remains to be seen what effect this development in the law will have on the reviewability of the

---

[1] See, for instance, *Modernising Procurement*, a Report by the Comptroller and Auditor General, HC 808/1998–9.
[2] Here we are concerned chiefly with contracts for the procurement of goods and services. The position regarding government employees is considered in 12.1.5.
[3] See 3.2.5.

common law contracting powers of central government.[4] Government procurement often raises policy issues which the courts may be unwilling to become involved in. This traditional lack of judicial control over central government contracting is matched by a lack of Parliamentary control.[5] Government contracting is also beyond the jurisdiction of the central[6] and local government ombudsmen.

A second important consequence of the freedom-of-contract approach is that the contracting powers of public functionaries may be used for any purpose which is not prohibited by law (including the rule that discretionary powers must not be fettered, which was discussed earlier (see 8.2.3) and is discussed further later in this chapter). Indeed, it has been said that 'whatever the Crown may lawfully do it may do by means of contract'.[7] Particularly in the case of central government, the constitutional implications of freedom of contract are considerable. Contracting may provide a viable alternative to legislation in a variety of situations as a means of achieving government policy objectives; indeed, this possibility underpins the use of contract as a technique of governance. In the extreme case, the use of contractual rather than legislative techniques may enable the government (for a time at least) to evade the effects of the rule that Parliament cannot bind its successors.[8]

One aspect of this freedom to use contracts to achieve any lawful purpose is the possibility of pursuing ('collateral' or 'secondary') goals other than procuring required goods or services of a particular quality at the best possible price.[9] This may be done by means of express contractual terms; for example, from 1891 until 1983 resolutions of the House of Commons (the so-called 'Fair Wages Resolutions') required the insertion into government contracts of terms requiring the payment of minimum wages; and current policy requires all government contracts to contain a 'prompt payment clause' requiring contractors to pay sub-contractors within thirty days of invoice. It may be done in other ways, too. For instance, governments may wish to award contracts with a view to easing unemployment in selected areas, or to favour British manufacturers over foreign, or small firms over large.[10] Another technique is to 'blacklist' potential contractors

---

[4] S. Arrowsmith, 'Judicial Review and the Contractual Powers of Public Authorities' (1990) 106 *LQR* 275; D. Oliver, 'Judicial Review and the Shorthandwriters' [1993] *PL* 214.
[5] See 12.2.2, 16.1.   [6] See 17.2.2.
[7] C. Turpin, *Government Procurement and Contracts* (London, 1989), p. 84.
[8] See 8.3.3.
[9] Turpin, *Government Procurement and Contracts*, pp. 73–9.
[10] Such policies may have anti-competitive effects: T. Sharpe, 'Unfair Competition by Public Support of Private Enterprises' (1979) 95 *LQR* 205.

who do not, for example, employ a certain proportion of handicapped people or people from ethnic minorities. A much-publicized example of blacklisting occurred in 1978 when the Labour government sought by this means to enforce its policy of limiting maximum pay increases.[11] The use of contracting powers in this way is objectionable if it is done (as it can be) without legislative support or without Parliamentary approval, especially if the policy being pursued is controversial.[12]

In the 1980s and 1990s, increased emphasis was put on efficiency and value-for-money in public procurement at the expense of the pursuit of collateral policies. This development was given legal force by a set of EC Directives that require public contracts[13] of a certain value to be awarded on narrow financial criteria—lowest price or most economically advantageous tender.[14] The main aims of these Directives are to prevent discrimination in the award of public contracts by contracting entities in one Member State against nationals of other Member States, and to ensure publicity, transparency, and the application of objective criteria in the process of inviting tenders and awarding contracts.[15] Although the Directives limit the potential of procurement as a means of promoting collateral social purposes, the precise nature and extent of the limitation is unclear. Decisions of the ECJ suggest that imposing contractual conditions that promote social policies is more acceptable than choosing contractors on social-policy grounds.[16]

---

[11] G. Ganz, 'Comment' [1978] *PL* 333.

[12] T. Daintith, 'Regulation by Contract: The New Prerogative' [1979] *CLP* 41. For some interesting (and relatively uncontroversial) uses of contractual techniques *in lieu* of law reform see R. Lewis, 'Insurer's Agreements not to Enforce Strict Legal Rights: Bargaining with Government and in the Shadow of the Law' (1985) 48 *MLR* 275.

[13] The scope of the directives is defined institutionally. Concerning the impact of privatization see E.R. Manunza, 'Privatised Services and the Concept of "Bodies Governed by Public Law" in EC Directives on Public Procurement' (2003) 28 *European LR* 273.

[14] The Directives are implemented by the Public Works Contracts Regulations 1991, the Public Services Contracts Regulations 1993, the Public Supply Contracts Regulations 1995, the Public Contracts (Amendments) Regulations 2000, the Utilities Contracts Regulations 1996, the Utilities Contracts (Amendments) Regulations 2001, and the Public Contracts (Works, Services and Supply) and Utilities Contracts (Amendments) Regulations 2003. In 2003 the European Commission published a new draft procurement directive that will in due course replace the existing directives.

[15] For an example of the application of the EC rules see *R v. Portsmouth City Council, ex p. Coles* (1996) 95 LGR 494. The regulations listed in the previous note also implement the Remedies Directive by providing for mechanisms and remedies in respect of breach of EC procurement rules: J. M. Fernández Martín, *The EC Public Procurement Rules: A Critical Analysis* (Oxford, 1996), pp. 255–66.

[16] S. Arrowsmith, 'The EC Procurement Directives, National Procurement Policies and Better Governance: the Case for a New Approach' (2002) 27 *European LR* 3, 12–13.

The contracting powers of public bodies other than the Crown (most notably, local authorities) are statutory, and although such powers are often drafted in extremely wide terms, thus preserving a great deal of freedom of action, contracts which do not fall within the limits of those powers will be *ultra vires* and unenforceable.[17] Moreover, the exercise of statutory contracting powers may be subject to judicial review in cases where a statutory power is exceeded or abused, or where a contract is made for purposes other than those envisaged by the empowering statute.[18] Another way of making these points it to say that contracting is not, as such, a function of local authorities, but rather a technique for performing statutory functions. The power to contract is subsidiary to the authority's specific functions.

The freedom of local authorities to pursue collateral policy objectives through contracting has been greatly curtailed by statute. Part II of the Local Government Act 1986[19] prohibits the publication by local authorities of material that appears to be designed to affect public support for a political party.[20] More directly, s. 17 of the Local Government Act 1988 prohibits local authorities (and a variety of other bodies) from exercising contracting powers (such as inviting tenders, awarding contracts, approving sub-contractors, and terminating contracts) on 'non-commercial' grounds.[21] However, express provision is made in s 18 to enable local authorities to comply with their statutory obligation to promote good race

---

[17] e.g. *Hazell v. Hammersmith and Fulham LBC* [1992] 2 AC 1 ('interest-rate swapping' agreements illegal); *Credit Suisse v. Allerdale BC* [1997] QB 306. But see Local Government (Contracts) Act 1997, which selectively modifies this rule. For more detailed discussion see I. Leigh, *Law, Politics and Local Democracy* (Oxford, 2000), pp. 38–62, 283–4, 298–9.

[18] *R v. Lewisham LBC, ex p. Shell UK Ltd* [1988] 1 All ER 938. In practice, one of the most important contexts in which this issue arises is land-use planning. Planning authorities have power to make contracts with developers, and such contracts are often used to obtain public amenities, such as parks, nurseries, and roadworks, at the developer's expense. The power is very wide and creates the danger that planning authorities may engage in a form of extortion. It enables authorities to achieve outcomes that could not be secured by the imposition of conditions on the grant of planning permission. Even so, such contracts must bear some relationship to planning objectives. See further T. Cornford, 'Planning Gains and the Government's New Proposals on Planning Obligations' [2002] *JPL* 796. It may be possible to challenge particular contract terms or the exercise of powers under existing contracts on the ground of *ultra vires*. See further Leigh, *Government Procurement and Contracts*, pp. 290–2.

[19] As amended by s. 27 of the Local Government Act 1988.

[20] H.F. Rawlings and C.J.C Willmore, 'The Local Government Act 1986' (1987) 50 *MLR* 52; Leigh, *Law, Politics and Local Democracy*, pp. 74–8.

[21] M. Radford, 'Competition Rules: The Local Government Act 1988' (1988) 51 *MLR* 747; Fernández Martín, *The EC Public Procurement Rules: A Critical Analysis*, pp. 46–53. See also Local Government Act 1999, s. 19.

relations. Section 20 imposes on authorities a duty, if asked, to give reasons for decisions made in exercise of contracting powers, and it makes provision for remedies. The EC Directives mentioned above also apply to local authorities, and they place even greater restrictions on contracting than does the 1988 Act by preventing even some commercial criteria being taken into account in the awarding of contracts.

A third important consequence of freedom of contract is that the common law has never developed any general principle allowing parties to a contract to obtain relief from what may be seen as unfair consequences of inequality of bargaining power. The government has very considerable bargaining power both by reason of its constitutional and economic strength[22] and because government contracts are often valuable and long-term. This power may enable it to secure more favourable terms and conditions than any private contractor could obtain (although, of course, large private corporations can also wield great bargaining power).

In practice, most government contracts are made in standard form.[23] There are two main sets of standard contract terms, one for construction contracts and the other for supply contracts. Contracts of central government typically contain a number of special terms (which may be seen as being designed to protect the public interest): for example, terms giving the government more control over performance than is usual in contracts between private parties, and giving the government certain powers of unilateral variation and termination. There are some statutory provisions which constrain government bodies in exercising their bargaining strength to the full. The provisions of the Unfair Contract Terms Act 1977 apply to public authorities (including central government) by virtue of the definition of 'business' in s. 14.[24] The Act renders ineffective certain contractual terms which purport to exclude or restrict liability for negligence or breach of contract. Public authorities (including central government) are bound in their contracting activities[25] to comply with the provisions of legislation which prohibits discrimination on grounds of sex or race.[26]

---

[22] For instance, the Ministry of Defence is the single largest customer of British industry: Turpin, *Government Procurement and Contracts*, p. 10.

[23] Turpin, *Government Procurement and Contracts*, pp. 105–11.

[24] The government is also bound by the EC-derived Unfair Terms in Consumer Contracts Regulations 1995.

[25] But not in legislating (*R v. Entry Clearance Officer, Bombay, ex p. Amin* [1983] 2 AC 818) unless the legislation conflicts with EC law or is incompatible with a Convention right.

[26] For instance, in the early 1990s the Ministry of Defence had to pay large amounts of compensation to women dismissed from the armed forces on becoming pregnant.

However, it should not be thought that the balance of contracting power is always in favour of the government. A common clause in government contracts makes provision for recovery of excess profits made by the contractor.[27] This type of clause is designed to protect the government in areas, such as defence procurement, where there may be very little choice of contractor and where, because of the highly advanced and innovatory nature of the work being done, it may difficult to assess tenders or to monitor performance. The mechanisms for preventing and detecting fraud and the making of 'excess' profits have often proved, in practice, to be ineffectual. Skill on the part of purchasing officers and sound management within purchasing units is crucial in ensuring that the government gets a good deal. Also important is the willingness of individuals (especially employees of contractors) to notify government of fraud, waste, and mismanagement on the part of contractors, especially in the defence industry. Legal protection for 'whistleblowers' is discussed in 15.3.

Despite the basically laissez-faire approach of the common law, the courts have developed a few constraints on the exercise of public contracting power. First, it will be recalled that licensing activities of monopolistic private contractual bodies have been subjected to judicial review for the sake, for example, of enforcing compliance with the rules of natural justice.[28] Since the effect of granting a licence in such cases would be to create a contractual relationship between the body and the licensee, such judicial control places a constraint on pre-contractual activity. Secondly, the common law has taken some notice of the fact that the pre-contractual activities of public authorities are usually conducted according to non-statutory rules, policies, and guidelines. In the case of central government, the Office of Government Commerce (within the Treasury) plays an important part in formulating such rules (etc.) as do purchasing departments themselves. Consultation with organizations representing contractors is also common.[29] Most local authorities adopt uniform standing orders published by central government and these contain provisions on tendering and contracting.[30] In addition, central government may issue circulars to local authorities recommending the adoption of particular contract terms. In practice, local authorities normally use a standard form of building contract published by the Royal Institute of British Architects. In *R v. Hereford Corporation, ex p. Harrower*[31] it was held that the

---

[27] Turpin, *Government Procurement and Contracts*, pp. 175–9.   [28] See 3.1.
[29] Turpin, *Government Procurement and Contracts*, pp. 61–6.
[30] See Local Government Act 1972, s. 135.
[31] [1970] 1 WLR 1424.

applicants were entitled to apply for mandamus to force the local authority to comply with its own standing orders regulating the process by which tenders for contracts were to be invited. We have also seen that the courts are prepared to review the substance, application, and interpretation of non-statutory rules on a variety of grounds. There is no apparent reason why this development should not apply to non-statutory rules dealing with contracting by public authorities. Government contracts are highly valuable assets, and the courts should be prepared to enforce standards of fairness on government in its dealings with tenderers and contractors.

Finally, we might note that failure to comply with a published tendering procedure may itself constitute a breach of contract;[32] and also that the Parliamentary Ombudsman may recommend that compensation be paid when a government body withdraws from contractual negotiations.[33]

12.1.3 THE FUNDING OF CENTRAL GOVERNMENT CONTRACTS[34]

In 1865 in *Churchward v. R.*[35] it was held that unless, at the time a contract was made on behalf of the Crown, sufficient funds had been voted by Parliament to meet the government's obligations under the contract, no valid contract came into existence. In other words, the existence of a valid contract was contingent upon the availability of funds for its performance. It followed that if funds had not been allocated, the government could not be sued or held liable for breach of contract if it did not perform its contractual obligations. Although there is no modern English authority on the point, it seems likely that English courts would accept the theory laid down in an Australian case[36] that the availability of funds is relevant to the performance of the contract and to the enforcement of any judgment for damages for breach, but that lack of funds does not prevent a valid contract being made.

12.1.4 THE LAW OF AGENCY

Contracts with public authorities are often made by an officer or agent acting on behalf of the authority. Indeed, the Crown can only contract through some natural or legal person acting on its behalf: the term 'the

---

[32] *Blackpool and Fylde Aero Club Ltd v. Blackpool BC* [1990] 3 All ER 25.

[33] P. Brown, 'The Ombudsman: Remedies for Misinformation' in G. Richardson and H. Genn, *Administrative Law and Government Action* (Oxford, 1994), pp. 325–6.

[34] Turpin, *Government Procurement and Contracts*, pp. 91–4.

[35] (1865) LR 1 QB 173.

[36] *New South Wales v. Bardolph* (1943) 52 CLR 455.

Crown' refers collectively to the executive branch of central government. However, when a duly authorized officer or agent of the Crown makes a contract on behalf of the Crown, that contract is made with the Crown.[37] The importance of this is that the contract attracts the privileges and immunities of the Crown.

In the ordinary law of agency the principal is bound by a contract made by the agent provided the latter actually had authority to enter the contract ('actual authority') or if the principal 'held out' (that is, represented by words or conduct) that the agent had authority which he or she did not actually have ('ostensible' or 'apparent' authority)[38] or, perhaps, if entering such a contract would usually be within the authority of someone in the agent's position ('usual' authority).[39] If the agent did not possess authority of any of these kinds, the principal is not bound but the agent can be sued for 'breach of (an implied) warranty of authority', that is, for holding out that he or she had authority. These rules apply to public authorities with one unjustifiable exception, namely that a Crown agent cannot be sued for breach of (an implied) warranty of authority.[40]

12.1.5 GOVERNMENT EMPLOYMENT

The relationship between many government bodies and their employees is an ordinary employment relationship. However, the position of Crown employees ('civil servants') is peculiar. It is not clear that the relationship between the Crown and its employees is contractual;[41] and the basic common law rule is that Crown employees are dismissable at will,[42] although this rule has been considerably modified by statute.[43] As we have seen, uncertainty about the status of civil servants has generated much litigation about the scope of judicial review.[44] While the legal position of civil servants may, in some respects, be precarious, in practice government

---

[37] *Town Investments Ltd v. Department of Environment* [1978] AC 359.

[38] The 'holding out' must be by the principal and not by the agent: *Attorney-General for Ceylon v. Silva* [1953] AC 461.

[39] G.H. Treitel, 'Crown Proceedings: Some Recent Developments' [1957] *PL* 321, 336–7.

[40] *Dunn v. Macdonald* [1897] 1 QB 401 and 555. Concerning the tort liability of an unauthorized agent see *Kavanagh v. Continental Shelf Company (No. 46) Ltd* [1993] 2 NZLR 648.

[41] For certain purposes it is deemed to be: Employment Act 1988 s. 30(1)(a). See generally S. Fredman and G. Morris, 'Civil Servants: A Contract of Employment?' [1988] *PL* 58; 'Judicial Review and Civil Servants: Contracts of Employment Declared to Exist' [1991] *PL* 485. In *Council of Civil Service Unions v. Minister for the Civil Service* [1985] AC 374 the power to employ civil servants was treated as a prerogative power.

[42] *Dunn v. R.* [1896] 1 QB 116; *Terrell v. Secretary of State for the Colonies* [1953] 2 QB 482.

[43] Employment Rights Act 1996, Part X and ss. 191–3.   [44] See 6.5.

jobs are relatively secure; although the appointment of senior civil servants (such as chief executives of executive agencies) for fixed terms is now common.

Like private individuals and corporations, public bodies are free (subject to legal limitations such as those contained in sex and race discrimination legislation) to employ or to refuse to employ whom they will. An allegation sometimes made, especially about central government in recent years, is that although public employees who advise politicians are meant to be politically neutral and not to allow their own political views to colour the advice they give, the political views of applicants for politically-sensitive posts have become a relevant factor in recruiting: The implication is that the government appoints people with views congenial to its own in the hope of receiving acceptable advice. In the very nature of the case, such allegations are almost impossible to substantiate; but it is, perhaps, worth noting that there are private vetting agencies that maintain lists of persons with certain political views which they make available to employers, and that the activities of such agencies have been investigated by the Employment Committee of the House of Commons.[45] Moreover, one of the major areas of investigation by the Nolan Committee on Standards in Public Life was appointment by the government to membership of executive non-departmental public bodies and NHS bodies. There was much concern about the criteria of appointment, and the Nolan Committee recommended that the overriding principle should be merit.[46]

It should also be noted that EC law prohibits discrimination against nationals of other Member States in recruitment to most civil service jobs.[47]

12.1.6 LIABILITY FOR BREACH OF CONTRACT

It is extremely rare for disputes arising out of the performance of government contracts to be the subject of litigation. Such disputes are usually resolved by informal negotiation between the government and the contractor or, if this does not succeed, by arbitration.[48] An important

---

[45] Second Report: Recruitment Practices (1990–1).

[46] Cm. 2850-I (1995). See also House of Commons Public Administration Select Committee, 'Government by Appointment: Opening Up the Patronage State', Fourth Report (HC 165, 2002/3).

[47] G.S. Morris, 'Employment in Public Services: The Case for Special Treatment' (2000) 20 *OJLS* 167, 176–7.

[48] Turpin, *Government Procurement and Contracts*, pp. 221–6.

reason for this is that the relationship between government and its contractors is often more in the nature of a long-term cooperative venture for mutual advantage than a one-off commercial deal. Within such a relationship, recourse to courts to settle disagreements will often seem inappropriate and possibly counter-productive. On the other hand, when contractual disputes are settled without recourse to a third party adjudicator, there is a danger that any inequalities of bargaining power between the parties may distort the outcome.[49] This may be one reason why, for example, governments have often had such difficulty in dealing with excess profit-making by contractors.

In general, the law governing the liability of public functionaries for breach of contract is the same as that governing the liability of private individuals and corporations. But a qualification must be added to this general position which is easy to state but not so easy to apply. Because public bodies have to consider the wider public interest in fulfilling their obligations under contracts, there may be circumstances in which the demands of public policy provide good grounds for a public body to refuse to perform its obligations to the other contracting party. In such cases the interests and rights of the individual contractor are subordinated to the demands of public policy. In other words, the law recognizes what might be called a public policy defence or immunity which public bodies can sometimes plead in actions against them for breach of contract. The difficulty is to define the scope of this defence or immunity, to specify when it will be available.

The other side of the same coin is that (as we have seen)[50] it is illegal for a public functionary to fetter its statutory discretion by contract or undertaking. It is important to note at this point that the principle against fettering refers to both contracts and (non-contractual) undertakings. Here we are concerned with contracts, but undertakings which are not contractually binding should not be ignored because we have already seen that failure to perform such undertakings can be illegal.[51] In *The Amphitrite*[52] the owners of a foreign ship unsuccessfully sued the government for failure to honour a promise to release the ship from British waters after it had discharged its cargo. The judgment of Rowlatt J is unclear as to whether the promise was contractually binding or not. If the case stands for the proposition that non-contractual undertakings can never be binding, it would now seem to be incorrect. It has long been

---

[49] Ibid. 236–9.   [50] See 8.3.3.
[51] See 8.3.4.   [52] [1921] 3 KB 500.

recognized that the courts are sometimes reluctant to find the requisite intention to create legal relations in the case of agreements between government and citizen. It does not follow from this that government bodies ought never to be prevented from going back on non-contractual undertakings which have raised legitimate expectations and induced reliance, when there is no good policy reason for allowing the government to dishonour its undertaking. Conversely, on the facts of *The Amphitrite*, it seems clear that a plea of the exigencies of war would be treated by a court as justifying the government going back on its promise regardless of whether it was contractual or not.

As we have already seen, the rule against fettering requires the court to make a value judgement about the relative claims of the individual contractor and the demands of public policy which the discretion is designed to serve, and in the light of this value judgement to decide whether the contract or undertaking is an illegal fetter on the proper exercise of the discretionary power. The question facing the court is not essentially different from that facing a court confronted with a plea of public policy in defence to an action for breach of contract. The only difference lies in the way the question is typically raised in practice. The fettering principle is usually relevant when a party seeks to force the public functionary to exercise its discretion, or seeks to challenge the exercise of a discretion which has been exercised in accordance with, or contrary to, the demands of a contract or undertaking. The plea of public policy as a defence typically arises in cases in which the contractor seeks to enforce the contract or to recover damages for breach of contract. It is important to realize that the same basic issue ties the two areas together, because it serves to show that any sharp division between the so-called public law obligation not to fetter the exercise of discretion and the private law contractual obligations of public bodies is unwarranted. The law of public contracts is basically an application of public law principles to the ordinary law of contract leading to certain modifications of private law principles in their application to public functions.

Most of the cases relevant to this topic have already been discussed.[53] Brief mention need be made of only two cases. *The Amphitrite*[54] has always been the source of much difficulty. In the first place, Rowlatt J seems to have thought that the public policy defence only applied to 'non-commercial contracts'; but this limitation would make it irrelevant to most cases. Secondly, the case might be taken to support the extreme

---

[53] See 8.3.3.   [54] [1921] B 500.

proposition that a defence of public policy can be established merely on the public body's word that the demands of public policy justify non-performance of its undertakings. However, such an interpretation is out of line with the case-law generally. It seems clear that the courts retain for themselves the final power to judge the validity of a plea of public policy. In some areas, such as the conduct of war, the courts will no doubt exercise their power in a very restrained way and will usually accept official certificates as to the demands of public policy on the ground that the exercise of the power to wage war is unreviewable in the courts (this explains *The Amphitrite*).

There is no general rule that pleas of public policy cannot be questioned and evaluated by the court. This emerges quite clearly from *Commissioners of Crown Lands v. Page*[55] in which it was held that the requisitioning of premises in 1945 could not be held to be in breach of the implied covenant of quiet enjoyment in the lease. Devlin LJ was clearly not prepared to allow decisions about the demands of the conduct of the war to become the subject of judicial inquiry, but denied that this created a general privilege to escape from any contract, which a public body happened to find disadvantageous, by pleading the public interest. The court will scrutinize the plea and if it feels competent to do so, will judge its merits. In one sense there is always a legitimate public interest in public functionaries not being bound to disadvantageous contracts, but against that interest must be weighed the contractual rights of the contractor. A contract is a technique by which parties can restrict their freedom of action in the future, and a party to a contract cannot be free to ignore that restriction as it wishes. In this context, it should also be noted that the ability of local authorities to terminate contracts for 'non-commercial' reasons has been severely curtailed by statute.[56]

Finally, it should be said that the public policy defence will frequently be of little relevance in practice because government contracts often contain express provisions conferring on the government a right to withdraw from the contract which would entitle it to give effect to the legitimate demands of public policy.[57] In French law there are several doctrines dealing with the termination and variation of public contracts, and it is sometimes suggested that English law would do well to adopt something like them.[58]

---

[55] [1960] 2 QB 274.
[56] Local Goverrnment Act 1988, s. 17(4)(c)(ii); see also s. 19(7)(b).
[57] Turpin, *Government Procurement and Contracts*, pp. 243–6.
[58] L.N. Brown and J. Bell, *French Administrative Law*, 5th edn (Oxford, 1998), pp. 206–10.

12.1.7 *ULTRA VIRES* AND LIABILITY FOR BREACH OF CONTRACT

What is the relationship between the doctrine of *ultra vires* and the common law rules of breach of contract? In the first place, it should be noted that the rule that public functionaries must not fetter the exercise of their discretionary powers by contract implies a legal limitation on the contracting powers of a public bodies that does not attach to the contracting powers of private individuals or corporations. Secondly, it should be recalled that if the contracting powers of the body in question derive from statute, the statute might impose limitations on those powers, and failure to observe those restrictions may mean that the body has exercised its contract-making power *ultra vires*. *Ultra vires* contractual provisions are, as a matter of contract law, void and unenforceable. However, the contract as a whole may not be void if it would, without the *ultra vires* provision(s), be one which a reasonable person would have entered into.[59] Moreover, money or property transferred under an illegal contract may be recoverable.[60]

More difficult to disentangle is the relationship between the doctrine of *ultra vires* and a plea of public interest in answer to a claim for breach of contract. It might be thought that as a matter of general principle, a public body could not be held liable in contract in respect of the exercise by it of its public powers unless that exercise of power was *ultra vires*. Clearly, if a breach of contract consists of the *ultra vires* exercise of a discretionary power, the public body would not be allowed to argue that its breach was justified by the public interest. But in many contract cases the exact problem is that there is a conflict between two valid exercises of different discretionary powers namely, the contract-making power and some other power. Only if the contract is declared to be a void (and thus *ultra vires*) fetter on the other discretionary power will no such clash arise. In such cases the question which the courts seem to ask themselves, when faced with a plea of public interest, is whether the public interest pleaded is of sufficient importance that it should be held to outweigh the interests of the private contractor. For example, in *The Amphitrite*[61] and *Commissioners of Crown Lands v. Page*[62] the defendant's plea involved an appeal to the exigencies of war, and it is a well-established principle that the courts will not review the exercise of the power of waging war. By contrast, in

---

[59] *In re Staines Urban District Council's Agreement* [1969] 1 Ch 11.
[60] *Westdeutsche Landesbank Girozentral v. Islington LBC* [1994] 1 WLR 938. See also *Westdeutcshe Landesbank Girosentral v. Islington LBC* [1996] AC 669.
[61] [1921] 3 KB 500. [62] [1960] 2 QB 274.

Dowty Boulton Paul Ltd v. Wolverhampton Corporation[63] and in the *Birkdale Electric Supply Company* case,[64] the court seems to have decided that the public interest pleaded was not sufficient to justify treating the public body differently from a private contracting party by allowing the interests of the private contractor to be overridden.

It is clear, therefore, especially from the *Dowty Boulton Paul* case (in which the decision of the local authority was directly challenged and held to be valid,[65] but was also held to amount to a breach of contract)[66] that a claimant who sues for breach of contract in respect of the exercise of a discretionary power need not prove that the exercise was *ultra vires*. Contractual rights may be deemed worthy of protection even against *intra vires* acts if the public interest being served by the exercise of the power is not seen as sufficiently important to justify infringing the strong principle that contracts ought to be performed.

12.1.8 THE EFFECT OF A PLEA OF PUBLIC POLICY

Perhaps the most contentious issue in this area is the effect of a plea of public policy. It is possible to approach this question in a technical fashion by seeking private law analogies. For example, it is possible to treat at least some cases (involving, for example, declaration of war after the contract was made) in terms of the doctrine of frustration. If this analogy is used, a re-adjustment of the affairs of the parties along the lines provided for in the Law Reform (Frustrated Contracts) Act 1943 would be justified: that is, restitution of benefits given and received subject to a claim for expenses incurred. If a contract is treated as containing an implied term entitling the public body to refuse to perform if public policy so demands (as in *Commissioners of Crown Lands v. Page*), the technically correct result may be to leave the losses where they fall.

Perhaps a better approach than searching for private law analogies would be one which, while recognizing that there may be good grounds of public policy which justify releasing public bodies from contractual obligations, deals with the questions of monetary compensation for the disappointed contractor more flexibly. Restitution of benefits conferred on the public body by the other party would be fair and reasonable to the extent that this is possible. It may be, too, that if a contracting party has

---

[63] [1971] 1 WLR 204.   [64] [1926] AC 355.
[65] *Dowty Boulton Paul Ltd v. Wolverhampton Corporation (No. 2)* [1976] Ch 13.
[66] [1971] 1 WLR 204.

incurred irrecoverable expenses in performance of the contract, that party should be entitled to compensation for such reliance losses. Should the contractor ever be entitled to damages for profits which were expected from performance of the contract? There might be an argument for saying that although a contractor should never be expected to bear actual losses for the sake of the public interest, the contractor should not be allowed to make a profit at its expense. The most flexible of all approaches would be to leave the question of the availability and amount of monetary compensation to be decided by the court in the light of the circumstances of each individual case and of the interests of both the public and the private contractor. However, courts are unlikely to be prepared to get involved in the fine discriminations and policy judgments that such an approach requires. It would probably be better if the legislature laid down some general principles.

The argument for monetary compensation for contractors whose claims are met by a successful plea of public policy is strengthened if it is recalled that often the action in breach of contract will be *intra vires*. The appropriate question is, who should bear the risk that the public interest may justify and demand non-performance? When the question is put in this way the answer, fairly obviously, is 'the public'.

12.2 CONTRACT AS A TECHNIQUE OF GOVERNANCE AND AN INSTRUMENT OF REGULATION

12.2.1 THE NEW PUBLIC MANAGEMENT

An important plank of government policy in the past twenty-five years has been to increase 'efficiency' in the delivery of services to the public by the use of contracts or contract-like techniques. This programme is sometimes compendiously referred to as the 'New Public Management' (NPM).[67] In its name, public utilities such as gas and electricity providers have been sold off to private investors ('privatized'), and the provision of services as diverse as garbage collection, legal advice and prison management have been 'contracted-out' (or 'out-sourced'), which means that while a public body remains ultimately responsible for the conduct of the activity, it is actually carried out by a private-sector entity under the

---

[67] G. Drewry, 'The New Public Management' in J. Jowell and D. Oliver (eds), *The Changing Constitution*, 4th edn (Oxford, 2000), pp. 167–89.

terms of a contract with the public body.[68] An alternative to contracting-out is market-testing under which the public body can (continue to) provide the service if it can beat off competition from the private sector. The resulting arrangement may be referred to as 'contracting-in', although it will not typically involve a legally enforceable contract.

Many governmental activities that have not been contracted-out are nevertheless conducted along contractual lines. For instance, the provisions of the National Health Service and Community Care Act 1990 create an 'internal market' within the NHS. Central to the operation of this market is the so-called 'NHS contract', by means of which units within the NHS ('providers') can sell services to other units within the service ('purchasers').[69] Schools can 'opt out' of local authority control; they can handle their own budgets and compete for students provided they meet agreed performance targets. Under the 'Next Steps' programme[70] (which was implemented not by statute but by contract-like 'framework documents' of unclear legal status)[71] the Civil Service has been roughly subdivided into two sectors which might (crudely) be called the 'policy-making sector' and the 'policy-executing sector'. Policy-makers remain in the traditional Whitehall departmental structure while policy-executives are hived off into executive agencies. Agencies are given budgets and are expected to use them as economically as possible to meet performance targets set by the department of which they are satellites. The main aim of this reform of the civil service was to increase efficiency and financial accountability in the running of government programmes and to put the delivery of public services on a more business-like footing while stopping short of privatization. The 'Public Service Agreement'[72] is another contractual technique used within government to regulate and exercise financial control over performance of public functions.

Yet another aspect of NPM is the 'private finance initiative' (PFI). PFI has been described as 'the subset of public service procurement or gov-

---

[68] For the story of contracting-out by local authorities see Leigh, *Law, Politics and Local Democracy*, pp. 217–21, 309–23.

[69] A. Davies, *Accountability: A Public Law Analysis of Government by Contract* (Oxford, 2001).

[70] The official history of the Next Steps programme is D. Goldsworthy, *Setting Up Next Steps* (HMSO, 1991). See also P. Greer, *Transforming Central Government* (Buckingham, 1994). Executive agencies employ some 227,000 staff—just over half of the home civil service. Collectively they spend some £18 billion a year: The Comptroller and Auditor General, *The Role of Executive Agencies* (HC 525, 2002/3).

[71] They are not ordinary contracts because such agencies remain part of the Crown, which, in law, is a single indivisible entity.

[72] D. Oliver, *Constitutional Reform in the UK* (Oxford, 2003), pp. 212–13.

ernment contracting which is characterized by the fact that it involves private sector provision of capital assets, the use of which is then, as it were, rented out by the private sector either to the public authorities or directly to the public, or both'.[73] For example, a private contractor might build a public road in return for the right to levy tolls on road-users. In addition to the search for 'efficiency', reduction of public spending is a widely acknowledged motivation for PFI arrangements.

One of the aims of the use of contractual techniques in the provision of public services is to subject those who provide the services to forms of 'market-based' as opposed to 'public' accountability. Classic forms of public accountability include elections, answerability to Parliament via the doctrine of ministerial responsibility, and judicial review. The hallmarks of the market are competition, consumer choice and the setting of prices for goods and services according to the balance of supply and demand. Some aspects of NPM—such as contracting-out and the NHS internal market—involve competition between service-providers, while others—the creation of executive agencies, for instance—do not. But all are informed by the basic market principle that satisfying customers is one of the chief criteria of, and the main route to, success. The 'Citizen's Charter' (launched in 1991) was part of the strategy of restructuring the public sector along market lines. Its main principles were that those who provide public services should be set published targets to meet, that information about the services should be freely available to consumers, and that adequate avenues of complaint and forms of redress should be available to dissatisfied customers.[74]

12.2.2 NPM AND ACCOUNTABILITY

Restructuring of the public sector along contractual lines involved separating responsibility for deciding what services will be provided (policy-making) from responsibility for the provision of those services

---

[73] M. Freedland, 'Public Law and Private Finance—Placing the Private Finance Initiative in a Public Law Frame' [1998] *PL* 288, 290. See also M. Elsenaar, 'Law, Accountability and the Private Finance Initiative in the National Health Service' [1999] *PL* 35.

[74] See A. Barron and C. Scott, 'The Citizen's Charter Programme' (1992) 55 *MLR* 526; G. Drewry, 'Mr Major's Charter: Empowering the Consumer' [1993] *PL* 248. Charter principles were applied to local government by Part I of the Local Government Act 1992. The successor to the Citizen's Charter was the Service First programme: C. Scott, 'Regulation Inside Government: Re-Badging the Citizen's Charter' [1999] *PL* 595. The principles underlying these programmes (as developed in a 1999 White Paper, *Modernising Government*) are now promoted by the Prime Minister's Office for Public Service Reform. See also G. Drewry, 'Whatever Happened to the Citizen's Charter?' [2002] *PL* 9.

(policy-execution). This process raises difficult and important issues about the balance of market forms of accountability and traditional public modes of accountability.[75] In the first place, the distinction between policy-making and policy-execution is not clear-cut. One result of this is that policy-makers may wish to interfere with the day-to-day running of public services even when this has been hived off to an autonomous entity. This is not a new phenomenon. In the days when there were a significant number of nationalized industries, the idea was that broad policy issues relevant to their activities would be decided by government but that their day-to-day activities should be conducted as if the industry was in the private sector. In fact, Ministers often sought to interfere in the daily minutiae of nationalized industry business.[76] Similar problems may arise in relation to executive agencies, for instance. In 1995–6 there was a major dispute between the Director-General (chief executive) of the Prison Service (an executive agency) and the Home Secretary as a result of allegedly excessive interference by the latter in the day-to-day running of the Service, thus undermining the ability of the Director-General to run prisons efficiently and economically and to meet the targets set for the Service by the government.[77] Because there is no clear line between making policy and executing it, those who make it cannot afford to leave service providers completely free to meet their 'contractual targets' in their own way.

A second problem concerns the impact of contractualization on the accountability for the making of the policy which service-providers execute. The 'contract' can provide a basis for holding service-providers accountable for the way services are delivered, but it does nothing to secure accountability for decisions about what services will be provided. Such decisions remain the responsibility of the public body which made the arrangements for provision of the services. In the market, the law of supply and demand determines not only how goods and services are provided but also what goods and services are provided. By contrast, the very reason why government takes responsibility for the provision of services to the public is so that they can be distributed by non-market criteria—so that, for example, free or subsidized services can be provided for people who could not afford to pay for them in the market. Whereas

---

[75] See e.g. C. Scott, 'Accountability in the Regulatory State' (2000) 27 *J of Law and Society* 38.

[76] T. Prosser, *Nationalised Industries and Public Control* (Oxford, 1986).

[77] Drewry, 'The New Public Management', 182–3; M. Moran, *The British Regulatory State: High Modernism and Hyper-Innovation* (Oxford, 2003), pp. 130–1.

market criteria may be suitable for judging the way public services are provided, traditional forms of public accountability are appropriate and necessary for controlling decisions about what public services are to be provided, to whom, and on what basis. Because the line between policy-making and policy-execution is unclear, some fear that contractualization may make it easier for policy-makers to deny responsibility for aspects of government policy, for which they ought to be accountable to Parliament, by saying that they are matters for the policy executant.[78] Another aspect of this 'accountability deficit' is a function of the contractual capacity of the Crown (see 12.1.2). Whereas the making of primary—and, to a lesser extent, secondary—legislation is formally subject to Parliamentary scrutiny, central government does not need Parliamentary approval to make contracts. It may, for instance, enter into PFI and out-sourcing arrangements without reference to Parliament. And although the NHS internal market was established by statute, the Next Steps programme was put in place as an entirely internal and non-legislative reorganization of the civil service. It is true that Parliamentary committees can and do investigate the operation of executive agencies and their relationships with sponsoring departments; but Parliament played no significant part in this fundamental transformation of the conduct of public business.

Thirdly, contractualization raises difficult questions about the accountability of the service-provider. Service providers (such as executive agenices) are, of course, accountable under their contracts with the public body responsible for procuring the services, but such accountability is essentially a matter between the two contracting parties. In relation to services the provision of which is contracted out, the 'consumer' may have contractual rights against the service-provider. However, in some instances the citizen will not be in such a contractual relationship. For example, a prisoner in a privatized prison has no contract with the corporation that runs the prison. Nor do citizens have contractual rights against executive agencies, for instance.[79] It would seem important, therefore, that there be public accountability for the way public services are delivered as well as for decisions about what public services ought to be provided. Attempts to use judicial review to regulate provision of contracted-out services have met with mixed success (see

---

[78] R. Baldwin, ' "The Next Steps": Ministerial Responsibility and Government by Agency' (1988) 51 *MLR* 622; G. Drewry, 'Next Steps: The Pace Falters' [1990] *PL* 322.
[79] I. Harden, *The Contracting State* (Buckingham, 1992), ch. 5. Judicial review and human rights law may provide resources for challenging decisions of private-sector providers of public services (see 3.2.2). See also 11.2.1.1, n. 23.

3.2.2). In the case of executive agencies, their chief executives are answerable to the Public Accounts Committee of the House of Commons and can be called before other select committees. Parliamentary questions about the day-to-day activities of agencies are referred to the relevant chief executive, and the answers are published in Hansard. The position in relation to other public entities is less satisfactory. This is particularly so in respect of a large number of unelected bodies established by central government to deliver services and implement policies which have traditionally fallen within the sphere of elected local government.[80] These bodies are sometimes referred to as 'the new magistracy'. This name is an allusion to the way the provision of public services was supervised by unelected magistrates before the creation of local authorities in the nineteenth century. Although these bodies are the local analogue of executive agencies, unlike the latter, they are not directly related to departments of central government and are free from many forms of public accountability.[81]

12.2.3 CONCLUSION

NPM has brought about enormous changes in the way public services are provided. By stressing the values of the market it has put many public activities more or less beyond the reach of traditional forms of political and legal control. Whether one finds this a cause for rejoicing or regret will depend partly on the observer's political ideology. From one point of view, the very rationale of NPM is to reduce the size of the public sector and the reach of public law. From another point of view, the legal category of contract is mere form which should not be allowed to conceal or displace the public interest in the activity being carried on under its aegis. On this latter view, contractual activities and relationships should be subject to public controls when this is necessary in the wider interests of society.

At the same time, the deficit in external legal and political accountability that many have detected is not the whole story about NPM. The use of more or less formal contractual techniques for the provision of public services has, ironically perhaps, led to a significant increase in

---

[80] S. Weir, 'Quangos: Questions of Democratic Accountability' (1995) 48 *Parl Aff* 306. See generally D. Oliver, *Constitutional Reform in the UK* (Oxford, 2003), ch. 17.

[81] The House of Commons Public Administration Select Committee has recently estimated that there are *at least* 567,000 appointed members of non-departmental public bodies in the UK ranging from members of the House of Lords to school governors: 'Mapping the Quango State', Fifth Report (HC 367, 2000/1); 'Government by Appointment: Opening up the Patronage State', Fourth Report (HC 165, 2002/3).

legal and law-like regulation of the performance of public functions. The privatized utilities are subject to strong legal regulation by external public agencies such as OFWAT (the water industry regulator) and Ofcom (the communications industry regulator). Provision of public services by executive agencies and local authorities is subject to strong financial and political control by central government. Customer service charters, framework documents, public service agreements, and NHS contracts are all designed to spell out the obligations of public-service-providers and the rights of public-service consumers in considerable detail. And so on. Such developments have been variously described in terms of a shift from 'club government', based on voluntary compliance with implicit rules and understandings by members of small ruling élites, to formalized, explicit, and coercive regulatory regimes;[82] in terms of the growth of 'regulation inside government' conducted by 'waste-watchers, quality police and sleaze-busters';[83] and in terms of the emergence of an 'audit society' obsessed with checking and inspection.[84] The common thread in these accounts of the transformation of governance structures in Britain in the past thirty years is a mapping of changing modes and patterns of regulation or, in other words, accountability for the provision of public services. Whether these changes represent a net reduction in accountability or, on the contrary, a net increase or, perhaps, no quantitative change at all, is extremely difficult to assess objectively. The way public services are provided and their provision is regulated has changed dramatically, but whether the amount and efficacy of such regulation has also changed is a different question.[85] Views about these developments are likely to depend on assessments of the perceived consequences of the changes in the light of understandings of what government is for, and of the desirable relationship between the public and private sectors and between governors and governed. In other words, whether accountability for the provision of public services is better or worse now than it was thirty years ago is, in part at least, a question of ideology.

[82] Moran, *The British Regulatory State*.
[83] C. Hood *et al.*, *Regulation Inside Government: Waste-Watchers, Quality Police and Sleaze-Busters* (Oxford, 1999).
[84] M. Power, *The Audit Society: Rituals of Verification* (Oxford, 1997).
[85] C. Scott, 'Accountability in the Regulatory State' (2000) *J of Law and Society* 38.

13

Restitution

A few words should be said about the application of restitutionary rules to public functionaries.[1] The law of restitution deals with situations in which the defendant has acquired some benefit at the expense of the claimant and it can be said that the benefit has been unjustly obtained. Suppose a public body charges a citizen for a service which it is under a duty to provide free of charge, or for some lesser amount than it actually charges. If the authority threatened to withhold the service if the charge was not paid, the law of restitution would consider that the charge had been unjustly extracted and would allow the citizen to recover it.[2] Similarly, if a public body made an unlawful tax demand and extracted the payment by applying unlawful pressure to the taxpayer, any payment might be recoverable.

But what if the body makes no threat or applies no pressure? Suppose that it believes, wrongly, that it is, as a matter of law, entitled to make the charge[3] and the citizen does not realize that it need not be paid. Or suppose that the Inland Revenue makes a wrongful tax demand thinking that, as a matter of law, the tax is due, and that the taxpayer pays it on the same basis. As a matter of public law, the tax or charge will be illegal[4] and recoverable in the law of restitution by virtue of the constitutional principle of 'no taxation without Parliamentary approval'.[5] Whereas *ultra vires*

---

[1] P. Birks, *Introduction to the Law of Restitution*, rev. edn (Oxford, 1989), pp. 294–9; A. Burrows, *The Law of Restitution*, 2nd edn (London, 2002), ch. 13; G Virgo, *The Principles of the Law of Restitution* (Oxford, 1999), ch. 14. Concerning restitutionary liability in EC law see T. Hartley, *Foundations of European Community Law*, 5th edn (Oxford, 2003), pp. 447–50.

[2] See *Congreve v. Home Office* [1976] QB 629 (threat to revoke TV licence unless extra licence fee paid).

[3] If an authority knowingly made a wrongful demand it could be sued for misfeasance in a public office.

[4] *R v. Inland Revenue Commissioners, ex p. Woolwich Equitable Building Society* [1990] 1 WLR 1400; *R v. Richmond upon Thames LBC, ex p. McCarthy & Stone (Developments) Ltd* [1992] 2 AC 48.

[5] *Woolwich Equitable Building Society v. Inland Revenue Commissioners* [1993] AC 70. Conversely, a public authority that makes an *ultra vires* payment can recover it by virtue of the constitutional principle of no public spending without Parliamentary authorization: A. Burrows, *The Law of Restitution*, pp. 420–3. A claim for restitution cannot be joined with a

conduct on the part of a public body will not give rise to a claim for damages,[6] it may give rise to a restitutionary claim. In some cases there may be a statutory provision for refund of an illegal tax or charge. If such a provision does not impose a duty to make a refund but only confers a power to do so, that discretion must be exercised reasonably and on the basis that a refund should only be refused if there is some good reason for refusal, such as the conduct of the person claiming the refund.[7]

The question of restitution of payments made to public bodies can also arise in 'private law' contexts; for example, if a public landlord makes an improper claim for rent. In such a case the principle that illegal taxes and charges can be recovered would probably be inapplicable and the ordinary 'private' law of restitution would apply. The mere fact that the public body had made a wrongful demand would not give rise to a claim for restitution. Such a claim would arise only if some other ground of restitution (such as duress or mistake of fact) could be found.

Sometimes a decision that a demand for payment was unlawful and unjust will have very wide effects, as similar payments may have been made by many citizens.[8] If an authority is required to repay a large number of small payments, the total impact on its finances might be very great. Is this a good reason to refuse restitution?[9] It is surely not a good reason to refuse to overturn unlawful decisions of the Inland Revenue that the impact on the public purse will be significant. The same should be true of wrongful demands for payment for a public service. The courts should not be sympathetic to an argument that to declare the demand invalid would damage public finances. They should leave it to the legislature to deal as it sees fit with any adverse impact on the public purse of judicial decisions awarding restitution.

Restitutionary claims may also arise in contexts other than wrongful demands for payment. For example, suppose a contract made by a public authority is held to be *ultra vires* and unenforceable, but only after it has

---

claim for judicial review under CPR Part 54. But it is not necessary to make such a claim in order to establish the illegality of the tax or charge—this can be done in a 'private law claim' to recover the payment: *British Steel Plc v. Customs and Excise Commissioners* [1997] 2 All ER 366. It has been argued that restitution of illegal taxes and charges would better be treated as a matter of public law than of private law: J. Alder, 'Restitution in Public Law: Bearing the Cost of Unlawful State Action' (2002) 22 *LS* 165.

[6] See 5.5.1.1.

[7] *R v. Tower Hamlets LBC, ex p. Chetnik Developments Ltd* [1988] AC 858.

[8] e.g. *Daymond v. South West Water Authority* [1976] AC 609.

[9] See *Air Canada v. British Columbia* (1989) 59 DLR (4th) 161; J. Beatson, 'Restitution of Overpaid Tax, Discretion and Passing-On' (1995) 111 *LQR* 375.

been performed (in whole or in part) by one or both of the parties. In private law the basic rule is that benefits transferred under an illegal contract are irrecoverable, although there are exceptions to this rule, most of which are designed to prevent a guilty party taking advantage of a party innocent of the illegality. By contrast, although an *ultra vires* contract made by a statutory authority will be void and unenforceable, money or property transferred to the authority by the other party under the terms of the contract may be recoverable (subject to an allowance for any benefits transferred by the authority to the other party). However, this does not apply in the case of a contract of loan because, it is said, to allow a creditor to recover money transferred to a statutory authority under such a contract would be tantamount to enforcing the void contract.[10]

---

[10] *Westdeutsche Landesbank Girozentral v. Islington LBC* [1994] 1 WLR 938. See further S. Arrowsmith, 'Ineffective Transactions, Unjust Enrichment and Problems of Policy' (1989) 9 *LS* 307; A. Burrows, 'Public Authorities, Ultra Vires and Restitution' in A. Burrows (ed.), *Essays on the Law of Restitution* (Oxford, 1991); M. Loughlin, 'Innovative Financing in Local Government: The Limits of Legal Instrumentalism—Part II' [1991] *PL* 568, 574–82.

Part III

Information

14

Information and Litigation

One of the greatest obstacles to effective accountability for the performance of public functions is public secrecy. It is difficult to exercise control, by whatever means, over public activity without accurate information about what public authorities are doing. British governments are notoriously secretive, and secrecy is often alleged to be justified 'in the public interest'. In this chapter we will consider the impact of public secrecy on the process of civil litigation;[1] and in the next chapter we will consider some wider issues of secrecy and freedom of information.

14.1 COLLECTING EVIDENCE

In cases where there is a trial, oral examination, and cross-examination of witnesses is an important way of collecting evidence. But not all litigation involves trials. In particular, in claims for judicial review under CPR Part 54, even when there is an oral hearing before a judge,[2] the evidence of witnesses is normally given in writing (in a 'witness statement' or by 'affidavit'). There is provision for witnesses who give evidence in writing to be cross-examined (CPR Rules 8.6(3), 32(7)), but oral cross-examination is exceptional. Unless the court gives permission, written evidence cannot be relied upon unless it has been served on the other party (CPR Rule 54.16(2)).

Although, in the British system, the purpose of adjudicating factual disputes is not to 'discover the whole truth', it is important that parties should be able to collect evidence relevant to their case and to do this, as far as possible, before any hearing or trial in order to prevent surprise. The main formal technique for doing this is 'disclosure and inspection of documents' (CPR Part 31). Disclosure involves revealing the existence of

---

[1] The rules discussed here also apply, *mutatis mutandis*, to criminal prosecutions. Concerning the latter see P. Birkinshaw, *Freedom of Information: The Law, the Practice and the Ideal*, 3rd edn (London, 2001), pp. 349–50.

[2] 'The court may decide the claim for judicial review without a hearing where all the parties agree': CPR Rule 54.18.

a document, and inspection involves revealing its contents. By means of disclosure and inspection a party can obtain access to documents in the control of the other party which are relevant to the case. Disclosure and inspection are designed to save time at trial; to enable a party to know, as fully as possible in advance, the case that may be presented by the other party and to prepare an answer as effectively as possible; and, if appropriate, to reach a settlement out of court. In claims for judicial review under CPR Part 54, disclosure is not required unless the court so orders (PD 54, 12.1).[3]

There are grounds on which a witness may be entitled not to answer a question or provide information. For example, a professional person, such as a doctor or solicitor, is entitled, in certain circumstances, to refuse to divulge information received in confidence in their professional capacity. There are analogous rules relating to disclosure and inspection. One of these rules is that in certain circumstances, a party may decline to disclose documents or to allow them to be inspected if it can be established that the public interest justifies or requires non-disclosure/non-inspection (CPR Rule 31.19). This is referred to as 'public interest immunity' (PII). For the sake of simplicity, the discussion in this chapter will be in terms of disclosure/inspection of documents even though it is also relevant to the giving of oral evidence.

14.2 CROWN PRIVILEGE OR PUBLIC INTEREST IMMUNITY?

The rule that disclosure of documents and inspection can be resisted on the ground of public interest used to be referred to by the phrase 'Crown privilege', signifying that the Crown had a privilege against disclosure.[4] The word 'privilege' was derived from the private-law rules of evidence; for example, the right of a solicitor not to disclose certain documents is called 'legal professional privilege'. The nature of this right as a 'privilege' has two corollaries in private law. First, the right of non-disclosure/non-inspection attaches not to the document but to the witness asked to give it. If some other person who does not enjoy such a right can be found who can disclose the required document, there is nothing to stop them doing so. Secondly, a party who enjoys the right of non-disclosure/

---

[3] This is because the claim for judicial review is not designed for cases raising significant factual disputes: see 6.2. This position may infringe the ECHR: see 6.8.

[4] The Crown's absolute immunity from disclosure (then called 'discovery') was abolished by s. 28 of the Crown Proceedings Act 1947.

non-inspection has a choice whether to claim it or not. If the party chooses not to exercise the privilege then there is nothing to stop the document being disclosed/inspected; only the privileged party can raise the issue of privilege. It has never been clear whether either or both of these corollaries also attaches to the use of the term 'privilege' in the public law context.

The term 'Crown privilege' is misleading and incorrect in a number of respects. First, the claiming of public interest immunity appears to be a duty, not a right.[5] However, contrary to the advice given by the Attorney-General to Ministers in relation to the notorious Matrix Churchill trials,[6] the duty is to claim immunity only when the public interest demands it.[7] A Minister should not sign a certificate claiming public interest immunity (a PII certificate) without first being satisfied that the public interest demands non-disclosure/non-inspection, even though it is ultimately for the court to decide whether or not disclosure/inspection should be ordered.[8] Secondly, once it has been decided that the public interest demands non-disclosure/non-inspection, immunity attaches to the document and not to the person in control of it (i.e. the Crown or other body from which disclosure/inspection is sought). If the public interest demands non-disclosure/non-inspection, the duty not to disclose or allow inspection cannot normally be waived—in principle at least; although in practice, no doubt, PII is not always asserted even in cases where, as a matter of law, it is available.[9] There appears to be at least one exception to the non-waiver principle. Bodies such as the Customs and Excise Commissioners and the National Society for the Prevention of Cruelty to Children (NSPCC) have successfully claimed immunity from disclosing the sources of their information on the ground that if

---

[5] *Makanjuola v. Commissioner of Police of the Metropolis* [1992] 3 All ER 617, 623 *per* Bingham LJ, approved by Lord Woolf in *R v. Chief Constable of the West Midlands Police, ex p. Wiley* [1995] 1 AC 274, 295–6.

[6] The collapse of which precipitated the Scott inquiry into the 'arms to Iraq affair' as to which see *The Scott Report* [1996] *PL* 357–527; A. Tomkins, *The Constitution after Scott: Government Unwrapped* (Oxford, 1998).

[7] The government has accepted this principle: G. Ganz, 'Volte-Face on Public Interest Immunity' (1997) 60 *MLR* 552.

[8] *R v. Chief Constable of West Midlands Police, ex p. Wiley* [1995] 1 AC 274. However, once it has been established that a particular class of documents is immune from disclosure/inspection, it might be that a minister would have no option but to claim immunity in respect of documents in that class and leave it to the court to waive the immunity if thought necessary: T.R.S. Allan, 'Public Interest Immunity and Ministers' Responsibilities' [1993] *Crim LR* 660. Concerning class claims see 14.5.

[9] C. Forsyth, 'Public Interest Immunity: Recent and Future Developments [1997] *CLJ* 51, 55–6.

confidentiality was not maintained, their sources of information would dry up. In such cases, the particular source being protected can waive the immunity because people will not be discouraged from coming forward if they know that it is only by their own choice that their identity may become known.[10]

A third reason why the term 'Crown privilege' is misleading is that any party to the litigation—not just the government—can raise an issue of public policy immunity, and the court can raise it of its own motion. On the other hand, if a Minister decides that the public interest does not require non-disclosure/non-inspection, a court is unlikely to question this conclusion. A court is more likely to consider ordering non-disclosure/non-inspection of its own motion if the decision not to claim immunity has been made by someone other than a Minister.[11] Fourthly, the term 'Crown' is inaccurate because it implies that public policy immunity only attaches to documents in the control of departments of central government. It is now clear, however, that the demands of 'public policy' can justify non-disclosure/non-inspection of material in the control of local government or other public functionaries. This development is an aspect of what I have called 'the functional turn in administrative law'.

14.3 INSPECTION TO DETERMINE RELEVANCE ETC.

To understand how PII claims are dealt with it is necessary to draw a distinction between two different questions: what might be called 'the disclosure question' on the one hand, and 'the immunity question' on the other. The disclosure question concerns whether a party is under a prima facie obligation to disclose a particular document[12] and whether, where such an obligation exists, the party may refuse inspection on some ground other than public interest immunity.[13] The immunity question concerns whether a party is entitled to claim immunity from disclosure/inspection on public interest grounds. In the present context, the disclosure question is essentially a private law question because the fact that the document is in the control of a public functionary does not, in theory,

---

[10] *R v. Chief Constable of the West Midlands Police, ex p. Wiley* [1995] 1 AC 274, 298–9. See also *Lonrho Plc v. Fayed (No. 4)* [1994] QB 749.

[11] *R v. Chief Constable of the West Midlands Police, ex p. Wiley* [1995] 1 AC 274, 296–7.

[12] Parties to litigation are obliged to make what is called 'standard disclosure' (CPR Rule 31.6). A court order is required to secure disclosure from a non-party: CPR Rule 31.17.

[13] CPR Rules 31.3(1)(a) and 31.3(2) respectively.

affect the issue of whether the conditions, for the existence of a prima facie obligation of disclosure or inspection, laid down in the CPR are satisfied. The immunity question, on the other hand, is a public law question because it turns on the balance between the public interest in the due administration of justice (which may require disclosure/inspection) and the public interest in non-disclosure/non-inspection.

The basic principle governing the disclosure question is that documents should be disclosed if they are relevant to questions in dispute.[14] A party to whom a document has been disclosed has a prima facie right to inspect it. There are two grounds on which the (correlative) obligation to allow inspection can be resisted: that the document is no longer in the party's control, and that to require inspection would be 'disproportionate to the issues in the case'. Only if the disclosure question is answered in favour of disclosure/inspection does any question of immunity arise. There is a difficulty here because, in order to know whether the conditions for disclosure/inspection are met in relation to any particular document, it is necessary to know what it contains. But if a claim of public interest immunity is made and is found to be justified, it would require the contents of the document not to be revealed. A solution to this problem would be to allow the court to examine the documents in private to ascertain whether the conditions for disclosure/inspection were met. It has been held that a judge should inspect documents for which immunity is claimed only if satisfied that they are more likely than not to contain material which would give substantial support to the contentions of the party seeking disclosure/inspection.[15] This is a high[16] standard, and it imposes a considerable restriction on the power of the court to inspect documents.

The importance of this restrictive attitude to inspection is not limited to the disclosure question. If a claim of public interest immunity is made, the only way the court can judge the strength of the claim without actually allowing the contents of the documents to be disclosed is to inspect the documents in private. If inspection is not allowed because the claimant has not passed the 'relevance threshold' for inspection, the court has no alternative but to accept the claim of immunity; otherwise it risks causing exactly that damage to the public interest which the government alleges will flow from the disclosure/inspection. Thus an unwillingness

---

[14] For a more detailed formulation see CPR Rule 31.6.
[15] *Air Canada v. Secretary of State for Trade* [1983] AC 624.
[16] But not insurmountable: e.g. *Re HIV Haemophiliac Litigation* [1990] *NLJ* 1349.

to inspect for relevance leads to an inability to question claims of immunity. It is important to realize that the upshot of a denial of discovery may not just be that some relevant documents are unavailable. If the essential elements of the claimant's case are buried in documents which the court refuses to inspect or refuses to allow the claimant to see, the case may never get off the ground, and a wrong may go uncorrected.

14.4 INSPECTION TO DETERMINE IMMUNITY

At one time the courts took the view that if a suitably senior government officer (usually a Minister) certified that the public interest required non-disclosure/non-inspection, such a certificate would be treated as conclusive by the court.[17] Since *Conway v. Rimmer*[18] the courts have been less prepared to accept the views of the executive as conclusive of the question of immunity: hence the practice of inspection in private by the court, this being the only way to adjudicate properly on a claim of immunity without revealing the contents of the documents. This change of attitude effected a shift of power from the executive to the courts. The courts took upon themselves the task of deciding what the demands of public policy were in respect of the disclosure/inspection of government information. The position now appears to be that no government document, however exalted in origin (e.g. Cabinet documents) is necessarily entitled to immunity, although the higher the origin of the document and the closer its connection with matters of high policy (as opposed to routine government administration), the less likely are the courts to question any claim for immunity made in respect of it.[19] Although it has never been spelt out, this change in the treatment of PII claims made by central government implies that a court should never defer to PII claims made by other public functionaries.

The task of the court when it inspects documents in order to adjudicate on a claim of immunity is to balance the alleged public interest in non-disclosure/non-inspection against the *public* interest in the due administration of justice (which, in an adversarial system, requires that all information having more than marginal relevance to the case be made available to the parties and the court), and to decide, on the basis of this balancing, whether the documents ought to be disclosed/inspected or not. It is important to note that what is weighed against the alleged public

---

[17] *Duncan v. Cammell Laird & Co Ltd* [1942] AC 624.   [18] [1968] AC 910.
[19] *Burmah Oil v. Bank of England* [1980] AC 1090.

interest in non-disclosure/non-inspection is not the interest of the individual litigant but the public interest in the due administration of justice. This is not to say that the interests of the litigant are irrelevant. The public interest can be measured only with reference to the strength of the claimant's case as a matter of law and fact, and the importance of the interest sought to be vindicated by the action. But at the end of the day, what the courts are seeking to uphold is the integrity of the legal process. This explains why the courts are prepared, in this area, to do the sort of balancing exercise which they are often not prepared to do. The courts are, in a special sense, guardians of the legal process, and their responsibility to protect it from encroachment by administrative action is greater than their responsibility to protect purely private interests from such encroachment.

As is the case with any balancing operation that requires detailed reference to the facts of particular cases, not all decisions will necessarily sit easily with one another. Consider, for example, the following two cases. In *Gaskin v. Liverpool City Council*[20] the claimant sought disclosure/inspection of documents relating to his behaviour and treatment when, as a child, he had been in the care of a local authority which he was now suing because of allegedly negligent maltreatment while he was in care. It was held that the proper functioning of the care services demanded that their records be kept confidential and should not be inspected by the judge. *Campbell v. Tameside MBC*[21] concerned disclosure/inspection of documents relating to the behaviour of a delinquent schoolboy, not in care, who assaulted a teacher. The teacher then sought to sue the local authority in negligence. It was held that the court was right to inspect the documents and decide, on the basis of their significance, whether the demands of justice outweighed the desirability that records of education authorities on individual problem children be kept confidential.

A close reading of these two cases suggests that the court was unsympathetic to Gaskin's claim but sympathetic towards Campbell's. We have noted that there is an unavoidable link between the strength of the claimant's case and the propriety of allowing disclosure/inspection.

---

[20] [1980] 1 WLR 1549. In the end, Gaskin was given access to documents on his file, the makers of which agreed to their disclosure/inspection. The ECtHR subsequently held that the makers of the documents should not have been given such a veto, and that there ought to have been some procedure under which the interests of Gaskin and the makers of the documents could have been balanced by an independent third party: *Gaskin v. UK* (1989) 12 EHRR 36. Facts similar to those in this case would now be covered by the Data Protection Act 1998, which is discussed in 15.4.

[21] [1982] QB 1065.

However, it is important that rules of disclosure/inspection should not be used to prejudge the merits of the case. It may be undesirable that complaints against care authorities of the relatively nebulous character of Gaskin's (he claimed that he had suffered psychological injuries and anxiety neurosis as a result of maltreatment) should be made in the courts given the complex nature of the relationship between child and care authority. If such actions are to be countenanced, they should not be frustrated by denying claimants access to their personal records.

14.5 CLASS AND CONTENTS CLAIMS

Unwillingness to accept official certificates that the public interest requires non-disclosure/non-inspection is also reflected in a greater scepticism about claims of immunity made on the basis that the documents in question belong to a class of documents that ought not to be disclosed/inspected (class claims), than about claims made on the basis that the documents in question contain sensitive material (contents claims).[22] The leading case is *Conway v. Rimmer*,[23] which involved an action for malicious prosecution by a former probationary constable against his one-time superintendent. The Home Secretary objected to the production of a number of internal reports on the conduct of the claimant during his probation, but this claim of immunity was rejected. This claim was a class claim, and the main argument for non-disclosure/non-inspection was based on candour and confidentiality: that internal reports on individual policemen would be less frank if the writer feared disclosure/inspection to the subject. The House of Lords asserted the right of the court, in all but the clearest cases, to assess for itself any claim of immunity, especially a class claim; and it encouraged scepticism towards the candour argument.

However, the history of the distinction between class and contents claims has been somewhat chequered, and not all judges take the same sceptical attitude to class claims. In *Air Canada*,[24] for example, Lord Fraser suggested that the court might be *less* well equipped to controvert a class claim than a contents claim because the court would not be in a good position to judge the importance of the particular class of

---

[22] Central government has said that it will not make class claims: G. Ganz, 'Volte-Face on Public Interest Immunity' (1997) 60 *MLR* 552, 553–4.
[23] [1968] AC 910.
[24] [1983] 2 AC 394, 436.

documents to public administration as a whole.[25] In *Ex p. Wiley*, Lord Slynn expressed the view that although class claims 'may sometimes have been pushed too far . . . on occasions in the past they have been necessary and justified, indeed valuable'.[26]

An area in which the courts are likely to be prepared to accept without question a claim of immunity, even if it is a class claim, is that of defence and foreign affairs. In *Duncan v. Cammell Laird*[27] a claim for immunity was upheld in respect of certain documents and plans relating to a submarine which sank during sea trials. Although the approach of deference to executive claims of privilege in this case has been in some degree departed from, the actual decision seems to be accepted as correct.[28] Although class claims are typically based on candour and confidentiality arguments, in the area of defence and national security a class claim may be made on the basis that all of the documents in the class contain material disclosure/ inspection of which might damage the public interest.

14.6 CONFIDENTIALITY

Another litmus test of the changing attitude of various courts and judges to the sanctity of executive claims of immunity is the approach taken to the issue of confidentiality. Claims of immunity (especially class claims, as we have just noted) often rest partly on the argument that desirable candour and frankness in the administration of government business will be discouraged if officials are aware that they risk disclosure/inspection of internal departmental documents.[29] Lord Keith in *Burmah Oil Ltd v. Bank of England*[30] was dismissive of such arguments and thought it 'grotesque' to suggest that 'any competent and conscientious public servant would be inhibited at all in the candour of his writings by consideration of the off-chance that they might have to be produced in litigation'. Such

---

[25] Inspection of documents may not assist in assessing the strength of a class claim because such claims do not relate to the contents of the documents. For this reason, too, the balancing exercise may be harder to carry out.

[26] [1995] 1 AC 274, 282.   [27] [1942] AC 624.

[28] See e.g. *Balfour v. Foreign and Commonwealth Office* [1994] 1 WLR 681.

[29] To the extent that the information has already entered the public arena, the confidentiality argument is weakened: *R v. Governor of Brixton Prison, ex p. Osman* [1991] 1 WLR 281, 290–1. Confidentiality is a relative, not an absolute, concept. This is reflected in the principle that documents disclosed for one purpose (such as use in particular litigation) must not be used for any other purpose, subject to some overriding public interest in the collateral use: e.g. *Re Barlow Clowes Gilt Managers Ltd* [1992] Ch 208.

[30] [1980] AC 1090, 1133.

views reflect the conventional wisdom that confidentiality as such is not a ground of immunity. The idea of 'confidentiality as such' is a very doubtful one. Confidentiality is always in aid of some end, and if the end is important enough and is likely to be jeopardized by lack of frankness, it can be said that immunity is protecting the end, not the confidentiality. At all events, some judges have shown themselves more sympathetic to the candour argument than Lord Keith. In *Burmah Oil Ltd* Lord Wilberforce said that he thought the candour argument had received an 'excessive dose of cold water'.[31]

It is certainly true that not all claims of candour and confidentiality are treated with equal suspicion by the courts. In *Alfred Crompton Amusement Machines Ltd v. Commissioners of Customs and Excise*[32] a claim of immunity was upheld in respect of a class of documents containing, amongst other things, information given voluntarily by third parties about the commission of excise offences. This was done in part so as not to discourage third parties from giving information for fear of being later identified. The same argument was important in *D v. NSPCC*[33] in which the House of Lords upheld a claim of immunity in respect of the identity of a person who had provided information to the Society. The claim for disclosure/inspection arose in connection with a claim for damages in negligence against an officer of the society for failure to investigate a complaint properly before confronting the claimant about it, thus causing her nervous shock.

With the *Crompton* and *NSPCC* cases can be contrasted *Norwich Pharmacal Co v. Commissioners of Customs and Excise*[34] in which the claimant sought an order requiring the defendant to reveal the names of illicit importers of a compound over which they had a patent. In this case the litigant's interest was strong and clear—to enforce its legal patent rights—and the argument for secrecy was weak because the identity of the importers was revealed by commercial documents supplied in the ordinary course of business and not some sensitive or confidential source. So there was no reason not to make the order sought.

The ambivalence of the courts to the candour argument is clear in cases concerning inquiries under s. 49 of the Police Act 1964, which

---

[31] Ibid. 1112.
[32] [1974] AC 405. See also *R v. Lewes Justices, ex p. Secretary of State for the Home Department* [1970] AC 388 (non-inspection ordered to protect informer despite allegations that the documents contained criminal libels against the applicant for a gaming licence); *Hassleblad v. Orbinson* [1985] QB 475 (public interest in not allowing information given by informer to be used as basis of a defamation action).
[33] [1978] AC 171.   [34] [1974] AC 133.

establishes an internal procedure for dealing with complaints of police malpractice. In *Neilson v. Laugharne*[35] and *Hehir v. Commissioner of Police*[36] it was held that demands of candour and public interest in the proper investigation of complaints against the police would generally support a claim of immunity against disclosure/inspection of records of a s. 49 inquiry in a civil action against any of the police officers involved. These cases were overruled in *Ex p. Wiley*[37] in which it was held that statements by complainants in such inquiries were not, as a class, immune from disclosure/inspection. Subsequently, however, the Court of Appeal has held that reports of officers conducting such inquiries are, as a class, immune from disclosure/inspection in order that they should 'feel free to report on professional colleagues or members of the public without the apprehension that their opinions may become known to such persons'.[38] On the other hand, such class immunity is subject to two qualifications: first, it protects documents and their contents, but it does not prevent a person who knows what the documents contain from using that knowledge, for instance to launch a ('collateral') defamation action against the investigating officer.[39] Secondly, the immunity would not prevent a judge ordering disclosure/inspection, in such collateral proceedings, of documents in a protected class if the public interest favouring disclosure/inspection *in those proceedings* outweighed the public interest in non-disclosure/non-inspection.[40]

The bottom line appears to be that there may, in certain circumstances, be a public interest in non-disclosure/non-inspection of documents based on considerations of candour and confidentiality, and that this interest may outweigh the public interest in disclosure/inspection to ensure the due administration of justice. But whether this is so or not will depend on the facts of individual cases.[41]

14.7 DISCLOSURE OF DOCUMENTS AND FREEDOM OF INFORMATION

The law of disclosure/inspection of documents for the purposes of litigation and the PII rules were developed against a background of

---

[35] [1981] QB 736.   [36] [1982] 1 WLR 715.   [37] [1995] 1 AC 274.
[38] *Taylor v. Anderton* [1995] 1 WLR 447, 465.
[39] *Ex p. Wiley* [1995] 1 AC 274, 306. A party to whom documents are disclosed for the purposes of particular litigation is under an obligation not to use them for any other purpose (such as instituting further litigation): *Taylor v. Serious Fraud Office* [1999] 2 AC 177.
[40] As occurred in *Ex p. Coventry Newspapers Ltd* [1993] QB 278.
[41] *Frankson v. Home Office* [2003] 1 WLR 1952.

government secrecy and control over information about the conduct of public affairs. As we will see in Chapter 15, the legal landscape has been significantly changed by the Freedom of Information Act 2000 ('FOI Act'), fully operational in 2005. The FOI Act creates a legally enforceable right, subject to a long list of exceptions, to be supplied with information by public authorities (as listed in the Act).

What impact will the FOI regime have on the law of disclosure? The first thing to note is that the FOI Act is concerned with access to 'information', whereas the law of disclosure relates to documents. The FOI Act does not create a right that public authorities disclose the existence of documents, or a right to inspect documents in the control of public authorities. Rather it creates a right to the 'communication' of information 'held' by public authorities. Nevertheless, the typical reason why a litigant seeks disclosure and inspection of documents is to gain access to the information they contain. In some cases, a litigant may be concerned to establish whether or not a particular document or class of documents exists. For this purpose, the law of disclosure will be more relevant than FOI law. But in the typical case, the FOI regime may provide litigants with a useful alternative or adjunct to disclosure/inspection.

In one respect, at least, the FOI regime has a significant advantage over the disclosure/inspection regime. Documents need not be disclosed unless they are relevant to litigation that is already under way. This rule prevents the law of disclosure/inspection regime being used to conduct 'fishing expeditions' designed to discover whether a public authority has in its control documents that may provide a basis for initiating litigation. By contrast, a person who seeks information under the FOI Act does not need to specify the purpose for which the information is sought, and so may be able to request information which, if it is held by a public authority, may provide grounds for commencing litigation against that or some other public authority or, indeed, against a private individual. The FOI regime may also be useful in cases where litigation has commenced but the public authority from whom information is sought is not a party to the litigation. Under the law of disclosure, a non-party (unlike a party) is required to disclose documents in its control only if a court so orders; and quite stringent conditions have to be satisfied before such an order will be made (CPR Rule 31.17). By contrast, information could be obtained from a non-party public authority under the FOI Act without the intervention of a court. The FOI regime is of even greater potential value in judicial review proceedings where disclosure, even by a party to the proceedings, is required only if the court so orders. A person making a claim for judicial review might be able to evade the need for court involvement by using the FOI regime.

Finally, note that whereas the public-interest limits of disclosure are specified by the common law rules of PII discussed earlier, the public-interest exemptions from the obligation to communicate information under the FOI regime are contained in Part II of the FOI Act. The common law PII rules are abstract and give the courts considerable discretion, whereas the exemptions under the FOI Act are formulated much more concretely. It is not clear what impact the statutory regime of exemptions will have on the formulation and application of the common law PII principles. One view is that 'the courts will be forced to modify substantially the doctrine of public-interest immunity, so as at least to parallel the statutory exemptions, or to limit them even further'.[42]

[42] R. Austin, 'Freedom of Information: The Constitutional Impact' in J. Jowell and D. Oliver (eds), *The Changing Constitution*, 4th edn (Oxford, 2000), p. 363.

15

Government Secrecy and Freedom
of Information

15.1 FREEDOM OF INFORMATION

A precondition of effectively holding public functionaries accountable is knowledge and information about their activities. Secret government is unaccountable government.[1] The traditional ethos of British government is reflected in the fact that legislation criminalizing the unauthorized disclosure of government-controlled information—the Official Secrets Act—predated freedom of information legislation by more than a century.[2] Nor was the common law much concerned to promote freedom of information. For instance, in a surprisingly recent case it was held that the parents of a soldier who died in an accident in the Falkland Islands were not entitled to disclosure of the report of the enquiry into his death even though the judge thought the refusal to disclose was *Wednesbury*-unreasonable.[3] For most of the twentieth century, British government was conducted, if not in the dark, at least in very dim light.

However, things began to change in the 1980s—first in local government. The Local Government (Access to Information) Act 1985 in essence gave the public access to meetings of local authorities and to agenda and other relevant documentation.[4] The operation of the Act was

---

[1] For an informal audit of the 'accountability and openness' of non-departmental public bodies see House of Commons Public Administration Select Committee, Fifth Report, HC 367, 2000–1, *Mapping the Quango State*, Part 2.

[2] The first Official Secrets Act was passed in 1889. Official secrets legislation (the current legislation was passed in 1989) and freedom of information legislation are not incompatible, of course, because there are important classes of information—relating to national security, for instance—which all governments (justifiably) want to keep secret no matter how committed they are in principle to openness. So protections for 'whistleblowers' under the Public Interest Disclosure Act 1998 do not apply to employees of the security and intelligence services (s. 11, amending s. 193 of the Employment Rights Act 1996). On the relationship between official secrets legislation and freedom of speech see *R v. Shayler* [2002] 2 WLR 754.

[3] *R v. Secretary of State for Defence, ex p. Sancto* (1992) 5 Admin LR 673. Subsequently, the Ministry changed its policy in favour of disclosing reports.

[4] See also Local Government Act 2000, s. 22; P. Birkinshaw, *Freedom of Information: The Law, the Practice and the Ideal*, 3rd edn (London, 2001), pp. 155–8, 227–34.

extended to other bodies such as community health councils.[5] Legislation was also passed dealing with access to information about the environment held by governmental agencies.[6] Related to the idea of freedom of information is that of transparency of government decision-making processes. As we have seen (see 12.1.2), this value is promoted (for instance) by rules regulating public procurement.

The cause of openness in government was significantly advanced by the Citizen's Charter (first introduced in 1991), one of the principles of which was provision of information about the delivery of public services. A 1993 White Paper on *Open Government*[7] was followed in 1994 by publication of a *Code of Practice on Access to Government Information*.[8] A non-binding code was chosen in preference to legally binding freedom of information legislation partly because it was considered that an informal approach would, in the long run, be more effective in creating an attitude of openness in government, and partly to prevent the courts becoming more heavily involved in scrutinizing the processes of government. Under the Code there was a general commitment to publish information about the processes of government, but not to make documents available. There was a long list of exemptions from the basic commitment. Information providers were allowed to charge, and suggestions were made that many government bodies charged excessively. The Parliamentary Ombudsman (see 17.2) was empowered to investigate complaints about failure to provide information or excessive charging. The Code applied only to bodies under the jurisdiction of the Ombudsman; but other bodies, such as the Local Administration Ombudsman (see 17.3), adopted codes modelled on the main Code.

The common law also made some advances in securing more open government. In *Birmingham City DC v. O*[9] a city councillor, who was not a member of the council's social services committee, sought access to that committee's documents about a particular adoption application because she had reason to believe that the adopting parents were unsuitable persons to be allowed to adopt a child. It was held that although the councillor

---

[5] Community Health Councils (Access to Information) Act 1988.
[6] J. Macdonald and C.H. Jones (eds), *The Law of Freedom of Information* (Oxford, 2003), ch. 16.
[7] Cm. 2290.   [8] Birkinshaw, *Freedom of Information*, pp. 238–50.
[9] [1983] 1 AC 578. For explanation of the background to this case and a more negative assessment of the principles it establishes see I. Leigh, *Law, Politics and Local Democracy* (Oxford, 2000), pp. 221–4.

had no right to see the documents, it was ultimately up to the council as a whole to decide whether a councillor who was not a member of a particular committee should have access to its papers. It was also held that the decision to allow access to the files was not an unreasonable one because, despite the sensitivity and confidentiality of the information, the councillor had made out a case for being allowed to see the documents. The Local Government (Access to Information) Act greatly improved access to local government information for both councillors and citizens, but the documents in this case would have been exempt from disclosure under the Act.

The principle underlying the *Birmingham City* case was that a member of a council was entitled to access to confidential information if he or she needed it in order properly to perform functions as a member of the council; in a nutshell, access was given on a 'need to know' basis. This principle was also applied to the question of whether a council member should be allowed to attend meetings of council committees of which he or she was not a member. The answer was 'yes', if attendance at the meeting was a reasonable way of obtaining information that the member needed to know.[10]

Despite these various developments, British citizens still lacked a legally enforceable right of access to information held by public authorities. This was finally achieved in the Freedom of Information Act 2000 ('FOI Act'), fully operational in 2005. The Act was preceded in 1997 by a White Paper, *Your Right to Know*, which foreshadowed a considerably more open regime than that which (after much consultation and debate) was eventually enacted. Indeed, one commentator has described the FOI Act as 'a sheep in wolf's clothing, masquerading as a Freedom of Information Act, yet in reality reserving to government near-absolute control over all sensitive governmental information'.[11] This judgment is partly based on the number and breadth of the exemptions from the obligation to disclose. Nevertheless, the Act does create, for the first time in Britain, a general right to be told, on request, whether a public authority holds information of a particular description and, if it does, to be given that information. In place of the legal principle, that unauthorised disclosure of 'official information' is unlawful, has been put the presumption that such information should be made available unless there is some good reason for non-publication.

---

[10] *R v. Sheffield CC, ex p. Chadwick* (1985) 84 LGR 563. For background to and further explanation of this case see Leigh, *Law, Politics and Local Democracy*, pp. 191–3.

[11] R. Austin, 'Freedom of Information: The Constitutional Impact' in J. Jowell and D. Oliver (eds), *The Changing Constitution*, 4th edn (Oxford, 2000), p. 371.

Here is not the place to consider the FOI regime in detail. However, a few points, particularly relevant to matters dealt with elsewhere in this book, are worth making. The first concerns the scope of the FOI Act. We have already seen that the scope of judicial review and of the HRA is defined in terms of the abstract concepts of 'public authority' and 'public function'.[12] By contrast, although the scope of the FOI Act is also defined in terms of 'public authorities', the meaning of this term is elaborated in a very long list of entities (both governmental and non-governmental) that are to be treated as public authorities for the purposes of the Act (Sched. 1).[13] Although this approach seems a little cumbersome, it has some advantage in terms of clarity and certainty.[14]

Secondly, as was noted in 14.7, the FOI regime may provide a valuable alternative to disclosure of documents as a means of gathering evidence for the purposes of litigation concerned with performance of public functions. More generally, greater openness will make it easier for citizens to hold public authorities to account for their conduct of public affairs, whether through the courts or other avenues, such as a tribunal or an internal complaints mechanism. Thirdly and, in some ways, much more importantly, the FOI Act imposes on public authorities an obligation to 'adopt and maintain' publication schemes (s. 19). A publication scheme specifies the types of information a public authority 'publishes or intends to publish'.[15] In adopting a publication scheme an authority is required to have regard to the public interest in allowing public access to information held by the authority and 'in the publication of reasons for decisions made by the authority'. The FOI Act[16] does not impose, as such, an obligation to give reasons for decisions (see 7.3.2.2.5); but it does, at least, suggest that when reasons are given, they should be communicated.

Publication schemes must be approved by the Information Commissioner, who may also prepare and approve model publication schemes

---

[12] See esp. 3.1 and 3.2.2.

[13] Central to the operation of the FOI regime in relation to entities performing public functions under contract are the exemptions in ss 41 and 43: S. Palmer, 'Freedom of Information: A New Constitutional Landscape?' in N. Bamforth and P. Leyland (eds), *Public Law in a Multi-Layered Constitution* (Oxford, 2003), pp. 240–5; M. McDonagh, 'FOI and Confidentiality of Commercial Information' [2001] *PL* 256.

[14] Entities can be added to the list of public authorities provided they satisfy the criteria laid down in s. 4(2).

[15] See e.g. the publication scheme of the Department of Constitutional Affairs, accessible at www.lcd.gov.uk/foi/publications/scheme.htm.

[16] Unlike the 1994 *Code of Practice on Access to Government Information* referred to earlier.

(s. 20). The real value of publication schemes does not lie in telling people what sorts of information are available on request, but rather in encouraging public authorities to make information available (on the Web, for instance) independently of any request that it be communicated. Identification of and access to unpublished material is facilitated by the Information Asset Register, managed by HMSO.[17]

A fourth point to note concerns the exemptions contained in Part II of the FOI Act.[18] The exemptions operate to relieve public authorities of the obligation to 'confirm or deny' the existence of information, or the obligation to communicate information, or both. Some of the exemptions protect classes of information (e.g. information held for the purposes of a public investigation: s. 30), while others are designed to avoid prejudice to a specified interest as a result of disclosure of information (e.g. the economic interests of the UK: s. 29). Some of the exemptions are absolute—those relating to national security and court records, for instance. Others are not absolute but apply if, 'in all the circumstances of the case', the public interest in secrecy outweighs the public interest in openness. The non-absolute (or 'conditional') exemptions, unlike the absolute exemptions, require the authority which holds the information[19] to do a balancing exercise similar to that involved in PII law, discussed in Chapter 14.

The number and width of the exemptions has led one commentator to observe that the FOI Act is more like a system of 'access to information by voluntary disclosure' than a 'legal right to information subject to specific exemptions'.[20] Amongst the most startling exemptions are those relating to information about the formulation of government policy (s. 35) and information likely to prejudice the effective conduct of public affairs (s. 36). The latter exemption is absolute so far as it relates to information held by either of the Houses of Parliament (s. 2(3)(e)). Otherwise, both exemptions are conditional. The former exemption is class-based whereas the latter is prejudice-based.

It has been said that these two exemptions 'reflect long-standing practice that advice to government should not be disclosed'.[21] It is certainly true that the policy-making process in Britain has traditionally been

[17] See www.hmso.gov.uk/copyright/guidance/gn_18.htm.
[18] The FOI Act regime is residual in the sense that information 'reasonably accessible' without recourse to the Act is exempt from its provisions: ss. 21, 39.
[19] Or, in the case of s. 36, a 'qualified person'.
[20] G. Ganz, *Understanding Public Law*, 3rd edn (London, 2001), p. 67.
[21] Macdonald and Jones, *Law of Freedom of Information*, p. 283.

secretive and subject to little or no legal regulation.[22] But participation by individuals and groups in the policy-making process has become a standard feature of the political landscape (see 19.2), and it may be questioned whether the approach adopted in these exemptions is necessary, desirable or even consistent with a serious commitment to 'open government'. Is it appropriate, for instance, to use the law to prevent publicity being given to differences of opinion amongst ministers (s. 36(2)(a))?[23] And what should we think about the argument underpinning s. 36(2)(b)—that people will only speak freely and frankly under a blanket of confidentiality—in the light of the judicial approach to this matter discussed in 14.6? It remains to be seen what impact these exemptions will have in practice. As a matter of principle, it would seem not unreasonable to conclude that legal entrenchment of the secrecy of the policy-making process is a retrograde step that represents the very antithesis of informational freedom.[24] This is not to say that all the processes of government decision-making can or should be conducted in the full glare of publicity. The question is whether these extremely broad exemptions define a legitimate sphere of State secrecy.

A final point to note about the FOI Act concerns the enforcement mechanisms in Parts IV and V of the Act. A person who is dissatisfied with the response of a public authority to a request for information is required first to use any internal complaints mechanism provided by the authority in question (s. 50(2)(a)). If still dissatisfied, the complainant can apply to the Information Commissioner. If the Commissioner decides that the authority has not dealt with the request in accordance with the provisions of the FOI Act, he can serve a 'decision notice' (s. 50(3)(b)) or

---

[22] See 7.6.2.2; P. Cane, 'The Constitutional and Legal Framework of Policy-Making' in C. Forsyth and I. Hare (eds), *The Golden Metwand and the Crooked Cord: Essays on Public Law in Honour of Sir William Wade* (Oxford, 1998).

[23] A. Tomkins, *Public Law* (Oxford, 2003), pp. 139–40.

[24] The government's own *Code of Practice on Written Consultation* (www.cabinet-office.gov.uk/servicefirst/index/consultation.htm) contains a principle that the results of consultations should be made widely available 'with an account of the views expressed, and reasons for decisions finally taken'. It elaborates by saying that 'individual responses [to consultations] should be generally made available to anyone else who asks for them. Failure to make material available may be incompatible with Open Government or Freedom of Information provisions'. In a proposed revised code published in September 2003 the elaboration is attached to a principle requiring agencies to 'give feedback regarding the responses received and how the consultation process influenced the policy'. See generally on consultation and citizen parrticipation in policy-making House of Commons Public Administration Select Committee, Sixth Report, 2000–1, HC 373, *Innovations in Citizen Participation in Government*.

an 'enforcement notice' (s. 52) on the authority specifying steps to be taken by the authority to comply with the law. Failure to comply with such a notice may constitute contempt of court (s. 54(3)), but cannot form the basis of a civil action against the authority (s. 56(1)). The complainant or the authority may appeal against a decision notice, and the authority may appeal against an enforcement notice, to the Information Tribunal. An appeal on a point of law lies from the Tribunal to the High Court (s. 59).

Decisions of the Tribunal would also, in theory at least, be amenable to judicial review; and the Tribunal is a public authority for the purposes of s. 6 of the HRA.[25] In this context, it is worth noting that the ECHR does not protect freedom of information, as such.[26]

15.2 PROTECTION OF SOURCES

As we have seen (see 14.6), one of the concerns underlying the confidentiality argument against disclosure of documents is a desire not to discourage candour, especially within government. Another is a desire not to discourage the supply of information, particularly to law-enforcement bodies, by persons who might fear that if their identity were made known they could become victims of reprisals. Law-enforcement bodies rely heavily on the activities of informers and 'whistleblowers'.

Protecting the anonymity of sources of information is also important for the operation of the media in general and the press in particular. In a free society the media play an important (though unofficial) part in keeping the public informed about the activities of government and in investigating alleged misconduct by government officials. 'Leaks' play a part in communicating information to the public about the activities of government. This was particularly so before the enactment of the FOI Act. As we have seen, however, the right to information created by the FOI Act is subject to many exceptions; and so leaking will continue to provide an important channel of communication between public authorities and citizens in relation to information not covered by the right to information. The informal communication of information to the media is often allowed or even initiated by the government itself. Our concern here is with unauthorized leaks.

---

[25] Note that courts and tribunals are not public authorities for the purposes of the FOI Act.

[26] Macdonald and Jones, *Law of Freedom of Information*, paras 21.39–53.

Information about sources of information is not, as such, an exempt category under the FOI Act. But many of the exemptions could be used to protect sources. Under s. 10 of the Contempt of Court Act 1981 no court may require the disclosure of sources of information unless such disclosure is necessary in the interests of justice, or national security, or the prevention of disorder or crime.[27] The section requires the court to balance the interest in anonymity of the source against the interest asserted by the party seeking disclosure. It creates a presumption in favour of non-disclosure[28] subject to the three stated qualifications, and on its face it embodies a powerful statement of the importance of maintaining a flow of information to the public *via* the media.[29] In practice, however, the attitude which the courts have taken to the section has somewhat weakened its force. For example, although it has been held that the government cannot simply assert that disclosure of the identity of a source is necessary in the interests of national security but must adduce adequate evidence of necessity, the majority in *Secretary of State for Defence v. Guardian Newspapers Ltd*[30] were prepared to accept as adequate evidence which the minority found inadequate. In general, the courts have shown themselves very deferential to claims that national security is at stake, and there is no reason to think that this attitude will not affect the approach of the courts to this provision.

It has also been held that the phrase 'for the prevention of . . . crime' does not refer just to the prevention of particular crimes but to the general project of deterring and preventing crime.[31] Similarly, the phrase 'in the interests of justice' does not refer only to 'the administration of justice in the course of legal proceedings in a court of law' but more widely to the freedom of persons to 'exercise important legal rights and to protect themselves from serious legal wrongs whether or not resort to

---

[27] The section says that the information must be contained 'in a publication', but it has been held that the section applies to information supplied for the purpose of being published: *X Ltd v. Morgan-Grampian (Publishers) Ltd* [1991] 1 AC 1. The principles contained in s. 10 have also been applied to other situations to which they are not strictly applicable: *Re an Inquiry under the Company Securities (Insider Dealing) Act 1985* [1988] AC 660.

[28] The party seeking disclosure must establish that it is 'necessary'.

[29] The principle underlying s. 10 is freedom of speech/freedom of the press (*Ashworth Hospital Authority v. MGN Ltd* [2002] 1 WLR 2033 at [38]), not freedom of information. This explains why it creates a qualified presumption against disclosure of information about the identity of sources whereas the FOI Act creates a qualified presumption in favour of disclosure of information including information about the identity of sources.

[30] [1985] AC 339. The ECHR does not protect freedom of information as such. A right of access to personal information has been read into Art. 8: *Gaskin v. UK* (1989) 12 EHRR 36.

[31] *Re an Inquiry under the Company Securities (Insider Dealing) Act 1985* [1988] AC 660.

legal proceedings in a court of law will be necessary to achieve these objectives'.[32] On the other hand, the mere fact that a party needs to know the identity of the source in order to take action against the source will not justify disclosure unless the interest, which the party seeking disclosure is trying to protect, is important enough to outweigh the presumption in favour of anonymity.[33] It appears that the interest in anonymity is more likely to prevail against an interest in asserting private legal rights than against either the interest in national security or the interest in the prevention of disorder or crime.

The House of Lords has also strongly reasserted the principle that a party ordered to disclose the identity of a source must do so on pain of punishment for contempt of court. A person who contests the correctness of an order for disclosure is not free to refuse disclosure pending appeal.[34]

15.3 BREACH OF CONFIDENCE

Not all informers, whistleblowers and 'leakers' of confidential information seek to remain, or succeed in remaining, anonymous. Those whose identity is or becomes known may open themselves to civil liability for breach of (an obligation of) confidence. The law of confidence can be used to protect not only private confidential information but also government secrets.[35] The most famous example of this is the *Spycatcher* litigation in which the government sued in various countries for injunctions to prevent the publication of the memoirs of ex-MI5 officer, Peter Wright. Because Wright lived abroad and his book was not published in Britain, the defendants to the actions in this country were newspapers

---

[32] *X v. Morgan-Grampian* [1991] 1 AC 1, 43 *per* Lord Bridge of Harwich.

[33] For instance, a health authority's interest in preserving the integrity of its patient records: *Ashworth Hospital Authority v. MGN Ltd* [2002] 1 WLR 2033

[34] *X v. Morgan-Grampian* [1991] 1 AC 1, criticised on this point by T.R.S Allan, 'Disclosure of Journalists' Sources, Civil Disobedience and the Rule of Law' [1991] *CLJ* 131. In this case a journalist refused to reveal the source of information about the financial affairs of the claimant company. The claimant obtained an injunction that prevented publication of the information in the press, but then sought the identity of the source. The journalist refused to reveal the source and disobeyed a court order that he do so. He was fined. The ECtHR subsequently held that the order for disclosure and the fine infringed Art. 10 of the ECHR because they were disproportionate, given that the injunction had protected many of the claimant's legitimate interests: *Goodwin v. UK* (1996) 22 EHRR 123. See also *Camelot Group Plc v. Centaur Communications Ltd* [1999] QB 124, esp. at [133]–[137] *per* Schiemann LJ.

[35] Information provided to a public authority, disclosure of which by the authority would constitute an actionable breach of confidence, is the subject of an absolute exemption under s. 41 of the FOI Act.

that wished to publish extracts from the memoirs. In this way the affair became overlaid with issues of press freedom,[36] and in a related case it was held that a newspaper might be in contempt of court if it published material that another newspaper had been ordered not to publish.[37] In the main litigation (*Attorney-General v. Guardian Newspapers Ltd (No. 2)*)[38] it was held that members of the security services are under a lifelong obligation of confidence in respect of secrets which they learn in their capacity as Crown servants. On the other hand, it was also held that when the government seeks to prevent the disclosure of confidential information it is not enough to show (at least where the publication is by a person other than the original recipient of the information) that the defendant was under an obligation to keep the information confidential. The government must also show that disclosure would be likely to cause some damage to the public interest.[39] It would then be open to the defendant to convince the court that there was a stronger public interest in disclosure such that the breach of confidence was justified.

The law of breach of confidence is complicated and in a state of development, and this is not the place to examine it in detail. Some points, however, need to be made. The first is that the common law recognizes that disclosure of confidential information may sometimes be in the public interest by providing a public-interest defence to an action for breach of confidence. So, for example, in one case it was held that employees of a company that manufactured breathalyser machines were justified, in the public interest, in disclosing information about the reliability of such machines which they had received in confidence in their capacity as employees.[40] In another case it was held that a doctor was justified in the public interest in releasing to the managers of a secure

---

[36] The ECtHR held that continuation of interlocutory injunctions restraining publication of extracts from Wright's book after its publication in the US constituted a breach of the ECHR: *The Observer and the Guardian v. UK* [1991] 14 EHRR 153.

[37] *Attorney-General v. Times Newspapers Ltd* [1992] 1 AC 191. There is an informal system, called the 'D-notice' system, by which the government seeks to regulate the publication of specific categories of information by newspapers: Birkinshaw, *Freedom of Information*, pp. 197–9; P. Sadler, *National Security and the D-Notice System* (Aldershot, 2001).

[38] [1990] 1 AC 109.

[39] Cf. the idea in the law of disclosure of documents that confidentiality is not *per se* a ground of non-disclosure. Matters relevant to the public interest in non-disclosure include the extent to which the information has already been published (see *Attorney-General v. Guardian* itself); and how long ago the events to which the information relates took place (*Attorney-General v. Jonathon Cape Ltd* [1976] QB 752).

[40] *Lion Laboratories Ltd v. Evans* [1985] QB 526.

hospital a confidential report which revealed that a patient had a long-standing and continuing interest in home-made bombs.[41]

Recognition that there may be a public interest in the disclosure of information supplied or acquired in confidence underpins statutory provisions that require auditors, in certain circumstances, to communicate to the Financial Services Authority information acquired in the capacity of auditor; and that relieve the auditor of any responsibility for breach of duty in so doing.[42] More generally, Part IVA of the Employment Rights Act 1996[43] protects workers, who (in good faith) blow the whistle on their employers by communicating certain classes of information[44] to specified recipients,[45] from being dismissed or subjected to other forms of detriment for having done so. Any confidentiality agreement between a worker and an employer that 'purports to preclude the worker from making a protected disclosure' is void (s. 43J).

A second point to note is that there is an important alternative to the civil law of confidence as a means of controlling the leaking of public information, namely a criminal prosecution under the Official Secrets Act 1989[46] or under one of a large number of other relevant statutes. It has been said that an action for breach of confidence should not lie in respect of public information the disclosure of which would not constitute an offence under official secrets legislation,[47] but it is not clear that the law will develop in this way. Unclear, too, is the relationship between the law of confidence and the FOI Act. Prima facie, one would expect that an action for breach of confidence would not lie in relation to information which a public authority would have an obligation to communicate on request. However, s. 41 of the FOI Act exempts from the obligations to confirm or deny and to disclose information the disclosure of which would constitute an actionable breach of confidence. This exemption is absolute, not conditional on disclosure being contrary to the public interest. This leaves the public interest issue to be dealt with in terms of

---

[41] *W v. Edgell* [1990] Ch 359.

[42] Financial Services and Markets Act 2000 (Communications by Auditors) Regulations 2001 and Financial Services and Markets Act 2000, s. 342(3) respectively.

[43] Inserted by the Public Interest Disclosure Act 1998. For a valuable analysis of the Act against the background of a discussion of the phenomenon of whistleblowing see J. Gobert and M. Punch, 'Whistleblowers, the Public Interest and the Public Interest Disclosure Act 1998' (2000) 63 *MLR* 25.

[44] Such as information that a criminal offence has been committed or that the environment is being damaged.

[45] Such as a Minister in a case where the employer is a public authority.

[46] S. Palmer, 'Tightening Secrecy Law: The Official Secrets Act 1989' [1990] *PL* 243.

[47] *Lord Advocate v. Scotsman Publications Ltd* [1990] 1 AC 812, 824 *per* Lord Templeman.

the public interest defence to an action for breach of confidence. As a result, the operation of the defence may be affected by decisions of the Information Commissioner and the Information Tribunal about the scope of the s. 41 exemption.

Use of the civil law has certain advantages for the government when compared with the criminal law. First, it removes the risk that a jury will acquit a person prosecuted for an offence under the official secrets legislation on grounds other than failure to prove the constituents of the offence beyond reasonable doubt: actions for breach of confidence are tried by a judge sitting alone. Secondly, an action for breach of confidence offers the prospect of preventing or restricting publication of the information in question by means of an injunction; and also the possibility of obtaining an 'account of profits', a remedy by which a person who has made a profit out of a breach of confidence can be required to 'disgorge' that profit.[48] Thirdly, because of the wording of s. 5(1) of the 1989 Act, it may be easier successfully to sue a subsequent recipient of information for breach of confidence than to bring a successful prosecution against the subsequent recipient for breach of the Act.[49] On the other hand, the 1989 Act contains no public interest defence; and under the Act it is an offence to disclose certain categories of information[50] even if the disclosure did not damage the public interest.

15.4 ACCESS TO PERSONAL INFORMATION

One of the important contributions of the 1980s to breaking down ingrained habits of secrecy was the first legislation designed to give people a legal right of access to files concerning themselves. The aim was to enable individuals to know what personal information was held, to have any inaccuracies corrected or erased, and, in the case of information held on computer, to obtain compensation for loss suffered as a result of inaccuracy. Concern about misuse of personal information initially focused on electronic files, but gradually spread to other forms of information

---

[48] Such an order was made against *The Times* newspaper in the *Spycatcher* litigation. In another action arising out of publication of the memoirs of a former spy, it was held that the government was entitled to the profits earned by the author from the publication, but on the basis of breach of contract, not breach of confidence (the information in question was no longer secret when the memoirs were published): *Attorney-General v. Blake* [2001] 1 AC 268.

[49] The section does not appear to apply to disclosure of information received from former civil servants.

[50] Those covered by ss. 1(1) and 4(3).

gathering and storage. A patchwork of legislative provisions was enacted in the 1980s and 1990s, and the matter is now dealt with comprehensively in the Data Protection Act 1998 (DP Act). As a result of s. 68 of the FOI Act, the scope of the DP Act is wider in relation to personal information held by public authorities than in relation to information held by private 'data controllers'.

Whereas freedom of information legislation promotes open government, data protection legislation promotes personal privacy and various other interests that individuals have in the collection and use of their personal details. Data protection legislation gives people access only to information about themselves. Section 40 of the FOI Act prevents individuals using the FOI regime as an alternative to the DP regime as a means of gaining access to information about themselves, and regulates the use of the FOI Act to gain access to personal information about other people.

Under the DP Act, data controllers must be registered, and must comply with eight 'data protection principles' when collecting and using data. 'Data subjects' have various rights, such as a right to prevent data-processing that is likely to cause substantial damage or distress, and a right to claim compensation from the data controller for damage or distress caused by any contravention of the Act. The operation of the Act is subject to various exemptions to protect national security, and the prevention or detection of crime, for instance. Responsibility for registration of data-controllers and for enforcement of the Act rests with the Information Commissioner (who also performs these functions under the FOI Act). There is a right of appeal to the Information Tribunal from enforcement decisions of the Commissioner; and a right of appeal on a point of law from the Tribunal to the High Court.

15.5 CONCLUSION

The main pieces of legislation discussed in this chapter—the Official Secrets Act, the Freedom of Information Act, the Public Interest Disclosure Act, and the Data Protection Act—and the common law of disclosure of documents discussed in Chapter 14, together form a dense and complex interlocking patchwork of legal rules designed to strike a balance between personal privacy, public secrecy and 'open government'. The broad landscape of information law in Britain has changed dramatically in the past twenty-five years. Only time will tell how the balance between these various interests will be struck in practice, and how the legal regimes we have examined will interact with one another. Information is the life-blood of accountability, and the growth of a complex body of information law in the past quarter century has greatly increased the role of law and legal institutions in promoting accountability for the performance of public functions.

Part IV

Non-Judicial Control

The focus so far in this book has been on judicial control of performance of public functions and exercise of public power through judicial review and civil liability. In this Part we now look briefly at various non-judicial forms of accountability. Chapter 16 looks at the role of Parliament, Chapter 17 at investigatory complaints-handling, especially by ombudsmen, and Chapter 18 at tribunals. The aim is to locate judicial control in the wider landscape of accountability of public functionaries.

16

Parliament

16.1 LEGISLATION

In order to understand the role of Parliament in scrutinizing the conduct of public functionaries it is necessary to draw a distinction between two different functions that Parliament performs. In the first place it is a legislative body. Parliament, of course, legislates on many matters that have nothing directly to do with the institutions and functions of governance. But many Acts of Parliament[1] are concerned with conferring and defining the administrative and legislative powers of central and local government and of other public functionaries.

One of the most striking features of the British Parliamentary system is the extent to which the legislative process (from the first stages of formulation of policy, through the drafting stage,[2] and right up to the final stage of voting on the third reading of a bill) is under the control of the government.[3] This is not to say that Parliament plays no part at the policy-formulation stage. Debates initiated by the opposition and debates on Green or White Papers issued by the government do allow policies to be aired before the proposals reach an advanced stage. Much more important, however, in the policy-formulation process is the well-established practice of all governments of engaging in extensive consultation with entities outside Parliament representing, or purporting to represent, groups of citizens who will be affected by the proposed legislation. Bodies, such as trade unions, employers' organizations, and business, consumer, and environmental organizations, are

---

[1] In the phrase 'Act of Parliament', 'Parliament' means the House of Commons, the House of Lords, and the Monarch acting together. The term 'Parliament' is also used to refer to the House of Commons and the House of Lords acting either separately or together (as in the case of a joint committee of both Houses).

[2] But see D. Oliver, 'The Reform of the UK Parliament' in J. Jowell and D. Oliver (eds), *The Changing Constitution*, 4th edn (Oxford, 2000), pp. 271–2.

[3] See generally T. Daintith and A. Page, *The Executive in the Constitution: Structure, Autonomy and Internal Control* (Oxford, 1999), pp. 241–58. Concerning the role of civil servants in the legislative process see E.C. Page, 'The Civil Servant as Legislator: Law Making in Public Administration' (2003) 81 *Pub Admin* 651.

constantly in touch with government seeking to influence the formulation of policy and legislation that will affect them.[4] (This is as true in relation to delegated as to primary legislation.)[5] Many MPs are 'sponsored' by, or have links with, extra-parliamentary interest groups and put forward views and interests of these groups in debates. It is also common for MPs to act as (paid) 'consultants' or 'advisers' to interest groups and lobby organizations.[6] In the House of Lords, where party loyalties are less important and many life peers are chosen specifically because of their knowledge of particular areas of social and economic

[4] This is a very large topic that cannot be explored here. A useful survey of theories and empirical evidence about 'interest group politics' is A.G Jordan and J.J. Richardson, *Government and Pressure Groups in Britain* (Oxford, 1987). Concerning the EU see S. Mazey and J. Richardson (eds), *Lobbying in the European Community* (Oxford, 1993). Underlying much of the literature on interest group politics are two competing theoretical models: a pluralist model and a corporatist model. Pluralists interpret interest group activity in terms of competition between groups for influence on government, whereas corporatists emphasize cooperation between government and selected sectional interests to achieve shared policy goals. Each model captures part of the reality. A third model is that of 'policy networks' (D. Marsh and R.A.W. Rhodes (eds), *Policy Networks in British Government* (Oxford, 1992). Unlike the other two models, it stresses that government and interest groups do not interact as two monolothic forces. Rather parts of government interact with sets of groups interested in specific policy areas such as agriculture, health or unemployment.

[5] E.C. Page, *Governing by Numbers* (Oxford, 2001), ch. 7.

[6] Links between outside organizations and MPs in their capacity as such are regulated by a Code of Conduct adopted in 1996 in response to the first report of the Committee on Standards in Public Life, which was established in the wake of a scandal involving payment of MPs in return for asking Parliamentary questions (for the history see M. Rush 'The Law Relating to Members' Conduct' in D. Oliver and G. Drewry (eds), *The Law and Parliament* (London, 1998), ch. VII). The Code is backed up by a detailed *Guide to the Rules Relating to Conduct of Members.* Complaints about non-compliance with the Code and the *Guide* are investigated by the Parliamentary Commissioner for Standards (PCS), an officer of the House of Commons. The decision about whether a breach has taken place and if so, what sanction to impose, lies with the Select Committee on Standards and Privileges. English courts have traditionally refused to become involved in Parliamentary self-regulation of the conduct of members (the PCS is not subject to judicial review: *R v. Parliamentary Commissioner for Standards, ex p. Al Fayed* [1998] 1 WLR 669); but there are reasons to think that the current system for handling complaints infringes Art. 6 of the ECHR: D. Oliver, *Constitutional Reform in the UK* (Oxford, 2003), pp. 183–6. The Committee on Standards in Public Life has recently recommended that the Select Committee establish an Investigatory Panel, chaired by a lawyer from outside the House, to inquire into serious, contested cases: *Standards of Conduct in the House of Commons*, Cm. 5663, 2002, ch. 6; R. James and R. Kirkham, 'Slow Progress in Parliament: The Eighth Report of the Committee on Standards in Public Life' (2003) 66 *MLR* 906. The Select Committee has rejected this recommendation, proposing instead that in such cases, the Commissioner's investigation should be assisted by a legal adviser and a senior member of the House (Second Report, HC 403, 2002/3, paras 23–42). See also D. Woodhouse, 'Delivering Public Confidence: Codes of Conduct, A Step in the Right Direction' [2003] *PL* 511. Concerning Parliamentary standards in the devolved assemblies see O. Gay, 'The Regulation of Parliamentary Standards After Devolution' [2002] *PL* 422.

life, the practice of putting forward the views of sectional interests is common.[7] Once the legislation is drafted and is before Parliament, the ability of peers and MPs to get the substance of the bill changed is very limited.[8] This is not to say that the government is never defeated when the Houses of Parliament vote on proposed amendments to a bill; but if the government has a comfortable majority in the House of Commons, defeats in that House are extremely unlikely. Defeats are more likely in the Lords. Nor is it true to say that the government is never persuaded to alter a bill as a result of opposition; but, once again, if it has a comfortable majority, such changes are more likely to be prompted by opposition from the government's own backbenchers than from the official opposition. Given that debates, both in standing committees (to which most bills are referred at the committee stage) and on the floor of the House, are conducted in an adversarial spirit rather than in a spirit of cooperative effort to achieve a good result, and given that voting is on party lines, the impact which Parliament can have on the shape of a bill is, at most, marginal.[9]

Does all of this have any relevance for administrative law? At first sight the answer must be negative. In English law there is a sharp distinction between primary and secondary legislation. The courts can invalidate secondary legislation on certain limited grounds, but primary legislation cannot be held invalid except on the ground that it conflicts with EC law. Under s. 4 of the HRA, primary legislation may be declared incompatible with the ECHR; but such a declaration does not affect the validity of the legislative provision(s) in question. Primary legislation is generally immune from legal challenge despite the fact that there are many elements in the Parliamentary process that might be thought to fall short of the ideal of representative democracy. These include the part played by the House of Lords;[10] the degree of control of the government over the legislative process; the fact that, in practice, sectional interest groups have much more to say at the drafting stage than do the elected representatives of the

---

[7] The House of Lords adopted a Code of Conduct in 2001. Allegations of non-compliance are investigated by a sub-committee of the Committee of Privileges.

[8] Even so, peers and MPs are the objects of considerable interest-group activity: M. Rush (ed.), *Parliament and Pressure Politics* (Oxford, 1990). On the role of individual MPs and committees in scrutinizing legislation see D. Feldman, 'Parliamentary Scrutiny of Legislation and Human Rights' [2002] *PL* 323.

[9] For a detailed discussion of the role of backbenchers in policy-making see J. Brand, *British Parliamentary Parties* (Oxford, 1992), esp. chs 1 and 10.

[10] Concerning progress with, and proposals for further, reform of the House of Lords see Oliver, *Constitutional Reform in the UK*, ch. 10.

people; and the strength of the party system in the House of Commons, which operates as a hindrance to searching bipartisan examination of proposed legislation. It might be argued, for example, that not only in the case of secondary legislation, but also in the case of primary legislation, the courts ought to be prepared to ensure that all interested groups get a chance to have their say in respect of the drafting of legislation. On the other hand, the introduction of judicial review into this context would involve the injection of a further non-representative element into what should be a highly democratic process. Much more desirable would be reforms of the legislative process itself in such a way as to increase the power of the House of Commons over the preparation and scrutiny of proposed legislation. If power over the legislative process is to shift from the government, it ought to shift to Parliament, not to the courts.

Another point worth making in this context is that under British constitutional arrangements, certain governmental activities must be supported by empowering legislation in order to be lawful. For example, taxation must be authorized by legislation; so too must public spending.[11] In theory then, and subject to what was said above, the government is forced to obtain Parliamentary approval for some of its actions (which are, therefore, subject to Parliamentary scrutiny and control); and it is, in this way, made accountable to Parliament for what it does. It should be remembered, however, that there are many activities that the government can engage in without seeking Parliamentary approval in the form of legislation.[12] For example, exercise of the government's contracting power is largely free of Parliamentary control. Government borrowing does not require legislation or even Parliamentary approval; nor does the declaration of war. Again, for example, the government exercises a great deal of regulatory power over the economy through the activities of the Bank of England; this does not involve the use of legislative coercion of financial institutions, but the exercise of *de facto* economic power. Even in cases where legislation is needed (e.g. to authorize public expenditure) the legislation is often purely formal, and the real decisions about spending are subjected to scrutiny by non-legislative Parliamentary procedures.[13]

---

[11] But see J. F McEldowney, 'The Contingencies Fund and Parliamentary Scrutiny of Public Finance' [1988] *PL* 232; 'The Control of Public Expenditure' in J. Jowell and D. Oliver (eds), *The Changing Constitution*, 4th edn (Oxford, 2000), pp. 197–201.

[12] T. Daintith, 'The Techniques of Government' in J. Jowell and D. Oliver (eds), *The Changing Constitution*, 3rd edn (Oxford, 1994), ch. 8.

[13] See generally Daintith and Page, *The Executive in the Constitution*, ch. 6.

Finally, it is worth noting that although most administrative and sub-ordinate legislative powers are conferred by legislation, such powers are often couched as broad discretions and in very vague terms. One result of this, it is often alleged, is that politically contentious issues as to how the powers will be exercised and to what ends, do not surface and are not debated. In this way Parliamentary control over governmental activity is weakened. Particularly controversial are so-called 'Henry VIII clauses' that empower Ministers to amend or repeal primary legislation by means of subordinate legislation. A noteworthy example of a 'prospective Henry VIII clause' is contained in s. 10 of the HRA, dealing with Acts of Parliament that have been declared incompatible with the ECHR.[14]

We can see, then, that in theory, legislative activity provides Parliament with important opportunities for scrutinizing and controlling government activity. In practice, however, Parliament's position is weakened by the fact that the government can, in a variety of ways, bypass the legislative process; and by the fact that even when it is used, it is too formalized to provide any real check on governmental policies and activities. Indeed, it has been argued that Parliament should not be seen as a governing institution but as a debating forum.[15]

16.2 SCRUTINY OF GOVERNMENT ACTIVITY

16.2.1 MINISTERIAL RESPONSIBILITY

Another function of Parliament is that of scrutinizing the day-to-day activities of government. The constitutional linchpin of this activity is the doctrine of individual ministerial responsibility (IMR).[16] According to this doctrine, Ministers are personally answerable to Parliament for the 'quality and success' of 'their policies, decisions, and actions, and for the policies, decisions, and actions of their departments'.[17] IMR is the key feature that distinguishes 'responsible government', in which Ministers (including the Prime Minister) are also members of the legislature, from 'presidential government' (exemplified by the US system of government) in which they (and the President) are not. IMR is a prime institution of

---

[14] See generally N.W. Barber and A.L. Young, 'The Rise of Prospective Henry VIII clauses and Their Implications for Sovereignty' [2003] *PL* 112 (arguing that such clauses perform a legitimate function in certain circumstances).

[15] J.A.G. Griffith and M. Ryle, *Parliament* (London, 1989), pp. 5–7.

[16] See further 19.1.3. Concerning collective ministerial responsibility see A. Tomkins, *Public Law* (Oxford, 2003), pp. 135–40.

[17] Ibid. 140.

what has become known (rather loosely) as the 'political constitution' as opposed to the 'legal constitution'. This distinction focuses on issues of accountability. In crude terms, the political constitution provides a framework for accountability to political institutions for policy failures, whereas the legal constitution provides a framework for accountability to courts and tribunals for breaches of public (and private) law.

Opinions differ about the efficacy of IMR as an accountability mechanism.[18] Three relevant issues deserve brief attention. The first concerns information. As noted in Chapters 14 and 15, information is a precondition of effective accountability. In this respect, one important factor is the willingness of the government of the day to allow and require ministers and civil servants to appear before Parliamentary committees; another is what restrictions are placed on the sorts of questions they may answer and the sorts of information they may give when they do appear.

A second issue concerns 'sanctions'. The typical requirement that IMR imposes is to give information about, and to explain, conduct of the Minister or the department. When things go wrong, a Minister may need to apologize and to undertake personally that steps will be taken to put things right. Only in very serious cases will a Minister be forced to resign in the name of IMR alone.[19] Pressure from the Prime Minister, the governing party, or the country (commonly expressed through the media), in addition to that exerted by Parliament, is usually necessary to secure a ministerial resignation. On the other hand, a Minister may be forced to resign by extra-Parliamentary pressure even if Parliament is not seeking that outcome.

A third issue relevant to assessing the efficacy of IMR concerns its scope. Ministers are obviously responsible for their own policies and conduct (their 'public' conduct, anyway).[20] In traditional constitutional theory, ministers are also responsible for the policies and public conduct of civil servants in their departments. This aspect of IMR goes along with the concept of an anonymous, independent, and politically neutral civil service made up of non-partisan functionaries doing the bidding of their political masters. Various developments in recent years have blurred this

---

[18] For an upbeat assessment see Tomkins, *Public Law*, pp. 140–59. For less optimistic accounts see Oliver, *Constitutional Reform in the UK*, 213–217; D. Woodhouse, 'Ministerial Responsibility: Something Old, Something New' [1997] *PL* 262.

[19] See generally K. Dowding and W-T. Kang, 'Ministerial Resignations 1945–97' (1998) 76 *Pub Admin* 411.

[20] The extent to which a Minister's private life attracts and should attract IMR is a different matter.

traditional picture. For example, many senior civil servants are now employed on short-term contracts, thus undermining the job-security traditionally associated with public service. Also, as a result of changes in modes of delivery of public services, individual heads of executive, non-departmental agencies now bear a significant measure of personal, financial, and administrative responsibility for the performance of public functions.[21] To the extent that such developments enable Ministers to resist the various demands of IMR, other accountability mechanisms might be needed. These may involve making senior civil servants directly answerable to Parliament, or utilizing investigatory procedures of the sort discussed in Chapter 17. In recent years, the increasing importance of law in British constitutional arrangements (as a result, for instance, of the enactment of the HRA and the FOI Act) has opened up avenues of non-political accountability that may be available to plug perceived gaps in the coverage of IMR. Of course, these various mechanisms differ in terms of the grounds of accountability, to whom the account has to be given, and how accountability is secured. For this reason, they may not be thought substitutable for one another. For instance, some might favour political accountability and, consequently, consider legal accountability to be an inadequate substitute for robust political scrutiny. Yet others might say that the processes of contractualization briefly mapped in 12.2.1 have built in to them 'managerial' accountability mechanisms that may (and were probably intended to) substitute for both legal and political techniques.[22]

16.2.2 QUESTIONS

Parliamentary questions are, of course, an integral part of enforcing IMR. But they deserve brief attention in their own right. Questions perform two main functions: to elicit information about the activities of government and to ventilate policy issues which arise out of the day-to-day conduct of government. By far the majority of questions (of which there are tens of thousands in each session) receive written answers, and this is the best medium for obtaining detailed information. Oral questions tend to be designed for political purposes rather than for getting information. Even if Ministers rarely resign as a result of revelations elicited by

---

[21] See also 12.2.2.
[22] C. Scott, 'Accountability in the Regulatory State' (2000) 27 *J of Law and Society* 38. For a discussion of the balance between managerial and political ('constitutional') account-ability see D. Woodhouse, 'The Reconstruction of Constitutional Accountability' [2002] *PL* 73.

Parliamentary questions, it is nevertheless true that governments can be embarrassed by questions and can be prompted to do something about the matters raised. Important, too, is the fact that the question is really the only Parliamentary procedure which has remained under the complete control of the back-bencher; and for this reason, if for no other, questions remain an important counterweight to government power and a constant, if minor, irritant.[23]

A major limitation on the usefulness of questions is that a Minister can only be asked, and need only answer, questions on matters over which he or she has control. In general, this prevents Ministers from being questioned about the day-to-day management and activities of non-departmental agencies and other governmental bodies which are, in theory at least, independent of direct ministerial control and direction in relation to their routine operations. In practice this limitation is generally, but not rigidly, observed. The result is that much governmental activity is protected from the scrutiny of Parliamentary questions. In the case of executive agencies, this 'accountability gap' is partly filled by the fact that the chief executives of agencies can be asked written questions the answers to which are published in Hansard.[24] The real problem, however, is that the line between routine operations, about which the chief executive can be asked, and matters of policy, for which the Minister is responsible, is blurred. This blurring may enable both the chief executive and the Minister effectively to avoid answering a question fully and properly.

Continuing tension in this area between successive parliaments and governments may be partly a result of confusion about the term 'responsibility'. The word may be understood rather legally as a rough synonym for 'liable'. Legal liability is basically of two sorts: liability to be punished (criminal) and liability to make reparation (civil). Legal liability is typically for one's own conduct. Occasionally a person may be vicariously liable for the conduct of another, but very rarely in criminal law. If political responsibility is understood as analogous to legal responsibility,

---

[23] The Public Administration Select Committee reports regularly on the topic of Parliamentary questions: e.g. Sixth Report, 2001/2 (HC 1086); First Report, 2002/3, HC 136 (Government Response). This report raises the important issue of the relationship between openness in answering questions and the freedom of information regime (see Ch. 15). In particular, the FOI Act will, in some cases, provide an enforcement mechanism in relation to government refusal to provide information requested by way of a Parliamentary question: B. Hough, 'Ministerial Responses to Parliamentary Questions: Some Recent Concerns' [2003] *PL* 211.

[24] P. Greer, *Transforming Central Government* (Buckingham, 1994), pp. 89–91; P. Leopold, 'Letters to and From "Next Steps" Agency Chief Executives' [1994] *PL* 214.

it is not surprising that Ministers want to minimize its scope. But political responsibility is not just about punishment and reparation. It is also about openness and explanation. It would not be reasonable to hold a Minister personally 'liable' to be 'punished' or to 'make reparation' for everything done in his or her department, let alone in non-departmental public bodies that operate in the same policy area. It does not follow, however, that the scope of responsibility in this narrow sense should also mark the boundary of the Minister's obligation to answer Parliamentary questions and generally to provide Parliament with information reasonably available to the Minister about the conduct of public business relevant to his or her portfolio.

16.2.3 SELECT COMMITTEES

Unlike standing committees, which consider legislation at the committee stage and operate in an essentially adversarial way as a microcosm of the House, select committees[25] are more investigative and usually less partisan, their membership consisting of backbenchers who are particularly interested in the area of operation of the committee. In 1979 the select committee system was rationalized and the number of committees was increased so that the operations of all of the major departments of State are now monitored by a committee. The function of these committees, which have wide powers to summon persons and papers and to initiate inquiries, is to maintain continuing scrutiny over the day-to-day running of government. Sometimes the committees investigate large policy issues and sometimes they probe more detailed current or continuing problems in the administration of government programmes. The terms of reference of the select committees are wide and enable them to investigate the activities not only of government departments, but also of non-departmental bodies.

Particularly worthy of mention is the Public Accounts Committee (PAC)[26] which, as its name implies, monitors the use of public money by government. This committee was first formed in 1861, and its investigations are now usually based on reports by the National Audit Office (NAO), which is headed by the Comptroller and Auditor General. The NAO conducts audits of two types. Certification audits are designed to check that taxes received and monies expended are properly accounted

---

[25] G. Drewry (ed.), *The New Select Committees*, 2nd edn (Oxford, 1989); Tomkins, *Public Law*, pp. 162–8; Oliver, *Constitutional Reform in the UK*, pp. 178–180.
[26] F. White and K. Hollingsworth, *Audit, Accountability and Government* (Oxford, 1999), pp. 122–7.

for, that appropriations are used for the right purpose, and that government business is conducted with propriety and probity. Value-for-money (VFM) audits are designed to judge whether government business is being conducted with 'economy, efficiency and effectiveness'. Such audits are not, in theory, concerned with matters of policy; but in practice it is difficult to pronounce on matters of economy, efficiency, and effectiveness without raising what could be seen as questions of policy. For this reason, VFM audits are controversial.[27] The PAC is not, of course, required to be silent about issues of policy, but it purports to confine itself to the issue of value-for-money. The departmental select committees, by contrast, are empowered 'to examine the expenditure, administration *and policy* of the principal government departments and associated public bodies'.

The select committee system is potentially a very important tool in scrutinizing governmental activity. It can provide much more thorough and systematic investigation than can questions, which are haphazard and often ill-informed. The back-bencher asks a question from a position of relative ignorance whereas the select committees have significant investigatory powers. An important practical constraint on the work of the committees is the fact that at the end of the day, a committee cannot force Ministers and civil servants appearing before them to answer particular questions or to answer them in a non-evasive way.

The effectiveness of the select committees[28] depends partly on what is done with their reports. Reports are presented to the House, but individual reports are rarely debated; publicity is the committees' main weapon. Much depends, too, on the ability of committees to act on the basis of consensus and in a non-partisan way;[29] and, most importantly of all, on the willingness of government departments to accept and act upon criticisms made by committees. The strength of the executive *vis-à-vis* Parliament imposes an inevitable and major constraint on what the committees can achieve by way of altering government behaviour or policy.[30]

It can plausibly be argued that select committees (like Parliament itself) operate 'on the sidelines of government'[31] because it is the executive

---

[27] J. McEldowney, 'The Control of Public Expenditure' in J. Jowell and D. Oliver, *The Changing Constitution*, 4th edn (Oxford, 2000), pp. 217–23. See also C. Scott, 'Speaking Softly Without Big Sticks: Meta-Regulation and Public Sector Audit' (2003) 25 *Law and Society* 203.

[28] 'Effectiveness' is a complex concept: Drewey (ed.), *The New Select Committees*, pp. 5–8, 397–8.

[29] Ibid. 362–5, 404–6, 408–11.   [30] Ibid. 372–6.   [31] Ibid. 426.

which runs the country.[32] On the other hand, reports of select committees contain large amounts of information about government activities which would probably not otherwise see the light of day; and in a governmental system as secretive as the British, this alone is a considerable achievement. At the same time, it does seem a pity that the expertise of members of select committees could not be more creatively harnessed to the job of formulating policy rather than just scrutinizing its execution.

16.2.4 CONTROL OF DELEGATED LEGISLATION

Another aspect of the scrutiny function of Parliament relates to delegated legislation. Most statutory instruments (SIs)[33] have to be laid before Parliament before they come into effect. In some cases, the statute under which the legislation is made only provides that the legislation shall be laid before the Houses (or the House of Commons only). In other cases, the statute provides that an instrument shall expire or not come into effect unless approved by resolution of the House(s) (the affirmative procedure). In yet other cases, the statute provides that after laying, the instrument will automatically come into operation unless either House (or the House of Commons only) resolves to the contrary (the negative procedure).[34] Statutory instruments can be subjected to both technical scrutiny and scrutiny on the merits.[35] The latter is concerned with the substance of the legislation and whether it is acceptable in policy terms; the former is more concerned with ensuring that the instrument does not exceed the powers of the maker (i.e. that it is *intra vires*) and that it is clearly and effectively drafted to achieve its stated purpose.

Views differ about the value and effectiveness of Parliamentary scrutiny of delegated legislation.[36] One theoretical advantage of Parliamentary

---

[32] [S]pare us government by select committee. This is a recipe for inertia and muddle': P. Riddell, 'The Rise of the Puppetocracy', *The Times*, 8 Feb 1993.

[33] See 3.2.3, 7.6.2.1.

[34] Under the negative procedure, a statutory instrument can be annulled but not amended. As a matter of self-imposed restraint, the House of Lords does not vote against statutory instruments. According to Page, of the SIs made between 1991 and 1999, 10 per cent were made by the affirmative procedure and 68 per cent by the negative procedure. Of the rest, 2 per cent were required only to be laid, while 19 per cent did not have to be laid: Page, *Governing by Numbers*, p. 26.

[35] J.D. Hayhurst and P. Wallington, 'The Parliamentary Scrutiny of Delegated Legislation' [1988] *PL* 547; Page, *Governing by Numbers*, ch. 8; House of Commons Select Committee on Procedure, *Delegated Legislation*, Fourth Report, 1996, HC 152.

[36] For an upbeat assessment see Page, *Governing by Numbers*, ch. 8.

control of delegated legislation, compared with judicial review,[37] is that it takes place before the legislation actually comes into force (but typically only after it has been drafted and the policies underlying it have been settled), or at least very soon after it comes into effect.[38] The fact that judicial review of legislation may take place a long time after the instrument has come into operation and despite the fact that it has been laid before and approved by Parliament (if the instrument is subject to the affirmative procedure),[39] probably acts as a disincentive to the courts to declare delegated legislation invalid, because this will mean that any acts done under it will be legally ineffective or unlawful. The courts can lessen the impact of such invalidation in some cases. For example, failure to consult a body required by statute to be consulted before legislation is made invalidates the legislation only as against that party.[40] If only one part of an instrument is invalid and can be easily severed from the rest of the instrument, then the remainder can be allowed to stand.[41]

Nevertheless, since delegated legislation usually affects very many people, it is a distinct disadvantage if, after it has been in operation for a long time, it can be struck down at the suit of an individual. The importance of this should not, however, be exaggerated. If the purpose of judicial review is to protect individuals, it cannot be a conclusive argument against invalidating delegated legislation that it has been in operation for some time and has had wide effects. In legal systems, such as that of the USA, in which statutes can be struck down because they are in conflict with a written constitution, people are much more used to the idea of invalidating legislative acts of wide importance in order to protect individual rights.

A second theoretical advantage of Parliamentary scrutiny over judicial review is that Parliament can concern itself more with the substance of the legislation. However, this raises a serious practical dilemma. One of the main reasons why so much rule-making is done by delegates of Parliament is that Parliamentary time is limited: the business of government is simply too multifarious and extensive to be regulated entirely by

---

[37] Successful legal challenges to delegated legislation that was also subject to Parliamentary scrutiny are extremely rare. Hayhurst and Wallington found only twelve instance between 1914 and 1986: [1988] *PL* 547, 568–9.

[38] The validity of acts done under a statutory instrument before it is revoked is not affected by revocation: Statutory Instruments Act 1946, s. 5(1).

[39] *F. Hoffman-La-Roche & Co AG v. Secretary of State for Trade* [1975] AC 295, 354 *per* Lord Wilberforce.

[40] *Agricultural Training Board v. Aylesbury Mushrooms Ltd* [1972] 1 WLR 190.

[41] *Dunkley v. Evans* [1981] 1 WLR 1522.

Parliament. Increasingly, primary legislation lays down only broad policy objectives, and delegated legislation is concerned not only with the detailed implementation of primary legislation but also with resolving important matters of policy.[42] Although the scrutiny of rules made by someone else may not take as long as making the rules in the first place, the Parliamentary timetable would simply not permit every instrument of major importance to be debated. In fact, only a very small proportion of statutory instruments is debated,[43] and since the Statutory Instruments Act 1946 came into operation only a handful of instruments subject to the negative procedure has been successfully 'prayed against'. An important reason why the affirmative procedure is relatively little used is that it necessitates a debate (which may take place in a standing committee).

So, whatever the defects of the actual procedures used in Parliament for scrutinizing instruments, it is unlikely that the level of scrutiny will ever be such as to make Parliamentary scrutiny an important means of control. The position of Parliament is also weak because there is no requirement that Parliament be consulted when delegated legislation is being drafted;[44] nor is Parliament in fact normally consulted. It should probably, therefore, be recognized that Parliament does not and never will play a significant part in scrutinizing delegated legislation or participating in its preparation. We should concentrate on increasing the power of Parliament in scrutinizing primary legislation[45] and develop other methods for increasing the democratic input into the making of delegated legislation.[46]

---

[42] For example, the Child Support Act 1991 contains more than 100 regulation-making powers in its fifty-eight sections. Concerning Henry VIII clauses, see n. 14 above and text. The House of Lords Delegated Powers Scrutiny Committee monitors statutory delegations of legislative power. In 2002 the Committee's Third Report concerned Henry VIII clauses.

[43] Page, *Governing by Numbers*, pp. 168–72.

[44] A very small proportion of statutory instruments must be laid before Parliament in draft.

[45] Parliamentary scrutiny of draft primary legislation is very rare: D. Oliver, 'The Reform of the UK Parliament' in J. Jowell and D. Oliver (eds), *The Changing Constitution*, 4th edn (Oxford, 2000), pp. 271–2.

[46] See e.g. House of Commons Public Administration Select Committee, *Innovations in Citizen Participation in Government*, Sixth Report, 2000/1, HC 373.

17

Investigating Complaints

In 7.2.1 we noted the distinction between adversarial and inquisitorial styles of fact-finding. The essential difference between them is that in the adversary system the fact-finder is presented with evidence whereas in an inquisitorial system the fact-finder collects evidence. The inquisitorial method of fact-finding can alternatively be called 'investigatory', and that is the term used in this chapter, which examines the use of formal investigatory techniques to resolve complaints against government. Investigating officials are often given the convenient, but unfortunately gender-specific, title of 'ombudsman'.

Designating someone within an organization, whether public or private, to deal with complaints is, of course, not a recent development; but the importance of making specific provision within government for handling complaints was reasserted in the early 1990s in the Citizen's Charter.[1] The appointment of complaints officers who are external to and independent of the organization complained against is also common both in the private[2] and public sectors. It began with the creation of the office of Parliamentary Commissioner for Administration (PCA) in 1967. The PCA—now called the Parliamentary Ombudsman (PO)—deals with complaints against central government; the Health Service Commissioner (HSC)—now called the Health Service Ombudsman (HSO)—with the National Health Service (this post is also held by the PO), and the Commission for Local Administration (CLA)—now called the Local Government Ombudsman (LGO)—with local government.[3] The EC has

---

[1] See 12.2.1.

[2] The legal position of private-sector ombudsmen may be more complex than that of their public-sector counterparts, and they may be more closely regulated by law. See, e.g., R. Nobles, 'Rules, Principles and Ombudsmen' (2003) 66 *MLR* 781.

[3] Concerning the Welsh ombudsmen see M. Seneviratne, 'Time for Change for the Ombudsmen in Wales' [2003] *PL* 656.

an ombudsman;[4] as does the House of Commons.[5] Our discussion of ombudsmen will give most attention to the PO.

17.1 INTERNAL COMPLAINTS MECHANISMS

As we will see later in this chapter, the practice of the three main public-sector ombudsmen is informed by a principle that complaints are best dealt with as close as possible to the source of the problem. On this basis, the first port of call for complaints ought to be within the relevant agency. An emphasis on internal complaints-resolution first emerged as an explicit principle of public administration in the Citizen's Charter in the early 1990s. Since then, internal complaints mechanisms have proliferated, and some have become quite elaborate and formalized.

The concept of 'internal review' is more complex than may at first appear. For instance, one of the potential problems of dealing with complaints at source is an appearance of lack of independence of the reviewer from the original decision-maker.[6] For this reason, complaints may be dealt with at some considerable 'distance' from the source even though by someone who is, in some sense, part of or under the control of the agency that is the object of complaint. For example, the Independent Review Service of the Social Fund is not part of the Benefits Agency, but it is subject to direction and guidance from the Secretary of State. In short, 'internal' is a relative term. Furthermore, internal review is valued not only because of its metaphysical proximity to the seat of the problem but also as a way of promoting relatively informal, cheap and speedy resolution of complaints, and of rationing access to more formal, expensive, and time-consuming grievance-handlers such as ombudsmen, tribunals, and courts, leaving them to deal with more serious cases. So it is better not to draw too sharp a distinction between 'internal' and 'external' review, but rather to think about review mechanisms in terms of various characteristics (such as informality, procedure, independence, and so on) needed for the resolution of complaints of various sorts and of varying complexity.

One of the most elaborate and highly developed public-sector complaints systems is that within the NHS. It was first established in 1996,

[4] K. Heede, *European Ombudsman: Redress and Control at Union Level* (The Hague, 2000); P.G. Bonnor, 'The European Ombudsman: A Novel Source of Soft Law in the European Union' (2000) 25 *European LR* 39.

[5] See 16.1, n. 6.

[6] e.g. Department of Health, *NHS Complaints Reform: Making Things Right* (undated), paras 3.35–41.

and in 2000–1 received 140,000 complaints. Its introduction changed the role of the HSO, who assumed a sort of appellate function in the system. In 2002–3, for instance, the HSO refused to investigate more than 41 per cent of complaints received because they were 'premature'— i.e. the complainant had not exhausted the NHS complaints system. The NHS complaints system has two stages, the first at local level and the second before an independent panel. An independent review of the system in 1999 argued that neither stage was working optimally.[7] The main concerns expressed about both stages were lack of impartiality and independence, lack of procedural fairness, and lack of training for complaints-handlers. The Department of Health subsequently conducted a review of the system, and it confirmed the validity of these concerns. An overhaul is planned that will involve, amongst other things, establishment of an 'independent' Commission for Health Care Audit and Inspection (CHAI). One of its functions will be to manage the second stage of the complaints process. It is not clear how the CHAI will interact with the HSO in what the HSO has called 'this somewhat crowded field'.[8]

This vignette of the NHS complaints system prompts a more general observation. There is a tension in the design of accountability mechanisms between informality, accessibility, speed, low-cost, and so on, on the one hand, and expertise, independence, due process, and so on, on the other. The establishment of the public-sector ombudsmen was, in part, a response to concerns about inadequacies in existing review institutions such as courts and tribunals (tribunals themselves having been, in their turn, partly a response to inadequacies of the courts). In practice, however, those very qualities that make 'new' complaints systems attractive may be seen as involving unacceptable departures from the standards of the pre-existing institutions. There is no easy or simple formula for resolving such tensions. Britain is experiencing a period of rapidly rising expectations about the way in which complaints against public bodies will be handled; and some of these expectations are more-or-less incompatible. People want cheap, quick, and accessible complaints systems that also display the traditional virtues of guaranteed independence and due process without their associated delay, cost and limited availability. In an increasingly legalistic and rights-oriented society, the pressure towards formality is hard to resist.[9] In principle, at least, what seems desirable is a

---

[7] Public Law Project, *Cause for Complaint? An Evaluation of the Effectiveness of the NHS Complaints Procedure* (London, 1999).

[8] HSO Annual Report, 2002–3, para. 1.7.

[9] Art. 6 of the ECHR lurks in the background.

mixed system that gives individuals choice between different review mechanisms which promote the various desired objectives in different ways and to different extents. In practice, it seems unlikely that people will be satisfied with an arrangement that requires them to exhaust a review mechanism, which they perceive to be inadequate, as a precondition of access to what is seen as a more acceptable process.

The relationship between 'internal' and 'external' review has been a subject of controversy amongst scholars.[10] 'Compulsory' internal review coupled with the option of external review in case of dissatisfaction with the outcome of the internal review, seems to provide a way of dealing with a large volume of relatively minor complaints cheaply and quickly, while still preserving values such as independence. On the other hand, it is argued that if internal review is made a prerequisite of access to external review, it will cease to be part of an administrative process of regulating and improving service-delivery and will become part of an adjudicative process of dispute resolution.[11] This, it is said, could have a negative effect on the quality of initial decision-making.[12] It is also argued that complainants are less likely to seek external review if they are required to engage the internal review process first. This argument is difficult to evaluate. There is plenty of evidence that most people who 'lose' at the internal review stage do not proceed to external review; but we do not know whether more people drop out after compulsory than after optional internal review. It is not surprising that most complainants do not proceed beyond internal review. More surprising are the results of an empirical study of internal reviews in homelessness cases.[13] Before 1996 the main formal avenue for challenging homelessness decisions was judicial review. In 1996 this was replaced by appeal to a county court. Internal

---

[10] M. Harris, 'The Place of Formal and Informal Review in the Administrative Justice System' in M. Harris and M. Partington (eds), *Administrative Justice in the 21st Century* (Oxford, 1999), ch. 2.

[11] See also S. Kerrison and A. Pollock, 'Complaints as Accountability? The Case of Health Care in the UK' [2001] *PL* 115. The relationship between resolving individual complaints and improving service quality (or 'standards') is a complex one. Internal review may be thought more likely than external review to contribute to quality improvements because of its proximity to the point of service delivery. This was one of the assumptions underlying the promotion of internal review by the Citizen's Charter: A. Page, 'The Citizen's Charter and Administrative Justice' in Harris and Partington (eds), *Administrative Justice in the 21st Century*. Ironically, the more complaints there are, the greater the likely contribution of complaints-handling to quality improvement by revealing systemic failures. It is also important that complaints be viewed as an opportunity and not just a problem.

[12] D. Cowan and S. Halliday, *The Appeal of Internal Review* (Oxford, 2003), pp. 208–9.

[13] Ibid.

review is a precondition of such an appeal. The authors of the study conclude that 'the take-up of rights to internal review . . . is actually quite low and comparable to the level of applications for leave to apply for judicial review prior to the 1996 Act'.[14] This low level of recourse to internal review is clearly not a universal phenomenon. As we have seen, there are some 140,000 formal complaints about the NHS each year. However, the research does suggest that the level of use of various grievance-handling mechanisms is affected by factors other than the nature of those mechanisms. The authors of the study suggest[15] that reasons for not seeking internal review of homelessness decisions may include ignorance of the existence of internal review, scepticism about its integrity, a perception that it is too 'rule-bound', 'applicant fatigue', and 'satisfaction' with the decision even though adverse. The researchers also found that some people 'pursued internal review unwittingly'.[16]

17.2 THE PARLIAMENTARY OMBUDSMAN

The office of the PCA was conceived, in part, as a way of making up for deficiencies and gaps in judicial and Parliamentary mechanisms for scrutinizing administrative activity. The PCA was seen as having two main functions: redressing genuine grievances; and, conversely, legitimizing the administrative process in cases where complaints were found to be unwarranted, and enabling civil servants accused of maladministration to clear their names.

As with judicial review, the volume of complaints handled by the PO is very small relative to the number of administrative decisions made every year. In 2002–3, 1,973 complaints were received via MPs (through whom complaints have to be channelled), down from 2,139 in 2001–2.[17] In 2002–3 only around 4 per cent of complaints received were outside the PO's jurisdiction. 136 complaints were formally investigated in full (with what is called a 'statutory investigation'), while around 2,000 were resolved more informally, either on the basis of the papers alone or as a result of an inquiry to the relevant department. More than half the complaints dealt with in 2002–3 were (on one ground or another) resolved adversely to the complainant. The public bodies that are most frequently

---

[14] Ibid. 37.					[15] Ibid., ch. 5.					[16] Ibid. 158.
[17] In 1993 the figure was 986. Surprisingly, the number of complaints has not risen steadily over the past decade but has varied significantly both up and down.

the subject of complaint are the Department of Work and Pensions[18] (38 per cent of all complaints in 2002–3) and the Inland Revenue. The PO can deal not only with decisions made by public officials but also with decisions made personally by Ministers. This happened, for example, in 1967 when the Foreign Secretary refused to allow certain compensation claims by ex-servicemen; and in 1974 when the Industry Secretary made misleading statements about the financial soundness of a tour operator. The PO deals with a wide variety of complaints: for example, about delay in the performance of public functions and the delivery of public services; about agencies that give false or misleading advice about citizens' rights, or unreasonably refuse or fail to give such advice;[19] about discrimination in the provision of social welfare or other benefits; about failure properly to apply departmental policy and procedural guidelines;[20] about refusal to pay compensation for injustice or loss inflicted by administrative action.[21] Conduct complained of ranges from arrogance, inefficiency, or incompetence to deliberate misconduct such as lying, personal bias, and suppression of information.

17.2.1 THE PO AND PARLIAMENT

The PO, as the name implies, is seen as an adjunct of Parliament. The PO makes frequent reports to Parliament (a report must be made at least annually), and the House of Commons Public Administration Select Committee (formerly the Select Committee on the PCA) monitors the PO's work and can investigate for itself and report to Parliament on matters arising from the reports of the PO. These activities of the committee can give extra impact to the work of the PO in cases where the additional publicity given by a report of a Parliamentary committee is thought to be useful in securing compliance with recommendations of the PO by a resistant department, or in prompting some change in administrative policy or practice. Another function which the select committee has exercised is to review the powers and working practices of the PO.

---

[18] The largest central government department.

[19] A.R. Mowbray, 'A Right to Official Advice: The Parliamentary Commissioner's Perspective' [1990] *PL* 68.

[20] A.R. Mowbray, 'The Parliamentary Commissioner and Administrative Guidance' [1987] *PL* 570.

[21] e.g. R. James and D. Longley, 'The Channel Tunnel Rail Link, the Ombudsman and the Select Committee' [1996] *PL* 38. This was one of the first cases in which the PCA adopted a test-case strategy for dealing with multiple complaints about the same issue. Investigating a representative complaint is now the standard technique for dealing with such cases: The Parliamentary Ombudsman, *Annual Report, 2002–3* (TSO), para. 1.7.

The committee has been very successful in helping the PO to enforce recommendations against departments, but it has been less successful in persuading governments to extend the jurisdiction and powers of the PO: governments do not welcome the scrutiny of the PO any more than they would willingly agree to significantly increased scrutiny powers for Parliament itself.[22] As a result of the fact that the PO is an adjunct of Parliament, the work of the PO is bound to be affected by the relative weakness of Parliament as a check on the exercise of power by governments.

It is ultimately the complainant's MP who decides whether the PO will be asked to investigate a particular complaint (either when the MP receives it directly or when it is referred by the PO), or whether the member personally will take some action, such as writing to a Minister or contacting an official. This is because constitutionally, the primary responsibility for defending the citizen against the executive is seen as resting with MPs. In fact, MPs deal personally with many more complaints than are referred by them to the PO.[23] Generally, only cases which are somewhat difficult, complex, or out of the ordinary are referred to the PO. Although a high proportion of MPs refer at least one complaint a year to the PO, it seems that most MPs view the work of the PO as marginal to their role as grievance-handlers.[24] There has long been a considerable body of opinion in favour of giving a right of direct access to the PCA/PO. A 1999 survey showed that only a bare majority of MPs favour retention of the 'MP filter'.[25]

The PO has very wide powers to call for and examine documents and persons, and is in a somewhat stronger position in this respect than select committees, which are ultimately more dependent on government cooperation. In one respect, too, the PO is in a stronger position than a

---

[22] R. Gregory, 'The Select Committee on the Parliamentary Commissioner for Administration, 1967–1980' [1982] *PL* 49. For more recent history see Select Committee on Public Administration, *Ombudsman Issues*, Third Report, 2002/3, HC 448 and the Government's Response (Cabinet Office, 2003), which is a masterpiece of evasion.

[23] A.C Page, 'MPs and the Redress of Grievances' [1985] *PL* 1; R. Rawlings, 'The MP's Complaints Service' (1990) 53 *MLR* 22 and 149. The fact that MPs are very active in dealing with complaints partly accounts for the fact that the PO deals with so few. It is generally believed that removal of the MP filter would significantly increase the number of complaints, as did the introduction of direct access to the LGO in 1988.

[24] Concerning the relationship between MPs and the PCA/PO see G. Drewry and C. Harlow, 'A "Cutting Edge"? The Parliamentary Commissioner and MPs' (1990) 53 *MLR* 745.

[25] P. Collcutt and M. Hourihan, *Review of the Public Sector Ombudsmen in England* (Cabinet Office, 2000), para. 3.38.

court in that public interest immunity cannot be pleaded in respect of documents to which the PO has access, nor do statutory limitations on disclosure of information avail against the PO. On the other hand, the PO has no access to Cabinet papers while the courts, as we have seen, claim the power in theory to inspect even Cabinet papers. The PO's investigations are protected by the law of contempt. Any act or omission that would be a contempt of court if the PO's investigation were a court proceeding, can be treated as a contempt of the investigation.[26]

The PO must conduct investigations in private,[27] whereas select committees normally operate in public. In other respects, the PO has very wide discretion about how to deal with cases. The PO's procedure can be more flexible than that of a select committee which, because of its nature and composition, is more or less restricted to formal interrogation of Ministers and senior civil servants. The PO can conduct much more personalized inquiries, which may get much closer to the seat of specific problems. On the other hand, investigations by the PO—especially full-scale statutory investigations culminating in a written report to Parliament—can take a long time. Things have improved over the years. In 1994 the average time taken for a full investigation was seventy weeks. Now, relatively few complaints are resolved by a statutory investigation. Only a very small proportion of cases take more than twelve months to complete, and most are resolved much more quickly than that. The PO cites foot-dragging and bad record-keeping by departments and other public bodies as hindrances to more speedy resolution of complaints. Throughput times have been considerably reduced by the adoption of various less-probing case-handling techniques. Such techniques are described in terms such as 'settlement' and 'conciliation' to distinguish them from 'investigation', which is understood as an elaborate procedure leading to a formal report. It is in performing such investigations that the PO mechanism most clearly displays its Parliamentary roots. The change in the PO's *modus operandi* in favour of more informal procedures makes the office look less like a Parliamentary select committee and more like one of the private-sector ombudsmen, whose focus is very much on dispute resolution, and which can be seen primarily as alternatives to courts.[28]

---

[26] Parliamentary Commissioner Act 1967, s. 9(1).

[27] Ibid., s. 7(1).

[28] R. James and P. Morris, 'The Financial Ombudsman Service: A Brave New World in "Ombudsmanry"?' [2002] *PL* 640, 640–1; Harris and Partington (eds), *Administrative Justice in the 21st Century*, pp. 136–41, 144–6

17.2.2 THE PO'S JURISDICTION

The PO has a discretion, reviewable by the courts,[29] whether to investigate any particular complaint or not.[30] The PO's jurisdiction is, in its terms, very wide: it covers any action taken by or on behalf of any of the departments and bodies listed in Schedule 2 to the Parliamentary Commissioner Act 1967 in exercise of administrative functions of the department or body.[31] The phrase 'or on behalf of' means that the PO can investigate actions of bodies to which the performance of administrative functions has been delegated by an entity subject to the PO's jurisdiction. Over the years, many additions have been made to the Schedule 2 list to take account of changing patterns of delivery of public services.

Certain areas are specifically excluded from the PO's jurisdiction. These include foreign affairs, diplomatic activity, the investigation of crime, action in matters relating to contractual or commercial activities, and the conditions of service of Crown servants. Some of these exclusions have been criticized, in particular that relating to complaints arising out of commercial transactions (especially the tendering process) and complaints about the conditions of service of Crown employees.

17.2.3 THE PO AND REMEDIES FOR MALADMINISTRATION

The PO has no power to award an enforceable remedy. Moreover, whereas a claim for judicial review can operate to suspend action on the matter complained of while the claim is being adjudicated, instigation of an investigation by the PO does not in any way affect the activities of the department or authority concerned.[32] However, this strict legal position masks a very different reality. The PO has persuasive power, partly because of the lack of coercive powers. Besides securing apologies, the PO frequently secures financial relief for a complainant[33] or persuades an

---

[29] *R v. Parliamentary Commissioner for Administration, ex p. Dyer* [1994] 1 All ER 375.

[30] In 2002–3 the PO exercised the discretion not to investigate in 2.5 per cent of the cases concluded.

[31] Before the full implementation of the FOI Act in 2005, complaints of non-compliance with the *Code of Practice on Access to Government Information* fall within the PO's jurisdiction (see D. Clark and J. Pearson, 'Regulating Open Government: A Comparative Study of the UK and Canadian Regimes' in Harris and Partington (eds), *Administrative Justice in the 21st Century*, ch. 7). From 2005 the FOI regime is policed by the Information Commissioner (see 15.1).

[32] Parliamentary Commissioner Act 1967, s. 7(4).

[33] M. Amos, 'The Parliamentary Commissioner for Administration, Redress and Damages for Wrongful Administrative Action' [2000] *PL* 21. The most spectacular example

authority to reconsider some decision made by it. Furthermore, in cases where the particular complaint is just a symptom of a wider problem, the PO can sometimes persuade an authority to change its general procedure for dealing with that type of case.[34] If a department proves to be resistant to the PO's suggestions or is guilty of repeated maladministration, the Select Committee can call the Minister before it and ask questions about the PO's findings, thus exerting considerable, unwelcome pressure.[35]

Should the PO be given coercive remedial powers? There are arguments against this. First, although the PO is required to give bodies or persons whose actions are the subject of complaint an opportunity to comment on the allegations made, the inquiry is informal and essentially investigative. Only very rarely does the PO conduct an oral hearing in an attempt to resolve conflicts of evidence that the investigators have been unable to reconcile. The PO is not bound by the rules of evidence and does not have to follow adversarial procedures. If the PO were to have power to award coercive remedies, justifiable demands could be made that the procedure followed in investigations should be more formalized so as to give the body subject to complaint a full chance to put its side of the case. The conferral of such power could also bring the PO's activities within the scope of the rules of natural justice and Art. 6 of the ECHR. Such legalization of PO investigations would inevitably add to the expense and length of inquiries.

Secondly, at present all the PO's investigations are private. An argument for privacy is that it helps maintain the anonymity of civil servants,[36] which the doctrine of ministerial responsibility is partly designed to protect by placing the responsibility for the efficiency of the administration on the

---

to date is provided by the PCA's investigation into the role of the Department of Trade and Industry in the collapse of the Barlow Clowes investment group. Although the government rejected the PCA's findings, it made *ex gratia* payments to investors of some £150 million in total.

[34] An example is the *Ostler* case, which will be considered below. See also P. Brown, 'The Ombudsman: Remedies for Misinformation' in G. Richardson and H. Genn (eds), *Administrative Law and Government Action* (Oxford, 1994), pp. 327–31.

[35] See B. Thompson, 'Administrative Justice: Towards the Millenium, Towards Integration?' in Harris and Partington (eds), *Administrative Justice in the 21st Century*, p. 466. In extreme cases, the PO can make a special report to both Houses of Parliament: Parliamentary Commissioner Act 1967, s. 10(3). This power is very rarely used.

[36] An important by-product of the activities of the PO has been a certain weakening of the principle of the anonymity of civil servants, because the PO's investigatory powers enable culpable civil servants to be identified. Concerning the naming of individuals in reports of the LGO see Local Government and Housing Act 1989, s. 32.

government rather than on individual civil servants. On the other hand, senior civil servants, such as chief executives of agencies, are being made increasingly responsible for the efficiency of government; and individual civil servants are increasingly being called to account before Parliamentary select committees. At all events, if remedies were to be available, at least some part, if not all, of the PO's investigations would need to be in public. Thirdly, the PO's decisions are not subject to review. If the PO had the power to give coercive remedies the possibility of review would be essential.

In short, that the PO is remarkably effective[37] despite lacking coercive remedial powers is ironically a function of the fact that the PO operates privately and informally. This informality also allows the PO a degree of remedial flexibility that courts and tribunals lack. All the POs have felt that they can do more by persuasion than they could hope to achieve by coercion. The independence of the PO is guaranteed—the holder of the office can be removed only by an address from both Houses of Parliament—and the fact that the PO is in this way equated with High Court judges gives the office, by association, much of the moral authority which attaches to the judiciary.

If, however, it were thought desirable to give the powers of the PO some coercive support, the Commissioner of Complaints Act (NI) 1969 might provide a suitable model. It empowers the county court to award damages, an injunction, or other relief in cases where the Commissioner has found maladministration; and in cases where there is evidence of continuing maladministration the Attorney-General can apply for an injunction. Perhaps this latter power could be given to the PO.

17.2.4 THE PO AND THE COURTS

Like the courts, the office of the PO is essentially an institution for rectifying complaints made by individuals. For example, the PO declined to investigate the complaints involved in the *Fleet Street Casuals* case[38] on the ground that the allegations of injustice in the administration of the tax system affected all taxpayers and, in a sense, the whole nation.[39] On the other hand, the PO would be prepared to investigate, for example, a complaint by an angling association that its fishing waters had been polluted by effluent from a Ministry of Defence factory. However, the PO

---

[37] For a list of major successes see P. Giddings, 'The Parliamentary Ombudsman: A Successful Alternative?' in D. Oliver and G. Drewry (eds), *The Law and Parliament* (London, 1998), p. 128.

[38] See 4.2.1. [39] Sir C. Clothier, (1984) 81 *LS Gaz* 3108.

will only investigate complaints that affect the complainant uniquely or affect a discrete class to which the complainant belongs (such as investors in a failed company or owners of property in the path of a proposed road or railway). The rationale of this approach is to draw a demarcation line between the activities of the PO and matters that ought properly to be dealt with by the political process. To this extent the PO takes a more restrictive approach than the courts, which are increasingly willing to entertain public interest actions.

Just as the decision of a court often has an impact beyond the actual litigants, so too the PO can, by securing satisfaction for a single complainant, at the same time indirectly help other potential complainants or, by prompting a change in administrative practice, improve the situation for others dealing with the particular department in the future. For example, an investigation in 1977 into an individual complaint of non-payment of a war pension led to a review of twenty-four similar cases and payment of the pension. This wider effect is an incidental by-product of an investigation into an individual's complaint. On the other hand, the PO does not perform an inspectorial function. Even if, in the course of investigating a particular complaint, the PO discovers some wider inefficiency in the administrative process, the PO does not investigate this personally. If further investigation is warranted, the PO can refer the matter to the select committee, which can inquire more generally into departmental rules and practice and, if appropriate, recommend wider administrative changes. Nor can the PO launch investigations into departmental procedures on her own initiative and without a complaint, simply because there is some reason to suspect bad administrative practice. A recent review of public-sector ombudsmen (see 17.5) recommended against giving the PO such a power on the ground that the PO's main function is to investigate individual complaints.

One particular feature of the institution of the PO that distinguishes it from the office of judge is its essentially personal nature. The volume of complaints with which the PO deals is small enough for the holder of the office to be able to supervise each one personally at some stage, and some people consider this very desirable. If the volume of complaints increased greatly, or if the PO's powers were greatly extended, then this individual, personalized element might be lost. A Complaints Commission would be a different institution from the PO.

There is clearly a conflict here. It may be true that the administration has greater faith in the PO institution because of its personalized nature (although it must be doubted whether many members of the public know that the office of the PO exists, let alone who its incumbent is). At the same time, it seems a poor justification for not advertising the PO more widely or for not extending the scope of an admittedly useful and successful institution that thereby the number of complaints might increase above the number which one person can supervise single-handedly. A number of individuals could achieve much the same effect if (as is the case in the LGO's office) they were given different areas of operation rather than arranged hierarchically under one super-Ombudsman. As it is, most of the actual spadework is done by assistants to the PO, as one would expect.

The most important boundary line (in theoretical terms, at least) between the PO and the courts is that whereas the latter deal with questions of legality, the PO deals with 'injustice as a consequence of maladministration'.[40] The classic formulation of the meaning of 'maladministration' is the famous 'Crossman catalogue' (which was formulated by the government spokesman in the course of a House of Commons debate on the 1967 Act): 'bias, neglect, inattention, delay,[41] incompetence, ineptitude, perversity, turpitude, arbitrariness and so on'. In his 1993 Annual Report,[42] the PCA published an updated list of examples of maladministration which included neglecting to inform a person, on request, of their rights, knowingly giving advice which is misleading or inadequate, failure by management to monitor compliance with adequate procedures, offering no redress or manifestly disproportionate redress, and failure to mitigate the effects of rigid adherence to the letter of the law where that produces manifestly inequitable treatment.

The Parliamentary Commissioner Act (PC Act) (s. 5(2)) provides that the PO shall not investigate a matter if the complainant could take or could have taken it to a court or tribunal, unless the PO thinks that it would not be reasonable to expect the complainant to take or to have taken this course.[43] This provision assumes, as seems to be clear from the

[40] Parliamentary Commissioner Act 1967, s. 5(1)(a).

[41] S.N. McMurtrie, 'The Waiting Game—The Parliamentary Commissioner's Response to Delay in Administrative Procedures' [1997] *PL* 159.

[42] Para. 7; see also Select Committee on the PCA, *Maladministration and Redress*, First Report, 1994/5, HC 112. The 'consolidated' definition can be found in Oliver and Drewry (eds), *The Law and Parliament*, p. 209.

[43] The alternative remedies rule of judicial review (see 5.6.2) is analogous. The LGO operates under a similar constraint, the effect of which was considered in *R v. Commissioner for Local Administration, ex p. Croydon LBC* [1989] 1 All ER 1033. An underlying concern is that a complaint to the PO/LGO should not be used to gather evidence preparatory to

expanded Crossman catalogue, that some administrative defects will be capable of being described not only as maladministration but also as *ultra vires* acts, or as civil wrongs, or as an exercise of discretion such as would justify an appeal to a tribunal.

Therefore, the definition of maladministration has to be read subject to the general qualification that the jurisdiction of the PO is residual. The PO will not normally investigate complaints solely about the content of discretionary decisions, nor complaints about delegated legislation. This restraint is reinforced by s. 12(3) of the PC Act, which provides that the PO may not question the merits of a decision taken without maladministration. This seems to assume that maladministration is procedural; but since the distinction between substance and procedure is not always easy to draw, the PO (on the urging of the select committee) does not interpret this restriction rigidly. If a decision is alleged to have been oppressive, unjust, discriminatory, or unreasonable, then the PO would be prepared to investigate it. The PO is also prepared to investigate cases in which some administrative rule has been properly applied but where it is argued that the rule itself is a bad one. The PO can recommend that the rule itself be changed; she can also recommend amendments to statutory regulations or to legislation. In this way the PO can perform a more positive and constructive role than the courts.

As a result there are certain types of administrative 'misbehaviour' that are sometimes dealt with by a court, sometimes by the PO; for example: unfair procedure, ignoring material relevant to the decision, unfair departure from announced policy guidelines or decisions favourable to the citizen, the giving of misleading or incorrect advice. There are also cases in which the PO has been able to secure (*ex gratia*) monetary compensation for an aggrieved citizen, some of which cases might fall within the rules of tort liability considered in Chapter 11.

The justification for avoiding undue overlap between the PO and courts or tribunals is clear: consideration of the same issue from different angles and in different ways, leading possibly to different results, is both wasteful of resources and undesirable in that it creates a possibility of conflicting decisions of bodies neither of which is subject to control by the other. It has been suggested that the PO should be given the power to

litigation. It seems that the practice of the LGO is generally to exercise the discretion to investigate favourably to the complainant: Harris and Partington (eds), *Administrative Justice in the 21st Century*, pp. 141–4. The high cost of going to court and the fact that the ombudsmen are free to the complainant are important considerations.

refer cases being investigated to the High Court if this seems appropriate.[44] On the other hand, the distinction between maladministration and the legality or substantive correctness of decisions is not always an easy one to draw. This justifies the PO in taking the view that if the complaint is such a minor one that it really does not warrant litigation, and if it seems unlikely that the complainant will litigate the complaint if the PO makes an adverse finding, the PO can investigate despite the fact that the complainant could litigate. An important point to bear in mind in this respect is that the services of the PO are free to the complainant whereas, of course, litigation can be extremely costly. So, for example, the PO would not expect a taxpayer worried about delay in issuing an amended tax assessment to go to court for an order of mandamus requiring the Inland Revenue to perform its duty. In a significant proportion of cases the PO exercises the discretion not to investigate on the ground that the complainant has a right of appeal to a tribunal.[45] The explanation may be that on the whole, tribunals are cheaper and less formal than the courts, and so the existence of a free and informal alternative is not as important in relation to tribunals as in relation to courts.

There have been some notable cases in which the same issue has been the subject both of investigation by the PO and proceedings before a court. In one case the Home Office threatened to revoke television licences bought by licensees before the expiry of their old licence in order to avoid an announced licence fee increase. The PCA investigated the Home Office's action on the assumption that it was lawful, and found that the Home Office had acted inefficiently and with lack of foresight in creating the situation in which people could buy overlapping licences and at the same time failing to explain the situation to the public; but he did not recommend a remedy. In later litigation by an aggrieved licence-holder the Home Office's action was held to have been unlawful and licensees who had paid the new higher fee were given a refund.[46] This case illustrates nicely the distinction between unlawfulness and maladministration.

Another example involved a case in which a landowner (Ostler) sought to challenge proposals for a trunk road, on the grounds of breach of natural justice and bad faith, after the statutory time-limit for challenges had expired. He alleged that there had been a secret agreement between the department and a third party, and that if he had known about it earlier

---

[44] Sir Harry Woolf, *Protection of the Public: A New Challenge* (London, 1990), pp. 87–92,
[45] In 2002–3, 3.7 per cent of concluded cases were rejected on the basis that the complainant had a right of appeal to a tribunal.
[46] *Congreve v. Home Office* [1976] QB 629; 7th Report of the PCA, 1974–5, HC 680.

he would have challenged the proposals when they were being considered at a public inquiry. The Court of Appeal held that the time-limit provision was effective to bar the challenge.[47] Ostler then complained to the PCA[48] and, as a result, the Department of the Environment made an *ex gratia* payment to Ostler to cover the reasonable costs of his court action. Also, as a result of the PO's investigations, new procedures were introduced to prevent a repetition of such a situation.

It can be seen, therefore, that sometimes the courts can provide a remedy where the PO fails to do so,[49] and sometimes vice versa.[50] The *Ostler* case raises a larger issue about compensation for loss inflicted by administrative action. In cases such as *Ostler* and in cases where authorities make *ultra vires* representations or give *ultra vires* assurances which it is not in the public interest to enforce by an estoppel, there is a strong argument for paying the injured party compensation. Recommendations by the PO that compensation be paid in such circumstances have often been accepted. On the other hand, it might be thought desirable that there should be a right to compensation in such cases rather than that it should depend on persuasion by the PO and the goodwill of the department concerned. More generally, the PO has been successful in securing *ex gratia* compensation for complainants in a variety of situations, and in this light it might be thought strange that the courts lack the power to require compensation to be paid in appropriate cases.

There is an argument that since the office of the PO was set up, the courts have become much more willing to hold that bad administrative action is illegal and to control the exercise of administrative discretion on both procedural and substantive grounds. As a result, many of the gaps in judicial review, which the PO was set up to fill, no longer exist. Therefore, the PO institution has to some extent outlived its purpose. The conclusion does not, however, necessarily follow, even if the premise is correct. Litigation is expensive and slow, and judicial adversarial techniques for

---

[47] *R v. Secretary of State for the Environment, ex p. Ostler* [1977] QB 122; 2nd Report of the Select Committee on the PCA, 1976/7, HC 223.

[48] 3rd Report of the PCA, 1976/7, HC 223.

[49] For other examples see Brown in Richardson and Genn (eds), *Administrative Law and Government Action*, pp. 323–5, 331–2, 336.

[50] See, e.g., D. Fairgrieve, *State Liability in Tort: A Comparative Law Study* (Oxford, 2003), p. 275. By contrast, in *R v. Commissioner for Local Administration, ex p. PH* (unreported, 21 Dec. 1998) it was held that the Commissioner had no jurisdiction to hear a complaint in respect of conduct that had already formed the basis of a successful claim for judicial review despite the fact that what the complainant sought by going to the LGO was compensation, which was not available by way of judicial review.

finding facts are not always as appropriate as the investigative techniques of the PO. Provided the PO and the courts are applying essentially the same principles of good administrative conduct,[51] a sensible division of labour is possible: the PO acting as a sort of troubleshooter while the courts deal with the really serious cases and those which raise important and novel issues of principle. It may be that the best way to distinguish between the courts and the PO is not in terms of the concepts of illegality and maladministration, but in terms of their differing roles and expertise in handling complaints and enforcing standards of good administrative conduct. The PO can, for example, deal with a minor case satisfactorily by securing an apology. Court action to secure such an outcome would be totally wasteful and unnecessarily provocative.

17.3 THE LOCAL GOVERNMENT OMBUDSMAN

The LGO performs essentially the same function, in respect of local government, as the PO performs in respect of central government.[52] The constitutional underpinning of this institution is slightly different from that of the PO in that there is no direct equivalent of ministerial responsibility at the local level. Complaints may be made in writing direct to a LGO, or via a member of the authority complained about or of any other authority concerned.

The LGO (like the PO) deals with a very small number of complaints relative to the number of public decisions within its jurisdiction. For example, in the year ending 31 March 2003, 17,610 complaints were received and 18,376 were determined. Of the latter, 3,857 cases were resolved favourably to the complainant. Only 122 of these cases involved a formal report. The rest were terminated by what is called a 'local settlement'.[53] Almost half of the complaints were on housing or planning matters, and the remainder on all the rest of local government services combined.

---

[51] For an analysis of the principles of good administration that have been established by the PO which suggests that they are 'similar to those that guide the courts' see D. Woodhouse, *In Pursuit of Good Administration: Ministers, Civil Servants and Judges* (Oxford, 1997), ch. 4 (the quoted phrase is at p. 89).

[52] The relevant legislation is the Local Government Act 1974, Part III as amended by the Local Government Act 1988, s. 29 and Sch. 3 and the Local Government and Housing Act 1989, Part II. Concerning the LGO's jurisdiction see LGO Annual Report 2002/3, pp. 31–4. In 2002–3, 12 per cent of complaints received were outside the LGO's jurisdiction.

[53] LGO Annual Report 2002/3, p. 30.

The Local Government Act 1974, s. 26(7) provides that the LGO may not investigate complaints that affect all or most of the inhabitants of a local authority's area. The idea behind this is that such complaints really concern 'the way the country is being run' and ought to be pursued through the political process. This reasoning also lies behind the POs willingness only to entertain complaints by individuals or small groups of individuals, even though not strictly limited to doing so by statute. This limitation preserves the nature of the LGO as essentially an *ex post facto* complaint or dispute-settling mechanism as opposed to a quality-control mechanism or an avenue for achieving political aims that the complainants have failed to achieve through the political process.

On the other hand, the LGO has been active in seeking to forestall complaints by improving local mechanisms for dealing with them. The LGO publishes quite detailed codes of practice for local authorities (available on the LGO web site) entitled *Running a Complaints System* and *Remedies*. The value of these codes is, no doubt, also reflected in the very high proportion of complaints to the LGO that is resolved by local settlement. The LGO has also developed a code entitled *Good Administrative Practice*, the aim of which is to assist councils to minimize complaints by improving the quality of their decision-making and service-delivery. The content of the latter two codes, in particular, suggests that the LGO perceives its role in resolving complaints primarily as a substitute for courts and tribunals. The statement, in the code on *Good Administrative Practice*, that 'failure to comply with legal requirements is one of the most common reasons for findings of maladministration' supports this interpretation.[54] So, too, does the declaration in the *Remedies* code that where the LGO finds 'that an injustice has been caused by maladministration, we seek a remedy that would, so far as possible, put the complainant back in the position he or she would have been in but for the fault'. At the same time, the high quality of the codes[55] and of other publications of the LGO shows that promotion of best practice is considered to be at least as important a part of the LGO's activities as dealing with complaints.

The LGO, like the PO, has no coercive powers. The ultimate 'sanction' is to publicize, in the local press and at the authority's expense, the fact

---

[54] The Code's 'Axioms of good administration' bear many similarities to the principles of judicial review.

[55] The codes are supplemented by annual digests of cases relating to the main areas of local authority activity. The digests are designed to illustrate pitfalls and how to avoid them, and are supplemented by an introduction that highlights widespread problems and issues.

that an authority has failed to take action recommended by the LGO. The authority may, if it wishes, publicize its reasons for non-compliance. This means that at the end of the day, the authority may simply assert that in its view there has been no maladministration. In this respect the LGO is in a weaker position than the PO, who not only decides conclusively whether there has been maladministration but can also enlist the aid of the Public Administration Select Committee (or Parliament) to put pressure on a recalcitrant department or authority. However, in practice it seems that local authorities rarely reject LGO recommendations, and that their lack of coercive force 'generally means that councils are open, co-operative and not defensive while the investigation is being carried out'.[56]

17.4 THE HEALTH SERVICE OMBUDSMAN

The constitutional position of the HSO is different again from that of either the PO or the LGO. Here, although the Minister is ultimately responsible for the functioning of the Health Service, the day-to-day running of it is largely in the hands of local health authorities and trusts, and there is no elected person with direct constitutional responsibility in relation to these authorities and trusts. So complaints can be made directly to the HSO, provided they have first been brought to the attention of the health authority. The HSO investigates complaints about the administration of the Health Service (including 'failures of service'); and, since 1996, can investigate matters of clinical medical judgment. In 2002–3 the HSO received 3,994 complaints against providers of NHS services but only 176 were accepted for investigation. Of the investigations completed in 2002–3, 86 per cent concerned matters of clinical judgment.[57] The main reason for non-investigation of complaints is that they are 'premature' because the complainant has not exhausted the internal NHS complaints procedure.

17.5 THE OMBUDSMAN SYSTEM

When the PCA was established in 1967, English administrative law was in its infancy. Since then, public and private sector ombudsmen have pro-

---

[56] LGO Annual Report 2002/3, p. 20.

[57] Such complaints acutely raise the issue of the relationship between the internal NHS complaints system, the HSO and the courts: HSO Annual Report, 2002–3, para. 1.8; Department of Health, *NHS Complaints Reform: Making Things Right* (undated), para. 3.27.

liferated, the courts have become much more active in supervising the performance of public functions, and internal complaints mechanisms have become widespread in both the private and the public sector and increasingly formalized. More-or-less legalized regulation of the performance of public functions, both internal and external, has grown exponentially in the past forty years. Whereas the PCA was a bold experiment in 1967, it is now a small part of a large and complex system of grievance mechanisms, both adjudicatory and investigative.

In this new world, the concept of the ombudsman as an extension of Parliamentary scrutiny of the executive seems less appropriate than it did in 1967. Parliament can now be seen as just one of many checks on various parts of the public sector. These checking mechanisms perform various functions: inspection, auditing, grievance-handling, quality control, promotion of 'best practice'. Some operate on adjudicative principles, others investigate, others advise. In short, in the past forty years regulation of the public sector has not only experienced huge growth, but also very significant specialization and division of labour. Against this background, it would make sense to recognize public-sector 'ombudsmanry' as a distinctive form of control, and to take a more systematic approach to its organization and functions.

In 2000 the Cabinet Office (as the result of a joint initiative by the PO, the HSO and the LGO) published a report of a *Review of Public Sector Ombudsmen in England.*[58] Amongst the report's recommendations was that the three main public-sector ombudsmen (but not other specialized offices such as that of the Prisons Ombudsman) should be amalgamated into a new 'collegiate' structure with a single point of entry for complaints. The MP filter for complaints to the PO would be abolished. The focus of the integrated Commission would be on redressing individual grievances rather than on any wider systemic function such as improving the quality of public decision-making. The Commission would be answerable to Parliament. The report made no recommendations for extending the jurisdiction of the Commission beyond the current jurisdictions of its constituent offices, but noted that it needed to be kept in line with changes in the organization and structure of the public sector. Within the new Commission, each ombudsman would specialize, but would be able to exercise the total jurisdiction of the Commission. This would make it easier to deal with complex complaints that cross the jurisdictional boundaries of one or more of the constituent elements

---

[58] B. Thompson, 'Integrated Ombudsmanry: Joined-up to a Point' (2001) 64 *MLR* 459.

of the Commission.[59] The authors of the report considered that the Commission should not be given coercive remedial powers.

The report represents a modest rationalization of the three major public-sector ombudsmen rather than a radical reappraisal of their role and place in the larger landscape of the 'administrative justice' system. Even so, the government has shown no inclination to implement its recommendations. In 2003 the Public Administration Select Committee again urged the government to act on the report, but the government's response leaves little doubt that appropriate legislation is not envisaged in the near future.

17.6 THE VALUE OF INVESTIGATORY TECHNIQUES

One way of viewing the ombudsmen we have examined is as relatively formal last resorts to be used when other informal avenues of complaint (such as internal complaints procedures or interventions by an MP) have been exhausted or seem unlikely to be effective. From this perspective, the main advantages of ombudsmen are that they are free to the complainant and that they add a weight to the complaint that it would not otherwise have.

When viewed in relation to courts and tribunals, ombudsmen play a role in dealing with complaints on matters that would not fall within the jurisdiction of such bodies. The fact that an administrative lapse may not constitute illegal behaviour does not mean that it is not worthy of rectification. As has been noted, however, instances of bad administrative behaviour can amount to *ultra vires* conduct, challengeable in a court. The value of ombudsmen in this type of case is that they provide a free and thorough means of redress for grievances which may not be serious enough to justify litigation. Some people initially feared that the activities of the ombudsmen might generate 'defensive administration', that is, elaborate, costly, and time-consuming precautions and procedures designed only to forestall and deflect criticism rather than to promote efficiency and effectiveness in the conduct of government business; and that they might discourage administrators from acting boldly and imaginatively for fear of adverse criticism if things went wrong. There is some evidence that if complaints investigators are too demanding, they

[59] e.g. complaints raising health and social services issues: HSO Annual Report 2003–4, paras 1.17–18.

can have these negative effects. They have to strike a compromise between, on the one hand, ensuring that citizens are not maltreated and, on the other, making demands on public functionaries that exacerbate some of the problems being complained about. From this point of view, a cooperative and non-coercive approach may be seen as advantageous and to be preferred to the approach of the courts, who are often criticized for being heavy-handed and lacking understanding of the realities of the public decision-making process.

Ombudsmen also provide a complement to government inspectorates (in particular the National Audit Office and the Audit Commission), which do not investigate individual complaints of maladministration but are concerned with general questions of the quality of government services. On the other hand, the concentration on individual grievances can be seen as a weakness because it may fail to notice or address wider administrative failings of which individual cases are but symptoms. If the ombudsmen were given some power to launch wider investigations prompted by individual complaints, this would undoubtedly add to the value of the institution. In this way greater progress might be made towards developing general principles of good administration appropriate to various government agencies.[60] Once such principles had been established, the role of ombudsmen in relation to individual complaints would be to ensure that authorities complied with the principles, which would constitute a sort of charter of 'citizens' administrative rights' analogous to the rules of natural justice and *ultra vires*. Investigative procedures are well suited to this type of wider role. It might, however, in some cases conflict with the function of resolving individual complaints. For example, individual complaints about delay in dealing with planning applications, or about discrimination in the allocation of council housing, might appear justified when viewed in isolation, but appear less so when the total resources available to a governmental agency or the interests of other applicants are taken into account. This is the problem of polycentricity, which we have considered before. It forces us to ask what the main function of commissioners for administration is: to protect individuals or to promote good administration?

Some would argue that ombudsmen need to be able to act coercively to be truly effective. To this end they could be given a power to instigate litigation on behalf of a complainant when this seemed the appropriate course. The Commission for Racial Equality and the Equal Opportunities

---

[60] C. Harlow, 'Ombudsmen in Search of a Role' (1978) 41 *MLR* 446.

Commission can do this. Such a power would enable an ombudsman to apply for interim relief to maintain the status quo pending the outcome of the investigation, and to obtain court orders against recalcitrant authorities that refuse to act upon an adverse report. It would, in addition, enable ombudsmen to help complainants with important cases that would be more appropriately dealt with by the courts (such a procedure could provide a sort of substitute for legal aid). In the television licences case discussed earlier, it might have been useful if the PCA could have applied to the court for a declaration as to whether the threatened revocation of licences was lawful or not. A decision that it was not would have done away with the need for further consideration by the PCA as to whether the Home Office's action, though lawful, amounted to maladministration.

18

Tribunals

18.1 WHAT ARE TRIBUNALS?

It is difficult to define the word 'tribunal'. It is not even the case that all
the bodies normally treated as deserving the description 'tribunal' or that
perform tribunal-like functions actually bear the name 'tribunal'. The
purpose of the following brief account is to describe the salient characteristics of tribunals. Some tribunals perform regulatory functions, such as
licensing. However, our main concern in this chapter is with appellate
tribunals, the function of which is to hear appeals[1] against decisions made
in exercise of public functions.[2] These are sometimes called 'court-
substitute tribunals'. There are many appellate tribunals dealing with a
wide variety of matters. For example, Social Security Appeal Tribunals
(SSATs)[3] and the Social Security and Child Support Commissioners
deal with social welfare benefits; there are immigration tribunals and
taxation tribunals, tribunals dealing with education, rent assessment, data
protection, pensions, the intelligence services, mental health,[4] and so on.

The case-loads of tribunals vary widely. Some tribunals have not heard
a case for years, and others are effectively defunct. In 2001/2 the Competition Commission Appeal Tribunal decided four cases while SSATs
decided more than 328,000 (about a quarter of all cases dealt with by
tribunals). In aggregate, tribunals greatly overshadow the courts as
checkers of the performance of public functions. Even so, the number of
decisions challenged in tribunals is a very small proportion of the number

---

[1] On the distinction between appeals and judicial review see 2.4.

[2] Including decisions of 'first-tier' tribunals. The Report of the Review of Tribunals by
Sir Andrew Leggatt, *Tribunals for Users: One System, One Service* (TSO, 2001) uses the
term 'appellate tribunals' to refer only to 'second-tier' tribunals (of which there are currently five) that hear appeals from first-tier tribunals.

[3] I am using this term slightly inaccurately as a convenient way of referring to the
tribunals that now form part of the unified appeals service constituted under the Social
Security Act 1998. These tribunals are managed by an executive agency called 'The Appeals
Service'.

[4] Mental Health Review Tribunals deal with decisions to detain people in mental
institutions: J. Peay, *Tribunals on Trial* (Oxford, 1989).

of decisions made. For example, less than 1 per cent of claimants who are denied a social security benefit appeal to an SSAT. Not all tribunals handle disputes about public decisions. For example, child support appeal tribunals[5] decide disputes between parents, and industrial tribunals decide disputes, concerning unfair dismissal and discrimination, between employers and employees in the private as well as the public sector. 'Domestic tribunals' (see 3.1) typically hear appeals from licensing and disciplinary decisions of private bodies such as the Jockey Club.

18.2 FUNCTIONS OF APPELLATE TRIBUNALS

The basic function of appellate tribunals is adjudication. A helpful way of thinking about first-tier appellate tribunals[6] may be to picture them as 'standing in the shoes' of the decision-maker whose decision is under appeal. What this means is that an appellate tribunal performs essentially the same decision-making function as the initial decision-maker but at the appellate level. Unlike courts exercising judicial-review jurisdiction, appellate tribunals are not limited to deciding whether decisions are 'lawful'. Nor, unlike public-sector ombudsmen, are they concerned with whether a decision was unjust by reason of maladministration. An appellate tribunal can substitute its decision for the decision appealed from and can reconsider any issue relevant to the initial decision. Thus, an appellate tribunal can decide issues of law, issues of fact and issues of policy. Moreover, it can substitute its decision on any of these issues for that of the initial decision-maker simply on the basis that it considers the decision appealed from to be 'wrong' in the sense of not being the decision that it, the appellate tribunal, would have made.

In deciding issues of law, appellate tribunals are, of course, bound by any relevant court decisions[7] and, possibly, by decisions of any superior

---

[5] These tribunals are included amongst the SSATs, most of which decide citizen/government disputes. Tribunals that handle citizen/citizen disputes are sometimes called 'party and party tribunals'.

[6] The powers of second-tier tribunals may be limited, for instance, to deciding questions of law.

[7] Subject to any ouster clause in the relevant legislation, tribunals are subject to judicial review. *Tribunals for Users* recommends creation of a general right of appeal on a point of law from all first-tier tribunals to a second-tier tribunal and the exclusion of judicial review from both first-tier and second-tier triibunals: paras 6.27–36. Judicial oversight of tribunals would be by way of an appeal on a point of law from a second-tier tribunal to the Court of Appeal.

tribunal. For instance, SSATs follow relevant decisions of the Social Security and Child Support Commissioners. Moreover, although tribunals are not strictly bound to follow their own earlier decisions, this does not mean that in practice tribunals do not do so. Following precedent is just a way of acting consistently, and basic fairness requires that every decision-maker should act consistently. However, it is really only possible to follow earlier decisions in any organized way if there is a reliable system for the recording and reporting of decisions.[8] In deciding issues of fact, appellate tribunals, unlike courts, are typically not bound by strict rules of evidence. But observation of SSATs suggests that in practice, they handle evidence in much the same way as a court.[9] So far as concerns issues of policy, because appellate tribunals are empowered to decide whether decisions are right or wrong as a matter of policy and stand, in a sense, in the shoes of the initial decision-maker, it has been said that they should not stick rigidly to earlier decisions or lines of precedent but should be prepared to consider each case on its own facts.[10] The tribunal's task is to ensure that the decision-maker's discretion was properly exercised given the particular circumstances of the case. This principle is analogous to that which limits the freedom of public functionaries to structure and confine their discretion by non-statutory rules (see 8.3.2). In this respect, appellate tribunals inhabit a sort of twilight world. On the one hand, ever since the report of the Franks Committee on *Administrative Tribunals and Enquiries* in 1957,[11] tribunals have been seen as part of the judicial branch of government—'machinery for adjudication' as the Franks Committee put it.[12] On the other hand, in reaching their decisions, first-tier appellate tribunals perform essentially the same tasks as the public functionaries against whose decisions they hear appeals.

18.3 THE INDEPENDENCE OF TRIBUNALS

This conclusion raises an important issue about the independence of tribunals. Independence is thought essential to the effective operation of

---

[8] *Tribunals for Users* recommends general adoption of a practice of designating certain decisions of second-tier tribunals as binding: paras 6.17–26.

[9] P. Rowe, 'The Strict Rules of Evidence in Tribunals: Rhetoric Versus Reality (1994) 1 *J of Social Security L* 9.

[10] *Merchandise Transport Ltd v. British Transport Commission* [1962] 2 QB 173.

[11] Cmnd. 218. 'Tribunals are an alternative to court, not administrative, processes': *Tribunals for Users*, para. 2.18.

[12] Cmnd. 218, para. 40.

courts as an external check on government decision-making. The independence of bodies that adjudicate 'civil rights and obligations' is protected by Art. 6 of the ECHR. Appellate tribunals, like courts, should be free from interference or direct influence by the government bodies from which they hear appeals; and on the whole, they are.[13] The mode of appointment of tribunal chairpersons and members (often by the Lord Chancellor) and the organizational structure of the tribunal system can help to foster independence.[14] The basically adversarial procedure of tribunals, in which the tribunal members act primarily as adjudicators taking relatively little part in the proceedings, may contribute to removing any appearance of bias towards the government position. On the other hand, most tribunals are staffed by employees of, and are administratively supported by, the agency whose decisions it reviews. Obviously this may create an appearance, if not the actuality, of bias.[15] The clerk to the tribunal often plays a considerable part in the more minor cases with which the tribunal deals. Moreover, the members of a significant number of tribunals are appointed by the agency whose decisions they monitor.[16] In principle, however, tribunals are meant to be fully independent, even if in practice they do not always appear to be (and perhaps are not) as independent as they might be.

That tribunals ought to be separate from and independent of the government departments whose activities they monitor is, to some extent, a matter of political choice. There is no intrinsic reason why public decisions ought not to be reviewed internally by more senior officials within a department or agency (see 17.1), or by a Minister, rather than by an external body. This is what happens in certain areas, perhaps the most notable being that of land-use planning, where appeals are decided by the Secretary of State for the Environment or by inspectors employed by the

---

[13] In 1989 the Treasury Solicitor wrote to the President of the Immigration Appeal Tribunal stating, in effect, that in his view a certain High Court decision (in an application for judicial review of a tribunal decision) was wrong. As a result of the political controversy that followed, the practice of the Treasury Solicitor of 'advising' the Tribunal concerning the outcome of judicial review applications was stopped.

[14] The presidential system under which a number of tribunals operate (see 18.5) is important in this respect: R. Sainsbury and H. Genn 'Access to Justice: Lessons From Tribunals' in A.A.S. Zuckerman and R. Cranston (eds), *Reform of Civil Procedure* (Oxford, 1995), p. 420.

[15] *Tribunals for Users*, paras 2.20–22.

[16] *Tribunals for Users* recommends that tribunal members be appointed by the same process as judges (para. 2.32). At the time of writing the government is consulting about proposals to establish a Judicial Appointments Commission which would be responsible for appointing tribunal members as well as judges. See *Tribunals for Users*, paras 7.7–12.

DoE rather than by an independent planning tribunal (see 7.7). Another example is provided by the arrangements for reviewing Social Fund decisions (see 8.1). Before the HRA came into operation, the legality of such arrangements had not been questioned, even though they caused dissatisfaction and were thought by some to be incompatible with basic constitutional—but legally unenforceable—principles. Now, they may be challengeable under Art. 6 of the ECHR. However, as we have seen, internal review mechanisms will not necessarily fall foul of Art. 6 of the ECHR, provided relevant decisions are subject to judicial review or appeal to a court (see 7.3.2.1). The scope of Art. 6 is further limited by the concept of 'civil rights and obligations'.

Even if independent external review of public decisions is not required by law, there are reasons why external review mechanisms might be established. Apart from the intrinsic value of independence, external review is more likely than internal review to make complainants feel that public power is subject to substantial check and to defuse individuals' feelings of having been treated unjustly or unfairly. Less 'respectable' motivations have been suggested as well. One is that setting up an independent tribunal may enable responsibility for potentially controversial decisions to be off-loaded onto a body immune from political criticism. It has also been suggested that the provision of an independent dispute-settling mechanism may make people more willing to accept changes in substantive rules they do not like.[17] The contentious nature of these reasons for establishing tribunals indicates that the decision to do so is sometimes itself a subject of political controversy. Arguments such as the desirability of retaining ultimate ministerial responsibility for decision-making, and that a right of appeal to a tribunal causes inflexibility and delay in the dispatch of government business, have also been used to resist creation of new tribunals. In situations where the requirements of Art. 6 do not apply, the decision whether or not to create a tribunal to handle disputes in particular areas of public activity can be made on the 'merits' of the case or political expediency rather than according to general principles about when external independent review is necessary or desirable.

---

[17] C. Harlow and R. Rawlings, *Law and Administration* (London, 1984), pp. 74–8; T. Prosser, 'Poverty, Ideology and Legality: Supplementary Benefit Appeal Tribunals and their Predecessors' (1977) 4 *Brit J of Law and Society* 39.

18.4 ADVANTAGES OF TRIBUNALS

18.4.1 COST, SPEED, AND INFORMALITY

For half a century at least, appellate tribunals have been seen as alternatives to courts for the adjudication of disputes between citizens and between citizens and government. In the past 100 years many more new tribunals have been created than new courts. What advantages are tribunals seen to have over courts? One factor is cost: the tribunal system is relatively cheaper for the government to run than the court system, partly because most members of tribunals are not paid as much as judges. Moreover, as noted below, legal aid is generally not available for representation before tribunals, and the government has repeatedly resisted calls from various quarters to extend legal aid for representation to tribunals.

Tribunals are also said to be good for claimants because it costs much less to appeal to a tribunal than to initiate court proceedings, and because tribunals deal with cases relatively quickly and informally. The cost advantage of tribunals is real, but has to be judged in light of the fact that legal aid is not available for representation before tribunals even in cases where paid representation would help the applicant (see below). Speed is not desirable in itself if it results in difficult and complex questions receiving inadequate consideration. Indeed, if speed[18] were the only relevant consideration, it might be better not to establish a tribunal at all but to rely on internal reviews. Tribunals can satisfy other important goals such as allowing complainants to participate in the decision-making process and providing an assurance of impartiality.[19]

As for informality, it may make tribunals somewhat less intimidating and more accessible especially for claimants who are poor and ill-educated.[20] This is obviously more important in the case of tribunals that deal with social security and social welfare benefits than tribunals that deal with commercial matters. Informality is relative, and the mode of operation of some tribunals is considerably more formal than that of others. The more legalized the issues with which a tribunal deals, the

---

[18] Or cost, for that matter: R. Sainsbury, 'Internal Reviews and the Weakening of Social Security Claimants' Rights of Appeal' in G. Richardson and H. Genn (eds), *Administrative Law and Government Action* (Oxford, 1994), pp. 302–3.

[19] Ibid.

[20] From one point of view, informality is only important if parties lack the resources to secure competent legal advice and representation: H. Genn, 'Tribunals and Informal Justice' (1993) 56 *MLR* 393, 398.

more formal its proceedings are likely to be, with lawyers playing an important part in presenting cases and with parties standing on their legal rights. Furthermore, it is important to distinguish between an informal atmosphere in a tribunal and informal procedure. Formality in procedure is usually associated with adversary adjudication, while alternatives to the adversary model such as investigation, mediation, and conciliation tend to be seen as more informal. The Council on Tribunals (see 18.5), which has general oversight of tribunals and their procedure, takes the view (reflected in its model rules of procedure for tribunals) that tribunal procedure ought to be basically adversarial. This is understandable given the similarities between the functions of appellate tribunals and courts: it is not within the remit of tribunals, any more than of courts, to mediate or conciliate or even to conduct ombudsman–like investigations.

Procedure before tribunals is very varied. Although many tribunals operate in a basically adversarial way, some tribunals follow less formal procedures. For instance, members of SSATs often take a somewhat active role in proceedings to help unrepresented applicants;[21] while officers responsible for representing the department before such tribunals typically adopt a passive or reactive stance rather than an aggressively adversarial approach.[22] Even so, in many cases before such tribunals the applicant will be at a disadvantage if only because of being unfamiliar with tribunal proceedings and with putting a case.[23] Moreover, the proceedings remain, at bottom, essentially a contest between two opposing positions. While the members of the tribunal may take steps to ensure that applicants feel at ease and are assisted in putting their case, the logic of the adversary model prevents the tribunal members taking too active a part to help the complainant. Nor is it clear that a very active tribunal would necessarily be desirable, because the success or failure of the application would then rest very heavily on the goodwill and competence of the members of the tribunal and on their attitudes towards claimants in general and the applicant before them in particular. In the words of one writer, informality of procedure may be positively disadvantageous to claimants because 'cases . . . may not be properly ventilated, the law may not be accurately applied, and ultimately justice may not be done'.[24] From this perspective, procedure should be as formal as is reasonably necessary to maximize the chance that a sound decision will be reached.

---

[21] J. Baldwin, N. Wikeley, and R. Young, *Judging Social Security* (Oxford, 1992), ch. 4.
[22] Ibid., ch. 7.   [23] Ibid., ch. 6.
[24] H. Genn, 'Tribunal Review of Administrative Decision-Making' in Richardson and Genn (eds), *Administrative Law and Government Action*, p. 263.

To the extent that procedure of appellate tribunals is basically adversarial, it is important that applicants before tribunals should be entitled to be represented by a lawyer or someone else who has some experience in presenting cases before tribunals.[25] The procedural rules of some tribunals give an unrestricted right of representation, and the Council on Tribunals encourages this.[26] As we have seen (see 7.3.2.2.4), it is unclear to what extent the common law recognizes a right to be represented before a tribunal or other public decision-maker. If a right to legal representation is to be truly effective, it must be possible for the applicant to pay a representative if necessary, particularly where the case raises legal or complex factual issues or where a great deal is at stake for the applicant. At present, applicants before most tribunals can get legal aid only to cover the cost of advice, not representation. Furthermore, most tribunals have no power to order the respondent to pay the applicant's costs.[27] In some cases this may not matter because representation by a social worker or a trade union official may be adequate and, as some evidence shows,[28] more effective than legal representation. However, lack of legal aid may put tribunal justice out of the reach of a significant number of applicants.

There is no doubt that informality, cheapness and speed are each, viewed in isolation, desirable goals both for courts and tribunals. It is also true, on the whole, that tribunals operate in a less formal way than courts and that appealing to a tribunal is cheaper and quicker than going to court. However, there are also other desirable goals, such as procedural fairness, claimant-participation, and high quality decision-making, that may require and justify procedures that are more formal, expensive, and lengthy, and which are more likely to vindicate claimants' legal rights and reasonable expectations of being treated fairly. Whether we call them courts or tribunals, our aim should be to establish adjudicative bodies that achieve a sound reconciliation of these various goals. Such an approach is also required by Art. 6 of the ECHR, at least in cases where civil rights and obligations are in issue.

---

[25] Ibid.

[26] *Tribunals for Users* is more guarded about legal aid for representation: paras 4.21–28. Making tribunals more user-friendly is the preferred option.

[27] An attempt to get around this rule failed in *Jones v. Department of Employment* [1989] QB 1.

[28] See 7.3.2.2.4, n. 103.

18.4.2 SPECIALIZATION

Tribunals are more specialized than courts in two ways.[29] First, tribunals typically deal with just one sort of issue (e.g. immigration or education matters). Many courts, on the other hand, deal with a very wide range of issues, and judges tend to be specialists in no more than a couple of areas of the court's jurisdiction. The creation of the Administrative Court has produced a degree of specialization in administrative law matters, but this is specialization more in the general principles of administrative law than in particular areas of public administration. As a result of jurisdictional specialization, tribunal members may be much more expert in the area of law, administration, and policy with which their tribunal deals than a judge who might hear an appeal from, or an application for judicial review of, a decision of the tribunal. This may and should lead the courts to be cautious in overturning or quashing decisions of tribunals.[30] On the other hand, specialized tribunals may lack a broader perspective, which might be of value in identifying claims that have a wider legal or administrative significance.

Secondly, while appellate tribunals are typically chaired by a lawyer (or consist of a legally trained person sitting alone), many tribunals[31] have a majority of members who are are non-lawyers.[32] Just as magistrates' courts provide a lay element in the criminal justice system, so tribunals provide a lay element in one sector of the civil justice system. Non-legal members of tribunals are usually appointed because they have relevant professional expertise (e.g. social workers may be chosen to sit on social security appeal tribunals) or knowledge and experience relevant to the subject matter of the tribunal's jurisdiction. The main advantages of 'non-legal specialization' are seen as being greater consistency in decision-making and a greater ability to give effect to the policy behind the legislation in a way that makes sense of the realities of the matters regulated by the legislation and reflects current social conditions. Knowledgeable lay persons may be more able than lawyers to foresee potential knock-on effects of their decisions, and as a result they may be able to

---

[29] For detailed consideration of this topic see S. Legomsky, *Specialized Justice* (Oxford, 1990).

[30] Tribunal expertise was one of the justifications for the decision in *Chief Adjudication Officer v. Foster* (see 6.6).

[31] But not, for instance, the Social Security and Child Support Commissioners: Commissioners must have the same qualifications as a High Court judge.

[32] See *Tribunals for Users*, paras 7.19–26.

avoid potential anomalies and inconsistencies in decision-making.[33] We also noted earlier (see 9.3) the argument that decisions on issues of law and fact may often be more rational and sensible if made with a thorough understanding of the area in which the questions arise. There is, however, another side to this second aspect of specialization. The knowledge and experience of lay members of tribunals is in the non-legal aspects of the tribunals' work. Even in areas where tribunals are reviewing discretionary powers not heavily structured by legal rules or formal policy guidelines, they operate within a framework of legal rules, and it is important that tribunal members understand these rules. Training of lay tribunal members is important in this respect; and, no doubt, after sitting on a tribunal for a period, some lay members acquire considerable knowledge of the relevant law (greater, perhaps, than that of lawyers who do not regularly deal with matters within the tribunal's jurisdiction). But lack of legal expertise in a tribunal may reduce the 'legal accuracy' of its decisions and can result in tribunal members who are not legally trained being marginalized and not making the contribution which they were appointed to make, while the tribunal's proceedings are dominated by the legal chair.[34]

Techniques for dealing with legal mistakes made by tribunals are to provide for appeals on points of law to a court (or second-tier tribunals consisting of lawyers), and to require tribunals to state reasons for their decisions that make clear the legal basis on which the decision was made.[35] The right-of-appeal solution is expensive and cumbersome. It is better to improve the quality of tribunal decision-making in the first instance by training tribunal members. However, once increased emphasis is put on legal correctness at the tribunal hearing stage, there is likely to be pressure to formalize procedure and to make it more adversarial. Lawyers may get more involved in representing claimants and tribunal proceedings may become more lengthy, expensive, and intimidating for the ordinary applicant. It may be that the price of informality is a certain amount of legal inaccuracy. However, once legal rights are defined, the beneficiaries of those rights are understandably and rightly inclined to insist on their strict observance and may not be willing just to use them as bargaining counters in informal negotiations.[36] This tendency

---

[33] M. Adler, 'Lay Tribunal Members and Administrative Justice' [1999] *PL* 616.
[34] Baldwin, Wikeley, and Young, *Judging Social Security*, ch. 5.
[35] See Tribunals and Inquiries Act 1992, ss. 10 and 11.
[36] Mental Health Tribunals seem to offer an exception to this observation: J. Peay, *Tribunals on Trial* (Oxford, 1989), pp. 222–3.

often has an ideological underpinning. For example, many see it as important, in order to preserve the dignity and individual worth of welfare claimants, that they should have clearly defined rights and not be subject to the discretion and mercy of the government or of tribunals, which might be inclined to take an establishment view of matters.

18.5 THE STRUCTURE OF THE TRIBUNAL 'SYSTEM'

There is a large number of tribunals and they have come into existence in a piecemeal and unsystematic way. Tribunals vary considerably in their organization, membership, and procedures. Some groups of tribunals, such as the SSATs, are organized on a 'presidential system' under which one person is responsible for the general administration of the tribunals in the system. This form of organization reinforces the independence of these tribunals. It has also led to improved facilities for the training of members of tribunals (both lay and legal) and has increased the consistency and quality of tribunal decision-making.

The Council on Tribunals plays some part in advising on the setting up of new tribunals, but attempts to persuade the government to simplify and rationalize the tribunal system have been unsuccessful.[37] According to the Council's own statement, its purpose is 'to keep under review, and report on, the constitution and working of the tribunals under its supervision, and where necessary to consider and report on the administrative procedures of statutory inquiries'.[38] The council publishes detailed model rules of procedure for tribunals, and a 'Framework of Standards'. These standards are based on the three principles of openness, fairness, and impartiality enunciated in the report of the Franks Committee on *Administrative Tribunals and Enquiries* (1957). Tribunals should be independent; provide open, fair and impartial hearings; be accessible to and focus on the needs of users; offer cost-effective procedures, and be properly resourced and organized. The Council's modest funding, and its lack of status and teeth, significantly limit the extent to which it can meaningfully monitor and coordinate (let alone expose defects in) the tribunal system. *Tribunals for Users* contains various recommendations

---

[37] C. Harlow and R. Rawlings, *Law and Admistration*, 2nd edn (London, 1997), pp. 467–71; Lord Archer of Sandwell, 'The Role of the Council on Tribunals' in Harris and Partington (eds), *Administrative Justice in the 21st Century*, ch. 24.

[38] Council on Tribunals, Annual Report 2001/2002, p. vi.

for making the council more important and effective.[39] More radically, it has been suggested that the council might be complemented or replaced by a more-generously funded independent research and advisory body (along the lines of the Australian Administrative Review Council)[40] to oversee the complex network of institutions (including the courts) and informal avenues for making complaints against government, and to make recommendations for reform.

In 2001 the Leggatt Review of Tribunals (in *Tribunals for Users*) recommended that most of the first-tier and second-tier adjudicatory tribunals dealing with citizen/public functionary disputes be integrated into a tribunal system with a unified administrative structure and a single point of access for all users. First-tier tribunals would be grouped together according to the subject matter of their jurisdictions, and each group would be provided with a second-tier tribunal to hear appeals on points of law from first-tier tribunals as well as acting as a first-tier tribunal for particularly complex cases. The second-tier tribunals would together form a single appellate division of the tribunal system. In March 2003 the government announced that it will implement the main recommendations of the Leggatt review.[41] At the time of writing it was unclear how many tribunals will be included in the new unified tribunals system.

18.6 CONCLUSION

Tribunals provide the main external forum for handling disputes between individual citizens and public agencies.[42] Tribunals are meant to provide relatively cheap, accessible, informal, speedy, and specialized justice. They were originally conceived as part of the executive rather than the judicial branch of government. The Franks Committee Report of 1957 reconceived them as machinery for adjudication rather than administration. The report of the Leggatt review reaffirmed that characterization, and recommended changes that would align tribunals even more closely with courts. In particular, tribunals would cease to be amenable to judicial review, and their decisions would be challengeable only for error of law. On this basis, tribunals would actually be subject to less judicial supervision

---

[39] *Tribunals for Users*, paras 7.46–55, 12.3.

[40] D. Pearce, 'Administrative Review Council' (2002) 35 *Australian Institute of Administrative Law Forum* 53.

[41] However, the 2003 Queen's Speech did not foreshadow legislation on this topic.

[42] Concerning the interface between internal and external review see *Tribunals for Users*, ch. 9.

that most courts. (At this point, it is worth recalling that in *Chief Adjudication Officer v. Foster*[43] the House of Lords held that the Social Security Commissioners (a second-tier tribunal) had jurisdiction to decide the validity of delegated legislation—a function traditionally assigned to the High Court in its judicial review jurisdiction.)

If fully implemented, the Leggatt proposals would go a long way to creating a separate system of public-law 'courts' connected to what Dicey called 'the ordinary courts' via appeals on points of law to the Court of Appeal. In such a system, the judicial review jurisdiction of the Administrative Court would be limited to public decisions that did not fall within the jurisdiction of a tribunal. The Leggatt proposals reinforce two significant constitutional developments of the past thirty years—the institutionalization of a public/private divide, and judicialization[44] and legalization of public decision-making. Given the increasing importance of Art. 6 of the ECHR, the latter trend is irreversible. The tribunal system contemplated in *Tribunals for Users* would be well designed to meet the requirements of the ECHR.[45]

---

[43] [1993] AC 754.

[44] See N. Wikeley, 'Burying Bell: Managing the Judicialisation of Social Security Tribunals' (2000) 63 *MLR* 475.

[45] C. Harlow, 'The ECHR and Administrative Justice' in M. Partington (ed.), *The Leggatt Review of Tribunals: Academic Seminar Papers* (Bristol, 2001).

Part V

Wider Perspectives on Judicial Control

19

Constitutional and Political Background

This book is mainly concerned with judicial control of performance of public functions, and in particular with judicial review. The aim of this final part is to discuss the constitutional, political, and administrative environment in which judicial control operates. This chapter considers some theoretical issues relevant to understanding the role of judicial control, while the next chapter discusses the impact of judicial control on the exercise of public power. Before we start, an important preliminary point needs to be made. This book has concentrated on courts[1] at the expense of other legal institutions (such as tribunals), on judicial review at the expense of the civil and criminal liability of public functionaries, and on general principles of judicial review at the expense of substantive areas of public law (such as immigration and housing). One result of this strategy has been to cast the spotlight on large issues of constitutional theory and institutional design at the expense of the everyday stuff of legal disputes about performance of public functions. The reality, of course, is that most such legal disputes are dealt with informally, or by internal complaints mechanisms, ombudsmen, tribunals, and so on, not by courts. They are of little or no constitutional significance beyond ensuring that particular public functions are performed and individual public decisions are made in accordance with relevant statutory provisions and relevant common law rules. This is not to underplay the value of ensuring that public functionaries comply with the law, but only to stress that the issues dealt with in this chapter are of little direct relevance to the daily conduct of public business. Rather they concern the broad institutional and constitutional framework within which public power is exercised.

More narrowly, the discussion in this chapter does not address the reasons why disputes about the performance of public functions find (or do not find) their way into a court or, for that matter, into an internal complaints system or tribunal, or to an ombudsman. It is not about the

---

[1] The Administrative Court in particular.

role of courts and judicial review in resolving individual disputes but rather about the constitutional and political significance of that role. Its focus is, in fact, still narrower than that, because not even all claims for judicial review have broader constitutional or political significance. Many (perhaps most) are concerned only with ensuring that individual exercises of public power comply with applicable legal rules. Our interest here is in the small proportion of decisions of superior courts that contribute to establishing constitutional ground-rules for the distribution, exercise, and control of public power.

19.1 CONSTITUTIONAL BACKGROUND

One of the concerns of administrative law is how the branches of government or, more broadly, various organs of governance, relate to one another. In the first place, it is concerned with the position of administrative agencies *vis-à-vis* Parliament, because most of the functions of administrative agencies are conferred and defined by statute, and because Parliament exercises control over the exercise of some public administrative functions. At the same time, the fact that actions of public administrators can be challenged in the courts makes the question of the proper relationship between the legislature and administrative agencies on the one hand, and the judiciary on the other, central to administrative law. There are several so-called 'constitutional doctrines' that bear on these relationships. They are: the supremacy (or sovereignty) of Parliament; ministerial responsibility; the separation of powers; and the rule of law. All of these doctrines are to a greater or lesser extent concerned with a central issue in constitutional theory, namely that of responsibility or 'accountability': how can those who wield public power best be made accountable for the way they exercise it? Accountability is a form of control. The courts are concerned mainly with control by the use of law, whereas Parliament is concerned with control by the exercise of political power. It is with the interaction between legal and political control that this section mainly deals.

19.1.2 SUPREMACY OF PARLIAMENT

The classic doctrine of the supremacy (or 'sovereignty') of Parliament[2] is contained in four main propositions, namely: (1) in case of conflict

---

[2] 'Parliament' in this context means the Monarch, the House of Lords, and the House of Commons acting in concert to produce primary legislation.

between statute law and common law, statute law prevails; (2) Parliament is free to enact whatever law it chooses; (3) no Act of Parliament can be challenged in the courts on the grounds of invalidity or lack of constitutionality (unless it is alleged to be inconsistent with EC law);[3] and (4) Parliament cannot bind its successors. For present purposes, the first proposition alone demands consideration.

Most of the powers and duties of public functionaries are statutory. It follows from the first proposition about Parliamentary supremacy that courts are bound to apply statutes according to their terms. Although this does not follow from the first proposition, traditional theory also says that indeterminacy and ambiguities in the language of statutes should be resolved, and gaps in them filled, by reference to the intention of the legislature. Thus, it is often said that the enforcement of statutory duties and the control of the exercise of statutory powers by the courts is ultimately justifiable in terms of the doctrine of Parliamentary supremacy: even though Parliament has not expressly authorized the courts to supervise governmental activity, it cannot have intended breaches of duty by governmental agencies to go unremedied (even if no remedy is provided in the statute itself), nor can it have intended to give administrative agencies the freedom to exceed or abuse their powers, or to act unreasonably. It is the task of the courts to interpret and enforce the provisions of statutes, which impose duties and confer powers on public functionaries, in the light of the principles of legality embodied in the grounds of judicial review. In so doing they are giving effect to the will of Parliament.

There are three main weaknesses in this theory of the basis of judicial control of the exercise of public functions. The first is relevant to statutory interpretation generally: it is unrealistic to treat the process of interpreting statutes, resolving ambiguities, and filling gaps, as always being a matter of discerning and giving effect to the intention of Parliament. Even assuming that we can make sense of the notion of intention when applied to a multi-member body following simple majoritarian voting procedures, there will be many cases in which Parliament did not think about the question relevant to resolving the indeterminacy or ambiguity, or filling the gap. In such cases the courts must act creatively in deciding what the statute means. The weakness of the intention theory of statutory interpretation is made clear by the notion of 'purposive interpretation'.

---

[3] A declaration that primary legislation is incompatible with a Convention right may be made under s. 4 of the HRA, but such a declaration does not affect the validity or operation of the legislation.

Especially (but not only) in the contexts of interpreting statutes passed to give effect to EC law and of protecting Convention rights,[4] courts may go beyond interpreting the words actually used in statutes and insert (or 'imply') into legislative provisions words or phrases needed to give effect to what the court perceives to be the true purpose or aim of the provision in question. It makes little sense to describe this process in terms of giving effect to what Parliament actually intended all along.

A technique for giving some meaning to the idea of the intention of the legislature is for courts to pay attention to what are called '*travaux preparatoires*', that is policy documents and statements that preceded the enactment of the relevant legislation and might throw some light on its intended meaning or, at least, the purpose for which it was enacted. In *Pepper v. Hart*[5] the House of Lords held that where a statutory provision is ambiguous or obscure or leads to an absurdity, a court required to interpret the provision can refer to clear statements, made in Parliament by a Minister or promoter of the bill, as to its intended meaning and effect, and to other Parliamentary material that might be necessary to understand such statements. This decision was of considerable constitutional significance because it implied that the relevant intention was not that of Parliament in enacting the legislation but rather that of the government in promoting it. It seemed to acknowledge the effective reality that Parliament does not legislate but rather legitimizes the government's legislation. In so doing, it further undermined the notion that in interpreting legislation, the courts were giving effect to the intention of Parliament. In an influential article critical of the decision in *Pepper v. Hart*, Lord Steyn made these implications explicit;[6] and in its wake the House of Lords has embarked on a process of re-interpreting *Pepper v. Hart* so that it does not undermine the principles that the job of interpreting legislation belongs ultimately to the courts, not to the government,

---

[4] Section 3 of the HRA imposes on courts an obligation, 'so far as it is possible' to 'read primary legislation in a way that is compatible with Convention rights'. On the meaning of 'so far as it is possible' see A.L. Young, 'Judicial Sovereignty and the Human Rights Act 1998' [2002] *CLJ* 53; G. Marshall, 'The Lynchpin of Parliamentary Intention: Lost, Stolen or Strained? [2003] *PL* 236.

[5] [1993] AC 593. In response to this decision, procedures were adopted for avoiding and correcting errors and ambiguities arising out of ministerial statements: HL Debs, Vol 563, col 26, 5 April 1995.

[6] J. Steyn, '*Pepper v Hart* A Re-examination' [2001] 21 *OJLS* 59; see also G. Marshall, 'Hansard and the Interpretation of Statutes' in D. Oliver and G. Drewry (eds), *The Law and Parliament* (London, 1998).

and that the question for the court is what the statutory words mean, not what the government or anyone else thinks they mean.[7]

A second weakness of the 'intention-of-Parliament' justification of judicial control of the performance of public functions is that it is at variance with the actual conduct of the courts. The mechanism, grounds, and remedies of judicial review were created and developed by the courts as means of controlling public power. The courts have shown themselves prepared to go a very long way to preserve their jurisdiction to supervise the exercise of public power by applying these principles. Perhaps the most striking modern example of this is the case of *Anisminic Ltd v. Foreign Compensation Commission.*[8] The main question in this case was whether a section in the Foreign Compensation Act, purporting to oust the jurisdiction of the court to review 'determinations' of the Commission, was effective to that end. The House of Lords held that the word 'determination' must be read so as to exclude *ultra vires* determinations. It then went on to extend considerably the notion of *ultra vires* as it applied to decisions on questions of law, the final result being to reduce the application of the ouster clause almost to vanishing point, despite the fact that it had arguably been meant to have wide effect.

A second example is provided by the attitude of the courts to the exclusion by statute of the rules of natural justice. In the face of legislative silence on the question of whether an applicant before an administrative body is entitled to the protection of these procedural rules, two approaches are possible. It could be said that the rules of natural justice will apply only if there is evidence of a legislative intention that they should; alternatively, it could be argued that silence should be construed as an invitation to the courts to apply common law procedural standards of natural justice. On the whole the courts, especially in recent years, have tended to the latter view, thus asserting the independent force of the rules of natural justice.

A third example is provided by cases, concerning powers given to a Minister, for example, 'to act as he sees fit' (see 9.8.2). Such phraseology appears to give the Minister unfettered discretion, but it has been held that such powers must be exercised reasonably in the light of the aims and purposes of the legislation conferring the power and of the relevant facts. In reality, the terms of the legislation may give very little guidance as to

---

[7] The leading cases are *R v. Secretary of State for the Environment, Transport and the Regions, ex p. Spath Holme Ltd* [2001] 2 AC 349; *Wilson v. Secretary of State for Trade and Industry* [2003] 3 WLR 568.

[8] [1969] 2 AC 147.

the way the power was meant to be exercised, even assuming that the Minister was not meant to be free to exercise his or her own best judgment. In effect, the courts are imposing standards of reasonable conduct on the Minister, irrespective of the question of legislative intent.

A third weakness in the statutory interpretation approach to judicial control of public power is that it does not justify judicial control of the performance of non-statutory functions. As we have seen (see 3.2.5), in the *GCHQ* case the House of Lords rejected the proposition that the common law (prerogative) powers of central government are immune from judicial review in favour of the proposition that the exercise of a common law power can be challenged provided only that the power or the circumstances of its exercise do not raise non-justiciable issues of policy. We have also seen (see 3.2.4) that the courts have extended the scope of judicial review to embrace the exercise, for public purposes, of *de facto* power which has no identifiable legal source either in common law or statute. Whatever the criteria that the courts will apply in reviewing the exercise of non-statutory powers, they cannot, by definition, be derived from a power-conferring statute.

If judicial control of governmental action cannot adequately be explained in terms of Parliamentary intention, how is it to be justified? Two lines of argument suggest themselves. First, despite the second proposition of Parliamentary supremacy stated above, it can be argued that there are certain features of our constitutional and political arrangements that are so basic to our system of government that it is not seriously thought that they could ever be subject to the whim of Parliament—for example, the right to vote in free elections. Parliament could, of course, pass legislation inimical to this right, but attempts to enforce it, whether in the courts or outside would, no doubt, either simply fail or else precipitate a constitutional crisis. Similarly, we might say, the right to seek judicial review of the exercise of public powers and to receive a fair hearing are of fundamental importance in a democratic society, and it is vital that these rights be protected from any but the most limited statutory abridgement.[9] A second line of argument that might support the refusal of the courts to be too deferential to Parliament is this: a vital underpinning assumption of Parliamentary supremacy is that Parliament is the most democratic governmental institution in our system. The political reality is that when the party in government has a comfortable

---

[9] This finds expression in Art. 6 of the ECHR which, in this respect, reinforces the established approach of English courts.

majority in the House of Commons, Parliament is almost as much under the control of the government as is the day-to-day conduct of government business. The implications of this line of argument will be considered more later (see 19.2).

The autonomy of judicial review has an important implication that ought to be made explicit, namely that in controlling the performance of public functions, the courts are asserting and exercising, in their own right and in their own name, a power to limit and define the powers of other public functionaries. Parliament allocates decision-making powers to public functionaries by virtue of its almost unlimited legislative power. The courts, by virtue of their inherent (i.e. self-conferred) common law power of judicial review of public functions, decide the legal limits of those allocations of power. In so doing they can not only castigate public functionaries for abuses or excesses of power but, equally importantly, they can legitimize controversial exercises of power by holding them to have been lawful. The courts, in short, perform an indirect power-allocation function. Once this is realized, it can be seen how important it is to understand the nature of this function and the justification for it, since it is clear that the courts are not detached umpires in the governmental process but that they play an integral part in deciding how it will operate.

On the other hand, it is important not to give undue emphasis to the autonomy of judicial review. In most cases, judicial review is concerned with the exercise of statutory powers and the performance of statutory duties. In exercising their independent judicial review function in such cases, the courts are inevitably constrained by the terms of the relevant statute. In other words, the statutory provisions provide the context in which the abstract principles of judicial review are given concrete content in individual cases (see 1.5).

In recent years, the matters discussed in this section have generated much debate about whether the doctrines of *ultra vires* and the supremacy of Parliament provide the basis of and justification for judicial review of the performance of public functions or whether they are to be found in 'the common law'.[10] In my view, the debate rests on a false dichotomy.

---

[10] Many of the leading contributions to the debate are collected in C. Forsyth (ed.), *Judicial Review and the Constitution* (Oxford, 2000). More recent contributions include M. Elliott, *The Constitutional Foundations of Judicial Review* (Oxford, 2001); N.W. Barber, 'The Academic Mythologians' (2001) 21 *OJLS* 369; P. Craig and N. Bamforth, 'Constitutional Analysis, Constitutional Principle and Judicial Review' [2001] *PL* 763; T.R.S. Allan, 'The Constitutional Foundations of Judicial Review: Conceptual Conundrum or Interpretative Inquiry? [2002] *CLJ* 87, 'Doctrine and Theory in Administrative Law: An Elusive Quest for the Limits of Jurisdiction' [2003] *PL* 429, 'Constitutional Dialogue and the Justification of

Historically it is certainly true that the courts did not acquire the judicial review function as a result of having it conferred on them by statute. It is a power the courts asserted for themselves. On the other hand, for the most part the performance of that function in individual cases is informed and constrained by the text of the statute that conferred the public function under review. The legislature and the courts are engaged in a sort of joint enterprise of creating and controlling the exercise of public powers. It has been argued that the issue at stake in this debate is whether the common law is in some sense morally superior to legislation.[11] It is certainly the case that in the past forty years, the part played by courts in controlling the performance of public functions has increased enormously in both size and significance. This is the result of developments such as British membership of the EU, reform of judicial review procedure, the enactment of the HRA and what might loosely be called a 'new judicial activism'. A common way of describing these changes is in terms of a shift from a 'political constitution'[12]—in which Parliament and other political institutions take the lead in checking and controlling the performance of public functions by the application of norms of politically acceptable conduct—to a 'legal constitution' in which courts and other legal institutions play a central role and in which legal norms impose significant constraints on the exercise of public power.

The idea that judge-made law is morally superior to law made by legislators may be one way of explaining and justifying this aggrandisement of the power of legal institutions, especially courts. More prosaically, it may simply be a function of distrust of politicians and the political process. Either way, the growing power of legal institutions raises serious and difficult questions about the identity of the people who staff these institutions and how they are chosen. An early sign of this problem was the controversy over Lord Hoffmann's participation in the *Pinochet* case.[13] Symptomatic, too, is the growing importance of the guarantee of the 'independence' of adjudicative institutions in Art. 6 of the ECHR; as are the moves towards a UK Supreme Court to replace the judicial House

---

Judicial Review' (2003) 23 *OJLS* 563; P Craig, 'Constitutional Foundations, the Rule of Law and Supremacy' [2003] *PL* 92.

[11] T. Poole, 'Back to the Future? Unearthing the Theory of Common Law Constitutionalism' (2003) 23 *OJLS* 435.

[12] This term was invented by J.A.G. Griffith, 'The Political Constitution' (1979) 42 *MLR* 1.

[13] D. Woodhouse (ed.), *The Pinochet Case: A Legal and Constitutional Analysis* (Oxford, 2000).

of Lords. As judicial power grows, so does the need to justify and legitimize its exercise. The courts might control public functionaries, but who controls the courts? The idea that courts or the common law occupy some sort of moral high ground in the constitutional landscape is, I think, one of which we should be very wary.

19.1.3 MINISTERIAL RESPONSIBILITY

As we have already seen,[14] individual ministerial responsibility (IMR)[15] is the constitutional foundation of political accountability of central government to Parliament. As a general accountability mechanism, IMR is limited in various ways. Much public decision-making and the activities of many public agencies do not fall within its scope. The sanctions attached to IMR are relatively weak. A government with a comfortable majority in the House of Commons can usually resist Parliamentary calls for the resignation of one of its number (unless the media also joins the chorus). Even so, IMR is the main symbol of the principle of responsible government according to which public agencies are politically accountable to representative institutions for the way they run the country.

In general, the stronger the mechanisms and institutions for holding public functionaries politically accountable, the less need there is for legal accountability through courts and other legal institutions. For many people, political accountability is preferable to legal accountability because it is more democratic. Sometimes the courts rely on the possibility of political accountability as a justification for not imposing legal constraints on the exercise of public power.[16] Various developments of the past fifty years—most notably, perhaps, British membership of the EU, devolution and the domestication of the ECHR—have greatly increased the role of law and courts, relative to political institutions, in holding public functionaries to account. This is not to say that institutions of political accountability are impotent, but only that relative to legal

---

[14] See 12.2.2, 16.2.1.
[15] G. Marshall, *Ministerial Responsibility* (Oxford, 1989); C. Turpin, 'Ministerial Responsibility' in J. Jowell and D. Oliver (eds), *The Changing Constitution*, 3rd edn (Oxford, 1994) (there is no chapter on this topic in the 4th edition because, the editors say, 'it can no longer be said . . . that it is a fundamental doctrine of the constitution: *The Changing Constitution*, 4th edn (Oxford, 2000), p. viii); D. Woodhouse, *Ministers and Parliament* (Oxford, 1994).
[16] e.g. the *Gouriet* case (see 3.1). The distinction between political and legal accountability also lies at the bottom of the 'political questions' version of the notion of non-justiciability (see 3.2.5).

institutions, they play a smaller role in holding public functionaries accountable than they did fifty years ago.

In reality, the distinction between legal and political accountability is not as clear-cut as this discussion might suggest. Accountability mechanisms vary on at least two dimensions—institutional and substantive. Paradigmatically, political accountability is enforced by a representative institution on the basis of non-legal norms of conduct. By contrast, paradigmatic legal accountability is enforced by appointed institutions on the basis of norms of conduct derived from statute or common law. Public sector ombudsmen, for instance, do not neatly fit either paradigm. The general point is simply that there are various ways of controlling public power. Law is only one of them. Understanding the role of administrative law and judicial review in this enterprise requires an appreciation of how they relate to other controlling mechanisms and to their limits as well as their potential.

19.1.4 SEPARATION OF POWERS

This doctrine (or, perhaps more accurately, 'value' or 'aspiration') has received various interpretations at different times and in different systems. The basic proposition underlying all versions of the doctrine is that excessive concentration of public power in the hands of a single agency is to be avoided because it encourages, or at least facilitates, abuse of power. For example, it is undesirable that the same agency should make laws and also adjudicate disputes about their application. To this end, powers are usually divided into legislative, administrative (or 'executive'), and judicial.

According to a strict version of separation theory, no agency should wield powers of more than one of these three types. This version of separation is not a feature of the British governmental system or, indeed, of any modern governmental system. For instance, the administrative branch of government not only 'executes' laws but also makes them (in the form of delegated legislation). Courts not only apply law, but also make it (common law). Parliament not only makes laws but also administers its own internal affairs and enforces rules of conduct on its members. A rather different interpretation distinguishes between different branches of government—the legislature, the executive, and the judiciary[17]— according to the type of power which is most prominent in the functions

---

[17] Adam Tomkins, *Public Law* (Oxford, 2003) argues that in the British constitutional system there are only two power blocs—the Crown and Parliament (the executive and the legislature). In his view, the judiciary sits (uneasily) in the Crown camp.

of each branch, and then forbids interference by any branch in the activities of any other branch. This version does not describe the British constitution either. On the contrary, the British system, at least in its classic form, could be said to be a system of checks and balances. Under such a system, abuse of power is guarded against not by avoiding the conferral of powers of different types on the one agency but by giving another entity, belonging to one of the other branches of government, the power to scrutinize the activities of the agency in order to prevent, or hold it accountable for, abuse of power. This interpretation of separation underlies the doctrine of ministerial responsibility and also, as we shall see, the notion of the rule of law.

Central to this version of separation of powers is the idea of the independence of the judiciary. In Britain, security of tenure and strong constitutional conventions effectively protect courts (and tribunals) from direct interference by other branches of government. One of these conventions is that the Lord Chancellor will defend judges from illegitimate 'politically motivated' attacks. This is ironical because it is the fact of being both the head of the judiciary and a member of the executive that enables the Lord Chancellor to perform this role. Some fear the abolition of the office of Lord Chancellor and its replacement by a Ministry of Constitutional Affairs may potentially weaken the independence of the judiciary at the very time that proposals to replace the judicial House of Lords with a UK Supreme Court are being made with a view to increasing the distance between the judiciary on the one hand and the legislature and the executive on the other.

Traditionally in the British system, the prime importance of judicial independence has been as a protection for citizens suing the government. Independence does not guarantee that judges will be impartial, but it does at least minimize the risk that those in power will be able to interfere with the judicial process to their own advantage. This aspect of judicial independence has been elevated from a constitutional convention and given legal status by Art. 6 of the ECHR. Independence is pivotal to the scheme of the ECHR because under it, human rights are conceived essentially as rights of individuals against governments. An important corollary of the legalization of judicial independence is the need to distinguish more clearly between judicial functions—to which the guarantee of independent performance attaches—and non-judicial functions which are not so protected. In Art. 6, this distinction is marked by the phrase 'determination of . . . civil rights and obligations or of any criminal charge', which defines the scope of the guarantee.

In what may be called 'multi-layered'[18] or 'complex' governmental systems such as federal States—Australia and the US, for instance— judicial independence is also recognized as critical for maintaining the power balance between the various components of government (State and federal, for example), especially when one component is economically or politically dominant. In Britain, this aspect of judicial independence assumed significance in the 1980s when increasing legalization (and souring) of relations between central and local government made litigation an attractive site for intergovernmental, financial, and ideological conflict. British membership of the EU and devolution within the UK have also increased the potential role of courts in holding the constitutional balance in an increasingly complex public domain. In the future, judicial independence and separation of powers are likely to become increasingly central ideas in English public law.

The metaphor of 'checks and balances' (that lies at the heart of the British version of separation of powers) is unstable because it rests on a hazy distinction between performing a function and checking someone else's performance of it. Some of the most fundamental concepts and principles of administrative law are concerned with policing the boundary between these two activities. The concept of *Wednesbury* unreasonableness and the distinctions between legality and merits, and appeal and review, are designed to prevent courts crossing the border between judicial and non-judicial functions. This issue has been highlighted by the enactment of the HRA, which significantly increases opportunities for judicial scrutiny of primary legislation. English courts are torn between their traditional respect for Parliament and its statutes and the more interventionist approach required by the ECHR and encapsulated, for instance, in the concept of 'proportionality' (see 9.8.3).

Recently, judicial responsibility for protecting human rights has led to decisions—in the area of immigration in particular—that have attracted strong criticism from the government in which some detect a real threat to judicial independence. More generally, the increasingly high profile of courts has lent new significance to what Griffith famously called 'the politics of the judiciary'.[19] The exercise of political power is subject to much more legal regulation than it was fifty years ago. More and more decisions of broad social, political, and economic significance are being

---

[18] See N. Bamforth and P. Leyland, *Public Law in a Multi-Layered Constitution* (Oxford, 2003).
[19] J.A.G Griffith, *The Politics of the Judiciary*, 5th edn (London, 1997); first published 1977.

made by judges, who have increasing opportunities to give effect to their own views about how society should operate. There has, in short, been a shift of political power to the courts. One reaction to this has been to insist that even the most senior judges should disqualify themselves from cases in which they have too strong a personal interest.[20] Another has been the proposal for the establishment of an independent Judicial Appointments Commission and increased emphasis in the selection process on procedural transparency, and criteria such as diversity and equality of opportunity.

We started out by noting that judicial independence is central to the British checks-and-balances version of separation of powers, in which public power is constrained by legal rules and principles applied by courts. As the power of courts increases, this very independence may come to seem problematic. Why should the courts, alone amongst public decision-makers, be exempt from the logic of checks and balances? How is the concern about legitimacy, which is fundamental to separation-of-powers theory, to be reconciled with freedom from external constraint?

19.1.5 THE RULE OF LAW

Perhaps even more than separation of powers, the rule of law is a contested concept, even if not quite 'all things to all people'. In English public-law theory, the most influential exposition of the concept has been that of A.V. Dicey in his *Introduction to the Study of the Law of the Constitution*, first published in 1885. For him, the rule of law meant three things. First, governors and governed should be bound by the same, not different, laws. Secondly, that law should be enforced, against governors and governed alike, by the 'ordinary courts'. Thirdly, the rights of the governed against the governors are better protected by the common law than by a statutory or constitutional bill of rights.

The first of these propositions was discussed at some length in Part II in relation to the civil liability of public functionaries. It is perhaps in relation to this proposition that public law today diverges most from Dicey's ideal. Dicey's rejection of a distinction between private law (applying to relations between citizens) and public law (applying to relations between citizens and government) was closely related to his second principle, which we will discuss in a moment. For him, a substantive public law/private law divide went hand-in-hand with an institutional

---

[20] *R v. Bow Street Metropolitan Stipendiary Magistrate, ex p. Pinochet Ugarte* [2000] 1 AC 119.

distinction between public law courts and ordinary courts. As we will see, the English legal system has remained more or less faithful to Dicey's second principle. But a substantive distinction between public law (roughly, the rules and principles of judicial review discussed in Section B of Part I) and private law (the law of tort and contract, for instance) has become firmly entrenched in English law in the past twenty-five years. Surprisingly, this was a result of the changes made to judicial review procedure in 1977, which had the effect of channeling most judicial review cases into the predecessor of the Administrative Court. From this developed the idea of 'public law claims' that were subject to public law rules, not private law rules. The substantive public/private divide has been reinforced by EC law (in which, for instance, the doctrine of the indirect effect of directives, and the rules about public procurement, apply only to 'organs of the State') and by s. 6 of the HRA, which applies only to acts of 'public authorities'. The stage has now been reached when it can be said, with only slight oversimplification, that in English law there are two regimes of rules: public law, which applies to public functions and acts, and private law, which applies to private functions and acts.

Understanding the second of Dicey's rule-of-law propositions requires some background to be sketched. One of the aims of the French revolutionaries in the late eighteenth century was to prevent judicial interference with the conduct of government business. To this end, judicial questioning of government decisions and actions was made a *criminal offence*. In 1799 a non-judicial body, called the *Conseil D'Etat*, was established to deal with citizens' complaints against the government. Until 1889, complaints to the *Conseil* could only be made through a government Minister. In 1879 thirty-eight members of the *Conseil* resigned or were dismissed as the result of a purge of members thought not to be 'in total agreement with the government'.[21] In this light, it is perhaps not surprising that Dicey was suspicious of the idea of special 'public law courts' such as the *Conseil*, and that he preferred to rely on judges for protection against governmental misconduct. Despite Dicey's strictures, the twentieth century saw the establishment of many tribunals to deal with citizen/government disputes. Such tribunals were originally characterized as part of the executive, not the judicial, branch of government. The report of the Franks Committee in 1957 re-characterized them as part of the judicial branch, and the report of the Leggatt review of tribunals in 2001 reaffirmed and reinforced this identification of tribunals as a species

---

[21] L.N. Brown and J.S Bell, *French Administrative Law*, 5th edn (Oxford, 1998), p. 5.

of court. Ironically, perhaps, 2001 also saw the establishment of the Administrative Court, the culmination of the process of development of the distinction between public law and private law traced above. The Administrative Court is, nonetheless, part of the 'ordinary' High Court.

Dicey's third rule-of-law proposition (that individual rights are better protected by the common law than by a bill of rights) was, in a way, a corollary of the other major plank of his constitutional theory, Parliamentary sovereignty. The common law is subordinate to statute, and the courts that make it are subordinate to Parliament. By contrast, a bill of rights—one that is constitutionally 'entrenched' at any rate—provides a basis on which courts can set themselves above the legislature by invalidating statutes. The first move away from the Diceyan proposition came with Britain's signature and ratification of the ECHR in 1950. In 1966 British citizens were given the right to petition the ECtHR about breaches of the ECHR. A head of steam for a domestic bill of rights began to build up in the 1980s. In the 1990s English courts made increasing use of the ECHR as a source of legal principles, and in 1998 the ECHR was domesticated by the enactment of the HRA, which finally came into operation in 2001. As we have seen throughout this book, the effect of the HRA is being felt in many areas of administrative law. In light of the earlier discussion of Parliamentary supremacy (see 19.2) three of aspects of the HRA regime deserve mention. First, although s. 3 of the HRA invites judges to take a robust, purposive approach to statutory interpretation, s. 4 empowers them only to make declarations of incompatibility, not to invalidate primary legislation. Secondly, the decision about what (if anything) to do in response to a declaration of incompatibility is left to the executive (s. 10), which can amend primary legislation by statutory instrument to remove the incompatibility. Thirdly, despite the domestication of the ECHR, the UK is still subject to the jurisdiction of the ECtHR. However, in the final analysis, the decision about how to respond to an adverse ruling by the ECtHR also rests with the executive.

Thus at the dawn of the twenty-first century, the institutional structure of the British constitution remains essentially Diceyan, despite huge changes. Parliament is still more-or-less sovereign; and Britain has nothing like a *Conseil D'Etat*, which has strong links with the executive branch of government.[22] Britain does have a bill of rights; but the chief

---

[22] J. Allison, *A Continental Distinction in the Common Law: A Historical and Comparative Perspective on English Public Law* (Oxford, 1996), pp. 146–9.

beneficiaries of the consequent shift of power have been the 'ordinary courts'. Britain also has an incipient system of public law courts (i.e. tribunals: see 18.5), but these are part of the judicial branch of government, not the executive. The principle that governors and governed should be equal before the law has certainly taken a battering. The substantive distinction between public law and private law is now well established. But even in this regard the situation may not be as anti-Diceyan as it appears at first sight. For instance, the Crown Proceedings Act 1947 abolished some long-standing legal immunities of government; and the *GCHQ* case[23] increased judicial control over the prerogative. There is no special English public law of contract and tort—nor is there likely to be. Distinguishing between governors and the governed is certainly objectionable if it results in institutions of governance enjoying unjustified legal protections and immunities, but not if it imposes additional obligations on those institutions in favour of its citizens. This is what the ECHR does—although ironically, some now argue that it should apply as much to citizens as to government (that it should have 'horizontal effect', in other words).

It is also important to observe that Dicey understood equality before the law institutionally—the government should be subject to the laws that bind its citizens. By contrast, the scope of public law is defined primarily in terms of the concept of 'public function'. This concept can be used to impose on non-governmental ('private') entities public-law obligations more onerous than those recognized by private law. The development of the substantive public/private distinction in English law can be interpreted as tending in precisely the opposite direction from that which Dicey feared, by imposing new obligations on private entities rather than relieving government of existing obligations. Not everyone would approve of the expansionist tendencies of modern English public law; but it is perhaps unlikely that Dicey would object.

19.1.6 CONSTITUTIONAL FRAGMENTATION

In modern times, the United Kingdom has been a unitary State. In essence, this means that there was only one legislature in the UK with power to make 'primary' legislation—the Westminster Parliament—and such legislation covered the whole nation. The constitutional principles we have considered in the previous sections developed against this background, and relate very largely to the national layer of government. The

---

[23] See 3.2.5.

fact that the UK was a unitary State did not mean that governmental power was concentrated entirely at the national level. Local government, in one form or another, has always played a significant role in public affairs, and in its modern form dates back to the nineteenth century. Administrative law is as much concerned with local as with national (or 'central') government. In strictly legal terms control of the activities of local authorities (that is, elected local councils) presents no constitutional issues different from those raised by the control of government activity generally.[24] On the other hand, the position of local authorities is somewhat special. Although they are subordinate in the government hierarchy to Parliament and to central government, they are nevertheless popularly elected and carry out functions of national importance such as providing housing, education and a wide variety of social-welfare services. If these activities were conducted by central government it could, within the limits of the law as laid down by Parliament and the courts, carry them out as it wished. Central government could integrate these activities into its management of the social and economic life of the nation as a whole. By contrast, local authorities are obviously concerned primarily to further the interests of their own areas. Many local authorities are under the control of political parties[25] which do not form the government at Westminster, and local authorities spend very considerable amounts of money (much of it raised by general taxation and provided by central government in the form of grants) partly, at least, according to their own priorities, rather than those of central government. For these reasons, local government presents central government with coordination problems, problems of integrating the activities of local government into the running of the nation as a whole.

---

[24] In one respect, members of local authorities used to be in a much worse position than other public functionaries in that they could be required to repay money spent or lost as a result of *ultra vires* conduct of the authority. This power to 'surcharge' was abolished in 2000 (Local Government Act 2000, s. 90).

[25] The influence and role of political parties in local government has increased greatly in the last thirty years. It was investigated by a government-appointed committee in the 1980s (the 'Widdicombe' Report on the Conduct of Local Government Business, Cmnd. 9797, 1986). On the legal significance of the politicization of local government see 7.3.2.1 n. 61, 8.3.5, 8.5.1, 12.1.2. It also provoked the provisions of the Local Government Act 2000 Part II (designed to strengthen the accountability of the local-government executive to the full council) and Part III (concerned with the conduct of members of local authorities). For discussion of the constitutional context of these provisions see I. Leigh, *Law, Politics and Local Democracy* (Oxford, 2000), ch. 7. For the view that Part II of the Act is motivated by 'efficiency' rather than 'democracy' see G. Ganz, *Understanding Public Law*, 3rd edn (London, 2001), pp. 82–3.

Tensions and conflicts between central and local government can and do arise, and in the 1980s and 1990s central government assumed much tighter legal, political, administrative, and financial control over local government than had previously been the case.[26] The general policy of the Conservative governments of that period was to emphasize the role of local authorities as service providers[27] rather than as democratic political institutions. Given that some 25 per cent of public expenditure is by local authorities, and that many of the services provided by them are basic social services, which should ideally be uniform throughout the country, a high degree of central control is inevitable. But the desire for, and the desirability of, local autonomy remain and argue against excessively tight central control. Local authorities are, after all, democratically elected, and political theorists in the past 150 years have put forward various arguments in favour of 'local democracy', emphasizing the educative and socializing value of participation in community decision-making.[28]

So far as administrative law is concerned, the most radical proposal for increasing local autonomy would be to loosen the fetters of judicial review and the doctrine of *ultra vires* and give local authorities more freedom in giving practical effect to the statutes under which they operate. Local authorities could be required to show that they were pursuing a defensible plan for local development in their area within the broad spirit of the empowering legislation, but not necessarily to show that they were complying with the letter of the statute.[29] In other words, whereas under the present law, local government has to cut its cloth to meet the demands of central government as expressed in empowering legislation, under this radical proposal central government would more often have to accommodate local government and leave people freer to do what they wanted in their local area. Even within the confines of the present law, if the courts were to adopt a presumption that statutes should, if possible, be interpreted so as to promote local autonomy, they could significantly enhance the independence of local government. In the end, however, radical change requires central government to relinquish more control of local affairs.

---

[26] M. Loughlin, 'Restructuring of Central-Local Government Relations' in J. Jowell and D. Oliver (eds), *The Changing Constitution*, 4th edn (Oxford, 2000), ch. 6.

[27] As a result of a programme called 'compulsory competitive tendering'—a form of contracting-out—local authorities became less involved in direct service-provision and more involved in arranging for services to be provided. The sale of many council houses greatly reduced the role of local authorities as providers of residential accommodation.

[28] D. Hill, *Democratic Theory and Local Government* (London, 1974).

[29] A concomitant of such an approach would be abolition of the fiduciary duty of local authorities (see 8.5.1).

Since 1997 the Labour government has embarked on a programme of reform designed to readjust the relationship between central and local government. The Local Government Act 2000 gives local authorities the power 'to do anything which they think is likely to' promote or improve the economic, social, or environmental well-being of their areas (s. 2(1)). However, this power is subject to 'any prohibition, restriction or limitation on their powers which is contained in any enactment (whenever passed or made)' (s. 3(1)). These provisions neither expressly nor impliedly loosen the fetters of the doctrine of *ultra vires*, and it remains to be seen how they will be interpreted and applied by the courts.[30] More importantly, local authorities continue to rely on central government for most of their income,[31] and they are subject to close and detailed financial regulation.[32] What seems certain is that however the relationship between central and local government develops in the years to come, it will be based more on law, and less on convention and agreement, than was the case in the mid-twentieth century.

Besides local authorities there are very many unelected bodies ('quangos') that operate at local level delivering services and implementing public policy. Many of these bodies have been established by central government, and their number has increased greatly since 1979 at the expense of the powers and functions of elected local authorities. As in the case of executive agencies, managerial and financial accountability and 'customer satisfaction' are seen as being the prime checks over the activities of such bodies, and external political controls are often weak. The activities of these bodies typically fall outside the scope of the doctrine of ministerial responsibility, and many fall outside the jurisdiction of the public-sector ombudsmen and the FOI regime. So far as legal accountability is concerned, a significant proportion of such bodies would, in theory at least, be subject to judicial review and human rights law.

Elected local authorities and quangos are not the only sites of constitutional authority outside Westminster and Whitehall. Diffusion and decentralization of political power increased significantly with UK membership of the EC. This added a supra-national element in the form of the legislative, executive, and judicial institutions of the EU. By virtue of the provisions of the European Communities Act 1972, conflicts between EC law and UK law (including Acts of Parliament) have to be resolved in

---

[30] Leigh, *Law, Politics and Local Democracy*, pp. 52–62.
[31] The Local Government Act 2003 gives authorities increased powers to borrow for capital projects.
[32] D. Oliver, *Constitutional Reform in the UK* (Oxford, 2003), pp. 300–3.

favour of EC law. Sub-national fragmentation was increased by devolution to Scotland, Wales, and Northern Ireland in 1998. Scottish devolution involves a division of legislative authority between the Scottish and Westminster Parliaments. The constitutional status of legislation of the Scottish Parliament is unclear. It is 'superior' to ordinary subordinate legislation such as is made by local authorities and Ministers of State. On the other hand, it does not count as 'primary legislation' for the purposes of the HRA. This means that if it is incompatible with Convention rights it is invalid. By contrast, although Acts of (the Westminster) Parliament can be declared incompatible with Convention rights, such incompatibility does not affect their validity. Moreover, the Westminster Parliament retains the power to pass legislation that applies to Scotland, even in areas in which the Scottish Parliament has legislative capacity. Scottish legislation is invalid to the extent of any inconsistency with Westminster legislation. The Privy Council has jurisdiction to entertain challenges to legislation of the Scottish Parliament on the ground that it is beyond power or inconsistent with Westminster legislation.

The Welsh Assembly has power only to make subordinate legislation. The effect of Welsh devolution is to create a national tier of local government in Wales. If devolved government were introduced in England, this is probably the form it would take. Both Welsh and Scottish devolution involve the creation of new executive branches of government that exercise many of the powers formerly exercised by the Secretaries of State for Wales and Scotland respectively.

The devolution statutes regulate many aspects of the operation of the devolved legislatures and executives. Devolution has added significantly to the role of law in constitutional arrangements. At the same time, agreements and concordats that are not meant to be legally enforceable also play a major role in regulating relations between the various layers of government. It remains to be seen how large a role courts will play in this new multi-layered constitution. Legalisation creates opportunities for judicialization. But, as illustrated by the recent history of relations between central government and local authorities in England, the extent to which such opportunities are exploited depends on the balance between cooperation and confrontation in dealings between the various governmental units. The greater the tensions, the more likely will recourse be had to the courts to resolve essentially political differences.

19.2 POLITICAL BACKGROUND

Constitutional and administrative law provide a framework for the exercise of political power, but only a framework. In any system, the exercise of high political power and its distribution between different governmental institutions tend to be regulated to a greater or lesser extent by agreements, conventions, understandings, and practices of no legal force. The most commonly advanced reason for this is that non-legal standards are more flexible than legal rules would be (although this argument is more compelling in respect of statutory than in respect of common law rules). It might also be argued that it is very difficult, and of little use, to attempt to prevent by law changes in the distribution of ultimate political power because, at the end of the day, the pattern of distribution of such power will operate satisfactorily only if it is acceptable to those competing for and wielding power, and to the nation generally. Conventions are rather like moral rules—when the people whose conduct they regulate no longer find them acceptable they are changed. Thus, for example, the convention that relations between central and local government should be regulated as much as possible by negotiation and agreement gave way, in the 1980s and 1990s, to an increasing use of legislation and courts to resolve often-acrimonious disputes between Whitehall and local authorities, especially those under the control of one of the opposition parties. It is important, therefore, to give some thought to the impact on constitutional theory and administrative law of the way the political system actually operates.

Two pillars of the British constitution are the principles of representation of, and responsibility to, the people.[33] Representation finds expression in the elected elements of government—the House of Commons, local authorities, the Welsh Assembly, and so on. Responsibility finds expression in scrutiny of the (elected and appointed) executive by elected representatives, and in the dependence of the (elected) executive on elected representatives for its continuation in power. However, both representation and responsibility are relatively weak principles. This is partly because much public power is exercised, and many public functions are performed, by entities that are neither representative nor responsible—the Monarch, the House of Lords, courts and tribunals, a host of national and local quangos, and so on. Another major cause of

---

[33] A.H. Birch, *Representative and Responsible Government* (London, 1964).

weakness is the party system. The main political function of elected representatives is to support the leadership and policies of their party, not to represent the people who voted for them, let alone the people who voted for a different candidate or did not vote at all. As a result of party discipline it is usually possible for the government to get legislation passed more-or-less unamended, and more-or-less to ignore criticism from select committees and the like. At all levels of government, although elected representatives play an essential formal role in law-making and in controlling the exercise of public power, they make a relatively small contribution to the development, formulation, and execution of public policy, whether that policy is implemented through law-making or in some other way (such as contract-making).

Rather than representation and responsibility, the main 'democratic' foundations of policy-making are participation and consultation. Policy is typically made outside representative forums in what political scientists call 'policy networks'—loose groupings of elected and unelected government officials, quangos, technical experts, and 'stakeholder' groups. Statute may impose on government an obligation to take advice and to consult stakeholders in the process of formulating policy. Large-scale public inquiries in the planning process (see 7.7.2) provide perhaps the clearest example of a formal, legalized system of public consultation and participation in the policy-making process. Another example is the obligation of local authorities under s. 4 of the Local Government Act 2000 to consult 'such persons as they consider appropriate' for the purposes of formulating a 'community strategy' for the promotion and improvement of the economic, social and environmental well-being of their areas. In the past twenty-five years, participation has also become a key concept in relation to the delivery of public services. Techniques such as contracting-out and the private finance initiative (see 12.2.1) have greatly increased the role of non-governmental entities in the performance of public functions, and have reduced the role of elected government in providing, as opposed to arranging for and regulating the provision of, public services.

From one point of view, the shift from representation and responsible government to participation and consultation is a very positive development because it gives those who want it a much larger role and stake in public affairs than can be had simply by voting for candidates put forward by one of the political parties or, indeed, by being an elected 'backbench' politician. From another perspective, however, the increasing role of the unelected and appointed in the formulation and implementation of public policy and the delivery of public services is deplorable. One cause for concern is the patronage dispensed by those who wield the power of appointment. How is this power to be regulated to ensure that public power is distributed in a way that promotes the interest of all and not just those of the patrons and the appointees?[34] Another concern is particularly pertinent to the role of 'stakeholder' interests in the policy-making process. Although the consultation process is to some extent regulated by statute and common law, it can certainly be argued that it is not sufficiently structured or controlled to ensure a diverse and varied input.[35] Rather, because of its informality and the extent to which it is controlled by the government, it offers much to those who have bargaining strength and 'loud voices', but little to the ordinary citizen or to groups unsympathetic or opposed to the government. Some interests are not sufficiently well organized to put their case forward; and anyway it is usually, in the end, up to the government to decide which groups will be consulted on any particular matter. Of course many stakeholder groups represent significant sections of the public, but nevertheless their function is to promote interests which are, by definition, sectional rather than broadly based in the community at large. This may not matter so long as the courses of conduct urged by these sectional interests are weighed properly against all other options. But it will matter if the influence of certain groups means that they can effectively discourage serious consideration of courses of action other than that which they propose.

Increasing participation of non-governmental agencies in the delivery of public services and the performance of public functions raise fundamental issues of accountability and control. To what extent should such bodies be treated as if they were part of government and subjected to public scrutiny? These issues have been discussed at various points in this book in the context, for instance, of the scope of judicial review and of the HRA, and of the use of contractual techniques as a regulatory instrument.

---

[34] See House of Commons Public Administration Select Committee, *Government by Appointment: Opening up the Patronage State*, Fourth Report, HC 165, 2002–3.
[35] P. Cane, 'The Constitutional and Legal Framework of Policy-Making' in C. Forsyth and I. Hare (eds), *The Golden Metwand and the Crooked Cord: Essays on Public Law in Honour of Sir William Wade* (Oxford, 1998).

19.3 LEGAL ACCOUNTABILITY IN CONSTITUTIONAL AND POLITICAL CONTEXT

In light of the discussion so far we can now consider the place of law and legal institutions generally, and of judicial review and courts in particular, in the constitutional and political landscape. We can begin by outlining four different functions that may be assigned to legal institutions (especially courts) in public decision-making processes.

19.3.1 PROTECTION OF STAKEHOLDER INTERESTS

Extra-Parliamentary and non-governmental interest groups play an important part in the policy-making process in Britain and, indeed, in all Western democracies. This fact has been used, especially in the United States, as a basis for suggesting that the primary role of the courts in reviewing the exercise of public power (especially rule-making) is the protection of significant sectional interests, particularly when the political system works in such a way as to deny them an effective voice in the legislative and governmental process. According to this view, the role of the courts is not primarily to ensure that public functionaries make the 'right' decisions, but to ensure that they make decisions in response to a set of diverse arguments and points of view. The role of judicial review is to ensure that all properly interested parties are given a chance to participate effectively in the public decision-making process. This approach implies that decisions made without some interested party being heard would be invalid.

Several points should be made about this approach. First, the prevalence of stakeholder consultation in the British system suggests that the political process is seen in part as a mechanism for reconciling competing and conflicting interests. Because political representation in England (at national as well as local level) is geographically based, whereas stakeholder groups often are not, such groups seek other methods of influencing government. Ways they do this include lobbying and briefing MPs, providing secretarial and research assistance to 'all party' committees of MPs, and 'sponsoring' MPs. Some form of proportional representation could facilitate greater stakeholder representation in Parliament, and has been adopted for elections to the Welsh Assembly and the Scottish Parliament. But the main method by which interest groups seek to influence government is direct communication with Ministers and civil servants. This practice is subject to very little publicity or outside control.

Interest groups are not accountable to the public for their lobbying activities, nor does the law have anything much to say about the internal structure of interest groups or their accountability to those whom they purport to represent. Furthermore, the government is not typically answerable, either at law or in Parliament, for the way it consults interest groups. The interest-protection approach to the function of courts deals with only one of these issues—that of ensuring that stakeholders are consulted. Whether the law in general, and the courts in particular, ought to be involved in regulating other aspects of the consultation process is a large question that cannot be considered in detail here. An argument could be made for treating interest groups as public and, therefore, publicly accountable, bodies performing public functions. Perhaps there should be legal rules dealing with the funding and internal organization of interest groups and regulating which groups are consulted by government and when. It is also important that there be clear published rules regulating the relationship between MPs and civil servants on the one side, and interest groups and the 'lobbying industry' on the other. This is one of the main issues dealt with in codes regulating the conduct of Members of Parliament.

Secondly, the interest protection view sees the law as primarily concerned with protecting the procedural right of groups to be consulted. It does not see the law as a suitable means of ensuring that sectional interests are protected by reviewing the substance of the decisions made after consultation. Such a function would be seen to involve undue judicial interference with public decision-making. In the British system it is generally thought that striking a balance between the competing interests of social groups is primarily a job for the political branches of government, not the courts. On the other hand, procedure and substance are not unrelated, and groups that use the law to assert procedural rights typically do so in order to increase their chance of securing a particular substantive result in the political process, if not in court.

A third point to note about the interest-protection view of judicial review is this: it might be argued that the cost and complexity of utilizing the judicial process would result in this approach providing wealthy and well-organized interest groups with yet another chance to influence government policy, rather than opening up the governmental process to a wider range of influences. From this perspective, the interest protection view might not be beneficial unless it were accompanied by other reforms, such as increased legal aid or rules that facilitated the bringing of class actions by relatively unorganized or disadvantaged groups.

Fourthly, it might be argued that the courts should not be used as a means of giving those who are disappointed with the political process a 'second bite at the cherry'. It would be better to reform the political process, making it responsive to a wider range of interests, than to involve the courts who might, by this involvement, risk jeopardizing their reputation for independence.

Fifthly, the common law, as it stands, interprets the right to participate in the administrative and political process predominantly in terms of the principles of natural justice which, as we have seen, are designed primarily to ensure individuals a hearing; they are not much use for promoting interest-group participation in public policy and decision making. Moreover, these rules do not apply to the legislative process, either Parliamentary or subordinate. The common law recognizes no general right of interested parties to be consulted before rules and decisions are made.

One feature of English judge-made administrative law which appears to embody a concern to enable interest groups to use the judicial process to control public decision-making are the rules of representative standing (see 4.2.2). Some interest groups, such as the Child Poverty Action Group, make regular use of the courts to challenge government action and to influence government policy. Groups which find it difficult to influence government directly because the government has no obligation, and chooses not, to consult them, are perhaps more likely to have recourse to the courts than are 'insider' groups favoured by the government of the day.

19.3.2 PROTECTING INDIVIDUALS

The idea that the courts should play a part in protecting group interests is, as we have noted, a view that reflects a 'pluralist' picture of the political process as, in part at least, a mechanism for reconciling and compromising conflicting interests. The classic picture of the British political process, on the other hand, sees politics more in terms of achieving collective goals and of furthering the public interest. Group interests are usually considered as subjective preferences of members of the group as to how society should run, whereas the public interest is seen as objective in some sense: it is not just an amalgam of or compromise between interests, but is something different from and superior to them.

This distinction between the public interest and private interests is implicit in the distinction between public law and private law, and it underlies the traditional idea of the role of judicial review (as well as of tribunals and other complaints mechanisms such as public-sector ombudsmen), namely to protect the rights of individuals against unlawful encroachment in the name of the public interest.[36] According to this view, the activities of government are being controlled in the name of law—the rights being protected are legal rights such as property rights. Many of these rights, for example the right to be treated fairly and in accordance with the rules of natural justice, are common-law rights 'invented' by the courts. The invention of legal rights by the courts is itself a political (as well as a legal) activity, just as the creation of legal rights by the legislature is a political activity. A legal right comes into existence when a political claim is given legal force by a law-making body.

Because the courts are primarily law-applying bodies, they must act in the name of legal rights. However, we should not allow the language of law to conceal the fact that some of these rights are created by the courts themselves, or to hide the fact that legal rights express and give legal effect to political claims. This can be seen clearly if we ask why we talk about the *rights* of individuals, but of the *interests* of groups. The reason is not that individuals do not have interests or that groups do not have rights. It is simply that in the British system, law tends to be used to protect the rights of individuals, whereas groups tend to use the political process to secure the enactment of laws or the adoption of policies that will protect the individual interests of their members or of others whose interests they seek to promote.

The 'protection of the individual' view of judicial review is, therefore, a view which asserts that political and governmental power ought to be exercised to further the public interest, but only so far as is consistent with those political claims of individuals which are embodied in individuals' legal rights or legally protected interests. It is, however, also the case that the power to protect individual rights against undue interference in the name of the public interest entails a power to decide that particular governmental action in the public interest does not constitute an undue encroachment on private rights. Ironically, the most common use of the notion of public interest in administrative law is as a device to resist claims by individuals that their rights have been improperly infringed. We have observed such use of the idea of the public interest in the principle that failure to give a person a hearing will not constitute a

---

[36] For an extreme version of this view of the role of judicial review see M.J. Detmold, *Courts and Administrators* (London, 1989). For a less extreme rights–based approach see T.R.S. Allan, *Law, Liberty and Justice* (Oxford, 1993). Views which emphasize the value of individuals usually have their political roots in some form of 'liberalism', or in some theory that attributes to human beings fundamental or natural rights by virtue of their humanity.

denial of natural justice if a hearing would do the person no good (see 7.3.2.2.1), or would unduly interfere with the efficient dispatch of government business (see 7.1); in the rule that alternative remedies must be exhausted before a judicial remedy can be sought (see 5.6.2), and in various other uses of remedial discretion (see 5.4); and in the unwillingness of the courts to allow tort actions against regulatory bodies (see 11.2.1).

The emphasis on individual rights in English public law was greatly increased by the enactment of the HRA. For instance, only victims can complain of acts incompatible with Convention rights. Groups purporting to represent victims apparently do not have standing under the HRA. It also finds expression in the idea that common law principles protecting fundamental individual rights may have a status and force greater than that of 'normal' judge-made rules and principles. This idea is one aspect of the glorification of the common law as the repository of basic and timeless social values and of courts as the guardians of such values.[37]

19.3.3 PROTECTING THE PUBLIC INTEREST

A third view of the function of judicial review occasionally surfaces in the cases. This might be called the 'public interest' view of administrative law.[38] According to this view, there are certain collective community interests and goals that (almost) everyone would accept because they are basic to our way of life. These interests may be 'shared'—the interest in clean air, for instance, or they may be 'aggregate' interests that each and every individual has—such as the interest in personal liberty. None of these public interests is absolute in the sense that we are prepared to pursue it no matter what the cost. For example, besides an interest in clean air we also have an interest in economic prosperity that may conflict with the interest in clean air; and as well as an interest in personal liberty we have an interest in protecting ourselves from criminal violence that may require restrictions on the liberty of the perpetrators of violence. It is the function of the political process, according to this view, to compromise

---

[37] T. Poole, 'Back to the Future? Unearthing the Theory of Common Law Constitutionalism (2003) 23 *OJLS* 435; J.A.G. Griffith, 'The Common Law and the Political Constitution' (2001) 117 *LQR* 42; Sir Stephen Sedley, 'The Common Law and the Political Constitution: A Reply' (2001) 117 *LQR* 68.

[38] C. Harlow, 'A Special Relationship? American Influences on Judicial Review in England' in I. Loveland (ed), *A Special Relationship? American Influences on Public Law in the UK* (Oxford, 1995), ch. 3.

and reconcile these conflicting community interests. The compromise position is then called 'the public interest'.

However, although we all have an interest in economic prosperity, for example, some have a greater interest in it than others. Manufacturers who pollute the air have less interest in clean air and more in economic growth than do others. Again, although we all have an interest in personal liberty, the police have a greater (professional) interest in depriving people of liberty than do others. There is a danger that in the process of reconciling conflicting public interests, undue weight may be given to one or the other of them because of the political influence of some sectional group which has a special concern with that interest. The public interest view of the judicial role would say that if a governmental body acts contrary to the public interest, any member of the public should be entitled to challenge that action in a court because action contrary to the public interest is illegal. In other words, this approach sees the courts as guardians of the public interest against undue encroachments in favour of sectional (or individual) interests. This view of the judicial role involves the courts in deciding whether governmental action is in the public interest. This is clearly a political function and it has the potential for leading the courts into areas of political dispute. But it does seem to underlie, for instance, liberalization of standing rules to allow 'public interest' actions (see 4.2.2).

19.3.4 ENFORCING THE CONSTITUTION

As we noted at the beginning of this chapter, most claims dealt with by courts, tribunals, ombudsmen, and so on have little significance beyond the facts of the particular complaint. However, part of the role of the judicial branch of government is to act as a sort of constitutional umpire, making sure that the various elements of the constitution are in equilibrium and that a satisfactory set of checks and balances remains in place. It is this constitutional umpiring role for which the judicial review jurisdiction of the Administrative Court is most suited and most important. The High Court occupies a 'higher' constitutional position than tribunals and ombudsmen, for instance. This high status brings with it the respect and power needed to handle disputes that have major structural or constitutional significance.

A good illustration of a court acting as a constitutional umpire is *M v. Home Office*, in which it was held that injunctions could be awarded against central government, and that Ministers could be held in contempt of court (see 5.2.5, 5.3.1). Another good example is the *Fire Brigades Union* case, in which it was held that the Home Secretary had acted illegally in attempting to use his prerogative powers to effect changes in the system of compensating victims of criminal injuries.[39] We might also cite *Chief Adjudication Officer v. Foster*, which held that a tribunal had power to decide whether subordinate legislation was *ultra vires* (see 6.6), and *R v. Parliamentary Commissioner for Standards, ex p. Al Fayed*, which held that the Commissioner is not amenable to judicial review (see 16.1, n. 6).

In the past thirty-five years the constitutional umpiring role of the courts (especially the superior courts) has been significantly enlarged by constitutional fragmentation (see 19.1.6). In a 'multi-layered' constitution some institution has to resolve disputes between the various layers about the division of public power between them. In the 1980s courts entertained major disputes between central and local government over the financial powers of local authorities. Courts may be called upon to decide the consistency of primary and subordinate legislation with EC law and with Convention rights; or the consistency of Acts of the Scottish Parliament with Acts of the Westminster Parliament. Statutory regulation of freedom of information and of political parties[40] provide other examples of legislation that gives courts power to decide disputes about matters of constitutional significance.

In the past forty years the 'administrative justice system' in England— of which judicial review and the courts form a part—has changed significantly. It is not fanciful to think that in the next decade or two it will change even more. A structure may emerge built on a general principle that individual citizens' complaints against public functionaries should be handled in the first instance by some form of internal review, with a right of appeal to an external body, such as a tribunal, and a further appeal on a point of law to a second-tier tribunal or a court. The role of the Administrative Court in such a system would be to provide external review in relation to decisions that did not fall within the jurisdiction of a tribunal, and to act as constitutional umpire dealing, for instance, with 'devolution issues', applications for declarations of incompatibility under the HRA, and so on.

19.3.5 LEGITIMIZING THE JUDICIAL ROLE

I am not suggesting that these four approaches to the constitutional role of courts and other legal institutions provide a framework for analysing

---

[39] *R v. Secretary of State for the Home Department, ex p. Fire Brigades Union* [1995] 2 AC 513; A. Tomkins, *Public Law* (Oxford, 2003), pp. 24–30.
[40] Political Parties, Elections and Referendums Act 2000.

the whole of administrative law. The point they bring out is that courts and other legal institutions are themselves political actors. The classification of courts and tribunals as public authorities under s. 6 of the HRA reflects the fundamental point that these institutions are just as much public functionaries as the various institutions they supervise and whose public decision-making they review. The focus of this book has been on the role of courts in holding other public functionaries accountable for the performance of public functions and the exercise of public power; and, in that way, providing them with a measure of legitimacy. But this leaves us with the issue of the accountability and legitimacy of the courts themselves and of other legal institutions that make up the public 'accountability industry'. *Quis custodies custodiet?* Who guards the guardians? This issue is most salient in relation to the superior courts because they sit at the top of the public accountability hierarchy. Most public power is, to some extent at least, subject to judicial scrutiny.

How is the political power of courts to be legitimized? First, we might say that a certain negative legitimacy is conferred on judicial decisions by· the possibility of legislative reversal. The only context in which the Westminster Parliament has no comeback against the courts is in relation to the enforcement of EC law. Even in relation to primary legislation declared incompatible with Convention rights, it is ultimately up to the government and Parliament to decide how to react subject, of course, to the obligations of the UK under the ECHR.

Secondly, while, from one point of view, the constitutionally protected independence of the senior judiciary from outside control or influence seems to make courts quite unsuited to perform political functions, from another point of view it could be argued that this very independence ideally equips courts to protect fundamental rights, interests, and constitutional structures. In this view, it is exactly because the judiciary is not popularly elected or politically accountable that it can constrain public functionaries from preferring their own interests or those of their supporters and promote enduring values that underpin a society's existence and identity. This argument lends legitimacy to the judicial role only to the extent that the rights, interests and structures protected, and the way they are protected in particular cases, command wide support in society as a whole. Courts jeopardize their legitimacy when they act in ways that generate significant controversy.

The demand that courts should be uncontroversial, however, creates a difficulty. Courts might avoid controversy by appealing to very abstract principles (such as 'individual freedom' or 'democracy') to which everyone would subscribe. But in practice they are asked to decide what such abstract principles require in concrete situations, and this is typically where controversy arises. People often disagree about the application of mutually agreed principles. They may also hold principles that compete with one another—openness and security, for instance—and may disagree about how the competition ought to be resolved. Courts, then, are faced with a dilemma: avoiding controversy may be desirable but extremely difficult. Perhaps the most we can expect of the judges is that they will attempt to be alert to the traditions and present values of society and to reactions provoked by their past decisions.

We should not, however, fall into the trap of thinking that because judicial decisions can be given some legitimacy by being rooted in widely accepted values, judges can make their decisions democratic by referring to the values of the community. Judicial review is not, and is not meant to be, a democratic institution. No matter how conscientious judges are in seeking to reflect community values, the difficulty of ascertaining what those values are and, in particular, the difficulty of ascertaining how they apply to the concrete situations with which the courts are confronted, makes it inevitable, to some extent, that the decisions which judges make will reflect their own views. And if we dislike the views of our judges then we should either appoint judges with views more to our liking or remove from the courts the powers which enable judges to give effect to their own views and allocate them to more 'democratic' institutions. To think that judges can resolve all the conflicts with which they are confronted by ascertaining fundamental community values is self-deception, because such shared community values as we have are neither detailed nor uncontested enough to solve all the questions that confront the courts.[41]

---

[41] P. Cane, 'Theory and Values in Public Law' in P. Craig and R. Rawlings (eds), *Law and Administration in Europe: Essays in Honour of Carol Harlow* (Oxford, 2003).

Functions and Effects of Administrative Law

20.1 TWO APPROACHES TO (THE FUNCTIONS OF) (ADMINISTRATIVE) LAW

There are (at least) two different, though related, ways of thinking about law in general and administrative law in particular. One involves analysing legal rules and principles in order to uncover the various values underlying them and to discover how those values interrelate. This might be called a 'normative approach'. The values underlying English administrative law include (but are certainly not limited to) representation, accountability, judicial deference, a public/private dichotomy, equality before the law, protection of the individual, transparency, and participation.[1] The normative approach seeks to understand administrative law as a system of rules and principles governing human behaviour and social interactions in accordance with such values. By contrast, we may approach law 'instrumentally'. The instrumental approach treats law and legal institutions as tools for influencing human behaviour and achieving desired social outcomes. Whereas the normative approach is primarily concerned with what the law says about how people should behave, the instrumental approach is primarily concerned with how and to what extent law and legal institutions influence and affect the way people actually behave. These two approaches are obviously not mutually exclusive or even antagonistic to one another. Both assume that law and legal institutions exist for a purpose—or, more accurately, for various purposes. Analysing legal rules and principles helps us to understand what those purposes are and is a useful basis for suggestions as to what they ought to be. Studying the actual operation and effects of law and legal institutions is a necessary part of determining whether and to what extent their purposes are achieved, and how they might be more fully achieved (whether by law or by some other means). As we will see in 20.2, the normative and

---

[1] See further P. Cane, 'Theory and Values in Public Law' in P. Craig and C. Harlow (eds), *Law and Administration in Europe* (Oxford, 2003).

instrumental approaches differ not over the issue of whether law is purposive, but rather over what its purposes or 'functions' are.

The idea that law is purposive naturally leads us to ask questions about how well it achieves its purposes, whatever we may consider them to be—in other words, about its 'impact'. In Britain, interest in the impact of administrative law in general, and judicial review in particular, can be traced back to the 1970s. In a path-breaking article, Carol Harlow discussed three techniques used by government to neutralize the impact of adverse judicial decisions: delaying tactics, making the same decision again but in accordance with the court's holding,[2] and legislating to nullify the effects of the court's judgment.[3] In an important essay published in 1987, Baldwin and McCrudden suggested that judicial review of decision-making by regulatory agencies has various adverse effects including discouragement of long-term planning and of the pursuit of radical policy options, increase in the use and influence of lawyers in administration, and the adoption of informal methods of working which are more immune to judicial review than more formal methods.[4] It is often argued, too, that judicial interference with the administrative process leads to the adoption of time-consuming 'defensive' administrative practices designed to minimize the risk that decisions will be successfully challenged rather than to improve the 'quality' of the decision.

Courts have shown themselves receptive to such arguments. For example, it seems that one reason for the development of the notion of procedural 'fairness' was to reduce the 'burden' which the rules of natural justice might impose on administrators (see 7.3.2.2.2); the prospect of administrative inconvenience may be taken into account in the exercise of remedial discretion (see 5.4); the risk of engendering undue caution and unhelpfulness in administrators has been used as a reason for not extending the doctrine of estoppel (see 8.3.1); and the danger of 'overkill' (i.e. of encouraging undue defensiveness on the part of decision-makers) has figured prominently in decisions denying the existence of a duty of care in the performance of regulatory functions (see 11.2.1.1). It has to be said, however, that typically such assertions about the potentially negative impacts of judicial decisions are based on intuition and anecdote

---

[2] Remember that judicial review does not usually involve the court substituting its decision for that of the original decision-maker, and that many of the grounds of judicial review leave open the possibility that the same decision may be made again when the original decision-maker reconsiders the case.

[3] C. Harlow, 'Administrative Reaction to Judicial Review' [1976] *PL* 116.

[4] R. Baldwin and C. McCrudden, *Regulation and Public Law* (London, 1987), pp. 60–1.

rather than hard evidence. In the 1970s and 1980s some work was done tracing the reaction of public decision-makers to individual major court decisions;[5] but it was not really until the 1990s that people started to study administrative law and judicial review systematically to discover how they actually work in practice and what their impact might be. There is now a small but growing body of relevant empirical research, mostly about judicial review (see 20.4). An initial difficulty in studying the impact of administrative law and judicial review is uncertainty about what is meant by 'impact'.[6] The basic point to note here is that because administrative law is purposive, a sound understanding of its impact will take account of its purposes (or 'functions'). So something has to be said about the functions of administrative law.

20.2 FUNCTIONS OF ADMINISTRATIVE LAW

It is important to stress at the outset that administrative law does not wear its functional heart on its doctrinal sleeve, as it were. Nor is it the case that by looking long and hard at the rules and principles of administrative law we could discover a definitive purpose or set of purposes of administrative law. Although any purpose attributed to law must be consistent with its rules and principles to be plausible, its purposes are to some extent in the eye of the beholder. People can and do disagree about what administrative law is for and what it should be doing.

The basic methodology adopted in this book has been to treat administrative law as a set of rules and principles about how public functions should be performed—the normative approach, in other words. At the highest level of abstraction, the function of administrative law implicit in this methodology is to embody and express a set of values about how public functionaries should behave. At a somewhat lower level of abstraction, the purpose of administrative law can be identified in terms of the grounds of judicial review. These grounds can be summarized in three

---

[5] e.g. T. Prosser, 'Politics and Judicial Review: The Atkinson Case and its Aftermath' [1979] *PL* 59; *Test Cases for the Poor* (London, 1983) ch. 5; L. Bridges, C. Game, O. Lomas, J. McBride, and S. Ranson, *Legality and Local Politics* (Aldershot, 1987); M. Loughlin and P.M. Quinn, 'Prisons, Rules and Courts: A Study in Administrative Law' (1993) 56 *MLR* 497.

[6] There are also issues about what is meant by 'judicial review': P. Cane, 'Understanding Judicial Review and Its Impact' in M. Hertogh and S. Halliday (eds), *Judicial Review and Bureaucratic Impact: International and Interdisciplinary Dimensions* (Cambridge, 2004). For present purposes, these can be ignored because the focus here is on judicial review as explained and analysed in this book.

principles: that fair procedures should be followed in the performance of public functions; that public functionaries should observe legal limits on their powers; and that they should respect the rights of individuals. The concept of fair procedure is encapsulated in the two principles of natural justice—the rule against bias and the fair hearing rule. The idea of 'legal limits' addresses substantive concerns: that public functionaries should act consistently with relevant laws, that they should resolve relevant issues of fact within tolerable margins of error, and that they should exercise their powers 'rationally' or 'proportionately' and for the purposes for which those powers were conferred. Respect for individual rights requires, for instance, that public functionaries should not disappoint legitimate expectations, and that they should act compatibly with fundamental human rights.

On this basis, we might say that the purpose of judicial review is to provide a mechanism for holding public functionaries accountable for having failed to comply with these three principles in their interactions with citizens and with other public functionaries. This is certainly the purpose implicit in accounts of judicial review that treat it primarily as a dispute-settling technique. On the other hand, we might want to say that judicial review (and other public accountability institutions such as tribunals and public-sector ombudsmen) are not only—or perhaps even primarily—concerned with correcting or repairing past departures from legal requirements, but also with generating standards for public functionaries to comply with in performing their public functions. We might then go one step further and say that as well as generating standards for the performance of public functions and holding public functionaries accountable for past failures to comply with them, it is also a function of accountability institutions such as these to secure future compliance with such standards by public functionaries generally.

To summarize, taking a normative approach to administrative law, we may identify three functions of judicial review: establishing standards for the performance of public functions, holding public functionaries accountable for particular failures to comply with such standards, and promoting general compliance with those standards. Each of these functions relates quite directly to the normative approach of treating administrative law as a set of rules and principles about human behaviour and social interactions.

An instrumental approach, by contrast, would treat administrative law and judicial review as means to some social end defined in terms other than the rules and principles of administrative law themselves. Thus we might say that the function of administrative law and judicial review is to promote 'good administration' understood in some sense other or wider than that embodied in the grounds of judicial review themselves.[7] A wider concept of good administration might, for instance, include values such as effectiveness and efficiency in implementing public programmes and delivering public services. The grounds of judicial review do not promote these values as such, and may, indeed, conflict with them. For instance, observing the requirements of procedural fairness and respect for human rights may reduce the ability of public functionaries to achieve their policy objectives quickly, cheaply, and comprehensively. This is not to say that the law gives no weight to effectiveness and efficiency. For example, the short time-limit on claims for judicial review is designed to prevent the performance of public functions being unduly delayed; public interest immunity from disclosure of documents and the many exemptions under the FOI regime are designed in part to promote effectiveness in public administration; the concept of procedural 'fairness' was developed partly in order to enable the rules of natural justice to be adapted to the needs of administrative efficiency; and a court may refuse a judicial review remedy on grounds of administrative efficiency even if the claimant has a good case on the merits. But effectiveness and efficiency are constraints on the promotion of the values underlying the grounds of judicial review rather than a positive aspect of the concept of good administration implicit in them.

Whereas under the normative approach the functions of judicial review are understood directly in terms of the substantive and procedural law of judicial review, under the instrumental approach, the function of judicial review is to make a contribution to a goal defined in broader terms. So, for instance, although the grounds of judicial review may capture part of what is meant by 'good administration', they do not exhaust that concept understood instrumentally. Similarly, although the mechanism of judicial review may make a contribution to promoting good administration, so may other institutions, such as Parliament, auditors, tribunals and public-sector ombudsman; and although adjudication of disputes between citizens and public functionaries may make such a contribution, so may other practices, such as investigation, auditing, strong management, and high-quality training of public functionaries.

---

[7] e.g. D. Woodhouse, *In Pursuit of Good Administration: Ministers, Civil Servants and Judges* (Oxford, 1997).

In the US administrative law literature, liberalism and republicanism provide competing interpretations of the point of administrative law.[8] For liberals, the prime goal of judicial review is the protection of individual rights and interests, whereas for republicans it is the promotion of rational public deliberation. Richard Stewart famously argued that the function of administrative law is to facilitate the participation of interest groups in administrative decision-making.[9] Perhaps the most influential—and certainly the most highly developed—instrumental theory of law is economic. Economic analysis of law emerged in the 1960s, and tort law was an early focus of interest. The economic theory of tort law rests on the idea that its function is to provide people with incentives to take cost-justified precautions against causing harm to others. Precautions are justified if the cost of taking them is less than it would cost to compensate for the harm they prevent. Underlying the economic theory is the idea that people decide how to behave by weighing the costs and benefits of various available courses of action. A 'rational' person (so the theory says) will take precautions to prevent harm if, but only if, the cost of doing so is less than the cost of compensating for the harm they prevent. According to the economic theory of law, the essence of rationality is self-interest. This idea, that people are motivated by self-interest, underpins the version of economic analysis applicable to public law. It goes by the name of 'public choice theory'. The normative foundation of public choice theory is that although it is acceptable and desirable for people to act out of self-interest in their private lives, it is neither acceptable nor desirable for public functionaries to act out of self-interest in performing their public functions. Public functions are functions that should be performed in the public interest, and not to further the interests of the functionary or of some particular individual or group.

From this point of view, the purpose of public law is to prevent self-seeking or partisan decision-making by public functionaries. An attempt to apply this idea to administrative law is built on the economics of principal and agent relationships—the 'agency-cost' approach.[10] According to this approach,

judicial review is designed for one purpose: to reduce to an optimal level the agency costs that arise when public officials are appointed as agents to carry out

---

[8] Mashaw, *Greed, Chaos and Governance: Using Public Choice to Improve Public Law* (New Haven, 1997), ch. 5, esp. pp. 111–18.

[9] R.B.Stewart, 'The Reformation of American Administrative Law' (1975) 88 *Harvard LR* 1699.

[10] W. Bishop, 'A Theory of Administrative Law' (1990) 19 *J Leg Stud* 489.

tasks for the benefit of their principals, where the principals are, in various contexts, the people, the legislature, or the ministry.[11]

Agency costs arise when public functionaries exercise discretion in their own interests, or in the interests of some individual or group, rather than in the interests of their political principals. Under this approach, courts are 'monitors of agency costs in government';[12] and their role is to reduce agency costs to an optimal level—i.e. to the point where any further reduction would produce no benefit to the public.

In terms of the three principles of judicial review identified above, it is easy to see how the agency-cost theory explains the principle that public functionaries should respect legal limits on their powers. Legal limits are imposed from above to regulate the performance of public functions; and so exceeding those limits represents a 'cost' to the 'principals' who imposed them. So far as procedural requirements are concerned, the rule against bias can obviously be interpreted as designed to reduce agency costs because a biased decision-maker is, by definition, one who gives illegitimate weight to some interest of their own or of a third party. The fair-hearing rule can be understood as a sort of adjunct to the rule against bias: it is only by hearing what a person has to say that their interests can be properly assessed and taken into account. The agency-cost approach does not accommodate the norm of respecting individual rights. Indeed, the agency-cost explanation of administrative law appears to be inconsistent with this norm because success in judicial review does not normally guarantee the complainant a positive outcome, but only provides another opportunity to obtain a favourable decision.[13] This gap between the agency-cost theory of administrative law and the law itself illustrates an important difference between the normative and instrumental approaches to the functions of judicial review. Under the normative approach, the functions of administrative law are read directly out of the law itself. As a result, there can be no 'explanatory gap' between the law and its functions. By contrast, under the instrumental approach, the functions attributed to administrative law are in some sense 'external' to and independent of the law. As a result, they may not succeed in explaining all the features of the existing law.

A puzzle about the agency-cost approach is why courts should be the monitors of agency costs. Because most public functionaries operate under statute, the immediate principal of a public functionary is typically the

---

[11] Ibid. 490–1.   [12] Ibid. 492.   [13] Ibid. 505–6.

legislature. Why should the legislature delegate the monitoring task to others who might be tempted to act in their own interests rather than in that of their principal?[14] The standard public-choice answer seems to be that 'judicial independence' minimizes the risk that judges will not act in the public interest.[15] By contrast, it has been argued that courts are more prone to be influenced by special interests than are the democratic branches of government.[16] Either way, the agency-cost approach throws interesting light on the relationship between legal and political accountability.

Both the normative and the instrumental approaches to the functions of administrative law view it primarily in terms of the public functionaries whose behaviour the norms of administrative law regulate. By contrast, we could adopt the perspective of the 'users' of the administrative law system—individuals and groups who make judicial review claims, complaints to ombudsmen, and so on. From their perspective, the functions of administrative law might include reversing an adverse decision of a public functionary, drawing attention to public misconduct, generating publicity for a cause or group, getting an issue on to the political agenda,[17] and so on. This approach focuses more on judicial review as a political or legal resource than as a tool for regulating the performance of public functions. We could also approach judicial review from the perspective of society as a whole and ask whether, for instance, one of its functions is to legitimize the exercise of public power by providing reassurance that public lawlessness can be uncovered and controlled.

20.3 STUDYING THE IMPACT OF ADMINISTRATIVE LAW

In principle, it might be possible to study the 'impact' of administrative law without making any assumptions about its function(s). Instead of

---

[14] The current debate amongst UK scholars about the constitutional basis of judicial review (see 19.1.2, n. 10 and text) can be understood as addressing this issue.

[15] Bishop, 'A Theory of Administrative Law', 491–2; R.D. Cooter, *The Strategic Constitution* (Princeton, 2000), pp. 195–8.

[16] F.B. Cross, 'The Judiciary and Public Choice' (1999) 50 *Hastings LJ* 355. See also E.R. Elhauge, 'Does Interest Group Theory Justify More Intrusive Judicial Review?' (1991) 101 *Yale LJ* 31.

[17] The classic study of this use of judicial review is T. Prosser, *Test Cases for the Poor* (London, 1983). See also C. Harlow and R. Rawlings, *Pressure Through Law* (London, 1992). For some Israeli research about the relative success of individuals and groups challenging public decisions see Y. Dotan and M. Hofnung, 'Interest Groups in the Israeli High Court of Justice: Measuring Success in Litigation and Out-of-Court Settlements' (2001) 23 *Law and Policy* 1.

asking how good administrative law is at achieving particular purposes, we might simply ask what (if any) impact it has on people's behaviour. In fact, most of the empirical literature about judicial review contains little or no explicit discussion of its functions. On the whole, researchers appear to be looking for effects of administrative law and judicial review rather than attempting to establish that, or how well or badly, they actually perform any specified function. To the extent that functions are acknowledged, they tend to be framed in broad terms such as promoting 'good decision-making',[18] 'bureaucratic justice',[19] and 'openness and participation in public decision making',[20] with little or no discussion of what these phrases mean. Indeed, it has been suggested that it is only when we understand the impact(s) of judicial review (what it does) that we can meaningfully engage in debate about its functions (what it is meant to do or should be doing).[21]

On the other hand, we might think that by choosing (even if subconsciously) to study particular impacts and not others, researchers (whether explicitly or implicitly) ascribe particular functions to judicial review and seek to discover how good it is at performing those functions. For instance, research so far has tended to focus on the impact of enforcement of administrative law through judicial review claims rather than on the impact of administrative law as such;[22] on cases in which the judicial review claimant has been successful; and on the impact of judicial review claims on public functionaries as opposed to claimants. Little systematic attention has so far been given to questions such as how much public functionaries know about administrative law and judicial review, and how this knowledge affects the way they perform their functions; why the majority of judicial review claims are settled or withdrawn before hearing; why people make (or do not make) judicial review claims; and so on.[23] Part of the explanation for this may be that researching the latter

---

[18] e.g. M. Sunkin and K. Pick, 'The Changing Impact of Judicial Review: The Independent Review Service of the Social Fund' [2001] *PL* 736, 745; G. Richardson and M. Sunkin, 'Judicial Review: Questions of Impact' [1996] *PL* 79, 100–1.

[19] S. Halliday, 'The Influence of Judicial Review on Bureaucratic Decision-Making' [2000] *PL* 110, 111–12; see also 121–2: 'just government'.

[20] Richardson and Sunkin, op cit. n. 18 above, 101.

[21] Ibid., n. 18 above, 80–1.

[22] This tends to put non-compliance rather than compliance with the law at the centre of attention.

[23] Considerably more research on such questions has been done in relation to personal injury tort law, for instance. See generally D. Dewees, D. Duff, and M. Trebilcock, *Exploring the Domain of Accident Law: Taking the Facts Seriously* (New York, 1996); H. Genn, *Paths to Justice: What People Do and Think about Going to Law* (Oxford, 1999).

group of issues would be much more difficult than investigating the former. Nevertheless, it is worth noting that because various functions can be ascribed to judicial review, and because it can be used for various purposes, there is no single sense in which we can speak of the 'impact' of judicial review. Moreover, any particular instance of judicial review may serve different functions for different interested parties, and more than one function for any one party. Just as there is no single perspective on the function of judicial review, so there can be no single perspective on its impact.

Besides complexity related to the various functions of judicial review, difficulty in studying its impact arises from two other sources. First, it is one thing to identify patterns or changes in the behaviour of public functionaries, but quite another to establish that they are causally related to judicial review. In a case where an agency reconsiders and changes an individual decision following a successful judicial review application by a person directly affected by the decision, the causal link may be easily enough established. But where the impact is a change in more general modes of working, the contribution of judicial review may be much harder to trace. It is a commonplace finding of research in this area that administrative decision-making is a product of various and diverse pressures and influences of which the law in general, and judicial review in particular, is only one. Hardest of all may be to trace the general impact of judicial review as an accountability institution as opposed to the impact of one or more individual judicial decisions.[24]

Secondly, even if it is established that a particular change in the behaviour of public functionaries is attributable to judicial review, there may be disagreement about whether the change provides an example of judicial review performing one of its (intended) functions or is, on the contrary, an unintended and undesirable side-effect. A good example is found in ongoing debates about the imposition of procedural requirements (such as the rules of natural justice) on public functionaries. It is widely accepted that regulating procedure in order to improve the quality of public decision-making is an appropriate function for judicial review,

---

[24] The research methodology that identifies a court decision on the one side and a decision-making practice on the other and seeks to link them causally is sometimes called 'positivist'. 'Interpretivism' is an alternative approach. The interpretivist's focus of study is on the decision-making process, and the aim is to identify the role played by law in that process. This is the methodology adopted by Halliday in the book discussed in 20.4. For more discussion of these two methodologies see M. Sunkin, 'Conceptual Issues in Researching the Impact of Judicial Review on Government Bureaucracies' in Hertogh and Halliday (eds), *Judicial Review and Bureaucratic Impact*.

but also that procedural requirements can be counter-productive if they reduce the efficiency of the decision-making process too much—by causing delays, for instance. There is less agreement about the optimum balance between procedural 'fairness' and efficiency. More importantly, it is unlikely that such disagreement could be resolved by empirical evidence about the impact of judicially imposed procedural requirements on agency behaviour because the concepts of quality and efficiency, and views about the optimum balance between them, are ultimately matters of value judgment rather than empirical evidence.

Another example is provided by Rosemary O'Leary's study of the impact of judicial review on the US Environmental Protection Agency,[25] which neatly illustrates the adage that one person's meat is another's poison. She distinguishes between 'positive' and 'negative' effects of judicial review. Amongst those she identifies as negative are 'increased power of legal staff' and 'decreased power and authority of scientists'. More pointedly, several of the effects she identifies appear in very similar form on both sides of the ledger. For instance, she cites reduction in the power of the Office of Management and Budget (a presidential auditing body) as a negative effect, and 'lifting of . . . prolonged OMB review' as a positive effect.[26] Redistribution of resources within the agency appears as a negative effect from the point of view of the losers, and as a positive effect from the point of view of the winners.

Uncertainty and disagreement about whether particular consequences are good or bad would not matter if our only interest in studying impact were descriptive. But because law is a purposive social institution, underlying many empirical studies of law and legal institutions is an evaluative or teleological agenda aimed at justifying and improving legal systems and practices. In other words, researchers are not merely interested in describing the impact of judicial review but also in assessing whether, in terms of its impact, judicial review is a good or a bad thing. The possibility that judicial review might be intended to serve various purposes at the same time, and that it might have negative effects, raises the possibility (for instance) that it might serve one of its intended purposes better than it serves the other(s), or that the costs of its negative effects may outweigh the benefits of its positive effects. Both possibilities complicate very considerably arguments about whether—judged by its consequences—

---

[25] R. O'Leary, 'The Impact of Federal Court Decisions on the Policies and Administration of the US Environmental Protection Agency' (1989) 41 *Admin LR* 549.

[26] Op cit. n. 25 above, 567.

judicial review is, on balance, desirable or not. Obviously, too, difficulty in tracing casual connections between particular effects and judicial review is highly relevant to assessing its value and desirability.

20.4 THE RESEARCH

As was noted in 20.1, early interest in the impact of administrative law and judicial review tended to focus on the reaction of public decision-makers to individual decisions or groups of decisions. Some of these studies concerned the impact of judicial decisions on policy-making while others were concerned with their impact on front-line (or 'street-level') service-delivery.[27] Interest in the actual and potential impact of judicial review on policy-making is part of a long tradition, especially in the US and particularly amongst political scientists, of study of the role of courts—relative to other institutions—in bringing about social change.[28] There is no doubt that judicial decisions can sometimes precipitate changes in policy, especially if they attract a lot of publicity or deal with issues of major public importance.[29] A limitation of research of this type is that it may be difficult to generalise from reactions to individual court decisions or groups of decisions to conclusions about the impact of judicial review as an institution. This is not, however, a problem unique to research of this sort. Empirical research about law and legal institutions is difficult, time-consuming, and expensive. Its focus is often necessarily quite narrow, and it may raise more questions than it answers. Even so, it is often tempting to extrapolate from what the research tells us to situations with which it does not deal or to conclusions that it does not support, directly at least. Given that for the foreseeable future, our knowledge about the impact of judicial review is likely to be patchy and incomplete, this is not necessarily a bad thing provided we recognize that once we go beyond the evidence, our judgments about the impact of judicial review are likely to be based on our views about the proper role of courts in controlling public functionaries. For example, if there is evidence that judicial review has had a good (or a bad) impact in particular

---

[27] For discussion of this distinction see L. Sossin, 'The Politics of Soft Law: How Judicial Decisions Influence Bureaucratic Discretion in Canada' in Halliday and Hertogh (eds), *Judicial Review and Bureaucratic Impact*.

[28] English studies in this tradition include Prosser, *Test Cases for the Poor* and C. Harlow and R. Rawlings, *Pressure Through Law*.

[29] A recent example is provided by the case of *R v. Lord Chancellor, ex p. Witham* [1998] QB 575 which elicited a positive response from the Lord Chancellor: HC Debs Vol. 292, Written Answers col. 366 (17 March 1997).

circumstances, and we extrapolate from this that judicial review is likely to have a similarly good (or bad) impact in other more-or-less similar circumstances, this conclusion is likely to be based partly on a value judgement that judicial review is generally a good (or a bad) thing; and this value judgement is likely to be based on approval (or disapproval) of the values promoted by judicial review rather than on its effects on behaviour.

A second body of research about judicial review, which is indirectly relevant to the issue of its impact, has studied patterns of judicial review claims.[30] Every judicial review claim is of direct relevance to the claimant and the defendant, and if the court's decision turns on the particular facts of the case, it may have no wider relevance. But at least some judicial review decisions have indirect relevance for public functionaries other than the defendant. The nature and extent of this indirect impact of a judicial review claim may depend on the subject matter of the claim. For example, a claim arising out of a type of decision that is made thousands of times a year is likely to have more indirect impact than one arising out of a unique or rare type of interaction between a citizen and a public functionary. Moreover, both the direct and the indirect impacts of judicial review as an institution will depend to some extent on the sorts of public functions and the types of issue that may become the subject of judicial review claims. For instance, judicial review is likely to have little or no impact on the performance of public functions that are non-justiciable. Or consider the example of decisions by local authorities about the housing of homeless persons. In the 1980s and 1990s challenges to such decisions constituted a very significant proportion of all judicial review claims. Now, however, judicial review in the Administrative Court has been replaced by an appeal on a point of law to a county court. As a result, the focus of any impact research in relation to homelessness decision-making will have to concern itself with appeals to the county court, not judicial review in the High Court.

In this respect, it is worth noting that to date, empirical research about the impact of administrative law generally (and not just in the homelessness area) has focused on judicial review and ignored appeals. But it cannot be assumed that the impact of appeals against decisions of public functionaries will be the same as the impact of judicial review. One important difference between the two, in theory at least, is that on appeal, but not on judicial review, the court can substitute its own decision for

---

[30] L. Bridges, G. Meszaros, and M. Sunkin, *Judicial Review in Perspective*, 2nd edn (London, 1995).

that of the original decision-maker. It is widely assumed that this puts the claimant for judicial review at a distinct disadvantage relative to the appellant because it leaves open the possibility that when the matter goes back, the original decision-maker will (have a strong incentive to) find a way of making the same decision again, consistently with the decision of the reviewing court, and that success in a judicial review claim is often (if not typically) pyrrhic. Recent Australian research casts some doubt on this assumption.[31] The researchers found that in about 60 per cent of cases in which the Federal Court of Australia set aside an agency's decision, the judicial review claimant ultimately obtained a favourable outcome. US research found that judicial 'remand' of decisions back to administrative agencies resulted in 'major changes' in the claimant's favour in 40 per cent of cases.[32] The proportion of cases in the two studies in which the claimant was successful at the judicial review stage was roughly the same. There is no way of knowing how the difference in ultimate success rates can be explained; and despite the difference, both sets of researchers think that the results of their respective studies seriously undermine the traditional assumption. However, whether a figure of 60 per cent ultimate 'success'—let alone 40 per cent—should be so assessed is itself a matter of opinion on which the empirical evidence casts little light. Furthermore, because some grounds of judicial review leave the original decision-maker with more discretion than others in reconsidering the initial decision, we would need to know much more about the cases in the research sample in order properly to assess the significance of the results.

Research of this type, which is concerned with the impact of judicial review as a dispute-resolution or grievance-handling mechanism can be contrasted with research concerned with the impact of judicial review as a mechanism for regulating decision-making procedures, methods and routines. Research of the latter type could be conducted either from a normative or an instrumental perspective. For example, there have been various empirical studies, from an instrumental perspective, of the enforcement of regulatory regimes in areas such as water pollution, health and safety at work, consumer protection, and so on. One of the issues addressed in such studies concerns the contribution law and legal processes can make

---

[31] R. Creyke and J. McMillan, 'The Operation Judicial Review in Australia' in Halliday and Hertogh (eds), *Judicial Review and Bureaucratic Impact*.
[32] P.H. Schuck and E.D. Elliott, 'To the Chevron Station: An Empirical Study of American Administrative Law' [1990] *Duke LJ* 984, 1059–60.

to the achievement of regulatory goals.[33] A few instrumentalist studies have focused more directly on the effects of judicial review on the operation of regulatory regimes.[34] By contrast, 'normativist' impact studies investigate the impact of judicial review in securing compliance with administrative law as embodied in the grounds of judicial review. Recall that from a normative perspective, judicial review can be said to have three functions: setting standards for the performance of public functions; holding public functionaries accountable for failure to comply with such standards; and promoting compliance with such standards. The first of these functions raises no interesting empirical questions because judicial review clearly does generate standards for the performance of public functions. The important questions about this function are normative—are the standards embodied in the grounds of judicial review good or desirable ones. Could they be normatively improved and if so, how?

The second 'normative' function does raise important empirical questions such as what proportion of breaches of administrative law standards result in a successful claim for judicial review? In the area of personal injury tort law, for instance, empirical research has shown that only a relatively small proportion of medical mishaps that could, in theory, give rise to a successful claim for negligence, are ever the subject of legal action. Although we know approximately how many judicial review claims are made and what they are about, no empirical research has been done that gives us any idea about the incidence of 'lawless' behaviour by public functionaries that could, in theory, give rise to a successful claim for judicial review.

It is the third 'normative' function of judicial review that has so far been the subject of empirical research from a normativist perspective. Studies in this category have looked at the activities of (for instance) housing authorities,[35] mental health tribunals[36] and 'internal' social

---

[33] K. Hawkins, *Law as Last Resort: Prosecution Decision-Making in a Regulatory Agency* (Oxford, 2002).

[34] C. Scott, 'The Juridification of Regulatory Relations in the UK Utilities Sectors' in J. Black, P. Muchlinski, and P. Walker (eds), *Commercial Regulation and Judicial Review* (Oxford, 1998).

[35] e.g I. Loveland, 'Housing Benefit: Administrative Law and Administrative Practice' (1988) 66 *Public Administration* 57; *Housing Homeless Persons: Administrative Law and the Administrative Process* (Oxford, 1995); S. Halliday, 'The Influence of Judicial Review on Bureaucratic Decision-Making' [2000] *PL* 110.

[36] G. Richardson and D. Machin, 'Judicial Review and Tribunal Decision-Making: A Study of the Mental Health Review Tribunal' [2000] *PL* 494.

security review bodies.[37] Some studies are concerned with the decision-making behaviour of public functionaries, whereas others have focused on their attitudes towards administrative law and judicial review.[38] A recurring theme of this literature is that administrative law is only one of a number of influences on the behaviour of public functionaries.[39] Other normative and institutional factors may operate independently of, and possibly in conflict with, the rules and principles of administrative law.

Researchers often discover that public functionaries routinely disobey the law either as a result of ignorance of the law's requirements or under the pressure of stronger competing influences. This phenomenon is obviously deeply problematic if the goal of judicial review is defined as securing compliance with administrative law norms. It is less problematic from an instrumental perspective in which law is only one of the possible instruments for achieving some broader goal.

Although studies such as these typically rest on an assumption that the function of judicial review is to secure compliance with administrative law norms as embodied in the grounds of judicial review, they necessarily deal with the application of these norms to specific public functions and, hence, with judicial decisions about specific public functions (such as homelessness decision-making by local authorities, or mental health decision-making by tribunals). We have already noted that the specificity of empirical impact research generates a 'gap' between the conclusions of individual research projects and conclusions about the impact of judicial review as an institution, and of administrative law, both of which operate (in theory at least) across a very broad field of public functions. In an important recent book Simon Halliday has suggested that the way to deal

---

[37] M. Sunkin and K. Pick, 'The Changing Impact of Judicial Review: The Independent Review Service of the Social Fund' [2001] *PL* 736. See also T. Buck, 'Judicial Review and the Discretionary Social Fund' in T. Buck (ed.), *Judicial Review and Social Welfare* (London, 1998).

[38] e.g. M. Sunkin and A.P. Le Sueur, 'Can Government Control Judicial Review?' (1991) 44 *Current Legal Problems* 161; Sunkin and Pick op cit. n. 37 above; R. Creyke and J. McMillan, 'Executive Perceptions of Administrative Law—An Empirical Study' (2002) 9 *Australian J of Admin L* 163. There seems little doubt that the past twenty-five years, both in the UK and in Australia, have witnessed increasing public concern with 'legality' in public administration. See, e.g., T. Daintith and A. Page, *The Executive in the Constitution: Structure, Autonomy and Internal Control* (Oxford, 1999), ch. 10; E. Willheim, 'Recollections of an Attorney-General's Department Lawyer' (2001), 8 *Australian J of Admin Law* 151. The precise contribution of administrative law and judicial review to this development is difficult to ascertain. On the whole, researchers have not investigated the impact of judicial review on the behaviour of the beneficiaries of the norms of administrative law as opposed to those subject to them.

[39] See esp. Loveland, *Housing Homeless Persons*, ch. 10.

with this gap is to use specific empirical impact studies to generate hypotheses about the broader impact of judicial review and administrative law.[40] Unlike assumptions based merely on intuition or anecdote, such hypotheses would have the advantage of being grounded in systematic empirical research. As such, they could provide a sound basis for further empirical research designed to test and either confirm or deny their validity. Given the difficulty of investigating the impact, of a human institution as complex as administrative law, on a range of activities as diverse as the tasks of governance in the twenty-first century, this incremental approach offers a promising framework for making real progress in understanding the role of law and the courts in controlling the performance of public functions.

According to Halliday, his research into local authority homelessness decision-making supports the following hypotheses about the impact of judicial review on the performance of public functions:

1 The more public functionaries know about administrative law, the greater its impact will be. This hypothesis raises the issue (about which we know very little) of how knowledge of administrative law is communicated to and disseminated amongst public functionaries and agencies.

2 The more conscientious public functionaries are about applying their legal knowledge to the performance of their functions, the greater will be the law's impact. To be legally conscientious is to be motivated to obey the law. Competing demands on decision-makers—such as the need to keep within a budget—may weaken this motivation if those demands conflict with the requirements of the law.

3 The greater the 'legal competence' of public functionaries, the greater will be the law's impact. 'Legal competence' is a complex concept. Essentially it refers to the ability to apply legal knowledge in such a way as to produce legally compliant outcomes. This may not merely involve mechanical application of legal rules to the facts of individual cases. Much public decision-making requires the exercise of discretion, and applying the rules and principles of administrative law properly typically involves a degree of interpretation of the law and individual judgment about its application to the particular case. This requires legal competence.

---

[40] S. Halliday, *Judicial Review and Compliance with Administrative Law* (Oxford, 2004).

4 The less competition there is between law and other influences on the behaviour of public functionaries, and the stronger the law's relative influence, the greater will be its impact. Halliday relates the law's strength to the ability of courts to enforce administrative law. He concludes that law is relatively weak because there is little that courts can do to ensure that public decision-makers comply with orders made and rules laid down in judicial review proceedings.[41]

5 The clearer and more consistent the law is, the greater will be its influence on the behaviour of public functionaries. Halliday argues that administrative law is 'riven by competing priorities' and sends out mixed messages to public decision-makers. This partly explains why its influence is often weak relative to other demands on decision-makers.[42]

I have stated these hypotheses in simplified form, and readers are encouraged to refer to Halliday's book for a fuller account of the research and of these hypotheses. Notice that the hypotheses make relative rather than absolute statements about the impact of administrative law. Notice, too, that they are relevant not only to understanding the role of court decisions in the public decision-making process, but also that of the rules

---

[41] The importance of this factor is illustrated by a recent study of the major role played by US federal courts in 'reforming' the prison system (M.M. Feeley and E.L. Rubin, *Judicial Policy-Making and the Modern State* (Cambridge, 1999). A significant part of the story is that courts not only laid down standards for the running of prisons but were also actively involved in ensuring that the standards were implemented. In effect, the courts in these cases operated as multi-functional regulatory agencies, setting standards for the performance of public functions, and monitoring and enforcing compliance with them.

[42] We might say that this hypothesis concerns the ideal 'form of law'. Instrumentalist discussions of this issue include R. Baldwin, 'Why Rules Don't Work' (1990) 53 *MLR* 321 and *Rules and Government* (Oxford, 1995), ch. 6; J. Black, ' "Which Arrow"? Rule Type and Policy' [1995] *PL* 94. A central hypothesis of instrumentalist regulatory theory is that law is more likely to promote regulatory goals if it is 'responsive'. The basic idea here is that people are more likely to work towards goals willingly when they have had some part in defining the goals and deciding how to promote them. Enlisting people's cooperation is more likely to be effective than simply telling them what to do, which may be counterproductive by encouraging evasion or merely technical compliance. In one respect, administrative law scores well in terms of responsiveness, because its open-textured principles give decision-makers considerable leeways of choice in performing their functions. Indeed, courts are often criticized for being too 'deferential' in applying these principles. On the other hand, it is often argued that courts are not responsive enough in formulating and applying the rules of natural justice, for instance, because they do not adequately understand and take sufficient account of the goals and values of those to whom the rules apply. An important distinction between the normative and the instrumental perspectives on the form of law arises from the fact that the normativist's goal is securing compliance with the law. For the instrumentalist, by contrast, compliance with the law is subsidiary to realization of some goal external to the law. So clarity and consistency of legal rules may not be as valuable to the instrumentalist as to the normativist.

and principles of administrative law as such. Furthermore, they are relevant to understanding not only why decision-makers fail to comply with administrative law, but also conditions that are likely to promote compliance. In terms of law's impact, understanding compliance is at least as important as understanding non-compliance. In any well-functioning legal system, most people comply with the law most of the time. Judicial review is a mark of non-compliance—of the pathology of the legal system, if you like. Whatever the impact of judicial review on the public decision-making process, it is perhaps unlikely that it holds the key to explaining why most public decision-makers comply with administrative law most of the time, or to promoting legality in public decision-making. Judicial review is an important technique (in qualitative if not in quantitative terms) for resolving disputes between citizens and public functionaries and, much more, for generating rules and principles to regulate the performance of public functions. By studying judicial review empirically we will better understand these two activities—i.e. dispute resolution and rule-making. But in order to understand why most interactions between citizens and public functionaries do not give rise to legal disputes, and to understand why public functionaries typically comply with the rules and principles of administrative law made by courts (and other rule-makers), a focus on courts is likely to be, at best, only a beginning. For this purpose, studying what public functionaries do is likely to provide much more illumination than studying what courts do. The role of courts in promoting compliance with the law is likely to be quite small.

Although other impact researchers have not, explicitly at least, followed the same methodology as Halliday, various other hypotheses can be extracted from their work. These include:

6 The impact of administrative law may vary as between different types of rules. For instance, it has been suggested that the impact of procedural rules may differ from that of rules concerning the substance of decisions.[43]

7 The likely impact of judicial review on a decision-maker's behaviour may be related to the amount of personal experience the decision-maker has had of judicial review.

8 The impact of judicial review on the work of a particular decision-maker may vary over time.[44]

---

[43] Machin and Richardson, op cit. n. 36 above.
[44] Sunkin and Pick, op cit. n. 37 above.

9 The more publicity a judicial-review decision attracts, the greater its likely impact.

10 Negotiatory and investigatory complaints procedures are likely to have more impact than adjudicatory procedures.[45] The underlying idea here is that decision-makers are more likely to understand what the law requires of them if they are involved in some sort of dialogue with the complainant and the complaint-handler about resolving the complaint. The impersonal and adversarial nature of judicial review militates against such dialogue.

The important point for present purposes is not whether these hypotheses will be shown to be true either generally or in relation to particular public functions or functionaries. Rather it is that because they are themselves derived from careful empirical observation of public decision-making processes, they provide valuable and reliable starting points for thinking about when judicial review is likely to have greatest impact and about how its impact might be increased, if this is thought desirable.

20.5 OTHER EMPIRICAL RESEARCH ABOUT ADMINISTRATIVE LAW

So far as concerns impact on the behaviour of public functionaries, judicial review is the only accountability mechanism that has yet attracted the sustained interest of empirical researchers. Little or no systematic work has yet been done on the impact of the activities of public sector ombudsmen[46] or of tribunals.[47] The internal operation of various tribunals has received some attention. For instance, there are studies of the impact of representation on the outcome of tribunal hearings;[48] and on the respective roles of adjudication officers who appear before, and legal

---

[45] M. Hertogh, 'Coercion, Cooperation and Control: Understanding the Policy Impact of Administrative Courts and the Ombudsman in the Netherlands' (2001) 23 *Law and Policy* 47 (study of the respective impact of courts and the ombudsman on policy-making).

[46] But see Hertogh, op cit. n. 45 above.

[47] For some discussion of the impact of social security tribunals see N. Wikeley and R. Young, 'The Administration of Benefits in Britain: Adjudication Officers and the Influence of Social Security Appeal Tribunals' [1992] *PL* 238, 250–9.

[48] H. Genn and Y. Genn, *The Effectiveness of Representation at Tribunals* (Lord Chancellor's Department, 1989); H. Genn, 'Tribunal Review of Administrative Decision-Making' in G. Richardson and H. Genn (eds), *Administrative Law and Government Action* (Oxford, 1994).

and non-legal members of, social security tribunals.[49] The working of internal complaints mechanisms, particularly within the NHS[50] and in local authority housing departments[51] has also been examined, but primarily from the point of view of accessibility and fairness to complainants rather than in terms of their impact on public decision-making. There has been quite a lot of research around the world into the impact (actual and potential) of tort liability in areas such as road and industrial accidents, but very little concerned specifically with the tort liability of public functionaries.[52]

20.6 CONCLUSION

At present we know relatively little about the impact of judicial review and administrative law on the performance of public functions. Our relative ignorance is likely to persist for quite a long time, and administrative law's impact may always remain a matter for more or less speculation. Does this matter? To what extent does the justification for judicial review and administrative law depend on their impact on behaviour? I have argued that normativists, as well as instrumentalists, think that influencing behaviour is at least part of the purpose of administrative law and judicial review. If they could be shown to have no impact at all, or if their only impacts could be shown to be undesirable, there would be no reason to keep them. But this has not been shown and, indeed, the contrary seems to be the case. Judicial review and administrative law, it seems, do sometimes influence behaviour in a desirable way. On the other hand, there is evidence that this impact is much less than lawyers often like to think. Furthermore, we do not know, and may never know, whether the beneficial effects of judicial review and administrative law outweigh their costs and any detrimental effects they may have.

If it were thought that the only way they could be justified was by showing that on balance they had a good impact on the performance of

---

[49] J. Baldwin, N. Wikeley, and R. Young, *Judging Social Security: The Adjudication of Claims for Benefit in Britain* (Oxford, 1992).

[50] H. Wallace and L. Mulcahy, *Cause for Complaint? An Evaluation of the Effectiveness of the NHS Complaints Procedure* (London, 1999).

[51] D. Cowan and S. Halliday, *The Appeal of Internal Review* (Oxford, 2003).

[52] For an English study see J. Hartshorne, N. Smith, and R. Everton, '*Caparo* under Fire: a Study of the Effects upon the Fire Service of Liability in Negligence' (2000) 63 *MLR* 502. Doctoral research is currently be conducted by Geoff Stewart-Richardson at the Australian National University into the impact of tort law and litigation on road-maintenance decision-making by local authorities.

public functions, our ignorance might cast serious doubt on the value of judicial review and administrative law. But normativists, at least, do not take such an uncompromisingly utilitarian approach to the law. For them, part of the function of administrative law is to embody and express certain values about the way society should run and the way public functionaries should behave. From this perspective, although the facts about the impact of judicial review and administrative law are certainly relevant to assessing their value, they cannot be conclusive because administrative law embodies values that deserve to be observed and promoted for their own sake. Law can be important not only on account of what it practically achieves but also on account of what it symbolically stands for. In law and politics, as in life, symbols can be important regardless of their actual impact on the world. Administrative law and judicial review can perform a non-instrumental symbolic function simply by existing and being available. Judicial review is symbolically important for the values it embodies and protects. From this perspective, judicial enforcement of administrative-law norms may have value independently of its impact on public decision-making.

Index